Negotiating Software Contracts

Fifth edition

Negotiating Software Contracts

Fifth edition

Robert Bond BA, CCEP

Bloomsbury Professional

**Bloomsbury Professional, Maxwelton House,
41–43 Boltro Road, Haywards Heath, West Sussex, RH16 1BJ**

© Bloomsbury Professional 2013

A CIP Catalogue record for this book is available from the British Library.

ISBN 978 1 78043 333 2

Typeset by Phoenix Photosetting, Chatham, Kent
Printed and bound in Great Britain by Martins the Printers, Berwick-upon-Tweed, Northumberland

**Bloomsbury Professional, Maxwelton House,
41–43 Boltro Road, Haywards Heath, West Sussex, RH16 1BJ**

© Bloomsbury Professional 2013

A CIP Catalogue record for this book is available from the British Library.

ISBN 978 1 78043 333 2

Typeset by Phoenix Photosetting, Chatham, Kent
Printed and bound in Great Britain by Martins the Printers, Berwick-upon-Tweed, Northumberland

Preface

This book provides an overview of the issues relating to negotiating and drafting software licences in the digital age. The book also provides an overview of the UK law relating to computer contracts

Although mass market software is capable of being delivered from the web, many software products are still delivered or installed by the software vendor, or bundled with hardware or developed as one-off solutions. This book, therefore, discusses many of the issues relating to the traditional software licences and support and maintenance agreements and many of the precedents relate to the traditional delivery of software solutions.

However, as the business of software licensing moves from traditional paper licences through to click-wrap contracts and as the concept of licensing object code only is now replaced by open licensing and the new licensing methods of the application service providers come to the fore, so these issues will also be addressed in this book.

There are already many excellent books covering in detail the subject matter of computer law and information technology law. This book is intended to complement such academic works by providing a general explanation of the law whilst covering in more detail the practical and commercial aspects of computer contract negotiations.

The text is divided into five Parts and Part I is divided into two chapters, with chapter 1 looking at the nature of software licensing and chapter 2 examining different types of software licence agreements.

Part II looks at the laws and regulations affecting software contracts, with chapter 3 addressing the different types of intellectual property laws and chapter 4 providing an overview of European Union law.

Part III deals with the issues of preparing for negotiations. Chapter 5 looks at negotiating principles, with chapter 6 looking at the preparations for negotiations carried out by both suppliers and buyers.

Part IV addresses the issues involved in preparing for drafting software licences agreements. Chapter 7 looks at the use of heads of agreement and memorandum of understanding and chapter 8 contains a check list of the contents of a typical software licence agreement.

Part V looks at some of the tactics and techniques of contract negotiation.

In the first edition of this book, the precedents covered a variety of software licensing scenarios from shrink-wrap and click-wrap, through standard licence and service to distribution, escrow and software development. In the second edition, a number of new precedents were added to cover software evaluation, IT services outsourcing, loan of hardware and software, data processing and trans-border data flow, as well as a computer games development licence. In this third edition, updates have been made to many chapters and additional precedents have been added.

We have been allowed to include the NCC Group's standard escrow agreements to which we have added some commentary. We acknowledge the copyright of NCC Group, and thank them for allowing us to use their material.

In addition, a glossary of software and web definitions are included in the book.

The law referred to is correct as at 1 January 2013.

Robert Bond
30 April 2013

Acknowledgments

Firstly, I would like to express my gratitude to all the staff at Bloomsbury Professional for their assistance and attention to detail. Secondly to my wife, Dr Patricia Bond, for her support and encouragement. Thirdly and finally, my clients over the past 34 years, without whose instructions, patience and loyalty I would not have gained such experience in this stimulating and changing field of law.

Robert Bond
30 April 2013

Contents

Preface   v
Acknowledgements   vii
Glossary   xv
Table of cases   xxxiii
Table of statutes   xxxvii
Table of statutory instruments   xxxix
Table of European legislation   xli
Table of international treaties and conventions   xliii

PART I   INTRODUCTION
1   Understanding software licence agreements   3
  1.1   What is a software licence agreement?   3
  1.2   What types of software and databases are distributed under
        contract and what laws protect them?   5
      1.2.1   Mainframe and minicomputer software   5
      1.2.2   Microcomputor software   6
      1.2.3   Commercially available software   6
      1.2.4   Commercially available databases   6
      1.2.5   Non-contract protection   7
  1.3   General comments   7
  1.4   Goals and purposes of parties to a software licence agreement   8
      1.4.1   In general   8
      1.4.2   Why are software licence agreements required by many
              software providers?   9
  1.5   Some differences between software sale, lease and licence
        transactions   11
      1.5.1   Legal concepts and characteristics   11
      1.5.2   Legal concept of sale   12
      1.5.3   Legal concept of lease   12
      1.5.4   Legal concept of licence   13
  1.6   Weaknesses of the software licence concept   14
2   Some general types of software licence agreements   17
  2.1   Developer-publisher licence agreements   17
  2.2   Publisher-distributor licence agreements   19
      2.2.1   Domestic distributors, OEMs and VARs   19
      2.2.2   Foreign distributors, OEMs and VARs   20
  2.3   User licence agreements   21

Contents

2.3.1   Signed licence agreements   21
2.3.2   Shrink-wrap licence agreements   21
2.3.3   Click-wrap licence agreements   24
2.4   Escrow and TTP agreements   25
2.5   Runtime licence agreements   26
2.6   Manufacturing licence agreements   27
2.7   Cross-licensing agreements   27
2.8   Joint venture licensing agreements   28
2.9   Core technology licence agreements   28
2.10   Software conversion agreements   28
2.11   Database and access software licence agreements   29
2.12   Maintenance service licence agreements   30
2.13   Facilities management agreements   31
2.14   Website agreements   31
2.15   Open source licences   32
2.15.1   Introduction   32
2.15.2   Historical analysis of the Open Source movement   33
2.15.3   The Open Source Definition   33
2.15.4   Examples of licences   36
2.15.5   Analysis of licences and their Open Source compliance   36
2.15.6   Choosing a licence   39
2.15.7   The future   40
2.16   Application service provider licences   42
2.17   Software as a service (SaaS)   42

PART II   LAWS AND REGULATIONS
3   Introduction to laws relevant to software contracts   47
3.1   Overview   47
3.2   Patent law   47
3.3   Copyright and database laws   51
3.4   Trade secret law   62
3.5   Trademark law   64
3.6   Contract law   65
3.7   Registered designs   66
3.8   Moral rights   67
4   European Union law   69
4.1   Overview   69
4,2   Competition law   69
4.3   EC Directive on the legal protection of computer programs   72
4.4   EC Directive on rental and lending rights and certain rights relating to copyright   73
4.5   EC Directive harmonising the term of protection of copyright and certain related rights   73
4.6   EC Directive on the legal protection of databases   73
4.7   EC Directive on unfair contract terms   74
4.8   EC Directive on e-signatures   75
4.9   EC Directive on distance selling of goods and services   77
4.10   EC Directive on data protection   78
4.10.1   Background to the Data Protection Acts of 1984 and 1998   78
4.10.2   Data security   80
4.10.3   Transfer of data overseas   81

4.10.4   US/EU Safe Harbor   81
4.10.5   Trans-border data flows   81
4.10.6   Article 26.1 of the Directive   82
4.10.7   Article 26.2 of the Directive   83
4.10.8   Trans-Border Data Flow (TBDF) agreements   83
4.11 EC Directive on Waste Electrical and Electronic Equipment
(WEEE Directive) (2002/96/EC) and EC Directive on the
restriction of the use of certain hazardous substances in electrical
and electronic equipment (RoHS Directive) (2002/95/EC)   87
4.11.1   Type of products affected   87
4.11.2   Key elements of the WEEE Directive   88
4.11.3   Key elements of the RoHS Directive   89
4.11.4   Key dates   90
4.11.5   Issues for the inbound and outbound supply chain   90
4.11.6   UK WEEE Consultation   91
4.11.7   EU WEEE Consultation   92

PART III   PREPARING FOR NEGOTIATIONS
5   Understanding negotiating principles   95
5.1   Introduction   95
5.2   What is negotiation   95
5.3   Why negotiate?   96
5.4   The give/get principle   97
5.5   What is a win-win deal?   97
5.6   Negotiating styles and ethics   98
5.7   Negotiating styles   99
6   Preparing for negotiations   101
6.1   Provider preparations
6.1.1   In general   101
6.1.2   Sales force training, customer qualification and
negotiating experience   101
6.1.3   Standard charges   102
6.1.4   Standard, printed, protective contracts   103
6.1.5   Pre-negotiation groundwork with customer   104
6.1.6   Internal deal structuring and negotiations   105
6.1.7   Preparation of substansive fall-back positions on open
points and early concerns   105
6.1.8   Inter-departmental meetings to plan negotiating strategy
and tactics   106
6.1.9   Preparation of contracts before negotiations
commence   106
6.2   Customer preparations   107
6.2.1   In general   107
6.2.2.   In-house needs analysis and procurement decision   107
6.2.3   Consultant-aided needs analysis and procurement
decision   108
6.2.4   Consensus view determination   109
6.2.5   Selection of acquistition structure and negotiating
strategy and tactics   113
6.2.6   Obtain management support   113
6.2.7   Select one team member as leader and interface   114
6.2.8   Know when to hire outside help   114

Contents

PART IV   PREPARING FOR DRAFTING
7   Preparing the contracts   117
    7.1   Pre-contractual documents and confidentiality   117
        7.1.1   Introduction   117
        7.1.2   Business secrets and confidentiality   118
    7.2   The use of heads of agreement   119
        7.2.1   Introduction   119
        7.2.2   Contract skeleton   120
        7.2.3   Drafting the heads   120
        7.2.4   Three golden rules   121
8   Checklist of the contents of a typical software licence agreement   125
    8.1   Overview   125
        8.1.1   Parties   125
        8.1.2   Recitals   126
        8.1.3   Definitions   126
        8.1.4   Payment(s)   127
        8.1.5   Licence grant   130
        8.1.6   Delivery   137
        8.1.7   Site and host preparation   137
        8.1.8   Installation   138
        8.1.9   Acceptance tests   138
        8.1.10   Term of the agreement   140
        8.1.11   Termination or expiration and result   142
        8.1.12   Service and updates maintenance   144
        8.1.13   Enhancements   144
        8.1.14   Escrow   145
        8.1.15   Training   145
        8.1.16   Consulting and developmental services   146
        8.1.17   Warranties in general   146
        8.1.18   Limited warranty   147
        8.1.19   Ongoing performance obligations   147
        8.1.20   Virus and error warranty   148
        8.1.21   European Money Union warranty   149
        8.1.22   Representations, warranties and indemnification
            regarding intellectual property rights   149
        8.1.23   Limitation of liability and remedy   150
        8.1.24   Limitation on recoverable damages   154
        8.1.25   Nature and scope of consequential damages
            exclusion   155
        8.1.26   Liquidated damages   156
        8.1.27   Most favoured customer   158
        8.1.28   Change control   158
        8.1.29   Availability of licensee's computer system to licensor for
            maintenance, training, and development purposes   159
        8.1.30   Recovery of lawyers' fees by prevailing party   159
        8.1.31   Statute of limitations   160
        8.1.32   Risk of loss or damage during transit   160
        8.1.33   Indemnities   160
        8.1.34   *Force majeure*   162
        8.1.35   Assignment of contract rights and obligations   163
        8.1.36   Notice provisions   163
        8.1.37   Entire agreement and variations   163

8.1.38   Severability   167
8.1.29   Confidentiality   168
8.1.40   Remote access   168
8.1.41   Data protection   169
8.1.42   Governing law and jurisdiction   170
8.1.43   Third party rights   173
8.1.44   Rights of audit   174
9   Necessary licence provisions   177
9.1   Key licence provisions from the provider's viewpoint   177
9.1.1   Introduction   177
9.1.2   What will I provide, when, and for how long?   177
9.1.3   What will I receive, when, and for how long?   178
9.1.4   What business and legal risks do I face that I should minimise or neutralise?   179
9.1.5   Other provisions   180
9.2   Key licence provisions from the customer's viewpoint   180
9.2.1   Introduction   180
9.2.2   Key questions   181
9.2.3   Other provisions   183
9.2.4   Clarity and precision   186

PART V   NEGOTIATING TACTICS AND TECHNIQUES
10   Creative problem solving   189
10.1   Introduction – reduce the issue to economics   189
10.2   Redefining the problem   189
10.3   Other techniques   191
10.3.1   Recognise opportunities   191
10.3.2   Borrow ideas   191
10.3.3   Look at the forest, not just the trees   191
10.3.4   Look for patterns   192
10.3.5   Don't ignore the obvious   192
10.3.6   Look at the difficulty differently   192
10.3.7   Ask: What if?   192
10.3.8   What rules can you break?   193
10.3.9   Combine or link ideas   193
10.3.10   Change names   193
10.3.11   Imagine how someone else would solve the problem   193
10.3.12   Notice the positive   193
10.3.13   Expect resistance and sell   194
11   The use of non-verbals in negotiation   195
11.1   Introduction   195
11.2   Silence – negotiating with yourself   195
11.3   Body language   196
11.3.1   Crossed arms   197
11.3.2   The hand over the mouth   197
11.3.3   The eyes   198
11.4   Personal space   199
11.5   Seating positions   200

Appendix   Precedents
1   Software evaluation licence and confidentiality agreement   205
2   Shrink-wrap licence   216

Contents

3   Click-wrap licence   223
4   Software licence agreement   229
5   Software licence agreement checklist   250
6   Software support and maintenance agreement   258
7   Memorandum of understanding in relation to negotiation of a formal joint venture and licensing agreement   281
8   Agreement for software development and licensing   288
9   Demo licence   308
10   Computer games development agreement   310
11   Heads of Agreement for software distribution   347
12   Software distribution agreement   354
13   Multimedia product licence and distribution agreement   374
14   Joint software development agreement   397
15   Reciprocal software licence agreement   411
16   Agreement for supply of hardware products   420
17   Hardware maintenance agreement   440
18   Agreement for loan of hardware and software products   459
19   Invitation to tender   477
20   IT services outsourcing agreement   489
21   Agreement for website hosting   511
22   Website software development, licensing and support agreement   518
23   Licence agreement for link between web sites   537
24   Trans border data flow agreement   547
25   Data processing agreement   558
26   Software licence code   567
27   Escrow agreements   572
     Development Single Licensee Software Escrow Agreement   573
     Escrow Secure – Single Licensee Software Escrow Agreement   584
     Holding Agreement   596
     Information Escrow Agreement   603
     Multi Licensee Software Escrow Agreement   613
     Single Licensee Software Escrow Agreement   625
     Single Licensee Website and Software Escrow agreement   636
28   Framework agreement   708
29   Software services agreement   734
30   Value added reseller agreement and licence   746
31   Standard contractual clauses (controller to processors)   760
32   Professional services agreement   772

Index   781

Glossary

3G   *Third generation.* A method of sending Internet information to mobile telephones at speeds of up to 2 kilobits per second, significantly faster than GPRS.

Access provider   An organisation that sells connectivity to the Internet. It provides a gateway into which users dial for connection. Agreements typically cover dial-in connectivity to their machine(s), which are host nodes on the Internet.

Acrobat   A programme from Adobe that allows the creation or reading of PDF files. PDF is a format that enables a reader to see the exact layout, graphics and typestyle of the document that the producer intended, without having to have the correct fonts installed on his machine. Users only need to have an Acrobat reader which is freely available from Adobe's web site. The format is useful for creating brochures to download.

ActiveX   Microsoft's answer to the Java technology from Sun Microsystems. It allows the creation of a self-sufficient program that can be run anywhere in an ActiveX network (whether Windows or Macintosh).

Address   An 'address' can mean the unique location of either an Internet server, a specific file or an email user. The server or IP address is the unique string of numbers of a particular server linked to the Internet (eg 194.72.83.225). This equates to a domain name such as hobsonaudley.co.uk. Individual files such as web pages have an address based on the domain name (eg www.hobsonaudley.co.uk/index.htm). This is known as the uniform resource locator (URL). Finally, individuals can have a mailbox linked to that domain name, providing them with their own virtual address.

ADSL *Asymmetric Digital Subscriber Line.* This provides fast access to the Internet. It is a standard which provides high bandwidth for data and voice connection. A problem many home users of the Internet encounter has been the low bandwidth (effectively the slowness of access and download). ADSL, a technology for transmitting digital information at high bandwidths on existing phone lines, could change that. BT is upgrading its exchanges to allow ADSL access, and service providers including AOL, Freeserve and Telewest are trialing high speed 'always on' services.

Agent or bot A program that collects information or performs some service in the background. It can be used, for instance, to create personalised search or news services. Also known as Intelligent Agents.

AI *Artificial Intelligence.* The simulation of the human intelligence processes by computers. A philosophical minefield, but also an important business area as firms look to develop AI or expert systems to provide initial legal advice, build first drafts etc.

Analogue technology This technology conveys data in the form of electronic signals of varying frequency together with carrier waves of a fixed frequency. Analogue technology is being replaced by digital technology.

Ananova *A virtual newsreader.* An interesting attempt to Create a 'person' who interacts with the visitor to the web site. As bandwidth increases, it becomes possible to create more user-friendly ways to access information or services, getting away from text boxes, search fields and, eventually, keyboards and mice.

Anonymous FTP Many hosts provide free information, which can be downloaded to your machine, using FTP. Where the information is free, an 'anonymous' facility is provided, as the system has no need to know who you are.

Application Service Provider (ASP) An authorised provider of its own as well as third-party software products to customers on an on-line rental/licence basis.

Archie A host-based program, which searches for specific files, stored on anonymous FTP sites.

Architecture The increasingly complex art (or science) of thinking out and specifying the interrelationships of computers, operating systems and networks.

ASCII *American Standard Code for Information Interchange.* The ASCII code table consists of 128 characters and is a way of representing ordinary text as a stream of binary numbers. The first 32 characters in the ASCII table are control codes and the last 96 characters are upper and lower case letters, numbers and special symbols. The most common format for text files in computers and on the Internet. Documents in ASCII (or plain) text are readable on almost any device.

Avatar

A computer-generated character or persona adopted by a user of an on-line environment. Another example of the attempt to create a more human feel to the online experience. In Hinduism, an avatar is an incarnation of a deity, hence an embodiment or manifestation of an idea or greater reality.

AVI file

Audio Visual Interleaves file. Microsoft's standard for sound and motion picture file. Apple has developed the Quicktime format that also plays on PCs. Users need a special player that may be included with a web browser to play the video and must download the complete file before playing, unlike streaming media formats that begin to play almost immediately.

Backbone

A central section of a network to which other networks connect. In the context of the Internet, it refers to the high-speed links between the main access providers.

Bandwidth

The capacity of a communications link between two nodes – the rate at which information can be transferred. A given message may travel through many nodes to reach its destination. However, the speed with which this is achieved is constrained by the slowest link, ie the one with the narrowest bandwidth. It is often referred to in Newsgroups where the writers of long and verbose messages may be accused of wasting bandwidth, ie the time taken to pass unnecessary information around the network.

Baud rate

The speed at which data is transferred between pieces of electronic equipment.

Blink

An activity performed by an off-line reader. A blink is the act of connecting to a host, downloading any new mail and posting messages or mail. The line is then disconnected. New mail and messages can then be read 'off-line' and responses composed for the next 'blink'. This approach minimises connect time and hence telephone charges.

Blog

A blog or web log is an internet diary made publicly available. Initially blogs were run by individuals without any commercial purpose but more recently businesses have set up marketing blogs and other similar blogs for commercial purposes.

Bluetooth

A short range wireless connection standard. Its aim is to link a wide range of computer, electronics and telecoms devices. The technology uses a low power two-way radio link which is built into a microchip.

Boot up

As you switch on your PC, it goes through the boot up sequence, which includes checking hardware for errors and loading DOS system files.

BPS

Bits per second. The unit used to measure baud rate.

Browser

A program which will allow your computer to download and display documents or pages from the World Wide Web. The most common program is Netscape, claiming 70% plus of the market.

Buffer

A small area of memory used to hold frequently accessed information, or data that will be needed at any moment.

Bulletin board (BBS)

Using a modem, you can hook up to an electronic bulletin board. From here you can chat to other people or download useful files (such as the latest software drivers for your video card).

CA

Certification Authority. A body which is set up to authenticate electronic signatures.

CcTLD

Country Code Top Level Domain. The part of the TLD which indicates the country of location, eg uk, .au, .ca, .fr.

Click-wrap

The description for and method of providing on-line or on-screen Licensing terms, for mass market software products and services, whereby a software licensing contract is intended to be entered into without necessarily being negotiated or signed by handwritten signature, but may be signed by electronic signature or where the terms may be accepted by the doing of some action such as the 'clicking' of a particular icon or button.

Client-Server Applications

Applications which run in two parts. Client applications, usually concerned with taking input and displaying information communicating with Server applications running on host machines.

Cookie

A small piece of computer code which transmits data about the user across the Internet. It might include data concerning the type of computer software and hardware being used, and other web sites visited by the user. Its value in market research terms is significant. Cookies are regulated in the EU.

Copyright
An intellectual property right, giving the copyright holder an economic right to control or prevent the unauthorised copying or reproduction of copyright material during the life of copyright, a term varying from jurisdiction to jurisdiction, and applying to the expression of an idea.

Cyberspace
A term used to refer to the place where the Internet resides. First use was by William Gibson in his book *Neuromancer* in 1984.

Database
A program used to store and access large amounts of information. The data may be stored in different forms such as text, sound and graphics.

DEFCONS
A series of standard contract terms and conditions issued by the UK Ministry of Defence in the acquisition of a variety of goods and services, including software. These are intended to override the provider's standard licensing terms and are heavily balanced in favour of the customer.

Dialup
A term used to describe on-demand access to the Internet. In other words, you dial up when you want access and 'hang-up' when you have finished. Larger organisations have permanent links.

Digital certificate
The equivalent of an Internet passport in that the certificate provides assurance of identity to an individual's digital signature. A digital certificate is a message which at least: (a) identifies the issuing certification authority; (b) names or identifies the individual; (c) contains the individual's public key; (d) identifies the terms of use of the certificate and (e) bears the digital signature of the certification authority itself.

Digital signature
A transformation of a message using an asymmetric encryption system and a hash function such that a person, having the initial message and the digital signers own public key can accurately determine: (a) whether the transformation was created using the private key that corresponds to the signer's public key; and (b) whether the initial message has been altered since the transformation was made.

Digital technology
Digital technology represents signals in the form of a series of binary numbers rather than as analogue electronic signals.

Disintermediation   The commercial process whereby intermediaries in a supply chain are bypassed or circumvented. In the travel industry, it applies to the process whereby Principals are seeking an increasing proportion of direct bookings from their ultimate clients, via various media, including the Internet.

Disk compression   Software that processes the files on the hard disk so they take up less disk space. Disk compression software can effectively double the size of most hard disks. Most files can be compressed, as they contain portions of identical data repeated throughout the file.

Dongles   Also known as keys, security devices and locks, these are made up of software and hardware and are intended to be a security device between the hardware equipment and the software program licensed by the provider. An authorised licensee only would have access to the dongle for attaching to the hardware input/output ports, without which the hardware would not allow the software to run. Usually a dongle is provided for every machine the software is to be run upon.

DOS   *Disk Operating System.* The software you need before you can get your computer to do anything. All other programs need the operating system to be loaded before they can work. The operating system is a bit like having a slave permanently at your disposal. If, say, you want a letter filed away, ask the operating system to put it somewhere and let it worry about how the hard disk stores the data.

Download   A method of copying a file from one computer to another, but most frequently used when referring to getting a file from the Internet.

Driver   A small program sitting between the operating system and hardware, which relays messages. For instance, the operating system tells the sound driver to play a note and the driver tells the soundcard to do it.

DTP   *Desktop Publishing.* Software used to create documents or publications.

E-Commerce   The facilitation of business relationships by electronic means.

E-mail address   A unique address which can be used to send e-mail directly. For example: robert.bond@speechlys.com is an e-mail address for Robert Bond within the domain speechlys.com

Emoticons	See Smilies
Emulation	Emulation makes a peripheral appear to an application as if it is another type of that peripheral. Take printer emulation as an example. Software publishers produce applications to work with a few popular printers, like the HP LaserJet, rather than making sure their product will work with every printer on the market. If other printer manufacturers make sure that their printer can mimic or 'emulate' a LaserJet, they know it will work with software compatible with the LaserJet.
Encryption technology	The means by which information is encrypted and decrypted using ciphers or codes in order to keep data confidential as well as to authenticate the identity of message senders and receivers.
EPOC	The operating system for wireless devices, such as the handheld organiser developed by Psion.
Escrow	The holding on deposit by a third party of confidential material on certain terms as to its release or control and use. In software terms it is often source code which is placed in escrow.
Extranet	A semi-private network of computers using a combination of fixed connections through both cables and the telephone system, via modems. The essential feature of an Extranet, which distinguishes it from an Intranet, is its more open nature. An Extranet is like an Intranet which has been opened up, to one degree or another, to one or more outsiders. For example, a law firm will set up an Extranet with a particular client, so that the lawyers and the clients can exchange information and documents freely and with more security than via the Internet.
FAQ	*Frequently Asked Questions.* Usually found in Newsgroups which contain collated answers to questions most commonly asked by new users. An invaluable source of information for 'newbies' – the Internet name for new users.
Firewall	A security system, which sits between computers on a local area network (LAN) and the point of connection to the Internet, designed to restrict access to the LAN from the Internet.
Flame	An abusive or personal attack against the poster of a message in a newsgroup. The Internet equivalent of losing your temper and the nearest you can get to

	thumping someone. Occasionally a flame might start a flame war with insults being hurled to and fro until common sense prevails.
Frames	The use of the structure of a particular web site to surround material derived from mother site, and make the entire page appear to be the creation of the host.
FTP	*File Transfer Protocol.* The basic way of transferring files across the Internet. An FTP 'client' program is required to run on your own computer. Products such as Netscape include this facility.
GIF	A standard way of storing graphics images, used extensively across the Internet. See also **JPEG**.
Gopher	As in Go-for. A menu-driven application that runs on your own computer to read documents and download files stored on hosts. The host computer must also be capable of running a Gopher server application.
GPRS	*General Packet Radio Service.* A method of sending Internet information to mobile telephones at high speed. GPRS will be capable of delivering information at a speed of up to 100,000 bits per second, compared to the 9600 bits which is currently the norm.
GSM	*Global System for Mobile Communications.* Common European standard for mobile telephones.
gTLD	*generic Top Level Domain.* A TLD which indicates the type of organisation, eg .net, .com, .gov, .edu.
Hard drive cache	A small area of memory dedicated as a buffer.
Hard drive controller	A chip responsible for operating the hard drive when given instructions by the PC's processor. The controller can have almost as much effect on PC speed as the hard drive itself.
Host	The computer you dial into at your service provider to get access to the Internet. It will have a unique Internet address.
HTML	*HyperText Mark-up Language.* The language used to create documents for the World Wide Web, and which enables them to link to one another.
HTTP	*HyperText Transfer Protocol.* The standard way of transferring HTML documents between Web Servers and Clients (browsers).
ICANN IDE	*International Corporation for Assigned Names and Numbers. Integrated Drive Electronics.* IDE hard disks are what you will find in most PCs today. They

have smart features such as built-in controllers and the ability to match the drive type specified in your PC's set-up. The latest IDE standard is known as Enhanced-1DE (E-IDE). E-IDE drives have a higher data throughput than conventional IDE drives. They also support more drives (two rather than four) and boast speeds that approach those of SCSL drives.

Intellectual Property Rights Also abbreviated as IPR, these are the bundle of legal rights or protections which include patents, copyright, trademarks, moral rights and trade secrets.

Internet The network of constantly changing connections between otherwise unconnected computers using modems and telephone lines.

Intranet A private network of computers using fixed connections normally using cables, usually all within the same building. The same effect can be achieved through the telephone system, via modems. The essential feature of an Intranet which distinguishes it from the Internet is its closed nature. An Intranet is a private network, most commonly confined within a particular organisation.

IP *Internet Protocol.* A layer of the set of protocols which devices on the Internet use to communicate with each other. It defines how packets of data get to their intended destination – often used with 'Transmission Control Protocol' in the form TCP/IP.

IP address The internal Internet address for a domain, expressed as a group of four numbers eg 158.152.34.2.

ISDN *Integrated Services Digital Network.* A fast digital communications infrastructure, which supersedes lower performance traditional analogue lines. If you have an ISDN line you can send digital information at speeds of up to 128Kb per second.

ISP Internet Service Provider. See **Access Provider**.

JANET *Joint Academic NETwork.* Links educational establishments in the UK.

JPEG A widely used way of compressing still images and video. See also **GIF**.

LAN *Local Area Network.* See also **Intranet**.

LDAP Lightweight Direct Access Protocol.

LINK A connection between one page on a web site and another page, either on the same site or on an entirely separate site, possibly hosted by a completely unrelated third party in a different part of the world. Links are most easily created by the use of HyperText Mark-up Language (HTML).

LISTSERV

An automated mailing list distribution system, used to distribute electronic newsletters.

LRA

Local Registration Authority.

Lurker

Someone who joins Newsgroups but does not contribute – the equivalent of a voyeur. However, it is usually best to lurk for a while to gauge the feeling of the group and accepted dialogue before making your own contributions.

Mail Gateway

A system which translates e-mail between different systems, for example, between Internet mail and your own Microsoft office mail.

M-Commerce

The facilitation of business relationships by the means of mobile communication devices.

Meta-tags

The embedding of key words or identifiers into the HTML script of a site, in order to generate as many visitors or 'hits' on a site, is called key meta-tagging. The result is that any user of a browser or search engine inputting a key word or phrase that is the same or similar to the key word or phrase in the HTML script on your site, will be led to your site.

MIME

Multipurpose Internet Mail Extensions. A method of encoding or decoding programs so that they can be sent as normal text e-mail messages.

Mirror sites

Heavily used sites, particularly FTP ones, are often replicated at other locations to relieve the load. These are mirror sites.

Modem

Modulator/DEModulator. The device that takes signals from your computer and translates them into a suitable form for the telephone system. The reverse procedure takes place at a modem on the host computer. The faster the speed of a modem, the better the response when transferring large amounts of information.

Moderator

The person who runs a newsgroup, conference or message area.

Mosaic

The first browser which increased the popularity of the World Wide Web.

Motherboard

The main circuit board in the PC. It accommodates the process, memory and expansion cards.

MP3	Software using sound compression technology which facilitates the transmission of sound signals via the web. See also **Real Player**.
MPEG	A type of video compression which makes it possible to have fullscreen, full-motion video on your PC.
MUG	Multi-User Game.
Multi-tasking	The ability of modern computers to carry out several functions at once.
Net Police	A (derogatory) term for those users who find it necessary to tell others how they should behave in Cyberspace.
Net Surfer	Someone who 'surfs' the Internet looking for interesting files, places to visit and people to talk to.
Netiquette	The supposed etiquette of the Internet community – for example avoiding the use of quoting, spamming and SHOUTING – use of capitals is taken as being the equivalent of shouting in real life.
Netscape	The most popular browser – claims 70% plus of the market.
Newbie	A new user – can also be used as a term of abuse.
Newsgroups	Internet Bulletin Boards. There are around 14,000 groups covering just about every subject imaginable. Most access providers run a newsgroup server which takes a feed of news from other servers, adds messages from its own users and passes it on to another server. The collective name for these newsgroup servers is the Usenet. Newsgroups are accessed using a newsreader program available from an Access Provider. The newsreader will give all new messages posted to groups to which they belong. They may start conversations with new messages or comment on current messages.
NNTP	*Network News Transfer Protocol*. The internal protocol used between news servers to exchange articles.
Node	Any device connected to the Internet, with an IP address, is a node.
Nominet	The UK 'not for profit' organisation – which oversees domain names ending with the following TLDs: – co.uk – org.uk – ltd.uk – plc.uk – net.uk

Object code	Computer code, derived by a computer or assembler program, from source code, into a form understandable by machine rather than human forms – also called executable and/or machine code.
OLR	*Off-Line Reader.* Enables information to be downloaded and read offline without maintaining a connection to the Internet. Material may also be prepared for mailing and then sent in a Blink. See **Blink**.
On-line	This term is actually used in association with using the Internet, referring to a service or information accessed through the telephone network via a modem.
Packet	A bundle of data that travels over the network. A message may comprise many packages. It contains information about its source, destination and an identifier for the recipient to understand how it relates to other packets.
Patent	An intellectual property right, granted by legislation, to the inventor of a novel idea or invention, and giving the inventor a monopoly for a limited period of time to control the exploitations of the patented idea or invention.
PC	*Personal Computer.* A computer substantially capable of operating in isolation from others, although it might be part of a network.
PDA	*Personal Digital Assistant.* Small, hand-held devices which typically integrate with computers. The Psion and Palm product ranges include examples. A portable organiser, increasingly with Internet access and e-mail functions.
PING	*Package INternet Groper.* A program used to test if Internet destinations exist and are operational.
PKI	A public key infrastructure comprising a set of technology components combined with practices, policies and a supporting legal framework which provide a highly trusted infrastructure. At its core is the application of asymmetric encryption techniques that ensure trust in the confidentiality and authentication of data and entities within electronic systems.
PoP	*Point of Presence.* A local access point provided by an Access Provider to give Internet access for the cost of a local call.
POP3	An e-mail transfer protocol.

Port	A term used for different points of entry into a single computer. For example, FTP, e-mail and WEB browsing may use different ports. However, the technicalities of ports are usually handled transparently as far as the user is concerned.
Post	To send an e-mail or a message to a newsgroup or conference.
Postmaster	The person responsible for e-mail handling at a domain.
PPP	*Point to Point Protocol.* Allows, amongst other things, IP connections between a computer and access provider. Any dial-up service used with an access provider will use PPP or SLIP, its predecessor.
Principal	The party which takes direct responsibility for the provision of travel arrangements to the client. This will include businesses commonly referred to as tour operators. Note that the term focuses on the activity in question, rather than a description of the type of business. Thus, many businesses will be both Principals and Retailers.
Protocol	Industry jargon for a standard rule or set of rules.
RA	Registration Authority.
RAM	*Random Access Memory.* Physical memory on your PC used to store and edit data which is cleared when the power is switched off.
Real Player	Software using sound compression technology which facilitates the transmission of sound signals via the web. See also **MP3**.
Reboot	When you restart your PC, by switching off and on, pressing the reset button (if you have one) or pressing Ctrl, Alt and Del simultaneously on the keyboard, the PC goes through a reboot process, wiping items from short-term memory and reading all your system files again.
Reformat	When you format a floppy or hard disk, the PC subdivides the whole magnetic disk into sectors for storing data. If a drive has been formatted once, it can be reformatted, which wipes the disk clean, and sets these sectors up again.
Refresh rate	The speed at which information on screen is updated. This takes place many times a second so the eye detects no screen flicker.

RFI	The abbreviation for Request for Information – a particular request issued by the customer in advance of negotiations for the acquisition of software, or hardware or both. The customer requests as much, or particular information as is required from the provider.
RFP	The abbreviation for Request for Proposals – a particular request from the customer often issued after receipt of an RFI, for the provider to complete answering specific enquiries of the customer for software, hardware or both.
Root directory	The starting point on a hard disk, the root directory, (eg c:\) displayed within DOS and Windows, contains all the files and directories that exist on your hard disk.
SCSI	*Small Computer Systems Interface.* A fast system that can be used to control many types of peripheral devices, such a hard disks, tape streamers and CD-ROM drives. All of these peripherals can be connected in a daisy chain to one SCSI controller card.
Server	A computer system on a network which provides services to Client applications. For example: a Gopher application requires both Client and Server applications which communicate with each other.
Shareware	A method of distributing software. Programs are provided free of charge or for a small handling fee, for the user to test for suitability. If, after 30 days, the product continues to be used, it should be registered with the author and paid for.
Shrink-wrap	The description for, and method of providing, printed software licensing terms, for mass-market software products, where a software licensing contract is intended to be entered into without necessarily being negotiated or signed.
Signature or sig	The personal tag used at the end of an e-mail message or posting. May include name, tel, fax, e-mail, business, etc. Anything from one to seven lines. Users with excessively large signatures, especially in relation to the text of their message, are often accused of having a low signal to noise ratio. In other words, the useful content is small, the noise, their sig, is large.
SIM	*Subscriber Identification Module.* Plastic card which is placed in the back of a mobile phone and allows you to store information on your phone.

SLIP	*Serial Line Internet Protocol.* Allows devices to use IP over communications links being superseded by PPP.
Smilies or Emoticons	Punctuation used to impart emotions within e-mail messages. Particularly in Newsgroups. When viewed at ninety degrees, they represent the human face. For example: :-) = happy, :-(= sad, :-o = amazement.
SMS	*Short Messaging Service.* Technology which allows text messages to be received and sent on mobile phones.
SMTP	*Simple Mail Transfer Protocol.* The Internet protocol for transferring mail.
Software	Computer programs which provide instructions to computer hardware, or other software, and which comprise data or information which may be stored in or upon a variety of media, and may be transmitted or disseminated by a variety of means.
Source Code	Instructions or statements written in eye-readable form in programmers' language (high level or assembly language) and capable of being compiled into object code.
Spam	Internet slang for posting the same message to several Newsgroups (also cross-posting) – an activity which is frowned upon.
Swapfile	Complex programs that handle many data, such as Windows, often require more memory than is available, so they use swap files. Data that is not needed immediately is transferred or 'swapped' into a temporary file on your hard disk.
System disk	A floppy disk that contains all the essential files needed to run DOS. If anything happens to your hard disk, you can start your PC using a system disk, helping you to fix the problem without losing any data.
System files	Special description files, which control how your PC starts up.
TCP	*Transmission Control Protocol.* A higher level of protocol than IP. IP is concerned with packets of data. TCP is concerned with messages which may comprise numerous packets. Almost universally used together and referred to as TCP/IP.
Telnet	A protocol which allows you to connect over the Internet to another computer in such a way as to appear as a local user of that computer. Requires the

use of a terminal emulator simulating your view of the remote computer. This is steadily being superseded by the WWW.

Title
Legal ownership of hardware or intellectual property rights in software. When title passes from seller to buyer it is usual for possession and risk for insurance purpose also to pass.

TLA
Three Letter Acronym.

TLD
Top Level Domain. The most general part of a web site or e-mail address, often indicating the type of organisation, country of location or both, eg org.uk

Trademark
A mark, image or identity applied to goods or services, registered or unregistered, which is unique to the business of its owner, but not necessarily descriptive of such business.

Trade secret
An intellectual property right, consisting of confidential information which may or may not be protectable by copyright or patent, but which is valuable as an asset to its owner.

Trolls
Trolling occurs when someone posts a message on the Internet and makes it appear as if the message came from someone else.

Trumpet
A Winsock-compatible Windows program that provides a dial-up connection to the Internet using the SLIP protocol.

TTP
The abbreviation for a Trusted Third Party; an independent individual, firm or company set up or licensed by the state to provide, amongst other things, escrow services and certification or verification services for public and private key algorithms or codes used in cryptographic software, and providing authentication services in respect of digital signatures used in e-commerce.

UNIX
A host operating system which supports multiple users sharing resources. Many host computers use UNIX Servers to provide their email, FTP and Web services.

URL
Uniform Resource Locator. An attempt to standardise address details of Internet resources. Most commonly used with www pages. For example, the home page for the Natural History Museum is: http://ww.nhm.ac.uk/

Veronica
Very Easy Rodent Oriented Net-wide Index to Computerised Archives! A catalogue of Gopher sites

	which allows you to search for menu items containing keywords, and then builds a menu of those sites.
VRML	*Virtual Reality Modelling Language. An* extension of HTML which gives virtual reality effects.
WAIS	*Wide Area Information Server.* Allows a client to perform searches simultaneously on multiple databases.
WAN	Wide Area Network.
WAP	*Wireless Application Protocol.* Intended to be an industry standard protocol and service profile for use with digital mobile phones, pagers, personal digital assistants and other wireless terminals. A standard to enable mobile device users to view web pages easily. It is intended to simplify wireless access to e-mail and voicemail and enable transactions to be carried out.
Web site	An individual's or company's presence on the World Wide Web; web sites are becoming highly interactive and consist of complex design and data content and are often developed and maintained by third-party developers and hosted on third-party servers.
Winsock	A standard interface within the Windows operating system, which resides between applications and network protocols. Used if you require access to the Internet from a Windows application.
WML	*Wireless Markup Language.* This allows web sites to tailor the information format to fit the screen and limited capacity of mobile devices.
WWW	*World Wide Web.* Also known as the Web. The generic name given to the entire interlinked HTML documents on the Internet, which are accessible via browsers such as Netscape. The part of the Internet which has single-handedly contributed to its major growth over recent years. First developed by an Englishman, Tim Berners-Lee.
XML	*Extensible Mark-up Language.* Similar to HTML in that it describes the contents of a web page. XML also enables the interpretation of the value or nature of the data being described.
ZIP	A way of compressing files to minimise transmission times over the Internet. Programs are available to ZIP files up (compress them) and UNZIP them (restore them to their original form) after transmission across the Internet.

Table of Cases

[All references are to paragraph number]

Aerotel/Macrossan, sub nom Aerotel Ltd (A Company Incorporated Under the Laws of Israel) v Telco Holdings Ltd, Telco Global Distribution Ltd, Telco Global Ltd [2006] EWCA Civ 1371; [2007] Bus LR 634; [2007] 1 All ER 225; [2006] Info TLR 215, CA 3.2

Alfred McAlpine Capital Projects Ltd v Tilebox Ltd [2005] EWHC 281 (TCC); [2005] BLR 271; 104 Con LR 39; (2005) 21 Const LJ 539, QBD 8.1.26

Anglo Group plc v Winther Browne & Co Ltd 72 Con LR 118; [1999-2000] Info TLR 61; [2000] ICTLR 559; [2000] Masons CLR 13; (2000) 144 Sol Jo LB 197, QBD (TCC) 8.1.9

Attheraces Ltd v The British Horseracing Board [2007] EWCA Civ 38; [2007] UKCLR 309; [2007] ECC 7; [2007] Info TLR 41; [2007] Bus LR D77, CA (Civ Div) 3.3

Beta Computers (Europe) Ltd v Adobe Systems (Europe) Ltd 1996 SLT 604; [1996] CLC 821; [1997-98] Info TLR 73; [1996] FSR 367; [1998] Masons CLR Rep 104, OH 2.3.2

British Horseracing Board v William Hill (Case C-203/02); [2004] ECR I-10415; [2009] Bus LR 932; [2005] 1 CMLR 15, CEC 3.3

British Sugar plc v NEI Power Projects Ltd (1997) 87 BLR 42; [1997-98] Info TLR 353; [1998] ITCLR 125; (1998) 14 Const LJ 365, CA (Civ Div) 8.1.25

Computer Associates International Inc v Altai Inc 23 USPQ 2d 1241 (2d Cir); amended 982 F 2d 693 (2d Cir 1992) 3.3

Cyprotex Discovery Ltd v University of Sheffield [2004] EWCA Civ 380; [2004] Info TLR 135; [2004] RPC 44; (2004) 148 SJLB 421, CA (Civ Div) 3.3

Decision of Courts of Appeal of Frankfurt am Main of November 3 1998 – 11U 20/98 .... 3.3

Decision of Courts of Appeal of Munich of February 12 1998 – 28U 5911/97 .... 3.3

Dunlop Pneumatic Tyre Co Ltd v New Garage and Motor Co Ltd [1915] AC 79; [1914-15] All ER Rep 739; 83 LJKB 1574; 111 LT 862; 30 TLR 625, HL 8.1.26

Fisher-Rosemount Decision (2009 18 May), IPO 3.2

Fraser v Thames Television Ltd [1984] QB 44; [1983] 2 WLR 917; [1983] 2 All ER 101; (1983) 133 NLJ 281; (1983) 127 SJ 379, QBD 3.4

Gates Rubber Co v Bando Chemical Industries Ltd 9 F 3d 823, 28 USPQ
2d 1503 (10th Cir 1993) 3.3

Harbinger UK Ltd v GE Information Services Ltd [2000] 1 All ER (Comm)
166; (2000) 2 TCLR 463; [2000] ITCLR 501, CA (Civ Div) 8.1.10.4
Hotel Services Ltd v Hilton International Hotels [2000] 1 All ER (Comm)
750; [2000] BLR 235, CA (Civ Div) 8.1.25

IBCOS Computers Ltd v Barclays Mercantile Highland Finance Ltd
[1994] FSR 275, Ch D 3.3

Jacobson v Katzer and Kamind Associates Inc 535 F 3d 1373 (2008), US
Ct of Appeals, Federal Circuit 2.15.3.4
John Richardson Computers Ltd v Flanders and Chemtec Ltd [1993]
FSR 497, Ch D 3.3

Kabushi Kaisha Sony Computer Entertainm ent v Edmunds (trading as
Channel Technology) [2002] EWHC 45 (Ch); [2002] All ER (D) 170
(Jan); [2002] ECDR 27; [2002] EMLR 34, Ch D 3.3

LAN Systems Inc v Netscout Service Level Corporation 183 F Supp 2d
328 (D Mass 2002) 2.3.3
Laurence Wrenn & Integrated Multi-Media Solutions Ltd v Stephen
Landamore [2007] EWHC 1833 (Ch D); [2007] All ER (D) 361 (Jul);
[2008] EWCA Civ 496; [2008] All ER (D) 134 (Apr), CA (Civ Div) 8.1.5.2
LIFFE Administration & Management v Pavel Pincava; De Novo Markets
Ltd [2007] EWCA Civ 217; [2007] Bus LR 1369; [2007] 4 All ER 981;
[2007] ICR 1489; [2007] RPC 30, CA (Civ Div) 3.2
Lotus Development Corpn v Borland International Inc 49 F 3d 807, 34
USPQ 2d 1014 (1st Cir 1995) 3.3

Magill TV Guide/ITP, BBC and RTE, Re [1989] OJ L78/43; [1989] 4
CMLR 757; [1990] FSR 71, Commission Decision 4.2
Merrill Lynch Inc's Application [1989] RPC 561, CA; [1988] RPC 1,
Patents Ct 3.2
Microsoft Corporation v Commission (T-201/04) [2007] ECR II-3601;
[2007] 5 CMLR 11, CFI 1.4.2
Morison v Moat (1851) 9 Hare 241; 68 ER 492 .... 3.4

Navitaire Inc v (1) Easyjet Airline Co Ltd (2) Bulletproof Technologies
Inc [2004] EWHC 1725 (Ch); [2006] RPC 3; [2005] ECC 30; [2005]
ECDR 17; [2005] Info TLR 1; [2006] RPC 3, Ch D 3.3
Nova Productions v Mazooma Games & Ors [2007] EWCA Civ 219;
[2007] Bus LR 1032; [2007] ECC 21; [2007] ECDR 6; [2007] EMLR
14; [2007] Info TLR 15; [2007] RPC 25; (2007) 30(5) IPD 30032, CA
(Civ Div) 3.3

Peabody v Norfolk 98 Mass 452 (1868) 3.4
PRO CD Inc v Zeidenberg No 95-C-0671-C; 86 F 3d 1447; 1996 US App
LEXIS 14951; 39 USPQ 2D (BNA) 1161; Copy L Rep (CCH) P27,529;
29 UCC Rep Serv 2d (Callaghan) 1109 (US 7th Cir CA, 20 June
1996) 2.3.2, 2.3.3

Saphena Computing Ltd v Allied Collection Agencies Ltd [1995] FSR
648, CA (Civ Div); affirming [1995] FSR 616, QBD 3.3
SAS Institute Inc v World Programming Ltd (case C-406-10); [2012] 3
CMLR 4; [2012] ECDR 22, CEC (Grand Chamber) 3.3

SAS Institute Inc v World Programming Ltd [2010] EWHC 1829 (Ch);
    [2011] RPC 1; [2010] ECDR 15; [2010] All ER (D) 151 (Jul), Ch D 3.3
SAS Institute Inc v World Programming Ltd [2013] EWHC 69 (Ch)........ 3.3, 4.3
South West Water Services Ltd v International Computers Ltd [1999]
    BLR 420; [1998-99] Info TLR 154; [1999-2000] Info TLR 1; [1999]
    ITCLR 439; [2001] Lloyd's Rep PN 353; [1999] Masons CLR 400,
    QBD (TCC) 8.1.9
St Albans City & District Council v International Computers Ltd [1996]
    4 All ER 481; [1997-98] Info TLR 58; [1997] FSR 251; (1996) 15 Tr
    LR 444; [1998] Masons CLR Rep 98; (1997) 20(2) IPD 20020, CA (Civ
    Div) .... 1.6, 3.3, 8.1.23, Apps. 4, 6, 8,
    16, 17, 18, 20, 21, 22
State Street Bank & Trust Co v Signature Financial Group Inc 149 F 3d
    1368; 47 USPQ 2d 1596 (Fed Cir Jul 23 1998); Cert denied 525 US
    1093 (1999) 3.2

Tetra Pak II, Re [1992] OJ L72/1; [1992] 4 CMLR 551; [1992] FSR 542,
    Commission Decision.. .... 4.2
Transport for Greater Manchester v Thales Transport & Security Ltd
    [2013] EWHC 149 (TCC) 8.1.44

UsedSoft GmbH v Oracle International Corp (case C-128/11), 3 July
    2012, CEC Grand Chamber... 1.6, 3.3

Watford Electronics Ltd v Sanderson CFL Ltd [2001] EWCA Civ 317,
    [2001] 1 All ER (Comm) 696; [2001] BLR 143; (2001) 3 TCLR 14;
    [2002] FSR 19; [2001] Masons CLR 57; (2001) 98(18) LSG 44, CA
    (Civ Div) .... 8.1.23, 8.1.37, Apps. 4, 6, 8,
    16, 17, 18, 20, 21, 22
Whale Associates Inc v Jaslow Dental Laboratories Inc 609 F Supp 1307;
    225 USPQ 156 (ED Pa 1985) 3.3

Table of Statutes

[All references are to paragraph number]

United Kingdom

Arbitration Act 1996 .... 8.1.42
Computer Misuse Act 1990.... 1.2.5, 3.4
  s 1(1) 3.4
Consumer Credit Act 1974 .... App 21
Contracts (Rights of Third
  Parties) Act 1999 .... 3.6, 8.1.43,
                Apps 1, 4, 6, 8, 10,
                12, 13, 14, 15, 16,
                18, 20, 21, 22, 24,
                25, 28, 32
Copyright Act 1956 .... 3.3
Copyright Designs and Patents
  Act 1988............. 1.2.5, 3.1, 3.8, 4.4
  s 26 .... 3.3
  s 50A....................... 8.1.5.11, App 18
  ss 77–79................................. 3.8
Data Protection Act 1998....... 2.16, 3.4,
            4.10, 4.10.1, 8.1.40,
            8.1.41, Apps 20, 21,
            24, 25, 29, 32
  s 1(1)........................ Apps 4, 6, 8, 10,
            16, 17, 18, 22
  s 68 .... Apps 6, 8, 10,
            16, 17, 18, 22
  Sch 1, Pt 1 .... 8.1.41
  Sch 12........................... Apps 6, 8, 10,
            16, 17, 18, 22
Income and Corporation Taxes
  Act 1988
  s 416 .... App 18
Patents Act 1977 .... 3.1
  s 1(2)(c)................................. 3.2
  s 40(1).................................... 3.2
Police and Justice Act 2006 ...... 3.4

Registered Design Act 1949
  s 1(2)..................................... 3.7
Sale of Goods Act 1979.............. 3.3
  s 12 .... App 29
  s 14 .... Apps 4, 18, 22
Supply of Goods and Services
  Act 1982......................... 3.3, 8.1.17
  s 2 .... App 29
Trade Marks Act 1994 .... 3.1, 3.5
Trade Union Reform and
  Employment Rights Act
  1993 .... App 19
Unfair Contract Terms Act
  1977 .... 8.1.23
  s 11 .... Apps 4, 16, 17,
            20

Germany

Copyright Act
  s 69 .... 3.3

United States

Commercial Code 3.1
Copyright Act 3.1
Patent Act................................. 3.1
Uniform Computer Information
  Transactions Act (UCITA).. 3.6
Uniform Trade Secrets Act 3.1

Table of Statutory Instruments

[All references are to paragraph number]

Consumer Protection (Distance
Selling) Regulations (SI
2000/2334) 4.9
Copyright (Computer
Programs) Regulations
1992 (SI 1992/3233) 4.3,
8.1.5.11, 8.1.5.12,
Apps 4, 6, 18
Duration of Copyright and
Rights in Performances
Regulations 1995 (SI
1995/3297) 4.5

Electronic Signatures
Regulations 2002
(SI 2002/318) 4.8
Transfer of Undertakings
(Protection of
Employment) Regulations
1981 (SI 1981/1794) .... App 19
Unfair Terms in Consumer
Contract Regulations 1994
(SI 1994/3159) 4.7

Table of European Legislation

[All references are to paragraph number]

Regulations

Reg 40/94 (Community Trade
  Marks) (OJ 1994 L11/1)..... 3.5
Reg 1103/97 (Introduction of
  the Euro) (OJ 1997
  L162/1)........................ Apps 4, 12
Reg 2790/1999 (Block
  Exemption for Vertical
  Agreements) (OJ 1999
  L336/21)
  Art 2(2).................................. 4.2
  Art 2(3).................................. 4.2
  Art 3 .... 4.2
Reg 6/2002/EC (Community
  Designs) (CDR) (OJ 2002
  L3/1).................................... 3.7
Reg 772/2004 (Technology
  Transfer Block
  Exemptions)('TTBER') (OJ
  2004 L123/11).................... 4.2
Reg 1907/2006 (Registration,
  Evaluation, Authorisation
  and Restriction of
  Chemicals) (REACH) (OJ
  2006 L220/1)...................... 4.11.6

Directives

Dir 91/250/EEC (Software
  Directive) (OJ 1991
  L122/42).................... 4.3, 8.1.5.11,
                          8.1.5.12, Apps 4,
                          6, 18
  Art 1(2)................................. 3.3
  Art 4(c) 3.3
  Art 5(3)................................. 3.3

Dir 92/100/EEC (Rental
  Lending Directive) (OJ
  1992 L346/61)..................... 4.4
Dir 93/13/EEC (Unfair
  Contract Terms) (OJ 1993
  L95/29)................ 2.3.3, 4.7, 8.1.23
Dir 93/98/EEC (Harmonising
  the Term of Protection of
  Copyright and Certain
  Related Rights) (OJ 1993
  L290/09)............................ 4.5
Dir 95/46/EC (Data Protection)
  (OJ 1995 L281/31)...... 4.10, 4.10.1,
                          4.10.1.1, 8.1.41
  Art 13(1)........................ Apps 24, 31
  Art 15(2)............................... App 24
  Art 25(1)............................... App 31
  Art 25(6)............................... App 24
  Art 26 .. .. 4.10.4
  Art 26(1)................... 4.10.6, 4.10.7
  Art 26(2)...................... 4.10.7, Apps
                          25, 31
  Art 26(4)............................... 4.10.8
  Art 29 .... 4.10.8
  Art 31 .... 4.10.8
Dir 96/9/EC (Legal Protection
  of Databases) (OJ 1996
  L77/20)........................... 1.2.4, 4.6
Dir 97/7/EC (Distance Selling)
  (OJ 1997 L144/19)........... 2.3.3, 4.9
  Art 6 .... 4.9
Dir 98/71/EC (Legal Protection
  of Designs) (OJ 1998
  L289/28)............................ 3.7
Dir 99/93/EC (E-signature
  Directive) (OJ 1999
  L013/12)............................ 4.8
Dir 2001/29/EC (Copyright
  Harmonisation) (OJ 2001
  L167/10)
  Art 2(a)................................. 3.3

Table of European Legislation

Dir 2002/95/EC (Restriction of the Use of Certain Hazardous Substances in Electrical and Electronic Equipment)(ROHS Directive) (OJ 2002 L37/19)........................ 4.11, 4.11.1, 4.11.3, 4.11.5, 4.11.6

Dir 2002/96/EC (Waste Electrical and Electronic Equipment) (WEEE Directive) (OJ 2002 L345/68)..................... 4.11, 4.11.1, 4.11.2, 4.11.4, 4.11.5, 4.11.6, 4.11.7

Dir 2012/19/EU (Waste Electrical and Electronic Equipment) (WEEE Directive) (recast) (OJ 2012 L197/38)..................... 4.11.7

Table of International Treaties and Conventions

[All references are to paragraph number]

Convention for the Protection
of Individuals with
regard to Automatic
Processing of Personal
Data (International Data
Protection Treaty) 4.10, 4.10.1
European Convention for the
Protection of Human
Rights and Fundamental
Freedoms 1950 .... 4.10
European Patents Convention
1973 .... 3.2
Art 52 .... 4.11

Geneva Act of the Hague
Agreement concerning the
International Registration
of Industrial Designs 3.7
Treaty of Rome
Art 81 .... 4.1, 4.2, 8.1.5.3
Art 82 ....1.4.2, 4.1, 4.2,
8.1.5.3
Treaty on the Functioning of
the European Union
Art 101 .... 4.1, 4.2, 8.1.5.3
Art 102 .... 4.1, 4.2, 8.1.5.3
Universal Copyright
Convention 1952 .... 3.3

Part I
Introduction

1 Understanding software licence agreements

1.1 WHAT IS A SOFTWARE LICENCE AGREEMENT?

At the core of software and software contracts is the legal concept of copyright. Copyright (as it applies to software) is the right for the owner or licensed proprietor to prevent anyone from copying their software without paying something for it. Since the use of software requires copying to occur, then any user of software must have permission to use and thereby copy such software.

A software licence agreement authorises someone to do something with software which would otherwise be an infringement of copyright. The party granting this authorisation is known as the 'licensor' while the party receiving the authorisation is known as the 'licensee'.

The licensor may own all rights to the software, or may have the permission of the owner to enter into licence agreements with others. The licensee may be:

— a user of the software;

— a distributor of the software;

— a publisher of the software;

— a website owner or host;

— a party who modifies, translates, or adds codes to the software;

— a party who makes copies of the software for its owner or a distributor;

— an original equipment manufacturer;

— a value added reseller;

— a joint venture partner;

— an independent maintenance company;

— a facilities management company;

— a technology escrow agent;

— an independent training company; or

— an independent sales representative or agent.

In general, if the software in question is protected by patent, copyright, or trade secret law, the licence agreement allows the licensee to deal with the software as specified in the licence grant provision of the agreement without infringing the licensor's copyright or patent rights, and/or without misappropriating the licensor's trade secrets. The agreement addresses other topics as well, such as payment and warranties. Sometimes maintenance and training will be addressed in the licence agreement and sometimes they will be covered by separate agreements. Whatever its other terms might be, the agreement will virtually always specify the rights conveyed to the licensee and the restrictions imposed on the licensee regarding the licensed software.

An agreement that licenses one or more copies of software is different from an agreement that sells one or more copies. When copies of software are sold, the purchaser takes title to the copies. One analogy is the purchase of a book at a bookshop. The purchaser can do many things with the purchased book, for example, he can resell the copy, lend it to a friend, or give it away. However, the purchaser cannot reprint the book, and cannot sell or make copies if the item is protected by an intellectual property law such as copyright. Such a reproduction and distribution would constitute copyright infringement if the purchaser did not have the permission of the copyright owner to reproduce the item and sell it commercially. Thus, when goods that are protected by copyright are purchased, title to the copy purchased does not give the purchaser complete freedom to do whatever he or she desires with the copy. There is an invisible, legal string attached to such goods that makes certain actions involving the purchased copy illegal.

In contrast, when copies of software are licensed, the licensee often does not obtain title to the licensed copy. Instead, the licensee obtains possession of one or more copies of the licensed software and gains certain specified rights to deal with the licensed copy or copies under the terms of the software licence agreement. There are exceptions to the general rule about the licensee not taking title to a licensed copy of software which are explained later. For this introduction, it is sufficient to note the general key difference between a software sale agreement and a software licence agreement: the former passes title while the latter does not. In addition, because licence agreements often contain limitations on the licensee's ability to deal with licensed software, the legal string mentioned above is usually stronger when affixed to licensed copies than it is on purchased copies of software.

One related point is important to our introductory discussion. There is a major difference between purchasing the intellectual property rights in software, on the one hand, and purchasing or licensing a copy of software, on the other. If the software is protected by copyright, to continue our book analogy, then the difference is between purchasing the copyright for the book and purchasing a copy of the book. In other words, the copyright owner can sell and you can buy copies of an item protected by copyright, but that purchase does not make you the copyright owner. Owning a copy of a book or software is not the same as owning the copyright for the book or software. Copyright is an asset of its owner and can be disposed of in the same manner as other assets, for example, when you sell assets of a company or sell all shares or stock in a company.

To continue further with the book analogy, if there is copyright in a book written by one author, then the writing on the pages is the expression of the idea or creativity behind the book but there is also copyright in the creativity or style if it can be expressed in writing. To this end the printed pages are like object code and the creativity, style and idea are like source code.

You should be aware that there is a difference between a software developer, a software publisher and a software distributor. A software developer is a party that creates software. A software publisher may create software, may acquire it from developers, or may do both. In any event the publisher will reproduce copies of the software or have them reproduced, will stock inventory of the software, and will promote its distribution. Most publishers distribute software as well. A software distributor acquires software from publishers and usually stocks an inventory, but always distributes copies by one or more methods, for instance, sales representatives, mail order, etc.

These differences have close parallels in the book publishing industry. A software publisher acquires its rights to the software in question from the developer just as a book publisher acquires its rights to books from authors. One difference between book publishers and software publishers is that book authors are rarely employed by the publishers of their books while it is more common for software developers to be individuals employed by the publishers of their software. It is also common for the developer to be an independent author like a typical book author. However, these independent developers are often corporations rather than individuals. Individual developers are most frequently found in the arena of home or school use microcomputer software. An independent software distributor is very much like an independent book distributor. Of course, there are exceptions to these general arrangements.

1.2 WHAT TYPES OF SOFTWARE AND DATABASES ARE DISTRIBUTED UNDER CONTRACT AND WHAT LAWS PROTECT THEM?

1.2.1 Mainframe and minicomputer software

Most mainframe computer and minicomputer software is distributed under a contract, and is also protected by trade secret law. In the United States patent law is used increasingly in lieu of trade secret law, and copyright law is infrequently used in conjunction with trade secret law and more reliance is placed upon copyright law, trade secret law and contract law. In the United Kingdom and the rest of the European Union, patent law is still not the primary source of intellectual property right protection. Contract law provides protection because such software is typically licensed to users.

1.2.2 Microcomputer software

Certain types of microcomputer software are distributed under contracts. Most microcomputer software is protected by copyright law. However, the laws and mechanisms selected to protect microcomputer software will vary; for example, some is licensed and hence protected by contract law if the licence agreement is valid and enforceable and some microcomputer software is sold, like books, without an accompanying user contract, and hence is not protected by contract law.

For example, very expensive or novel microcomputer programs may be protected by trade secret law, or patent law might be used, but copyright protection combined with trade secret protection is common. Usually such software is marketed under a licence agreement signed by the end user.

For typical microcomputer business applications, copyright and trade secret law are often used in combination. Such software is usually marketed under a licence agreement that is not signed by the user. The enforceability of these agreements in the absence of validating legislation is questionable. In the United States some patent protection for parts or all of these programs is evident in the marketplace.

For home, educational or entertainment programs, copyright law is often used in combination with some effort to protect through trade secret and trademark law. Such software is usually marketed by selling copies, not through licensing copies. Such sales can be compared to selling copies of books except that trade secret protection is not available for commercially published books. In addition, there is a significant volume of unprotected 'freeware' or 'public domain' software available through libraries, electronic e-bulletin boards, trade publications and other sources.

1.2.3 Commercially available software

Trademark and unfair competition law are important to the businesses of software, computer and database providers, for example, to their identity, quality image, and sales; but trademark law and unfair competition law do not directly protect the content or expression of products as do patent, copyright and trade secret law, except perhaps in some misappropriation situations, for example, the misappropriation and publication of news in a database before it is published by the source of the news.

1.2.4 Commercially available databases

Databases generally available to the public for a fee are protected by various bodies of law and contracts depending upon circumstances such as the method of dissemination, the value, user rights, etc, for example:

- If microfiche is the medium, copyright protection often is used exclusively. Often copies of the microfiche and its data content are sold, sometimes the data is licensed under a licence agreement.

- If printed copies or reports are marketed, copyright protection often is used exclusively. If the data is licensed, trade secret and contract protection may be attempted.

- If a computer tape, a disk or a CD-ROM is the medium, often copyright and trade secret protection are used, especially if the data access code is recorded on the tape, disk or CD-ROM. Usually the data is licensed under the terms of a licence agreement.

- If the data is made available through a closed telecommunications network with a host computer, usually copyright protection is used and usually the data is licensed. Trade secret protection may be attempted.

- If the data is made available through the internet or online networks usually copyright protection is used and usually the data is licensed under contractual terms and conditions often contained in a click-wrap contract. Trade secret protection may be attempted.

EC Directive 96/9 on the Legal Protection of Databases[1] introduced a new *sui generis* right of protection of 15 years in addition to copyright. This Directive will be discussed in Part II, SECTION 4.6.

1   OJ 1996 L77/20.

1.2.5   Non-contract protection

Tort law and/or criminal law offer some redress for the theft, disruption or destruction of software or databases under certain circumstances. For example, many jurisdictions have adopted computer virus legislation that makes a variety of types of computer tampering a criminal offence. In the UK the Computer Misuse Act 1990 specifically addresses the question of hacking in that three offences exist namely:

—   unauthorised access to computer material;

—   unauthorised access with intent to commit or facilitate the commission of further offences; and

—   unauthorised modification.

Further civil and criminal law remedies for infringement of copyright in computer programs is available under the Copyright Designs and Patents Act 1988.

1.3   GENERAL COMMENTS

While the primary focus of this work is software licence agreements in the context of a major acquisition, distribution arrangement, development project, or conversion project, many comments are offered regarding computers and databases accompanied by licensed software. Advice is given in relation to other types of computer contract such as maintenance and support agreements, outsourcing agreements and escrow, and numerous parallels are drawn between software providers on the one hand and computer and database providers on the other. The term 'provider' is preferred in this work because software is available from different types of sources: developers, publishers, distributors, retailers, mail order houses, computer vendors, database publishers, bulletin boards, etc. 'Provider' encompasses all sources. As used in this work, either the type of provider in question will be clear from the context, or the term will have a typical meaning of publisher, distributor, computer vendor that distributes software, etc.

References in this work to a customer's 'technical staff' or 'technical personnel' are meant to refer to members of a company's data processing staff, programming staff, consultants in technical areas, or management information services department, and are intended to encompass their managers, directors, etc. 'Customer' is used in this book rather than 'user', except on occasion, because customer has a broader meaning. For example, a publisher may be a customer for a software developer, but not a user of the developed software. The context in which 'customer' is used should make its meaning clear. 'Price' as used herein is meant to include purchase price, licence fee, service charge, etc, depending on the context.

1.4 GOALS AND PURPOSES OF PARTIES TO A SOFTWARE LICENCE AGREEMENT

1.4.1 In general

The goals and purposes of the parties to a software licence agreement vary according to a number of factors, but some generalisations can be made. Software providers in Western countries are motivated by profit. Software costs money to develop and distribute. A new microcomputer business application may cost half a million pounds or many times that amount to develop and market. Mainframe programs often cost even more.

Software licensees are not uniform in their goals and purposes. Commercial users of application programs, operating systems, databases, and computers, generally want results. That is, such users have more or less specific results in mind when they acquire a new application, or switch to a new operating system. The desired results may be processing customer orders faster, inventory control, e-mail, improved secretary efficiency, improved response times, a more capable system that does new things, reduction of current processing costs, etc. These desired results are the business and/or technical reasons for licensing commercially used software. Of course, many commercial users also desire maintenance-free software that requires little or no operator training and hope for a good relationship with the software provider, but some problems in these and other areas usually will be tolerated if the more specific major business or technical results are produced.

In contrast, the traditional position of both software and computer providers is that they provide solutions which the customer is responsible for selecting and operating so as to produce whatever results are desired. The goal of the commercial customer to receive results and the purpose of software, database, and computer providers to furnish a solution are inconsistent even though some solutions sometimes provide the desired result. This insight is important to your understanding of software, database, and computer transactions.

Licensee-distributors have different goals from licensee-users. A distributor falls into the category of profit-motivated software providers. Like others in this group, the licensee is interested in moving products out of the door and into the hands of the user. Thus, you can see that the goals and purposes of all licensees are not the same because different types of licensees deal with software in different ways.

Another major goal of parties to a software licence agreement merits attention. Software providers want to minimise potential liability. A liability determination in litigation may lead to bad publicity that hurts business. Damage awards can wipe out profits and push a company into bankruptcy. Minimising the risk of legal liability is a goal of the software provider in software licence agreements.

In contrast, a software user wants to quietly enjoy his licensed software free of any concerns about liability arising from its operation. Sophisticated software users ensure that their licence agreement makes the software provider responsible for the most likely risks of legal liability arising from the exercise of the users' licensed rights.

There are other goals and purposes that could be mentioned, but these suffice to illustrate the differences in the parties' outlooks.

In general the software provider wants to make profit from supplying a solution to the customer's needs (with software being the medium and the object of the solution) and without incurring the burden of ongoing responsibility and liability to the customer. The customer wants to get his needs satisfied fully by the software he is obtaining and paying for with the maximum performance and ongoing support from the provider.

1.4.2 Why are software licence agreements required by many software providers?

As we observed earlier, software is an asset. It can be protected by contract provisions, patent law (sometimes), copyright law (often), and trade secret law (fairly often). Assuming the software in question is protected by copyright law, the owner of a copy is allowed to transfer that copy to others without the copyright owner's permission or knowledge. If all software were sold, the owner of each copy could deprive the copyright owner of much needed revenue by transferring his copy to another after a period of use. If the software could not be transferred, the second user would have to acquire a copy in the marketplace, thereby improving the copyright owner's profits. The only way the copyright owner can prohibit such a transfer under current law is by means of contract restrictions on a licensee. The desire to maximise revenue leads a copyright owner to license his software rather than sell copies.

In addition, if object code is distributed rather than source code, the owner can claim trade secret protection for his program. Unfortunately for the owner, trade secret law allows reverse engineering through disassembly or decompilation. The trade secret owner can, subject to certain statutory exceptions in EU member states, prohibit reverse engineering of distributed copies through restrictions in licence agreements. The desire to prohibit reverse engineering leads the owner to license his software rather than sell copies.

This desire to prohibit reverse engineering is prompted by the realisation that the ideas discovered from a decompiled or disassembled program can be used by a current or future competitor in a competing product, and can be disseminated to users by trade publications or on bulletin boards, any one of which reduces the owner's revenue flow. The software business is hard enough without giving away your trade secrets.

While there are other reasons, such as minimising legal risks through protective contract provisions, these are two of the main reasons why software licence agreements are required by many software providers.

In the case of *Microsoft Corporation v Commission case T-201/04*,[1] the Court of First Instance rejected the appeal by Microsoft against the European Commissioner's decision in 2004 that Microsoft had abused its dominant position under Article 82 of the Treaty of Rome.

The case originated from a complaint from Sun Microsystems that Microsoft had refused to provide it with interoperability information which Sun required in order to develop its server products so as to operate effectively with Microsoft's Windows PC operating system. After several years of investigation, the Commission adopted a Decision, finding that Microsoft had abused its dominant position in the marketplace and in particular that Microsoft's refusal to make available interoperability information was anticompetitive. Microsoft, amongst other things, was fined €497,192,304 and ordered to cease its anticompetitive practices.

Microsoft's appeal to the Court of First Instance was based on a number of points but in essence Microsoft claimed that the Commission had been incorrect in its assessment of the law relating to interoperability and bundling and further, that the imposition of a fine was illegal.

For the computer industry, the issues surrounding the abuse of dominant position and also that of interoperability data are important.

At a time when many software companies are moving to more open solutions, it is unusual for a major software vendor to totally ring-fence its products and use intellectual property rights as a mechanism to prevent competitors or perceived competitors from interfacing their products.

The right to reverse analyse where interoperability data is necessary is an enshrined right under European law and arises because the European Commission recognised many years ago that dominant technology companies could stifle competition and innovation by ring-fencing their technology and refusing to make interoperability data available to other developers. Microsoft's refusal to make data available to Sun was in itself anticompetitive as confirmed by the Court of First Instance.

The recent court decision requires detailed analysis but in the short term it is sufficient to say that the licensing practices of software companies continue to require audit and analysis in order to ensure compliance with EU law.

While there are other reasons, such as minimising legal risks through protective contract provisions, these are two of the main reasons why software licence agreements are required by many software providers.

1   [2007] ECR II-3601.

1.5   SOME DIFFERENCES BETWEEN SOFTWARE SALE, LEASE AND LICENCE TRANSACTIONS

1.5.1   Legal concepts and characteristics

As the introduction explained, there are significant differences between software sales and software licences. A software lease is also different from both. It is important that you understand the basic differences and similarities of these transactions. The following chart summarises their fundamental characteristics and compares them to similar transactions.

Subject Matter Activity	Sale	Lease	Licence
Property	Legal title, risk and possession passes	Leasehold title, risk and possession passes; freehold does not	Limited right of use granted only; risk and possession passes
Equipment	Legal title, risk and possession passes	Possession and risk passes, but the title does not	Limited right of use granted only; risk and possession passes
IPR	Legal title to copyright, trademarks, patents and risk and possession passes	N/A	Limited right of use granted only; risk and possession passes

Subject Matter Activity	Sale	Lease	Licence
Copy of Software Product	Legal title and risk in the media and possession passes, but IPR and title in software remains with setter/owner	Possession and risk passes on strict terms for a fixed period subject to regular payments	Limited right of use of copy granted only; risk and possession passes

1.5.2 Legal concept of sale

Nature: a sale conveys title or ownership, which is a property interest. The rights to possess and use the purchased item are part of the ownership rights, as are the rights to resell or otherwise dispose of the purchased item.

● **Sell equipment:** title passes to purchaser.

● **Sell intellectual property rights:** title to copyright, patent, trademark, or trade secret passes to purchaser.

● **Sell a copy of software:** title to the copy passes to the purchaser, but the seller retains ownership of the intellectual property rights in the copy, for example, patent, copyright, trademark, etc.

1.5.3 Legal concept of lease

Nature: a lease conveys the right to possess and use, but not to resell or otherwise distribute the leased item. No title passes. A lease is primarily a financing arrangement that conveys property interests. Thus it could be argued that a lease is a mixed property law and financing concept.

● **Property lease:** transfers a leasehold title to property giving the right to occupy the premises upon payment of rent. Title does not pass but an option to purchase the freehold may be included in the lease.

● **Equipment lease:** conveys a personal property right to possess and use the leased equipment upon payment of rent. Title does not pass but an option to purchase may be included in the transaction.

● **Software lease:** conveys a personal property right to possess and use the leased software upon payment of rent. Title does not pass as a part of the lease transaction. If the software is protected by copyright and trade secret law, the lessee should also have an express or implied intellectual property right licence to possess and use the intellectual property or protected technology in the software. The lessee often obtains this licence directly from the intellectual property right licensor who may or may not be the lessor as well. Independent, third-party software lessors are increasingly noticeable in the marketplace, as are financing companies who finance software licence fees receivable.

The personal property right to possess and use a copy of software under a lease is theoretically different from a right to possess and use all intellectual property in the software. This may sound like a difference without a distinction. If the lessor and the licensor are the same party, or the lessor has permission from the licensor to license the software to the lessee-licensee, then the theoretical difference is not noticeable as a practical matter. Also, a lease can be viewed as conveying an implied licence. To illustrate, assume that the software is a mainframe program protected by trade secret law and that the lessee-user finances possession and use of the software under a lease, but does not obtain the trade secret owner's permission to possess and use the trade secrets in the software under a licence. The very existence of a lease can easily be viewed to imply that it conveys to the lessee-user both personal property and intellectual property rights to possess and use the leased software. Also, the lessor may convey both types of rights expressly or by implication in the lease. If the lessor owns the trade secrets or has the permission of the trade secret owner to grant the user licence, then there is no problem. However, independent lessors who convey express or implied licences must be careful to obtain permission to do so.

One situation where the trade secret licensor may argue that the lessee has no right to possess and use its intellectual property in the leased software arises when the original lessee-licensee-user subleases the software to a third party, for example, a company spun off from the lessee-licensee, with the approval of an independent lessor, but without the knowledge or contractually required approval of the trade secret licensor. Generally speaking, the owner of trade secrets must know who has copies and grant permission for their possession and use in order to preserve their status as trade secrets.

1.5.4 Legal concept of licence

A licence conveys a personal privilege or right to do one or more things with the licensed item, for example, to possess it; to use it; to make or reproduce it; to distribute one or more copies by specified means (for example, sale, license, etc); publicly to display or operate the licensed item; to prepare modified versions or translations of the licensed item; etc. A licence agreement usually incorporates payment terms and hence is like a financing arrangement, but it can be used to convey more than the rights to possess, use, resell or otherwise dispose of the licensed item. For example, a licence of software can convey to the licensee the right to prepare a foreign language translation of the software, or a right to make many copies of the software and distribute them commercially. In the absence of a licence grant authorising them, the purchaser or the lessee of a copy of copyrighted software cannot do these things without infringing the copyright in the software.

● Property licence: grants limited right to use and not possess, real property. No property right is conveyed as a part of this privilege of use. This privilege is revocable but unassignable except for prior written agreement.

- Software licence: assuming the software is protected by intellectual property law, the licence grant conveys permission for possession and specified conduct with respect to the software. Use may or may not be allowed, depending on the type of licence agreement. For example, a distributor may be licensed to distribute copies supplied to him, but not licensed to use a copy of the software in his business.

1.6 WEAKNESSES OF THE SOFTWARE LICENCE CONCEPT

Many legal concepts are defeasible concepts. In other words, they are capable of being defeated by certain circumstances. For example, the concept of a contract is defeated if there is no consideration to support the parties' agreement. The concept of a software licence embedded in a contract called a software licence agreement is likewise defeated, or nullified, if the agreement is not valid. Generally speaking, an offer, its acceptance, and consideration are required to create a valid contract.

The existence of a software licence can also be destroyed by other circumstances. A software licence agreement may qualify as a valid and enforceable contract in every legal sense, but it may be characterised by a court as a valid and enforceable sale contract rather than a valid and enforceable licence agreement. For example, a licence grant in a software licence agreement can be adulterated to the point of destruction by sale language in the agreement. In its pristine form the concept of a licence does not pass title. A sale passes title. If a software licence agreement contains the terms 'sale' or 'purchase' or 'purchaser', the licence concept underlying the licence grant is adulterated. One, or more, uses of such terms anywhere in a software licence agreement may cause a court to characterise the contract as a software sale agreement.

Another example of massive licence grant and underlying concept adulteration is a perpetual term in a software licence agreement. If the licensee can keep the software forever after payment of a fee, a court may decide that there is no substantive difference between the so-called licence agreement and a sale agreement as will be discussed later in this section in the case of *UsedSoft GmbH v Oracle International Corp.*[1]

Mass-market software such as shrink-wrapped business software and leisure or entertainment software often contain licence grant terms such as 'a perpetual royalty free non-exclusive transferable licence' and is 'sold for a once only retail price'. Notwithstanding that the only part of the product which is a 'good' is the media upon which or within which the software is embodied, to all intents and purposes the whole item is perceived as a 'good' which in consumer terms involves a number of implied statutory rights which might not be included in a 'supply' or true licensing situation.

Similarly, a licence grant can be destroyed by the actions of the licensor. If the licensed software is advertised or promoted as software that is sold or purchased, such advertising or promotion is inconsistent with the legal concept of a licence that underlies the grant provision in a software licence agreement. It serves as a notice that the licensor really believes he is selling copies, and creates customer expectations that title to a copy will be acquired when a copy is acquired. Almost any advertising or promotion of sold or purchased copies contaminates the licence grant sufficiently that a court might characterise the software licence agreement as a software sale agreement.

Courts pay heed to substance over form, and substance includes more than the title given to a contract. The case of *St Albans City and District Council v International Computers Ltd*[2] has amongst other things, decided that software is 'goods' as much as the media upon or within which the software program is supplied, unless the language of the licence agreement clearly specifies that the media is 'sold' and the program and the user manual is 'licensed and supplied' only.

Thus, in order for a software licence agreement to be analysed by a court as such, the agreement must be a valid, unadulterated, and uncontaminated contract. The legal concept of a sale is stronger than the legal concept of a licence and they are inconsistent concepts. The concept of a licensed copy of software will be overcome by the concept of a sold copy of software if the software licence agreement is invalid (defeated), adulterated (not genuine), or contaminated by actions outside of the agreement's terms (not pure, ie not treated as a software licence transaction).

In contrast, the concept of a software lease is consistent with the concept of a software licence. Where the licence is a licence to possess and use, a software lease is virtually identical to a software licence. The lease conveys a personal property right to possess and use the leased item and the licence conveys an intellectual property right to possess and use the licensed intellectual property. Both finance or may be viewed as financing the acquisition and use of the software, especially if a licence agreement calls for more than one payment. The very existence of such a lease may be interpreted to convey such a licence. However, the concept of a software licence is broader than the concept of a software lease because the licence concept is not limited to usage: it can cover reproduction, distribution, etc. In addition, a software licence agreement is not always a financing vehicle. Royalty-free licences are granted in some situations where non-monetary consideration is involved.

In mass-market software products the language of the transaction and marketing invariably includes the words 'sale', 'product', 'sale price', 'goods' and as a consequence a court will more likely than not imply statutory rights attaching to the sale of goods rather than the supply of resources and materials.

As referred to above, the judgment in *UsedSoft GmbH v Oracle International Corp* confirms that the author of software cannot oppose the resale of 'used' licences allowing the use of such programs downloaded from the internet. The exclusive right of distribution of a copy of a computer program covered by such a licence is exhausted on its first sale. Briefly the facts were that Oracle developed and distributed online computer programs functioning as 'client/server software'. The customer of such a program was entitled to download it on the basis of a licence agreement for an unlimited period exclusively for the customers' internal business purposes. UsedSoft was a German business which marketed software licences acquired from customers of Oracle by which customers of UsedSoft were able to download a copy of the program from Oracle's website after acquiring a 'used' licence. Oracle brought proceedings against UsedSoft in the German courts seeking an order for it to cease its marketing and sales practices.

In its judgment the European Court of Justice explained that 'the principle of exhaustion of the distribution right applies not only where the copyright holder markets copies of his software on a material medium (CD Rom or DVD) but also where he distributes them by means of downloads from his website. Where the copyright holder makes available to his customer a copy – tangible or intangible – and at the same time concludes, in return for payment of a fee, a licence agreement granting the customer the right to use that copy for an unlimited period, that right holder sells the copy to the customer and thus exhausts his exclusive distribution right'.

The case above indicates, amongst other things, that perpetual licences will almost certainly be perceived as a sale rather than a licence and software owners should consider licensing on a fixed-term basis in order to prevent the exhaustion of the distribution right.

1 Court of Justice of the European Union 3 July 2012 judgment in case C/128/11.
2 [1996] 4 All ER 481.

2 Some general types of software licence agreements

2.1 DEVELOPER-PUBLISHER LICENCE AGREEMENTS

A developer-publisher licence agreement is an important type of software licence agreement for all categories of software: mainframe, minicomputer, and microcomputer. In the microcomputer software arena, these contracts are commonplace but vary in their approach to significant terms. For example, the licence grant may transfer the developer's copyright interest to the publisher, or the publisher may acquire an exclusive licence to distribute the software during the term of the licence agreement. Often such agreements cover several programs and it is not unusual for such agreements to cover several machine types or versions of each program, for example, a Mac and an IBM version of each program developed.

Sophisticated developers require minimum royalty payments in these agreements plus an advance royalty payment that is returned at a rate of less than 100% of all royalties earned so that the developer receives some incremental revenue from initial copies distributed. Sophisticated developers will limit the geographical scope of the licence grant and reserve the right to market some machine types, media types, or foreign language translations directly or through other publishers.

Sophisticated publishers will set milestones for the development of each version of each program and insist that royalty advances are divided into payments that are tied to the milestones, for example, that become due only upon the publishers' acceptance or approval of the developers' work product or progress required by the milestones. Negotiations also occur over advance payments that are not recoverable as advance royalties.

In these agreements publishers must be careful to obtain the rights they need to distribute the programs as planned, to obtain warranties on all programs, to address maintenance responsibilities, to address enhancement development, etc. Developers must be careful to retain rights to their libraries or 'tool kits' of software. For example, a developer may write a component of a program known as an 'engine' for use in many programs, intending for each program ordered by various publishers to contain the engine. This component should be licensed on a non-exclusive basis so that it can be licensed to many publishers. An exclusive licence or assignment precludes multiple uses of such a component.

In the mainframe software arena, computer vendors often assume the role of software publishers contracting with developers and customers for publication rights. Mainframe computer users commonly write or have their computer vendor's programmers write or assist in the development of unique applications or utilities. Sometimes the computer vendor will desire marketing rights for such programs in order to enlarge its libraries of software offered to other customers. Here the customer almost always retains ownership of the new program and grants distribution rights to the vendor. The vendor may pay a royalty, but more often provides the customer with 25-50% discount on future purchases up to a specified ceiling of discount pounds or for specified equipment or service purchases.

There are many other situations, patterns, and exceptions in the general area of software development and publishing. Changes in these patterns occur from time to time and these customs are not uniform throughout the world. In general, however, developer-publisher licence agreements exist because one party develops or contracts for the development of software but has no interest in attempting to market the software developed, while another party wants to market new programs as part of its mainstream business but would not undertake internal development of the program in question for one or more reasons.

Remember that development projects are seldom completed on schedule, that they often generate disputes, and that litigation often arises in relation to failure to deliver on time or failure to match specification. Developer-publisher arrangements are complex transactions that call for careful thought, attention, and negotiations by both parties. It is highly desirable to build dispute resolution mechanisms into the software development agreement rather than ignore the potential for problems in developer-publisher relationships. Also, acquiring outside help in negotiating and drafting your agreement is often prudent and well worth the cost.

Finally, it is important to ensure from the customer's point of view that the contract contains a rolling transfer of the ownership during and after development of the program where it is agreed title to the program will pass. If the publisher needs ownership of IPR in the program it needs this in the part-developed program as well as the finished program, because if the publisher has to terminate the contract before the program is completed, say for persistent failure of the developer to 'hit milestones' then the publisher needs title to the part-developed program in order to get the work completed elsewhere. To the extent that core technology of the developer will never be released, perhaps a source code escrow needs negotiating so that underlying technology can be used to complete the program.

2.2 PUBLISHER-DISTRIBUTOR LICENCE AGREEMENTS

2.2.1 Domestic distributors, OEMs and VARs

UK software publishers typically distribute copies of software through various means. Mainframe software publishers employ representatives to market their products directly to users.

Microcomputer software publishers can afford the overhead costs of an extensive in-house representative force only if many of their products are relatively expensive. Such programs might have licence fees ranging between £5,000 and £30,000, for example. Most microcomputer software publishers market less expensive products and hence cannot support many, if any, in-house representatives. As a result of this factor and others, such as an understandable desire to maximise market penetration, recover research and development costs, and maximise profit, many microcomputer software publishers market their products through original equipment manufacturers ('OEMs'), value added resellers ('VARs'), and distributors with their own sales forces. National accounts are also of major importance to many microcomputer software publishers. Large retailers with chains of outlets in several regions are the typical account for such publishers. In fact, one of the major decisions facing such publishers in the context of marketing strategy is whether to distribute their products exclusively through distributors, through distributors and OEMs or VARs, through national accounts as well as distributors, OEMs and VARs, through mail order, through independent sales representatives, or through some other mechanism or combination of means.

One of the recurring legal problems arising from the use of multiple distributors, OEMs, VARs, national accounts, independent sales representatives and combinations of these and others to market software is the publisher's failure to keep the contracts with each of these parties consistent. Contracts are written so that national accounts encroach on distributors' territories, so that OEMs and VARs violate sales representatives' exclusive rights to market to specified types of customers, etc. In the EU certain exclusive distribution arrangements may be in breach of competition laws. Often these inconsistencies arise because of a lack of attention to such details by management, but they are notorious as the source of problems for microcomputer software publishers, microcomputer manufacturers, CD-ROM database publishers, etc. In-house or outside legal and administrative personnel can help maintain consistency in such agreements and cost less than the damages awarded or settlements paid when no one oversees contract consistency.

Another major area of concern in domestic distribution arrangements of many types is protection of the publisher's intellectual property rights. Without a carefully drafted software licence agreement for the arrangement, a publisher could find the trade secrets embedded in his code entering the public domain, he could lose his rights in his trademarks on the product, and he could lose the ability to recover copyright infringement damages from software pirates. Intellectual property law protections available for the protection of software assets function under specific conditions, limitations and restrictions. Software publishers who desire to protect their assets should gain a basic understanding of these legal protections and employ competent help to safeguard their software assets.

Distributors have their own legal concerns, such as ensuring proper calculation and receipt of payment through clear payment terms in their agreements with publishers. One of the growing items of concern for distributors, OEMs, VARs, and others who market software published by others is the possibility of product liability claims against the distributor as well as the publisher in connection with certain types of software, for example, software that operates medical examination or treatment equipment, software used to design buildings, etc. Product liability insurance and carefully drafted contracts that protect the distributor from such claims as much as possible are increasingly important.

2.2.2 Foreign distributors, OEMs and VARs

UK software publishers often have the opportunity to distribute their products abroad during the first few years of operation. Mainframe software publishers vary in their approach to international distribution. Some companies work through agents, distributors, or joint ventures in foreign countries.

Microcomputer software publishers use widely diverse means to distribute their products abroad. Only a small percentage of such publishers can afford to pay a sales staff in foreign countries so it is common for UK microcomputer software to be distributed to foreign nationals by mail, telecommunications, distributors, agents, OEMs, VARs, joint ventures, etc.

Another factor unique to foreign distribution arrangements is the impact of the laws of the countries of the software users and of some international treaties on the validity of international distribution contracts, on the effectiveness and operation of specific terms and conditions, and on the protection of UK publishers' intellectual property rights in their software. Patent, copyright and trademark treaties can help UK software publishers protect their programs in countries that are signatories to the treaties provided the requirements of local laws are satisfied. The United Nations Convention on the International Sale of Goods can influence not only computer and software sales, but also some software distribution and user licence agreements. In general, UK software publishers can be unpleasantly surprised by foreign laws and the operation of treaties on their international transactions as easily as they can be pleasantly surprised if they do not learn how these laws and treaties affect their business before they distribute their products abroad.

Other major factors that may influence foreign disseminations of software in some countries include foreign tax requirements, statutory requirements for extra-contractual termination payments, restrictions on the repatriation of funds, and limitations on the validity of exclusive relationships, to name a few.

2.3   USER LICENCE AGREEMENTS

2.3.1   Signed licence agreements

User licence agreements typically give a computer user a conditional right to use the licensed software and no right to distribute it. The common conditions on continued use include timely licence fee payments, continued compliance with a prohibition on reverse engineering, continued compliance with restrictions on the transfer of the licensed copy, use of the software on only one computer, at only one computer site, etc. Mainframe software publishers typically require signed licence agreements with their customers before they deliver programs. These agreements may be negotiated on one or more points prior to customer acceptance, and they are often valid and enforceable contracts. Even if these contracts are pre-printed documents that are signed unchanged, they will normally be enforceable against a mainframe computer user. Of course, there are noteworthy exceptions to this general rule.

2.3.2   Shrink-wrap licence agreements

Many microcomputer software publishers distribute their products under different types of contracts. Publishers of expensive microcomputer programs can afford to have employees call on prospective customers, negotiate terms, and obtain signatures on contracts.

More common business applications, educational and entertainment programs rarely generate sufficient revenue to support a nationwide field sales force. Such programs are generally marketed through sales staff, distributors, VARs, OEMs, etc. Attempts to have retail clerks obtain signatures on licence agreements were failures. Users shopping in retail stores usually preferred to acquire another package whose publisher did not require a signed licence agreement, or to acquire the same package in another store whose assistants did not insist upon a signed contract as a condition to its acquisition. To increase the likelihood of research and development cost recovery, to maximise licence fees, and in an attempt to maximise legal protections, publishers of business applications and utilities employed 'shrink-wrap' licence agreements. The most common version of a shrink-wrap licence agreement appears on the outside of the box or container for the software and can be read through a clear plastic wrapper around the box or container.

In contrast, most publishers of educational and entertainment software programs elected to sell copies of their software and ignored the use of a shrink-wrap licence agreement. Thus, you can buy copies of such programs in the same way you can buy copies of books in a book store. Such programs are typically distributed in object code and protected by copyright law. The use of software locks, keys and dongles as an added safeguard against piracy is common.

Shrink-wrap licence agreements attempt to accomplish many of the same things that signed licence agreements attempt to accomplish. Payment terms, restrictions on usage, and prohibitions on licensee transfers, loans, rentals, etc, of the licensed copy of software are common to both types of agreements. Prohibitions on reverse engineering, limited warranties, limitations of liability, consequential damages exclusions, and limitations on recoverable damages are also common to both types of agreements. The major difference between a signed licence agreement and a shrink-wrap licence agreement is that the latter is not signed by the user, hence the validity of the shrink-wrap licence agreement is more open to question than the typical signed licence agreement.

Shrink-wrap licence agreements typically provide that opening the package or using the software constitutes acceptance of the agreements' terms and conditions. The problem with this concept is not that one's actions cannot signify contract acceptance, rather that there is probably no 'meeting of the minds' between the licensor and the user. Users typically believe they are purchasing copies of software bearing shrink-wrap licence agreements. At least some users would not acquire such software if they thought they were not purchasing the copy acquired. Actions signifying a meeting of the minds between two parties can constitute contract acceptance, but generally the actions must clearly signify that meeting of the minds before a valid contract is formed.

Another traditional criticism of shrink-wrap licence agreements is that they are contracts of adhesion. In other words, when one party has a far superior bargaining position and can force contract terms on the other by adopting a take-it-or-leave-it stance, a court may decide it is against public policy to enforce such a contract of 'adhesion'. Such decisions are most common when the party in the inferior bargaining position is a consumer and the party in the superior bargaining position is a merchant. Because the party acquiring microcomputer software bearing a shrink-wrap licence agreement is sometimes an individual who has no opportunity to negotiate the agreement, the possibility of an adhesion contract analysis was foreseen.

In an attempt to avoid meeting-of-the-mind and adhesion contract attacks on shrink-wrap contracts, many microcomputer software publishers allow customers to return unopened packages for a full refund. Nevertheless, conventional wisdom among computer law practitioners is that the simple shrink-wrap licence, unsupported by statute or other mechanisms, is likely to be deemed a sale agreement upon judicial analysis.

In the absence of validating legislation, some microcomputer software publishers have adopted the tactic of repeating the licence agreement's terms and conditions on initial screens of the microcomputer software program and requiring the user to press the return or enter key to signify his acceptance of the terms and conditions. This approach may not be sufficient to create a valid and enforceable contract. For example, if the licence agreement is placed on 'optional' screens that can be avoided by the operator, or that do not appear unless the operator selects a menu item that makes them appear, then the operator is likely to avoid the licence agreement-bearing screens and never signify acceptance to its terms and conditions. Even if the screens are 'mandatory' or cannot be avoided, a user could press the return or enter key without reading or accepting the terms and conditions. Sophisticated software publishers will not only place the licence agreement's terms and conditions on mandatory initial screens following the 'splash' or first screen, but will also require the user to add a statement to the effect that he has read and accepted the terms and conditions and require the insertion of the user's name. If either is not inserted, the user should not be able to move on to the main menu or next screen. While this approach is not foolproof, it seems to be the best variation of the screen approaches.

Sophisticated software publishers will not stop here, however, in their attempts to ensure the validity of their shrink-wrap licences. Another approach that can be adopted is to include a response card with the microcomputer software program that addresses not only the availability of enhancements and other programs, but also states that by signing the response card the user accepts the terms and conditions of the shrink-wrap licence agreement. Signing of the card is couched as an alternative to the other actions of opening the package or using the software, any one of which signifies acceptance. Of course, one problem with this approach is that the user can nullify it by simply failing to sign and return the response card. Screens bearing the shrink-wrap licence (two or more are usually needed to capture all of the terms and conditions) and response cards are not the only options available to microcomputer software publishers to validate their shrink-wrap licence agreements. Whenever an organisation desires numerous copies of the software, the publisher can supply a signed master agreement covering all copies acquired. Such an agreement could be complete as to every detail, repeating and superseding relevant provisions of the shrink-wrap licence agreement as well as adding others, in which case the agreements packaged with any copy received by the user might be irrelevant. On the other hand, the master agreement could leave the shrink-wrap licence agreements' terms and conditions operational by simply incorporating them by reference as parent of the master agreement, in which case the user organisation's execution of the master agreement would signify acceptance of both the master agreement and the provisions of the shrink-wrap licence agreements accompanying copies of the software received by the user organisation.

Two cases in 1996, *Beta Computers (Europe) Ltd v Adobe Systems (Europe) Ltd*[1] under Scots law, and *PRO CD Inc v Zeidenberg*[2] under US Law have both reinforced the validity of shrink-wrap licence agreements provided the customer has the opportunity to read and, if necessary, reject the terms by returning the product within a reasonable period.

Of course, the reality that returns might so occur must be an issue addressed between the provider and the dealer who actually distributes the product to the customer.

1   [1996] FSR 367.
2   No 95-C-0671-C (US 7th Cir CA, 20 June 1996).

2.3.3   Click-wrap licence agreements

These are digital variations of the shrink-wrap licence agreements and are becoming more common in electronic e-commerce, cybertrade and web-site shopping where no paper contract precedes or follows the making of a contract by the provider and customer.

Where demonstration software, databases, e-journals, or internet shopping malls are accessible in a provider's web-site the customer must scroll through an on-screen licence agreement and can only make a purchase after reaching the end of the licence and signifying acceptance by e-mailing acceptance to the provider or sending his credit card details or clicking a particular key, this confirming agreement to the licence terms.

Because such click-wrap licence agreements are in standard forms and are accessed remotely by the customer, there is little or no room for negotiation. The EC Directive on Distance Selling[1] (discussed in part II, **section 4.9**) will also apply as will the EC Directive on Unfair Contract Terms[2] so that suppliers will have to ensure such agreements are clearly written, contain no unfair terms and provide 'cooling off' periods.

The US case of *i.LAN Systems, Inc v Netscout Service Level Corporation*[3] has confirmed that a click wrap licence agreement is enforceable but, under Massachusetts law would be interpreted under the Uniform Commercial Code.

In addressing the case Chief Judge Young said:

> 'Has this happened to you? You plunk down a pretty penny for the latest and greatest software, speed back to your computer, tear open the box, shove the CD ROM into the computer, click on "install" and, after scrolling past a license agreement which would take at least fifteen minutes to read, find yourself staring at the following dialog box: "I agree." Do you click on the box? You probably do not agree in your heart of hearts, but you click anyway, not about to let some pesky legalease delay the moment for which you've been waiting. Is that "click wrap" licence agreement enforceable? Yes, at least in the case described below.'

Of interest in this case was that i.LAN Systems were a reseller of Netscout's products. i.LAN had signed a detailed value added reseller agreement. i.LAN having signed the VAR agreement, then placed a purchase order for software products. The software products as delivered to i.LAN were subject to a click-wrap agreement which included language to the effect that nothing in the click-wrap agreement would affect any pre-existing agreements between Netscout and its licensee.

The click-wrap agreement contained the usual limitation of liability clauses and limited warranty clauses which the court held i.LAN had accepted when it clicked 'I agree'. In reaching this decision the court followed the leading US case on enforceable shrink-wrap contracts, namely *ProCD, Inc v Zeidenberg.*

1   97/7 OJ 1997 L144.
2   93/13 OJ 1993 L95.
3   183 F.Supp.2d 328.

2.4   ESCROW AND TTP AGREEMENTS

Software or technology escrows sometimes involve a licence agreement. Software escrows historically become important when the software user licenses an important or critical application in object code and there is no commercially available substitute that could be acquired and placed in use on short notice and at a reasonable cost. If the software publisher fails to maintain and enhance the software as required by the licence agreement, or if the publisher falls into bankruptcy, the user would need the program's source code and technical information about the source code in order to continue to maintain and enhance the important or critical program. The frequency with which software publishers have liquidated or fallen into bankruptcy over the past decade helps to give rise to such concerns.

Of course, users are not the only parties who demand the creation of software escrows. Distributors, OEMs, VARs, joint venture partners, and others worry about the non-performance, liquidation or bankruptcy of software publishers. Any of these parties could inquire about or demand a source code escrow arrangement.

Software escrows are a subset of a broader type of escrow known as the technology escrow. The major difference between the two is that a software escrow arrangement is limited to software and related items including updates, enhancements, technical documentation, user documentation, flow charts, etc; while technology escrows are used for non-software as well as software technology. Technology escrows are used by inventors and participants in research and development joint ventures to substantiate the creation of their inventions and the timing of those inventions, by government contractors to comply with the demands of procurement RFPs, and by others. The inventions or technology of such parties may or may not involve or include software.

There are various approaches to software escrows. The software publisher may establish an escrow in advance of customer demand, or in response to customer demand. The escrow may serve more than one customer or only a particular customer. The escrow agent may be one of the party's banks, insurance companies, accountants or attorneys, or it may be an independent escrow company whose primary business is escrow service. Generally speaking, sophisticated users prefer an independent escrow provider to an agent of one of the parties.

The escrow arrangement typically requires the software publisher to transfer a copy of source code to the escrow service provider who is required by contract to deliver a copy of the source code to one or more users upon the failure of the publisher to maintain the program licensed by the user(s) in executable code form, or upon the bankruptcy of the publisher. The escrow service provider may hold a copy of the source code under a licence agreement with the publisher, or may take title to a copy of the source code. The user may receive a copy of the source code from the escrow service provider under a licence from the provider, or under the terms of the user's executable code licence agreement. Alternatively the user may own the copy of the source code received from the source code provider, or other arrangements could be worked out. In any event, licence agreements between publishers and escrow service providers, and licence agreements between escrow service providers and software users are both considered escrow licence agreements.

Of course, one option to a source code escrow arrangement is for the publisher to give the user a copy of the source code, but many publishers are understandably reluctant to do so. Another alternative is for the user to plan on acquiring a commercially available substitute program if the original program crashes and is not fixed or otherwise becomes unusable in part or in whole. This approach makes an escrow unnecessary but requires confidence by the user that such substitutes will be available and capable of being quickly utilised whenever the need for them arises.

The UK's leading escrow agency, the National Computing Centre,[1] has published a range of escrow agreements on its website,[2] that they have kindly allowed us to incorporate in this book.

Trusted Third Party (TTP) agreements are a variation upon escrow agreements and are becoming used in the area of cryptography and e-commerce. In order to provide certification or authentication of cryptographic keys and digital signatures used in cybertrade transactions a number of corporations and bankers are offering their services as TTPs who hold in escrow algorithms and keys of the cybertraders in order to provide if requested a verification service.

The terms upon which they are licensed to hold such information and materials are contained in a TTP agreement.

1 National Computing Centre and NCC Escrow International Ltd, Manchester Technology Centre, Oxford Road, Manchester M1 7ED.
2 www.nccglobal.com.

2.5 RUNTIME LICENCE AGREEMENTS

Runtime licence agreements typically arise in the context of a microcomputer software developer or publisher developing a new program that incorporates a component or elements from another developer, for example, the code comprising the 'engine' of the program. Copies of the new program containing code from both developers will be distributed to users. The engine, which enables the new program to operate on a microcomputer, is licensed from its developer in an agreement that allows the new program creator to use the engine in his development work and then to reproduce and distribute copies of the new program containing the engine and the creator's code. This licence agreement also allows the new program creator's customers to operate or 'run' the engine portion of the new program under the creator's standard user licence agreement for the entire program. Sometimes the engine developer will require all users to sign a separate licence agreement with the engine developer in addition to licensing the remainder of the program from its creator under a signed or shrink-wrap licence agreement. Some engine developers do not require a separate user's agreement but insist that the program creator's standard user agreement contain certain protective provisions that benefit the engine developer as well as the program creator. In any event the engine developer often charges a royalty for every copy of the new program distributed as well as a fee for the program creator's acquisition, use, and reproduction of the engine code.

2.6 MANUFACTURING LICENCE AGREEMENTS

A manufacturing licence agreement can be distinguished from a typical user licence agreement in that the former allows the licensee to make or reproduce numerous copies while the latter allows the user to operate or use a single copy of the licensed product and may allow the user to make one or a few backup copies.

The manufacturing licence agreement was used long before software was invented and is still used by patent owners for all types of patented devices and formulas. The patent owner would license another party to make the patented invention and perhaps to sell units as well. When patent attorneys and inventors of patented devices talk about licence agreements they often mean this type of manufacturing licence agreement. If a patented device includes software, then software reproduction and perhaps distribution is covered by such a licence.

For non-patented software the closest thing to a manufacturing licence agreement is a licence from a software publisher to a 'reproduction house' or distributor to reproduce copies of the software on magnetic or other media such as CD-ROM. A reproduction house is the equivalent of a printer printing copies of a book which are forwarded to the publisher's order fulfilment warehouse. In contrast a distributor will reproduce, stock, and distribute copies of the software.

In each context the right to make or reproduce copies of the item in question is separate from the right to sell or otherwise distribute copies of the item and the licence will have only those rights granted in the licence agreement.

2.7 CROSS-LICENSING AGREEMENTS

Cross-licensing agreements traditionally arise in the context of two or more patent owners licensing other(s) to make, use, or sell their respective patented inventions. Such agreements can also arise in the context of patented or non-patented software, for example, where two software publishers license the other to distribute their respective programs to a type of customer or in a territory that the licensor has not penetrated.

The key to a cross-licensing agreement is that part or all of the consideration for the agreement is the reciprocal licence grant for each party's products. Cross-licensing agreements may be most common where the parties are located in different countries or have a different customer base in the same country, but they typically arise where the parties' respective rights block the other in the marketplace or where both parties want to distribute the other's products.

2.8 JOINT VENTURE LICENSING AGREEMENTS

Joint venture licensing agreements often arise where one party has a distribution capability for a product which its developer lacks, or where two or more parties join in a research and development effort to create new technology that both can use and/or distribute. In the former context, the parties share costs and profits in some defined manner. Thereby the agreement is distinguishable from a simple distribution arrangement where there is little if any cost sharing and the distributor typically receives a fee regardless of the publishers' profits or lack thereof.

In the context of a research and development joint venture, mutual investment and established technology contributions are commonplace. The new technology developed by the joint venture's personnel is usually shared by the investors for their use and often may be incorporated in their products. Cost and risk sharing are key elements in this context.

2.9 CORE TECHNOLOGY LICENCE AGREEMENTS

The core technology of a company is the technology that generates or allows the generation of the bulk of the company's revenue. A core technology licence agreement typically allows another party to either use or distribute the core technology. The licence agreement must be carefully negotiated and drafted and the consideration paid to the licensor should justify the risks inherent in licensing core technology. Sometimes government agencies insist on such licences. Also, these licences are found most frequently where the technology in question is near the end of its useful or market life, or where the licensor is desperate for funds or plans to sell his company.

2.10 SOFTWARE CONVERSION AGREEMENTS

Software conversion agreements arise in various contexts and may involve virtually any type of software. Conversions from one computer to an incompatible computer fairly often involve both data and software conversions from one data format and software operating system environment to another.

Data conversions are virtually inescapable in this context, but the user can avoid a software conversion by deciding to utilise new software on the new computer.

Software conversions also arise where the user retains an existing computer but wants to acquire a program that will not operate on the existing computer. Here the user may contract for the conversion work. Another context in which conversion work is common is in the development context. For example, a microcomputer software developer might be asked to develop a new program that would operate on an IBM PC and other, incompatible computers such as a Mac PC or in the case of games software for Sega, Sony or Nintendo. In this context, the developer might develop one program and convert the others from the first. The other programs are frequently called 'conversions'. In contrast, in the mainframe software arena, the process of changing the software and/or data is known as the 'conversion'. Thus, in some contexts a conversion means a program, and in others a conversion means a transaction.

Conversion transactions are among the most complex transactions involving software. They rarely progress without glitches. They often generate heated disputes and cost overruns. Carefully planned conversion transactions that are captured in carefully drafted contracts are most likely to be successful, and minimise the risk of cost overruns and disputes. Conversion transaction agreements are thrown in file drawers after execution like most other contracts, but conversion agreements rarely stay in the file because they are working project documents, because of the extreme likelihood of cost overruns and because of the frequency of disputes.

2.11 DATABASE AND ACCESS SOFTWARE LICENCE AGREEMENTS

Databases distributed on floppy disks or compact disks such as CD-ROMs are often accompanied by access programs that permit the user to gain access to their contents. Commercially available online databases also require access codes, and such programs are distributed separately or are built into custom-made terminals supplied by the database publisher.

These access programs are often distributed under shrink-wrap licence agreements for a nominal charge. While online database providers do not necessarily want competitors to reproduce and distribute portions or all of their access code, many feel that copies should be distributed freely or at a nominal charge in the hope or expectation that usage of their databases might increase. Hence, some are willing to give away unlicensed copies of their access programs or dispense with the traditional shrink-wrap licence agreement and employ an online agreement purportedly accepted by some action of the user.

Publishers of databases distributed on floppy disks, compact disks, or tapes are usually more concerned about protecting their access programs. They may require a signed licence agreement that covers both their databases and their access software. Reverse engineering of their access software or its piracy is a sensitive issue for these publishers because their major assets, the databases, may become accessible by competitors or unlicensed users if the access software is penetrated and used in an unauthorised manner. If the databases are recorded on compact disks, and the data is arranged in a proprietary format, the access code can take considerable time and money to develop and may be a major asset of the database publisher.

2.12 MAINTENANCE SERVICE LICENCE AGREEMENTS

It is common for the software owner to license the software and also provide maintenance service. However, independent maintenance providers have slowly grown in importance to software users for several reasons. Sometimes these service providers offer a lower cost alternative to the vendor's maintenance service. In addition, many software companies have gone out of business and hence are not available to provide maintenance service. Independent maintenance service providers may fill the void, especially when the user's data processing staff has neither the time nor the knowledge required to maintain the system.

Software providers commonly discontinue standard maintenance on old releases of programs at or near the end of their market life. The alternatives for users of such programs are either to try to maintain the systems themselves, pay the software provider for maintenance service on a time and material basis or contract with an independent maintenance house for the service. The last alternative may be the most sensible and economical, assuming a suitable escrow agreement is already in place.

The same situation arises concerning old releases of a program still marketed in a current release several steps advanced from the user's old release. Software providers will offer a standard maintenance contract and fee for the current release and perhaps the one or two latest releases before the current edition of the software, but will not indefinitely continue to offer standard maintenance service and charges for early releases of the program. Here again the independent maintenance service provider may fill the void.

Whatever may trigger the use of an independent software provider, maintenance will be virtually impossible without a copy of the source code for the program. The independent maintenance service provider will need to obtain a copy of the source code from someone, either the user, an escrow agent or the software provider. If the source code is obtained from the latter source, the software provider is likely to license its use to furnish maintenance service. If the source code is obtained from an escrow agent, the agent may require the maintenance company to sign a licence agreement. Such agreements are examples of maintenance service licence agreements.

2.13   FACILITIES MANAGEMENT AGREEMENTS

Facilities management ('FM') or outsourcing agreements have become more common in the last two years within the computer industry particularly as companies have 'downsized' during the recession or have 'returned to their core activities'.

Many companies have decided it is more cost effective and more manageable to sub-contract to a third party some or all of the information technology services previously handled in-house.

Many computer providers have for years offered bureaux services and indeed a number of companies built their entire reputation upon such services and then diversified to other areas.

The facilities management agreements are either negotiated during the life of an existing computer system so that the hardware and software as they exist are transferred to the FM company with or without all of the transferor's personnel or are negotiated at the start of the installation of a new system where the outsourcing service is often provided by the provider itself.

Often the more crucial part of a facilities management agreement relates to the level of service to be provided by the FM company but inevitably the issue of intellectual property rights and software licensing becomes part of the negotiations and where outsourcing takes place during the life of an existing software agreement, problems will occur where the existing software licence does not provide for the right to assign and the FM company therefore cannot get the right that it needs in order to carry out the service that it has sought to negotiate for.

Facilities management agreements and outsourcing agreements in general are a complex area and are subjects worthy of entirely separate consideration from this book. However, many of the legal and commercial issues relative to software licensing are as equally relevant to facilities management agreement negotiations.

2.14   WEBSITE AGREEMENTS

As more businesses engage third-party developers and internet service providers to build and manage interactive websites for the internet, so licence agreements are becoming more sophisticated in relation to the development of the site and its interactivity, the licensing rights and the provision of ongoing maintenance and support.

In complex websites where the full range of audiovisual material is used, the developer may be required to procure third-party rights to use certain material, may develop specific application software programs and incorporate third party authorising tools, all of which the customer will require licensing to.

In the event that the developer fails adequately to maintain the website or goes into liquidation, then the customer will require an escrow agreement in respect of source code.

2.15   OPEN SOURCE LICENCES

2.15.1   Introduction

What if you had the right to get a free upgrade whenever your software needed it? What if, when you switched from a Mac to a PC, you could switch software versions without incurring an additional charge? What if the software does not work or is not powerful enough, you can have it improved or even fix it yourself?

What if the software was maintained even if the company that produced it went out of business? What if you could use your software on your office workstation, your home desktop computer, and your portable laptop, instead of just one computer? These are some of the rights that Open Source gives you.

The Open Source Definition is a bill of rights for the computer user. It defines certain rights that a software licence must grant you to be certified as Open Source. Programs like the Linux operating system and Netscape's web browser have become extremely popular, displacing other software that has licences that are more restrictive. Companies that use Open Source software have the advantage of its very rapid development, often by several collaborating companies, and much of it contributed by individuals who simply need an improvement to serve their own needs.

Programmers feel comfortable contributing to Open Source because they are assured of the following rights:

— the right to make copies of the program, and distribute those copies;

— the right to have access to the software's source code, a necessary preliminary before you can change it; and

— the right to make improvements to the program.

These rights are important to the software contributor because they keep all contributors at the same level relative to each other. Anyone who wants to is allowed to sell an Open Source program, so prices will be low and development to reach new markets will be rapid.

Anyone who invests the time to build knowledge in an Open Source program can support it, and this provides users with the option of providing their own support, or the economy of a number of competing support providers. Any programmer can tailor an Open Source program to specific markets in order to reach new customers. People who do these things are not compelled to pay royalties or licence fees.

2.15.2   Historical analysis of the Open Source movement

Richard Stallman has popularised free software as a political idea since 1984, when he formed the Free Software Foundation and its GNU Project. Stallman's premise is that people should have more freedom, and should appreciate their freedom. He designed a set of rights that he felt all users should have, and codified them in the GNU General Public Licence or GPL. Stallman christened his licence the 'copyleft' because it leaves the right to copy in place. Stallman himself developed seminal works of free software such as the GNU C Compiler, and GNU Emacs.

The Open Source Definition started life as a policy document of the Debian GNU/Linux Distribution. Debian, an early Linux system and one still popular today, was built entirely of free software. However, since there were other licences than the copyleft that purported to be free, Debian had some problem defining what was free, and they had never made their free software policy clear to the rest of the world.

2.15.3   The Open Source Definition

The Open Source Definition is not itself a software licence. It is a specification of what is permissible in a software licence for that software to be referred to as Open Source. The Open Source Definition was not intended to be a legal document. To be Open Source, all of the terms below must be applied together, and in all cases. They should be applied to derived versions of a program as well as the original program. It's not sufficient to apply some and not others, and it is not sufficient for the terms only to apply some of the time.

Open Source does not simply mean access to the source code. The distribution terms of an Open Source program must comply with the following criteria:

2.15.3.1   Free redistribution

The licence may not restrict any party from selling or giving away the software as a component of an aggregate software distribution containing programs from several different sources. The licence may not require a royalty or other fee for such sale.

This means that you can make any number of copies of the software, and sell or give them away, and you do not have to pay anyone for that privilege. The 'aggregate software distribution containing programs from several different sources' was intended to fit a loophole in the Artistic Licence, a rather sloppy licence originally designed for Perl. Today, almost all programs that use the Artistic Licence are also available under the GPL.

2.15.3.2   Source code

The program must include source code, and must allow distribution in source code as well as compiled form. Where some form of a product is distributed without source code, there must be a well-publicised means of downloading

33

the source code, without charge, via the internet. The source code must be the preferred form in which a programmer would modify the program. Deliberately vague source code is forbidden. Intermediate forms such as the output of a pre-processor or translator are not allowed.

Source code is a necessary preliminary for the repair or modification of a program. The intent here is for source code to be distributed with the initial work, and all derived works.

2.15.3.3   Derived works

The licence must allow modifications and derived works, and must allow them to be distributed under the same terms as the licence of the original software.

The intent here is for modification of any sort to be allowed. It must be allowed for a modified work to be distributed under the same licence terms as the original work. However, it is not required that any producer of a derived work must use the same licence terms, only that the option to do so be open to them. Various licences speak differently on this subject – the BSD licence allows you to make modifications private, while the GPL does not.

2.15.3.4   Integrity of the author's source code

The licence may restrict source code from being distributed in modified form only if the licence allows the distribution of 'patch files' with the source code for the purpose of modifying the program at build-time.

Some authors were afraid that others would distribute source code with modifications that would be perceived as the work of the original author, and would reflect poorly on that author. This gives them a way to enforce a separation between modifications and their own work without prohibiting modifications. Some consider it un-aesthetic that modifications might have to be distributed in a separate 'patch' file from the source code. Linux distributions like Debian and Red Hat use this procedure for all of the modifications they make to the programs they distribute.

Note also that this provision says that in the case of patch files, the modification takes place at build-time. This loophole is employed in the Qt Public Licence to mandate a different, though less restrictive, licence for the patch files, in contradiction of section 3 of the Open Source Definition. There is, however, a proposal to clean up this loophole in the Definition while keeping Qt within Open Source.

The licence must explicitly permit distribution of software built from modified source code. The licence may require derived works to carry a different name or version number from the original software.

This means that Netscape, for example, can insist that only they can name a version of the program Netscape Navigator™ while all free versions of the program must be called Mozilla or something else.

We generally accept that when we have to pay for a licence to use software then we are bound to observe the software licence and acknowledge the copyright of the software owner. However, it is often presumed that if software is free then copyright and licence terms are no longer applicable.

That is not the case and indeed has recently been confirmed in the US in the case of *(1) Jacobson v Katzer* and *(2) Kamind Associates Inc*, 13 August 2008. The above case from the US Appeals Court confirms that where a royalty free open source software product was used in breach of its licence the breach was not only of contract but also of copyright. The court rejected the argument that because the software was distributed on a royalty free basis the copyright owner had no economic rights to enforce and confirmed that the law of copyright applies to open source licences as much as it does to freeware.

This US case highlights that whilst copyright in software generally denotes the licence to use copyright in return for some economic benefits, it does not preclude the economic benefit from being generated other than by money. In other words, open source licences which allow royalty free use in return for the ability to generate market share through brand awareness or reputation need to be supported by not only contract terms but also the law of copyright.

2.15.3.5   No discrimination against persons or groups

The licence must not discriminate against any person or group of persons.

2.15.3.6   No discrimination against fields of endeavour

The licence must not restrict anyone from making use of the program in a specific field of endeavour. For example, it may not restrict the program from being used in a business, or from being used for genetic research.

2.15.3.7   Distribution of licence

The rights attached to the program must apply to all to whom the program is redistributed without the need for execution of an additional licence by those parties.

The licence must be automatic, no signature required. Unfortunately, there has not been a good court test in the US of the power of a no-signature-required licence when it is passed from a second party to a third. However, this argument considers the licence in the body of contract law, while some argue that it should be considered as copyright law, where there is more precedent for no-signature licences.

2.15.3.8   Licence must not be specific to a product

The rights attached to the program must not depend on the program's being part of a particular software distribution, if the program is extracted from that distribution and used or distributed within the terms of the program's licence. All parties to whom the program is redistributed should have the same rights as those that are granted in conjunction with the original software distribution.

This means you cannot restrict a product that is identified as Open Source to be free only if you use it with a particular brand of Linux distribution, etc. It must remain free if you separate it from the software distribution it came with.

2.15.3.9 Licence must not contaminate other software

The licence must not place restrictions on other software that is distributed along with the licensed software. For example, the licence must not insist that all other programs distributed on the same medium must be Open Source software.

2.15.4 Examples of licences

The GNU GPL, BSD, MPL, X Consortium, and Artistic licences are examples of licences that are considered conformant to the Open Source Definition.

2.15.5 Analysis of licences and their Open Source compliance

To understand the Open Source Definition, we need to look at some common licensing practices as they relate to Open Source.

2.15.5.1 Public domain

A common misconception is that free software is public domain. This happens simply because the idea of free software or Open Source is confusing to many people, and they mistakenly describe these programs as public domain. The programs, however, are clearly copyrighted and covered by a licence, a licence that gives people more rights than they are used to.

A public-domain program is one upon which the author has deliberately surrendered his copyright rights. It cannot really be said to come with a licence; it is the holder's personal property to use as he sees fit.

If you are doing a lot of work on a public-domain program, consider applying your own copyright to the program and re-licensing it. For example, if you do not want a third party to make their own modifications that they then keep private, apply the GPL or a similar licence to your version of the program. The version that you started with will still be in the public domain, but your version will be under a licence that others must heed if they use it or derive from it.

You can easily take a public-domain program private, by declaring a copyright and applying your own licence to it or simply declaring 'All Rights Reserved'.

2.15.5.2   *Free software licences in general*

One can be forgiven for the mistaken belief that programs on a Linux disk are your own property. That is not entirely true. Copyrighted programs are the property of the copyright holder, even when they have an Open Source licence like the GPL. The licence of the program grants you some rights, and you have other rights under the definition of fair use in copyright law.

It is important to note that an author does not have to issue a program with just one licence. You can GPL a program, and sell a version of the same program with a commercial, non-Open Source licence. Many people who want to make a program Open Source and still make some money from it use this exact strategy. Those who do not want an Open Source licence may pay for the privilege, providing a revenue stream for the author.

All of the licences have a common feature: they each disclaim all warranties.

2.15.5.3   *The GNU General Public Licence*

This licence is simple: everyone is permitted to copy and distribute verbatim copies of this licence document, but changing it is not allowed. An important point here is that the text of the licences of Open Source software are generally not themselves Open Source. Obviously, a licence would offer no protection if anyone could change it.

The provisions of the GPL satisfy the Open Source Definition. The GPL does not require any of the provisions permitted by paragraph 4 of the Open Source Definition, Integrity of the Author's Source Code.

The GPL does not allow you to make modifications private. Your modifications must be distributed under the GPL. Thus, the author of a GPL-ed program is likely to receive improvements from others, including commercial companies who modify his software for their own purposes.

The GPL does not allow the incorporation of a GPL-ed program into a proprietary program. The GPL's definition of a proprietary program is any program with a licence that does not give you as many rights as the GPL.

There are a few loopholes in the GPL that allow it to be used in programs that are not entirely Open Source. Software libraries that are normally distributed with the compiler or operating system you are using may be linked with GPL-ed software; the result is a partially free program. The copyright holder (generally the author of the program) is the person who places the GPL on the program and has the right to violate his own licence. However, this right does not extend to any third parties who redistribute the program – they must follow all of the terms of the licence.

In early 2007 The Free Software Foundation published a discussion draft of version 3 of the GPL (and of LGPL – see below) in order to address certain commercial issues arising from an agreement between Microsoft and Novell under which Microsoft agreed to refrain from asserting its patent rights against Novell customers in the event that Microsoft patents were found in Novell's software.

2.15.5.4 *The GNU Library General Public Licence*

The LGPL is a derivative of the GPL that was designed for software libraries. Unlike the GPL, a LGPL-ed program can be incorporated into a proprietary program. The C-language library provided with Linux systems is an example of LGPL-ed software – it can be used to build proprietary programs, otherwise Linux would only be useful for free software authors.

An instance of an LGPL-ed program can be converted into a GPL-ed one at any time. Once that happens, you cannot convert that instance, or anything derived from it, back into an LGPL-ed program.

The rest of the provisions of the LGPL are similar to those in the GPL – in fact, it includes the GPL by reference.

2.15.5.5 *The X, BSD and Apache licences*

The X licence and its relatives the BSD and Apache licences are very different from the GPL and LGPL. These licences let you do nearly anything with the software licensed under them.

The most important permission, and one missing from the GPL, is that you can take X-licensed modifications private. In other words, you can get the source code for a X-licensed program, modify it, and then sell binary versions of the program without distributing the source code of your modifications, and without applying the X licence to those modifications. This is still Open Source, however, as the Open Source Definition does not require that modifications always carry the original licence.

Many other developers have adopted the X licence and its variants, including the Berkeley System Distribution (BSD) and the Apache web server project. A feature of the BSD licence is a provision that requires you to mention (generally in a footnote) that the software was developed at the University of California any time you mention a feature of a BSD-licensed program in advertising.

Keeping track of which software is BSD-licensed in something huge like a Linux distribution, and then remembering to mention the University whenever any of those programs are mentioned in advertising, is somewhat of a headache for business people. The Debian GNU/Linux distribution contains over 2,500 software packages, and if even a fraction of them were BSD-licensed, advertising for a Linux system like Debian might contain many pages of footnotes! However, the X Consortium licence does not have that advertising provision.

2.15.5.6 *The Artistic Licence*

Although this licence was originally developed for Perl, it has since been used for other software.

Section 5 of the Artistic Licence prohibits sale of the software, yet allows an aggregate software distribution of more than one program to be sold. So, if you bundle an Artistic-licensed program with another of the licensed program you can sell the bundle. This feature of the Artistic Licence was the cause of the 'aggregate' loophole in paragraph 1 of the Open Source Definition.

The Artistic Licence requires the programmer to make modifications free, but then gives a loophole (in section 7) that allows modifications to go private or even place parts of the Artistic-licensed program in the public domain!

2.15.5.7 The Netscape public licences and the Mozilla public licence

NPL was developed by Netscape when they made their product Netscape Navigator Open Source. Actually, the Open Source version is called Mozilla; Netscape reserves the trademark Navigator for their own product.

An important feature of the NPL is that it contains special privileges that apply to Netscape and nobody else. It gives Netscape the privilege of re-licensing modifications that you have made to their software. They can take those modifications private, improve them, and refuse to give you the result. This provision was necessary because when Netscape decided to go Open Source, it had contracts with other companies that committed it to provide Navigator to them under a non-Open Source licence.

Netscape created the MPL, or Mozilla Public Licence, to address this concern. The MPL is much like the NPL, but does not contain the clause that allows Netscape to re-license your modifications.

The NPL and MPL allow you to take modifications private.

Many companies have adopted a variation of the MPL for their own programs. This is unfortunate, because the NPL was designed for the specific business situation that Netscape was in at the time it was written, and is not necessarily appropriate for others to use.

2.15.6 Choosing a licence

2.15.6.1 Do you want people to be able to take modifications private or not?

If you want to get the source code for modifications back from the people who make them, apply a licence that mandates this. The GPL and LGPL would be good choices. If you do not mind people taking modifications private, use the X or Apache licence.

2.15.6.2 Do you want to allow someone to merge your program with his own proprietary software?

If so, use the LGPL, which explicitly allows this without allowing people to make modifications to your own code private, or use the X or Apache licences, which do allow modifications to be kept private.

2.15.6.3 Do you want some people to be able to buy commercial-licensed versions of your program that are not Open Source?

If so, dual-license your software. Use the GPL as the Open Source licence; then find a commercial licence appropriate for the code you add to the program.

2.15.6.4 Do you want everyone who uses your program to pay for the privilege?

If so, perhaps Open Source is not for you.

The table below gives a comparison of licensing practices:

Licence	Can be mixed with non-free software	Modifications can be taken private and not returned to you	Can be re-licensed by anyone	Contains special privileges for the original copyright holder over your modifications
GPL	NO	NO	NO	NO
LGPL	YES	NO	NO	NO
BSD	YES	YES	NO	NO
NPL	YES	YES	NO	YES
MPL	YES	YES	NO	NO
Public Domain	YES	YES	YES	NO

2.15.7 The future

IBM has joined the Open Source world, and the venture capital community is discovering Open Source. Intel and Netscape have invested in Red Hat, a Linux distributor. VA Research, an integrator of Linux server and workstation hardware, has announced an outside investor. Sendmail Inc, created to commercialise the ubiquitous Sendmail e-mail delivery program, have announced six million dollars in funding. IBM's Postfix secure mailer has an Open Source licence, and another IBM product, the Jikes Java compiler, has a licence that tries but does not quite meet the intent of the Open Source Definition. IBM appears to be willing to modify the Jikes licence to be fully

Open Source, and is collecting comments from the community as the present work is in preparation.

Two internal Microsoft memos, referred to as the Halloween Documents, were leaked to the online public. These memos clearly document that Open Source and Linux threaten Microsoft, and there is a school of thought that suggests Microsoft will launch an offensive against them to protect its markets.

It is likely that Microsoft will use two main strategies: copyrighted interfaces and patents, they may also extend networking protocols, including Microsoft-specific features in them that will not be made available to free software. They, and other companies, will aggressively research new directions in computer science and will patent whatever they can, before others can first use those techniques in free software.

In the second Halloween document, a Microsoft staff member comments on the exhilarating feeling that he could easily change part of the Linux system to do exactly what he wanted. Additionally, it was so much easier to do this on Linux than it was for a Microsoft employee to change NT!

Microsoft may attempt to circumvent the Open Source program by releasing a lot of software that is just free enough to attract users without having the full freedoms of Open Source. It is conceivable that they could kill off development of some categories of Open Source software by releasing a 'good enough', 'almost-free-enough' solution.

System administration is the next frontier: while Linux-conf partially addresses this issue, it falls far short of being a comprehensive system-administration tool for the naive user. If Caldera's COAS system is successful, it could become the basis of a full solution to the system administration problem. However, Caldera has had trouble keeping sufficient resources allocated to COAS to finish its development, and other participants have dropped off the bandwagon due to the lack of progress.

The plethora of Linux distributions appears to be going through a shake-up, with Red Hat as the perceived winner and Caldera coming in second. Red Hat has shown a solid commitment to the concept of Open Source so far. A new president and rumours of an Initial Public Offering (IPO) could mean a weakening of this commitment, especially if competitors like Caldera, who are not nearly as concerned about Open Source, make inroads into Red Hat's markets.

If the commitment of commercial Linux distributors to Open Source became a problem, it would probably spawn an effort to replace them with pure Open Source efforts similar to Debian GNU/Linux. Alternatively, at the very least it is more directed to the commercial market than Debian has been.

Open Source allows software to be shared easily. Businesses are adopting the Open Source model because it allows groups of companies to collaborate in solving a problem without the threat of an anti-trust lawsuit. Moreover, because of the advantage they gain when the computer-programming public contributes free improvements to their software, some large corporations have adopted Open Source as a strategy to combat Microsoft and to assure that another Microsoft does not come to dominate the computer industry.

However, the most reliable indication of the future of Open Source is its past. In just a few years, it has gone from nothing to a robust body of software that solves many different problems and is reaching the million-user count.

2.16 APPLICATION SERVICE PROVIDER LICENCES

At the end of the last century a new phenomenon in the field of software licensing was the development of the application service provider concept ('ASP'). Computer software owners began licensing their products to independent intermediaries who then loaned or rented for specific periods and/or specific purposes the original licensor's software to end users.

An ASP enables customers to avoid the expense of purchasing licences for indefinite periods when they might only want to use the licensed product for a short period. For example, a user might permanently require Microsoft Office products such as Word and PowerPoint but might only occasionally require Excel or Publisher.

In a strict ASP scenario the licensor, the software owner, usually licenses the ASP the right to provide customers with the right to use on a 'rented' basis, the licensor's software. This is almost a 'pay as you go' concept.

A number of ASPs have found themselves in breach of the owner's rights, because they have not put in place appropriate licences from software owners to rent out the use of the software to customers.

In many ASP scenarios, the customer may uplift its data to the ASP's website and, using the ASP server, carry out data processing tasks. One of the difficulties here is that the processing activities will be carried out on the ASP server and not the customer's server and may, therefore, put the customer in breach of any obligations it may have under the Data Protection Act 1998 in relation to personal data that is being processed by or on third-party systems.

Other than the hosted aspect of the ASP licence terms and the payment mechanisms, most of the ASP licence terms will be the same as in any other software licence agreement.

2.17 SOFTWARE AS A SERVICE (SaaS)

In the past ten years or so there has been a move from customers outsourcing their licensed software management to third parties (such as applications service providers) offering their solutions on a hosted basis to customers.

SaaS has itself moved into the Web 2.0 community where applications can be used on an almost 'pay as you go' basis with customers using services hosted outside their office environment, small software vendors providing hosted services through large application providers such as Google and providers such as Google offering hosted services to corporations large and small. This complex web of software services is often referred to as 'cloud computing'.

Many SaaS solutions are provided on a 'one too many' basis and as a consequence many of the solutions are generic and not tailored to individual users' requirements. The mass market nature of SaaS means that licences are standardised and negotiation is limited to key issues.

Whereas outsourcing did not preclude tailoring of software and services, SaaS solutions are generally not bespoke but therein lies a risk. The 'day-by-day' nature of many SaaS solutions means that the concept of a fixed product does not exist and the importance of support becomes critical. The software and solutions that SaaS providers make available are regularly updated and intellectual property rights remain with the SaaS provider.

Whereas in outsourced arrangements the software remained in the 'ownership' of the customer, in a SaaS situation ownership remains with the SaaS provider and on termination of any contractual arrangement the customer has little or no opportunity to 'port' to another solution. Back-up is therefore critical as are issues over data protection and information security. The following checklist may be useful to consider for SaaS/Cloud agreements:

- Basic charges

- Licence fees

- Charge per user

- Configuration and integration

- Consultancy issues

- Support and maintenance

- Escrow

- Data protection

- Information security

- Transfer of services

- Applicable law

- Warranties and indemnities.

Part II
Laws and regulations

3 Introduction to laws relevant to software contracts

3.1 OVERVIEW

Every jurisdiction has its own national laws which vary for protecting intellectual property rights. In the UK the law which applies includes the Copyright Designs and Patents Act 1988, the Patents Act 1977, and the Trade Marks Act 1994. In the US the Patent Act, the US Commercial Code, the Copyright Act, the Uniform Trade Secrets Act and various state laws all apply to intellectual property in computer programs.

Intellectual property is a bundle of rights including patents, copyright, design rights, trademarks, service marks, registered designs and topographies for semiconductor products as well as confidential information or trade secret law and such rights attach to a variety of inventive or creative efforts such as music, literary works, designs and, amongst other things, computer programs.

On occasions some, if not all, of the bundle of intellectual property rights may relate to a software licence and the major areas of law which apply domestically and internationally to software licence agreements and other software contracts are discussed below.

3.2 PATENT LAW

Most foreign countries have an absolute novelty standard that requires the patent application in that country to be filed before any sale of the invention or offer to sell it, and before any publicity, advertising, or distribution of promotional literature that describes the invention sufficiently to disclose it to the public. Disclosing the invention without a confidentiality agreement also nullifies your ability to obtain a patent in many of these countries. Note that these disclosures may be in the US or elsewhere, not only in the foreign country in question, and they will be sufficient to preclude you from obtaining a patent in the foreign country. Also, in most foreign countries the first to file the application for an invention or discovery will obtain the patent, unlike the US 'first-to-invent' system where a subsequent filing claiming an earlier discovery or invention date will obtain the patent.

It is often said that you can patent an idea (or invention) but you can only copyright the expression of the idea (or invention). The idea or the invention to be patentable must be new, involve an inventive step, be capable of industrial application and must not be one of the statutory exceptions of which a 'computer program' is one and 'a method of doing business' is another.

Whilst patent protection in the UK has not always been regarded as appropriate for computer software, there have been a number of applications. However, these have generally been unsuccessful because the Hearing Officer has either regarded the application as being in respect of a computer program and thereby excepted, or the result of the use of the program is merely a method of doing business, thereby being also excepted (see Merrill Lynch's Application (1989)).

Following the US case of *State Street Bank & Trust Co v Signature Financial Group Inc*,[1] it has become important to consider the value of patenting software.

In the *State Street Bank* case the court addressed Signature Financial Group's patent which was directed to a data processing system for its 'hub and spoke financial services configuration' which was an investment structure in which mutual funds ('Spokes') pooled together assets in an investment portfolio ('Up') which operated as a partnership. It was claimed that the structure achieved economies of scale and the tax benefits of a partnership. When negotiations for a licence between the State Street Bank and Signature Financial broke down, the bank sued to have the patent declared invalid on the basis that it was 'a method of doing business' which under US Patent Law was an invalid subject matter for a patent.

The Federal Circuit in abandoning the 'method of doing business' exemption found that since the software produced a useful concrete and tangible result, it was inventive enough to be the subject matter for a patent application.

With so many web products being driven by software technology it becomes important to view patent protection as a more valid route than was previously the case. It becomes equally as important for any business to carry out patent searches to establish at as early a date as possible the fact that their developments do not infringe already filed patent applications for third parties.

The European Patents Convention enables a single application to be made for designated patents in signatory countries or to the European Patents Officer in Munich which permits patents for software where its application has a novel technical effect although its members may not all permit such patents under their national laws. In the European Patent Office guidelines it is stated that, amongst other things, 'a computer program claimed by itself or as a record on a carrier is unpatentable irrespective of its content. The situation is not normally changed when the computer program is loaded into a known computer but patentability should not be denied merely on the ground that a computer program is involved in its implementation'.

The UK Patents Act 1977 provides patent protection for 20 years and for countries which are signatories to the European Patent Convention the term is for the same period. Whilst it may appear harder and, therefore, less desirable to obtain patent protection in the UK than it may be in other countries such as the US, this is still no reason to discount patent protection as a means of securing suitable rights for software.

The Court of Appeal recently delivered an important judgment on the rights of employers to claim ownership of employee inventions. The decision in *LIFFE Administration & Management v Pavel Pincava (1) and De Novo Markets Ltd (2)*[2] is the first Court of Appeal judgment on the employee invention provisions in nearly 30 years. It is of particular relevance given the widespread development of inventions which may not be patentable as such in the UK, notably computer software, business methods and so-called 'blue sky' research. The importance of these types of inventions to business is increasing given the increased reliance on computer software and automated business processes which were of course of significantly less importance to business when the Patent Act 1977 came into force. The current case demonstrates the importance of careful drafting of employment contracts and employment policies for businesses in relation to employee inventions, intellectual property and confidentiality provisions.

The UK Patents Court recently ordered compensation of £1.5 million to be paid to two employee inventors as compensation for the outstanding benefit of the patent to the employer.

Section 40(1) of the Patents Act 1977 provides that compensation may be awarded to an employee where it appears to the court that:

'(a)   the employee has made an invention belonging to the employer for which a patent has been granted,
(b)   having regard among other things to the size and nature of the employer's undertaking, the invention or the patent for it (or the combination of both) is of outstanding benefit to the employer, ...'

Many employers assume that all inventions by employees (during the course of their employment and within their normal duties) belong to the employer but this is not necessarily so.

—   Even where there is a contract of employment granting intellectual property rights from the employee to the employer, this will be overridden where the employee applies to the court in the case of a patent of 'outstanding benefit'.

—   The 'outstanding benefit' does not have to relate to the invention of the employee but more to the benefit of the patent itself.

—   The level of compensation is not necessarily related to the remuneration of the employee.

In this particular instance, the employees concerned were research scientists who discovered a radioactive imaging agent which was subsequently patented and which became a highly successful product for their employer sold under the trade mark MYOVIEW.

The level of compensation was calculated on the value of the patent taking account of generic competition. In this instance the court considered a figure of 3% of the benefit was appropriate compensation which translated to £1 million for one employee and £500,000 for his colleague, but also, interestingly, represented about three days of the profits from MYOVIEW.

Talented and creative employees are extremely valuable to many companies and employers use not only contractual controls and restrictions on those employees to ensure that their creativity benefits the employer, but also induce loyalty by share option schemes, incentive schemes and compensation arrangements, particularly in the field of research and development. What is interesting is that the level of compensation payable to an employee as a result of a patent of outstanding benefit may be in addition to any existing employee benefits.

On 18 May 2009 the Intellectual Property Office published a Decision under the Patents Act 1977 in favour of Fisher-Rosemount Systems, Inc on the issue as to whether or not four particular patent applications numbered GB 0419580.6, GB 0419583.0, GB 0724070.8 and GB 0724072.4 were excluded from patentability as a program for a computer by s 1(2)(c) of the Patents Act 1977.

The four applications related to reconfiguring a process control system associated with a process plant. The process control system of the invention included workstations which stored and executed applications used to configure and monitor a process plant, a configuration database which stored configuration data generated at the workstations and the number of process devices throughout the process plant.

The Patents Act 1977 indicates that a patent may be granted only for an invention in respect of which the grant of patent is not excluded by s 1(2) (c) – namely that invention must not be 'a scheme, rule or method for performing a mental act, playing a game or doing business, or a program for a computer'.

The general approach to deciding whether an invention is excluded from patentability is the four-step test laid down by the Court of Appeal in *Aerotel / Macrossan*[3] namely:

1.   properly construe the claim;

2.   identify the actual contribution;

3.   ask whether it falls solely within the excluded matter; and

4.   check whether the contribution is actually technical in nature.

In the *Fisher-Rosemount* decision the hearing officer, applying the four step test, reached the conclusion that the use of the computers did not exclude the inventions from patentability and in particular that the invention, albeit utilising computer software, made a technical contribution.

The *Fisher-Rosemount* Decision continues to reinforce the fact that computer generated inventions or inventions that rely upon computer programs should seriously be considered for patent protection notwithstanding the relatively restrictive regime in the UK.

1   149 F 3d 1368 (Fed Cir 1998); Cert denied 1999.
2   [2007] EWCA Civ 217, [2007] RPC 30.
3   Sub nom *Aerotel Ltd (A Company Incorporated Under the Laws of Israel) v Telco Holdings Ltd, Telco Global Distribution Ltd, Telco Global Ltd* [2006] EWCA Civ 1371.

3.3   COPYRIGHT AND DATABASE LAWS

Copyright is at the core of intellectual property right protection for computer software and globally is recognised as the main protection for the rights of the owner.

Copyright arises in the expression of an idea whereas patents arise in the idea itself. Therefore, the concept or idea behind a piece of software may not necessarily be protected by copyright until such time as it is reduced to written form.

Until recent years in many countries computer software was not specifically referred to in statutes as having its own right to protection for copyright purposes. Certainly in the UK in the Copyright Act 1956 there was no mention of computer programs and therefore copyright was deemed to apply to computer programs because they were 'written' and therefore might well be regarded as 'literary works' which were specifically referred to in the Copyright Act 1956.

The Copyright Designs and Patents Act 1988 (CDPA 1988) replaced previous UK copyright statutes. CDPA 1988 specifically refers to computer programs as being a literary work and, therefore, being entitled to copyright protection. However, copyright only subsists under CDPA 1988 if the work is original, whether or not the work is generated by human or computer provided that there is writing which is defined as 'any form of notation or code', whether by hand or otherwise and regardless of the method by which, or medium in or on which, it is recorded!

The author, that is the person who creates the work, is generally regarded as the copyright owner except that, where the software program is made by an employee in the course of his employment, the employer is the first owner of copyright.

If the work is created by an employee under a contract of employment but outside the normal course of his employment, the work may not necessarily belong to the employer and if the work is created by a sub-contractor, such as a freelance programmer, then since that person is not an employee again ownership will remain with that freelance programmer. It is, therefore, extremely important to ensure that there is some contractual arrangement whereby work which is carried out by an employee outside of his normal duties or is commissioned as between software publisher and freelance programmer is vested in the employer, otherwise difficulties may occur in the future. There is an assumption that where a company commissions the writing of computer software upon payment of the appropriate fee, title in the computer work vests in the commissioner. This is not the case, as has been learnt to the cost of many businesses.[1] Programmers who are contracted to major companies and institutions through agencies are usually signed to agreements whereby all intellectual property rights are owned by the company but as more and more work is 'done on the move' or by means of 'teleworking' there is always the risk that work created outside the usual company's offices may not always belong to the company but may remain with the programmer.

It should be remembered that copyright prevents third parties from copying the work of the copyright owner and copyright will attach to the work, not to the idea that underlies the work. It should, therefore, be remembered that where the idea for a particular piece of software is generated the idea as such does not have the benefit of copyright protection until it is reduced to written form.

The case of *Kabushi Kaisha Sony Computer Entertainment v Edmunds (trading as Channel Technology)*[2] shows that UK copyright law in the guise of the CDPA 1988, s 26 will enable copyright owners to successfully prevent copy protection devices from being used in the UK. In this case, Sony successfully obtained summary judgment against the defendants on the ground that they were importing into the UK from Russia a computer chip which allowed users to circumvent the copy protection codes implemented in Sony's Playstation 2 consoles.

On an international basis it is important for the provider and the customer to have agreed specific contractual licensing provisions because the degree of protection afforded to software varies from jurisdiction to jurisdiction. The Berne Convention is the most widely observed international treaty relating to copyright. No formalities are necessary to obtain copyright protection.

The Universal Copyright Convention is another international treaty where, for protection to exist, a copyright notice must appear on published works and in certain jurisdictions a deposit of the work or its registration is necessary before protection applies.

In the 1990s a number of EU member states introduced a voluntary registration system for software programs, namely, Italy, Spain and Portugal, where deposit of a software program in its object code form and upon payment of a small fee may provide the copyright holder with certain presumptive rights of ownership which may be of use in infringement proceedings.

A voluntary registration scheme has existed in the UK since 1911 whereby a copy of the copyright work (the program) may be deposited upon payment of a fee with the Register of Copyright at Stationers' Hall in London and a certificate is issued to the copyright holder thereby asserting his copyright. This scheme has become more popular in recent years with the increase in piracy and as a means of further reassurance for the copyright owner in infringement proceedings. At the beginning of 2000 Stationers' Hall ceased to offer its registration scheme.

Whilst it is not necessary to display any statement or wording regarding copyright on a software product it is generally felt good practice to display a copyright statement as an assertion of copyright ownership and statement to the world at large as well as to the licensed user. Therefore, where the owner of a computer program wishes to assert or further enforce copyright ownership, the statement that is usually suggested is as follows:

'© [name of copyright owner] [year of first publication]'.

Often the words 'all rights reserved' are added to the copyright statement. These words are intended to mean that apart from copyright, all other intellectual property rights are reserved or retained by the copyright owner.

The usual places to display the above copyright statement are:

— on all packaging for the software product;

— on the front cover or inside front cover of any accompanying documentation and user manuals;

— as an opening page on the first loading of the program so that the copyright statement is clearly displayed as the program is 'scrolled through'; or

— physically on the media within which or upon which the program is embedded or incorporated.

The extent to which copyright arises in the 'look and feel' of a computer program or part of a computer program has been the subject of much litigation in the US, although no Supreme Court rulings have been given on the issue. There have, however, been a considerable number of Circuit Courts of Appeal decisions but their analyses have not been uniform.

In the US, copyright protection extends to the literal elements of a computer program such as the source code and object code but there is no clear decision on how much of the non-literal 'look and feel' of a computer program can be protected by copyright.

The first test, a simple 'sweat of the brow' test was applied in the case of *Whale Associates Inc v Jaslow Dental Laboratories Inc*,[3] but this test was subsequently replaced by the 'abstraction-filtration-comparison' test developed by the Second Circuit in *Computer Associates International Inc v Altai Inc*.[4] This test employs, first, a consideration of the computer program at all levels of abstraction, thus permitting a detailed analysis of all of the structural components of the program from the general functions of the program to specific line by line coding. Secondly, the test also involves a filtration step to attempt to define elements which are protectable for copyright purposes as being expressions of an idea from those elements which comprise the concept of the idea of the program itself. Finally, the comparison test compares the protected expression of the idea within the computer program to the allegedly infringing program using a 'substantial similarity' test.

The Computer Associates test found favour in the Tenth Circuit case of *Gates Rubber CO v Bando Chemical Industries Ltd.*[5]

The First Circuit's decision in *Lotus Development Corpn v Borland International Inc*[6] took a slightly different view of testing what is capable of copyright protection and proposed that, first, one should analyse and identify the idea, concept and methodology involved in the program and thereafter examine to see which of those elements were essential to the expression of the idea and which were not. The court then proposed that it should be considered whether or not the unessential elements were capable of copyright protection.

Under UK law the first 'look and feel' decision was given in the case of *John Richardson Computers Ltd v Flanders and Chemtec Ltd*[7] where the US approach was followed, drawing on the *Computer Associates* test. However, in the case of *IBCOS Computers Ltd v Barclays Mercantile Highland Finance Ltd,*[8] the reliance upon US tests was criticised by the court and the test to be applied as laid down by Jacob J is:

(1)   what are the work(s) in which copyright is claimed?;

(2)   is each work original?;

(3)   was there copying from that work?;

(4)   if there was copying, has the substantial part of that work been reproduced?

The European Court of Justice (ECJ) decision in *British Horseracing Board v William Hill*[9] has narrowed the *sui generis* database right, the right which protects database owners against unlawful extraction and manipulation of the contents of databases. The right exists where there is 'a substantial investment in obtaining, verifying, or presenting the contents of the database'.

The ECJ has ruled that an 'investment … in obtaining … the contents' of a database refers to 'resources used to seek out existing materials and collect them in the database'. Crucially, 'it does not cover the resources used for the creation of materials which make up the contents of a database'. 'Substantial' must now be assessed qualitatively as well as quantitatively in relation to the investment placed in that acquisition for the right to exist and is relative to the database from which data is being taken.

This could affect all databases viewed outside the business (either by licence or published in the public domain). In order to ensure the commercial value of such databases is fully protected, it may be wise to seek alternative means, such as:

—   electronic rights management;

—   rigorous licences/agreements;

—   separating data collection and database creation (management between arm's-length commercial entities).

It would also be prudent to consider the means of audit trailing in cases where data 'theft' is suspected.

The major issue exists in relation to the 'ownership' of the data placed into the database. The database right exists only if there was substantial investment in the obtaining, verifying or presenting data forming the contents of the database. The investment is at the stage of the creation of the database and not the original creation of the data (whether prior or subsequent to that).

In terms of infringement, the amount extracted or re-utilised, has to be 'substantial' for the right to be infringed. 'Substantial' in this instance is measured against the database from which the data is taken. When measured against the database from which extraction or re-utilisation occurred, what is taken may be insubstantial but of significant economic value relative to the remnant. This could affect the value of the database as an asset, which may be disastrous for smaller publishers. The *sui generis* right would no longer offer protection.

There are two main courses of action:

— increasing the likelihood of successful litigation with the rights currently available; or

— prevention.

Although the decision has reduced the potential protection available under the *sui generis* database right there are other sources of protection. Under the CDPA 1988 databases are expressly protected under copyright as a literary work, using the same definition as for the database right. Despite the new classification of originality imposed, the right subsists for longer (the author's life plus 70 years) and is supported by a body of case law.

The careful drafting of end user agreements, licences and contracts dealing with the database or a part thereof can aid in the control of the use of data, ensuring its value to the owner.

Digital Rights Management is becoming of great importance to many industries. The means of controlling access to certain sources of data, permitting particular modes and time of access (from mere viewing through to download) and even the control of its use post-download has grown with the explosion of electronic data management. This may involve additional expense but is a relatively robust mechanism.

Finally, if the separation of data creation and acquisition with the aim of constructing a database is the key, then the separation could be achieved by ensuring an arm's-length relationship, perhaps by the creation of a new subsidiary company to undertake database creation and management, with associated agreements as to the rights. However, this is not a tested route and subsequent ECJ judgments or jurisdiction interpretation may decide otherwise (or confirm it as an option).

One low cost option is the use of auditing processes by which infringements can be traced. This at its simplest may consist of seeding data.

In a decision[10] that will be of interest to data-owners and data-users, the Court of Appeal has ruled that the British Horseracing Board (BHB) was not in breach of competition laws aimed at preventing abuse of a dominant position, by insisting on a licence agreement put in place for the supply of data, despite the fact that the data (or at least some of it) was not protected by database rights.

Attheraces Ltd (ATR) and the BHB entered into negotiations for a licence for the supply of data, including pre-race data. At the same time a dispute arose between the BHB and William Hill in which the BHB alleged that William Hill was infringing BHB's database rights in the pre-race data that was the subject of the negotiations with the ATR. That dispute was ruled in favour of William Hill and the effect of the judgment was to deny BHB database rights in the pre-race data. The decision undermined the ATR/BHB negotiations and BHB threatened to cease to supply ATR unless ATR entered into a licence and paid sums claimed to be due. In April 2005 ATR brought proceedings, claiming amongst other things that the BHB was abusing its dominant position by refusing to supply it data.

The High Court initially found in favour of ATR, ruling that the BHB's refusal to supply ATR data amounted to an abuse of its dominant position. The BHB appealed against the finding of abuse (but not that it had a dominant position). The Court of Appeal found in favour of the BHB and found that there was no abuse.

When considering the intellectual property aspects of ATR's claim (ie that the BHB's insistence on a licence to access data was unjustified in light of the decision in the *William Hill* case that the pre-race data was not protected by database rights), the Court of Appeal examined the draft agreements that were in negotiation between ATR and the BHB. It noted that at no time during the negotiations had ATR raised the issue as to whether the definition of 'data' should only include data in which the BHB had database rights. Had ATR raised these sorts of arguments, and the BHB been adamant or unreasonable in its response (perhaps by refusing to remove pre-race data from the definition of 'data'), then the outcome might have been different. However, ATR had not done so and in the overall context of the case, ATR had not established that the BHB's insistence on a licence constituted an abuse of a dominant position.

ATR was in an unusual position in this case as it was able to rely on a decision directly relating to the issue of whether database rights existed in specific data or not. In most cases it will be difficult to advise with absolute certainty whether database rights exist in specific data. Therefore, data-owners are best advised to continue to insist on licences to use their data, although where they have a particularly large market share they will need to pay heed to arguments from licensees that certain data is not protected by database rights or risk a competition law claim. Even where there are no database rights, however, there may be perfectly valid reasons for requiring a licence (eg the data being of a confidential nature) and legal advice should be sought. It is the abuse of a dominant position with which the law is concerned, not the creation and holding of the dominant position itself.

In the case of *Navitaire Inc v (1) Easyjet Airline Co (2) Bulletproof Technologies Inc*[11] Navitaire claimed that Easyjet and their software developers had infringed copyright in Navitaire's ticketless booking program by developing a similar system based on their computer language, computer commands, screen layouts, icons and business logic.

Although Navitaire did not suggest that the new Easyjet ticketless booking program had copied the underlying software of Navitaire's system they did claim that copyright had been infringed by, amongst other things, non-textual copying.

The court held that under the CDPA 1988, computer languages were not in the copyright protection afforded to computer programs and that ad hoc languages such as user command interfaces were not protected by copyright either. In addition, the court held that, as a matter of policy, business logic of a computer program should not be protected through literary copyright.

The court did find, in this instance, that Easyjet's computer development partners, Bulletproof Technologies Inc, had infringed copyright in certain icon drawings which had been copied exactly by Bulletproof Technologies Inc.

The Court of Appeal Judgment in *Nova Productions v Mazooma Games & Ors*[12] will be of immense interest and potential concern to software developers and the owners of copyright in computer programs. In its judgment, the Court of Appeal, following the *Easyjet* decision, confirmed that:

— it is not an infringement of copyright to make a computer program which emulates another program (including its look and feel) but which does not copy the other program's code or graphics;

— ideas which underlie computer programs are not protected by copyright; and

— no additional copyright protection, over and above protection as individual graphic works, is given to a series of images displayed in a computer program.

If a computer program is protectable by copyright but other aspects of it including computer language and commands and business logic are not so protected by copyright then, perhaps, other methods of protection should be considered, such as, patent, trade secrets and stricter licensing terms.

In the case of *Cyprotex Discovery Ltd v University of Sheffield,*[13] the UK Technology and Construction Court was faced with deciding on who was the owner of copyright in a computer program that was developed by an employee of Cyprotex as part of a Research Agreement with the University of Sheffield.

The University had developed a database known as Simcyp and in 2000, Cyprotex and the University agreed to collaborate in the creation of an improved software program based on Simcyp, but utilising more user friendly operating systems such as Windows. As part of the funding for the program Cyprotex provided the services of one of its employees. The contract that the parties entered into was poorly drafted and there was no clear definition as to who was to be the owner of copyright in not only the finished developed program, but also the developments themselves. When relationships between the parties broke down, a dispute over ownership arose, since each of the parties argued the terms of the Research Agreement gave them copyright in the program.

Part of the difficulty that the court faced was that the Research Agreement clearly expressed that copyright ownership would vest in the improvements to the computer program and also indicated that the University was allowed to license third parties and sponsors to use the resulting intellectual property in the computer program. To this extent, no statement was made about who would have ownership in the computer program itself, as opposed to the improvements to it.

The court stated that notwithstanding the common law position (that in the absence of an agreement to the contrary copyright vests in the party developing the work, in this case Cyprotex), the intention of the parties must clearly have been that the developed program and the program itself would belong to the University and therefore, were satisfied that either by virtue of the express terms of the Research Agreement or by necessary implication, ownership of copyright of the software vested in the University.

Following the court's decision, Cyprotex appealed to the Court of Appeal but once again the Court of Appeal held that the Research Agreement contemplated and indeed required that the University should recruit a programmer to produce the software, and whether or not the work was carried out by an employed programmer or a sub-contracted programmer the intention of the parties must have been that ownership would pass to the University.

It would be wise not to rely upon a court making such a decision in the future. Businesses are urged to define as clearly as possible, where ownership of copyright and all other intellectual property rights will vest under any research development or programming agreement. Moreover, businesses should remember that unless work is carried out by an employee in the course of employment, then ownership of intellectual property rights will vest in the person that carries out the work. Given the amount of use of third party developers, designers, consultants and outsourced companies, it is most important to ensure that ownership is addressed by a properly drafted and legally enforceable contract.

Following the UK case of *St Albans City & District Council v International Computers Ltd*[14], the High Court held that a computer disk containing intangible software fell within the description of 'goods' to the same extent as the tangible medium on which the software was supplied. After drawing an analogy between the tangible hardware (the disk) on which the intangible program (the software) was delivered, Sir Iain Glidewell stated that 'If the disk is sold ... but the program is defective ... there would prima facie be breach of the terms as to quality and fitness for purpose implied by the 1979 Act or the 1982 Act'. It follows that the mode employed to deliver the software ie encoded onto a disk, is just as important as the software licence terms which govern the use of the software by the licensee.

This classification has since been echoed in a number of European jurisdictions, notably by the Finnish Supreme Court[15] and in two German Courts of Appeal decisions.[16]

The legal concept of copyright is pivotal to software and software contracts. Copyright law provides the mechanisms for the controlled commercial exploitation of an author's work whilst ensuring the extensive circulation of the copyright work.

Products rich in intellectual property rights which are sold are subject to both the Sale of Goods Act 1979 and the Copyright Designs and Patents Act 1988.

In certain circumstances, the Supply of Goods and Services Act 1982 will govern the contractual relationship between the software supplier and the end-user. This would be the case where software has been designed and developed as a result of a commissioned project. A contract of this type would be for the provision of services as opposed to the sale of goods and the supplier in this scenario would have to comply with the implied terms under the Act as well any explicit contractual terms in the supply agreement.

An important distinction needs to be drawn between the sale of intellectual property rights in the software as opposed to the sale or licence of the copy version of the software. The distinction becomes apparent between the sale of a tangible product such as a CD-ROM versus the sale of the copyright in the CD-ROM. The pivotal issue to this distinction is one of ownership of the copyright.

What is the status of software? The judiciary across the European Union appear unanimously to agree that software may indeed be classified as 'goods', as exemplified in the cases cited at the beginning of this chapter. The apparent 'consensus of the judiciary' to decree that software may be classified as goods is an alarming development for software vendors and the software industry as a whole. 'According to at least one English judge, sheer commercial expediency dictates that software be treated as "goods" lest it fall through the cracks in consumer protection legislation'.

Nevertheless, the intangible status of software can work to a software vendor's benefit and avoid the goods classification, providing the delivery mechanism of the software is addressed. If the software is delivered in a downloadable intangible form or is installed by the supplier on the customer's server, and the terms of the software licence uses language that indicates licence and supply, then the classification of software as goods is avoided.

If judicial consensus for classification of goods as software is a growing trend, what is the impact of the doctrine of exhaustion of rights on software distribution? Most companies will be at the mercy of this doctrine due to its significant influence over the 'extent to which the distribution of goods protected by their intellectual property can be controlled'.

The doctrine is founded on the premise that the intellectual property right holder 'exhausts' his or her right following the first sale of the software product. The doctrine operates on three distinct platforms: national exhaustion, regional exhaustion and international exhaustion.

The 'regional exhaustion' applies to the confines of the European Union and states that the intellectual property right holder cannot obstruct any subsequent resale of that software copy after the initial sale has been concluded.

In the recent decisions of the Courts of Appeal of Frankfurt am Main and Munich, the courts based their opinion on section 69c, no. 3 of the German Copyright Act which is the result of the direct implementation of Article 4(c) of the EU Computer Software Directive 1991 (The Directive). The Directive states that the first approved sale of a software copy, by the intellectual property right holder within the European Union, exhausts any further distribution rights of the intellectual property right holder in relation to that software copy. The exception to this is the right to control subsequent rental of the software copy.

Software vendors supplying into the European Union need to re-examine their standard end user licences to ensure that their software does not fall foul of being classified as 'goods'. Furthermore, delivering software in an intangible form or installing as part of commissioning is crucial to ensuring that the goods classification is not applicable. Such a classification will almost certainly open up Pandora's box and the grasp of the doctrine of exhaustion will not be far behind.

The European Court of Justice (ECJ) decision in *British Horseracing Board v William Hill* has narrowed the *sui generis* database right, the right which protects database owners against unlawful extraction and manipulation of the contents of databases. The right exists where there is 'a substantial investment in obtaining, verifying, or presenting the contents of the database'.

Two recent cases have further explored the application of copyright to software and software contracts. The first case is the case of *UsedSoft GmbH v Oracle International Corp*[17] (discussed in more detail in Part 1 Section 1.6).

The second case and indeed ongoing litigation is *SAS Institute Inc v World Programming Ltd* [2013] EWHC 69 (Ch).[18] In 2009 the SAS Institute, creators of the SAS system, brought litigation against World Programming Ltd (WPL) on the basis that WPL had infringed copyright of SAS in both its software program and accompanying manuals. WPL did not dispute the fact that it had obtained a licensed copy of the program but relied upon the fact that, in producing a competing program that achieved the same functionality of that of SAS, it had not infringed copyright since there was no copyright in the underlying ideas of the SAS program. The case was first heard in the High Court of England and Wales[19] where it was held that WPL infringed copyright in the SAS manuals by substantially reproducing them in the WPL manual but had not infringed copyright in the SAS software. The matter was referred to the Court of Justice of the European Union where full judgment was handed down on 2 May 2012.[20] In essence the ruling from the EWHC was that 'Article 1(2) of Council Directive 91/250/EEC' – of 14 May 1991 on the legal protection of computer programs must be interpreted as meaning that neither the functionality of the computer program nor the programming language and the format of data files used in a computer program in order to exploit certain of its functions constitute a form of expression of that program and, as such, are not protected by copyright in computer programs for the purposes of that Directive. Further 'Article 5(3) of Directive 91/250' must be interpreted as meaning that a person who has obtained a copy of a computer program under a licence is entitled, without the authorisation of the owner of the copyright, to observe, study or test the functioning of that program so as to determine the ideas and principles which underlie any element of the program, in the case where that person carries out acts covered by that licence and acts of loading and running necessary for the use of the computer program, and on condition that that person does not infringe the exclusive rights of the owner of the copyright in that program. Further 'Article 2 (a) of Directive 2001/29/EC' of the European Parliament and of the Council of 22 May 2001 on the harmonisation of certain aspects of copyright and related rights in the information society must be interpreted as meaning that the reproduction, in a computer program or a user manual for that program, of certain elements described in the user manual for another computer program protected by copyright is capable of constituting an infringement of the copyright in the latter manual if:

– this being a matter for the National Court to ascertain – that reproduction constitutes the expression of the intellectual creation of the author of the user manual for the computer program protected by copyright.

1 *Saphena Computing Ltd v Allied Collection Agencies Ltd* [1995] FSR 616.
2 [2002] All ER (D) 170 (Jan).
3 609 F Supp 1307,225 USPQ 156 (ED Pa 1985).
4 23 USPQ 2d 1241 (2d Cir); amended 982 F 2d 693 (2d Cir 1992).
5 9 F 3d 823,28 USPQ 2d 1503 (10th Cir 1993).
6 49 F 3d 807, 34 USPQ 2d 1014 (1st Cir 1995).
7 [1993] FSR 497.
8 [1994] FSR 275.
9 (C-203/02) [2009] Bus LR 932.
10 *Attheraces Ltd v The British Horseracing Board* [2007] EWCA Civ 38.
11 [2004] EWHC 1725 (Ch).
12 [2007] EWCA Civ 219 (14 March 2007).
13 [2004] EWCA Civ 380.
14 [1996] 4 All ER 481.
15 (KKO 2003:88).
16 Decision of Courts of Appeal of Munich of February 12 1998 – 28U 5911/97 and the Decision of Courts of Appeal of Frankfurt am Main of November 3 1998 – 11U 20/98.
17 Court of Justice of the European Union 3 July 2012 judgment in case C/128/11.
18 *SAS Institute Inc v World Programming Ltd* [2013] EWHC 69(Ch).

19 [2010] EWHC 1829(Ch).
20 *SAS Institute Inc v World Programming Ltd* case number C-406-10.

3.4 TRADE SECRET LAW

Trade secret protection may have originated in the 1851 English case of *Morison v Moat*,[1] and later it may have been first recognised in the US in a Massachusetts case, *Peabody v Norfolk*.[2] One goal in the judicial development of trade secret law has been to discourage unfair competition and trade practices. A second goal has been to encourage research and innovation.

Trade secret and the law of confidence are not designed to protect secrecy so much as to protect against the misappropriation of a secret exploited in commerce and the effort or investment required to develop the secret.

Historically the question of how mass-marketed software could be distributed to thousands without the loss of its trade secrets was among the first generation of legal issues faced by computer law practitioners. Publishers of such software quickly decided to distribute executable code, not source code, and to attempt to license their programs just like their colleagues who published minicomputer and mainframe software.

In theory the life of a trade secret can be permanent so long as the elements of the relevant statutory or common law definition continue to be satisfied. The types of items that may contain trade secrets and be protected by trade secret law include algorithms, source code, and private databases as well as the more traditional business plans, customer lists, etc. Trade secret protection has been recognised for software, printed program instructions and magnetically recorded information.

The inadvertent disclosure of a trade secret may destroy its status as a secret as easily as an intentional disclosure might, and either may result in the loss of trade secret protection.

Of course, trade secrets can be preserved through the use of valid licence agreements. Trade secret law allows reverse engineering by a party that legitimately acquires an item containing the secrets. Reverse engineering the item to discover its embedded trade secrets is a well-used practice in many industries and is used by some regarding software. A valid licence agreement with confidentiality obligations and perhaps a reverse engineering prohibition serves to preserve the status of the trade secrets as secrets.

Many foreign countries do not have trade secret laws, and some who have such laws have only a very weak version of them in comparison to the UK and US. Thus contract protection for trade secrets is important in international transactions. In the UK trade secret law and confidential information applies to a wide variety of matters but computer programs, algorithms, designs for hardware, user manuals and expressions of ideas may all be regarded as being confidential information provided they are not already in the public domain and, further, that when such matters are communicated the person wishing to have the protection of trade secret laws conveys to the other party an indication that the matters concerned are treated by him as being confidential.

As has been previously stated, in the UK as well as in the US, copyright does not necessarily extend to the idea behind the software but only to the software itself whereas trade secret law may apply to the idea as well as to the expression of it. For example, an employee who creates a program during the course of employment will be bound under his common law duty of good faith to his employer to maintain the idea as confidential as well as the expression of the idea, namely the resulting computer program, and will have created a copyright protection which, generally speaking, will pass to the employer. For confirmation that the obligation of confidence covers concepts or ideas see *Fraser v Thames Television Ltd.*[3]

As has previously been stated, the importance of the role of contractual protection as a means of controlling trade secrets law cannot be understated and wherever trade secrets or confidential information are being imparted it is extremely important to indicate clearly that such matters are regarded as being secrets and confidential information.

Despite the existence of the common law concept of trade secrets, in the software industry there has been a difficulty in recent years in preventing unauthorised access to computers or 'hacking' as it is commonly known and, whilst the Data Protection Act 1984 in the UK did much to address the issue of protecting the confidentiality of computer stored information about individuals, it was not until the Computer Misuse Act 1990 became statute that criminal law protection against the unauthorised access to confidential information stored on computer was provided.

The Police and Justice Act 2006, amongst other things, amended the Computer Misuse Act 1990 extending the scope of a number of computer misuse offences.

The Computer Misuse Act 1990 was drafted at a time when hacking was hardly a word in common use and when denial-of-service attacks and similar activities were not envisaged.

The Police and Justice Act 2006:

— extends the scope of the hacking offence by amending the Computer Misuse Act, s 1(1) to read 'A person is guilty of an offence if (a) he causes a computer to perform any function with intent to secure access to any program or data held in any computer *or to enable any such access to be secured*; (b) the access he intends to secure, *or to enable to be secured*, is unauthorised...';

— provides for a person found guilty of hacking to be subject on summary conviction to imprisonment for a term of up to 12 months or a fine not exceeding the statutory maximum or both and on indictment, up to two years' imprisonment or a fine or both;

— amends the Computer Misuse Act 1990 to make it an offence to carry out any activity with the requisite intent or knowledge which causes an unauthorised modification of the contents of any computer (note that this wording falls short of what many security experts require to address denial-of-service attacks or the distribution of malicious code);

— provides for a new offence of making, supplying or obtaining articles for use in activities of computer misuse.

One of the difficulties, not only in the UK but on a more global basis, for businesses is that as systems become more 'open' the instances where confidential information can be easily accessed become almost limitless and whilst there is little UK litigation on this area of the law, at present, there undoubtedly will be more in the future.

1   (1851) 9 Hare 241.
2   98 Mass 452 (1868).
3   [1984] QB 44, [1983] 2 All ER 101.

3.5   TRADEMARK LAW

Trademark rights arise from commercial use or the intention to use them commercially followed by commercial use. Trademarks may be registered or not, but registration gives some advantages and is usually preferable to not registering your mark. If a mark is registered, the registration must be renewed from time to time. The duration of trademark protection is potentially unlimited. The trademark owner's exclusive rights to use the mark with respect to certain goods and services may continue as long as the trademark owner uses the mark in commerce; uses it correctly, for example, as a trademark rather than a generic name; controls the quality of the products bearing the mark; and as long as customers continue to perceive the mark as an indicator of source or sponsorship of the products bearing the mark.

While it is beyond the scope of this book to discuss trademarks and trademark law at length, it should be noted that trademark rights may be lost through abandonment or misuse of the mark.

In the UK trademarks and service marks are protected by statute under the Trade Marks Act 1994.

Under the existing law trademarks may be applied for in respect of computer programs generally speaking under Class 9 for the program itself and under Class 16 for accompanying user manuals. One difficulty which many software houses have is that they tend to use descriptive marks as trademarks which may be unregisterable although the Trade Marks Act 1994 is considerably more lenient than the previous UK legislation. It is now possible to register not only names and words but also distinctive shapes and configurations.

One of the difficulties with trademark protection is that whereas in some countries trademarks may have protection even if unregistered in other countries there may be no protection at all and, therefore, whilst a prudent company may wish to register trademarks in connection with a particular program, this can be an expensive process since it may be necessary to register a trademark in every jurisdiction.

The Community Trade Mark ('CTM') which applies to member states of the EU came into force in 1996.[1] The Community Trade Mark Office is based in Alicante, Spain, and provides a harmonised trademark application system by means of one application for all member states.

1 Council Regulation (EC) (No 40 of 20 December 1993).

3.6 CONTRACT LAW

As previous sections of this work indicate, contract law is very important to software licences and the differences between software sale, lease, and licence agreements.

The rules as to whether a contract is validly formed differ between jurisdictions. What constitutes an enforceable contract under one legal system may not apply in another. A new area that is emerging particularly relates to digital signatures since many contracts are now being formed through e-commerce where no handwritten signature exists at all.

In English law it is generally necessary for there to be some consideration passing between the parties as well as there being an offer and acceptance. A promise to carry out a contract where there is no other consideration may not lead to a valid contract under English law. However, whilst agreeing to keep an offer open for a certain length of time would not be binding under English law it would be in other legal jurisdictions such as Scotland.

The Contracts (Rights of Third Parties) Act 1999 applies in the UK to contracts which are entered into on or after 11 May 2000. The Act enables a third party to enforce contractual rights as if it were a party to the contract. This is a big leap forward for customers who wish to seek the benefit of warranties in third-party licensed products as well as in reseller and integration contracts where many of the software products licensed are licensed on a 'back-to-back' contract basis. The parties to a software contract need now to consider when and whether third parties are to have rights or not. If third-party rights are to be excluded then such exclusion must be expressly referred to in the contract terms.

In the US where the transaction relates to a sale, then the Uniform Commercial Code applies and in many parts of Europe specific civil codes apply to contracts for sale. However, in Scotland, many European countries and parts of the US such rights can be conferred. This is significant where software is distributed by OEMs, VARs and other resellers appointed by the original provider. Care needs to be taken if the provider is to create a right to enforce rights against a licensee or receive the protection of any limits of liability in the sub-licence.

In 1999 the US passed the Uniform Computer Information Transactions Act (UCITA) which a number of states have now adopted. UCITA is intended to clarify the issues of online software contracting and provide statutory guidance as to how a click-wrap contract can be effectively made. More importantly UCITA is intended to clarify how the law applies to relationships between the software publisher and the end user. UCITA is, however, only of value when it is enforced as part of state legislation. At the beginning of 2002 UCITA was the subject of continued criticism and is the subject of redrafting, particularly in relation to sections of the legislation which presently allow software vendors to install disenabling devices into the software which are activated when licence fees are not paid or are not kept up.

3.7   REGISTERED DESIGNS

Directive 98/71/EC of the European Parliament and of the Council of 13 October 1998 on the legal protection of designs (OJ L289, 28.10.1998) was implemented throughout the EU by virtue of the Community Design Regulation (CDR) (OJ L3, 05.01.2002). At the end of 2006 the European Council confirmed that the EC will become a signatory to the Geneva Act of the Hague Agreement concerning the International Registration of Industrial Designs, and this will then allow applicants to obtain registered designs across the EU as well as in non-EU countries that are also signatories of the Geneva Act.

In the UK the CDR caused amendments to the Registered Design Act 1949 and has now generally made the registration as designs of computer icons, graphical user interfaces and web pages, a real opportunity for software developers and program owners.

Before the CDR, the UK, like many other member states, defined 'design' in terms of 'features of shape, configuration, pattern or ornament applied to an article by any industrial process ...' and the definition of 'article' was defined as 'any article of manufacture and includes any part of an article if that part is made and sold separately'. This set of definitions meant that computer generated images and icons were prevented from being protected.

Under the Registered Design Act 1949 (before amendment) in the United Kingdom, the narrow definitions of registered designs meant that in the case of computers, icons and symbols could only be protected if they were displayed directly as a result of information used to define and generate those symbols and therefore icons produced by software such as word processing programs were not capable of registration as they were not an integral part of the computer. Apple computers were successful in obtaining UK registered design no. 2094032 for 'computer display screens with computer generated icon' but this was after an appeal tribunal hearing.

The CDR as now implemented means that the definition of design under s 1(2) of the UK Registered Designs Act 1949 as amended reads '... the appearance of the whole or a part of a product resulting from the features of, in particular, the lines, contours, colours, shape, texture or materials of the product or its ornamentation'. Moreover, product is now defined as 'any industrial or handicraft item other than a computer program: and in particular, includes packaging, get up, graphic symbols, typographic typefaces and parts intended to be assembled into a complex product'.

The UK law and no doubt laws in other EU member states are now able to provide greater registered design protection for computer designers and computer vendors. It is possible to register all sorts of images generated by computer, displayed on screens, mobile phones, digital watches, digital cameras and MP3 players.

It has been suggested that the range of examples of what may be included within the definition of 'product', including 'get-up', 'graphic symbols' and 'typographic typefaces' shows that the term is to be interpreted broadly. Whilst computer programs are excluded from the definition of product this is only as regards the computer programs themselves (ie the lines of code and the functionality). Specific graphics which are produced by computer programs, such as icons, are likely to be considered protected as symbols.

It must be remembered that for graphics or symbols to be registered they must also be new and have individual character. This means that the design must not be identical to an existing design but there are no barriers to the registration therefore of new computer icons, graphical user interfaces, webpage designs or other computer generated symbols which were previously unregistered on the grounds that they were not applied to an article.

A registered design once granted lasts for 25 years and is an aggressive method of protection.

3.8 MORAL RIGHTS

Many jurisdictions which recognise that the inventive and intellectual efforts of authors are entitled to legal protection divide that protection between economic rights on the one hand and moral rights on the other. Whilst economic rights are intended to provide the means for the inventor or author to secure remuneration for exploitation of his works, the moral rights are concerned with the author's personal and professional reputation and are seen as quite separate to, for example, copyright.

France introduced express copyright protection for computer software in 1985 and, at the same time, modified the application of moral rights to this type of copyright work. Moral rights include first, the right to control disclosure of the work, secondly the right to determine when and in what matter the work is to be attributed to the author, thirdly the right to withdraw the work from publication and fourthly, the right to prevent modification of the work and to prevent its destruction.

In the UK moral rights were first introduced into our statutory law by the Copyright Designs and Patents Act 1988, ss 77–79.

Moral rights do not apply to computer programs in the UK but they will apply to other material accompanying computer programs, such as user manuals, specifications and so on, and since quite often works produced by employees for employer licensors or by sub-contracted programmers will be vested in the licensor then it is certainly necessary to provide, for contractual provisions, to deal with the question of moral rights which will not necessarily pass over to the employer or commissioner. The best protection for the employer or commissioner is to ensure that the employee/freelance programmer waives moral rights but where such a waiver cannot be obtained then specifically there must be agreement as to precisely what moral rights are to be exercised or may be exercised.

Since moral rights is still a relatively new area for computer software licences and related matters there is not, as yet, a body of legislation in the UK and this is an area where, no doubt, further developments will occur in the future.

4   European Union law

4.1   OVERVIEW

At the core of the laws of the EU is the Treaty of Rome (now replaced by the Treaty on the Functioning of the European Union (TFEU), or Lisbon Treaty), which provides for the establishment of a common European and economic market and each member state of the EU is subject to the Treaty of Rome and the laws which emanate from the European Commission.

When the UK joined the EC various laws were immediately incorporated into UK law without further parliamentary legislation and now certain European laws automatically override UK law and certain European Directives have to, ultimately, be implemented in the UK as our law.

Many of the competition laws and other laws of the EU are applicable to member states of the EEA.[1]

One of the main areas of EU law which affects computer contracts is in the field of competition where the TFEU, arts 101 and 102 (formerly Treaty of Rome, arts 81 and 82) relate to agreements between companies which, in effect, are distorting competition by creating monopolies or where the parties abuse their dominant position within the market place.

1   Ie the member states of the EU plus Norway, Iceland and Liechtenstein.

4.2   COMPETITION LAW

The Competition Rules of the EU are interpreted and applied by the European Commission so as to further the general economic and political policies of the member states to the ultimate benefit of the consumer. They are applied to distribution agreements, know-how agreements, joint ventures, mergers, acquisitions, patent licences etc.

Article 101 of the TFEU prohibits agreements which distort competition, for instance, where a licensor attempts to specify prices at which goods may be resold or imposes obligations on a licensee to automatically hand back to the licensor improvements made by a licensee during the course of an agreement. However, Regulation 2790/1999 (OJ 1999 L336/21, 22 December 1999) provides a general block exemption for vertical agreements if market share of the relevant market is no greater than 30% (art 3). There is also a turnover threshold of:

1. €100 million where competing undertakings enter into a non-reciprocal vertical agreement (art 2(2)).

2. €50 million where an association of retailers enter into vertical agreements with their members or suppliers (art 2(2)).

The same Regulation also provides an exemption to vertical agreements where intellectual property rights are assigned or licensed to a buyer, provided such rights:

—   are not the primary object of the agreement;

—   are directly related to the use, sale or resale of goods by the buyer or its customers; and

—   the contract's clauses do not contain provisions having the same object or effect as vertical restraints not excepted (art 2(3)).

Importantly for software vendors, it is now possible to impose 'non-compete' clauses on resellers provided the term does not exceed five years! However, there are certain minimal agreements to which the TFEU, art 101 (formerly Treaty of Rome, art 81) will not apply where, for example, the goods or services that the agreement relates to, together with the parties' similar goods or services, are less than 5% of the total market affected by the agreement and the parties' aggregate annual turnover does not exceed €300m. The above rule (applying to minimal agreements), known as the 'de minimis' rule, is the subject of review and it is proposed to raise the market share threshold for vertical agreements to 10% and to remove the turnover threshold. The de minimis rule arises as a result of the European Commission Notice on Agreements of Minor Importance which do not fall under article 81.1 of 3 September 1986,[1] as amended by the Commission Notice of 23 December 1994.[2] In addition to the exemptions listed above, an agreement can also be exempted from art 101 either under individual or under block exemptions issued by the European Commission if certain conditions are met.[2]

A block exemption is a regulation which automatically confers exemption on a particular type of agreement which complies with the terms of the exemption. For example, there is a block exemption relating to exclusive distributorships which, amongst other things, permits restrictions in exclusive distribution agreements to the effect that distributors are prevented from seeking customers outside their territory. However, if a distributor receives an unsolicited request from outside its territory it is entitled to respond. However, in an exclusive distribution agreement where there was a statement that a distributor 'shall not sell nor export whether directly or not the products to other countries and the territory without the "principal's" consent in writing', it was held that this was not protected by the block exemption since the terms of the wording were such that the distributor was effectively prevented from himself distributing outside the territory or indeed allowing anyone else to. This contravened the EU concept of free trade within the whole Community.

The European Commission has introduced a new Regulation to apply to technology transfers. Technology transfers have been subject to European competition rules for many years, but have had the benefit of certain 'clearances' which automatically apply if the agreements either meet existing competition laws, or are of relatively minor importance and therefore do not materially affect free trade within the European Union.

The Technology Transfer Block Exemption Regulation ('TTBER') provides a 'safe harbour' to businesses whose market share thresholds fall below certain levels – 20% combined for licensing agreements between competitors and 30% each for agreements between non-competitors. In other words, even if the terms of a licensing agreement could be seen as anti-competitive the agreement may not be subject to competition rules if the parties' market shares fall below the above levels.

In addition to the market share (or de minimis) exemption the TTBER provides a blacklist of hardcore anti-trust violations.

The TTBER affects not only patent and know-how licensing but also technology transfer agreements relating to design right and software. It does not, however, apply to R&D, technology pooling and sub-distribution agreements.

The TFEU, art 102 (formerly Treaty of Rome, art 82) seeks to prevent abuse of dominant position within the marketplace where, for example, a dominant company forms cartels, refuses to supply or creates elements of over-charging.

In 1984 IBM was investigated by the European Commission who applied the Treaty of Rome, art 82 to the situation where IBM was found to have a dominant position in the supply of central processing units and basic operating and system software for IBM computers 360 and 370 on account of IBM's significant market share in the central processing unit market. It was alleged that IBM had abused its power because it had not provided other manufacturers with the technical information they needed in order for them to make competitive products compatible with 360 and 370 products. Proceedings by the Commission were suspended after IBM gave certain undertakings to supply the necessary interface information and to make available certain formats and protocols to third parties.

Two decisions are of relevance to aspects of the computer industry and, in particular, contractual provisions within the industry, because it is clear that the European Commission will not tolerate dominant companies maintaining a monopoly or abusing their power by restricting competition or the movement of goods and services within the EU (*Re Magill TV Guide/ITP, BBC and RTE*,[3] and *Re Tetra Pak II*[4]).

In relation to the Treaty of Rome, arts 81 and 82 it has only been possible to touch the surface of this complex area. However, the question of aspects of a software licence which might distort the opportunity of competition or restrict the movement of goods within the Community should be borne in mind, whether the parties are both within the UK or whether only one of the parties is within the EU.

There are often conflicts between the intellectual property rights monopoly that an owner has over its products on the one hand and the requirements of competition law for there to be free movement of goods on the other hand.

As a general principle, compulsory licensing of intellectual property rights is contrary to the notion of monopoly conferred by intellectual property rights, but on occasions the European Court of Justice recognises that there may be an obligation to grant licences where an intellectual property right either relates to an essential facility or is otherwise required for development of new markets.

1   OJ 1986 C231/2.
2   OJ 1994 C368/6.
3   [1989] 4 CMLR 757.
4   [1992] 4 CMLR 551.

4.3   EC DIRECTIVE ON THE LEGAL PROTECTION OF COMPUTER PROGRAMS

The Software Directive[1] (officially known as the Directive on the legal protection of computer programs) harmonises copyright protection for computer programs throughout the EU so that there can be a more internationally effective basis for protection. The Software Directive requires computer programs to be protected by copyright as if they were literary works, following what is already the case in the UK and is understood in the Berne Convention. The period of copyright protection is for the life of the author plus 50 years or, where the program is owned by a company as employer, then 50 years from the time of publication of the program. In addition, the copyright holder is entitled to prevent unauthorised copying, but a licensee of the program is permitted to carry out any form of copying which is necessary for the program to be used or in order to make a security back-up, and is also allowed to carry out error correction for the purpose of enabling the program to run correctly. Furthermore, reverse engineering or decompilation is now possible where the licensee needs to understand the underlying code, copy and translate the program and investigate the functionality of the program in order to understand its ideas and principles and no consent of the copyright holder is here required provided, of course, that such information is not already available to the licensee.

The Software Directive is embodied in UK law by the Copyright (Computer Programs) Regulations 1992.[2]

The Software Directive has recently been the subject of judicial opinion and analysis in the case of *SAS Institute Inc v World Programming Ltd* (see discussion in 3.3).[3]

1   91/250 OJ 1991 L122.
2   SI 1992/3233.
3   *SAS Institute Inc v World Programming Ltd* [2013] EWHC 69(Ch).

4.4   EC DIRECTIVE ON RENTAL AND LENDING RIGHTS AND CERTAIN RIGHTS RELATING TO COPYRIGHT

This Rental Lending Directive,[1] which came into force in 1994, introduced a right for the creators of copyright work to authorise or prohibit the rental and lending of originals and copies of copyright works. The Directive is implemented in the UK under the CDPA 1988.

1   92/100 OJ 1992 L346.

4.5   EC DIRECTIVE HARMONISING THE TERM OF PROTECTION OF COPYRIGHT AND CERTAIN RELATED RIGHTS

This Directive[1] harmonised the term of copyright protection as from July 1995 where the term is set at 70 years after the death of the author or after the work is made available to the public and for related rights 50 years from the point at which the copyright term begins. This is now in force from 1 January 1996 in the UK by virtue of the Duration of Copyright and Rights in Performances Regulations 1995.[2]

1   93/98 OJ 1993 L290.
2   SI 1995/3297.

4.6   EC DIRECTIVE ON THE LEGAL PROTECTION OF DATABASES

This Database Directive[1] intended to harmonise, throughout the EU, the legal protection of electronic and manual databases.

The Directive defines a database as 'a collection of works, data or other independent materials arranged in a systematic or methodical way and capable of being individually accessed by electronic or other means'. Not only does the Directive contemplate electronic and digital databases, but it also states that protection under the Directive should also extend to non-electronic databases, thereby including paper databases within the Directive.

The Database Directive creates protection of both structure and content of the database with copyright protection applying to the structure and a *sui generis* right applying as a method of protection for the content.

For the structure as well as the content of the database to be protected by copyright, the creator of the database must have used skill and judgment in the selection of the content. The period of copyright protection is to be 70 years from the date of creation or publication. The *sui generis* right will apply where the content has been compiled without necessarily involving skill and judgment and its period of protection is 15 years, but renewable in the event of any major change to the database content.

It should be noted that the copyright protection will apply to the structure of the database notwithstanding that individual elements of the content of the database may also be subject to their own copyright protection.

Because of the EEA-centric nature of the Directive non-EEA database makers or database owners cannot benefit from the *sui generis* right.

A UK company which sub-contracts database development outside the EEA is still regarded as the database maker and therefore has full protection.

A US company which acquires a database from a UK database maker will on the one hand purchase the database but on the other hand may not have any rights to enforce the *sui generis* right in the EEA.

Often, this EEA-centric issue is not a problem because foreign companies purchasing databases from the EEA do so as a result of a share acquisition and therefore the database rights holder remains an EEA resident entity. However, where a foreign company makes an asset purchase (as opposed to a share purchase) the rights will be assigned to the foreign entity which, if copyright protection does not apply, will no longer be able to enforce the *sui generis* right within the EEA.

It is important that companies which are making acquisitions or taking licences of EEA created databases should carry out due diligence as to the rights of the database maker in such databases (eg whether copyright or *sui generis* or both). Where the database being transferred is protected by *sui generis* rights then the foreign company should consider making such acquisition through an EEA subsidiary.

1   96/9 OJ 1996 L77/20.

4.7   EC DIRECTIVE ON UNFAIR CONTRACT TERMS

This Directive,[1] which came into force at the end of 1994, protects consumers from unfair terms in pre-printed or standard form contracts. In the UK we already have the Unfair Contract Terms Act 1977 which has similar intentions but the European Directive is now in force in the UK by means of the Unfair Terms in Consumer Contract Regulations 1994[2] and relates to a number of terms which may be considered unfair in contracts with consumers.

This Directive and the UK Regulations are of particular interest to software suppliers who operate on standard terms of sale or supply and to sizeable purchasing companies who operate on standard terms and conditions of purchase in that where the parties are of considerably unequal bargaining power, and particularly where the other party is a consumer or end-user, then any ambiguity in the standard terms will be interpreted against the person who drew them up or, in the event that the terms are deemed to be unfair, then they will be struck out of the contract.

1 93/13 OJ 1993 L95.
2 SI 1994/3159.

4.8 EC DIRECTIVE ON E-SIGNATURES

In e-commerce and e-procurement it is important to be sure that any online contracts and licences are validly made and furthermore that the parties making them can be authenticated.

The E-signature Directive[1] was the result of various EU communications and research, in particular work carried out by DG XI11 and is an indication of the EU's desire to lead in the initiatives for globally secure e-commerce.

The Directive was a reaction to the demands and initiatives of business communities including the work of UNCITRAL, OECD, ICC and others.

The Directive has as its aim first, the framework for providing legal validity to e-signatures and, secondly, a framework for a hierarchy of certification authorities.

Since not all signatures which are created electronically are digital signatures (as later defined) the Directive accepts that there may be a need to define digital signatures and e-signatures separately (and indeed does so).

The Directive also addresses the issue of certification authorities. In paper contracts where high levels of authentication or verification are required, then the signature of the party to be bound to a contract is often witnessed and/or notarised. In electronic transmissions there is no automatic form of witness or notarisation and indeed there is usually an absence of this act or performance. Recently this lack of authenticity has been addressed by the use of certification authorities who attest to the identity of the person signing electronically and where such signature is achieved using a digital signature then the facility exists for a digital certificate to be supplied by a certification authority, giving further certification or verification to the e-signature as well as the message.

'E-signature' is defined so as to include digital signature but to include other 'data in electronic form'. The Directive recognises that there are other methods of e-signature such as biometric technology or signature digitisation technology which provide methods of authentication.

Where an e-signature is to be given force of law by being verified by a certification service provider, it is easier in the area of digital signatures to see how this can occur than it is in other forms of digitised signature because, in general, the creation of a digitised signature is carried out with the use of technology, whereas the creation of a digital signature is effected by technology itself.

The definitions of 'e-signature' and 'advanced e-signature' compare favourably with other definitions in circulation.

The Directive also defines what is meant by 'certification service provider' as an accredited person or entity providing certification services. These services are not spelt out but would be likely to include not only the provision of e-certificates but also date and time stamping and other archiving and storage services, but not key escrow services where the private key, as opposed to the public key, is held by the certification service provider.

The accreditation of a certification service provider is left to member states to set up, but guidance is given within the Directive on the types of accreditation schemes to be made available and definitions for those schemes and accreditation bodies are given in the Directive. In the UK, the Department of Trade and Industry carried out a consultation exercise during 2001 in relation to its proposed regulations on the implementation of the Directive. On 25 January 2002 the Department issued a second Consultation Paper on its proposed regulations, particularly in relation to, first, the liability that a certification service provider may be obliged to accept in relation to those who rely upon digital certificates and, secondly, the data protection obligations to be placed on certification service providers.

The UK government implemented the Electronic Signatures Regulations 2002.[2]

The reality is that the take-up of digital signatures themselves has not been great and indeed there has not been as harmonised an approach to the use of these signatures and authentication methods as was expected by both technology providers and governments.

The continued growth of online communication and the value to the European Union of the digital economy has raised the question as to what consumers and technology providers see as valuable in electronic signatures and electronic identification. In launching the public consultation Neelie Kroes, European Commission Vice President for the Digital Agenda said 'I welcome everybody's views on how we can best verify people's identities and signatures when we buy, sell or undertake administrative procedures online but need to be highly secure. I want to help all Europeans get online without feeling that they will fall victim to data frauds or scams.'

The consultation seeks feedback on:

- citizens' and businesses' expectations of EU rules on electronic signatures, identification and authentication;

- the ICT sector's view on how these signatures can be best tailored to face the forthcoming challenges triggered by technological progress;

- the common set of principles which should guide the mutual recognition of e-identification and

- e-authentication in Europe;

- the potential contribution of research and innovation to the development of new e-identification and

- e-signature for authentication, such as alternatives to current public key infrastructure (PKI) technology used for digital signatures.

The results of the consultation will be used to make necessary changes to the current e-signatures regime.

1   99/93 OJ 1999 L013.
2   SI 2002/318.

4.9   EC DIRECTIVE ON DISTANCE SELLING OF GOODS AND SERVICES

The Distance Selling Directive[1] on the protection of consumers in respect of distance contracts was published in June 1997.

It should be noted that the Distance Selling Directive does not apply to contracts relating to financial services including banking and insurance.

The Distance Selling Directive applies to any contract concerning goods or services concluded between a supplier and a consumer under an organised distance sales or service scheme run by the supplier, who, for the purpose of the contract, makes exclusive use of one or more distance communications, up to and including the moment at which the contract is concluded. The Distance Selling Directive specifically lists mediums by which such distance sales can take place which include digital transmissions via PC or television.

The Distance Selling Directive requires the supplier to give certain information to the consumer before a contract is concluded, including:

—   the identity of the supplier;

—   the supplier's address;

—   description of the goods or services;

—   details of payment;

—   delivery costs;

—   a right of cancellation; and

—   for alternative conditions to be in clear and intelligible language.

Article 6 of the Distance Selling Directive[2] lays down requirements relating to the right of withdrawal, including a 'cooling-off period' and this Distance Selling Directive is a clear example of where consumers' rights are dictated by their own country's law and cannot be waived through an online contract.

The Distance Selling Directive was implemented into English law by the Consumer Protection (Distance Selling) Regulations[3] on 31 October 2000.

4.10   EC DIRECTIVE ON DATA PROTECTION

There is no general constitutional nor statutory right to privacy in the UK and the UK courts have not sought to develop a common law right of privacy.

There are, however, a number of initiatives that have originated from the European Commission which seek to give individuals the equivalent to rights of privacy and these have included not only the European Convention on Human Rights, but, more particularly, the EC Directive on Data Protection.[1]

The UK brought into force the Data Protection Act 1984 (DPA 1984) to enable the UK to ratify the Council of Europe's Convention for the Protection of Individuals with Regard to Automatic Processing of Personal Data. In order to understand DPA 1984 it is necessary to understand the Convention and the international initiatives that led up to that Convention.

1   95/46 OJ 1995 L281/31.

4.10.1   Background to the Data Protection Acts of 1984 and 1998

In 1974 the Organisation for Economic Co-operation and Development (OECD) set up a Data Bank Panel, and a group of experts that succeeded the Data Bank Panel put together what have become known as the OECD Guidelines. These were a set of guidelines rather than compulsory regulations and they placed importance on:

—   the need to harmonise the data protection laws of different countries;

—   the need to ensure a free flow of information; and

—   the necessity of guaranteeing rights where privacy and personal data were concerned.

Separately from the OECD the Council of Europe in the 1970s worked, amongst other things, on the preparation for an International Data Protection Treaty which was adopted on 28 January 1981 under the title of the Convention for the Protection of Individuals with regard to Automatic Processing of Personal Data. The Convention came into force on 1 October 1985 and is binding upon those member states who have signed or ratified the Convention.

The UK, having ratified the Convention, incorporated its basic principles into the DPA 1984 which came into force in 1988.

The EC Directive on Data Protection (the 'Directive'),[1] provides regulations as to the responsibilities of businesses which store, control and transfer data held about individuals and the data concerned may be automated or manual and may consist of personally identifiable sounds and images. Furthermore, the definition of use includes 'collection, recording, organisation, storage, adaptation or alteration, retrieval, consultation, use, disclosure by transmission, dissemination or otherwise making available, blocking, erasure or destruction'.

Given that the cost of notification under the UK Data Protection Act 1998 (DPA 1998) is £35 per annum, it seems surprising that any company should not look carefully at its requirements to notify.

Companies who obtain data from their website and then wish to use that data for marketing purposes and pass such data on to marketing or mailing list companies certainly need to reconsider their data protection registrations since they will need to draw to the attention of the data subject the reasons for which they are holding and obtaining and transmitting such data.

DPA 1998 reflects the requirements of the Directive and one of the main changes from DPA 1984 is that the law applies to paper records as well as e-records.

The UK law requires any business which processes data about living individuals to be notified with the Information Commissioner except in certain circumstances where the use of the data is only for the direct use of the business in relation to control of employee information, customer records and the like.

For businesses which are in the financial services, banking and credit reference sectors, as well as legal and consultancy services, there are no exemptions and notification is compulsory.

Failure to comply with the law in some instances brings not only civil liability but also criminal liability and there may be personal liability for directors and officers too!

Compliance with DPA 1998, irrespective as to whether exceptions are available or not, extends to the adherence to the eight Data Protection Principles laid down by the Directive.

The eight Data Protection Principles are:

1. Data must be processed fairly and lawfully with the express consent of the individual unless processing is necessary to comply with a contract with that individual.

2. Data must be obtained for one or more specified and lawful purposes and may not be further processed in any manner incompatible with those purposes.

3. Data shall be adequate, relevant and not excessive in relation to the purpose for which the data is processed.

4. Data shall be accurate and kept up to date.

5. Data shall not be kept for longer than is necessary.

6. Data shall be processed in accordance with the rights of the data subject under DPA 1998.

7. Appropriate technical and organisational measures should be taken against unauthorised or unlawful processing of data as well as against accidental loss, destruction or damage to such data.

8. Data shall not be transferred outside the EEA unless the recipient country provides an adequate level of protection in line with the European Data Protection Directive.

4.10.1.1 Rights of individuals

The individuals' rights under the Act relate to 'personal data'. Personal data is data which relates to a living individual who can be identified:

— from those data;

— from those data and other information;

— and includes any opinion about an individual and an indication of the data controller's intention towards that individual.

The various individual rights include:

1. Subject access rights.

2. The right to prevent processing likely to cause damage or distress.

3. The right to prevent processing for purposes of direct marketing.

4. Rights in relation to automated decision taking.

5. The right to take action for compensation if the individual suffers damage as a result of a breach of the Act by the data controller.

6. The right to take action to rectify, block, erase or destroy inaccurate data.

7. The right to make a request to the Commissioner for an assessment as to whether or not any provision of the Act has been contravened.

1   95/46 OJ 1995 L28/31.

4.10.2 Data security

It is difficult for a business which does not have in place adequate data security procedures to argue that it is in compliance with the Seventh Data Protection Principle. The Seventh Principle states:

> 'Appropriate technical and organisational measures shall be taken against unauthorised or unlawful processing of data as well as against accidental loss, destruction or damage to such data.'

The key words in the Seventh Principle, in this instance, are 'appropriate technical and operational measures'.

'Appropriate technical measures' might include the use of firewalls to keep out hackers, virus checkers to reduce the risk of infectious software entering the corporate network and encryption technology to provide confidentiality and authentication.

'Appropriate operational measures' will include the use of suitable policies, practices and procedures in order to ensure compliance with data security standards as well as safe use of the previously mentioned technological measures.

Businesses are advised to consider the implementation of the generally accepted security standard, set up by the British Standards Institute and endorsed by the Information Commissioner and the Department of Trade and Industry, BS 7799.

4.10.3 Transfer of data overseas

The Eighth Data Protection Principle states:

> 'Personal data shall not be transferred to a country or territory outside the European Economic Area unless that country or territory ensures an adequate level of protection for the rights and freedoms of data subjects in relation to the processing of personal data.'

4.10.4 US/EU Safe Harbor

With the passage of legislation implementing the Directive, it has effectively become illegal to transfer personal data from the EU to the US unless *one* of the Article 26 exceptions applies (see below). To avoid an international trade crisis, the European Commission, working with the US Department of Commerce, developed a 'safe harbour' for US organisations engaged in transatlantic business. US organisations that choose to join the safe harbour are deemed to provide an 'adequate level of protection' for personal data and, therefore, may receive personal data from the EU.

US 'safe harbor compliant' businesses must abide by certain principles which mirror the EU Data Protection Principles.

4.10.5 Trans-border data flows

In order to comply with the 'safe harbour' principles, a business in the private sector has to be monitored by its supervisory authority (such as a trade body or regulatory authority) and be certified as compliant. Companies that participate in Safe Harbor are identified on a website maintained by the US Department of Commerce. Although the programme is strictly voluntary, any company that signs on will be subject to government enforcement or private litigation if they fail to honour their commitment.

4.10.6 Article 26.1 of the Directive

Article 26.1 of the Directive requires member states to provide several exceptions to the general rule prohibiting the transfer of personal data to a country that does not provide 'an adequate level of protection'.

1. *Consent.* Transfers may be made with the 'unambiguous' consent of the data subject. The consent must be specific and informed. It can be made a condition for the provision of a non-essential service, but consent is unlikely to be valid if the data subject has no real choice but to give his/her consent. For example, if an existing employee is required to agree to the international transfer of data, his or her consent is unlikely to be valid if the penalty for withholding consent is dismissal. In so far as possible, the reasons for the transfer and the countries involved should be specified. Particular risks should be identified.

2. *Contract performance.* Trans-border transfers are permitted where certain types of contracts are in place or contemplated:

   — a contract between the data controller and the data subject, *and* the transfer is necessary for performance of the contract *or* the transfer is a necessary part of pre-contractual steps taken by the data controller at the request of the data subject;

   — a contract between the data controller and someone other than the data subject, *and* the contract is entered into at the data subject's request or in his/her interests and the transfer is necessary for performance of the contract or the transfer is necessary for conclusion of the contract.

   In this context, contracts are not restricted to goods and services. These provisions will, for example, be relevant in the case of employment contracts.

   Whether a transfer is 'necessary' for the performance of a contract depends on the nature of the goods, services, etc, provided under the contract rather than the business structure of the data controller. A transfer is not 'necessary' if the only reason it is needed is because of the way a data controller has chosen to structure its business.

3. *Important public interest.* This exception is most likely to apply in areas such as crime prevention and detection, national security and tax collection.

4. *Legal claims.* This exception applies if the transfer is necessary for the establishment, exercise or defence of legal claims.

5. *Vital interests.* This exception applies where the transfer is necessary to protect the vital interests of the data subject, that is, in matters of life or death.

6. *Public register.* This exception applies if the transfer is made from a register which according to law is intended to provide information to the public.

4.10.7 Article 26.2 of the Directive

In addition to the exceptions provided under Article 26.1, Article 26.2 of the Directive provides that member states may authorise a trans border data transfer where the 'data controller adduces adequate safeguards ... from appropriate contractual clauses'. In other words, personal data may be transferred from a member state to a country without 'adequate protection', if the member state's laws permit the parties to ensure the adequate protection of the data by means of appropriate contract provisions.

In determining what amounts to an adequate level of data protection, the following will have to be taken into consideration:

— The nature of the personal data.

— The country of origin of the information contained in the data.

— The country of final destination of that information.

— The purposes for which and period during which the data are intended to be processed.

— The law in force in the country or territory in question.

— The international obligation of that country or territory as well as any relevant codes of conduct or other rules which are enforceable in that country.

— Any security measures taken in respect of the data in that country.

The Directive provides that the EU Commission can decide whether or not a certain country outside the EEA ensures an adequate level of data protection. The EU currently has stated that Canada, Guernsey, Jersey, Isle of Man and Switzerland have an adequate level of data protection.

4.10.8 Trans-Border Data Flow (TBDF) agreements

European Commission Model Clauses. Because of the importance of TBDF agreements to the uninterrupted flow of data, the European Commission has published its Decision approving standard contractual clauses that, in its judgment, provide adequate protection for data transferred to countries that do not, by law, provide adequate protection. The legal effect of the Decision is to oblige member states to recognise as providing adequate safeguards contracts corresponding to the clauses approved in the Decision.

Non-standard TBDF agreements. Notwithstanding the Decision, businesses are free to develop and use their own non-standard TBDF agreements which may be based on the model clauses. The difference is that by using a non-standard TBDF agreement, the data controller takes the risk that there could be a subsequent challenge as to whether the contract used did in fact ensure adequacy.

Prior approval of non-standard TBDF agreements. In most member states, there is no system of prior approval by the local Commissioner. Rather, it is for the data controller to determine how it ensures compliance with applicable data protection laws and to be able to defend its actions should it be called on to do so subsequently.

With regard to such clauses, Art 26(4) provides that the Commission may decide that certain standard contractual clauses offer sufficient safeguards. This provision is the legal basis for the Decision on the Model Clauses for transferring data to a data controller in a third country published by the Commission on 15 June 2001 and which came into force on 3 September 2001, as well as the Decision on the Model Clauses for transferring data to a data processor in a third country of 27 December 2001.

ICC Model Agreement. The International Chamber of Commerce (ICC), in 1997, began preparing Model Trans Border Data Flow Clauses, which were then submitted to the European Commission. Although their clauses were not approved, the EU Model Clauses, published in 2000, were remarkably similar!

In 2003, the ICC (which, since 1997, had been drafting a more 'business-friendly' set of clauses) in conjunction with the Confederation of British Industry, the International Communications Round Table, the Federation of European Direct Marketing, the Japanese Business Council in Europe and the European Industry Association of Information Systems Communication Technologies and Consumer Electronics published a second version of their proposed standard contractual clauses which were submitted to the Article 31 Committee and Article 29 Working Party of the European Commission responsible for EU Data Protection. After lengthy negotiations a final version was submitted for approval in September 2003.

On 5 January 2005 the European Commission approved the ICC Model Contract to take effect from 1 April 2005.

Binding corporate rules. On 3 June 2003 the Article 29 Data Protection Working Party of the European Commission published a working document which proposed that as an alternative to the EU Model Clauses on trans-border data flows, it may be possible for multinational corporations to utilise their binding corporate rules in order to meet the 'adequacy test' with regard to trans border data flows of personal data.

The working document is available at http://europa.eu.int/comm/internal_market/privacy/workingroup/wp2003/wpdocs03_en.htm.

The working document recognises that many multinational companies would like to adopt codes of conduct for international transfers of personal data along the same lines as other binding corporate codes which they use for items such as protection of confidential information, prohibition and misuse of corporate assets, implementation of ethical business practices and the like.

The Article 29 Working Party make it clear that they do not see binding corporate codes as being an indication that the EU Model Clauses have been superseded but rather that they see codes of conduct sitting alongside other trans border data flow solutions. Whilst this working document is an encouraging step in the right direction for ensuring free movement of personal data cross-border, it should be made clear that any binding corporate code of conduct must take into account the fact that:

— data subjects should be made third party beneficiaries of such codes of conduct;

— such codes of conduct should be subject to national legislation applicable to members of the corporate group;

— to that extent some existing codes of conduct may go part of the way to being acceptable, they will, however, need further work to bring them in line with the Article 29 proposals.

Several Data Protection Authorities, including the Information Commissioner's Office in the UK, have expressed considerable interest in promoting the use of binding corporate rules (BCR). The UK, Austria, Germany and the Netherlands and four others are currently examining BCR submitted by several multinationals, and it may well be that if such BCR are approved that this will put pressure on all Data Protection Authorities to view BCR as a viable alternative to TBDF agreements.

The ICC BCR Working Party has completed a review and report to promote the use of BCR and explain the enforceability or 'binding nature' of BCR under national laws.

On 14 April 2005 the Article 29 Data Protection Working Party published two working documents which positively support BCR.

Working document WP 108 provides a checklist for companies to use when developing BCR to enable those companies to speed up the process of approval with national regulators.

Working document WP 107 outlines a proposed cooperation procedure for allowing the approval by one national regulator to create a 'domino effect' approval for other national regulators.

Until now, companies have had to submit different application forms to each EU member state when asking data protection authorities to approve their BCRs – corporate codes which set measures to ensure data protection in transfers from one country within the EU to a country outside it. To help businesses demonstrate their compliance, the ICC took the initiative to standardise the process across all 27 EU countries by way of a single BCR application form. The standardised form was submitted to the Article 29 Working Party for discussion and I was involved in drafting and liaising with the UK ICO and Irish DPA.

Divided into eight sections, the ICC form guides companies through the application process, ensuring all the necessary information is included, and explains what conditions exist and what obligations need to be met. The

EC has now published a standard application form for the approval by data protection authorities in the EEA of BCR to regulate the transfer of personal data cross-border which is very similar to that which the ICC form.

The standard application form is intended to provide a one stop track mechanism for companies to obtain approval in all member states of their BCR, as an alternative solution to the use of EU approved Model Clauses for adducing adequacy of protection in relation to personal data when it is transferred from within the EEA to third countries.

eBay is another multinational that has developed BCR as a mechanism to protect the data and privacy rights of individuals in the event that their personal data is transferred to third countries outside the European Economic Area. eBay has taken just 12 months to develop and gain approval of its BCR which apply to both employees' and customers' personal data.

For many businesses with limited global data transfers it may be sufficient to contemplate the use of either safe harbour or the EU Model Clauses, but for others with complex corporate structures and a web of cross-border data transfers BCR seems the holy grail if not the reality!

Data controller to data processor agreements. In a move to standardise and speed up transfers of international data worldwide, the International Chamber of Commerce has submitted to the European Commission (EC) a proposal covering flows of personal data from data controllers to data processors.

Since the EC published its set of controller to processor clauses in 2001, the business community has recognised the need for a more pragmatic set of clauses that takes into account the rapidly-evolving climate for data processing. As global sourcing progresses and more and more businesses transfer data processing to companies that process data subject to an agreement with and under the control of the original data controller, the need for more pragmatic clauses has increased. On 5 February 2010, after many years of consultation and negotiation with leading trade organisations such as the International Chamber of Commerce, the EC published updated standard contractual clauses to allow transfer of personal data by controllers in the EU to processors outside the EU.

The new Model Clauses took effect from 15 May 2010. They allow processors to sub-process transfers that will be helpful for many global entities and service providers, and is an acknowledgement of the complexities of data management and processing today, not envisaged when the Data Protection Directive was drafted nearly two decades ago.

The Decision is available at:http://eur-lex.europa.eu/LexUriServ/LexUriServ. do?uri=OJ:L:2010:039:0005:0018:EN:PDF.

In December 2012 the Article 29 Data Protection Working Party announced the implementation effective on 1 January 2013 of BCR for processors. The new BCR for processors enables a data processor for itself and the data controller to comply with the EU data protection rules without having to negotiate safeguards and conditions each time a contract is entered into. Working Party Document 195 sets out the proposals for a BCR for processors and an application for it has now been published to enable a BCR to be submitted by a processor. The application procedure for a processor BCR will be the same as for BCR for controllers which 'means it will be based on a process with a lead DPA and a system of mutual recognition involving a substantial number of European DPAs'.

4.11   EC DIRECTIVE ON WASTE ELECTRICAL AND ELECTRONIC EQUIPMENT (WEEE DIRECTIVE) (2002/96/EC) AND EC DIRECTIVE ON THE RESTRICTION OF THE USE OF CERTAIN HAZARDOUS SUBSTANCES IN ELECTRICAL AND ELECTRONIC EQUIPMENT (RoHS DIRECTIVE) (2002/95/EC)

The objective of the WEEE Directive is to increase and encourage the amount of recycling of WEEE within the EU while minimising the disposal of WEEE as unsorted municipal waste. Manufacturers are encouraged to design products that can be easily disassembled, recycled and reused and that have minimal environmental impact. Broadly this is achieved by making producers of WEEE responsible for its collection and recycling and environmentally sound disposal.

The RoHS Directive goes hand in hand with the WEEE Directive in limiting the amounts of specified potentially hazardous substances that may be contained in electronic equipment, since the content of hazardous components in electronics is seen as a significant barrier to recycling of WEEE.

Individual member states are responsible for implementing the Directives and it will be these local laws that must be complied with. As both Directives grant member states some discretion in how they may transpose, it is expected that local differences will pose a major challenge for businesses operating across different member states.

4.11.1   Type of products affected

The WEEE Directive applies to a wide range of electrical appliances, provided that they do not form part of another type of equipment that is not covered by the Directive, intended both for consumers and business users which are in ten broad categories:

— Large household appliances.

— Small household appliances.

— IT and telecommunications equipment.

— Consumer equipment.

— Lighting equipment.

— Electrical and electronic tools (with the exception of large-scale stationary industrial tools).

— Toys, leisure and sports equipment.

— Medical devices (with the exception of all implanted and infected products).

— Monitoring and control instruments.

— Automatic dispensers.

The RoHS Directive covers eight of the ten categories listed under the WEEE Directive but does not include medical devices and monitoring and control instruments (although the possible inclusion of these two categories will be reviewed) but also covers electric light bulbs and household luminaries. The RoHS Directive does not apply to spare parts for the repair of EEE placed on the market before 1 July 2006 or to the reuse of EEE placed on the market before that date.

4.11.2 Key elements of the WEEE Directive

A 'producer' of WEEE, according to the Directive is any person who:

— manufactures and sells EEE under his own brand;

— resells EEE produced by other suppliers under his own brand; or

— imports or exports EEE on a professional basis into a member state.

Under a notion of Individual Producer Responsibility, in each EU member state 'producers' will, *inter alia*, be responsible for:

— registering with the appropriate authorities;

— providing annual data on the quantity and category of EEE that they put onto the market;

— ensuring the equipment is marked with a crossed-out wheelie-bin symbol (this signals that the product is EEE for the purposes of the WEEE Directive and was placed on the market after 13 August 2005) and bears the mark of the producer;

— financing the collection, treatment, recycling etc of household WEEE from central collection facilities;

— financing the collection, treatment, recycling etc of non-household WEEE placed on the market before 13 August 2005 when supplying replacement products;

— financing the collection, treatment, recycling etc of non-household WEEE;

— demonstrating evidence that targets of recycling and reuse are being met;

— providing information to those involved in the collection, treatment, recycling and environmentally sound disposal of WEEE to enable them to identify various components and any hazardous substances;

— providing financial guarantees in respect of household EEE (by way of participation in a collective financing scheme, a recycling insurance or a blocked bank account).

Retailers and distributors of EEE to household consumers are required to provide free in store take-back to domestic customers when those customers are placing like-for-like replacement equipment.

It will be an offence and penalties will be imposed on those firms who fail to meet their responsibilities under the implementing member state law.

It is open to producers to comply individually or through a compliance scheme or a collective scheme which would handle registering and reporting as well as collecting, treating and recycling the waste according to the producer's needs.

4.11.3 Key elements of the RoHS Directive

While, in essence the WEEE Directive makes the WEEE producer 'responsible' for what he places on the market, the RoHS Directive places strict limits on the amount of lead, cadmium, mercury, hexavalent chromium and both polybrominated biphenyl (PBB) and polybrominated diphenyl ether (PBDE) flame retardants. Again, this responsibility falls on the 'producer' but will in practice be up to the manufacturer to ensure that the products are marketable in the EU.

In broad terms, producers of electronics will be prohibited from placing on the EU market EEE products which are non-compliant with the maximum concentration values. Failure to comply will be an offence (although there will be a defence of due diligence) and fines will be imposed by the regulatory authorities.

There are also numerous exemptions from RoHS (which will be reviewed every four years) for specific applications such as lead in glass of cathode ray tubes and fluorescent tubes, lead as an alloying element, lead in electronic ceramic parts, mercury in particular categories of fluorescent lamps, hexavalent chromium as an anti-corrosion of the carbon steel cooling system in absorption refrigerators. The European Commission is considering further possible exemptions for specific applications.

Although self-declaration will be the basis for compliance, producers must be able to demonstrate this by supplying enforcement agencies with technical information, when requested, as to the contents of the EEE. This information must be retained by the producer for a period of four years after the EEE is placed on the market. Failure to supply this information when requested will also be an offence.

4.11.4 Key dates

13 August 2005 was a key date in the EU in respect of WEEE – any products placed on the market after this date must bear the crossed-out wheelie-bin symbol and carry the producer's mark. The key date for RoHS was 1 July 2006. EEE products placed on the EU market after that date must comply with the RoHS maximum concentration values.

4.11.5 Issues for the inbound and outbound supply chain

The WEEE and RoHS Directives have a combined impact on the entire supply chain. Component suppliers, OEM manufacturers, manufacturers, importers, distributors and business end-users are likely to be affected. The intended effect is that in order to comply with WEEE more easily, manufacturers will be encouraged to produce EEE that is durable and can be easily treated, reused or recycled. Important decisions at the design stage will therefore reduce end-of-life costs associated with WEEE.

In a typical scenario, a manufacturer of IT equipment that is sold in the EU will need to ensure that his component suppliers supply RoHS compliant components (this could involve a vast number of suppliers). The head manufacturer will require materials information and certificates of compliance. Manufacturers should also review their contractual relationships with suppliers to take account of the question of RoHS compliance. Likewise first tier suppliers will require certificates of compliance and materials information from their suppliers and so on. Information on the contents of components will be important in order to meet the RoHS requirements but also to be able to provide that information to recyclers and treatment facilities when those products reach end-of life as required by WEEE.

The IT manufacturer will have to adopt measures to comply with WEEE in individual EU member states – his approach will depend on how the products are sold (whether directly or via resellers or distributors) across the EU and whether the end-users are household consumers or businesses. As per RoHS considerations, the manufacturer will also need to review existing and proposed contracts with resellers/distributors and business end-users. This will involve collaborating with outbound supply chain participants, establishing company policies concerning WEEE and RoHS as well as making important business decisions.

Failure to take up the compliance challenge promptly will result in damaging consequences: suppliers of non-RoHS-compliant parts risk being removed from supplier lists, non-RoHS-compliant products will be banned from sale in the EU and producers that have not addressed WEEE compliance will therefore be at a competitive disadvantage in the marketplace.

4.11.6   UK WEEE Consultation

On 7 April 2009 the Department for Business, Enterprise and Regulatory Reform (BERR) published a consultation paper on the European Commission's proposed changes to the WEEE and RoHS Directives. The WEEE Directive (Waste Electrical and Electronic Equipment Directive (2002/96/EC)) places responsibilities on producers and distributors to pay for collection and disposal schemes for WEEE. The regulations on WEEE have been in force for some time in the UK and have led to 'take back systems' for products that incorporate the crossed wheelie bin sign.

But this has also led to an increase in administrative burdens for authorities and manufacturers. The proposed changes to the WEEE Directive and its implementation in the UK are intended to:

—   reduce administration and bureaucracy;

—   encourage re-use of WEEE;

—   require producer registration to be limited to one member state only in order to reduce savings;

—   increase enforcement; but

—   encourage producers to finance all the cost of WEEE collection throughout the whole waste chain;

—   give more information to users of EEA products in order to enable them to make informed purchasing choices.

The RoHS Directive (Restriction on Use of Certain Hazardous Substances in Electrical and Electronic Equipment Directive (2002/95/EC)) prohibits the marketing of new EEE that contains more than prescribed levels of certain hazardous substances including heavy metals and flame retardants. The RoHS Directive is intended to minimise the impact on the environment when EEE is treated or disposed of and the proposed changes are intended amongst other things to bring RoHS in line with other environmental initiatives such as WEEE and the REACH Regime (Regulation) EC (No.1907/2006) for the use of chemicals.

The amendments will for the first time include medical devices and monitoring and control instruments as being categories of equipment subject to the RoHS Directive.

Until now medical device, control and monitoring instrument manufacturers and suppliers have been excluded from the requirements of RoHS and will no doubt have concerns about the practicalities and costs of their equipment now being included.

4.11.7 EU WEEE Consultation

On 17 April last the Department for Business Innovation and Skills (BIS) launched the UK Government's consultation of implementing the recast WEEE Directive 2012 (Directive 2012/19/EU on waste electrical and electronic equipment (WEEE) (recast)) and on changes to the Waste Electrical and Electronic Equipment (WEEE) Regulations 2006.

The consultation closes on 21 June 2013 and is a key part of the process to introduce the revised WEEE Regulations that are expected to come into force from 1 January 2014.

The consultation is relevant to:

- Producers;

- Retailers;

- Distance sellers;

- Distributors;

- Local authorities;

- Waste management companies and treatment operators; and

- Re-use organisations.

The recast WEEE Directive introduced a number of changes of which the main ones are:

- The introduction of higher member state collection and recovery targets and a changed methodology for calculating the WEEE collection rate;

- A wider scope for the range of products covered by the Directive;

- Lowering the regulatory and cost burdens on business through the introduction of an 'authorised representative' who can fulfil the obligations of the producer;

- Better controlling of the illegal international trade in WEEE; and

- A requirement for retailer take-back of very small WEEE in certain circumstances.

Part III
Preparing for negotiations

5   Understanding negotiating principles

5.1   INTRODUCTION

All of us negotiate on a daily basis because negotiation is an aspect of daily life.

We negotiate at home over what TV programme to watch, over what's for supper, over what we are doing at the weekend. We negotiate in the workplace with our superiors and our assistants, we bargain for pay rises and improved work conditions, we negotiate over when we can take holidays. We strike business deals both large and small and we negotiate when we buy a car, electrical goods, property and so on.

We are all capable of negotiation but not all of us are natural negotiators. We can, however, improve our negotiating skills by training and experience.

There are many excellent books and training courses on various aspects of negotiation and the fact that there is a proliferation of these indicates that the art of negotiation is of increasing importance.

Negotiation is as much a business practice as are team skills, management and quality control and, inevitably, aspects of negotiation find their way into many other business practices and management skills.

5.2   WHAT IS NEGOTIATION?

Negotiation is the process between two or more opposing parties to a deal or transaction by which each party seeks to obtain the maximum benefits and rewards from the deal that is struck or agreement that is reached.

Negotiation is a process which occurs in bargaining situations with no guarantee that a bargain will be reached.

Successful negotiation inevitably involves elements of compromise by the bargaining parties.

Negotiation occurs when we want something that someone else already has and may or may not be prepared to give to us.

Remember that there are some occasions where negotiation could occur but does not. Often this happens when someone introduces to us the opportunity to get something which we never knew we even needed and where, because of lack of preparation and lack of information, we are induced or bamboozled into buying something we had never contemplated. Opportunist sales, such as insurance, time-share, satellite dishes and the like, are examples of where experienced sales people will seek to strike a bargain with the innocent customer who, through lack of skill and preparation, is persuaded that the thing that is for sale is the very thing they have always wanted.

Perhaps the earliest negotiating and non-negotiating process occurred when the serpent persuaded Eve that the apple was the thing that she and Adam really wanted and poor old Adam ate the apple without ever inquiring about the terms of the deal, or attempting to negotiate a get-out clause.

5.3 WHY NEGOTIATE?

Why not negotiate! Unless you believe that you cannot improve the terms of the bargain that you are seeking to strike then there must be value in negotiating. Usually the other side are expecting you to negotiate anyway.

In many cases the other party is disappointed and even anxious if there is no element of negotiation in the deal.

Negotiation can be positive for both parties since, as compromise is reached and terms are disclosed, each party will learn positive information about the other and the deal reached may be better than either party had anticipated.

If you never try for the maximum you are never going to know how much you could achieve. The art of negotiation is to understand how to push for the maximum benefits, and at what point to push no further in case no deal is struck at all.

Shimon Peres said recently that 'all known solutions are dead ones. The art of negotiation is to invent and create and not to hang from the cliff of yesterday'. He also once said 'This is not a negotiation of give and take because [we have] something to give but nothing to take'.

5.4 THE GIVE/GET PRINCIPLE

METHOD 1

PARTY A GIVE/GET	Both parties are willing to give up points at issue in negotiation in order to get what they respectively want. This is a positive approach to reaching a compromise although the concessionary areas will be subject to variation. Since both parties have an attitude of compromise this method is likely to result in a good bargain for both sides.	PARTY B GIVE/GET

METHOD 2

PARTY A GIVE/GET	Here Party A approaches the negotiation with a willingness to give up in concessionary areas in return for something it wants. However, Party B is intending only to give up points if Party B gets what it wants. Party A may eventually revert to Party B's method and create a stalemate. Likewise Party B may keep getting without any intention of giving too quickly and create a stalemate again by forcing Party A to take a less positive approach.	PARTY B GET/GIVE

METHOD 3

PARTY A GET/GIVE	In this example neither party comes to the table prepared to give until a point is first won or received. This is confrontational aggressive positioning by both parties and unlikely to lead to a lasting solution. Indeed there is a real risk that both parties will have to walk away rather than conclude a deal.	PARTY B GET/GIVE

5.5 WHAT IS A WIN-WIN DEAL?

Much emphasis is placed on achieving a win-win situation and many attempts have been made to define what makes for a win-win. A win-win occurs when both parties feel that not only have they achieved as good a result as possible, but that they have also helped each other achieve such a satisfactory result. If the parties genuinely believe that each party has gained more than lost, then they may be anxious to ensure that the agreement realises its potential during the life of the agreement. To be able to achieve a win-win both parties must understand the needs and goals of the other. This does not mean that the bottom line must be revealed by both sides, but that they should negotiate towards a mutual compromise and not a confrontational result. If either one or both sides intend to win at any cost or to 'score points' then it is unlikely that a win-win will be achieved.

It is important to appreciate that the real win-win deal must be capable of lasting throughout the life of the agreement. I have seen many situations where the parties to negotiation leave the table, both feeling that a satisfactory win-win agreement has been struck, only to find that six months down the line it is a win-lose deal at best and, at worst and more often than not, it is a lose-lose. This scenario often occurs when the parties are seeking to strike a 'point in time' deal where because of lack of flexibility, lack of long-term planning and short-term objective criteria the parties reach an agreement which they perceive a win-win at the time but which was never built to last.

Benjamin Franklin once said: 'Trades would not take place unless it was advantageous to the parties concerned.' Of course, it is better to strike as good a bargain as one's bargaining position admits. The worst outcome is when by overriding greed, no bargain is struck, and a trade that could have been advantageous to both parties, does not come off at all.

5.6   NEGOTIATING STYLES AND ETHICS

Your negotiating style is a combination of the personality and attitude you display during negotiations together with the approaches you adopt towards those negotiations. Your attitude and approach may remain consistent during negotiations, or one or both may change from issue to issue, from day to day, and so on. The following chart illustrates the interplay of attitudes and approaches often adopted. Some personality and attitude types are listed across the top of the chart, while common approaches appear in the left column. A discussion of ethics in negotiations follows the chart.

5.7 NEGOTIATING STYLES

PERSONALITY AND ATTITUDE TYPES			
A P P R O A C H E S	Co-operative/ Pleasant/ Professional/ Diplomatic/Polite	Coercive/ Combative/ Aggressive/ Arrogant/Stubborn/ Confrontational/ Sarcastic	Mixed – Varies With Issue
Straightforward and honest			
Subtle, secretive or clever, but honest			
Slightly dishonest and/or somewhat devious			
Dishonest or dishonourable, and devious			
Mixed – varies with issue			

Many of these categories are self-explanatory, but a few require illustration. A dishonourable style of negotiation becomes evident when one party to the negotiations makes major, unqualified commitments and then refuses to honour them. Imagine a salesperson who gives a customer an unauthorised 'side letter' containing major concessions or assumptions of responsibility. Then imagine his employer refusing to honour the letter.

Another example is a party's negotiating team that agrees to positions on issues, and then reopens and renegotiates many of the issues, perhaps several times for some of them.

Other evidence of a dishonourable style is one party ignoring the content of the signed contract and continuing to negotiate as though no contract had been signed. Of course, this style is occasionally used by business people in emerging nations, not because these business people are dishonourable but more because few of them have any real experience of how Western-style business is conducted.

Dishonesty may or may not be detected in negotiations, but dishonourable behaviour will be noticeable as a general rule.

Perception plays a role in recognising your own negotiating style. For example, fairly often a dishonourable, devious, sarcastic and confrontational negotiating style used by one party's team in negotiating a major transaction or alliance will be perceived by that team as a straightforward, honest and co-operative style.

Those with a straightforward, honest and co-operative style have the tendency to feel that anyone with any other style is unethical or unprincipled. In fact, only those who are dishonest or dishonourable are generally perceived as unethical, and some who are slightly dishonest or devious might still be perceived as ethical. Literally speaking, all negotiators have principles, but those principles may or may not lead to ethical behaviour. Your feeling of trust for the other party, your perception of whether or not you obtained a fair win-win deal and your assessment of whether the other party is ethical may or may not coincide.

You might trust the other party to take only those actions that are in its short-term and long-term best interest, but you might feel that the other party is slightly unethical in its negotiating style.

A fair win-win deal can be obtained from an unethical or untrustworthy party if you know what you are doing before, during and after negotiations and if you have sufficient leverage at the negotiating table to get the concessions and the deal that you want.

The bottom line regarding ethics in negotiations is that each person decides whether or not to be completely ethical, or to engage in slightly or materially unethical conduct, and sometimes your perception of what constitutes ethical behaviour will not be shared by the other party.

It must be recognised that negotiation is unique and culture-specific. For example, in the UK we tend to negotiate on the basis of proposal and counter proposal, whereas in Asian and Far Eastern countries negotiations tend to solve problem areas from the information available. In the UK we will often accept a less than perfect position.

6 Preparing for negotiations

6.1 PROVIDER PREPARATIONS

6.1.1 In general

The degree to which some suppliers prepare for negotiations of major transactions is not well recognised by customers. In certain industries where there is a degree of ongoing maintenance and support, service revenue provides an increasingly large share of the suppliers' gross revenue, but even in these industries major transactions usually contribute most of the sellers' revenues as well as the bulk of sales commissions. Hence sales personnel, senior management, financial and treasury departments and staff and support groups and most hi-tech providers are oriented towards pursuing and securing major transactions. New accounts occupy a special place in the hearts of most suppliers because of their contribution to revenue growth and because new customers often become repeat customers. Discounts on add-on orders often are not as great as those on initial orders unless there has been careful negotiating by the customer. Hence new accounts are valued for likely future orders as well as the initial order. Sales personnel often receive bonuses and promotions based in part on their success in landing new accounts. With these incentives both new and existing customers who are major deal prospects are given much attention and thought.

6.1.2 Sales force training, customer qualification and negotiating experience

Long-established suppliers train new sales people in product characteristics, sales techniques and company policies. These new personnel are then assigned to a sales supervisor or manager, given a list of existing accounts and told to service the existing accounts and bring in new business through cold calls, referrals, existing contacts or prospects already identified. Periodic reviews of progress are conducted by the supervisor or manager, who usually visits any new or existing customer that contemplates any measurable order through the new sales representative. Large orders trigger a visit by the supervisor's or manager's superior. Each prospect for any measurable or significant order is continuously 'qualified', meaning that a series of stages are identified leading from an expression of interest to a signed contract, and the prospect is guided from one stage to the next by the sales staff. Each stage tests the continued interest of the prospect. Supervisor and manager visits are part of the testing process, which may also include product demonstrations, discussions with reference accounts, and sometimes a trial use of the desired product or an off-site benchmark test. Of course, some of these steps are also used by the prospective customer to 'qualify' the supplier.

When the time comes to close a major transaction the sales representative, his supervisor, and his manager may all attend the closing to help ensure contract signing. A contract administrator or in-house solicitor may join the sales personnel. Generally, the attention a transaction receives will depend upon its size. Most often the sales supervisors and managers, and any accompanying staff or support personnel, at negotiating sessions or closings are experienced, sophisticated negotiators. Their experience and skill usually exceeds the negotiating skill and experience of all licensee personnel. Thus the supplier almost always has an advantage in negotiations. One way a customer can neutralise that advantage is to bring an experienced negotiator into the negotiations.

Some suppliers in the IT sector train their negotiators to use unusual techniques. A few software publishers train their female sales representatives and contract negotiators to say 'Help me', whenever a deadlock or stalemate is reached. Opposing, older, male negotiators often treat the younger female as they would treat their daughters and communicate the 'bottom line' of the customer that must be satisfied if the deal is to close. Usually the bottom line had not been disclosed prior to that point. Sometimes the older male on the customer's negotiating team goes further and suggests some creative problem-solving solution to the deadlock or stalemate. At least one US software publisher goes one step further and trains their female representatives or negotiators to cry and feign stomach illness when the customer gives a negative reaction to some important request by the licensor or when a deadlock or impasse is reached.

6.1.3 Standard charges

Virtually all substantial electronic and telecoms providers will publicly list their standard fees and charges for all off-the-shelf products and standard services. These fees and charges are calculated to provide profit and some room for discounts in appropriate situations. A 25%–50% profit margin in standard fees and charges is to be expected, but a 60% or greater margin is not unheard of, and each product will have a break-even quantity for recovery of development costs before it generates a profit. Standard fees and charges are usually accepted by prospective customers as a starting point for discount negotiations. Hence the provider has the advantage of being able to determine the starting point for financial discussions, and being able to concede modest or reasonable discounts while still making a profit on the transaction. Of course, this method of operation is standard in the computer and database industries as well as others, and is generally accepted as reasonable.

6.1.4 Standard, printed, protective contracts

Prudent sellers prepare and employ standard, printed, protective contract forms and offer them to customers for virtually all of their transactions. While a number of companies use typewritten contracts as standard forms, most use printed forms with small print. Small type makes these agreements much shorter than they would be if typed. Thus they appeal to business people who prefer short contracts. More important to suppliers is the impact of such forms on negotiations and doing business. Blank lines or schedules will be used for product identification and statements of charges, but virtually no room is left for changes in contract terms, thereby creating an 'official' looking and intimidating document that discourages negotiation of non-price terms. Many business people have no interest in reading legal documents in general, much less documents in small print, thus review and negotiation of non-price terms is discouraged by the small print. Further, if a provider's form agreement is used, its general business policies, risk protections, and explanations of the transaction contained therein are likely to be accepted. Since providers do business with many customers, standardisation of contract terms is a logical administrative step and tends to minimise expenditures for contract administration. Custom-made contracts with many customers makes contract administration and its cost a major problem. Finally, provider form agreements give the provider an advantage in negotiations. The starting point for negotiations of many non-price terms in these form contracts will be slanted to some degree in favour of the provider, for example, by giving the provider flexibility in satisfying performance obligations. Thus there are many advantages inherent in the use of standard form contracts.

A customer must really want to negotiate before the time and energy necessary to review, analyse, discuss, and negotiate a fine-print contract is expended. Then changes, except for deletions, must be added via an addendum. Of course, the customer can insist upon the right to prepare a custom-made contract for its deal, and some do so, but these agreements are expensive and time consuming for the customer to prepare. Few customers have them prepared in advance, and even if they are prepared in advance or for a particular transaction, the customer must have sufficient bargaining power to insist successfully on the use of its form as the basic contract. Hence, most customers accept standard, printed, provider-protective contract forms and any changes are usually made via an addendum to the form. Of course, vendor printed-form contracts are used in many industries and are generally accepted as a reasonable way to do business.

Customers or buyers who engage in expensive transactions on a regular basis, or who license technology or services that are very important to their business more than a few times per year, should prepare and require most suppliers to use the buyer's standard form agreement. It can be difficult and time consuming to make all of the business decisions that are captured in these standard-form contracts, but the result is worthwhile for a number of reasons, for example, using the customer's standard-form contract helps to level the negotiating table that is otherwise slanted heavily in the seller's favour.

6.1.5 Pre-negotiation groundwork with customer

By the time the salesperson presents the provider's standard contract for a major transaction, he has had the opportunity for numerous meetings and telephone conversations with the customer's business or technical personnel, and these personnel are usually convinced that the proposed deal captured in the standard contract is the solution to their company's needs or problems. A member of senior management will normally sign major transaction contracts.

If the contract is forwarded to the company's lawyer before execution, it is typically forwarded with the message that some individual or group within the company wants to sign the document and has already negotiated the fee or charge to his or their satisfaction. If the company lawyer raises objections or concerns upon review of the contract, he may be viewed as an obstacle or 'deal killer'. While this is not true in every company, it is true in a measurable number of companies and providers are well aware of the perception. Providers prefer to have the contract signed without prior review by the company's lawyer for obvious negotiation and delay-avoidance reasons. Nevertheless, if it is sent to the company's lawyer prior to execution, providers realise that it will often be sent with the message that the contract is ready for signature by the company's business people, hence the lawyer should not delay its progress. Encouraging this message when the contract is sent to the company's lawyer is part of the groundwork done by the salespeople to minimise negotiations and hasten closing.

Providers are careful to develop one or more 'internal salesmen' or 'internal champions' as one of their standard sales techniques during their pre-negotiation groundwork with the customer. The internal champion is a vocal advocate for the acquisition of the goods or services. Usually he is the individual who is convinced the seller's products are the solution to a company need or problem and the individual who has interacted with the licensor's salesperson for some time.

By developing an internal champion who is sold on the transaction, providers hope to gain three things. First, support. A company employee in a responsible position will support contract execution by senior management, field any questions by senior management, and work to persuade senior management to sign the contract.

Secondly, pressure. The internal champion will bring pressure to bear on the company's lawyer for a quick and mild response to the contract either expressly, indirectly through a 'senior management is ready to sign the contract' message, or subtly by feeding the lawyer's apprehension about being perceived as a deal killer or obstacle if significant objections are raised. In-house counsel are more likely to feel this pressure than an outside counsel whose career is not affected by the company's politics, and even in-house counsel may feel sufficiently secure that he can review the agreement without feeling pressure to approve it quickly with little or no objection. However, sometimes that pressure is felt and it works to the provider's advantage in minimising or eliminating lawyer objections or negotiation demands. The pressure applied by the internal champion makes it expedient for the in-house counsel to apply a 'rubber stamp' approval to the contract.

Thirdly, help with negotiations. If negotiations are conducted, the internal champion is a friendly force that helps the provider at the negotiating table.

In the realm of company politics, the provider and the internal champion are now connected for better or for worse. The benefits of having an internal champion are well recognised by providers of software, computers, telecommunications equipment, databases, and related services.

6.1.6 Internal deal structuring and negotiations

Provider sales personnel are the provider's primary connection with customers and must inform the provider's management about any concessions required to close a major transaction. Because deviations from standard charges or fees and from standard contract terms are deviations from standard provider policies, the salesperson must argue for the concessions he feels are necessary and obtain management's blessing or alternative input regarding acceptable concessions. The credibility of the salesperson within his company plays a role in these internal negotiations and transaction structuring responses from management. Many salespeople feel that internal negotiations are more difficult than customer negotiations. Often the salesperson becomes an advocate for the customer in these internal discussions. After all, his commissions and bonuses will depend upon completed transactions.

6.1.7 Preparation of substantive fall-back positions on open points and early concerns

During the course of pre-negotiation groundwork by the salesperson it sometimes becomes apparent that a prospective customer for a major acquisition is determined to negotiate some points in the contract or has strong concerns about some aspects of the transaction. At this early stage the salesperson, and perhaps his supervisor, manager, and director, will confer with provider organisation staff and support groups affected by the points or concerns to discuss and plan responses. Some topics may be sufficiently sensitive to warrant preparation of immediate responses and one or more fall-back positions, and may warrant an early visit to the customer by a member of a staff or support group. For example, if the customer wants discounted 24-hour, seven-day on-site maintenance coverage by provider engineers, the regional director of the provider's engineer organisation is likely to visit the customer site prior to contract execution, and discuss his responses to the customer's request with the salesperson and others in the provider's sales organisation. Initial and fall-back positions on the pricing and details of this service will be planned in advance.

These situations can arise at any stage of the salesperson's interaction with the prospect. Providers are generally apprehensive about making concessions early in the sales cycle because they worry about having to make additional concessions of an as yet unknown nature at closing in order to obtain the business. For example, if a 'best price' is offered early in the cycle, a better price could be demanded at closing as a final condition to contract execution.

6.1.8 Inter-departmental meetings to plan negotiating strategy and tactics

Where negotiations are necessary, the supplier can usually reduce the number of open points and concerns raised during the sales cycle to a number that could be addressed at a transaction closing, or at least in one or two meetings after which the provider could reasonably hope to receive a signed contract. At this point the provider's management or sales force may call a formal meeting of staff and support groups affected by the open points or concerns to plan a negotiating strategy and one or more tactics. Any previously communicated positions and previously identified but unused fall-back positions will be reviewed. New positions will be formulated on open and likely discussion topics. These meetings can be intense when a staff or support group clashes with the sales force, but they usually generate successful strategies, tactics and positions. By the time these meetings occur, the prospective customer is almost always totally committed to doing business with the provider and is simply delayed by some final concerns or attempts to maximise concessions.

6.1.9 Preparation of contracts before negotiations commence

Sophisticated sellers prepare and deliver standard contracts for execution after the primary customer contact is sold on the transaction. Fees or charges may or may not be negotiated at this point, but other terms usually are not negotiated at this stage. Hence the preparation of the contract amounts to filling in a few blank spaces. Providers often do not wait, in other words, for a request for contracts, or give the customer much of an opportunity to think about preparing a contract. Where some industries typically negotiate a number of points before drafting or presenting a contract, software providers are ready with contracts after agreement on fees and charges, and sometimes before. This approach expedites contract signing and minimises the possibility of negotiations or 'buyer's remorse', which is a change of mind about a deal after deciding to accept it. Software provider contracts appear on customer desks before or immediately after an agreement on fees or charges.

6.2 CUSTOMER PREPARATIONS

6.2.1 In general

This section of the report addresses customer preparations for the negotiation of a major transaction. In general, customers will think about preparing for a very large transaction, but give less thought to preparations for transactions that are perceived as less than huge or very important deals. While understandable, this approach to major transactions often sets the stage for problems that could have been avoided. For example, if a software conversion or development project for a critical or very important enhancement or module of a program is projected to cost only a few thousand dollars, problems can be expected unless the project is planned well and some negotiations occur. As another example, FT 500 companies might view a software licence transaction projected to cost £100,000 as a modest transaction requiring little forethought, planning and negotiation. If the company has a well thought out, well drafted master agreement with the software and related service provider, this reaction may be appropriate. If not, planning and negotiations are highly recommended. Such a 'modest' transaction is in reality a major acquisition if the software is important to the customer, regardless of the customer's perception of its cost.

In general, customers do not always plan enough for negotiations. They leave themselves open to avoidable problems as a result. Sales managers love un-negotiated major transactions.

This criticism does not suggest that every possible concession, or every 'ounce of blood', must be extracted at the negotiating table. More and more legal actions are threatened and take place each year as a result of poorly negotiated or drafted contracts. Like most legal cases, many of these claims are settled out of court. However, litigation is expensive and disruptive. Also, management, sales, purchasing and in-house legal personnel may be fired or have their careers negatively affected by problems in major software transactions. Trade publications report these events on a regular basis, and countless cases and terminations go unreported. Major transactions are serious business. A problem prevention orientation is highly advisable in these transactions. Suppliers recognise the wisdom of this orientation and act accordingly. Most customers need to focus on and recognise the importance of this orientation more than they do now.

6.2.2 In-house needs analysis and procurement decision

While an increasing number of customers employ outside consultants to analyse their technology needs and recommend a solution, it is probably safe to say that most customers make their own needs analysis either independently or with the help of a provider, and their own solution selection decision.

One of the common problems in an in-house analysis and selection decision process is a failure to see the big picture and prepare a master plan. For example, a customer with a data processing or management information services staff should have a master operational and growth plan that contains an acquisition procedure element, a development work procedure element, a staff training element, a maintenance service element, a disaster plan element, and so on, as well as anticipating hardware needs, setting downtime goals, deciding on distributed versus centralised capability and deciding whether to outsource service. Many customers lack a clear procedure for the acquisition of significant software, or its development, or its conversion. Such a plan should require communication between the customer's technical staff, the group that will benefit from the software or related services and senior management. Requiring senior management to sign contracts for major transactions is not enough. Senior management must be asked its expectations regarding a major transaction. In particular, senior management must communicate the results expected from the transaction in terms of business goals, business needs to be satisfied and business concerns to be solved. The master plan must call for this type of communication. While it can occur without a master plan or procedure, a written checklist containing this requirement helps to ensure that the communication will occur. If this communication does not occur, the success of a major transaction, as measured by senior management, is less likely than if the communication does occur.

Why, you may ask? One answer is because the background and mindset of a customer's technical staff typically has a technical and resource orientation. Like providers, customer personnel tend to focus on the technical capability of goods and services and of providing that capability to their employer's various departments. Senior management and the departmental users of such goods and services tend to focus on results that they will produce. Misunderstandings between these groups are common, and often leave the technical staff with a vague, incomplete or inaccurate understanding of the business goal, need or concern motivating the major transaction. Selecting the wrong solution or an inadequate solution often results. Only a minority of technical personnel, like a minority of lawyers or other professionals, can grasp, remain focused on and be driven by the overriding business purpose for a major transaction. Many negotiators tend to focus on the trees (details) rather than the wood (big picture business purpose). Of course, it may be necessary to focus on both the trees and the wood. To have the chance of creating this multiple focus in a major transaction, the business purpose for the transaction must be communicated to and understood by the involved technical personnel.

In summary, it is essential to synchronise management and technical personnel on the business needs, expectations and concerns that justify and motivate a major transaction in order to maximise its likelihood of success.

6.2.3 Consultant-aided needs analysis and procurement decision

6.2.3.1 Survey of senior management

Many outside or independent contractor consultants do a good job of helping their clients in major transactions. One of the first steps of these consultants is to meet with several members of the senior management team to survey their business goals, needs and concerns underlying a forthcoming major transaction. Another focus of their survey is to inquire about how the transaction fits within the company's short-term and long-term business plans. A third line of inquiry might be whether the contemplated transaction was recommended by the company's independent auditors, by another independent consultant's report, by a parent company, by a strategic alliance participant, or others. Any relevant business plans, reports, etc, will need to be reviewed by the consultant. Because some of the information in these documents, as well as some information conveyed verbally, is confidential and proprietary to the company, consideration should be given to requiring the consultant to sign a non-disclosure agreement.

6.2.3.2 Survey of technical personnel

Another initial step of an independent consultant in helping his client in a major transaction is to meet with the customer's senior or assigned technical personnel to survey their perceptions of their needs, goals and concerns. Preliminary thoughts of the technical personnel about the forthcoming transaction will be shared at this time. Details of the customer's current systems, equipment, facilities and staff may also be conveyed in these meetings.

6.2.3.3 Review of relevant business plans and goals, RFP preparation and evaluation

After the initial meetings, the outside consultant will review the relevant business plans, reports, and notes of his discussions with senior management and technical personnel. A plan of action will be formulated that often includes the consultant's preparation of a request for proposals ('RFP') from established providers with the types of products or services that may be needed by the customer. Often the RFP will ask the provider to propose solutions based on the factual information contained in the RFP. Further discussions with management, user departments and technical personnel normally follow. The consultant normally helps evaluate the proposals received and may help with subsequent negotiations.

6.2.4 Consensus view determination

Regardless of whether an outside consultant is employed to help with the task, it is very important for the involved parties within the customer's organisation to reach and recognise a consensus view of the need, goal or concern that should be addressed by the major transaction. This need, goal or concern may be obvious and understood by all involved parties at the outset of planning for the transaction. Almost invariably each individual involved presumes all others involved in the transaction share his view. Unfortunately, different views are the norm. Communication between technical personnel and senior management is vital to the long-term success of a major transaction. Senior management may impose a 'consensus' view of the need, goal or concern to be addressed, but technical personnel will not be certain of management's view without communication on the subject. The individuals who suffer the consequences of a different view are usually the technical personnel. Staff personnel such as an in-house lawyer who will join the negotiating team or review contracts need to understand the goal or concern motivating the major transaction, and it must be clearly explained in advance.

The immediate result of different views of a transaction may be delays in contract execution. A subsequent likely result may be delays and cost overruns in implementation. The third likely result is problems following implementation that make it clear that a mistake was made prior to contract execution. For example, if a customer needs to establish communications between recently ordered minicomputers that will be installed at remote locations and the customer's mainframe or selected microcomputers at the company's headquarters, technical personnel will tend to focus on the best software solution given the types of equipment then employed. Senior management wants the communications link, but may also want to ensure that it will work when new equipment for the headquarters' site is acquired in a year or two. The technical personnel charged with the responsibility of acquiring or developing communications software that will enable communications between remote and headquarters' computers may or may not be aware of the possibility that the headquarters' equipment will be replaced in the foreseeable future. Even if the technical personnel are aware of this possibility, or that it is probable, the future plans can easily be overlooked or forgotten by a technical evaluator charged with the responsibility of acquiring or developing software to establish the communications link as quickly as possible after the remote site minicomputers are delivered in a few weeks or months.

If there is insufficient or no communication with senior management prior to software acquisition, three events are immediately probable. First, senior management will not express the need for the new software to work on both current and future equipment. Secondly, the technical staff will not explain to senior management that only certain types of new equipment will be compatible with the communications software and may be acquired in the future if the company's long-term need is to acquire a communications program that works now and in the future on different equipment. Thirdly, the company's staff reviewing the software contract will probably not be informed of the long-term need and are unlikely to require assurances in the contract that the program acquired will work with certain types of new equipment likely to replace the current headquarters' equipment in the foreseeable future.

A possible delayed consequence of not addressing future compatibility prior to contract execution is that incompatible replacement equipment will be ordered for the headquarters' site in one or two years. When senior management is informed of the need for new communications software at that point, the reaction is likely to be negative unless the software licence fees for the current communications program were not paid in a lump sum and the licence agreement can be terminated quickly. Few senior managers like to pay twice for the same type of software in a relatively short time span. Technical personnel have been fired, demoted or received smaller than normal raises in similar situations. This is only one of countless examples of how unsynchronised views of a customer's needs, goals or concerns can create problems for the customer.

6.2.4.1 Focus on personnel

Few customers recognise the importance of key provider personnel and key customer personnel to some transactions. Provider and customer personnel are key resources in software development and conversion transactions. Customers should consider identifying key provider personnel in such projects and requiring them to remain at the customer's site until the project is completed. Providers are reluctant to make such commitments in contracts but may be persuaded in a major transaction.

In a different vein, customer personnel should be selected in advance for the key roles they will play in the transaction, for example, for the negotiating team, a project manager, etc.

6.2.4.2 Focus on necessary services

The services provided in a major transaction may be critical to the success of the transaction as a whole. If independent, third-party service providers seem likely to provide better or equivalent services at a lower cost, they should be considered in pre-negotiation planning. One important question in this regard will be whether the independent service supplier needs access to the proprietary material provided by another provider to the customer.

6.2.4.3 Line up political support

One of the mistakes commonly made by the leader of the customer's negotiating team is the failure to line up political support for his role in the forthcoming negotiations. Appointment to the role and ascertaining senior management's desired results are not enough. Senior management should be willing to stand behind the decisions, strategy and tactics of the negotiating team and should make that commitment in advance of negotiations. Providers are masters at going around obstacles in negotiations by persuading the customer's senior management to order their removal. Providers also sense a lack of senior management support or neutrality very quickly and use that situation to their advantage at the negotiating table. A united customer tends to help the customer's negotiating team.

6.2.4.4 Form negotiating team

As mentioned earlier, the best people available should be selected to form an interdisciplinary negotiating team for major transactions. A leader should be designated as the main spokesperson and liaisor with senior management. Obviously a small company engaging in a major transaction might not form a team for negotiations. Personnel in small companies tend to wear several hats, or have several areas of responsibility. In theory, one person can represent a customer as well as several in the context of negotiations whether the customer is large, small or somewhere in between. However, the best approach to negotiating a major transaction is often the interdisciplinary team approach because it involves personnel from various interested disciplines from the outset of negotiations, it permits them full knowledge and decision-making opportunities and it generally ensures that they 'buy into' the transaction. A one-man approach creates the risk that the other groups in the customer organisation will present their concerns, or argue that their needs were not met by the transaction, after negotiations are completed. Even worse is the possibility that the other groups may argue that aspects of the transaction required their prior approval which was not obtained. The single negotiator may have intentionally or inadvertently ignored the approval requirement of the other groups, but in any event the post-negotiation negative reactions of other groups may slow down contract execution, may kill the deal and may embarrass the single negotiator. Sometimes such negative post-negotiation reactions are simply based on the perception that the individual negotiator encroached on another group's 'turf' or area of responsibility. Sometimes these reactions are based on legitimate concerns that the individual negotiator overlooked or ignored and that will be difficult or impossible to address following negotiation completion.

An obvious variation of the single man approach is to have the single negotiator tell the provider(s) that deal approval is required by other groups before the contract is signed. This approach can work well in small, relatively unimportant transactions. At least two problems arise when it is employed in major transactions. First, there is usually some delay in closing the deal while the reviewing groups review and learn about the transaction. Secondly, it can be difficult to obtain changes in the contract(s) for the transaction at this stage. A small number of unimportant changes are commonly accepted at this stage, but providers tend to become disturbed by significant changes requested after negotiations have been completed with the customer's primary negotiator. With some justification providers can question the customer's good faith and seriousness of interest in the transaction under these circumstances. The provider's complaints can create pressure on the reviewing groups to retract or modify their request. Whether or not important changes are made, the reviewing groups may become irritated at the sole customer negotiator and the customer's relationship with the provider may become strained. A solo negotiator runs political risks in this approach to negotiating a major transaction whether or not those risks are perceived in advance. More than a few solo negotiators of major transactions have had their careers negatively impacted because representatives of other groups were not parties to the negotiation of the deal. Nevertheless, this approach is used with some frequency.

The best negotiating team usually includes a technical person, a legal representative and someone from a financial or controllers group. Of course, the degree of importance of the transaction affects the customer's judgment on the parties involved. A financial person may not be needed as long as budget constraints are not exceeded. Alternatively, a member of senior management may participate in the negotiations.

Sophisticated customers always involve their legal group in negotiations. Not being involved in negotiations of a major transaction from the outset is a major complaint of customer solicitors. If one is involved early in the negotiations, a customer's lawyer can help structure the deal in a logical manner, can raise important legal issues early, and can protect the customer's interests while the parties are engaged in give and take discussions. Also, the legal group will seldom object to a deal if one of its people were involved in the negotiations from the outset. Delays can be minimised if a legal person is involved with negotiations, contrary to the perception of many businesspeople. Where the legal group is not included in the negotiating team, the potential for significant delays is maximised rather then minimised.

6.2.5 Selection of acquisition structure and negotiating strategy and tactics

After the negotiating team is selected, prior plans should be reviewed and incorporated as basic elements in the structural plan for the transaction, and in the strategic and tactical plans of the team. Discussion of the other elements of the structure, strategy and tactics should then occur. A master plan should be agreed upon at this time. As with any 'game plan', adjustments may be required later. Nevertheless, a sophisticated customer will spend time and invest careful thought in a master plan for forthcoming negotiations.

Another step that may be taken by the team is practice negotiation sessions. If the basic contract(s) for the transaction are in the customer's possession prior to its negotiation, practice sessions can be helpful in finalising the customer's negotiating plans. If not, these sessions may still be helpful to some degree.

6.2.6 Obtain management support

After the master plan for the pending negotiations is completed to the negotiating team's satisfaction this plan should be reviewed in some detail with one or more members of senior management. Helpful suggestions are often the result of these meetings. In addition, they give senior management the opportunity to confirm that the plan is consistent with the company's needs, goals or concerns. Equally as important is the blessing of senior management on the plan. If the senior manager 'buys into' the plan, three benefits normally result. First, it is unlikely that a contract or result consistent with the plan will be criticised following negotiations. Secondly, delays because of senior management review of a transaction prior to contract execution become unlikely or are minimised in length. Thirdly, if the provider tries to solicit support from senior management during negotiations on a topic or position rejected by the negotiating team, the provider's attempt to go around the team is more likely to fail as long as the team is acting in accordance with the approved master plan. The substantive and political support of senior management for the negotiating team can be very important to the team's success in negotiations.

6.2.7 Select one team member as leader and interface

Often a negotiating team leader will be selected in the normal course of planning for the forthcoming negotiations. If this selection has not been made prior to commencement of negotiations, it should be an item on a planning checklist that is resolved at this stage. One spokesperson is important to the progress of negotiations. Other team members may contribute on topics in their areas of responsibility, but one leader is necessary to prevent a disorganised negotiation. Failure to agree upon a team leader sets the stage for disagreements or irritations among team members that providers can exploit. A united front is important in team negotiations. Providers are extremely perceptive of opportunities to play one team member against another at the negotiating table.

6.2.8 Know when to hire outside help

Some customers are sensitive to the need for outside consultants or lawyers in their negotiations of major transactions, but most are not. Customers usually need outside help more often than providers because providers employ sophisticated negotiators and normally approach negotiations from a superior bargaining position. Outside help can neutralise the provider's superior position and skill in negotiations, or at least minimise both, providing the consultant or solicitor is an experienced expert. If outside help is employed, it is better to involve the helper at the pre-negotiation planning stage than to rush him in at the start of negotiations. The money saved and concessions gained, through the help of outside experts, frequently exceeds the value of the service they provide.

Part IV
Preparing for drafting

7 Preparing the contracts

7.1 PRE-CONTRACTUAL DOCUMENTS AND CONFIDENTIALITY

7.1.1 Introduction

In the course of negotiations or discussions leading towards a contract the parties demonstrate considerable elements of trust at a time when they do not know enough about each other for trust to really exist.

There is often an assumption that until the contract is signed, neither party is in any way bound to the other. This is not necessarily the case. During the course of negotiations the parties will not only exchange information which may be regarded as confidential, but will also create contractual obligations so that at the point of dispute, whilst there may not be a signed contract, there are often contractual obligations.

When parties are exchanging information they should clearly state whether they intend the information to be legally binding or not. This applies as much to exchanges of information by e-mail as it does to exchanges of information in paper form. The parties should use protective language to ensure that no contractual obligation exists, unless, of course, they wish their exchange of information to create binding obligations.

Before a contract is signed, the exchanges between the parties may be formalised in a number of ways:

- a term sheet;
- a letter of intent;
- a comfort letter;
- a Memorandum of Understanding;
- heads of terms;
- heads of agreement.

The terminology used is less important than the binding or non-binding nature of the document. These pre-contractual documents will be discussed later.

7.1.2   Business secrets and confidentiality

Whether or not the parties enter into a pre-contractual agreement it is usually the case that in the course of negotiations, one party will reveal to the other information that is confidential. It is important to ensure, as early as possible, that the parties agree how to deal with business secrets and other confidential information and issues such as this are best dealt with by the use of confidentiality letters or agreements often called 'confidentiality agreements' or 'non-disclosure agreements' or 'NDAs'.

Even if the NDA is kept short and is executed in the form of a letter it is still essential that a number of key issues are addressed and these are as follows:

—   *The parties.* The parties to the NDA should clearly be defined and it should be considered carefully as to whether or not a party that is a group company should be defined as a specific company rather than the group as a whole. The risk of sharing information for the benefit of an entire group is that many of the group companies may be in jurisdictions where an enforcement of the agreement may be difficult and expensive and in any event the wider that confidential information is shared, the greater the risk.

—   *Consideration.* For a contract to be legally binding, it is usual for there to be some form of consideration whether in the form of monetary value or by way of performance. In mutual NDAs there are often obligations passing both ways and therefore consideration is achieved. In one-way confidentiality agreements consideration may not pass between the parties and therefore the disclosing party may wish to include some form of nominal consideration with the other party.

—   *Obligations of confidence.* Even if the NDA is not binding, common law may imply a duty of confidence if it is clear that the nature of the information being exchanged was obvious to the parties as confidential. It is, however, better to have express terms of confidentiality in the agreement.

—   *Term.* Some confidentiality agreements are open ended. This may be useful if the parties accept that confidentiality should last in perpetuity but it is usual to try and put a limit on the obligations of confidentiality dependent upon the nature of the information being exchanged.

—   *Subject matter.* The parties should clearly define what items are the subject of confidentiality and how information should be flagged as being confidential. In addition, the parties should define the circumstances in which confidential information is to be disclosed and used.

— *Exceptions*. The parties need to state clearly when confidential information is not to be treated as confidential. Typically this arises when the information in question is either already in the public domain or comes into the possession of the recipient via a third party or was already known to the recipient prior to disclosure.

— *Restrictions on use*. The parties should indicate how confidential information is to be protected and used and what obligations are to be placed on a disclosing party to ensure that sufficient steps are taken to maintain the proprietary value of the information. For example, an author who wishes his work to be analysed by a company with the view to publication should take responsibility for protecting his intellectual property at all times.

— *Duties of the parties*. Once confidential information has been disclosed the NDA needs to define the obligations of the disclosing party and the recipient during the period of disclosure. In addition, there needs to be a formula as to how confidential information is dealt with on termination of the NDA or on the confidential information ceasing to be of use to the recipient.

— *Law and disputes*. The parties need to agree on the applicable law of the NDA and on mechanisms as to how any disputes are to be dealt with.

7.2 THE USE OF HEADS OF AGREEMENT

7.2.1 Introduction

There are occasions when the parties negotiate upon a standard form of conditions of the licensor and it may be that many of those terms remain intact, complete and unchanged and only a few clauses are changed, for example, those relating to pricing, delivery dates and ownership of intellectual property rights, to name a few.

In many cases very little of the provider's standard terms and conditions are used and larger companies and corporations use the provider's terms and conditions or standard forms as a starting point only.

There are, however, occasions, particularly where the deal relates to bespoke software, where the parties start negotiations with a blank sheet of paper and create a final contract based around each other's specific requirements within the deal. There are standard terms which will always be necessary in any form of software licence but how do the parties in negotiation construct a satisfactory contract from a blank sheet of paper with or without their lawyer being present throughout the deal making? Perhaps by the use of Heads of Agreement or a Memorandum of Understanding.

7.2.2 Contract skeleton

There are essential elements in any form of contract and the who, what, when, where, why and how process is applicable here. In other words, you need to agree on who the parties are; what the product is and the other essential elements of the deal are; when delivery is to take place and when other milestones are to be achieved; where delivery is to take place, where the software is to be located, where the territory is to be in terms of distribution; why certain obligations of the parties arise and why this particular contract is being formed; and, finally, how will certain obligations be performed, certain disputes settled and how will the contract come to an end or be terminated.

In building the contract there are certain logical places for certain specific terms to be included. Without stating the obvious, the first portion of the contract should deal with the date of the contract, the details of the parties, the reasoning for the contract being entered into and the definitions. So, first, you will have outlined the effective date of the contract, who the contract is being made between, why it is being entered into and, finally, what all the subsequent specific terms and words in the contract will mean.

In effect the next portion of the contract is the major portion, which includes the essential terms such as the nature of the program, the duration of the contract, the rights granted and excluded, the obligations of the parties, the warranties, the ownership of intellectual property rights, acceptance tests and so on.

The next major portion of the contract comprises what in the UK are known as 'boiler plate' clauses, such as severability, arbitration, governing law and jurisdiction, *force majeure*, notices and so on.

Finally, there may be schedules which give the opportunity for the parties to list detailed and specific items such as milestones, detail on the software products, list of intellectual property rights attaching to them such as trade names, trademarks, patents and so on.

7.2.3 Drafting the Heads

The Heads of Agreement or Memorandum of Understanding forms not only an *aide-memoire* during the course of negotiations but also registers in plain language the terms agreed.

Heads of Agreement are not prepared with the intention that they are the contract itself but rather that they are the precursor to the full form contract which the parties' lawyers will finalise.

As to whether the Heads of Agreement are in themselves contractually binding will depend upon the nature of the wording of the Heads of Agreement, but it is the writer's opinion that Heads of Agreement should be 'subject to formal contract' and certainly signed with the wording 'Subject to board approval' or 'Subject to final contract'. In this way whilst the terms negotiated and agreed by the negotiating teams are reduced to written form, neither party is bound by the Heads of Agreement but will only be bound at the point that the final agreement is signed, dated and exchanged.

When producing the Heads of Agreement, keep the language simple and plain but cover the essential points. It is often difficult in the computer industry to avoid jargon but, where jargon is used, it may be worthwhile defining it (particularly where the customer is not experienced but the licensor is) and even if both parties understand the jargon remember that the purpose of Heads of Agreement is to record the negotiated deal in case of a breakdown and where a breakdown occurs it may be a lay person who will have to decide the precise interpretation of jargon.

Keep the clauses short and clear. Heads of Agreement are precisely that – they are bullet points or headings and are not intended to be lengthy clauses – that is something for the final agreement.

Try to use consistent numbering or phrasing so that whoever prepares the final agreement can logically follow through and interpret the particular bullet points and their subheadings.

Be sure that words are correctly spelt. A typing error can have a dramatic effect. For example, 'the Licensee is *not* entitled to more than one free copy' means something entirely different from 'the Licensee is *now* entitled to more than one free copy'.

7.2.4   Three golden rules

During the course of negotiations, although the parties may agree on points, certain assumptions may have been made, and the licensor and the licensee may have an entirely different view of what has been agreed.

The first golden rule applicable to drafting contractual documents, whether Heads of Agreement or not, is:

- *Those who think they have agreed generally have not*

Where the negotiating teams have gained mutual respect and believe that they are working towards the same common goal the second golden rule applies:

- *Those who think that they get on well will generally fall out*

Finally, whether negotiations take a matter of hours, a matter of days or a matter of months and nothing has been reduced to final contract form but the parties are already dealing with each other as if there were contracts, the third golden rule applies:

- *An oral agreement is not worth the paper it is written on.*

The following is a list of do's and don'ts for the initial stages of negotiation. Act reasonably and in a friendly manner as the object of negotiations is to reach agreement and not to win an argument.

When a written statement has been submitted by your opposite number (OPPO), do:

(a) enquire about each significant point asking why it is made unless it is obvious;

(b) appear ignorant, even if this is not true, in order that a particular statement that you do not agree with can be explained at length;

(c) note points with which you disagree and reserve your position;

(d) make certain each point has been fully understood even if this means going over the ground twice – this applies particularly if the languages are not the same;

(e) test out the strength of OPPO's view of each point of significance so that at a later time one can assess how far a particular point is a sticking point or is negotiable;

(f) be aware of the interrelationship between different contract points and the possible counter-arguments which will be developed if success is achieved on any particular one;

(g) correct your OPPO if he is proceeding on a false belief as to a factual position for which you are responsible.

Do not:

(a) speculate on OPPO's reasons or put words into his mouth;

(b) show the depth of your knowledge by answering questions put to your OPPO by another member of your team;

(c) agree significant points immediately, even if agreement will be reached in the end;

(d) snatch at what appears to be a favourable bargain or interpretation of OPPO's views;

(e) be drawn into lengthy arguments on any individual point for which it may be difficult to withdraw;

(f) betray feelings by showing anger, surprise or delight at OPPO's remarks;

(g) improve OPPO's judgment unless it is advantageous.

When you have submitted a written proposal, do:

(a) limit answers to questions to the minimum necessary;

(b) test out the strength of OPPO's suggestions by seeing if he will withdraw them without requiring any corresponding concessions.

Do not:

(a) elaborate at length on motives;

(b) concede anything or be drawn into trade-off negotiations before all points have been discussed.

When no written statement has been submitted by either side, do:

(a) identify all the points to be discussed;

(b) cover each point in sufficient depth for both sides to be aware of each other's position;

(c) keep the discussion explanatory;

(d) correct your OPPO if he is proceeding on a false belief as to a factual position for which you are responsible;

(e) be aware of the interrelationship between different contract points and the possible counter arguments which will be developed if success is achieved on any particular one.

Do not:

(a) let the discussions ramble on without any defined order;

(b) concentrate the discussion on one point to the exclusion of all others;

(c) be drawn into definite commitments either in the form of making a firm concession or taking up a position from which it may be difficult later to withdraw.

In the course of initial negotiations it may be necessary to reveal confidential information to your OPPO, which you will necessarily need to protect should the deal not proceed, and I suggest either a letter of confidentiality is entered into or if the circumstances dictate a more comprehensive non-disclosure agreement is signed.

8 Checklist of the contents of a typical software licence agreement

8.1 OVERVIEW

It is a truism in the computer and software industries that everything is negotiable if the deal is big enough to warrant the discounts or risks required to obtain the business. This maxim has limits: for example, sophisticated providers will avoid unprofitable transactions and pay heed to legal limitations on their ability to make price and non-price concessions. Nevertheless, because many points may be negotiated in a major software licence transaction, this section of the book briefly comments on various types of provisions commonly found in several types of licence agreements for a major software transaction. Some standard contracts employed in such transactions are contained in the Appendix to this book. These agreements may be referenced for examples of provisions that capture many of the types of terms noted below. It should be remembered, however, that contract terms appropriate in one major software transaction may not be appropriate in another.

It is perhaps an obvious piece of advice, but one that is often overlooked, that it is extremely useful for software contracts to be given a title or heading so that as a matter of good practice and administration, it is easy upon picking up a contract to understand what its content is likely to be about. In other words, the agreement should be described as what it is, for example, a software licence agreement or a distribution agreement or a development agreement and so on.

8.1.1 Parties

It is worthwhile considering whether the parties to the contract are the correct contracting parties.

From the provider's point of view, the provider should be sure that it is using the correct supplying or trading company as the contracting party and, furthermore, that that contracting party is capable of giving all of the warranties and guarantees that may be set out later in the agreement.

From the customer's point of view, it is essential that the customer is sure that the customer's contracting entity is that which the customer actually requires to be party to the contract. The customer may need to make sure that its company is described as including its subsidiaries and associated companies, all of whom may wish to have the benefit of the licensed software.

Many providers 'ring fence' their intellectual property rights by placing ownership of software and other assets into non-trading holding companies which may be situated offshore or in other jurisdictions separate from the jurisdiction in which the trading or supplying-provider company is actually based. If ownership of intellectual property rights and other assets are vested in such a manner, then the customer needs to be sure that the provider company with whom it is contracting is capable of making the guarantees and warranties in the agreement and is also in a position to control source code if it is placed in escrow. If the contracting provider's company is not the owner of the software then the customer may need to ask for some further assurances from the provider that the true owner of the software can provide the necessary escrow arrangements and performance warranties which only the true owner can give.

In the case of small software developers, often the developer company is no more than the corporate embodiment of one or two essential programmers and the customer may want to contract not only with the developer company, but also with its director/shareholder programmers in order to obtain the maximum guarantees and warranties as to performance, quality and the like of the services being provided.

8.1.2   Recitals

Some software contracts recite or state at the outset the reasons as to why the contract is being entered into and often describe the background or knowledge of the parties concerned. For example, 'the licensor is experienced in the provision of software solutions for the higher educational sector'.

Such a recital may well be an accurate description of the expertise of the licensor but it may also, in the case of litigation, be used by the customer as an argument (in the event of a failure of the software to perform) that the licensor was representing an expertise which it did not in fact have.

In some cases, where standard software contracts are used to apply to non-standard situations, the incorporation of standard recitals may be highly inappropriate and therefore whilst recitals at the outset of the contract may be of use, their precise wording should be carefully considered by both parties.

8.1.3   Definitions

Definitions may be relatively unimportant in minor software transactions such as the acquisition of a single copy of pre-written microcomputer software from a retail outlet, but they become very important in many major software transactions. Why? There are several answers. First, technical terminology is not always consistently used by provider and customer technical personnel, much less their business or staff personnel. One reason for such inconsistency is that all technical personnel do not have the same level of knowledge, experience and understanding. A definition of key technical terms helps to reduce the chances of a misunderstanding among personnel.

Secondly, software and related service providers are not totally consistent in their use of non-technical terms in their standard form agreements. Software is not always called software. A customer using software from four different sources could encounter four different generally descriptive names for the providers' products, for example, programs, program products, tools, conversion tools, software tools, software programs, source code, utility programs, spreadsheets, operating systems, productivity aids, courseware, microcode, executable programs, etc. The likelihood of confusion among customers increases as providers wax eloquent in their use of vague names for their various services, especially where some services are bundled and some are not, but their names are virtually identical. Clear definitions would help almost every provider's standard form agreements: vague definitions, few definitions, or no definitions are more common.

Thirdly, providers and customers alike tend to forget or overlook the potential audiences for their contracts. Judges and arbitrators may understand clear definitions of key technical or business words common in the type of transaction reflected by the parties' agreement, but they are not likely to understand such words except with clear definitions.

This analysis does not suggest that every term capable of being misunderstood or that might be foreign to a judge or jury must be defined. Rather, it suggests that key words call for definitions.

Definitions can be inserted in a contract in several ways. The introduction to the contract and statement of the parties' desires may contain defined terms. The first section of the agreement may define additional terms. Sometimes definitions are located in an appendix to the agreement. The other major approach to definitions is to define terms the first time they are used in an agreement. These approaches can be combined in an agreement.

8.1.4 Payment(s)

8.1.4.1 Amount(s)

The amount(s) paid in a software licence agreement are the business heart of the contract. From a businessperson's standpoint, payment(s) should be clearly stated even if nothing else in the contract is clear.

The amount(s) payable can be couched in various forms. For example, some software licence agreements require payment of a one-time, lump-sum licence fee. Others require annual or monthly licence fee payments. In development projects, payments may hinge on satisfaction of milestone requirements during the project. Some portion of a licence fee may be conditional upon acceptance. Countless payment schemes are used in different situations and the scheme employed helps to dictate the amount(s) payable at one or more points in time.

The location of the payment(s) provision in a software licence agreement also varies. It may be contained in the licence grant, in an attached schedule, or in a separate provision. Alternatively, the amount(s) due may be stated in a provider's standard price or fee schedule or list and incorporated in the agreement by reference. Generally speaking, it is preferable from a clarity standpoint to specify the amounts due somewhere in a software licence agreement. There are exceptions to this principle, however, such as the amount due for a microcomputer software program distributed under a shrink-wrap licence agreement. Here a price tag may be affixed to the container for disks bearing the software.

8.1.4.2 Due date(s)

The due date(s) for payment will vary according to the payment scheme adopted in the software licence agreement or necessitated by the type of transaction. For example, mail order software is usually paid for in advance of receipt via credit card.

The due date(s) for payment are frequently negotiated in a major software transaction. Much time may be devoted to the timing for payments in discussions between the software provider and customer. This attention is especially common in software development and conversion transactions, but is also fairly common in other types of transactions involving a software licence, such as distribution arrangements. The timing of payment and mechanisms to ensure payment are very important in international distribution arrangements. The larger the international transaction, the more likely it is that letters of credit will be employed to ensure payment by a point in time.

8.1.4.3 Increases and caps

Software users paying an annual or other periodic payment may sign agreements allowing the provider to increase licence fees, maintenance fees, etc over the life of the contract. Sophisticated users will attempt to negotiate a 'cap' or limit on such increases in any given year or other period during the agreement's term. In a major transaction many providers will agree to a reasonable ceiling on their increases per period.

8.1.4.4 Cure period for late payments

A cure period for late payments is a contract provision that allows a payment to slip past its due date without creating a breach of contract, provided the payment is made during the specified extension or 'cure' period. The provider is sometimes required to notify the customer of the provider's failure to receive a timely payment before the cure period is triggered. A cure period for late payments is worded differently from an extension of invoice payment time from 30 to 45 or 60 days which moves the due date for payment backward. The cure period does not move the provider's originally requested due date backwards, although that can be the practical effect, rather the cure period is a grace period intended to allow occasional, limited flexibility in the customer's, distributor's, etc payment performance, and a mechanism for inadvertent payment oversights to be corrected.

8.1.4.5   Interest on late payment

Customers who are slow to pay their invoices are a problem for software providers as they are in any business. Some software providers will attempt to discourage late payments by including an interest charge on outstanding overdue balances in their standard software licence agreements that call for multiple periodic payments. This practice is common in many industries. In certain jurisdictions excessive amounts of interest charged may be viewed as unreasonable, usury or a 'penalty' thus invalidating the provision.

8.1.4.6   Reductions in charges or fees

Software providers infrequently, but occasionally, reduce their standard licence fee for a product and convey the savings to customers. Competitive pressures sometimes force such reductions. They also occur on occasion when older products are being phased out in favour of newer, improved products although these reductions may be offset by increases in standard maintenance charges for the older products.

In the context of software development or conversion transactions, reductions in specified charges may appear as contingencies built into the parties' agreement that are triggered by failure to complete the project, or a portion of the work, by a specified date or within a specified period after an event. Obviously a customer must negotiate for such a plan prior to contract execution. Such reductions appear more often in contracts with government departments than in a commercial customer context. Here the reductions may be accomplished by the department filing a claim against a performance bond required of the provider, even if no specific sum was identified as the proper reduction in project cost for failure to satisfy a milestone or meet a completion date.

8.1.4.7   Bonus

In the same context of software development or conversion transactions, and occasionally in the context of a facilities management, maintenance, service bureau or distribution agreements, the customer will agree to pay the service provider a bonus for some performance in excess or advance of that required by the parties' agreement. Service providers must negotiate for such a plan prior to contract execution, but the door may be opened in negotiations by a customer who desires a reduction in charges upon a failure to meet a deadline or satisfy milestone criteria after several attempts. One natural response to such a customer is to request bonuses at least as numerous and significant as the requested reductions.

8.1.4.8 Retention against acceptance

In development and conversion transactions, in major software acquisitions, in turnkey equipment and software acquisitions, and some other software-related arrangements it is usually prudent for the party making the payment(s) to attempt to negotiate a 25% or greater retention from the agreed upon fees or charges until acceptance occurs. While providers of software or related services do not like to concede such a partial withholding of agreed upon payment(s), such concessions can be reasonable and obtainable through negotiations. To make such a request reasonable the criteria for acceptance must be clear and mutually acceptable. Many customers feel that a reserve for acceptance mechanism in their agreement keeps providers motivated to fix problems and to work hard to prevent them from happening, for example, delivery delays, acceptance test failures, etc.

8.1.5 Licence grant

The licence grant in a software licence agreement is one of its most important provisions. The grant provision defines the rights of the customer-licensee with respect to the software licensed and usually contains the restrictions or limitations imposed by the licensor on the licensee's rights. As a general rule, rights not granted expressly or by implication in the grant clause are not conveyed by the licence agreement. Of course, rights are sometimes conveyed and restrictions are fairly often located in other sections of a licence agreement. Also, additional rights may be conveyed verbally after contract execution, implied through the parties' course of dealing with one another, or added to a contract in an addendum. The following discussion explores the rights and restrictions commonly found in the grant clauses of software licence agreements for major software transactions.

Note that the licence grant contains a mixture of business considerations addressed in more or less legal sounding terminology.

8.1.5.1 Exclusive or non-exclusive

A key point of any licence grant is whether it is exclusive or non-exclusive. 'Exclusive' can be understood to mean 'only'. When a copyright owner grants an exclusive licence to all of his copyright rights, he actually transfers ownership of the copyright for the duration of the grant and within the confines of the grant's limitations. Exclusive licences are more likely to be granted by developers to publishers or publishers to distributors than they are to be conveyed from publishers to software users. By definition, only one user could have an exclusive licence grant for a particular protected right without the publisher breaching a contract by giving a second user the same right. Publishers would go bankrupt if they could grant only one licence.

A non-exclusive licence is the opposite of an exclusive licence in that it means 'one of (potentially) many'. The licensor of software under a non-exclusive licence has discretion to license hundreds or thousands of copies, or only one copy. Non-exclusive copyright licences do not automatically, by definition, convey ownership of any right as do exclusive copyright licences. Non-exclusive licences are frequently granted to commercial software users.

8.1.5.2 To use; make or reproduce; distribute by sale, lease, rental, loan, gift, or licence; publicly display; publicly perform

A second key point of any licence grant is the rights conveyed to the licensee. The variety of the possible rights conveyed illustrates the breadth of the legal concept of a software licence and the various uses of a software licence agreement. For example, a software user-licensee obtains possession of a copy of software and the right to use the copy either expressly or by implication in a software licence grant. The user may also receive the right to reproduce the copy received for backup or archive purposes. In contrast, a software conversion or reproduction house normally receives only the right to reproduce copies of a program for a publisher or distributor. A distributor normally receives the right to distribute copies of a program by sale, lease or licence; and may receive the right to reproduce copies, directly or through a subcontractor, or the right publicly to display the operation of the program in the course of marketing efforts, for example, to display the operation of a microcomputer program at trade shows, in training classes, etc and to allow dealers or retailers to display its operation to potential customers. If the program is a game or entertainment program, the distributor and its dealers may receive the right publicly to perform the game in the course of marketing efforts.

Of course, if a program is sold to a user or distributor, that party can treat the copy purchased as a book may be treated, assuming copyright protection. For example, the purchaser could resell the copy, rent or lease it to another, modify the program as necessary to make it operate on his computer, etc. However, this discussion focuses on licensed software and presumes a valid and enforceable software licence agreement. Such agreements may prohibit user-licensee modifications, reproductions, transfers, etc or may prohibit a distributor from modifying and using the program while allowing its distribution.

In general, a licensee of software protected by copyright law will infringe the owner's copyright if the licensee's actions exceed the scope of its licence grant. The licensor need not expressly retain rights not granted, in other words, in order to prohibit unlicensed actions. Copyright licence grants will be interpreted as prohibiting actions not otherwise expressly allowed.

The decision in the case of *Laurence Wrenn & Integrated Multi-Media Solutions Ltd v Stephen Landamore* [2007] EWHC 1833 (Ch) demonstrates that where computer software is commissioned it is essential to clarify in the contract rights of ownership and licence terms.

In the case in question, where the commissioning company and its sole director, Mr Wrenn, commissioned Mr Landamore to develop certain software programs there was no initial contract and whilst there did not appear to be any dispute over the fact that ownership of the programs remained with the programmer, Mr Landamore, when the parties fell out with each other and tried to confirm their legal rights and obligations by subsequent contract the issues of ownership and right became more confused.

Ultimately the UK High Court held that although the software programs were commissioned by Mr Wrenn and his company there was no need to imply an assignment of copyright in order for Mr Wrenn and his company to commercialise the software and therefore an exclusive licence was a satisfactory solution.

In addition, the court held that for Mr Wrenn and his company to make use of the software, it was necessary to have access to the source code even though ownership remained with Mr Landamore.

With hindsight, the parties would have been better to have reduced their respective understandings to contract at the earliest possible stage. The complexity of code in programs means that an assignment of outright ownership is unlikely to work and the parties need to carefully construct licensing and source code access arrangements.

8.1.5.3 Territory, host(s) and site(s)

Often a licence grant specifies a limitation on the licensee's actions regarding the licensed software in the nature of a territorial, system or location statement. For example, a distributor might have the territory within which it may distribute copies of software specified in the licence grant. A user might be told by the licence grant that it may use the licensed copy on a single computer, a single network or at a single site.

Of course, there are variations on this theme. A user-licensee may be informed by the licence grant provision of a software licence agreement that it may use the software at any company-owned location, or that the use allowed is limited to use in connection with information from one company location. The latter right is designed to prohibit processing information from remote locations. Licence agreements with a government department may allow use by any government department. Even if such agreements are intended to be limited to a specific department or user within a department, DEFCONS (which are incorporated into such agreements) may override these provisions. Knowledgeable counsel is a necessity for software providers doing business with departments if they wish to retain control of their intellectual property rights in their software products.

In a similar vein, the laws of foreign countries may nullify or override attempts to provide exclusivity of territory. For example, the Treaty on the Functioning of the European Union (or Lisbon Treaty), arts 101 and 102 (formerly the Treaty of Rome, arts 81 and 82) may, subject to certain exceptions, prevent attempts to provide exclusivity which create or may create a monopoly. Once again, any lawyers knowledgeable in this area can assist software providers in maintaining control over their rights and products and in avoiding unenforceable or illegal contract provisions.

8.1.5.4   Duration-limited, evergreen, perpetual, unspecified

The duration of the licence grant is usually stated in the grant clause and varies with the type of software and situation in question. Microcomputer software is fairly often licensed on a perpetual basis, raising the question of whether the licence agreement is really a sale agreement. Poorly drafted licence agreements may not specify the duration of the licence grant. This omission is easily avoided either by an express statement, or by an express or implied connection between the term of the licence grant and the term of the licence agreement.

Minicomputer and mainframe computer software licence grant provisions are more likely to be limited in duration but renewable under an 'evergreen' clause that continues the life of the licence until it is terminated by the licensor or licensee. Once again the licence grant in these agreements may have a specified duration or may track the life of the licence agreement.

8.1.5.5   Relationship of licence term to term of contract

The duration of the licence grant does not always coincide with the duration of the software licence agreement. For example, the licence agreement may be signed by the parties and the software may be delivered subsequently with its licence term commencing upon its acceptance. The term of such an agreement may commence upon contract execution rather than acceptance of the program. The same contract may serve as the licence agreement for a second program acquired months or years after contract execution. The second program could be brought under the terms and conditions of the agreement via a letter or schedule signed by the parties. The two programs would then be licensed under the same licence agreement, but the duration of their individual licences may be inconsistent with each other and with the duration of the licence agreement. The licence for either of the programs may be terminable without terminating the licence agreement. Sometimes the licences of all programs used or distributed under one licence agreement will be terminated but the parties will continue the life of the agreement expecting it to be given new application to another program licensed in the future.

Microcomputer software is commonly licensed under an agreement whose licence grant expires contemporaneously with the life of the agreement, and mainframe and minicomputer program licences can be structured to have a contemporaneous term. Where equipment is leased and several programs are licensed at the same time, the user may negotiate to make the lease term and licence terms contemporaneous so that the software can be replaced when the equipment is replaced.

8.1.5.6 Number of copies licensed

Grant of licence provisions in software user licence agreements normally specify the number of copies of each program licensed. In distribution agreements a quantity of each program distributed may be stated as a quota, or the distributor may be required to maintain a specified minimum inventory. A site licence or company licence may give a user the right to reproduce and use at the site or throughout the company a specified quantity of copies, a maximum number of copies or an unlimited number of copies of the licensed software.

8.1.5.7 Types of code licensed object, source, etc

With the exception of software mass-marketed under shrink-wrap licence agreements, it is common for software licence agreements with users to specify in their grant provisions that object code is being licensed to the user and that source code is only made available pursuant to a separable source code licence. Where source code is licensed it is common for the licence grant to identify this fact.

8.1.5.8 Transferable or non-transferable rights

Grant provisions in user licence agreements often specify that the licensed rights are non- transferable, meaning that the user may not unilaterally transfer the software to another party without the licensor's permission. Violating this limitation on the licence grant may subject the user to a claim that it has infringed the licensor's right to control the distribution of his software. Some software providers who also furnish equipment will allow a user to transfer its licence to a subsequent purchaser of the equipment provided they are notified of the transfer in advance and have the option to approve or disapprove the subsequent licensee. This approval option is normally considered important in a licence agreement calling for ongoing fee payments because the subsequent user may be a credit risk. Even if there is no ongoing fee, the licensor may want to impose or transfer charge, or recover any taxes imposed on the transfer. Also, if the new user is a known software pirate, the licensor may want a new agreement with the new user or may be reluctant to approve the transfer.

Government regulations or foreign laws may nullify or override the restriction on transfers that a non-transferable licence grant conveys.

8.1.5.9 Payment type: one-time fee, fixed periodic royalty, royalty free or other

As discussed earlier, the payment schemes evident in software licence agreements vary considerably. Where the licence is granted on a royalty-free basis or one lump-sum payment, this fact may be conveyed in the licence grant provision. Where multiple or periodic payments are required in user, distributor, development or other agreements involving software, the payment terms are often stated in a separate provision or in an attached schedule. As noted in SECTION 8.1.4.1, price tags or mail order catalogues may convey the cost of mass-marketed software.

8.1.5.10 Software defined to include documentation, updates and enhancements

Some software licence grants will encompass not only the initially delivered program, but also its updates, enhancements and user documentation. These items may be addressed separately in other provisions, but the customer should ensure their receipt and the licensed rights to deal with updates and enhancements in the same manner that he is authorised to deal with the originally delivered program, be it for personal use, distribution or some other right.

Copies of user documentation are usually sold or provided at no charge as items bundled with the software. Sophisticated user-licensees will define the software to include the documentation for warranty and indemnification purposes, or require the documentation to be mentioned separately in licensor warranty and indemnification provisions. Software licensors who desire to license the use of documentation rather than sell or give away copies may include the user documentation in a definition of the licensed software.

8.1.5.11 Number of copies that can be reproduced

Licence grants sometimes specify that a user-licensee may make one or more archive copies of the licensed software. This right may be conveyed elsewhere in the licence agreement, but the important point is to ensure that the right is stated somewhere or that backup copies are unnecessary because of maintenance coverage or for some other reason. In the UK restrictions on backup are now invalid as a result of the Copyright (Computer Programs) Regulations[1] resulting from the EC Directive on the Legal Protection of Computer programs.[2] The Regulations and the Directive, incorporated in an amendment to the Copyright Design and Patents Act 1988,[3] state that a lawful acquirer, a licensee of the program, is permitted to carry out any form of copying which is necessary for the program to be used and in order to make a security backup without having to obtain express consent. There is even a stated right that error correction will be permitted but this is only for the purpose of enabling the program to run correctly. It will not affect the requirement for maintenance and support contracts to be entered into.

Even if maintenance coverage seems to make a backup copy unnecessary, a disaster might leave a user-licensee unable to recover a copy of software from a non-operative computer so that it could be removed to a hot site. Hot sites are discussed further in SECTION 8.1.5.13 below. Hence, backup copies are important in most situations.

1   S1 1992/3233.
2   91/250 OJ 1991 L122/42.
3   Copyright, Designs and Patents Act 1988, s 50A.

8.1.5.12 Modifications or maintenance by licence allowed and rights regarding modified version

If the user-licensee desires to perform maintenance on licensed software, the grant clause should express the right to modify the program to make corrections and fix defects. The same principle applies if the user-licensee desires to improve the licensed program. Generally, the right to make changes in a program protected by copyright law is an exclusive right of the copyright owner. However, the previously mentioned Copyright (Computer Programs) Regulations[1] allow maintenance to the extent of error correction.

In addition it is worth mentioning at this point that, under English law, reverse engineering or decompilation had previously been regarded as an infringement of copyright but the Regulations mentioned above, as a result of the EC Directive on the Legal Protection of Computer Programs,[2] now allow a lawful licensee to analyse the underlying code, copy and translate the program and investigate the functioning of the program in order to evaluate and understand its ideas and principles without the need to obtain consent of the copyright holder, but only for the purpose of achieving inter-operability of an independently created program with the licensed software subject to a number of conditions. This is an implied right which may not be excluded by licensing arrangements within the EU.

In addition, if the user-licensee desires to own modifications or improvements he makes in the licensor's program, that ownership should be specified in the licence agreement. Some agreements contain standard provisions making all modifications or improvements the property of the licensor. Licensors often wish to incorporate valuable user modifications in their standard product. Where the licensor's programmers will make the modifications or improvements under a service contract, their ownership should be negotiated if the user-licensee pays for the work. Even if the user-licensee has no desire to own or market the changes he paid for, their ownership may be used as a bargaining chip in negotiations. For example, their use and distribution by the licensor could justify price concessions or royalties.

1   SI 1992/3233.
2   91/250 OJ 1991 L122/42.

8.1.5.13 Use of copy at a hot-site or cold-site allowed

If the user-licensee has a hot-site or cold-site arrangement, live and backup server arrangements or a mirrored server arrangement, or believes he may make such arrangements in the future, then he needs flexibility in his licence grant to transfer the original copy or a backup copy of the licensed software. Some provider standard forms allow movement of the licensed copy or a backup to another location in the event of a disaster, but most do not. Hence the point often requires negotiation.

8.1.5.14 Use, reproduction, and modification of source code and technical information received from escrow agent

Unless a separate agreement or an addendum to the licence agreement allows the use, reproduction and modification of source code and technical information received by a user-licensee from a source-code agent, the licence grant needs to address the user's right to so deal with these items. The typical user licence grant covering executable code will not allow the use of source code. The user who insists on a source code escrow arrangement needs to ensure that he has the rights to deal with the source code as necessary upon its receipt from the escrow agent.

8.1.5.15 Grant subject to other terms of contract

The typical well-drafted licence grant in a software licence agreement will include the concept that the grant is made subject to the other terms of the software licence agreement. All of the desired qualifications on a licence grant may not fit well into one or even a few paragraphs. Some of them may be most conveniently expressed elsewhere in the agreement. Also, the licensor may intend to allow the grant to continue only so long as all conditions are complied with. For all of these reasons, and others, it is prudent for a software licensor to so draft its licence grant provisions.

8.1.6 Delivery

Delivery is an important element in many major software transactions. As a general rule, the licensor will not specify in the licence agreement a firm delivery date or deadline, and the licensee must negotiate for clarification and written commitments on this point if it is important to him. The same is true regarding computer acquisitions.

8.1.7 Site and host preparation

Standard licensor form agreements sometimes require the licensee to prepare the site and host computer for software installation, perhaps according to the licensor's specifications. This site preparation requirement is more common with respect to computers.

The site and host are important in this context for several reasons. First, computers and software operating on them can be affected by the environment.

Prudent users will require the provider in a major transaction to inspect and approve the site prior to computer installation.

Secondly, software must be compatible with its host computer environment in order to operate on the computer. Prudent users will take steps to ensure that compatibility before expending large sums in major software transactions.

8.1.8 Installation

Some software providers install licensed software without cost, some demand an installation charge and some tell users they must install the program themselves. If the licensor installs a program, it is common for his installers to run diagnostic tests upon installation in order to confirm proper loading and operation of the program. After these tests are passed, the licensor gives or sends the user an invoice for the software. If the user wants the opportunity to confirm the functionality of the program before an invoice issues, he must negotiate for an acceptance test.

8.1.9 Acceptance tests

The acceptance test is another key element of a software licence agreement in a major software transaction. As indicated above, software providers often use installation tests as the acceptance standard. If the user-licensee desires another arrangement, he must negotiate for it. Whatever type of subjective or objective acceptance test is negotiated, customers should be careful to also negotiate the consequences of an acceptance test failure and to include these consequences in the parties' contract.

It is important for both parties to communicate clearly to each other, agree upon and then express in the contract precisely what the parties intend the software and system to do. If the supplier warrants that its product will perform in accordance with its own documentation, then this is substantially in favour of the supplier because it is hardly likely to warrant that its own product will not perform in line with documentation which it, the supplier, has already prepared. On the other hand, customers are all too often willing to rely upon the supplier to provide performance criteria and performance specifications. In many cases the definition of the performance and functionality of the software is no more than a schedule of hardware and software descriptions and technical serial numbers. In other words, there is still nothing in the contract that really explains what solution and interpretation the software is intended to perform or give effect to.

In the case of *Anglo Group plc v Winther Browne & CO Ltd*,[1] the court held that customers have a responsibility to communicate adequately to their suppliers their particular needs for the product that is being supplied to them. In this case, the dispute centred on a system which was subsequently found to have bugs in it. The judge ruled that not only was there a responsibility on the customer to choose the most suitable system for its own business needs, but there was also a duty on the customer to co-operate with the supplier and accept reasonable solutions to any problems that might arise.

The effect of this court decision is that suppliers should prepare adequate specifications of their requirements and needs and ensure that these are integrated into the contract documents as well as into the actual acceptance procedures for the work product.

The *Anglo Group* case does not, however, absolve the supplier from its obligations to deliver software of satisfactory quality or services of satisfactory quality. In the case of *South West Water Services Ltd v International Computers Ltd*,[2] the court held that South West Water was entitled to terminate a software integration contract because of persistent failure by International Computers Ltd to meet the customer's specification.

In the *South West Water* case the customer had agreed a specification with the supplier, but the supplier had vastly underestimated the amount of work necessary to meet that specification and, in addition, the supplier had misrepresented its ability to comply with the contract terms.

1   (2000) 144 Sol Jo LB 197.
2   [1999] BLR 420.

8.1.9.1   *Offsite benchmark test*

One step a software user can take in requiring satisfaction of an acceptance test prior to (initial) payment is to negotiate an offsite benchmark test of the software. In fact, this test can be required before the parties' agreement is signed, and this test is most often employed by government agencies. In this test, an offsite host computer such as the provider's must operate the desired program under some normal operating conditions, for example, an 'actual-work' processing requirement. If the test is satisfied according to the subjective or objective criteria established by the parties, then the user will sign the agreement or accept delivery, as the case may be.

8.1.9.2   *Onsite ready for use*

A declaration that a program is 'ready for use' by a software provider is nothing more than a statement that the provider's installation tests have been satisfactorily completed. No user acceptance test is involved where the customer pays for software declared ready for use by the software provider unless a user test requirement is negotiated.

8.1.9.3   *Onsite objective criteria*

One form of user acceptance tests for software licensed in a major acquisition is an onsite test requiring the operation of the desired program under identified work conditions and the satisfaction of agreed upon objective criteria for user acceptance. If the software passes the test, the user will sign an agreement or accept delivery if an agreement is already signed.

Generally speaking, objective standard acceptance tests are more reasonable and even-handed than subjective evaluation acceptance tests. The only difficulties with objective standard tests are things like user difficulty in deciding on standards, provider and user difficulty in reaching agreement on objective standards, difficulty in drafting the standards clearly, difficulty in interpreting the standards, the degree to which subjective evaluation of the satisfaction of objective standards creeps into the test, etc.

8.1.9.4 Onsite subjective standard

The major alternative to an objective acceptance test is a subjective standard for acceptance, although some tests contain mixtures of objective and subjective elements. Customers, especially as an opening position in negotiations, fairly often demand a totally subjective acceptance test for the program in question. The same is true in computer acquisitions. Then the burden is on the software provider to negotiate for an objective test or to refuse an acceptance test altogether. Much time can be spent on the negotiation of acceptance tests, but the time spent can be worthwhile. At a minimum, an acceptance test can help a user-licensee ensure that he is acquiring a product that will produce the desired business result, and furnish such an indicator before the product is paid for.

Software providers in major transactions increasingly respond to acceptance test demands with an offer of a trial usage period. This is a reasonable counteroffer, but it also gives the provider a slight advantage over his position in an acceptance test. The provider knows from experience that after a program has been installed for 30, 60 or 90 days it is unlikely that the customer will order it removed. Even if the program does not generate the desired business result, it usually generates sufficient business and/or technical improvements that the customer will conclude it is worthwhile keeping.

Whichever tests or standards are adopted, it is important to involve those with technical expertise in defining the criteria for the acceptance tests. Furthermore, it must be remembered that, unless the licence says otherwise, any use of the software may be deemed to be acceptance of such software.

8.1.10 Term of the agreement

Many of the most important details about the term of a software licence agreement are discussed below. From a business standpoint it is obviously important to know and possibly negotiate the duration of a transaction over which periodic revenue may be received, and to know and possibly negotiate when the parties' obligations are satisfied. This section and the next section on termination set the stage for such determinations and negotiations.

8.1.10.1 Commencement before software is delivered

As indicated earlier, the term of a software licence agreement may commence upon its execution, upon the delivery or installation of a product licensed under an agreement or upon some other event. The term of a licence agreement in a major software transaction need not coincide with the term of the licence grant for software licensed under the agreement. In fact, software licence agreements often serve as the parties' basic agreements for several programs licensed at different points in the agreements' lives.

It is important to recognise that the term of a software licence agreement and the term of a licence grant for a particular program acquired pursuant to the agreement are separate but related topics in contract negotiations. These topics are related chiefly because the term of a licence grant normally expires when the agreement expires, unless an event or clause that allows continued life for the licence grant, for example, a clause allowing continued use for a short period, or transferring the licence grant to another agreement. These topics are also rated because the licensee may want all licence fee payment obligations to start or stop at the same point regardless of how long the software has been licensed for or installed, for example, to stop when leased equipment hosting the software is replaced. It makes no sense to continue paying application program licence fees after the only computer that can host the software is replaced with an incompatible machine.

Licensees are well advised to co-ordinate the life of their software grant and the life of their agreement in a manner that makes sense in the transaction in question.

8.1.10.2   Limited term expires unless parties renew

One approach to an agreement's life is to give it a fixed, limited term after which it expires unless an agreement between the parties renews it. This approach can be favoured in agreements with foreign distributors and representatives as a means of avoiding termination penalties imposed in some foreign countries. This approach will not nullify such penalties in every country, but it will in some. In some jurisdictions, particularly the Middle East, the duty to compensate a distributor will arise even on a failure to renew or extend a fixed-term agreement.

8.1.10.3   Evergreen clause term automatically renews indefinitely

Under an evergreen clause arrangement, the term will be fixed, but will automatically renew, or extend on an annual basis until one of the parties terminates the agreement. Many software providers prefer this approach regarding major agreements with users. Both parties are normally given only a narrow window of opportunity to terminate such an agreement each renewal period. This window can easily close unnoticed. If the term of the software licence grant also renews under a separate evergreen clause with a narrow window for termination, or under the agreement's evergreen clause, users must be observant and plan ahead or they can be locked into licence fees for another period after deciding a program is no longer required. Of course, such clauses also allow the provider to administer thousands of user licence agreements at a lower cost than if all users could terminate at will after an initial licence period.

8.1.10.4 Perpetual term

A perpetual term gives 'forever' life to a contract, and it is much more common in shrink-wrap licence agreements than in signed licensed agreements. A perpetual term raises the question of whether the licence agreement is really a sale agreement.

In the case of *Harbinger UK Ltd v GE Information Services Ltd*[1] the Court of Appeal had to consider the effect of a support and maintenance obligation provided in perpetuity. The licensor in this case had granted a distribution agreement together with support and maintenance obligations which were expressed to be 'in perpetuity'.

The licensor terminated the distribution agreement and delivered that its obligations to support and maintain were also thereby extinguished. The court, however, held that the obligation to support and maintain should exist for so long as the distributor was also obliged to support and maintain the software for its own customers.

1 [2000] 1 All ER (Comm) 166.

8.1.10.5 Unspecified term until agreement is terminated

An unspecified contract duration gives the agreement an indefinite term and means the agreement's life will end only when the agreement is terminated by one of the parties. Such an arrangement is more often the result of sloppy legal drafting, or non-legal contract drafting, than it is the result of intelligent planning.

8.1.10.6 Grace period

A grace period extends all or part of a contract's life for a fixed or identifiable period. Such provisions are more common in distributor licence agreements than in user licence agreements. Grace periods allow distributors the ability to clear out their remaining inventory and/or the inventory held by dealers, and prevent breach of contract and copyright infringement claims for unauthorised post-termination distribution.

8.1.11   Termination or expiration and result

Sometimes a distinction is drawn between a termination and a cancellation. A termination can mean an imposed end of the contract's life that is allowed by its terms. A cancellation is an imposed ending that is not allowed by contract terms and that may or may not be allowed by law. An expiration always means a natural death, that is, an end of the contract specified by its terms. For our purposes it is sufficient to use 'termination' to mean either an allowed or an unanticipated ending to a contract's life imposed by one of the parties. Note that parties to a contract may agree to end its life for unplanned or unanticipated reasons. Contract termination does not always result from one party imposing an end or from a planned expiration.

8.1.11.1 Termination upon breach

One of the most common types of termination results from a breach of contract obligations by one party. The breach is often a non-performance of a required obligation, but it may be an inadequate performance as well. If the breach is material, contract law may well allow termination. On the other hand, in some foreign countries any minor breach may allow termination.

Litigation is common after a termination for a breach of contract. The defendant usually counterclaims as well as defending against the claimant's claims. If the claimant is not faultless in the parties' business dealings, both parties may end up partial winners and partial losers.

8.1.11.2 Termination without cause

Some contracts allow one or all of the parties to terminate 'at will' or without a breach of contract by another party. This right may be exercisable at any time without prior notice, only with prior notice of a specified period, or only at specified points with or without notice. This is the type of termination that most often gives rise to penalties when foreign distributors or sales representatives are terminated.

8.1.11.3 Expiration at end of term

As indicated earlier, the expiration of an agreement at the end of its initial term is a natural death for a contract in the sense that it is preordained by the agreement's terms. If the agreement contains an option to renew that is not exercised, the expiration is still anticipated and planned for in the agreement. In contrast, if the agreement automatically renews subject to termination, then the end of the contract results from a termination, not its expiration.

8.1.11.4 Expiration upon lapse of intellectual property rights

A variation on the theme of a natural expiration can be found in some technology licences where the technology is protected by an intellectual property law. In this variation, the contract may call for its expiration upon the end of the protected life of the intellectual property. For example, a patent licence may specify the end of the patent's life as the end of the licence agreement, and copyright licences may terminate at the end of the period of copyright.

8.1.11.5   Consequences

From a business standpoint and from the standpoint of protecting intellectual property rights in software, the consequences of the termination or expiration of a licence agreement should be specified in the agreement and negotiated if necessary. User-licensees should be required to return licensed software or erase it. Certificates of destruction help preserve trade secret protection and may be helpful in litigation over software piracy by an ex-licensee. Distributor-licensees should be required to stop distribution upon or at some point after termination or expiration of a software licence agreement. Sometimes distributors are allowed to return an inventory for a refund or credit against final payments from a publisher, and some are allowed a 'remaindering' or 'sell-off' period for 90 days after termination.

8.1.12   Service and updates maintenance

Some software providers include maintenance terms in their licence agreement which call for copies of updates containing several defect corrections as they are made generally available to customers. Others cover maintenance in a separate agreement, or in a rider or appendix to a licence agreement.

User-licensees should pay particular attention to the interplay of maintenance and warranty provisions, especially regarding their coverage and commencement, so that they are not surprised by maintenance charges for service, or by a lack of coverage at a time when the warranty was expected to provide no-charge, complete protection.

Detailed aspects of a service level agreement or support and maintenance agreements are not the subject of this work, but suffice to say that the value of the licensed software is often dependent upon the value or level of service, support and maintenance offered by and enforceable under a service level or maintenance agreement.

It is essential to define clearly what is or is not included in standard charges; whether the provider is giving full training or merely 'training the trainers'; whether the customer is obligated or not to take up new releases; and whether what may appear to be generous maintenance terms by the provider may just be a means of reducing original 'fit for purpose' warranties in the software licence.

8.1.13   Enhancements

Enhancements are usually regarded as major improvements in software functionality. Some software providers charge for enhancements, some do not, and some will charge only for especially significant enhancement. Whatever the case may be, user-licensees need to ensure that enhancements are addressed in their software licence agreements, and to attempt to negotiate any unsatisfactory arrangement for enhancements.

8.1.14   Escrow

A source code escrow is deposit of source code with a party with the intention to have the code released to a user of executable code, or a joint venture partner, etc, upon one or more events such as a failure to provide timely maintenance service. In the context of user licence agreements, source code escrows address two fundamental concerns: that a provider will not furnish satisfactory maintenance service; or that a provider will liquidate or fall into bankruptcy. In either event, the user will need a copy of the provider's source code in order to have a chance of successfully maintaining the licensed program. Technical information regarding the program will also be required.

User-licensees should consider requiring a licensor of executable code to either furnish a copy of source code, or establish a source code escrow for the user's benefit whenever the software in question is critical or very important to the user's business and when there is no similar substitute for the program readily available in the marketplace. The substitute should be compatible with the user's equipment and likely to be available in the foreseeable future. A program at the end of its lifecycle may not be available in the marketplace for long.

Many licensors have established an escrow to service all of their customers requesting one. User-licensees should ensure that established escrows meet their needs, as they should with an escrow created in response to their request. The escrow should call for the deposit of source code, technical information and user documentation for the originally supplied program. User verification or independent verification of the materials supplied should be a feature of the escrow assuming the software in question is important or critical to the user's business. Source code deposits of updates and enhancements should be required and verified before deposit. The triggering events for release of the deposited materials should be identified. The user's rights regarding the licensed materials should be specified, including the right to prepare and utilise altered code and modified versions of the program. Responsibility for payment for the escrow should be assigned. A mutually acceptable independent escrow agent should be utilised. Conflict of interest problems may arise if the user's or provider's bank, insurance company or solicitor serve as the escrow agent. These are not all of the issues that should be addressed, but they serve as illustrations of the important issues in source code escrow arrangements. Source code escrows are a type of technology escrow arrangement utilised in various technology-based industries. Ideally, the source code escrow arrangement will be negotiated simultaneously with other contract terms, and made a part of the parties' licence agreement.

8.1.15   Training

Training seldom receives as much attention as it deserves. Adequate user training can have a significant impact on the success of a software licence transaction. The amount and cost of training should be identified in the parties' agreement. Training charges are one of the most easily negotiated charges in a software licence arrangement. User-licensees usually prefer onsite, as opposed to the provider's site, training sessions. The location of the training sessions should be negotiated and specified in the parties' contract.

8.1.16 Consulting and development services

Major software licence transactions often involve a small amount of provider consulting and/or development services. Minor customising work on pre-written programs may be adequately covered in the parties' agreement. In contrast, significant consulting or development work necessitates a separate agreement or at least an appendix to the licence agreement. Writing interface code and menus or shells may or may not require major effort, but they justify a separate agreement or appendix or both so that all of the important issues they raise can be addressed.

Consulting and development services are often major software transactions. New software development projects are rarely completed without problems of some sort. Hence, they deserve negotiation and a carefully drafted contract. System selection consulting, and system analysis or design projects by independent consultants, may focus on important or critical programs, or cost enough, to justify a separate, negotiated agreement or appendix.

While it is beyond the scope of this book to discuss the issues idiosyncratic to these transactions, detailed specifications are very important to successful major development projects. Customers are well advised to apportion payment for these projects among milestones requiring well-identified deliverables. A portion of the project payment should be reserved for system acceptance.

8.1.17 Warranties in general

As a general rule suppliers will seek to warrant their goods and services to the minimum and it is usual for the customer to have to negotiate in extended express warranties to cover their particular requirements and needs.

The more mass market, high volume, low value the software the more usual it is for the software to be warranted on an 'as is – as available' basis or WYSIWYG (What you see is what you get).

The more complex the solution delivery is the more likely it is that the warranties will be broken down into warranties for hardware, software, third party products, professional consultancy and programming and the like.

There has already been much discussion as to whether or not software is 'goods' for the purposes of implied warranties under the Sale of Goods Act 1979 in the UK and on the whole, the more mass market the software, the more it is likely to be seen as 'goods'. The more the software is delivered on an integration and commission basis the more likely it is that the software will be treated as 'services', thereby weakening the degree of implied warranties.

In general, the more that a customer negotiates extended warranties into a contract the more the supplier will seek to limit the impact of those warranties under the Limitation of Liability Clauses (which will be discussed later).

On an increasing basis now, where warranties are divided up between hardware, software, third party products, consultancy and the like, the more it becomes important to balance each express warranty against each express limitation of liability clause and, indeed, each insurable aspect of the risk associated therewith. In other words, when negotiating and drafting software contracts in the area of warranties, it is essential to consider at the same time those other clauses that impact upon warranties such as limitations of liability, indemnity and insurance.

Set out hereafter are a series of the types of express warranty that might well be included in a computer contract.

8.1.18   Limited warranty

Limited warranties are standard provisions in software licence agreements. Some warranties address only the media for the software and indicate the software is provided without any warranty. Some warranties submit that the software will satisfy licensor specifications. Others focus on defects in material and workmanship. In a major software licence transaction, as in a major computer acquisition, a user is best served by a warranty that the acquired product will furnish the user's desired business results. Software providers are reluctant to provide such warranties, but they can be negotiated in some deals. Reasonable qualifications can be added to such warranties to protect software providers against events beyond their control causing a violation of such a warranty.

8.1.19   Ongoing performance obligations

Ongoing performance obligations are most often found in agreements with government agencies even though they can be helpful to commercial user-licensees. These provisions require software to meet specified performance standards over the life of the licence agreement or for a long period, in contrast to the short duration of most limited warranty provisions.

If time has been spent in defining a detailed specification and functionality for the software solution, then by incorporating such specification and functionality description into the contract, the customer particularly will set a standard against which performance warranties can be matched. Ongoing performance warranties can apply equally to hardware as to software and usually for software a warranty that it will 'comply with supplier specification or manual' will be of value provided that such specification or manual is satisfactorily incorporated into the contract.

In the case of ongoing service performance the customer should require that the supplier warrants compliance with service description but this in turn places an obligation upon the customer to ensure that the service description is accurate in terms of what is required.

If the solution being provided by the supplier relates to a total integration package where software, hardware and consultancy is being provided for the customer, then the customer may wish to negotiate a general ongoing performance warranty for the total solution ('the System').

An example of such a warranty might be:

> The supplier warrants that [upon installation] [for a period of [X] months from the Acceptance Date] the System will provide the functionality and performances specified in the Schedule.

8.1.20 Virus and error warranty

In so far as viruses, bugs and latent defect errors are not already covered under any undertaking and warranties of the provider or are not specifically items included in any specification to which the provider is obligated to deliver matching software, it may be wise for customers to require specific undertakings or warranties to be given by providers.

No provider will usually guarantee that software is error or bug free, but, equally, customers will not want to acquire software solutions that are flawed. It may also be reasonable for a customer to accept that the provider does not warrant that the software will be free from minor interruptions or errors.

Many providers will provide limited warranties for the software after delivery or acceptance but will expect subsequent errors or defects to be cured under ongoing maintenance and support arrangements. From the provider's point of view, unusual defects which are outside of acceptance tests or specifications, or which indeed were never contemplated by either of the parties at the time the transaction was entered into, would be unusual error corrections provided under the maintenance agreement, but as additional expense to the customer and not within the standard maintenance fee.

An example of such a warranty might be:

> (i) The provider shall ensure that it and its employees, consultants, agents and sub-contractors take all reasonable precautions to ensure that no known viruses for which detection and antidote software is generally available are coded or introduced into the buyer's software when the provider is supplying any hardware or software or any services under this Agreement.
>
> (ii) In the event that the provider identifies a computer virus on the buyer's system it shall immediately notify the buyer.
>
> (iii) The provider undertakes to remove, at its own expense, any virus whose presence on the buyer's system should have been prevented by the provider had it properly discharged its duties pursuant to clause (i) above and, where

> necessary, pay for the cost of reconfiguring the System and installing virus-free software at no cost to the buyer.
>
> (iv) If a virus is identified on the buyer's system, notwithstanding the use by the provider of reasonable precautions as defined under clause (i) above, all subsequent remedial work undertaken by the provider shall be paid for by the customer on a time and materials basis.

8.1.21 European Monetary Union warranty

Although there is still some uncertainty as to whether or not the Euro currency will be implemented under the European Monetary Union Policy as planned, the generally accepted view is that almost all but the smallest businesses should prepare for the implementation of the Euro and develop an ability to process Euro transactions, regardless of whether or not, or indeed when the Euro is implemented or whether or not or when the UK joins the European Monetary Union.

There are a number of reasons for this, including the fact that many companies already trade in or deal with businesses who trade in the 11 'in' member countries who have already indicated they will be participating in European Monetary Union, and many have indicated they wish to do business in Euros anyway. In addition, during the transactional dual currency period, all conversions to EC currencies must be paid first into the Euro and then into the relevant European currency. This conversion process is referred to or known as the 'Triangulation Rule'. Conversion must also be made using six significant figures and other special conversion and rounding conversions will have to apply. It is unlikely that many businesses will have these facilities built into their software unless their software was written very recently.

The following warranty is a suggestion only:

> The Supplier warrants that the system will:
>
> (a) Recognise and manage directly all single and multiple currency changes necessitated by the implementation of EMU and the Euro in part or all of the EU, such functionality to be available for use by the customer regardless of whether or not, or when, the UK or any other country joins the EMU Group of Nations; and
>
> (b) Correctly implement all conversion, rounding, triangulation and other technical requirements for all stages of implementation of the Euro as laid down by EU law.

8.1.22 Representations, warranties and indemnification regarding intellectual property rights

User-licensees and distributor-licensees alike hope to enjoy the benefits of their licensed rights peacefully. Neither would enjoy having the exercise of those rights enjoined by a third-party action against the licensor. Nor would they enjoy being named in a damages suit against the licensor for copyright infringement or trade secret misappropriation.

For such reasons, sophisticated licensees require representations and warranties regarding the ownership or right to license the software in question, and indemnification regarding a damages award against them as a result of exercising their licensed rights. Many software licensors provide part, but not all, of these assurances. For example, trade secret rights are sometimes omitted from standard intellectual property representations, warranties and indemnification provisions. While these omissions address a legal topic rather than a business topic, they can give rise to business disruption. Hence they are worthy topics for negotiation by business as well as legal personnel in a customer organisation.

8.1.23 Limitation of liability and remedy

The limitation of liability and remedy provision is an important legal protection in many contracts across many industries. Typically this provision attempts to safeguard the provider of goods and services against certain types of legal liability. Providers typically limit liability by providing only a limited warranty and then excluding all other warranties, in the alternative, no warranty at all may be provided and all warranties may be excluded. An example of provisions that reflect this plan in a US provider's standard software licence agreement is set out below.

The Customer is responsible for selecting equipment, software, and services suitable for the Customer's needs. No prior statement or promise by the Licensor relating to the services or Products provided hereunder shall be deemed an express warranty or part of the basis of this Agreement.

The Software, Documentation and all services provided hereunder are provided 'AS IS' with no warranty whatsoever. The Licensor does not warrant that the functions contained in the Software will meet the Customer's needs, or that the operation of the Software will be uninterrupted or error free, or that defects in the Software will be corrected.

THERE ARE NO WARRANTIES, EXPRESS OR IMPLIED, BY OPERATION OF LAW OR OTHERWISE, OF THE PRODUCTS OR SERVICES FURNISHED HEREUNDER. THE LICENSOR DISCLAIMS ANY IMPLIED WARRANTY OF MERCHANTABILITY OR FITNESS FOR A PARTICULAR PURPOSE. THE ENTIRE RISK AS TO THE QUALITY AND PERFORMANCE OF THE SOFTWARE IS WITH YOU. SHOULD THE SOFTWARE PROVE DEFECTIVE, YOU ASSUME THE ENTIRE COST OF ALL NECESSARY SERVICING, REPAIR, OR CORRECTION.

The Customer assumes responsibility for the supervision, management and control of the Equipment and modifications and revisions thereto including, but not limited to: (1) assuring proper configuration of the Equipment for Software installation,

---

audit controls and operating methods; (2) implementing sufficient procedures and checkpoints to satisfy its requirements for security and accuracy for input as well as restart and recovery in the event of malfunction; (3) accomplishing the productive utilisation of the Equipment in the use of the Software in processing of the Customer's work.

Where the agreement contains a limited warranty or some other provisions that provide remedies addressing various types of problems the provider may attempt to exclude all types of remedies and damages other than out-of-pocket expense reimbursement damages. An example of provisions that reflect this plan in a US provider's standard software licence agreement is set forth below.

— The licensor's entire liability and customer's sole and exclusive remedy for any and all liability or claims in connection with or arising out of this agreement or the existence, non-delivery, furnishing, functioning, or the customer's use of products or services provided under this agreement, for any cause whatsoever, and regardless of the form or nature of the liability or claim, whether in contract or in tort, including, without limitation, claims of negligence or strict liability, is set forth in paragraph 2.

— If the licensor fails, after repeated attempts, to perform any of its obligations or to provide the remedies set out in this agreement, the licensor's liability shall be the customer's actual, direct damages such as would be provable in a court of law, but not to exceed the software licence fee stated herein which the customer has paid for the specific item that caused the damage. Notwithstanding the provisions of any applicable statute, the remedies available to the customer in this agreement are exclusive remedies, and all other remedies, statutory or otherwise, with respect to the matter hereof, are hereby expressly waived by the customer.

— In no event shall the licensor be liable for: (1) any incidental, indirect, special or consequential damages whatsoever, including, but not limited to, damages for business interruption, loss of business information, loss of software use, loss of goodwill or loss of revenue or profit, even if the licensor has been advised, knew, or should have known of the possibility of such damages; or (2) damages caused by the customer's failure to perform its obligations and responsibilities under this agreement; or (3) claims, demands, or actions against the customer by any other party.

In the UK and within the EU as a result of the UK's Unfair Contract Terms Act 1977 and the EC Directive on Unfair Contract Terms,[1] first any ambiguity in a clause which attempts to limit liability with a customer, the end-user, will be interpreted against the person imposing it (the licensor) and, secondly, any attempt to exclude liability for death or personal injury arising out of the negligence of the person imposing such clause (the licensor) will be invalid. Therefore, the clauses which are outlined above might find some lack of favour within the UK and thus an example of a more appropriate attempt to limit liability is set out below:

— The Licensor will indemnify the customer for direct physical injury or death caused solely either by defects in the programs or by the negligence of the Licensor's employees acting within the course of their employment and the scope of their authority.

— The Licensor will indemnify the customer for direct damage to property caused solely either by defects in the programs or by the negligence of its employees acting within the course of their employment and the scope of their authority. The total liability of the Licensor under this sub-clause will be limited to £1,000,000.00 or the contract price for any one event or series of connected events whichever is the greater.

— Except as expressly stated in this clause and elsewhere in this Licence Agreement, any liability of the Licensor for breach of this Agreement will not exceed in the aggregate of damages, costs, fees and expenses capable of being awarded to the customer the contract price paid or due to be paid by the customer under this Agreement.

— Except as expressly stated in this Agreement, the Licensor disclaims all liability to the customer whether in contract tort or otherwise in connection with the Licensor's performance of this Agreement or the customer's use of the programs and in no event will the Licensor be liable to the customer for special, indirect or consequential damages including, but not limited to, loss of profits or arising from loss of data or unfitness for user purposes.

It should be noted that where limitations on liability are imposed in contract terms between a supplier and customer then statutory provisions may override attempts to limit liability but if the customer is, in fact, an intermediary distributor and not 'the man in the street' then the Unfair Contract Terms Act 1977 may not apply since both the parties will be deemed to be in the business of dealing with software products and this can lead to a greater need for contract negotiation.

However, since the case of *St Albans City and District Council v International Computers Ltd*[2] it has become clear that where a customer suffers loss as a result of faulty software and no terms and conditions vary the implied terms of merchantability or fitness for purpose, then any attempt by the supplier to limit its liability for such loss below what is deemed to be a reasonable figure (perhaps such a figure being linked to the suppliers' insurance cover for such losses) will be avoidable or even void as an unfair contract term.

As a consequence customers are more likely now to demand that any limit of liability in favour of the supplier for losses other than indirect should be linked to a reasonable sum of at least £1,000,000 (the usual minimum limit for which insurance cover would be granted under a suitable policy).

Alternative limitation of liability clauses could be the following:

— *100% approach*. Except as provided above in the case of personal injury, death, and damage to tangible property, Supplier's maximum liability to Customer for any cause whatsoever (whether in the form of the additional cost of remedial services or otherwise) will be for direct costs and damages only, and will be limited to the price paid to Supplier for the product or the annual charge for the service that is the subject of Customer's claim, OR

— *125% approach*. Except as provided above in the case of personal injury, death, and damage to tangible property, Supplier's maximum liability to Customer for any cause whatsoever (whether in the form of the additional cost of remedial services or otherwise) will be for direct costs and damages only, and will be limited to a sum equivalent to the price paid to Supplier for the products or services that are the subject of Customer's claim plus damages limited to 25 per cent of the same amount for any additional costs directly, reasonably and necessarily incurred by Customer in obtaining alternative products and/or services, OR

— *Approach reflecting insurance cover*. Except as provided above in the case of personal injury, death, and damage to tangible property, Supplier's maximum liability to Customer for any cause whatsoever (whether in the form of the additional cost of remedial services or otherwise) will be for direct costs and damages only, and will be limited to the greater of: (a) [amount linked to value of insurance cover eg one million pounds]; or (b) a sum equivalent to the price paid to Supplier for the products or services that are the subject of Customer's claim, plus damages limited to 25 per cent of the same amount for any additional costs directly, reasonably and necessarily incurred by Customer in obtaining alternative products and/or services, OR

— *Actual Insurance Recovery approach*. Except as provided above in the case of personal injury, death, and damage to tangible property, Supplier's maximum liability to Customer for any cause whatsoever (whether in the form of the additional cost of remedial services or otherwise) will be for direct costs and damages only, and will be limited to either: (a) where the event is covered by Supplier's insurance policies, the amount which Supplier actually recovers from its insurers under those policies, to a maximum of one million pounds; or (b) in all other cases, a sum equivalent to the price paid to Supplier for the products or services that are the subject of Customer's claim, plus damages limited to twenty-five per cent of the same amount for any additional costs directly, reasonably and necessarily incurred by Customer in obtaining alternative products and/or services, AND

— *Maximum liability*. Except as provided above in the case of personal injury, death, and damage to tangible property, Supplier's maximum liability to Customer for any cause whatsoever (whether in the form of the additional cost of remedial services or otherwise) will be for direct costs and damages only, and will be limited to a sum equivalent to the price paid to Supplier for the products or services that are the subject of Customer's claim plus damages limited to 25 per cent of the same amount for any additional costs directly, reasonably and necessarily incurred by Customer in obtaining alternative products and/or services.

However in the 2001 UK case of *Watford Electronics Ltd v Sanderson CFL Ltd*[3] it was held that provisions in a contract for the supply of computer software that both excluded the supplier liability for indirect loss, as well as limiting the damages recoverable to the amount paid by the customer under the contract, satisfied the reasonable test under the Unfair Contract Terms Act 1977, s 11. On appeal the court decided that the contract had been negotiated between experienced businessmen of equal bargaining power and skill and, as such, the supplier limitation clause was reasonable.

1   93/98 OJ 1993 L290.
2   [1996] 4 All ER 481.
3   [2001] EWCA Civ 317, [2001] 1 All ER (Comm) 696.

8.1.24   Limitation on recoverable damages

A limitation on recoverable damages provision states a maximum compensatory damage award limitation. In cases where a user-licensee wins a judgment of liability against a provider on a tort claim of misrepresentation, this clause will not limit the court's ability to award damages that exceed the contract's limitation. In cases where a user-licensee wins a judgment of liability against a provider on a breach of contract claim, this clause will limit the court's ability to award damages that exceed the contract's limitation absent unusual circumstances, for example, a determination that the contract is invalid, or that the provision is drafted in such a way that it does not apply to the breach in question.

Limitations on recoverable damages are reasonable provisions from a provider's standpoint. Several lawsuits resulting in large damage awards for breaches of contract can quickly drain the corporate treasury of small companies and dent the earnings of mid-sized and large companies. Bankruptcy is sometimes caused by large damage awards. Small companies can seldom afford to set aside large sums as contingent reserves for possible damage awards. Limitations on recoverable damages run to the heart of any corporation, its treasury.

On the other hand, customers can argue that the best way to avoid large compensatory damage awards in breach of contract claims is for the provider to perform as required by the contract. Simply do not breach the contract and you need not worry about large damage awards.

Providers can counter that the question of whether or not a contract is breached can be a matter of interpretation, especially where common law requires reasonable and not perfect performance, as a general rule.

The debate can go on and on, and much time can be wasted. One course of action can be for the customer to explore what insurance may be available to buyers of software systems (for example, loss of business insurance). It may be cheaper to purchase such insurance rather than to attempt high limits of liability from the provider. The essential point for our purposes is that prudent providers will insert such provisions, and sophisticated customers at least sometimes attempt to raise the limitation, or to delete the clause altogether. By inserting this provision in its standard form agreement the provider puts the customer in the position of one who must argue for its removal or change, a disadvantageous position. If the customer drafts a tailor-made agreement for the transaction or requires use of a standard customer form agreement, then the provider is normally in the position of having to argue for the addition of such a provision, which is a non-favoured position.

An example of a provision that limits recoverable damages in a provider's standard software licence agreement is quoted below.

XYZ's liability for actual damages from any cause whatsoever will be limited to the greater of (1) £100,000 or (2) the one-time charge paid for, or any charges which would be due for 12 months' use of, the individual Program that caused the damages or is the subject matter of, or is directly related to, the cause of action. Such charges shall be those in effect when the cause of action arose and shall include any upgrade, initial or process charges paid to XYZ. This limitation will apply, except as otherwise stated in this Section, regardless of the form of action, whether in contract or in tort, including negligence.

Again the clause shown above might well be acceptable within the US but within the UK and the EU would be subject to the same limitations as previously discussed (see SECTION 8.1.22) in that it may be impossible to limit liability where the claim is for damages for personal injury or death resulting from negligence.

8.1.25 Nature and scope of consequential damages exclusion

Software providers like to exclude the possibility of consequential damages arising from a breach of contract claim. Consequential damages can be simply defined as damages that arise from the consequences of a breach of contract on the claimant's business other than any actual, identifiable out-of-pocket expenses or losses that compensatory damage awards reimburse. Consequential damages can be very large monetary awards and cover such items as lost profits or the loss of goodwill.

Sophisticated customers may accept an all encompassing consequential damages exclusion by a provider, or they may argue that the provision must be reciprocal, that is, it must be written so as to benefit both parties equally. Another possible reaction of a sophisticated customer is to argue that a provider should not be able to exclude its exposure to either actual or consequential damages suffered by the customer as a result of suits by third parties based on a claim of intellectual property infringement or misappropriation. The customer's rights to deal with software as allowed in its licence agreement stem from the licensor's ownership or right to license intellectual property rights in the software. If the licensor does not have the ability to grant the licensed rights and the customer is enjoined or must pay damages as a result, the customer's lost profits resulting from the injunction order to stop use of the software, as well as the customer's out-of-pocket damages, should be recoverable from the provider according to this argument. This argument is based on the concept that licensees should not bear losses arising from fundamental defects in the very thing the customers paid for, whether or not they are out-of-pocket losses. While providers may argue that no transaction can be made risk free, the customer has a reasonable point in this context.

An example of a provision that excludes consequential damages in a provider's standard software licence agreement is quoted below.

In no event will XYZ be liable for any damages arising from performance or non-performance of the Program during the Program testing period or for any damages caused by your failure to perform your responsibilities. In addition, XYZ will not be liable for any lost profits, lost savings, incidental damages, lost data or other economic consequential damages, even if XYZ has been advised of the possibility of such damages. Furthermore, XYZ will not be liable for any damages claimed by you based on any third-party claim.

Several cases, including *British Sugar plc v NEI Power Projects Ltd*[1] and *Hotel Services Ltd v Hilton International Hotels*[2], have highlighted the fact that an attempt to exclude all loss apart from direct loss by using catch-all words such as 'indirect loss or other consequential damages' may have the opposite effect. Care should be taken to draft such an exclusion clause so as to include or exclude specific types of anticipated damage. Where it is desired to exclude liability for a loss which flows directly from a breach then it may be better to use a catch-all phrase such as 'all other direct losses'. If it is necessary to keep the use of the word 'consequential', care should be taken when listing specified damages and then adding the words 'or other indirect or consequential losses', as this may be interpreted to allow the courts to include a loss which might otherwise have been excluded.

1 (1997) 87 BLR 42.
2 [2000] BLR 235.

8.1.26 Liquidated damages

A liquidated damages clause is often used in contracts as a means of ensuring that the parties know up-front what the consequences will be of a breach of the agreement and are thus a contractually agreed pre-estimate of damages that would otherwise be awarded by a court of law.

Liquidated damages can be applied to contractual breaches such as delay in the performance of an obligation, failure of timely supply, breach of agreed service levels or breach of time critical delivery.

Liquidated damages are often referred to by the parties as 'penalties' but this is precisely what they should not be! A court will uphold a liquidated damages clause if satisfied that the parties have taken steps to genuinely estimate the anticipated loss following a breach. Whilst courts generally do not interfere in the commercial arrangements between parties to a contract they will refuse to enforce a liquidated damages clause because it is a 'penalty' or an instance of 'usury' if the pre-determined sum is considered to be an unreasonable estimate of the probable loss or it has been used by one party as a means of pressure or oppression on the other.

The leading UK cases on liquidated damages are generally in relation to construction or engineering contracts but whilst the 2005 case of *Alfred McAlpine Capital Projects Ltd v Tilebox Ltd*[1] confirms that a court will be slow to interfere with an arm's-length negotiated liquidated damages clause, the older case of *Dunlop Neumatic Tyre Co. Ltd v New Garage and Motor Co. Ltd*[2] sets down the guidelines as to the distinction between liquidated damages and penalty clauses namely that:

1.   Clause titles are irrelevant and a liquidated damages clause labelled as 'a penalty clause' may still be enforceable as the court will look beyond the clauses title and interpret its substance.

2.   The essence of a liquidated damages clause is that it should be a genuine pre-estimate of damage.

3.   The essence of a penalty clause is that it operates by way of a threat.

4.   It is a matter of construction as to whether or not the clause in question creates liquidated damages or a penalty and the courts will interpret the clause as a result of all the facts surrounding the negotiations at the time the contract was entered into.

In negotiating and drafting the parties should take into account the guidelines above so that the clause is enforceable and thus worth all the time spent on negotiation and in order to do this it is suggested that:

1.   The liquidated damages should be based on genuine pre-estimates of loss.

2.   Where it is difficult to pre-estimate loss then the parties should document the methodology for the mechanism they use in the clause for estimating damages or service credits.

3.   Wherever possible the liquidated damages should be expressed in precise terms based on documented examples of failure or breach and not on generic formulas.

4. If the parties intend liquidated damages to be the exhaustive remedy then this should be clearly stated as otherwise the aggrieved party can seek unliquidated damages whether or not there is a liquidated damages clause in the contract.

5. Liquidated damages may well be more enforceable if the amount of the damages is calculated on a scale linked to the seriousness of the breach in question.

In addition to the above points it should be remembered that a liquidated damages clause needs to be negotiated and drafted in parallel with all complementary clauses relating to warranties, limitations of liability, intellectual property infringement, indemnities and insurance.

1 [2005] EWHC 281 (TCC), [2005] BLR 271.
2 [1915] AC 79.

8.1.27 Most favoured customer

In the US, and now in the UK, some institutions, government agencies and authorities are seeking to include a 'most favoured customer' clause. This is an undertaking by the provider that it has offered no better terms to any other third party at the time of the contract with the customer, and/or that if it offers better terms to any other third party in the future it will offer the same terms to the customer.

Most providers seek to avoid such a clause or at least agree that it only applies to charges such as training, call-out fees and incidentals. Examples of such clauses are as follows:

The Licensor represents that the charges, fees, costs, other payments and discounts set forth in this Agreement are no less favourable to the Licensee than the most favourable terms offered or received to or by any other customer of the Licensor as of the time this Agreement is signed by the Licensee.

If, during the term, the Licensor signs any contract for similar software that contains payment terms, discounts, charges, fees or costs that are more favourable to another customer, then these more favourable provisions will immediately be extended to the Licensee.

8.1.28 Change control

Unless the delivery is of a simple software product the chances are that in the course of commissioning and acceptance and, indeed, if not before that date, the parties will make changes to their deliverables and/or requirements.

It is important to consider putting into the contract a clause which sets out the formula by which such changes can be mutually agreed. An example of such a change control clause is as follows:

1. Any change or variation to the scope of work or nature of services or products to be supplied pursuant to this Agreement will be referred to as a 'Change' and will be subject to a Change Notice in accordance with the following Change Procedure. Both parties agree that it is in their best interests to implement Changes as quickly and as efficiently as possible.

2. If either party considers that a Change is necessary, or that a Change is in effect being forced upon it by the other party, it shall serve a Change Notice on the other party. A Change Notice can be in any form but must provide reasonable details of the Change and, if possible, the party's estimate of the effect (if any) of the Change on the contract price or rates, its impact on delivery dates or supply times, and any other effect which it is considered the Change will have.

3. The other party will respond in writing by return if possible, but in any event within seven calendar days of receipt of the Change Notice, indicating whether or not it accepts the proposed Change, and giving its own estimate of the effects which the Change will have, including any costs expected to arise in connection with evaluating the proposed Change.

4. Each party shall respond to all further correspondence by return if possible, but in any event within seven days of receipt of previous correspondence, until agreement on the proposed Change is reached and recorded in an Agreed Contract Amendment signed by both parties.

5. Neither party shall be under any obligation to accept any Change that is not subject to an Agreed Contract Amendment [which just states the position under the law of contract].

8.1.29 Availability of licensee's computer system to licensor for maintenance, training, and development purposes

A standard clause in the provider's licence agreement forms requires the licensee to make its host computer available to the provider from time to time for purposes of training the licensee's employees in the licensed program's operation, in order to perform software development work or software diagnostic tests, or so that the provider may repair or enhance the software. The timing of such availability is usually vague in a provider's standard form agreement and should be clarified. Customers can be disrupted, and providers can be taken advantage of, if a reasonable plan cannot be agreed upon and captured in contract language.

8.1.30 Recovery of lawyers' fees by prevailing party

In the UK the prevailing party in civil litigation can recover its lawyers' fees, but in the US and many European courts this is not the case. Hence, many standard form agreements contain provisions allowing the recovery of reasonable lawyers' fees. Relatively few laws allow their recovery so the concept seems reasonable provided the provision is sufficiently qualified. For example, it might be made reciprocal or come into play only after the last appeal of the other party's loss is either denied or lost.

8.1.31   Statute of limitations

A statute of limitations is a rule that limits the time within which a lawsuit may be filed. The length of time varies with the type of legal claim. Parties to a contract may agree to shorten the period allowed by law in many commercial contexts. Thus it is common to see a one- or two-year window for litigation specified in standard form licence agreements. Generally such limitations will be enforced against breach of contract claims filed after the specified period has elapsed.

One of the difficulties some customers are facing with the Year 2000 compliance issue is that if software was installed and accepted more than six years ago, then if the claim is under UK law that the software is not 'fit for purpose' and is unable to function beyond 1999, then such claim may fail since the period within which claims should be brought is six years.

8.1.32   Risk of loss or damage during transit

It is not within the scope of this book to explain terms like 'CIF' and 'FOB'. The point here is that the risk of loss or damage during transit may become important in a software licence agreement. Remember that where reference to terms such as 'CIF' and 'FOB' are used it is worthwhile linking such terms to their specific definition within *ICC INCOTERMS*.[1] For example, where software is shipped to a foreign distributor, the risk of loss or damage to inventory shipped from a UK publisher is as important as it is in agreements for other exported products of the same value.

The ICC published *INCOTERMS 2000* in September 1999 which contains provisions for electronic delivery and appropriate amendment of standard INCOTERMS to take account of e-commerce.

1   1990 edn.

8.1.33   Indemnities

In a number of contracts, particularly US style agreements, warranty clauses are phrased as indemnities. There is often confusion as to the role of an indemnity clause as opposed to a warranty clause.

Broadly speaking, whereas a warranty clause identifies those breaches in respect of which the defaulting party is liable to pay damages or make compensation, an indemnity clause, more often than not, requires the indemnifying party to compensate the aggrieved party for losses that it has directly suffered as a result of the indemnifying party's breach, usually where the loss has been generated through a third party claim.

Whilst warranties are usually drafted in respect of specific breaches and as such the contract provides for limitations of liability, in the case of indemnity clauses they are often drafted in relation to unspecified breaches and with neither a limit on the amount claimable nor any involvement by the indemnifying party in the third party claims, settlement of such claims or resulting litigation.

Under English law, the courts often take a wider view of what will be recoverable under an indemnity claim as opposed to a warranty claim and in particular will not restrict the loss to direct damages. The almost 'blank cheque' nature of the liability of the indemnifying party results from the fact that the beneficiary of the indemnity clause is often under no obligation to mitigate its loss.

Although indemnity clauses are usually in relation to losses arising through breach of IPR or trade secrets there is no reason why indemnity clauses cannot also be used for other areas where the beneficiary suffers loss including loss or misappropriation of information and personal data, wilful or malicious conduct or fraud, damage to tangible property and breach of relevant laws and regulations.

Given all of the above comments, the negotiating and drafting of an indemnity clause requires considerable attention. The areas in respect of which an indemnity claim can be made need to be carefully considered by both parties and particular attention needs to be given to the mechanism by which the indemnifying party can take control of any claim in respect of which the beneficiary is entitled to subsequently claim.

Since an indemnity clause is another contractual mechanism whereby the indemnifying party will have to pay out damages or perhaps be forced by specific injunction to perform services over and above those which it anticipated, there is no reason why there should not be a limitation on the damages under an indemnity clause just as there are limitations of liability under warranty clauses.

On some occasions indemnity clauses are expressed to be the sole and exclusive remedy and where this is the case the beneficiary needs to take care that by accepting such a clause it has not denied itself the opportunity to make other claims and has not denied itself the opportunity of terminating the contract for breach. An example of an indemnity clause is as follows.

Owner warrants that it has the right to enter into and perform its obligations under this Agreement and will indemnify CUSTOMER against any loss or expense (including reasonable lawyer's fees and expenses) as a result of any claim that the normal use or possession of PRODUCT and associated documentation infringes the intellectual property rights of any third party, provided that the claim does not arise as a result of the use of PRODUCT and associated documentation otherwise than in accordance with the terms of this Agreement or the PRODUCT Licence Agreement and subject to the following conditions:

CUSTOMER must promptly notify Owner in writing of any allegation of infringement.

CUSTOMER must make no admission without Owner's consent.

CUSTOMER must, at Owner's request, allow Owner to conduct and/or settle all negotiations and litigation and must give Owner all reasonable assistance at Owner's expense. The cost incurred or recovered in such negotiations and litigation will be for Owner's account.

Owner will have the right to change all or part of PRODUCT and associated documentation or to grant or obtain licences for the use of all or part of the PRODUCT in order to avoid litigation.

Failure of CUSTOMER to notify Owner under this clause shall not relieve Owner of its obligations hereunder except to the extent that Owner is prejudiced by such failure. CUSTOMER may participate in its own defence at its own expense.

8.1.34 *Force majeure*

A *force majeure* provision is intended to recognise that Acts of God may disrupt performance, and to allow a grace period for performance where an Act of God causes a delay, for example, a flood. In many industries this concept is stretched to include man-made events beyond the reasonable control of a party that delays performance, for example, labour disputes. Some software providers further stretch the concept to cover events within their control, for example, an exhausted inventory of software.

Another aspect of *force majeure* provisions is how long they shield non-performance from becoming a breach of contract. A fixed period may be specified, for example, up to six months, or the period may be indefinite.

An example of a *force majeure* provision in a provider's standard software licence agreement is quoted below.

The Licensor is not responsible for failure to fulfil its obligations hereunder due to labour disputes, fire, flood, government rules or regulations, temporary shortages of parts or Software, unavailability of Software, or any other similar or dissimilar causes beyond the Licensor's reasonable control that directly or indirectly delay or prevent the Licensor's timely performance hereunder. Dates or times by which the Licensor is required to render performance under this Agreement shall be postponed automatically to the extent that the Licensor is delayed or prevented from meeting them by such causes.

The customer may wish to specifically exclude certain events from the *force majeure* clause, such as default of the provider's sub-contractor, or lock-outs.

8.1.35　Assignment of contract rights and obligations

Software providers like to have the flexibility of transferring their rights and obligations to purchasers of their companies and other parties without the customer's consent. Some standard provider agreements specify this right and some are silent, reasoning that silence on this topic will be interpreted by a court as allowing assignment.

Conversely, most software providers do not want the customer assigning software licence agreements without express permission. Providers need to retain control over their software trade secrets in order to preserve their status as trade secrets. Also, the assignee may be a poor credit risk or an unsavoury character. Thus, many standard software provider agreements prohibit assignment of the licence agreement as a whole and all software licences except with the express, written permission of the provider except where the assignee is an associate of the licensee or the assignment is a result of reconstruction or amalgamation.

Some customers may want to negotiate a specific right to assign licences to companies within their corporate group or to assign licences to the purchaser of the entire business of the licensee.

8.1.36　Notice provisions

A notice provision addresses all of the notices that are required by the agreement. Some notice provisions specify the names of individuals in the parties' organisations, their addresses and the allowable types of mail or couriers. Others refer to the address of the parties in the introductory paragraph of the agreement. Still others are silent as to addresses or individual addressees. Another factor sometimes addressed in these provisions is the effective date of the notice, for example, the date of depositing a letter in the mail, the date of its receipt, etc. Customers need to ensure that an acceptable and practical arrangement is stated in these provisions, or, if not, to negotiate changes. For large customer companies it may be desirable to have notices addressed to both: (a) the project manager; and (b) the company secretary in order to deal with staff turnover. Job titles are safer than individual names.

Most agreements prohibit modifications except those agreed upon in writing and signed by the parties. Separately, it is normal for the parties to agree that they may change their addresses for notices upon a verbal or written notice which the other party will not sign. Few agreements reconcile these differences and expressly carve an exception in the first clause which recognises that notice address changes may be unilateral.

8.1.37　Entire agreement and variations

Following discussions and negotiations where the terms are reduced to written form it is important that the parties to the final contract know what has been finally agreed and where the parameters of that contract exist.

During negotiations many representations and statements may have been made by the parties, either verbally or in writing, and the party receiving such representations may or may not have placed reliance upon them in ultimately agreeing to deal.

For this reason the final agreement should include a clause which confirms that the agreement being signed is the complete agreement and that any prior representations are not relied upon.

An example of such a clause is set out below.

This Agreement supersedes all prior agreement arrangements and undertakings between the parties and constitutes the entire agreement between the parties relating to the subject matter hereof. No addition to, or modification of, any provision of this Agreement should be binding upon the parties unless made by a written instrument signed by a duly authorised representative of each of the parties.

Beware of automatically using this form of clause without considering whether prior agreements should be overridden. In a case in which the writer was involved a substantial contract ended up in arbitration and one of the mistakes that had been made by the licensor was that in the course of negotiations the licensor's standard agreement had been continually amended and that when the final agreement was signed two years after the commencement of negotiations it was, in fact, the eighth version of the licensor's original standard contract. Every contract that had been entered into contained an entire agreement clause thereby nullifying each prior agreement in succession so that when the final agreement was signed (being substantially different from the original and biased more in favour of the licensee than prior versions), the entire agreement did away with certain terms which the licensor subsequently claimed always had been intended to have been included by the parties. The licensee was entirely happy with the final version since it matched precisely the licensee's needs and it was the licensor (whose negotiating team had changed on several occasions during the two-year period) that found themselves receiving substantially less royalties than they were likely to receive during the term of the contract as against those which they had anticipated receiving under the terms of the original standard form. The lesson to be learnt from this is that you should be sure that where an entire agreement clause is used, if there are terms from earlier agreements that you do not wish to nullify these should be brought in to the final agreement or you do not use an entire agreement at all.

The same problems can occur where, in a software licence deal, there are collateral agreements which are fundamental to the main software licence agreement, such as maintenance and support agreements and escrow agreements, because, although each are separate agreements, they all interrelate and may all have been entered into at different times and dates and consequently entire agreement clauses must be carefully thought through.

Following the decision in *Watford Electronics Ltd v Sanderson CFL Ltd*[1] an entire agreement clause cannot be used as an exclusion clause.

The Sanderson standard terms and conditions contained an entire agreement clause, that stated 'no statement or representation made by either party have been relied upon by the other in agreeing to enter into the contracts', and a limitation clause, that stated 'neither the company nor the customer shall be liable to the other for any claims for indirect or consequential losses whether arising from negligence or otherwise'. The bespoke system supplied did not perform satisfactorily and Watford sued for damages.

On appeal the Court of Appeal held that the limitation clause could be split into two – the first part covering 'indirect or consequential losses' and the second part covering the cap on liability. Each of these could be read and applied separately and were reasonable in the circumstances.

The effect of the entire agreement clause was to acknowledge non-reliance of representations made before the contract. The court stated that there were two good reasons to allow these clauses in a commercial contract: (1) that the parties, who were of equal bargaining power, were entitled to some commercial certainty; and (2) that it was reasonable to assume that the price paid reflected the commercial risks taken by both parties.

The acknowledgement of non-reliance did not purport to prevent a party from proving a representation was made but did prevent them from relying on it. The court stated that the fact that the acknowledgement did not achieve its purpose did not make it an exclusion clause.

Therefore the first part of the limitation clause (the limit of losses) has to be looked at in connection with the entire agreement clause, on the basis that the whole agreement was to be incorporated into the document which they signed and that no one should rely on anything else. There was no reason why the parties should have intended to include the liability of any negligent pre-contract misrepresentation.

A case of 28 May 2002 between BCT Software Solutions Ltd, a software support and maintenance provider and Arnold Laver & Co Ltd, a timber company licensing the said software, highlighted some important issues and potential hazards of incorporating a document into a contract by reference. The dispute arose after Arnold Laver terminated their contract for BCT's ongoing support and maintenance of their Great Plains financial software package. BCT claimed that by terminating the support and maintenance agreement, Arnold Laver had also terminated their right to license the software from BCT, as stated in the standard Terms and Conditions referred to in the agreement. Arnold Laver argued that during negotiation of the agreements and subsequent provision and billing of the two services, it was understood that the software licence and the support and maintenance were separate services and as such were not dependent on each other.

The case relied on the extent to which both parties had incorporated the BCT's standard terms and conditions. These terms and conditions had been significantly revised by BCT after the commencement of the negotiations between BCT and Arnold Laver. The old terms and conditions had stated that purchase of the software licence would comprise a one-off payment for unlimited use, with the support and maintenance services being charged separately on an annual basis according to the number of software licences supplied. The new terms and conditions indicated that the licence fee would cover both the software licence and the support and maintenance services, but charged out monthly.

This alteration created an entirely different regime, particularly regarding the way in which the use of the software was licensed. Under the old terms and conditions, the client would pay an initial sum for the licence of the software and could continue to use it regardless of whether they required the support and maintenance services. Under the new terms and conditions, the software licence only lasted as long as the customer continued to pay for the support and maintenance services. Importantly, throughout this negotiation period, the BCT salesman involved in setting up the Arnold Laver agreements claimed to be unaware of the changes in the terms and conditions and continued to refer to, and negotiate with, the old conditions in mind. This, despite being unintentionally misleading, led to Arnold Laver signing a final contract that referred to the new terms and conditions, whilst believing that the old terms and conditions still applied. Arnold Laver claimed never to have been shown a copy of the new terms and conditions and not to have had them brought to their attention.

An accounting irregularity later caused BCT to go into receivership. BCT's intellectual property and book debts were purchased by Electronic Data Processing (EDP) who had previously been in acquisition talks with BCT. As a result of the receivership, Arnold Laver terminated its agreement with BCT, no longer requiring support and maintenance services and believing that it had the licence to continue running the Great Plains software package. EDP then demanded that under the standard terms and conditions of the agreement between BCT and Arnold Laver, Arnold Laver must terminate using the software which was to be re-claimed by EDP.

The law states clearly that when one party signs a document to accept an offer made in the document, in this case the terms of the agreement, it is taken that he accepts those terms regardless of whether he reads them or not. This also applies to terms incorporated by reference. Previous rulings however have highlighted the importance of the court reviewing all of the evidence to see what bargain was struck between two parties. It has also been noted that, in the case of new terms conflicting with those previously agreed – the original terms must prevail. After reviewing the case, Deputy High Court Judge Kevin Garnett QC concluded that only one payment for the software licence was required from Arnold Laver and that their continued use of the software was not conditional on payment of BCT's support and maintenance service.

This case highlights the importance of the contract negotiators being fully aware of the terms of any documents that are being incorporated into an agreement by reference. Always read the small print when you sign an agreement, whether it be a new contract or a renewal of a long-standing agreement and review all documents referred to in the agreement.

It is essential that staff are fully briefed of any changes in the working environment that may affect them. This is particularly important in a sales environment where they will have to be aware of terminology alterations and changes in negotiation tactics. Do not rely on sending staff updated documents to read or for them to install on their computers as they may not be actioned, as in the BCT case.

1   [2001] EWCA Civ 317, [2007] 1 All ER (Comm) 696.

8.1.38   Severability

As software providers know and customers are also aware, statutes, regulations and court decisions change from time to time during the life of a contract. Terms which may have been included in a software agreement may be valid at the time that the agreement is entered into but may at some point in the future become void, illegal, invalid or unenforceable and the effect of the invalidity of those terms is that the whole agreement fails.

Consequently, it is wise to include a severability clause in a contract to ensure that where only a portion of the contract becomes unenforceable or invalid that only that portion is extracted from the contract and the remainder of the contract continues in force as was the intention of the parties.

An example of a severability clause is shown below.

If any of the provisions of this Agreement are judged to be illegal, invalid or unenforceable then the continuation in full force and effect of the remainder of this Agreement will not be prejudiced unless the substantive purpose of this Agreement is then frustrated in which case either party may terminate this Agreement forthwith by notice in writing to the other party.

One of the most crucial areas where this clause can be effected is where the parties unwittingly use wording in respect of pricing policy, discounts, exclusive territories, intellectual property rights and activities which in some way breach the competition laws of the parties' jurisdictions. The writer is aware of situations in Europe where parties have entered into software licences that in some way conflict with the competition rules of the Treaty of Rome and if at some point in the future the validity of the contract were called into question by the European Commission DG IV then a severability clause might prove useful in terms of enabling the majority of the software licence to remain in force.

8.1.39 Confidentiality

Notwithstanding that a confidentiality agreement or non-disclosure agreement may have already been entered into between the parties prior to the negotiation and drafting of the software contact itself, it is important to provide a confidentiality clause in order that the parties clearly understand what business secrets should be dealt with.

Although confidentiality clauses are regarded as 'standard' they do require more attention than is often given.

A typical confidentiality clause normally stipulates that information which the parties state or mark as confidential and pass to each other shall be treated as confidential except where the receiving party can show that the confidential information was already in the public domain or had been acquired by it from a third party or is regarded by the receiving party for one reason or another as not being confidential. It is, however, better to describe in some detail precisely what type of information should be marked or treated as confidential. A party receiving confidential information might well find that its ability to carry on research in a particular field is hampered by the fact that it has signed an agreement containing a confidentiality clause under which it has received from the supplier information which is similar to information which it had already developed itself, but which it cannot now use. One way of solving this is to split confidential information between that which is commercial and in respect of which the restrictions are all embracing and confidential information which is merely technical, where the restrictions may be slightly more relaxed.

8.1.40 Remote access

In order for customers to comply with good IT security practices it may be prudent to consider what risk may be associated with the fact that many suppliers are given modem or other remote access to the customer's networks for the purposes of error correction and 'patching'.

Many software suppliers as part of their service level agreements, request and, indeed, almost automatically implement, modem links so that minor problems can be corrected without the supplier having physically to attend the customer's premises.

One of the risks here is that such remote access implementations mean that the security of the customer's network is potentially breached.

As a consequence the following clause is suggested.

If the Supplier[1] has remote dial-up or modem access to any part of the User's Equipment in the course of performing its obligations under this Licence the following provisions of this Clause [...][2] shall apply additionally. The Supplier:

1. will (a) only use a remote access method approved by the User (such approval not to be unreasonably withheld or delayed), (b) provide the User with the name of each individual who will have remote access to the User's Equipment and the phone number at which the individual may be reached during dial-in, (c) ensure that any computer used by its personnel to remotely access the User's Equipment will not simultaneously access the internet or any other third-party network while logged on to the User's Equipment;

2. further warrants and agrees that its personnel will not remotely access the User's Equipment from a networked computer unless the network is protected from all third-party networks by a firewall that is maintained by a 7 x 24 administrative staff. Said firewall must be certified by the International Computer Security Association (ICSA) (or an equivalent certification as determined by the User) if the connection to the User's network is an ongoing connection such as frame relay or TI line;

3. will restrict remote access by the Supplier to only the User's test and/or training systems and nothing in this Clause shall entitle the Supplier to have access to the User's live production copy of the Scftware unless the parties have expressly agreed in writing that such access is to take place and the User has given written confirmation of the date on which such access was implemented. The Supplier shall report in writing when such access takes places detailing all activities and actions taken during such access;

4. will comply at all times with the Data Protection Act 1998 in relation to any processing of personal data as a data processor on behalf of the User and will indemnify the User for any liability that the User incurs as a result of a breach of this warranty.

---

1   Change terms like 'supplier' or 'user' to reflect the actual terms used in the contract, for example, 'licensor' or 'licensee'.
2   Insert correct clause number as appropriate to the contract in question.

8.1.41   Data protection

The Data Protection Act 1998 and the EC Directive on Data Protection[1] both impose a requirement upon the controller of personal data to comply with certain data protection principles. Amongst those principles are the obligations for a data controller to protect the integrity of personal data both in its processing and in its transfer.

Where a company outsources its technology or utilises third parties to support its business offsite (in the case of disaster recovery or website hosting) it is necessary for the data controller to impose risk controls on those third parties.

Where a consultant, or an integration company or an Internet Service Provider or a web development company, might have access to the systems and thereby the personal data in the control of a customer, the customer might wish to include the following clause in its contracts:

> The Supplier warrants that it is compliant with the Data Protection Act 1998 and will indemnify the Customer from and against all costs, claims, liabilities and demands arising out of any breach by the supplier of its obligations to keep data secure and to adhere to the Eight Data Protection Principles[1] of the Data Protection Act 1998.

Other examples of processors representations and warranties are as follows.

> Representation
>
> The Supplier and its subsidiaries have, in all material respects, processed the data in accordance with all applicable laws and regulations. Without limiting the foregoing, the data have been collected and further processed, in all material respects, in accordance with all notice and consent requirements of such laws and regulations and have been processed only for the purposes for which such data were collected or to which the data subject subsequently consented. The terms 'processing', 'process', and 'processed' shall mean any operation or set of operations which is performed upon data, whether or not by automatic means, such as collection, recording, organisation, storage, adaptation or alteration, retrieval, consultation, use, disclosure by transmission, dissemination or otherwise making available, alignment or combination, blocking, erasure or destruction.
>
> Warranty
>
> The Controller warrants that it has obtained all necessary consents from individuals whose personal data Controller supplies to the Processor, and the Controller and the Processor warrant to each other that they are respectively compliant with the Data Protection Act 1998.

If the recipient of the data is not a company within the EU, then the supplying customer will need to be even more cautious about the supplier having access to personal data because of the obligations laid down in the Eighth Data Protection Principle. The Eighth Data Protection Principle places severe restrictions upon the transfer of personal data outside the EEA[2] to a recipient in a jurisdiction which is deemed not to have the same levels of privacy protection as within the EEA. Examples of data export and data processing agreements are provided as Precedents to this book.

1 See Data Protection Act 1998, Sch 1, Pt I.
2 Ie the member states of the EU plus Norway, Iceland and Liechtenstein.

8.1.42 Governing law and jurisdiction

Because of the increase in international trade, a supplier is likely to sell throughout the world and it therefore becomes important for the agreement to indicate what law applies to the interpretation of the contract and what legal jurisdiction will apply to the settlement of disputes.

Where the parties are based in the UK there will be an assumption that English law will apply and, in the absence of any agreement to the contrary, this is likely to be the case since the contract will have been entered into in the UK and UK law is the law most applicable. Where, however, one party only is based in the UK and the other party is in another jurisdiction then the choice of law becomes a point for negotiation.

The seller will naturally wish to use the law which he understands and which is most applicable to the location of his business, but the customer will have the same requirements.

Within the US there is quite a variation between certain states as to applicable laws. The state law in California is substantially different from that in Louisiana, but, then, in the UK there are differences between English and Scots law.

US companies generally insist upon the law of their state applying to the contract and for a particular county to be the jurisdiction for litigation. When a UK customer is faced with this imposition, on occasions, he may give way, but this can be unwise without first understanding the precise implications of the US state law to future disputes.

If there is a deadlock then, on occasions, the parties may choose neutral ground and opt for a third-party law and jurisdiction.

In an agreement entered into between a US licensor and a Turkish licensee the language of the contract was English, the applicable law was the Swiss Code of Obligation but the jurisdiction was Zurich Canton, Switzerland. This was a balance between the needs of the two parties in that the Americans were happy with English language and Swiss law because many aspects of Swiss commercial law are similar to US law and, from the Turkish point of view, English language was acceptable and since Turkish law is based on German law and the Swiss Code of Obligation, in turn, is similar to German law, there were substantial comparisons.

Several institutions now operate arbitration facilities within the UK and there are, of course, international arbitration bodies, such as the International Chamber of Commerce and the American Arbitration Association, who have substantial experience in the field of dispute settlement.

In choosing the method of arbitration and the body to act as arbitrators it is necessary to have some understanding of the particular rules and requirements of each method. For example, arbitration provided by an expert appointed through the British Computer Society may be a relatively informal procedure, whereas arbitration under the UK Arbitration Acts which have specific procedures may be slightly more complex and, at the other end of the scale, arbitration through the International Chamber of Commerce Court of Arbitration or under UNCITRAL Rules may be extremely expensive although highly appropriate in the more substantial deals.

Apart from litigation and arbitration many companies are now insisting that all disputes are referred to Alternative Dispute Resolution (ADR) before the parties get to court. ADR is a voluntary mediation service which has gained considerable popularity in Canada and the US, where the ADR procedure and mediator's decision is often agreed upon to be binding on the parties.

In the software industry, as well as many other sectors, ADR offers an attractive method of resolving disputes because the parties want a quick, cost-effective and conciliatory procedure which ADR can provide, more so than litigation or arbitration proceedings. In the UK one of the leading ADR service providers, the Centre for Effective Dispute Resolution (CEDR) suggests that ADR has several advantages, of which the following are examples:

— *Speed.* ADR proceedings can be set up as quickly as the parties require and the actual 'hearing' may only take a day or two.

— *Confidentiality.* Unwanted publicity is avoided as proceedings are confidential and held in private.

— *Cost.* The costs and expenses usually associated with litigation or arbitration are substantially reduced by use of ADR.

— *Control.* As ADR is voluntary and the parties agree upon the process, they have more control than in other dispute procedures.

— *Business relations.* ADR is not intended to be adversarial. ADR is intended to assist the parties to reach a negotiated compromise which helps to preserve relationships.

The Arbitration Act 1996 has introduced power for a court to 'stay' proceedings until matters have first gone to ADR or arbitration, if that is what the parties had contractually agreed. In other words, if the contracts contain an ADR clause then if only one party proceeds straight to litigation in court, the court has the right to refer the dispute to ADR before hearing the case further.

An example of an escalating ADR clause is as follows:

The following procedures will be adhered to in all disputes arising under this Agreement:

1. Each party recognises that the other party's business relies upon the protection of its intellectual property rights and other proprietary information and trade secrets (IPR) and that, in the event of a breach or threatened breach of IPR, the other party will be caused irreparable damage and such other party will therefore be entitled to injunctive or other equitable relief in order to prevent a breach or threatened breach of IPR.

2. With respect to all other disputes which are not IPR-related pursuant to (1) and its special rules the following procedures in (2) to (6) shall apply. Where there is a dispute, the aggrieved party shall notify the other party in writing of the nature of the dispute with as much detail as possible about the deficient performance of the other party. A representative from senior management ('representatives') of each of the parties shall meet in person or communicate by telephone within five business days of the date of the

---

written notification in order to reach an agreement about the nature of the deficiency and the corrective action to be taken by the respective parties. The representatives shall produce a report about the nature of the dispute in detail to their respective boards and, if no agreement is reached on corrective action, the chief executives of each party shall meet, in person or by telephone, to facilitate an agreement within five business days of a written notice by one to the other. If the dispute cannot be resolved at board level within a further five business days, or if the agreed upon completion dates in any written plan of corrective action are exceeded, either party may seek its legal remedies as provided below.

3. If the parties cannot resolve a dispute in accordance with the procedure in (2) above, then they shall, with the assistance of the Centre for Effective Dispute Resolution in London, seek to resolve the dispute or difference amicably by using an Alternative Dispute Resolution (ADR) procedure acceptable to both parties before pursuing any other remedies available to them.

4. If either party fails or refuses to agree to or participate in the ADR procedure or, if in any event dispute or difference is not resolved to the satisfaction of both parties within 90 days after it has arisen, the matter shall be sealed in accordance with the procedure below.

5. The parties shall irrevocably submit to the exclusive jurisdiction of the English Courts for the purposes of hearing and determining any dispute arising out of this Agreement, if the parties cannot resolve such dispute by the procedure set out above.

6. This Agreement and all matters arising from it and any dispute resolutions referred to above shall be governed by and construed in accordance with English law, notwithstanding the conflict of law provisions and other mandatory legal provisions.

8.1.43 Third party rights

Before the Contracts (Rights of Third Parties) Act 1999 (the Act) it was the case that a person who was not a party to a contract (a third party) could not enforce any right under the contract. Similarly, a contract could not impose any obligations or liabilities on a third party.

However the Act attempts to draw a balance between the freedom of the parties to vary a contract and the interests of the third party. The Act means that a contractual clause benefiting a third party (eg the promisee's subsidiary company or sub-contractor or employee) will be straightforwardly enforceable by that third party if:

—   the contract expressly provides that he may; or

—   where a term in the contract purports to confer a benefit on him (unless on a proper construction of the contract it appears that the parties did not intend the term to be enforceable by the third party).

It is therefore prudent to include a clause to the effect of excluding the provisions of the Act. By doing so it ensures that any rights of third parties are not deemed to be enforceable by them. This is particularly the case where the parties are companies and may have subsidiaries or conversely parent companies.

An example of such a clause might be:

> The parties recognise that this Agreement is intended to benefit and shall so benefit (insert name of third party) for the purposes of the Contracts (Rights of Third Parties) Act 1999 and, subject to that, the parties confirm their intent not to confer any rights on any other third parties by virtue of this Agreement.

8.1.44   Rights of audit

It is increasingly common for technology contracts to include audit rights to protect both the supplier and the customer.

Suppliers may need to audit that customers are complying in all respects with the licence terms in respect of numbers of copies of software, notices displayed on back-up copies, access rights to network usage and so on. Customers will require an audit of the supplier in respect of hosted services, for example, where the customer needs to ensure the service provider is complying with data security regulations.

Audit rights are not necessary for every software licence or data transfer agreement and in many cases audit clauses can require considerable negotiation. From a point of inconvenience as well as the practical issue of confidentiality some suppliers will resist customer audits or insist that independent third parties carry out the audit under strict terms of confidentiality.

Audit rights can apply in a number of situations including:

— ensuring compliance with contractual requirements;

— ensuring that services are being supplied by the agreed level of personnel;

— checking the technical and organisational measures for security in place;

— ensuring that business continuity and disaster recovery measures are being met;

— establishing compliance with the parties' respective obligations under relevant legislation including data protection, financial services for authority requirements and health and safety;

— checking that specific issues in respect of the licence usage of software are complied with;

— establishing that agreed insurance coverage is in place.

Where audit rights are required there will, as has already been indicated, be a need to manage such rights including:

— limiting the frequency of audits within a particular period;

— requiring advance notice for an audit;

— implementing confidentiality in non-disclosure procedures;

— limiting the scope of an audit;

— requiring the use of independent third parties;

— ensuring audits do not disrupt business;

— ensuring auditors comply with onsite legal and regulatory requirements;

— agreeing who pays the cost of audit.

A recent High Court decision provides useful guidance on what information or materials are likely to be disclosable under an audit right clause and what may be reasonably withheld. In the case of *Transport for Greater Manchester v Thales Transport & Security Ltd*, the court granted specific performance in respect of the majority of the documents that the TGM had requested Thales to provide under a clause which committed TGM to request documents 'relating to ... the carrying out of any of the supplier obligations' or in order to 'audit' any of that information.

Although the case related to the construction industry it is valuable as it addresses what might reasonably be disclosable under an audit clause and in this instance indicated that the term 'audit' described a process of checking and verifying and was not limited to financial audit. As a consequence the following documents were found to be within the scope of the rights under the audit clause – namely board meeting minutes, reports produced by external advisors, internal reviews of the contract and issues arising from it, sensitive commercial information and documents that review the obligations sometime after problems had occurred.

Specific performance was refused in respect of certain documents where the categories of documents were too imprecise or the documents were covered by legal privilege or where the documents were being used as a 'fishing expedition'.

This case highlights that when drafting or negotiating an audits right clause care needs to be taken on too wide a clause for the recipient or too generic a clause from the party relying upon it. The more that legal privilege can be applied to documents the less disclosure there will be and overall as normal, precision needs to be taken in the use of language.

9 Necessary licence provisions

9.1 KEY LICENCE PROVISIONS FROM THE PROVIDER'S VIEWPOINT

9.1.1 Introduction

Vendors and licensors in English-speaking countries are somewhat more consistent and predictable than their customers in terms of their feelings toward contract clauses. This is not to say that all vendors and licensors recognise the same contract terms as 'absolutely necessary', or even that all or nearly all recognise the importance of contracts. Also, some key provisions in some UK and US contracts might be illegal and unenforceable in other countries. The point here is that, when compared with customers as a whole, most software providers who have survived or will survive their first decade in the industry are attuned to the importance of contracts and three fundamentally necessary categories of contract provisions. These categories are discussed below and examples of key terms from the licensor's viewpoint are included in the discussion.

9.1.2 What will I provide, when, and for how long?

Answers to this question are key terms that should always be found in a contract for a major software transaction. A lack of clarity or full information on this topic simply sets the stage for confusion, unhappy customers, disputes and possible litigation. All goods and services provided should be identified to some reasonable level of detail, and specified in the quantity or for the duration or project agreed upon.

There should be no difficulty in identifying off-the-shelf software or other products. Smart custom-software developers-licensors also recognise the importance of detailed specifications for their projects. Most major projects are carried out on a fixed price or 'not to exceed' basis rather than on an unlimited time and expenses basis. In this context specifications are a two-edged sword, but also a two-sided benefit. They state requirements which the developer-licensor must satisfy, define products which the customer desires and expects and state the standard by which a failure or possible breach of contract may be measured. In addition, specifications define the limits of responsibility, or the maximum obligation, beyond which the developer-licensor can require additional compensation. Since the specifications for most customising projects and most custom-made software development projects are altered, supplemented or redefined by the customer, the developer-licensor can reasonably utilise the specifications ('specs') and desired changes as the basis for add-on revenue requirements.

If no specifications are developed, the developer-licensor opens the door to a situation where it can be taken advantage of by a customer who changes its mind about the definition of the deliverable and thereby requires additional work without increasing the project's fixed price or ceiling. From the developer's standpoint, specifications and a mechanism that allows increased billings for changes in specs are prudent and even essential elements of a large development project. From the customer's standpoint, specifications and a mechanism that allows mutually agreed upon changes in the specs for a major software development or customising project are equally essential because the clear definition of deliverables which specifications state are the heart of the project, and because the change mechanism gives the customer flexibility.

The 'when?' issue directs us to delivery commitments. The standard, printed form contracts of many software providers, like those of many of their equipment provider cousins, do not stipulate a timeframe for delivery and installation. The question of 'When must I deliver the software?' is intentionally not raised in these agreements. The burden is on the customer to require delivery and installation dates or timeframes, or a project completion schedule with this information. Usually the provider benefits slightly from an unspecified delivery and installation deadline. The lack of such a requirement in the parties' agreement gives the provider flexibility and may help the provider avoid a breach of contract for a delayed delivery or installation, whether it was unavoidable or subject to the provider's control.

Recommendation: in a major deal the customer should insist upon clear delivery and installation deadlines in the parties' agreement(s).

Of course, such deadlines may be conditional on such factors as the suitability of the environment for the delivered software, access to the customer's equipment, the availability of the customer's personnel to test the delivered product, or other reasonable conditions. Also, the delivery deadlines can take the form of specified dates, specified events, a specified number of days after an event, or some other form.

9.1.3 What will I receive, when, and for how long?

This question boils down to: 'When and how will I be paid?' The answers are always necessary in a contract for a major software transaction. Most business people understand this point very well, hence it will not be examined closely. If a licensor's standard form contract is clear about nothing else, the answers to this question are usually very clearly stated.

A related topic that sometimes triggers discussion is the question of whether a cure period for correction of failures to perform in accordance with the contract should apply to late payment requirements. This topic can be important to all sides of a major transaction and it has some potential to become a 'deal breaker'. The cure period commences at some point after a deadline is missed and it delays a breach of contract until the period expires. The problem-solving compromise in some negotiations over whether to apply the cure period to late payments is to allow the cure period but to agree upon interest for late payments. A variation is to allow a reduced cure period to apply to late payments and a longer cure period to apply to other breaches of the parties' contract. Of course, some vendors and licensors require interest on late payments and refuse to allow any cure period. However, few providers are ready to terminate a customer immediately after a payment's due date. As a practical matter most customers will receive the benefit of a short grace period on payments, at least during their first transaction with a provider.

9.1.4 What business and legal risks do I face that I should minimise or neutralise?

This third category of fundamentally important contract terms, from the licensor's viewpoint, contains provisions that are common in contracts for various transactions in many industries.

Liability safeguards: most licensors who are or will be survivors in their markets recognise early in their history that there are three basic, conventional, ways to safeguard against liability: to incorporate, to buy insurance, and through protective contract provisions. Incorporating and contract language usually cost less than insurance such as a general liability policy, a product liability policy, or an errors and omissions policy. Incorporation is a common first step for a new software provider. Smart entrepreneurs usually develop standard, protective contracts within the first few years of their business life. Failure to insure may result in a court decision that an exclusion of liability is unreasonable, if appropriate insurance was available at a reasonable price.

Risks: business people tend to worry about revenue, cash flow, return on investment, and market share and other business worries, but the greatest risks anticipated are usually litigation and disputes that would (a) raid the company's accounts, or (b) throw it into bankruptcy, or (c) generate so much bad publicity that the business would be hurt badly or wither and die. These risks are generally perceived as risks which the provider should always strive to minimise or eliminate.

Protective contract terms: the standard protective clauses found in most UK and US vendor contracts, as well as in those of UK and US software licensors, include: (a) an exclusion of consequential damages; (b) a limited warranty with a specified exclusive remedy (such as the repair or replacement of a defective unit) and an alternate exclusive remedy of the refund of money paid or part of the money paid; (c) an exclusion of other express warranties; (d) a disclaimer of all implied warranties; and (e) a limitation on recoverable damages to some specified amount, to part of the sum paid, or to the entire payment for the item(s) giving rise to the dispute or litigation. Examples of these provisions were provided in Chapter 8. While these provisions can be overdone, in most software agreements some variation of these provisions is reasonable and makes good business sense. Of course, other types of liability limitations or exclusions are sometimes demanded by software providers. The reasonableness and importance of each of these provisions must be analysed on a case-by-case basis.

9.1.5 Other provisions

Depending on the nature of the software transaction other contract provisions may assume the status of a key clause. Source code licences are usually sensitive transactions for the software provider claiming trade secret law protection for some or all of a product's source code. A provider may reasonably insist on protective clauses in source code licence agreements that supplement or toughen those normally found in executable code licence agreements. For example, disclosure of the source to non-employees may be absolutely prohibited, only those licensee employees with a need to access the source in the course of their assigned duties may be allowed to use a copy, and use of the source may be specifically limited to the agreed upon purpose for which the licensee intends to employ the code. Also, sign-out and sign-in logs for all copies of source may be required, together with an audit provision. Removal of source from the building in which it is housed may be prohibited. These provisions or some variation of them are generally considered to be reasonable and essential in the context of a source code licence agreement where the source is a valuable asset of the licensor and it has not previously fallen into the public domain.

One argument for not providing an escrow source code is that the code for well-known products will normally have a commercial value and will be an asset realisable by a liquidator. The purchaser is likely to be a third-party maintainer wanting to do business in maintaining the well-known product.

9.2 KEY LICENCE PROVISIONS FROM THE CUSTOMER'S VIEWPOINT

9.2.1 Introduction

The provisions, topics and considerations surrounding major software transactions can be categorised in several ways. For example, customers often divide issues for negotiation into 'financial', 'technical', 'legal' and 'other business needs' categories, and then negotiate the categories in some selected sequence. In addition, customers often search for and attempt to identify for negotiation purposes the 'key' provisions. However, customers are not as consistent as providers in their identification of key contract terms.

The 'key' software licence provisions from the customer's viewpoint will vary to some degree, but not completely, from one major software transaction to another. Customers tend to see two general groupings of key terms, but thereafter the number and nature of key terms will vary from customer to customer and deal to deal. The major variables that affect the classification of a contract provision as a key clause in your licence agreement are listed in SECTION 9.2.3. Of course, reasonable people may disagree about the importance of any contract clause or topic. The variables listed in the second half of this chapter explain some of the reasons for such disagreements.

9.2.2   Key questions

Regardless of whether the customer and supplier employ one contract or several agreements to capture a transaction, regardless of whether the customer is an end-user or a middleman and regardless of whether software or some software-related service is provided, the customer can ascertain a number of key contract terms by asking the questions listed in SECTIONS 7.2.2.1 and 7.2.2.2.

9.2.2.1   What do I receive, when, and for how long?

Answers to this question are terms that are always necessary in a contract for a major software transaction. Some of these answers could be conveyed by implication. For example, if you purchase equipment, purchase and transfer of title language imply that you can keep the equipment forever if you wish, assuming you pay for it in full and on time. None the less, the acquiring party should always know what is being acquired, when it will be delivered and installed, and how long it may be used, distributed, modified, displayed, and so on, before it must be returned, destroyed or discarded, if ever. Some examples of answers to this question follow.

The goods and/or services you will receive should be identified in clear detail. Vaguely identified deliverables often create problems for customers. Some examples of deliverables that should be specified clearly and in detail in your contract include:

- equipment, by manufacturer or private label; by model, quantity, characteristics, specifications, and serial number (as soon as the serial number is available);

- off-the-shelf software by name, characteristics, specifications, and quantity of copies;

- custom-made and tailored systems ('CMATS');

- mutually acceptable functional and technical specifications for the CMATS;

- mutually acceptable design and acceptance criteria for the CMATS;

- a detailed, mutually acceptable implementation plan for the CMATS;

- an incremental payment plan, or other mutually acceptable payment arrangement, for the CMATS; and

- custom-made database designs, report designs, screen designs, screen and data nomenclature and definitions, interfaces and access protocols, all according to clear, detailed specifications and a detailed implementation plan thereof, both of which are created, reduced to writing, and agreed upon before work begins, as should be the case with the CMATS deliverables.

What you receive in terms of ownership of the deliverables, or in rights to use, reproduce, distribute, modify, display, relocate or transfer the deliverables, should be clearly and precisely stated in complete detail. Surprises on these topics after a contract is signed may be hazardous to your career, not just to your organisation. Some examples of these contract provisions are listed below:

- title to equipment (when does it pass to you or is it never acquired?);

- title to the copy of software operating on the equipment, or your rights under your software agreement's licence grant provision and the limitations on those rights, which are often scattered in several contract provisions; and

- ownership of the intellectual property rights in custom-made software, or your rights to use, reproduce, distribute, modify, display, relocate or transfer this software to other equipment, to different sites, to different users, and so on.

9.2.2.2   What do I pay, when, and for how long?

Answers to this question should always be essential contract provisions from a customer's viewpoint. Common sense demands this information in addition to business and legal requirements. It is rare for a customer to have a good business reason to be indifferent about the price, when it must be paid, or when payments must commence, their frequency, and their duration. All required and contingent payments should be clearly specified in the parties' agreement. The timing of all payments should be clearly set out, for example, due dates and any cure period for late payments. Conditions on the payments must be identified, for example, passage of acceptance tests. Some examples of these payments follow:

- equipment prices, instalment payments or lease charges and any buy-out option price for leased equipment;

- software licence fees or purchase prices, listed separately unless there is some advantage to the customer to accept a bundled cost, for example, operating system software bundled with the equipment purchase price (insisting on an unbundled cost is likely to produce a higher total cost);

- maintenance charges, unbundled so that you can control them through negotiated discounts and a ceiling or cap on periodic increases; and

- other service charges such as vendor programming, design, or analysis service charges, separately specified.

9.2.3 Other provisions

In addition to the foregoing, a few other contract terms are likely to be perceived as essential in most major software transactions. Almost any contract term can become critical to the customer's success under circumstances that elevate its importance. The following variables identify some of these circumstances and some of the contract provisions they make necessary.

9.2.3.1 The nature of the transaction

The nature of the transaction can play a major part in your deciding whether a contract term is essential. For example, in an off-the-shelf software licence agreement, the licence-grant clause is absolutely necessary. However, in a facility management deal, customer personnel may not be the authorised user of any software, and hence the customer may not need a licence grant. Similarly, a customer might feel that a data processing service provider need not warrant its internally used software against defects, but a software licensor is often required to provide such a warranty.

9.2.3.2 Needs, goals and concerns, and your sense of urgency

The customer's needs, goals and concerns, and the urgency of its specific needs, are all primary factors determining which contract provisions are essential in a software or related service transaction. For example, if the customer has an urgent need, there may be no time for negotiations and the customer may be willing to sign any licensor document as stands. In this situation, getting the product is the absolute need, not the contract terms. Of course, this thinking can be dangerous and unpleasant surprises sometimes result from ignoring or treating lightly the content of contracts, for example, if you find out your licence grant does not let you do what you need to do with the licensed software after you have signed the agreement.

If you have a critical need to avoid downtime, then the ability to move software to a disaster recovery location may be a necessity, or you may decide you must have onsite spare parts and three-shift, onsite maintenance service, or you may decide you must self maintain your licensed software and/or equipment. In the latter event, access to source code is an absolute necessity, and either sending your employees to the vendor's maintenance personnel training courses or hiring vendor maintenance engineers probably becomes a necessity as well.

Are you concerned about the financial strength of your licensor and the possibility of its bankruptcy? In this case, obtaining source code or a source code escrow may be perceived as absolutely necessary.

Does your 'enterprise view' require the acquisition of software that will support your data designs and data flow in your internal databases? If so, then it may be absolutely necessary to develop some interface software when some new off-the-shelf software is acquired from a new supplier. By extension, contract provisions addressing this interface development project become absolutely necessary.

Are you concerned about whether a new system will be compatible with your existing systems? If so, a benchmark test, or an acceptance test, a trial use period, and/or a compatibility requirement and warranty might be considered essential.

9.2.3.3 Budget

Is your budget for the acquisition or alliance more than adequate, inadequate or barely adequate? This variable could make instalment payment terms, or deferred payment language, critical to the success of the deal.

9.2.3.4 Policies

Your organisation's policies sometimes dictate the importance of contract terms. For example, your law department may have a policy of requiring your country's law as the law which governs the contract.

Your organisation's policies may require you to develop and use standard contracts in lieu of the supplier's standard contracts. In this situation more than a few contract terms are necessities. Standard contracts contain numerous business decisions and limitations on risks. At least some of the provisions that capture these concepts will typically be considered absolutely necessary and 'sacred cows' that are unchangeable.

In addition, your organisation may have a policy that requires tailor-made, detailed and thorough acceptance tests for each major acquisition. Contract provisions that capture and require the application of such acceptance criteria then become necessities.

Does your organisation have a policy requiring ongoing standards of performance, or performance bonds? If so, then these provisions become extremely important.

Your organisation may require a ceiling on maintenance service charge increases. This 'cap' provision then becomes a necessity.

Do you require the flexibility to terminate ongoing payments for some or all of the software you licenSe if your budget is reduced? If so, contract terms giving you this flexibility are vital.

Suppose you are about to acquire a new switch and you need onsite spare parts for this telecommunications system. Further, suppose that you want to buy used parts from other sources because they are significantly cheaper than new parts from the vendor. Now assume that the vendor insists upon inspecting and testing these parts to ensure that they do not short circuit the new system covered by the vendor's standard maintenance policy. If the vendor charges a very small fee for this inspection and testing, then you may not object. However, you may have a firm policy against payment of expensive inspection, testing and 'certification' charges for the vendor's approval and coverage of these spare parts under its standard maintenance policy. Avoiding expensive certification charges may be important to a customer, and a refusal to pay them has killed more than one multi-million-pound acquisition.

Many other examples could be cited, but these few should illustrate the importance of organisation policies in ascertaining the key contract terms in your deals.

9.2.3.5 Culture

The environment in which you function can dictate the necessity of some contract terms as well as your attitude toward suppliers. Your organisation's style of doing business may require you to be aggressive and demanding with suppliers, or even handed, or easy going and friendly. If your organisation's culture requires aggressive negotiations in a major deal, a 'most-favoured customer' provision may be an absolute necessity in your contract.

If your organisation is fast-moving, decisive and willing to take risks, you may not hesitate to make unqualified commitments to a supplier. On the other hand, if your organisation is slow-moving and careful, or is highly political in nature, then contract provisions giving you flexibility to make changes after the contract is signed, and/or numerous protective provisions, may be practical necessities or politically prudent.

9.2.3.6 History

Your organisation's history in dealing with a particular supplier may dictate the necessity of some contract terms, for example: warranties and representations against shut-down, slow-down, or use limitation devices in software; or a clause requiring responses to maintenance problems within a specified period. Of course, provisions like these are appropriate in contracts for major acquisitions absent a negative history with a supplier, but they become more important after a bad experience.

9.2.3.7 The individual

The position of the individual within the organisation and his risk-taking orientation are major factors in determining the absolutely necessary terms of a particular deal. To illustrate, in many companies junior and middle management personnel tend to focus on their individual concerns or the interests of their unit, department, section or group. The best interests of the organisation as a whole may not be their primary consideration. The paradigm examples are (a) the lawyer who focuses only on protecting the organisation against risk, and (b) the techie who focuses only on the technical evaluation of the licensed software. Such a focus is not necessarily 'wrong', but it helps to dictate the contract provisions that these individuals will deem absolutely necessary. Of course, some techies and some lawyers see the big picture as well as the trees and are business oriented. Hence, in some transactions the needs of the organisation will be understood and well served by these individuals.

The risk-taking orientation of the individual may help to dictate vendor selection as well as the number and variety of protective provisions that are deemed 'absolutely necessary'. Examples of such protective contract provisions include liability limitations, source-code escrows, credits for downtime, flexibility in termination, or other forms like bid bond or performance bond requirements.

9.2.4 Clarity and precision

From the customer's viewpoint, clarity and precision in contract language are as necessary as the key terms we have reviewed. Vagueness and ambiguity almost always favour the licensor, whether or not the licensee recognises the ways in which vague provisions can be harmful. For example, some customers insist upon vague, subjective acceptance language in the parties' contract, reasoning that it gives them control and discretion regarding acceptance of the items delivered. Perhaps these customers also feel they have insufficient time to identify and negotiate objective acceptance criteria. One difficulty with this reasoning is that a subjective acceptance mechanism invites disagreement over whether the supplier's product or service should be, or should have been, accepted. Except for some major, glaring deficiency in the product or service supplied, the supplier can claim that its product or service should be accepted as easily as the customer can claim it should not be accepted. Of course, such disagreements sometimes lead to a strained relationship, a loss of future business for the supplier, a loss of a valuable supplier to the customer or a law suit. Such disagreements are needless and many can be avoided through the use of objective acceptance criteria. In general, vagueness and ambiguity in the parties' agreement should be tolerated by the licensee only if it helps the licensee in some significant manner.

Part V
Negotiating tactics and techniques

10 Creative problem solving

10.1 INTRODUCTION – REDUCE THE ISSUE TO ECONOMICS

Inevitably situations will arise in which no fallback position and no tactic or other negotiating tool will generate a mutually acceptable resolution of an issue. One fairly well recognised 'last-resort' approach to this situation is for the provider(s) to reverse their positions and claim to be willing to make the concessions demanded for a price. This approach is usually employed only if the provider is seriously interested in obtaining the business in question, and the price is usually high. The foundation for this approach to problem solving is the reasonable belief that industry-standard, customary, reasonable or modest risks should be assumed at standard price or discount levels, but that greater risks or extraordinary performance requirements should be assumed only if greater rewards are available, or at least possible, under reasonable criteria. If the provider's standard risk assumption level is reasonable, this 'greater reward for greater risk' suggestion is also reasonable. Of course, the price may be reasonable or not, and affordable or not, however reasonable this approach to the problem may be. Solutions that are less well known are suggested in the following pages of this chapter.

10.2 REDEFINING THE PROBLEM

Of all of the creative problem solving techniques known to man, the one that may be best known is the technique of redefining the problem. Some real-life situations will illustrate this technique.

CASE STUDY

Assume you are about to open negotiations for a custom-made computer program that your organisation believes will solve a major operational problem, for example, slow customer billings. Furthermore, assume that this project will be extremely expensive. You know the preferred developer's opening, fixed price quote will far exceed your budget. Tough negotiations are expected because of

---

the degree to which you will have to ask the developer to cut its price in order for you to obtain Board approval of the contract. Regardless of whether or not you are successful, your boss, the Managing Director of your organisation, has told you that he wants to recoup the development project expense by obtaining ownership of all rights in the new program and distributing it, for a fee, to other organisations like yours. Consequently, he advised you that it is 'absolutely necessary' for you to obtain ownership of the program from the independent contractor-author.

At the pre-planned time during the first face-to-face negotiating session with the developer, you explain that you will need to obtain all rights to the software, its design documents and technical and operator documentation, and its specifications, all of which will be prepared solely by the developer and approved by you prior to their acceptance. The developer responds by pointing out that it is going to own the rights to these items under current copyright law, subject to appropriate contract provisions to the contrary. The developer adds that you did not make this demand in your request for proposals, hence it is a major surprise. Furthermore, your requirement for ownership entails an asset purchase from the developer, not the anticipated non-exclusive software user licence for the developed program in executable code form. If the developer were willing to sell the asset, it would sell only the new application code and not its proprietary driver or 'engine' code in the program that has been and in the future will be built into other custom-made applications for other customers. The price of the application code sale would be at least five times the price of a paid-up licence fee for the executable code version of the program. In addition, the developer questions your ability to maintain and market the program. You have no internal or external software sales staff at the moment.

You respond that you would be willing to contract with the developer for maintenance and enhancement support, but you cannot afford the sale price. In fact, you cannot afford the quoted executable code licence fee.

After a break requested by the developer, you are told that the developer does not want to sell its rights to the program to you. You explain that you must acquire all rights to the program. Together, you and the developer explore whether additional budget monies are available from other budget categories or from anticipated future budgets that would allow you to pay for a standard licence, if not a more expensive asset purchase. You find a way to structure the payments for the standard non-exclusive licence to use the executable code, but no additional funds to apply toward the asset purchase price.

The developer repeats its refusal to sell the rights to the program and points out that you could not afford to buy the rights even if the developer were willing to sell them. You try every tactic you can think of and employ all of your pre-planned fallback positions, but to no avail.

You change strategies following a break which you request, but the developer argues that it makes no sense from a business standpoint to change its position. The developer plans to distribute the new program as a new standard product and nothing you have said convinces the developer to change its position. You are deadlocked on this ownership issue. You must have the program, and own it. Everyone in your organisation who is involved with this transaction feels strongly that this developer should write the program. What can you do?

Possible solutions: creative problem solving rides to the rescue. Try redefining the problem. The Managing Director really wants revenue from distribution of the program. Why not negotiate for a royalty from the developer on other customer licences based on the argument that you are paying for the development project and hence are entitled to a return on your 'investment'. You will have to explain the reasonableness of this alternative plan to the Managing Director, but the idea is worth exploring and it could solve your problem. Ownership becomes a much less important issue in this approach and might be easily agreed upon if a satisfactory royalty arrangement, with or without minimum payments, can be negotiated. In fact, you might even waive your demand for ownership under these circumstances.

10.3 OTHER TECHNIQUES

Numerous other creative problem-solving techniques can be applied in different situations arising during the negotiation of a major transaction. The following non-exhaustive list may give you some ideas that you could employ to help you move closer to a signed contract. Note in passing that some of these ideas should be helpful during the planning stage prior to negotiations. Some of them suggest good habits to develop when planning any action in any field. Using imagination you should be able to find other contexts in which some of the following suggestions could be helpful.

10.3.1 Recognise opportunities

During the course of the negotiations of most major transactions, the other party's negotiator or a negotiating team member will say something that opens the door to a possible benefit. If you recognise this opportunity, and if you feel it is worth pursuing, you may be able to obtain this benefit simply by discussing it. An important part of creative problem solving is recognising and taking advantage of opportunities that the other side gives you. You need to listen carefully and digest what you hear in order to use this technique.

10.3.2 Borrow ideas

Ideas that helped you or someone you know resolve a problem may be helpful in negotiating a contract. These ideas may have been used in the same type of deal or in an entirely different context. Take a moment to ask yourself what impasse-solving solutions you have seen or heard of others using, as well as what ideas you have used successfully in the past, and consider their application to difficult-to-resolve issues in your current negotiation.

10.3.3 Look at the forest, not just the trees

Try to step back from the details of the topic you are attempting to negotiate and view the big picture, for example, senior management's goals and expectations for the deal, the overall consequences of the transaction for your organisation, and other events which are contingent upon closing the deal. Is the other side's position reasonable when considered as a part of the whole transaction? Is your need in this topic area absolutely necessary because of its importance to the big picture of the entire transaction? Perhaps explaining this view will help you solve the problem at hand.

10.3.4 Look for patterns

Looking for patterns can be a very helpful habit in negotiations. Patterns of behaviour by the other side's negotiating team may tip off undisclosed information. Often neither party discloses its bottom line on important issues. If the other side repeats a concept several times in a manner you believe might be sincere, then the observed pattern of this return to the same position or concept may mean that it lies close to the other side's bottom line.

Often these patterns of behaviour are discernible only if you read body language. For example, if the provider's other team members often cover their mouths while the provider team's lead negotiator makes a new proposal, and you have observed this pattern of behaviour in the past whenever a proposal was one or two levels away from the provider's bottom line on the issue then in question, you could logically infer that the provider may be willing to give you more than the current proposal offers.

10.3.5 Don't ignore the obvious

Sometimes the solution to your problem is obvious and apparent, but for some reason it is overlooked or ignored as options are explored or points are expressed at the negotiating table. Try stepping back mentally and asking yourself if there is an obvious solution available. Once in a while the surprising answer might be 'yes'.

10.3.6 Look at the difficulty differently

This suggestion can take various forms. It could amount to redefining the problem as has been suggested before. Alternatively it could suggest looking at the other side's reasoning for not accepting your proposal in a different way in order to ascertain flaws. Are there any inconsistencies between the other side's position on the issue at hand and its position on other issues? Can required performance be assured in another manner besides delivery of one initially specified item? Can you assure yourself that acceptable services will be provided in some other manner, for example, through credits against billings if the services are not acceptable?

10.3.7 Ask: What if?

What if you accepted the other side's position? What would the consequences be? Are they acceptable? What if you altered your position slightly? Could you accept the consequences? What if you halted negotiations and sought another supplier or walked away from this prospective provider? Would this provider return with a more acceptable proposal? (Often, but not always, the answer is 'yes'.) Do you have sufficient time to use this technique, or will you get into trouble if you do?

10.3.8   What rules can you break?

Breaking rules can be politically dangerous, and the results can be positive or negative. In the case study presented in SECTION 10.2 the proposed solution required the customer's negotiator to violate explicit, direct orders from the Managing Director. Obviously the negotiator should seek the Managing Director's approval for the altered plan, but a solution that broke the rules was essential to a successful closing.

10.3.9   Combine or link ideas

Sometimes each party will have rejected some proposals of the other that are considered important. Perhaps if you combine one of your important proposals with one of the other side's important proposals both sides can benefit. This approach is not 'horse trading' one concession for another. Rather, it involves a linkage of ideas that were previously raised as separate topics. The combination may be acceptable to both parties because of the mutually beneficial result created by or perceived in the combination.

10.3.10   Change names

Technical, legal, and even business terminology is not always consistently used by all people. Moreover, some people have a negative reaction to some names or labels. You may be able to defuse negative emotion or eliminate misunderstandings simply by suggesting a different name for the item in question and consistently using that new name.

10.3.11   Imagine how someone else would solve the problem

Sitting back and trying to picture how another person might resolve your problem, someone like your boss, might help you find a way to close the issue at hand.

10.3.12   Notice the positive

Some people, perhaps most, tend to reject new ideas proposed by another person, either because of a 'not-invented-here' negative bias, or because one aspect of the idea seems flawed, so the entire idea is rejected. A diplomatic and sometimes helpful approach to a new problem solving proposal from the other side is to notice and comment on the positive aspects of the other side's idea, if you can find any, before you comment on the negative aspects. This simple technique encourages the other party to fix the negative aspects of its proposal and the use of the revised idea to solve your problem, provided the negative aspects of the proposal are capable of being fixed.

10.3.13　Expect resistance and sell

Whenever you propose a new problem solving idea you should expect resistance from the other side of the negotiating table. If you anticipate and plan for this resistance by developing persuasive arguments supporting your proposal, you may avoid a 'knee-jerk' negative reaction. The one limitation on this technique is to recognise when the other side has bought your proposal and immediately to stop selling. The danger in continuing to sell your idea is that you will say something the other side had not thought of that will trigger a rejection.

This technique of supporting your proposals with persuasive arguments will complement praise for the positive aspects of the other party's proposals before you give negative feedback. By using these two simple techniques in combination, you can expedite problem solving and deal closings more than you might expect.

11 The use of non-verbals in negotiation

11.1 INTRODUCTION

In the last 20 years, and, particularly, in the last ten years, there has been a great deal of research into and use of non-verbal communication within negotiation.

In this chapter we will consider the use and threat of silence in negotiation, the value of appreciating body language and its signals in negotiating situations and also the issues relating to personal space.

All of these matters are variable depending upon culture and, to some extent, individual characteristics but, broadly speaking, there are some clear consistencies within the use of silence and the awareness of body language and personal space when negotiating at the table, or even discussing transactions in an informal 'cocktail party' environment.

11.2 SILENCE – NEGOTIATING WITH YOURSELF

Silence can be a very effective negotiating tool for customers, or for providers who feel no pressure to accept customer proposals at the negotiating table. Many of us abhor lapses in conversation and feel compelled to fill in gaps. Also, in the UK, silence is perceived as a negative reaction in the context of negotiating business transactions. If a customer's negotiator says nothing after the provider's negotiator explains his position on an issue, the provider's negotiator will be strongly tempted to start talking and soften the stance or sweeten the proposal just explained. Only the most experienced negotiators will resist this urge and let the silence continue. The typical response of immediately offering some concession in order to appease the silent party and get him talking again amounts to making a concession without a request or demand for the concession. In other words, if you respond to silence this way, you are negotiating with yourself. Oriental negotiators use silence very effectively, especially against US, UK, Canadian and Australian opponents.

11.3 BODY LANGUAGE

Many of us do not realise just how much use non-verbal communication has in discussions and negotiations with other people. We use body language unconsciously and yet, with training and observation, it is possible not only to learn the feelings of other people from their non-verbal reactions, but also to use body language as a positive means within negotiation.

Students of body language often qualify their analyses by explaining that body language is culturally dependent. One must be aware of possible differences in body signal meaning when observing someone from another culture. For example, a gesture or movement by an Italian may have a different meaning when it is made by an Englishman. On the other hand, foreign signal meanings often become assimilated into the local culture for one reason or another. Hence, people reading this book are likely to understand the body language of some foreigners even if the readers have never left their home town.

Some students of body language attempt to supplement their understanding by self-analysis and projection. The feelings you have when you are doing something with your hands, feet, legs, arms, head or eyes might be the same feelings another person has when he moves in the same way. The obvious danger of projecting your feelings on someone else is that you may be wrong regardless of the identical body language being displayed. The way to overcome this potential pitfall is to question the individual displaying the signal and try to confirm the accuracy of your signal reading through his answers. Of course, your questions may be subtle, or not, depending on the delicacy of the situation.

Also, you should be aware that some sophisticated negotiators will intentionally signal attitudes and feelings that are not real in the hope of evoking the reaction they desire from you. The more experienced a negotiator is, the more careful you must be to confirm your reading of his body language.

With these introductions, three examples of body language used in the course of negotiating are set out in SECTIONS 11.3.1–11.3.3 below.

Understanding non-verbal communication is extremely useful in all walks of life, but particularly in negotiations, since much can be gleaned about the feelings or reactions of the other side by observing body language.

The way in which you interact with the other side in negotiations may be enhanced by synchronising your body language with that of the person that you are negotiating with, or by adopting more attentive sitting positions, or by making the seating arrangements at the negotiating table less adversarial.

For example, discussions in a round table arrangement are often more informal than those which are conducted face to face across a wide table, since there is an invisible barrier created between the parties down the centre of such a table.

Observing and adapting to body language differences, particularly when those differences arise culturally, is a distinct advantage in negotiation but is only part of the answer. As we have seen above, the non-verbals that are apparent in certain situations may not be entirely indicative of the feelings or emotions of the person displaying those verbals and therefore further questioning by the observer will clarify whether the body language observed is truly indicative of the feelings that may be underlying such body language.

11.3.1 Crossed arms

Some body language is situation dependent, not just culture dependent, and some signals can also be gender dependent. For example, crossed arms can have a different meaning in a social setting than at the negotiating table, and women and men often signal different things when they cross their arms. An American woman crossing her arms is usually signalling that she is cold; she is simply trying to increase body warmth. An American man crossing his arms at a social gathering may do so simply for comfort or because he is bored; on occasion he will be having a gas attack and indigestion.

On the other hand, a man attempting to work out the details of an important deal signals something entirely different when he crosses his arms at the negotiating table. Here crossed arms will usually mean a negative reaction of some sort to a statement by the other side, perhaps a feeling of defensiveness, or a signal that his mind is made up and closed – he is rejecting the other side's request or demand. If the man leans back in his chair, pushes away from the table, and crosses his legs as well as his arms, then he is totally uninterested in the speaker's message and is probably 'tuning out'.

A woman at the table may signal the same feelings in the same ways, but caution is required here lest you misread the woman's signals. Remember she may be cold, or she could be cold and bored if the topic is not in her area of responsibility. You should ask questions before you finish your analysis, for example, 'Does it feel chilly in this room?', or 'I'm cold, are you?', or 'Are you cold?'. The total verbal and non-verbal response should enable you to determine whether she is cold or whether her crossed arms have another meaning.

11.3.2 The hand over the mouth

In the context of discussing and negotiating major transactions, a hand over the mouth of a person on the opposite side of the negotiations is an important body language signal. The lips must be covered for this signal to have the meaning about to be ascribed. It does not matter whether the lips are covered by one finger or the entire hand, or by one hand or two, as long as they are completely covered. Then this signal, in the context under discussion, will convey a wealth of information.

It will aid our discussion to label the person flashing the hand over the mouth signal as 'A', and the observer as 'B'. Assume B is the speaker and A is listening. Remember that A and B are on opposite sides of the negotiation. When B observes A's hand over A's mouth in the context under discussion, B knows that B has credibility. B is being believed as he speaks. Whatever point B is trying to make, B has succeeded, at least with A, the person flashing the signal. In addition, A conveys a feeling of inadequacy when A flashes this signal. This feeling is often accompanied by a feeling of anxiety and uneasiness, and it usually arises because of a lack of knowledge about, or experience with, the topic being addressed by B. Alternatively, this feeling could arise from uncertainty about how a problem can be resolved, or from a lack of memory about a past event under discussion. Any aspect of the topic about which A has less than adequate knowledge and experience will almost always trigger at least a momentary hand over the mouth signal unless, of course, A is trained to avoid giving this signal. In this writer's experience in our context of major transactions, B's credibility and A's feeling of inadequacy on the topic under discussion always accompany one another when this signal is flashed, even though the two are obviously not absolutely necessary partners. The same meaning for the hand over the mouth body language is apparent in many other contexts, but they remain beyond the scope of this book.

The hand over the mouth signal is usually gender, age and culture neutral, and it retains its meaning in many contexts beyond that of our focus.

Within the scope of our examination, the hand over the mouth signal can have a different meaning when it appears among the speaker's negotiating team members as the speaker makes a proposal or suggestion. The speaker's team members may be signalling that the speaker's proposal or suggestion is not his bottom line on the issue in question. Also, a hand over the mouth of one or more speaker team members while the speaker makes a proposal or suggestion can make the other side suspicious: the speaker's team can be viewed as hiding something or being devious. As a result, the other party's trust and confidence in the speaker's organisation can weaken.

11.3.3   The eyes

If you knew your opponent was telling you a lie, how much would that information help you? Obviously it could be very helpful. The eyes sometimes give away a lie. While your opponent is talking, look for his eyes to dart to the right, that is, to his right. The eyes should return from this super-fast shift after less than a second. If you see this movement, the speaker is probably telling a lie.

Several points of this explanation require clarification. First, no head movement is involved with this body-language signal. The head does not move at all. Secondly, this glance to the right is truly super fast. This is not a casual glance to the right. Nor is it a glance at the window to a speaker's right to see some birds flying by, or a glance at someone walking in a door to the speaker's right.

Thirdly, this signal is not, and does not include, a glance up, down or to the speaker's left. Those movements have other meanings. For example, a look down accompanied with the head moving down indicates strong emotion about the topic which the speaker is addressing, at least usually. Alternatively, it might simply indicate fatigue.

Fourthly, on occasion a speaker will attempt to observe the reaction to his words by an opponent sitting to his right, or attempt to signal a colleague sitting to his right to speak up in support of the statement he is making, or simply attempt to sneak a quick glance at an attractive member of the opposite gender sitting to the speaker's right. Obviously no lie is indicated by any of these glances. The lesson from these examples is that you must be alert to distractions from or communications to those sitting to the speaker's right before you attach meaning to his eye movement.

How else can you tell when a glance to the right does not mean a lie? You ask questions, subtle, direct, or in between, in an attempt to corroborate your impression. You may need some imagination to formulate a question whose answer can make you satisfied that you have detected a lie, but one or more questions can be helpful in this regard. Every lie is not accompanied by a glance to the speaker's right, and perhaps less than 10% of all lies are accompanied by such body language. Nevertheless, you may be able to use this information to your benefit. The first time you catch an opponent in a lie through recognition of this eye-shift body-language signal, you might want to take a break in order to recover from the shock and decide how you are going to respond.

11.4 PERSONAL SPACE

Some discussions occur while both sides are standing up rather than sitting at a negotiating table. In this situation, understanding personal space can be important to your success.

As a general rule women tend to stand 12–18 inches apart when they converse while standing up. Their business conversations are more intimate, from a space standpoint, than those of men in most English-speaking countries. For example, American, Canadian, English and Australian males tend to stand about 18 inches apart when discussing business while standing. In addition, men from these parts of the world normally stand about 18 inches from a woman who is not a 'significant other'. If they approach closer, they may be viewed with suspicion by the female.

If a man, call him 'A', moves closer than 18 inches to another man ('B'), or to another woman ('C'), then A may be perceived in several negative ways by an American, Englishman, Australian or Canadian, for example, as overly aggressive, possibly as having a personal agenda, as intimidating and/or as unpleasant. B or C will feel at least uncomfortable at A's encroachment on B's or C's personal space. Obviously, if A wants to sell something to B or C, then A should not encroach on their personal space.

Drill sergeants in the military have long understood that one way to intimidate a recruit is to stand nose to nose and yell. The violation of the recruit's personal space coupled with yelling succeeds in intimidating most recruits. The same result is common without yelling. Usually only those who have been warned of what to expect or those with a cultural background in which nose-to-nose exchanges are commonplace will not feel threatened or at least somewhat apprehensive by a nose-to-nose encounter.

Cultural backgrounds are important to business and social conversations in several ways, one of which is noticeable when Western business people converse with Arab or Japanese business people while standing. In some Arab cultures it is commonplace for men to stand nose to nose while discussing business. Westerners unfamiliar with this custom encounter it the first time they do business with Arabs who have not been 'Westernised'. The common result is for the Western business person to back up as the Arab moves within the Westerner's personal space. The backing up can continue until the Westerner is backed into a corner, which is a ludicrous but far too common result. The consequences are not only the uneasy, unhappy feelings of the Westerner about the invasion of his personal space and being backed into a corner, literally speaking. The Arab usually believes the Westerner is weak and inadequate or easily taken advantage of. No business, or low-quality business, may result.

In contrast, Japanese business people prefer to stand about two feet apart, largely to allow room for bowing. If a Westerner approaches within the two-foot personal space, he runs the risk of offending the Japanese. The possible negative ramifications are obvious. One of the most interesting social gatherings includes Japanese and Arabs. The Japanese tend to back up even faster than the Americans.

11.5 SEATING POSITIONS

When it comes to getting around the table it is worth remembering that the seating and positioning of the parties can help or hinder negotiations.

If the table is oblong and narrow, then one party sitting close to the table will achieve a dominant but potentially aggressive position, because the other party will feel their personal space invaded and keep a position of sitting back from the table. If, of course, they also sit up to the table then the atmosphere may become very confrontational.

On the other hand, a round table tends to break down the invisible barrier which can exist down the middle of a rectangular table, although it is still possible to create such a division.

Another example of the use of positioning occurs where there is an uneven number of negotiators between one party and the other. If the numbers are equal then usually all parties will be involved in the negotiation whether the tables are oblong or round, as shown in the diagram below.

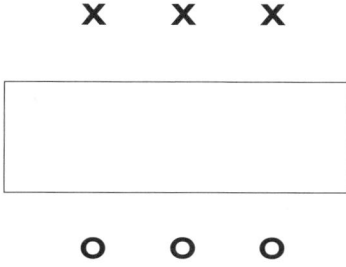

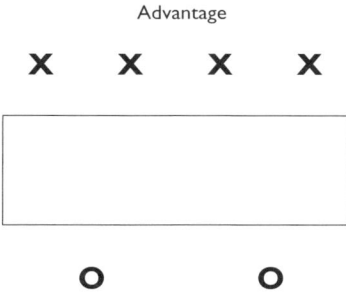

However, if the numbers are unequal one party may be at a disadvantage.

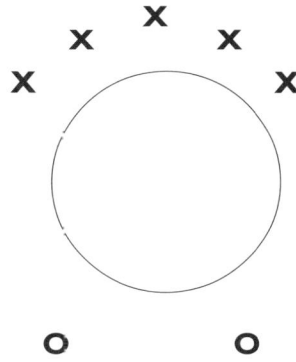

Then again the party with the smaller number can use this to its advantage by positioning the team members in order to isolate at least one of the other team's members if this is tactically sound.

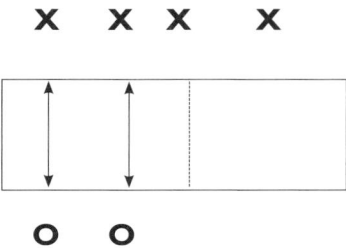

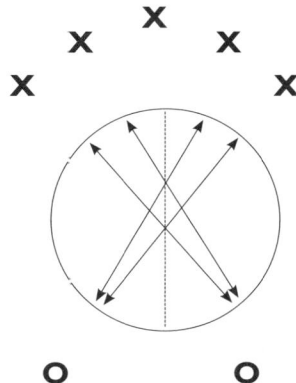

Recommended reading list

Bainbridge, D, *Software Copyright Law* (Butterworths, 1999).

Burnett, R, Klinger, P, *Drafting and Negotiating Computer Contracts* (Tottel Publishing, 2005).

Morgan, R, Burden, K, *Computer Contracts* (Thomson, 7th edition, 2005).

Rennie, M T, *Computer Contracts Handbook* (Sweet & Maxwell, 1989).

Rennie, M T, *Further Computer Contracts* (Sweet & Maxwell, 1989).

Appendix
Precedents

1 Software evaluation licence and confidentiality agreement[1]

This Software Evaluation Licence and Confidentiality Agreement ('Agreement') is entered into effective on [   ] by and between,

[   ] with its registered office at [   ] ('the Licensor'),

and

[   ] with its principal offices at [   ] ('the Licensee').

RECITALS

A.   The Licensor has released and is continuing to develop [*please insert description of function of software*].

B.   The Licensor is prepared to disclose to the Licensee certain Licensor software components listed in the attached SCHEDULE A and as added to by the Licensor from time to time in source code form and/or object code as stated in SCHEDULE A and/or the associated technical documentation listed on the following terms and conditions. Together the software components and the documentation shall be referred to as the Materials.[2]

C.   The Materials are supplied to the Licensee for the sole purpose of internally testing and evaluating the Materials as further described in SCHEDULE A ('Evaluation').

1. PROVISION OF MATERIALS

The Licensor shall deliver the Materials in such form as are currently available to the Licensor. Any details of further Materials provided by the Licensor for the Evaluation shall be recorded in an addition to SCHEDULE A (in the form attached) signed by both parties.

2. USE AND LICENCE OF MATERIALS

2.1   Subject to the terms and conditions of this Agreement, the Licensor hereby grants to the Licensee a non-exclusive, non-transferable, limited licence to use one copy of the Materials internally at [*specify address of location(s) where the Materials will be used*] solely for the purposes of the Evaluation. The Licensee may only copy the Materials as is reasonably necessary for the purpose of back-up.

2.2   All copies of the Materials provided by the Licensor and any copies made by the Licensee, including all intellectual property rights including all patents, inventions, copyrights, database rights, design rights (whether registered or not), trademarks, trade names, logos, trade secrets, know how, semiconductor topography rights and all rights to sue for passing off or unfair competition and all applications for the same and all rights of a similar nature existing anywhere in the world ('Intellectual Property Rights') therein, are and shall remain the exclusive property of the Licensor.

2.3   The Licensee shall not distribute, sell, supply, modify, adapt, amend, incorporate, merge, or otherwise alter, the Materials. The Licensee shall not attempt to decompile, reverse-engineer or otherwise disassemble any part of the Materials. The Licensee acknowledges that the Materials are to be used solely for reference purposes when carrying out the Evaluation. Nothing in this Agreement shall be construed as a representation that the Licensee will not independently pursue similar opportunities related to the Evaluation of software applications which may provide equivalent functionality to the Materials provided by the Licensor under this Agreement.[3]

2.4   The Licensee acknowledges that the Materials, the related Intellectual Property Rights including its object and source code and related proprietary information embodied therein or related thereto ('Proprietary Information'), contain valuable trade secrets of the Licensor and are also protected by the copyright and patent laws of various countries. The Licensee agrees that it will keep the Proprietary Information in strict confidence and will not in any way:[4]

2.4.1   disclose or make available the Proprietary Information or any portion thereof to any person or entity, except employees and representatives of the Licensee to whom such disclosure is strictly necessary for Evaluation who are bound by confidentiality obligations. Each of the Licensee's employees or representatives who will have access to any Proprietary Information shall execute a non-disclosure agreement undertaking to keep the Proprietary Information confidential in favour of the Licensor, on terms no less stringent than those contained herein in a form acceptable to the Licensor, which prohibits the unauthorised use or disclosure of any Proprietary Information;

2.4.2   copy, reproduce or duplicate the Proprietary Information or any portion thereof in any form or medium, except as provided in this Agreement.

The Licensee's confidentiality obligations under this CLAUSE 2 shall survive termination of this Agreement for any reason whatsoever.

2.5[5]   The Licensee shall maintain the Proprietary Information and any copies thereof in a secure fashion and will take all reasonable measures consistent with the highest standards of security generally used in the industry for the protection of valuable source code in order to protect the Proprietary Information and any copies thereof from theft, copying, reproduction, or unauthorised distribution, disclosure, dissemination or use. Without limiting the foregoing, the Licensee shall (i) use at least the same level of security for the Proprietary Information that it uses for its own most valuable trade secrets and source code; (ii) use the Proprietary Information only in a secure area and workstation; (iii) limit use of the Proprietary Information to specific individuals to whom such disclosure is strictly necessary to complete the Evaluation and from whom confidentiality undertakings in writing providing no less stringent protection than agreed to in this Agreement have been obtained and who are not (and who will not be) assigned to work on the development of products that compete with the Materials, during the Evaluation and for a period of two (2) years commencing on the completion of the Evaluation; and (iv) store all copies of the Proprietary Information in a safe (or equally secure storage place) when it is not being used by the Licensee for the Evaluation.

2.6   The Licensee shall immediately notify the Licensor of any unauthorised use or disclosure of, or of any unauthorised access to, or of any theft or loss of any copies of the Materials or other Proprietary Information which it suspects or which comes to its attention.

2.7   The Licensee shall reproduce and include any copyright or other proprietary rights notices on all copies of the Proprietary Information and partial copies thereof.

2.8   To the extent permitted by the law, the Materials are supplied as is, including any faults. To the maximum extent permitted by the law, the Licensor excludes all warranties, conditions or other terms that may be implied into this Agreement whether by law, statute or otherwise. The Licensor gives no condition, warranty or other term whatsoever, either express or implied including, without limitation, any condition, warranty or other term as to the condition of any code, or as to merchantability, satisfactory quality, fitness for a particular purpose, non- infringement, or use of reasonable care and skill. To the extent permitted under applicable law, the Licensor shall not be liable in contract, tort or otherwise for any loss or damage, howsoever arising in connection with the Materials or this Agreement. The Licensor shall not be liable for any indirect, special, or consequential damages, whether such damages or losses are known, foreseen, foreseeable or unforeseen. Nothing in this Agreement shall limit the Licensor's liability for negligently caused death or personal injury or fraud.[6]

2.9   Except for the rights and licence granted hereunder, nothing contained in this Agreement shall be construed to grant to the Licensee any right, title or interest in or to the Materials. The Licensor expressly reserves all right, title and interest in and to the Materials which are not specifically granted to the Licensee hereunder.

2.10   The Licensee shall maintain complete and accurate books and records of its use of the Materials hereunder. The Licensor shall have the right to inspect and audit the facilities and all the relevant books and records of Licensee to ensure that Licensee is fully complying with its obligations hereunder. Any such audit shall be upon at least twenty-four (24) hours prior written notice and shall be conducted during normal business hours no more than twice per calendar year.

3. BREACH

3.1   The provisions of this Agreement are necessary for the protection of the business and goodwill of the parties and are considered by the parties to be reasonable for such purpose. The Licensee agrees that any breach of this Agreement may cause the Licensor substantial and irreparable damages and, therefore, in the event of any such breach, in addition to other remedies which may be available, the Licensor shall have the right to seek specific performance and other injunctive and equitable relief.

4. TERMINATION

4.1   The Licensee may terminate the Licence at any time by giving at least [30] days' prior written notice to the Licensor.

4.2   The Licensor may terminate the Licence forthwith on giving notice in writing to the Licensee if:

   4.2.1   the Licensee commits any serious breach of any term of this Agreement and (in the case of a breach capable of being remedied) shall have failed, within [30] days after the receipt of a request in writing from the Licensor to do so, to remedy the breach (such request to contain a warning of the Licensor's intention to terminate); or

   4.2.2   the Licensee permanently discontinues the use of the Licensed Program Materials.

4.3   Save as expressly provided in CLAUSE 4.2 or elsewhere in this Agreement the Licence may not be terminated.

4.4   Forthwith upon the termination of the Licence, the Licensee shall return to the Licensor the Licensed Program Materials and all copies of the whole or any part thereof or, if requested by the Licensor, shall destroy the same (in the case of the Licensed Programs by erasing them from the magnetic media on which they are stored) and certify in writing to the Licensor that they have been destroyed. PROVIDED THAT the Licensee may extract and store any Licensee data upon a separate media for continuity purposes.

4.5   Any termination of the Licence or this Agreement (howsoever occasioned) shall not affect any accrued rights or liabilities of either party nor shall it effect the coming into force or the continuance in force of any provision in this Agreement which is expressly or by implication intended to come into or continue in force on or after such termination.

5. INTERPRETATION

5.1 In this Agreement unless the context otherwise requires:

5.1.1 words importing any gender include every gender;

5.1.2 words importing the singular number include the plural number and vice versa;

5.1.3 words importing persons include firms, companies and corporations and vice versa;

5.1.4 references to numbered clauses and Schedules are references to the relevant clause in or Schedule to this Agreement;

5.1.5 reference in any Schedule to this Agreement to numbered paragraphs relate to the numbered paragraphs of that Schedule;

5.2 the headings to the clauses, Schedules and paragraphs of this Agreement will not affect the interpretation;

5.2.1 any reference to an enactment includes reference to that enactment as amended or replaced from time to time and to any subordinate legislation or byelaw made under that enactment;

5.2.2 any obligation on any party not to do or omit to do anything is to include an obligation not to allow that thing to be done or omitted to be done;

5.2.3 any party who agrees to do something will be deemed to fulfil that obligation if that party procures that it is done.

6. AMENDMENTS

This Agreement may not be released, discharged, supplemented, interpreted, amended, varied or modified in any manner except by an instrument in writing signed by a duly authorised officer or representative of each of the parties hereto.

7. ANNOUNCEMENTS

No party shall issue or make any public announcement or disclose any information regarding this Agreement unless prior written consent has been obtained from the other party.

8. ASSIGNMENT

8.1 This Agreement is personal to the parties and, subject to CLAUSE 8.2 below, neither this Agreement nor any rights, licenses or obligations under this Agreement, may be assigned by either party without the prior written approval of the other party.

8.2   Notwithstanding the foregoing, either party may assign this Agreement to any acquirer of all or of substantially all of such party's equity securities, assets or business relating to the subject matter of this Agreement or to any entity controlled by, that controls, or is under common control with a party to this Agreement. Any attempted assignment in violation of this clause will be void and without effect.

9.   ENTIRE AGREEMENT

This Agreement supersedes all prior agreements, arrangements and undertakings between the parties and constitutes the entire agreement between the parties relating to the subject matter of this Agreement. However the obligations of the parties under any pre-existing non-disclosure agreement shall remain in full force and effect insofar as there is no conflict between the same. The parties confirm that they have not entered into this Agreement on the basis of any representation that is not expressly incorporated into this Agreement.

10.   FORCE MAJEURE[7]

Neither party shall have any liability under or be deemed to be in breach of this Agreement for any delays or failures in performance of this Agreement which result from circumstances beyond the reasonable control of that party. If such circumstances continue for a continuous period of more than [6 months], either party may terminate this Agreement by written notice to the other party.

11.   NOTICES

11.1   Any notice to be given under this Agreement shall be in writing and shall be sent by first class mail or air mail, or by fax (confirmed by first class mail or air mail), to the address of the relevant party set out at the head of this Agreement or such other address as that party may from time to time notify to the other party in accordance with this CLAUSE 11.1.

11.2   Notices sent as above shall be deemed to have been received three working days after the day of posting (in the case of inland first class mail), or seven working days after the date of posting (in the case of air mail), or on the next working day after transmission (in the case of fax messages, but only if a transmission report is generated by the sender's fax machine recording a message from the recipient's fax machine, confirming that the fax was sent to the number indicated above and confirming that all pages were successfully transmitted).

11.3   In proving the giving of a notice it shall be sufficient to prove that the notice was left, or that the envelope containing the notice was properly addressed and posted, or that the applicable means of telecommunication was addressed and despatched and despatch of the transmission was confirmed and/or acknowledged as the case may be.

12. SCHEDULES

The provisions of SCHEDULE A to this Agreement shall form part of this Agreement as if set out here.[8]

13. SEVERANCE

If any provision of this Agreement is prohibited by law or judged by a court to be unlawful, void or unenforceable, the provision shall, to the extent required, be severed from this Agreement and rendered ineffective as far as possible without modifying the remaining provisions of this Agreement, and shall not in any way affect any other circumstances of or the validity or enforcement of this Agreement.

14. SUCCESSORS AND ASSIGNEES

14.1   This Agreement shall be binding upon, and enure to the benefit of, the parties and their respective successors and permitted assignees, and references to a party in this Agreement shall include its successors and permitted assignees.

14.2   In this Agreement references to a party include references to a person:

14.2.1   who for the time being is entitled (by assignment, novation or otherwise) to that party's rights under this Agreement (or any interest in those rights); or

14.2.2   who, as administrator, liquidator or otherwise, is entitled to exercise those rights;

14.2.3   and in particular those references include a person to whom those rights (or any interest in those rights) are transferred or pass as a result of a merger, division, reconstruction or other reorganisation involving that party. For this purpose, references to a party's rights under this Agreement include any similar rights to which another person becomes entitled as a result of a novation of this Agreement.

15. WAIVER

No delay, neglect or forbearance on the part of either party in enforcing against the other party any term or condition of this Agreement shall either be or be deemed to be a waiver or in any way prejudice any right of that party under this Agreement. No right, power or remedy in this Agreement conferred upon or reserved for either party is exclusive of any other right, power or remedy available to that party.

16. COUNTERPARTS

This Agreement may be executed in any number of counterparts or duplicates, each of which shall be an original, and such counterparts or duplicates shall together constitute one and the same agreement.

17. TIME IS OF THE ESSENCE

Time shall be of the essence in this Agreement as regards any time, date or period mentioned in this agreement or subsequently substituted as a time, date or period by agreement in writing between the parties.

18. SUB-CONTRACTING

With the prior written consent of the Licensor (such consent not to be unreasonably withheld or delayed) the Licensee may perform any or all of its obligations under this Agreement through agents or sub-contractors, provided that the Licensee shall remain liable for such performance and shall indemnify the Licensor against any loss or damage suffered by the Licensor arising from any act or omission of such agents or sub-contractors.

19. LANGUAGE

This Agreement is made only in the English language. If there is any conflict in the meaning between the English language version of this Agreement and any version or translation of this Agreement in any other language, the English language version shall prevail.

20. COSTS AND EXPENSES

Each party shall bear its own legal costs and other costs and expenses arising in connection with the drafting, negotiation, execution and registration (if applicable) of this Agreement.

21. THIRD PARTIES'

[The parties confirm their intent not to confer any rights on any third parties by virtue of this Agreement and accordingly the Contracts (Rights of Third Parties) Act 1999 shall not apply to this Agreement.]

Or

[The parties recognise that this Agreement is intended to benefit and shall so benefit (insert name of third party) for the purposes of the Contracts (Rights of Third Parties) Act 1999 and, subject to that, the parties confirm their intent not to confer any rights on any other third parties by virtue of this Agreement.]

22. PROPER LAW AND JURISDICTION

22.1   This Agreement and all matters arising from it and any dispute resolutions referred to below shall be governed by and construed in accordance with English Law notwithstanding the conflict of law provisions and other mandatory legal provisions save that:

22.1.1 The Licensor shall have the right to sue to recover its fees in any jurisdiction in which the Licensee is operating or has assets; and

22.1.2 The Licensor shall have the right to sue for breach of its intellectual property rights and other proprietary information and trade secrets ('IPR') (whether in connection with this Agreement or otherwise) in any country where it believes that infringement or a breach of this Agreement relating to its IPR might be taking place. For the avoidance of doubt, the place of performance of this Agreement is agreed by the parties to be England.

22.2 Each party recognises that the other party's business relies upon the protection of its IPR and that in the event of a breach or threatened breach of IPR, the other party will be caused irreparable damage and such other party may therefore be entitled to injunctive or other equitable relief in order to prevent a breach or threatened breach of its IPR.

22.3 With respect to all other disputes which are not IPR related pursuant to CLAUSES 22.1 and 22.2 above and its special rules the following procedures in CLAUSES 22.3 to 22.5 shall apply. Where there is a dispute the aggrieved party shall notify the other party in writing of the nature of the dispute with as much detail as possible about the deficient performance of the other party. A representative from senior management ('representatives') of each of the parties shall meet in person or communicate by telephone within five business days of the date of the written notification in order to reach an agreement about the nature of the deficiency and the corrective action to be taken by the respective parties. The representatives shall produce a report about the nature of the dispute in detail to their respective boards and if no agreement is reached on corrective action, then the chief executives of each party shall meet in person or by telephone, to facilitate an agreement within five business days of a written notice by one to the other. If the dispute cannot be resolved at board level within a further five business days, or if the agreed upon completion dates in any written plan of corrective action are exceeded, either party may seek its legal remedies as provided below.

22.4 If the parties cannot resolve a dispute in accordance with the procedure in CLAUSE 22.3 above, then they shall with the assistance of the Centre for Alternative Dispute Solution, seek to resolve the dispute or difference amicably by using an Alternative Dispute Resolution ('ADR') procedure acceptable to both parties before pursuing any other remedies available to them. If either party fails or refuses to agree to or participate in the ADR procedure or if in any event the dispute or difference is not resolved to the satisfaction of both parties within [90] days after it has arisen, the matter shall be settled in accordance with the procedure below.

22.5 If the parties cannot resolve the dispute by the procedure set out above, the parties shall irrevocably submit to the exclusive jurisdiction of the Courts of England and Wales for the purposes of hearing and determining any dispute arising out of this Agreement.

The parties have caused this Agreement to be executed by their duly authorised representatives, effective as of the day and year first written above.

Signed on behalf of the LICENSOR   Signed on behalf of the LICENSEE

By: [   ]   By: [   ]

Name: [   ]   Name: [   ]

Title: [   ]   Title: [   ]

Date: [   ]   Date: [   ]

SCHEDULE A

MATERIALS LICENSED

SOFTWARE:

COMPONENT	SOURCE CODE PROVIDED

DOCUMENTATION:

Together with updated versions of all or part of the Materials provided to the Licensee at the Licensor's discretion during the term of the Agreement.

DESCRIPTION OF THE EVALUATION:

Initialled on behalf of the LICENSOR [   ] dated [   ]

Initialled on behalf of the LICENSEE [   ] dated [   ]

1   This Agreement is intended to apply to a situation where the licensor has proprietary software which it is prepared to licence on a limited evaluation basis to a licensee so that the licensee may evaluate the software in case the licensee may wish to utilise it in its own or bundled with its own products.

2   In this particular Agreement, it is envisaged that the licensor may licence the software in both source code as well as object code form.

3   Because of the highly confidential nature of the licensor's technology, the licensor attempts by this clause to limit as much as possible the licensee's use. If the licensor is licensing source code, the licensee in fact has considerable ability to analyse the software and for this reason the usual reference to 'reverse analysis' is not included.

4 Because of the confidential nature of the licensor's software, the licensor seeks to keep the licensee and its employees bound by confidence.

5 Because of the confidential nature of the licensor's software the licensor seeks by this clause to impose strict security on the licensee and its possession of the licensor's software.

6 Because of the confidential nature of the licence and the fact that the software is in development, the licensor reasonably seeks to limit its liability and minimise warranties.

7 This force majeure clause is short and general. It may be appropriate to insert a more detailed force majeure clause such as:

'Notwithstanding anything else contained in this Agreement, neither party shall be liable for any delay in performing its obligations hereunder if such delay is caused by circumstances beyond its reasonable control (including without limitation any delay caused by any act or omission of the other party) provided however that any delay by a sub-contractor or supplier of the party so delaying shall not relieve the party from liability for delay except where such delay is beyond the reasonable control of the sub-contractor or supplier concerned. Subject to the party so delaying promptly notifying the other party in writing of the reasons for the delay (and the likely duration of the delay), the performance of such party's obligations shall be suspended during the period that the said circumstances persist and such party shall be granted an extension of time for performance equal to the period of the delay. Save where such delay is caused by the act or omission of the other party (in which event the rights, remedies and liabilities of the parties shall be those conferred and imposed by the other terms of this Agreement and by law):

- any costs arising from such delay shall be borne by the party incurring the same;
- either party may, if such delay continues for more than 10 weeks,
- terminate this Agreement forthwith giving notice in writing to the other by reason of such termination.

8 As many contracts are varied or amended during their life cycle it is important that all Schedules are agreed to and signed or initialled by the parties so that there can be no dispute as to the totality of the contract and its contents.

9 Before the Contracts (Rights of Third Parties) Act 1999 (the Act) it was the case that a person who was not a party to a contract (a third party) could not enforce any right under the contract. Similarly, a contract could not impose any obligations or liabilities on a third party.

However the Act attempts to draw a balance between the freedom of the parties to vary a contract and the interests of the third party. The Act means that a contractual clause benefiting the third party (eg the promisee's subsidiary company or sub-contractor or employee) will be straightforwardly enforceable by that third party if:

- the contract expressly provides that he may; or
- where a term in the contract purports to confer a benefit on him (unless on a proper construction of the contract it appears that the parties did not intend the term to be enforceable by the third party).

It is therefore prudent to include a clause to the effect of excluding the provisions of the Act. By doing so it ensures that any rights of third parties are not deemed to be enforceable by them. This is particularly the case where the parties are companies and may have subsidiaries or conversely parent companies.

2 Shrink-wrap licence

I. LICENCE

In consideration of your agreement to the terms of this Agreement, we grant you (the individual or entity whose name and address appears on the Registration Card) a perpetual, non-exclusive right to use the Software in accordance with CLAUSE 2 below.[2] This licence is personal to you as the purchaser of the Software and the licence granted herein is for your benefit only.

2. PERMITTED USE

As purchaser of the authorised copy of the Software, you may, subject to the following conditions:[3]

2.1   load the Software into and use it on a single computer (of the type identified on the package) which is under your control;[4]

2.2   copy the Software for backup and archival purposes and make up to two copies of the documentation (if any) accompanying the Software, provided that the original and each copy is kept in your possession and that your installation and use of the Software does not exceed that allowed by this Agreement;[5]

2.3   transfer the Software, on a permanent basis only, to another person by transferring all copies of the Software to that person and/or destroying copies not transferred. The other person must agree to the terms of this Agreement and on such a permanent transfer, the licence of the Software to you will automatically terminate.[6]

3.   RESTRICTIONS ON USE

You may not nor permit others to:[7]

3.1   load the Software into two or more computers at the same time. If you wish to transfer the Software from one computer to another, you must erase the Software from the first hard drive before you install it onto a second hard drive;

3.2   sub-license, assign, rent, lease or transfer the licence or the Software or make or distribute copies of the Software except as permitted by this Agreement;

3.3   translate, reverse engineer, decompile, disassemble, modify or create derivative works based on the Software except as permitted by law;

3.4   make copies of the Software, in whole or part, except for back-up or archival purposes as permitted in this licence;

3.5   use any back-up copy of the Software for any purpose other than to replace the original copy in the event that it is destroyed or becomes defective;

3.6   copy the written materials (except as provided by this Agreement) accompanying the Software;

3.7   adapt, modify, delete or translate the written material accompanying the Software in any way for any purpose whatsoever;

3.8   vary, delete or obscure any notices of proprietary rights or any product identification or restrictions on or in the Software.

4.   UNDERTAKINGS

You undertake to:

4.1   ensure that, prior to use of the Software by your employees or agents, all such parties are notified of this licence and the terms of this Agreement;

4.2   reproduce and include our copyright notice (or such other party's copyright notice as specified on the Software) on all and any copies of the Software, including any partial copies of the Software;

4.3   hold all drawings, specifications, data (including object and source codes), software listings and all other information relating to the Software, confidential and not at any time, during this licence or after it's expiry, disclose the same, whether directly or indirectly, to any third party without our consent.

5. TITLE

As licensee you own only the diskette or medium on which the Software is recorded or fixed. You may retain the media on termination of this Agreement provided the Software is erased. We shall at all times retain ownership of the Software.

6. WARRANTY

Subject to CLAUSE 6.2, we warrant that for a period of [90] days from the date of your purchase of the Software ('the Warranty Period'):[8]

6.1   the medium on which the Software is recorded will be free from defects in materials and workmanship under normal use. If the diskette fails to conform to this warranty, you may, as your sole and exclusive remedy, obtain (at our option) either a replacement free of charge or a full refund if you return the defective diskette to us or to your supplier during the warranty period with a dated proof of purchase;

6.2   the copy of the Software in this package will materially conform to the documentation that accompanies the Software. If the Software fails to operate in accordance with this warranty, you may, as your sole and exclusive remedy, return all of the Software and the documentation to us or to your supplier during the warranty period, along with dated proof of purchase, specifying the problem, and we will provide you either with a new version of the Software or a full refund (at our option).

6.3   We shall not be liable under the warranties given in CLAUSE 6.1 above if the diskette or the Software fails to operate in accordance with the said warranty as a result of any modification, variation, or addition to the Software not performed by us or caused by any abuse, corruption or incorrect use of the diskette or Software, including use of the Software with equipment or other software which is incompatible.

7. DISCLAIMER

We do not warrant that this Software will meet your requirements or that its operation will be uninterrupted or error free. We exclude and hereby expressly disclaim all express and implied warranties or conditions not stated herein (including without limitation, loss of profits, loss or corruption of data, business interruption or loss of contracts, so far as such exclusion or disclaimer is permitted under the applicable law. This Agreement does not affect your statutory rights.

8. LIABILITY[9]

8.1   Our liability to you for any losses shall not exceed the amount you originally paid for the Software.

8.2   In no event will we be liable to you for any indirect or consequential damages even if we have been advised of the possibility of such damages. In particular, we accept no liability for any programs or data made or stored with the Software nor for the costs of recovering or replacing such programs or data.

8.3   Nothing in this Agreement limits liability for fraudulent misrepresentation or our liability to you in the event of death or personal injury resulting from our negligence.

8.4   You hereby acknowledge and agree that the limitations contained in this clause are reasonable in light of all the circumstances.

9. TERMINATION

9.1   The Agreement and the licence hereby granted to use the Software automatically terminates if you:[10]

9.1.1   fail to comply with any provisions of this Agreement;

9.1.2   destroy the copies of the Software in your possession;

9.1.3   voluntarily return the Software to us.

9.2   In the event of termination in accordance with CLAUSE 9.1 YOU must destroy or delete all copies of the Software from all storage media in your control.

10. SEVERABILITY

In the event that any provision of this Agreement is declared by any judicial or other competent authority to be void, voidable, illegal or otherwise unenforceable or indications of the same are received by either you or us from any relevant competent authority, we shall amend that provision in such reasonable manner as achieves the intention of the parties without illegality or, at our discretion, such provision may be severed from this Agreement and the remaining provisions of this Agreement shall remain in full force and effect.

11. ENTIRE AGREEMENT

YOU have read and understand this Agreement and agree that it constitutes the complete and exclusive statement of the Agreement between us with respect to the subject matter hereof and supersedes all proposals, representations, understandings and prior agreements, whether oral or written, and all other communications between us relating thereto.[11]

12. ASSIGNMENT

This Agreement is personal to you and you may not assign, transfer, sub-contract or otherwise part with this Agreement or any right or obligation under it without our prior written consent.[12]

13. WAIVER

Failure or neglect by either party to exercise any of its rights or remedies under this Agreement will not be construed as a waiver of that party's rights nor in any way affect the validity of the whole or part of this licence nor prejudice that party's right to take subsequent action.[13]

14. LAW AND DISPUTES

This Agreement and all matters arising from it are governed by and construed in accordance with the laws of England and Wales whose courts shall have exclusive jurisdiction over all disputes arising in connection with this Agreement and the place of performance of this Agreement is agreed by you to be England.[14]

If you have any questions about this Agreement, please contact (*give details*).

15. SOFTWARE LICENCE REGISTRATION CARD

> I have read and fully understand and agree to be bound by and comply with the Agreement, a copy of which is printed overleaf.[15]
>
> Signed: [   ]
>
> Dated: [   ]
>
> Printed Name: [   ]
>
> Title: [   ]
>
> On behalf of: [   ]
>
> Company: [   ]
>
> Address: [   ]

1   This document is a single user licence agreement provided in shrink-wrap form and usually applicable to mass market software. Where the software is provided in a boxed fashion, usually the shrink-wrap licence is printed on the outside of an envelope in which

the disk or CD-ROM is placed. The intention is that by the breaking of the seal of the envelope, as well as the loading of the software onto a PC, the user is bound by the licence terms. The emboldened section at the beginning of the document is designed to bring sufficiently to the attention of the user the essential licence terms as well as the procedures for acceptance and rejection.

2   This is a statement of fact and draws to the attention of the user the fact that the software is being licensed on a limited basis and not 'sold'. It also confirms that the right is perpetual (ongoing) and non-exclusive.

3   These licence restrictions are typical for mass market software.

4   This clause allows the software to be loaded onto and used on a particular PC for which the software is written as well as on a PC controlled by the licensee. This language is intended to define that the PC must be owned by the user and therefore specific to the user.

5   This clause provides for the software to be copied for limited purposes and only within the general terms of the licence.

6   This clause provides for the transfer of the software to another person by the transfer of all copies to that person and destroying copies not transferred. The other person must however agree to the terms of the Agreement. Once it has been transferred the licence will terminate as regards the transferor.

7   These restrictions are typical for mass market software.

8   It is usual in shrink-wrap and click-wrap contracts to limit the warranty both by time and as to performance. In this instance the warranty clause also includes a limited indemnity in respect of matters which under United Kingdom law could not be excluded in any event.

9   Having already limited the usual warranties this agreement also seeks to limit liability of the licensor to the licensee. Because the limitations are unilateral given the nature of the agreement, it is important to recognise that for the terms and conditions to be binding on a consumer they must be fair and reasonable. It is equally important that the consumer agrees to their reasonableness.

10 The licence is deemed to automatically terminate on the happening of specific events but other than this the licence term would be perpetual subject to the expiration of copyright. It may be appropriate to express in a shrink-wrap agreement the term of the licence grant in words such as:

    'The software is licensed on a non-exclusive perpetual basis, subject only to termination in accordance with CLAUSE 8',

    or alternatively:

    'The software is licensed on a non-exclusive basis for the full term of copyright therein subject only to earlier termination in accordance with CLAUSE 8'.

11 Following discussions and negotiations where the terms are reduced to written form it is important that the parties to the final contract know what has been finally agreed and where the parameters of that contract exist.

    For this reason the final agreement should include a clause which confirms that the agreement being signed is the complete agreement and that any prior representations are not relied upon.

    Beware of automatically using this form of clause without considering whether prior agreements should be overridden.

12 Software providers like to have the flexibility of transferring their rights and obligations to purchasers of their companies and other parties without the customer's consent. Some standard provider agreements specify this right and some are silent reasoning that silence on this topic will be interpreted by a court as allowing assignment.

    Conversely most software providers do not want the customer assigning software licence agreements without express permission. Providers need to retain control over their software trade secrets in order to preserve their status as trade secrets. Also, the assignee may be a poor credit risk or unsavoury character. Thus, many standard software provider agreements prohibit assignment of the licence agreement as a whole and all software licences except with the express, written permission of the provider except where the assignee is an associate of the Licensee or the Assignment is a result of re-construction or amalgamation.

    Some customers may want to negotiate a specific right to assign licences to companies within their corporate group or to assign licences to the purchaser of the business of the licensee.

13 A waiver clause is useful to ensure that the fact that one party has not previously enforced a right under the contract does not prevent it from doing so in the future.

14 Because of the increase in international trade, a supplier is likely to sell throughout the world and it is important for the agreement to indicate what law applies to the interpretation of the contract and what legal jurisdiction will apply to the settlement of disputes.

15 There is always the risk that a shrink-wrap licence may be difficult to enforce given its unilateral nature and also the fact that it is often drawn to the attention of the licensee after the licensee has 'purchased' the licensed product. As a result some suppliers also attach a software licence registration card to the shrink-wrap licence in the hope that by completing the card and returning it to the supplier the customer is providing further evidence of its intention to be bound by the shrink-wrap licence terms.

3   Click-wrap licence[1]

PLEASE READ THIS CAREFULLY BEFORE USING MATERIALS

A.   PROPERTY OF LICENSOR:

YOU MAY OBTAIN A COPY OF THIS SOFTWARE PRODUCT EITHER BY DOWNLOADING IT REMOTELY FROM OUR SERVER OR BY COPYING IT FROM AN AUTHORISED DISKETTE, CD- ROM OR OTHER MEDIA ('HARD MEDIA'). THE COPYRIGHT, DATABASE RIGHTS AND ANY OTHER INTELLECTUAL PROPERTY RIGHTS IN THE PROGRAMS AND DATA WHICH CONSTITUTE THIS SOFTWARE PRODUCT ('THE MATERIALS'), TOGETHER WITH THE HARD MEDIA ON WHICH THEY WERE SUPPLIED TO YOU, ARE AND REMAIN THE PROPERTY OF THE LICENSOR ('THE LICENSOR'). YOU ARE LICENSED TO USE THEM ONLY IF YOU ACCEPT ALL THE TERMS AND CONDITIONS SET OUT BELOW.

B.   LICENCE ACCEPTANCE PROCEDURE:

BY CLICKING ON THE TWO ACCEPTANCE BUTTONS WHICH FOLLOW THIS LICENCE AGREEMENT (MARKED 'DO YOU ACCEPT THESE TERMS AND CONDITIONS?' AND 'ARE YOU SURE THAT YOU WISH TO ACCEPT THESE TERMS AND CONDITIONS?'), YOU INDICATE ACCEPTANCE OF THIS LICENCE AGREEMENT AND THE LIMITED WARRANTY AND LIMITATION OF LIABILITY SET OUT IN THIS LICENCE AGREEMENT. SUCH ACCEPTANCE IS EITHER ON YOUR OWN BEHALF OR ON BEHALF OF ANY CORPORATE ENTITY WHICH EMPLOYS YOU OR WHICH YOU REPRESENT ('CORPORATE LICENSEE'). IN THIS LICENCE AGREEMENT, 'YOU' INCLUDES BOTH THE READER AND ANY CORPORATE LICENSEE.

C.   LICENCE REJECTION PROCEDURE:

YOU SHOULD THEREFORE READ THIS LICENCE AGREEMENT CAREFULLY BEFORE CLICKING ON THE TWO ACCEPTANCE BUTTONS. IF YOU DO NOT ACCEPT THESE TERMS AND CONDITIONS,

YOU SHOULD CLICK ON THE 'REJECT' BUTTON, DELETE THE MATERIALS FROM YOUR COMPUTER AND PROMPTLY (AND IN ANY EVENT, WITHIN 14 DAYS OF RECEIPT) RETURN TO THE LICENSOR OR A LICENSED RESELLER

(A)   THE DISKETTE OR OTHER MEDIA;

(B)   ANY OTHER ITEMS PROVIDED THAT ARE PART OF THIS PRODUCT; AND

(C)   YOUR DATED PROOF OF PURCHASE. ANY MONEY YOU PAID TO THE LICENSOR OR A LICENSOR RESELLER FOR THE MATERIALS WILL BE REFUNDED, ALONG WITH ALL COSTS OF POSTAGE AND PACKING.

D.   OTHER AGREEMENTS:

IF YOUR USE OF THESE PROGRAMS AND DATA IS PURSUANT TO AN EXECUTED LICENCE AGREEMENT, SUCH AGREEMENT SHALL APPLY INSTEAD OF THE FOLLOWING TERMS AND CONDITIONS.

LICENCE AGREEMENT AND LIMITED WARRANTY

1.   OWNERSHIP OF MATERIALS AND COPIES

The Materials and related documentation are copyrighted works of authorship, and are also protected under applicable database laws. The Licensor retains ownership of the Materials and all subsequent copies of the Materials, regardless of the form in which the copies may exist. This licence is not a sale of the original Materials or any copies.

2.   LICENCE

Provided that you have paid the applicable licence fee, the Licensor grants to you a limited, non-exclusive licence to:

2.1   Use and copy the Materials for use on any computer system owned, leased and/or controlled by you or any member of your corporate group, which expression includes Corporate Licensee, Corporate Licensee's majority-owned subsidiaries, any parent company having a majority-owned interest in Corporate Licensee, and such parent's majority-owned subsidiaries;[2]

2.2   Make copies of the Materials for back-up, archival or other security purposes.

3.   LICENCE RESTRICTIONS

You may not use, copy, modify or transfer the materials (including any related documentation) or any copy, in whole or in part, including any print-out of all or part of any database, except as expressly provided for in this licence. If you transfer possession of any copy of the materials to another party except as provided above, your licence is automatically terminated. You may not translate, reverse engineer, decompile, disassemble, modify or create derivative works based on the materials, except as expressly permitted by the law of this agreement. You may not vary, delete or obscure any notices of proprietary rights or any product identification or restrictions on or in the materials.[3]

4. NO TRANSFER

The materials are licensed only to you. You may not rent, lease, sublicense, sell, assign, pledge, transfer or otherwise dispose of the materials, on a temporary or permanent basis, without the prior written consent of the Licensor.[4]

5. UNDERTAKINGS

You undertake to:

5.1   ensure that, prior to use of the Materials by your employees or agents, all such parties are notified of this licence and the terms of this Agreement;

5.2   reproduce and include our copyright notice (or such other party's copyright notice as specified on the Materials) on all and any copies of the Materials, including any partial copies of the Materials;

5.3   hold all drawings, specifications, data (including object and source codes), software listings and all other information relating to the Materials confidential and not at any time, during this licence or after it's expiry, disclose the same, whether directly or indirectly, to any third party without the Licensor's consent.

6. LIMITED WARRANTY

6.1   Subject to the limitations and exclusions of liability below, the Licensor warrants that (a) the diskette(s) on which the Materials are furnished will be free from material defects under normal use; and that (b) the copy of the program in the package will materially conform to the documentation which accompanies the package. The Warranty Period is ninety (90) days from the date of delivery to you.

6.2   The Licensor will also indemnify you for personal injury or death solely and directly caused by any defect in its products or the negligence of its employees.

6.3   The Licensor shall not be liable under the said warranty above if the Materials fail to operate in accordance with the said warranty as a result of any modification, variation or addition to the Materials not performed by Licensor or caused by any abuse, corruption or incorrect use of the Materials, including use of the Materials with equipment or other software which is incompatible.

7. NO OTHER WARRANTIES

The foregoing warranty is made in lieu of any other warranties, representations or guarantees of any kind, either expressed or implied, including, but not limited to, any implied warranties of quality, merchantability, fitness for a particular purpose or ability to achieve a particular result. You assume the entire risk as to the quality and performance of the materials. Should the materials prove defective, you (and not the Licensor nor any licensed reseller) assume the entire cost of all necessary servicing, repair or correction. The Licensor does not warrant that the materials will meet your requirements or that its operation will be uninterrupted or error free.

8. LIMITATION OF LIABILITY

The Licensor's entire liability and your exclusive remedy shall be:

8.1   the replacement of any diskette not meeting the Licensor's 'Limited Warranty' and which is returned to the Licensor together with dated proof of purchase, or

8.2   if, during the Warranty Period, the Licensor is unable to deliver a replacement diskette which is free of material defects, you may terminate this Agreement by returning the Materials to the Licensor and any money you paid to the Licensor for the Materials will be refunded, along with the cost of postage and packing.

9. EXCLUSION OF LIABILITY

Except in respect of personal injury or death caused directly by the negligence of the Licensor, in no event will the Licensor be liable to you for any damages, including any lost profits, lost savings, loss of data or any indirect, special, incidental or consequential damages arising out of the use of or inability to use such materials, even if the Licensor has been advised of the possibility of such damages. Nothing in this agreement limits liability for fraudulent misrepresentation.[5]

10. YOUR STATUTORY RIGHTS

This licence gives you specific legal rights and you may also have other rights that vary from country to country. Some jurisdictions do not allow the exclusion of implied warranties, or certain kinds of limitations or exclusions of liability, so the above limitations and exclusions may not apply to you. Other jurisdictions allow limitations and exclusions subject to certain conditions. In such a case the above limitations and exclusions shall apply to the fullest extent permitted by the laws of such applicable jurisdictions. If any part of the above limitations or exclusions is held to be void or unenforceable, such part shall be deemed to be deleted from this Agreement and the remainder of the limitation or exclusion shall continue in full force and effect. Any rights that you may have as a consumer (ie a purchaser for private as opposed to business, academic or government use) are not affected.[6]

11. TERM

The licence is effective until terminated. You may terminate it at any time by destroying the Materials together with all copies in any form. It will also terminate upon conditions set forth elsewhere in this Agreement or if you fail to comply with any term or condition of this Agreement or if you voluntarily return the Materials to us. You agree upon such termination to destroy the Materials together with all copies in any form.

12. EXPORT

You will comply with all applicable laws, rules, and regulations governing export of goods and information, including the laws of the countries in which the Materials were created. In particular, you will not export or re-export, directly or indirectly, separately or as a part of a system, the Materials or other information relating thereto to any country for which an export licence or other approval is required, without first obtaining such licence or other approval.[7]

13. GENERAL

13.1   You agree that the Licensor shall have the right, after supplying undertakings as to confidentiality, to audit any computer system on which the Materials are installed in order to verify compliance with this software licence.

13.2   Each party hereby irrevocably agrees that the courts of the country of registration of the Licensor, its subsidiary office, or reseller which issues an invoice for this licence, shall have exclusive jurisdiction to resolve any controversy or claim of whatever nature arising out of or in relation to this Agreement and the place of performance of this Agreement shall be that country and that the laws of that country shall govern such controversy or claim.

13.3   This Agreement constitutes the complete and exclusive statement of the Agreement between the Licensor and you with respect to the subject matter of this agreement and supersedes all proposals, representations, understandings and prior agreements, whether oral or written, and all other communications between us relating to that subject matter.

13.4   Any clause in this Agreement that is found to be invalid or unenforceable shall be deemed deleted and the remainder of this Agreement shall not be affected by that deletion.

13.5 Failure or neglect by either party to exercise any of its rights or remedies under this Agreement will not be construed as a waiver of that party's rights nor in any way affect the validity of the whole of part of this Agreement nor prejudice that party's right to take subsequent action.

13.6 This Agreement is personal to you and you may not assign, transfer, sub-contract or otherwise part with this Agreement or any right or obligation under it without the Licensor's prior written consent.[8]

Should you have any questions concerning this Agreement you may contact *(insert details)*.

1 This document is intended to be a licence to enable the download of software for evaluation purposes for a limited period from the software owner's web site. It can be adapted for use in the case of value added resellers or application service providers, except that, where necessary, amendments should be made to state clearly who is the owner of the original software.

2 It may be appropriate to limit the use even further to one user, but this may be impractical to police.

3 The licence restrictions are typical and, in so far as the limitations cannot be overridden by applicable law, it is usual for the licensor to limit, as much as possible, the use which the consumer can make of the evaluation software. In particular in this case, since the evaluation software is encryption software, the limitation of use is specifically expressed to allow encryption of other material which may be transferred over networks, whilst at the same time limiting the transfer of the encryption software itself.

4 Many software licences limit the use of the software to a particular person or entity and seek to prevent transfer. In this case, because the software is evaluation software only, it is essential to express that transfer is not permitted.

5 As to limitations generally see Paragraph 89 [2619] et seq ante and see Form 5 note 4 [2777.33] ante.

6 Because the licensor may not be able always to identify who will be downloading the agreement and the software that accompanies it, it is advisable to include wording which seeks to reinforce the rights of the consumer, notwithstanding any other terms that may have been included to try to reduce those rights. In this instance, the evaluation agreement is intended to be used on a global basis and so wording has been included to indicate that where local laws override terms in the agreement, they should be specifically allowed to do so, so as not thereby to cause the rest of the agreement to be void.

7 Because the nature of the software envisaged by this agreement is encryption software and thereby on occasions controlled as to export by certain countries, this agreement includes an export control clause. This is not applicable to all products and situations and needs to be evaluated on a transaction by transaction basis.

8 Many standard software provider agreements prohibit assignment of the licence agreement as a whole and all software licences except with the express, written permission of the provider, unless the assignee is an associate of the Licensee or the Assignment is a result of re-construction or amalgamation. Some customers may want to negotiate a specific right to assign licences to companies within their corporate group or to assign licences to the purchaser of the business of licensee.

4 Software licence agreement

THIS AGREEMENT is made the [ ] day of [ ]

BETWEEN:[1]

(1)   (*licensor*) whose [registered office *or* principal place of business] is at (*address*) and whose facsimile ('fax') number is (*number*) ('the Licensor') and

(2)   (*licensee*) whose [registered office or principal place of business] is at (*address*) and whose facsimile ('fax') number is (*number*) ('the Licensee')

RECITALS

A.   The Licensor has developed and owns or has licensed from third parties certain computer software applications that will (*insert description of function of software*).

B.   The Licensor has agreed to deliver to the Licensee and install on the Licensee's computer the above computer programs and to grant to the Licensee a non-exclusive licence to use such programs and their associated documentation.

NOW IT IS AGREED as follows:

1.   DEFINITIONS

In this Agreement, unless the context otherwise requires, the following expressions have the following meanings:

1.1   **'Acceptance Date'** means the date on which the Licensed Programs are accepted (or deemed to be accepted) by the Licensee pursuant to CLAUSE 7;

1.2   **'Delivery Date'** means the delivery date specified in SCHEDULE D or such extended date as may be agreed by the Licensee;

1.3   **'Equipment'** means such computer equipment as may be specified by the Licensee from time to time and is as presently listed in SCHEDULE A;

1.4 **'Intellectual Property Rights'** means all vested contingent and future intellectual property rights including but not limited to copyright, trademarks, service marks, design rights (whether registered or unregistered), patents, know-how, trade secrets, inventions, get-up, database rights and any applications for the protection or registration or these rights and all renewals and extensions thereof existing in any part of the world whether now known or in the future created to which the Licensor may be entitled;

1.5 **'Location'** means the computer room where the Equipment is to be installed as specified by the Licensee from time to time and as listed in SCHEDULE E;

1.6 **'Licence'** means the licence granted by the Licensor pursuant to CLAUSE 2.1;

1.7 **'Licence Fee'** means the fee for the Licence provided under this Agreement as specified in SCHEDULE C;

1.8 **'Licensed Program Materials'** means the Licensed Programs, the Program Documentation and the Media;

1.9 **'Licensed Programs'** means the systems, applications and computer programs of the Licensor specified in SCHEDULE B and all releases and versions thereof;

1.10 **'Media'** means the media on which the Licensed Programs and the Program Documentation are recorded or printed as provided to the Licensee by the Licensor specified in SCHEDULE F;

1.11 **'Program Documentation'** means the operating manuals, user instructions, technical literature and all other related materials in eye-readable form supplied to the Licensee by the Licensor for aiding the use and application of the Licensed Programs;

1.12 **'Specification'** means the specification of the Licensed Programs describing the facilities and functions thereof, a copy of which is annexed to this Agreement as SCHEDULE G;

1.13 **'Use the Licensed Program Materials'** means to read all or any part of the Licensed Programs from magnetic or other storage media, to load the Licensed Programs on the Equipment for the storage and running of the Licensed Programs, to read and possess the Program Documentation in conjunction with the use of the Licensed Programs and to possess the Media.

2. GRANT OF LICENCE[2]

2.1 The Licensor hereby grants to the Licensee a non-exclusive licence to Use the Licensed Program Materials on and in conjunction with the Equipment subject to the terms and conditions contained in this Agreement.

2.2 The Licensee shall Use the Licensed Program Materials for processing its own data for its own internal business purposes only.

2.3 The Use of the Licensed Program Materials is restricted to use on and in conjunction with the Equipment save that:

2.3.1 if the Licensed Program Materials cannot be used with the Equipment because it is inoperable for any reason then the Licence shall be temporarily extended without additional charge to use with any other equipment until such failure has been remedied provided that such equipment is under the direct control of the Licensee. The Licensee shall promptly notify the Licensor of such temporary use and of the commencement and cessation thereof;

2.3.2 the Licensee may with the prior written consent of the Licensor (such consent not to be unreasonably withheld) Use the Licensed Program Materials on and in conjunction with any replacement equipment (to be specified by type and serial number) if the Use of the Licensed Program Materials on and in conjunction with the Equipment is permanently discontinued. Upon such consent being given the replacement equipment shall become the Equipment for the purposes of the Licence.

2.4 The Licensee shall not without the prior written consent of the Licensor Use the Licensed Program Materials in any location except the Location.

2.5 The Licence shall not be deemed to extend to any programs or materials of the Licensor other than the Licensed Program Materials unless specifically agreed to in writing by the Licensor.

2.6 The Licensee hereby acknowledges that it is licensed to Use the Licensed Program Materials only in accordance with the express terms of this Agreement and not further or otherwise.

3. TERM

The Licence shall commence on the Acceptance Date and shall continue [for a period of (insert number of years)] from year to year thereafter until or unless terminated in accordance with any of the provisions of CLAUSE 16or any other clause of this Agreement.[3]

4. PAYMENT

4.1 The Licence Fee shall be paid by the Licensee as provided in SCHEDULE C.[4]

4.2 The Licence Fee and other charges payable under this Agreement are exclusive of any applicable VAT and other sales tax which shall be payable by the Licensee at the rate and in the manner prescribed by law against submission of a valid tax invoice.

4.3 Any charges payable by the Licensee under this Agreement in addition to the Licence Fee shall be paid within [30] days after the receipt by the Licensee of the Licensor's invoice therefor.

4.4   The Licensor shall have the right to charge interest on overdue invoices at the rate of [4%][5] per annum above the base rate of (insert name of bank) Bank Plc, calculated from the date when payment of the invoice becomes due for payment up to and including the date of actual payment whether before or after judgment.

5.   DELIVERY AND INSTALLATION

On the Delivery Date the Licensor shall deliver the Licensed Program Materials to the Licensee and install the Licensed Programs on the Equipment at the Location.[6] The Licensed Programs so delivered shall consist of one copy of the object code of the Licensed Programs in machine-readable form only, on the Media.[7]

6.   RISK

Risk in the Media shall pass to the Licensee on delivery. If any part of the Media shall thereafter be lost, destroyed or damaged the Licensor shall promptly replace the same (embodying the relevant part of the Licensed Programs or Program Documentation) subject to the Licensee paying the cost of such replacement.

7.   TESTING AND ACCEPTANCE

7.1   The Licensee shall supply to the Licensor immediately after installation of the Licensed Programs, test data which in the reasonable opinion of the parties is suitable to test whether the Licensed Programs are in accordance with the Specification, together with the results expected to be achieved by processing such test data using the Licensed Programs. The Licensor shall not be entitled to object to such test data or expected results unless the Licensor can demonstrate to the Licensee that they are not suitable for testing the Licensed Programs as aforesaid, in which event the Licensee shall make any reasonable amendments to such test data and expected results as the Licensor may request. Subject to the receipt of such test data and expected results, the Licensor shall process such data, in the presence of the Licensee or its authorised representative, on the Equipment using the Licensed Programs by way of acceptance testing within [7] days after such receipt at a time mutually convenient to both parties.

7.2   The Licensee shall accept the Licensed Programs immediately after the Licensor has demonstrated that the Licensed Programs have correctly processed the test data by achieving the expected results.

7.3   In the event of failure of the Licensed Programs to pass the tests referred to in CLAUSE 7.1 the Licensor shall and in any event not later than [3] days following notification of the relevant failure at its own expense correct the errors in the Licensed Programs and notify the Licensee that it is ready to repeat the tests and such tests shall be repeated within [7] days after such notice at a time mutually convenient to both parties.

7.4 In the event of failure of the Licensed Programs to pass the repeat tests referred to in CLAUSE 7.3 the Licensee shall be entitled to terminate this Agreement or, by notice to the Licensor within [3] days require the Licensor to correct the errors in the Licensed Programs in which event the provisions of CLAUSE 7.3 shall, mutatis mutandis, apply.

7.5 Notwithstanding the above, installation of the Licensed Programs shall be deemed to be completed and the Licensed Programs shall be deemed to be accepted upon successful execution of the tests referred to above or when the Licensed Programs have been put into operational use, whichever is the earlier.

8. COPYING

8.1 The Licensee may make only so many copies of the Licensed Programs as are reasonably necessary for operational security and use.[8] Such copies and the media on which they are stored shall be the property of the Licensor and the Licensee shall ensure that all such copies bear the Licensor's proprietary notice. The Licence shall apply to all such copies as it applies to the Licensed Programs.

8.2 No copies may be made of the Program Documentation without the prior written consent of the Licensor. The Licensor shall provide the Licensee with [2] copies of the Program Documentation containing sufficient information to enable proper use of all the facilities and functions set out in the Specification. If the Licensee requires further copies of the Program Documentation then these may be obtained under licence from the Licensor in accordance with its standard scale of charges from time to time in force.

9. RESTRICTIONS ON ALTERATIONS[9]

9.1 The parties acknowledge that the Licensed Programs are to be modified by the Licensor in order to integrate and operate with third party software as identified in SCHEDULE H.

9.2 Subject to CLAUSE 9.3, the Licensee undertakes not to translate, adapt, vary, modify, disassemble, decompile or reverse engineer the Licensed Program Materials without the Licensor's prior written consent.[10]

9.3 Notwithstanding CLAUSE 9.2, in the case of reverse analysis where permitted by applicable law, the Licensee may incidentally decompile the Licensed Programs only if it is essential to do so in order to achieve interoperability of the Licensed Programs with another software program or hardware ('Permitted Purpose') and provided the information obtained by the Licensee during such decompilation is only used for the Permitted Purpose and is not disclosed or communicated to any third party without the Licensor's prior written consent and is not used to create any software which is substantially similar to the expression of the Licensed Program Materials nor used in any manner which would be restricted by copyright.

9.4 Notwithstanding CLAUSE 9.3, the Licensee undertakes to first consult the Licensor regarding any data the Licensee requires in order to achieve interoperability or to deduce underlying ideas and principles so that the Licensor may consider making the same available to the Licensee (without the Licensee having to rely on CLAUSE 9.3) subject to the restrictions on disclosure set out in CLAUSE 9.3.

10. SECURITY AND CONTROL

The Licensee shall during the continuance of the Licence:

10.1 effect and maintain adequate security measures to safeguard the Licensed Program Materials from access or use by any unauthorised person;

10.2 retain the Licensed Program Materials and all copies thereof under the Licensee's effective control;

10.3 maintain a full and accurate record of the Licensee's copying and disclosure of the Licensed Program Materials and shall produce such record to the Licensor on request from time to time.

11. PROPRIETARY RIGHTS

11.1 The Licensed Program Materials and the Intellectual Property Rights of whatever nature in the Licensed Program Materials are and shall remain the property of the Licensor.

11.2 The Licensee shall notify the Licensor immediately if the Licensee becomes aware of any unauthorised use of the whole or any part of the Licensed Program Materials by any person.

12. INTELLECTUAL PROPERTY RIGHTS

12.1 The Licensor shall defend at its own expense any claim brought against the Licensee alleging that the Use of the Licensed Program Materials infringes the Intellectual Property Rights of a third party ('Intellectual Property Claim') and the Licensor shall pay all costs and damages awarded or agreed to in settlement of an Intellectual Property Claim provided that the Licensee:

12.1.1 furnishes the Licensor with prompt written notice of the Intellectual Property Claim;

12.1.2 provides the Licensor with reasonable assistance in respect of the Intellectual Property Claim;

12.1.3 gives to the Licensor the sole authority to defend or settle the Intellectual Property Claim.

12.2 If, in the Licensor's reasonable opinion, the use of the Licensed Program Materials are or may become the subject of an Intellectual Property Claim then the Licensor shall either:

12.2.1 obtain for the Licensee the right to continue using the Licensed Program Materials which are the subject of the Intellectual Property Claim; or

12.2.2 replace or modify the Licensed Program Materials which are the subject of the Intellectual Property Claim so they become non-infringing.

12.3 If the remedies set out in CLAUSE 12.2 above are not in the Licensor's opinion reasonably available, then the Licensee shall return the Licensed Program Materials which are the subject of the Intellectual Property Claim and the Licensor shall refund to the Licensee the corresponding portion of the Licence Fee, as normally depreciated, whereupon this Agreement shall immediately terminate.

12.4 The Licensor shall have no liability for any Intellectual Property Claim resulting from the Use of the Licensed Program Materials in combination with any equipment (other than the Equipment) or programs not supplied or approved by the Licensor or any modification of any item of the Licensed Programs by a party other than the Licensor or its authorised agent.

13. WARRANTIES[11]

13.1 The Licensor warrants that for [90] days following the Acceptance Date:

13.1.1 the Licensed Programs will provide the facilities and functions set out in the Specification when properly used on the Equipment;

13.1.2 the Program Documentation will provide adequate instructions to enable the Licensee to make proper use of such facilities and functions;

13.1.3 the Licensed Programs will operate fully with any third party software referred to in SCHEDULE H.

13.2 The Licensor warrants that in providing its obligations hereunder it will attain standards of care and skills as high as any currently available in the software industry and that all personnel will have qualifications and experience appropriate for the tasks to which they are allocated.

13.3 The Licensor shall ensure that itself and its servants, agents and sub-contractors take all reasonable precautions to ensure that no known viruses for which detection and antidote software is generally available are coded or introduced into the Licensed Program.

13.4 The Licensor warrants that neither the performance nor functionality of the Licensed Programs is affected by dates prior to, during and after the year 2000.

13.5 The Licensor warrants that regardless of whether or not or when the United Kingdom becomes a participating country in the process commonly known as European Monetary Union, the Licensed Programs:

13.5.1 are capable of performing all functions set out in its specification for any number of currencies and for any common currency adopted by members of the European Union ('the Euro');

13.5.2 will comply with all legal requirements now and hereafter applicable to the Euro in any jurisdiction including but not limited to the rules on conversion, triangulation and rounding set out in Council Regulation Number 1103/97 and any subsequent or similar regulation or law;

13.5.3 are capable of accepting displaying and printing and will incorporate in all relevant screen layouts all symbols and codes adopted by any government or any other European Union body in relation to the Euro or any other currency;

13.5.4 do and will comply with all laws and regulations applicable in the United Kingdom (including those applicable to the introduction of the Euro) or any country of the European Union.

13.6 If the Licensor receives written notice from the Licensee after the Acceptance Date of any breach of the said warranties then the Licensor shall at its own expense and within [4] weeks after receiving such notice remedy the defect or error in question.

13.7 When notifying a defect or error the Licensee shall (so far as it is able) provide the Licensor with a documented example of such defect or error.

13.8 The said warranties above shall be subject to the Licensee complying with its obligations under the terms of this Agreement and shall also be subject to the limits and exclusions of liability set out in CLAUSE 14 below. In particular, the said warranties shall not apply to the extent that any defect in the Licensed Programs arose or was exacerbated as a result of:

13.8.1 incorrect use, operation or corruption of the Licensed Programs;

13.8.2 any unauthorised modification or alteration of the Licensed Programs;

13.8.3 use of the Licensed Programs with other software or on equipment with which it is incompatible.

13.9 To the extent permitted by applicable law, the Licensor:

13.9.1 disclaims all other warranties with respect to the Licensed Programs, either express or implied, including but not limited to any implied warranties relating to quality, fitness for any particular purpose or ability to achieve a particular result;

13.9.2   makes no warranty that the Licensed Programs are error free or that its use will be uninterrupted and the Licensee acknowledges and agrees that the existence of such errors shall not constitute a breach of this Agreement;

13.9.3   does not give any warranty in respect of third party products listed in SCHEDULE H. The Licensor will pass on to the Licensee the benefit of any third party warranty supplied by a third party manufacturer or supplier.

14. LIABILITY

14.1   The Licensor shall during the term of this Agreement maintain employer's liability, third party liability, product liability and professional negligence insurance cover in respect of its liabilities arising out of or connected with this Agreement, such cover to be to a minimum value of [ONE MILLION POUNDS] and with an insurance company of repute. The Licensor shall on request supply copies of the relevant certificates of insurance to the Licensee as evidence that such policies remain in force. The Licensor undertakes to use reasonable commercial efforts to pursue claims under such insurance policies.

14.2   The Licensor shall indemnify the Licensee for personal injury or death caused by the negligence of its employees in connection with the performance of their duties hereunder or by defects in any product supplied pursuant to this Agreement.

14.3   The Licensor will indemnify the Licensee for direct damage to tangible property caused by the negligence of its employees in connection with the performance of their duties hereunder or by defects in any product supplied pursuant to this Agreement. The Licensor's total liability under this clause shall be limited to [£500,000] for any one event or series of connected events.

14.4   Save in respect of claims for death or personal injury arising from the Licensor's negligence, in no event will the Licensor be liable for any damages resulting from loss of data or use, lost profits, loss of anticipated savings, nor for any damages that are an indirect or secondary consequence of any act or omission of the Licensor whether such damages were reasonably foreseeable or actually foreseen.

14.5   Except as provided above in the case of personal injury, death and damage to tangible property, the Licensor's maximum liability to the Licensee under this Agreement or otherwise for any cause whatsoever (whether in the form of the additional cost of remedial services or otherwise) will be for direct costs and damages only and will be limited to the greater of:

14.5.1   the sum for which the Licensor carries comprehensive insurance cover pursuant to CLAUSE 14.1 above; or

14.5.2   a sum equivalent to the price paid to the Licensor for the products or services that are the subject of the Licensee's claim, plus damages limited to 25% of the same amount for any additional costs directly, reasonably and necessarily incurred by the Licensee in obtaining alternative products and/or services.

14.6   The parties hereby acknowledge and agree that the limitations contained in this CLAUSE 14 are reasonable in light of all the circumstance.[12]

14.7   The Licensee's statutory rights as a consumer (if any) are not affected. All liability that is not expressly assumed in this Agreement is hereby excluded. These limitations will apply regardless of the form of action, whether under statute, in contract or tort including negligence or any other form of action. For the purposes of this clause, the 'Licensor' includes its employees, sub-contractors and suppliers who shall all have the benefit of the limits and exclusions of liability set out above in terms of the Contracts (Rights of Third Parties) Act 1999. Nothing in this Agreement shall exclude or limit liability for fraudulent misrepresentation.

15.   CONFIDENTIAL INFORMATION

15.1   Both parties to this Agreement undertake, except as provided below, to treat as confidential and keep secret all information marked 'confidential' or which may reasonably be supposed to be confidential, including, without limitation, information contained or embodied in the Licensed Program Materials, the Specification and other information supplied by the Licensee or Licensor (in this Agreement collectively referred to as 'the Information') with the same degree of care as it employs with regard to its own confidential information of a like nature and in any event in accordance with best current commercial security practices, provided that, this clause shall not extend to any information which was rightfully in the possession of either party prior to the commencement of the negotiations leading to this Agreement or which is already public knowledge or becomes so at a future date (otherwise than as a result of a breach of this clause).

15.2   Both parties shall not without the prior written consent of the other party divulge any part of the Information to any person except:

15.2.1   to their own employees and then only to those employees who need to know the same;

15.2.2   to either parties' auditors, HM Inspector of Taxes, HM Customs and Excise, a court of competent jurisdiction, governmental body or applicable regulatory authority and any other persons or bodies having a right duty or obligation to know the business of the other party and then only in pursuance of such right duty or obligation;

15.2.3   any person who is for the time being appointed by either party to maintain the Equipment on which the Licensed Programs are for the time being used (in accordance with the terms of the Licence) and then only to the extent necessary to enable such person to properly maintain the Equipment.

15.3   Both parties undertake to ensure that persons and bodies referred to in CLAUSE 15.2 are made aware prior to the disclosure of any part of the Information that the same is confidential and that they owe a duty of confidence to the other party.

15.4   Each party to this Agreement shall promptly notify the other party if it becomes aware of any breach of confidence by any person to whom it divulges all or any part of the Information and shall give the other party all reasonable assistance in connection with any proceedings which the other party may institute against such person for breach of confidence.

15.5   The foregoing obligations as to confidentiality shall remain in full force and effect notwithstanding any termination of the Licence or this Agreement.

16. TERMINATION

16.1   The Licensee may terminate the Licence at any time by giving at least [30] days' prior written notice to the Licensor.

16.2   The Licensor may terminate the Licence forthwith on giving notice in writing to the Licensee if:

16.2.1   the Licensee commits any serious breach of any term of this Agreement and (in the case of a breach capable of being remedied) shall have failed, within [30] days after the receipt of a request in writing from the Licensor to do so, to remedy the breach (such request to contain a warning of the Licensor's intention to terminate); or

16.2.2   the Licensee permanently discontinues the use of the Licensed Program Materials.

16.3   Save as expressly provided in CLAUSE 16.2 or elsewhere in this Agreement the Licence may not be terminated.

16.4   Forthwith upon the termination of the Licence, the Licensee shall return to the Licensor the Licensed Program Materials and all copies of the whole or any part thereof or, if requested by the Licensor, shall destroy the same (in the case of the Licensed Programs by erasing them from the magnetic media on which they are stored) and certify in writing to the Licensor that they have been destroyed. PROVIDED THAT the Licensee may extract and store any Licensee data upon a separate media for continuity purposes.

16.5   Any termination of the Licence or this Agreement (howsoever occasioned) shall not affect any accrued rights or liabilities of either party nor shall it effect the coming into force or the continuance in force of any provision in this Agreement which is expressly or by implication intended to come into or continue in force on or after such termination.

17. DATA PROTECTION

The parties hereby undertake to comply with the provisions of the Data Protection Act 1998 and any related legislation insofar as the same relates to the provisions and obligations of this Agreement.[13]

18. INTERPRETATION

18.1 In this Agreement unless the context otherwise requires:

18.1.1 words importing any gender include every gender;

18.1.2 words importing the singular number include the plural number and vice versa;

18.1.3 words importing persons include firms, companies and corporations and vice versa;

18.1.4 references to numbered clauses and Schedules are references to the relevant clause in or Schedule to this Agreement;

18.1.5 reference in any Schedule to this Agreement to numbered paragraphs relate to the numbered paragraphs of that Schedule;

18.1.6 the headings to the clauses, Schedules and paragraphs of this Agreement will not affect the interpretation;

18.1.7 any reference to an enactment includes reference to that enactment as amended or replaced from time to time and to any subordinate legislation or byelaw made under that enactment;

18.1.8 any obligation on any party not to do or omit to do anything is to include an obligation not to allow that thing to be done or omitted to be done;

18.1.9 any party who agrees to do something will be deemed to fulfil that obligation if that party procures that it is done.

18.2 In the case of conflict or ambiguity between any provision contained in the body of this Agreement and any provision contained in any Schedule, the provision in the body of this Agreement shall take precedence.

19. AGENCY, PARTNERSHIP

This Agreement shall not constitute or imply any partnership, joint venture, agency, fiduciary relationship or other relationship between the parties other than the contractual relationship expressly provided for in this Agreement.

20. AMENDMENTS

This Agreement may not be released, discharged, supplemented, interpreted, amended, varied or modified in any manner except by an instrument in writing signed by a duly authorised officer or representative of each of the parties hereto.

21. ANNOUNCEMENTS

No party shall issue or make any public announcement or disclose any information regarding this Agreement unless prior written consent has been obtained from the other party.

22. ASSIGNMENT

22.1 This Agreement is personal to the parties and, subject to CLAUSE 22.2 below, neither this Agreement nor any rights, licenses or obligations under this Agreement, may be assigned by either party without the prior written approval of the other party.

22.2 Notwithstanding the foregoing, either party may assign this Agreement to any acquirer of all or of substantially all of such party's equity securities, assets or business relating to the subject matter of this Agreement or to any entity controlled by, that controls, or is under common control with a party to this Agreement. Any attempted assignment in violation of this clause will be void and without effect.

23. ENTIRE AGREEMENT

This Agreement supersedes all prior agreements, arrangements and undertakings between the parties and constitutes the entire agreement between the parties relating to the subject matter of this Agreement. However the obligations of the parties under any pre-existing non-disclosure agreement shall remain in full force and effect insofar as there is no conflict between the same. The parties confirm that they have not entered into this Agreement on the basis of any representation that is not expressly incorporated into this Agreement.

24. FORCE MAJEURE[14]

Neither party shall have any liability under or be deemed to be in breach of this Agreement for any delays or failures in performance of this Agreement which result from circumstances beyond the reasonable control of that party. If such circumstances continue for a continuous period of more than [6 months], either party may terminate this Agreement by written notice to the other party.

25. NOTICES

25.1 All notices hereunder shall be in writing.

25.2 Notices shall be deemed to have been duly given:

25.2.1   when delivered, if delivered by courier or other messenger (including registered mail) during normal business hours of the recipient; or

25.2.2   when sent, if transmitted by fax or e-mail and a successful transmission report or return receipt is generated; or

25.2.3   on the fifth business day following mailing, if mailed by national ordinary mail, postage pre-paid; or

25.2.4   on the tenth business day following mailing, if mailed by airmail, postage pre-paid, in each case addressed to the most recent address, e-mail address, or facsimile number notified to the other party.

26. SCHEDULES

The provisions of SCHEDULE[S] *(A–H)* to this Agreement shall form part of this Agreement as if set out here.[15]

27. SEVERANCE

If any provision of this Agreement is prohibited by law or judged by a court to be unlawful, void or unenforceable, the provision shall, to the extent required, be severed from this Agreement and rendered ineffective as far as possible without modifying the remaining provisions of this Agreement, and shall not in any way affect any other circumstances of or the validity or enforcement of this Agreement.

28. SUCCESSORS AND ASSIGNEES

28.1   This agreement shall be binding upon, and enure to the benefit of, the parties and their respective successors and permitted assignees, and references to a party in this Agreement shall include its successors and permitted assignees.

28.2   In this Agreement references to a party include references to a person:

28.2.1   who for the time being is entitled (by assignment, novation or otherwise) to that party's rights under this Agreement (or any interest in those rights); or

28.2.2   who, as administrator, liquidator or otherwise, is entitled to exercise those rights;

and in particular those references include a person to whom those rights (or any interest in those rights) are transferred or pass as a result of a merger, division, reconstruction or other reorganisation involving that party. For this purpose, references to a party's rights under this Agreement include any similar rights to which another person becomes entitled as a result of a novation of this Agreement.

29. WAIVER

No delay, neglect or forbearance on the part of either party in enforcing against the other party any term or condition of this Agreement shall either be or be deemed to be a waiver or in any way prejudice any right of that party under this Agreement. No right, power or remedy in this Agreement conferred upon or reserved for either party is exclusive of any other right, power or remedy available to that party.

30. COUNTERPARTS

This Agreement may be executed in any number of counterparts or duplicates, each of which shall be an original, and such counterparts or duplicates shall together constitute one and the same agreement.

31. TIME IS OF THE ESSENCE

Time shall be of the essence in this Agreement as regards any time, date or period mentioned in this agreement or subsequently substituted as a time, date or period by agreement in writing between the parties.

32. SUB-CONTRACTING

With the prior written consent of the Licensor (such consent not to be unreasonably withheld or delayed) the Licensee may perform any or all of its obligations under this Agreement through agents or sub-contractors, provided that the Licensee shall remain liable for such performance and shall indemnify the Licensor against any loss or damage suffered by the Licensor arising from any act or omission of such agents or sub-contractors.

33. LANGUAGE

This Agreement is made only in the English language. If there is any conflict in the meaning between the English language version of this Agreement and any version or translation of this Agreement in any other language, the English language version shall prevail.

34. COSTS AND EXPENSES

Each party shall bear its own legal costs and other costs and expenses arising in connection with the drafting, negotiation, execution and registration (if applicable) of this Agreement.

35. SET-OFF

Where either party has incurred any liability to the other party, whether under this Agreement or otherwise, and whether such liability is liquidated or unliquidated, each party may set-off the amount of such liability against any sum that would otherwise be due to the other party under this Agreement.

36. THIRD PARTIES[16]

Subject to CLAUSE 14.7 above, a person who is not a party to this Agreement has no right under the Contracts (Rights of Third Parties) Act 1999 to enforce any term of this Agreement but this does not affect any right or remedy of a third party which exists or is available apart from such Act.

37. PROPER LAW AND JURISDICTION[17]

37.1   This Agreement and all matters arising from it and any dispute resolutions referred to below shall be governed by and construed in accordance with English Law notwithstanding the conflict of law provisions and other mandatory legal provisions save that:

37.1.1   the Licensor shall have the right to sue to recover its fees in any jurisdiction in which the Licensee is operating or has assets, and

37.1.2   the Licensor shall have the right to sue for breach of its intellectual property rights and other proprietary information and trade secrets ('IPR') (whether in connection with this Agreement or otherwise) in any country where it believes that infringement or a breach of this Agreement relating to its IPR might be taking place. For the avoidance of doubt, the place of performance of this Agreement is agreed by the parties to be England.

37.2   Each party recognises that the other party's business relies upon the protection of its IPR and that in the event of a breach or threatened breach of IPR, the other party will be caused irreparable damage and such other party may therefore be entitled to injunctive or other equitable relief in order to prevent a breach or threatened breach of its IPR.

37.3   With respect to all other disputes which are not IPR related pursuant to CLAUSES 37.1 and 37.2 above and its special rules the following procedures in CLAUSES 37.3 to 37.6 shall apply. Where there is a dispute the aggrieved party shall notify the other party in writing of the nature of the dispute with as much detail as possible about the deficient performance of the other party. A representative from senior management ('representatives') of each of the parties shall meet in person or communicate by telephone within five business days of the date of the written notification in order to reach an agreement about the nature of the deficiency and the corrective action to be taken by the respective parties. The representatives shall produce a report about the nature of the dispute in detail to their respective boards and if no agreement is reached on corrective action, then the chief executives of each party shall meet in person or by telephone, to facilitate an agreement within five business days of a written notice by one to the other. If the dispute cannot be resolved at board level within a further five business days, or if the agreed upon completion dates in any written plan of corrective action are exceeded, either party may seek its legal remedies as provided below.

37.4   If the parties cannot resolve a dispute in accordance with the procedure in CLAUSE 37.3 above, then they shall with the assistance of the Centre for Alternative Dispute Solution, seek to resolve the dispute or difference amicably by using an Alternative Dispute Resolution ('ADR') procedure acceptable to both parties before pursuing any other remedies available to them. If either party fails or refuses to agree to or participate in the ADR procedure or if in any event the dispute or difference is not resolved to the satisfaction of both parties within [90] days after it has arisen, the matter shall be settled in accordance with the procedure below.

37.5   If the parties cannot resolve the dispute by the procedure set out above, the parties shall irrevocably submit to the exclusive jurisdiction of the Courts of England and Wales for the purposes of hearing and determining any dispute arising out of this Agreement.

37.6   [While the dispute resolution procedure above is in progress and any party has an obligation to make a payment to another party or to allow a credit in respect of such payment, the sum relating to the matter in dispute shall be paid into an interest bearing deposit account to be held in the names of the relevant parties at a clearing bank and such payment shall be a good discharge of the parties' payment obligations under this Agreement. Following resolution of the dispute, whether by mediation or legal proceedings, the sum held in such account shall be payable as determined in accordance with the mediation or legal proceedings, and the interest accrued shall be allocated between the parties pro rata according to the split of the principal sum as between the parties.]

38.   NON POACHING OF STAFF

The Licensee covenants with the Licensor that it shall not either during the term of this Agreement or within a period of 6 months thereafter directly or indirectly entice away or endeavour to entice away from the Licensor any person who has during the previous 12 months been employed by the Licensor to perform this Agreement.

39.   COMPLIANCE WITH RELEVANT LAW

[Both parties will comply with all applicable laws, rules and regulations in respect of all activities conducted under this Agreement.]

AS WITNESS etc

SCHEDULE A

THE EQUIPMENT

SCHEDULE B

LICENSED PROGRAMS

SCHEDULE C

LICENCE FEE

SCHEDULE D

DELIVERY DATE

SCHEDULE E

LOCATION

SCHEDULE F

MEDIA

SCHEDULE G

SPECIFICATION AND FUNCTIONALITY

SCHEDULE H

DETAILS OF THIRD PARTY SOFTWARE

(signatures of (or on behalf of) the parties)

1   It is worthwhile considering as to whether the parties to the contract are the correct contracting parties. Many providers 'ring fence' their intellectual property rights by placing ownership of software and other assets into non-trading holding companies which may be situated off-shore or in other jurisdictions separate from the jurisdiction in which the trading or supplying-provider company is actually based. If ownership of intellectual property rights and other assets are vested in such a manner, then the customer needs to be sure that the provider company with whom it is contracting is capable of making the guarantees and warranties in the agreement and is also in a position to control source code if it is placed in escrow. If the contracting provider's company is not the owner of the software then the customer may need to ask for some further assurances from the provider that the true owner of the software can provide the necessary escrow arrangements and performance warranties which only the true owner can give.

In the case of small software developers, often the developer company is no more than the corporate embodiment of one or two essential programmers and the customer may want to contract not only with the developer company, but also with its director/ shareholder programmers in order to obtain the maximum guarantees and warranties as to performance, quality and the like of the services being provided.

2   As a general rule, rights not granted expressly or by implication in the grant clause are not conveyed by the licence agreement. Of course, rights are sometimes conveyed and restrictions are fairly often located in other sections of a licence agreement. Also, additional rights may be conveyed verbally after contract execution, implied through the parties' course of dealing with one another, or added to a contract in an addendum.

3   The term of a software licence agreement may commence upon its execution, upon the delivery or installation of a product licensed under an agreement, or upon some other event. The term of a licence agreement in a major software transaction need not coincide with the term of the licence grant for software licensed under the agreement.

It is important to recognise that the term of a software licence agreement and the term of a licence grant for a particular program acquired pursuant to the agreement are separate but related topics in contract negotiations.

Licensees are well advised to co-ordinate the life of their software grant and the life of their agreement in a manner that makes sense in the transaction in question.

4   The amount(s) payable can be couched in various forms. For example, some software licence agreements require payment of a one-time, lump-sum licence fee. Others require annual or monthly licence fee payments. In development projects, payments may hinge on satisfaction of milestone requirements during the project. Some portion of a licence fee may be conditional upon acceptance. Countless payment schemes are used in different situations and the scheme employed helps to dictate the amount(s) payable at one or more points in time.

5   In certain jurisdictions excessive amounts of interest charged may be viewed as unreasonable, usury or a 'penalty' thus invalidating the provision.

6   As a general rule, the licensor will not specify in the licence agreement a firm delivery date or deadline, and the licensee must negotiate for clarification and written commitments on this point if it is important to him.

7   Licence grant provisions in software user licence agreements normally specify the number of copies of each program licensed.

8   In the United Kingdom restrictions on back-up are now invalid as a result of the Copyright (Computer Programs) Regulations 1992, SI 1992/3233 resulting from the European Union Directive on the legal protection of computer programs, 91/250 EEC OJ 1991 L122/42. The Regulations and the Directive are incorporated in an amendment to the Copyright Design and Patents Act 1988, s 50A, which states that a lawful acquirer, a licensee of the program, is permitted to carry out any form of copying which is necessary for the program to be used and in order to make a security back-up without having to obtain express consent. There is even a stated right that error correction will be permitted but this is only for the purpose of enabling the program to run correctly. It will not affect the requirement for maintenance and support contracts to be entered into.

9   If the user-licensee desires to make improvements to the licensed software, the grant clause should express the right to modify the program to make corrections and fix defects. Generally, the right to make changes in a program protected by copyright law is an exclusive right of the copyright owner.

10 Under English law reverse engineering or decompilation had previously been regarded as an infringement of copyright but S1 1992/3233, as a result of the European Directive on the legal protection of computer programs, 91/250 EEC OJ 1991 L122/42, now allows a lawful licensee to analyse the underlying code, copy and translate the program and investigate the functioning of the program in order to evaluate and understand its ideas and principles without the need to obtain consent of the copyright holder. Such analysis is only for the purpose of achieving interoperability of an independently created program with the licensed software subject to a number of conditions. This is an implied right that may not be excluded by licensing arrangements within the European Union.

11 There has already been much discussion as to whether or not software is 'goods' for the purposes of implied warranties under the Sale of Goods Act 1979, s 14 and on the whole, the more mass market the software, the more it is likely to be seen as 'goods'. The more the software is delivered on an integration and commission basis the more likely it is that the software will be treated as 'services', thereby weakening the degree of implied warranties.

In general the more that a customer negotiates extended warranties into a contract the more the supplier will seek to limit the impact of those warranties under the Limitation of Liability Clauses.

12 Since *St Albans City and District Council v International Computers Ltd* [1996] 4 All ER 481, CA, it has become clear that where a Customer suffers loss as a result of faulty software and no terms and conditions vary the implied terms of merchantability or fitness for purpose, then any attempt by the supplier to limit its liability for such loss below what is deemed to be a reasonable figure (perhaps such a figure being linked to the suppliers' insurance cover for such losses) will be unavailable or even void as an unfair contract term. As a consequence Customers are more likely now to demand that any limit of liability in favour of the supplier for losses other than indirect should be linked to a reasonable sum of at least £1,000,000 (the usual minimum limit for which insurance cover would be granted under a suitable policy). As to limitation of liability generally see Paragraph 89 [2619] ante.

However in *Watford Electronics Ltd v Sanderson CFL Ltd* [2001] EWCA Civ 317, [2001] 1 All ER (Comm) 696, CA, it was held that provisions in a contract for the supply of computer software that both excluded the supplier liability for indirect loss, as well as limiting the damages recoverable to the amount paid by the customer under the contract, satisfied the reasonable test under the Unfair Contract Terms Act 1977, s 11. On appeal the court decided that the contract had been negotiated between experienced businessmen of equal bargaining power and skill and as such, the supplier limitation clause was reasonable.

13 United Kingdom law requires any business which processes data about living individuals to be notified with the Data Protection Office. Under the Data Protection Act 1998, s 1(1) (the Act) data is defined as information which:

(a) is being processed by means of equipment operating automatically in response to instructions given for that purpose;

(b) is recorded with the intention that it should be processed by means of such equipment;

(c) is recorded as part of a relevant filing system or with the intention that it should form part of a relevant filing system; and

(d) does not fall within paragraph (a), (b) or (c) but forms part of an accessible record as defined in section 68 of the Act.

Accessible records are health records, educational records and accessible public records defined in SCHEDULE 12 to the Act.

14 This force majeure clause is short and general. It may be appropriate to insert a more detailed force majeure clause such as:

'Notwithstanding anything else contained in this Agreement, neither party shall be liable for any delay in performing its obligations hereunder if such delay is caused by circumstances beyond its reasonable control (including without limitation any delay caused by any act or omission of the other party) provided however that any delay by a sub-contractor or supplier of the party so delaying shall not relieve the party from liability for delay except where such delay is beyond the reasonable control of the sub-contractor or supplier concerned. Subject to the party so delaying promptly notifying the other party in writing of the reasons for the delay (and the likely duration of the delay), the performance of such party's obligations shall be suspended during the period that the said circumstances persist and such party shall be granted an extension of time for performance equal to the period of the delay. Save where such delay is caused by the act or omission of the other party (in which event the rights, remedies and liabilities of the parties shall be those conferred and imposed by the other terms of this Agreement and by law):

• any costs arising from such delay shall be borne by the party incurring the same;

• either party may, if such delay continues for more than 10 weeks,

terminate this Agreement forthwith giving notice in writing to the other by reason of such termination.'

15 As many contracts are varied or amended during their life cycle it is important that all Schedules are agreed to and signed or initialled by the parties so that there can be no dispute as to the totality of the contract and its contents.

16 Before the Contracts (Rights of Third Parties) Act 1999 (the Act) it was the case that a person who was not a party to a contract (a third party) could not enforce any right under the contract. Similarly, a contract could not impose any obligations or liabilities on a third party.

However the Act attempts to draw a balance between the freedom of the parties to vary a contract and the interests of the third party. The Act means that a contractual clause benefiting a third party (eg the promisee's subsidiary company or sub-contractor or employee) will be straightforwardly enforceable by that third party if:

- the contract expressly provides that he may; or
- where a term in the contract purports to confer a benefit on him (unless on a proper construction of the contract it appears that the parties did not intend the term to be enforceable by the third party.)

It is therefore prudent to include a clause to the effect of excluding the provisions of the Act. By doing so it ensures that any rights of third parties are not deemed to be enforceable by them. This is particularly the case where the parties are companies and may have subsidiaries or conversely parent companies.

17 An example of another dispute settlement clause is:

'Any dispute which may arise between the parties concerning this Agreement shall be determined as follows:

(1) If the dispute shall be of a technical nature relating to the functions or capabilities of the Licensed Program Materials or any similar or related matter then such a dispute shall be referred for final settlement to an expert nominated jointly by the parties or failing such nomination within Fourteen (14) days after either party's request to the other therefore nominated at the request of either party by the President for the time being of the British Computer Society. Such expert shall be deemed to act as an expert and not as an arbitrator. His decision shall (in the absence of clerical or manifest error) be final and binding on the parties and whose costs shall be borne between the parties in equal shares unless he determines that the conduct of either party is such that such party should bear all of such fees.

(2) In any other case the dispute shall be determined by the High Court of Justice in England and the parties hereby submit to the exclusive jurisdiction of that Court for such purposes.'

5 Software licence agreement checklist

Most of the time a Software Licence Agreement ('Agreement') is made for complex and costly services. Therefore it is important to carry out due diligence and a needs analysis. As part of this research you can use this checklist. This checklist is based on the assumption that you are the Licensee.

Scope of Licence/Use	Criteria to Apply
Appropriate Licensee Entities Covered	• Ensure that all entities (contemplating usage or needing access to the software are covered (including sites, affiliates, customers, vendors, etc. if appropriate). • As appropriate, licence should be multi-year or perpetual (in 'term' section of the Agreement). • If application is to be accessed over the Internet or via other externally hosted environment, special care must be taken for issues of content ownership, security and system back-up/business interruption.
Exclusive/non-exclusive	• Software was uniquely developed for you, the Licence grant should be exclusive. For standard of 'off the shelf' software, non-exclusive will suffice.
Appropriate Geography Covered	• The geographic area in which the software will be used must be authorised in the Agreement. • Other optional descriptions include 'Domestic' or 'International', as applicable.
Appropriate Languages Covered	• The applicable language should be identified.
Transferable	• As appropriate licence should be transferable.
Appropriate Modules/Functionality Covered	• The functionality that you are licensing must be listed and described in detail, most often as comprehensive attachments to the licence.

Scope of Licence/Use	Criteria to Apply
	• Options for attachments that describe functionality include: RFP responses; product literature or brochures; minutes from appropriate meetings; hardware/non-functional specs. • Scope of use should be broad enough (eg seats/users, countries) to cover anticipated use. • As appropriate licence (or the service agreement) must include upgrades, updates and new versions. • As appropriate licence should include access to source codes (subject to release upon triggering events) without limitations (escrow).
Appropriate Materials/Devices/Media Covered	
Licence Covers Custom Deliverables Generated from Licensor Services	• Licensee to have the right to customise and combine the software with other products. • Design and functionality of custom deliverables must be defined in detail. • Whenever possible deliverables should be included in software upgrades, system maintenance, and pricing considerations (when re-use/resale of custom work/enhancements is possible). • Deliverables, they must be included in any software escrow (source code). • Finally, intellectual property ownership of custom work/enhancements must be clearly defined (including, when appropriate, rights to sub license, proper assignment of intellectual property, waiver of moral rights).
Adequate Quantity of Copies Provided	• Quantity of software copies should include a minimum of 2 copies per 'entity' operating the software. • One copy for non-production, back-up purposes; one copy as 'pilot' to test functionality (especially, newly added functionality/enhancements/customisations). • These are minimum recommendations; additional copies may be appropriate.
Acceptable Method and Definition of Delivery	• Delivery must be clearly defined (eg when, how, who) as it is typically the milestone that 'starts-the-clock' for items such as payment, warranty, etc. • Delivery must include a successful installation and operational test of the software on your environment (acceptance criteria). Such environment should be that recommended and warranted by vendor.

Scope of Licence/Use	Criteria to Apply
	• It is vital that Delivery includes as much of the functionality as possible. • If the need for multiple deliveries exists, that should be reflected on attendant payments and warranty schedules. • Ensure that internal team recognises significance of delivery, and is properly prepared.
Licence Extends to Appropriate Data (eg Non-Licensee)	• Ensure there are not restrictive (or contravening) covenants regarding what data can reside on/pass through the system (eg non-licence third party vendors). • Additionally, allowances for use of such data by third party may be needed.
Product Specs/Configs Attached and Incorporated into Agreement	• Non-functional specifications (hardware requirements, additional third party software, etc) must be clearly outlined and warranted by vendor, and made a part of the Agreement.
Web Enabled Version/Internet Use/ Firewall Responsibility	• Special care in the Agreement for web/ internet versions in the areas of firewall responsibility, general security, content ownership, etc.
Licence Fees	
Rate is Reasonable/Discount off Retail	• Pursue aggressive discounting with MFN (Most Favoured Nation) clauses; the right to audit pricing of vendor's client base at large; lock-down price for future functionality at current discount and pricing for minimum of one year. Keep in mind enhancement/ customisations and their ownership, re-sale value, pricing.
Most Favoured Nation Pricing	• Question whether the Vendor has offered better pricing to others and add language warranting that you are in receipt of the best pricing offered by vendor.
Lock for 12 Months on Pricing of Future Modules	• Include language that locks in pricing for additional Vendor modules for reasonable time period (eg one year).
Fee Includes Pre-Go-Live Fixes	• Vendor should warrant that all fixes prior to end of software acceptance period/'Go-Live' shall be provided at no additional charge.
Payment of Fee Tied to Key Milestones	• All payments should be tied to key (successful) milestones. For example: significant portion of licence fees within 'x' days of 'Delivery'.

Scope of Licence/Use	Criteria to Apply
Late Payment Terms are Reasonable	• Keep late payment terms to a minimum, and only for items not disputed.
Late Payment Only Applies Where Fees are Not in Dispute	• Late payment terms are only applicable when fees are not in dispute.
Warranty	
Licensor has Ownership, Title, and Right to License in Geography	• Vendor must warrant that it possesses undisputed ownership of the software (or right to license) and all items licensed (non-infringement and right to license).
Product Will Operate Per Published Specs (attached to Agreement)	• Warranty must include operability of functionality licensed. This functionality must be clearly defined and made part of the Agreement. • Further, warranty provisions should apply to all enhancements and customisation to the software. • Non-functional specs (hardware, third party software, etc) should be representative of client environment and warranted by Vendor.
No Bugs, Trojan Horses, Back Doors, Worms, Time Bombs, etc...	• Vendor must warrant that there are no disabling devices resident in software.
Term is Reasonable and Extends for Reasonable Period After Go-Live	• Ensure that warranty terms is long enough after 'go-live', and will be suspended (and extended accordingly) until any critical defects are repaired. • Ensure adequate additional remedies are available in the event of failure to cure defects (especially critical defects).
Types of Defects are Categorised (critical v non-critical)	• Add a table that describes the various levels and categories of defects, including 'system halting' and other terms of art.
Clarity of Required Response and Response Time for Each Category	• Clearly define type of response and response times required to address each type of defect. • Ensure adequate notice procedures for defects are in place.
Warranty Period Suspended While Critical Defects are Repaired	• Add language that suspends the warranty period for as long as a critical defect exists and remains uncured.
Reasonable and Clear Warranty Exclusion	• Ensure clear language around warranty exclusions (eg solely caused or under the exclusive control of Licensee; amount unpaid are 'undisputed'; functionality/operability outside the scope of the published specs).

Scope of Licence/Use	Criteria to Apply
Remedies	
Adequate Remedy for Failure to Cure Categorised Defects	• Tie specific remedies to each category of defect that remains uncured.
Recovery of Fees Upon Failure to Cure Critical Defect	• Require sufficient fee recovery (eg 2x fees) for failure to remedy 'critical defects'. Further protection via insurance or Vendor liability may be appropriate for business interruption concerns.
Indemnity Conditions are Reasonable	• Ensure a strong indemnification provision which includes replacement of infringing components or whole systems; right to choose defence strategy (vendor pays legal fees); adequate notice by vendor in the event of infringement; indemnification for personal injury and property damage (data loss); etc
Maintenance **(If Maintenance is in Scope of Agreement)**	
Verify Consistency with Warranty Section	• If Maintenance services are referenced in the Agreement, ensure consistency of timing, fees, service levels, etc.
Scope of Maintenance Services is Clear and Adequate	• Insist on tight language around maintenance services and levels. • For example, application may require 24hr availability for mission criticality. • Clearly delineate maintenance level responses tied to criticality of problem. • Error resolution by telephone, email, etc. • Tie penalties to non-compliance. • Maintenance (or the licence) should include systems fixes, enhancements and upgrades, new versions made generally available to clients. • Further, include a clear pathway for maintenance of client specific custom work and enhancements along with reasonable platform migration (eg Client Server to internet) if desired.
Coverage Period Reasonable and Adequate	• Include language that adequately cover the timeline of your business operations and requirements (commitment of maintenance for a certain period of time). • Ensure that warranty claims are not paid for under the maintenance agreement (unless warranty has expired).
Term Commences on Go-Live	• Ensure that term commences upon 'go-live'/ system acceptance versus Delivery of software.

Scope of Licence/Use	Criteria to Apply
	• If significant enhancements are being delivered incrementally, build pricing/term of maintenance to reflect their delivery timeline.
Fee is Reasonable (15–18%)	• Keep fees as reasonable percentage of licence fees. If possible apply percentage to discounted licence fees with first payment on go-live date.
First Payment Only Upon Go-Live	• Require first maintenance payment only upon go-live date. • If feasible, a multi-year payment scheme may be appropriate to secure greater discounting.
Fee Increase	• Keep annual increased capped or linked to a suitable index (eg RPI)
Delivery and Receipt of Maintenance Services is Reasonable	• If desire, use language that requires a periodic maintenance log from vendor to corroborate the maintenance services received.
Licensee May Cancel with Reasonable Notice with Pro-Rata Rebate	• Ensure provision for reasonable cancellation of maintenance services, to include a pro-rata refund for all pre-paid fees.
Licensor is Locked In and May Not Cancel for Reasonable Period	• Ensure the maintenance agreement has specific renewal provisions, versus an 'evergreen' auto-renewing dynamic • Preferably the renewal should be annual and without any significant administrative burden.
Reinstatement Fee is Reasonable	• Ensure a reasonable maintenance reinstatement dynamic is in effect. • For example, if there has been no significant software updates by vendor, reinstatement should be minimum. • At maximum, reinstatement should only require approximately three months value of back fees.
Enhancements	
Automatic Updates for Regulated Information Without Charge	• Include language for system enhancements provided to vendor's client base to be included in updates (at your option) received under maintenance agreement. • There should be no additional charge for these enhancements. • Additionally, ensure that enhancements/ customisation you are installing are considered as part of Maintenance Agreement. • Further, any significant technology migration should be priced reasonably (MFN)

Scope of Licence/Use	Criteria to Apply
Migration to New Platform Allowed	• Migration to new platform should be allowed and should be priced reasonably.
Training	
Scope of Training Clearly Defined/ Menu of Options Attached	•
Fee/Cost Structure Fixed and Clearly Defined	•
Payment Terms Reasonable and Clearly Defined	•
Training Location Clearly Defined	•
Training Materials Clearly Defined and Adequate	•
Indemnity for Infringement for Training and Materials	•
Warranty for Skilled Trainers	•
Licensee May Pre-Approve Trainer's Quals and Require Replacement	• Add language that enables you to review and pre-approve any training staff assigned to your implementation.
Most Favoured Nation Pricing/Lock in for Additional Training Fees	•
Consulting Services	
Scope of Services Clearly Defined	•
Deliverables Clearly Defined	•
Fee is Fixed and Clearly Defined	•
Payment Tied to Milestones	•
Warranty for Skilled Staff	•
Licensee May Pre-Approve Staff Qualifications and Require Replacement	•
General Provisions	
Assignment Provision Reasonably Allows Licensee for Assignment	•
Confidentiality/NDA	• Agree on a separate confidentiality and/or non disclosure agreement including employee compliance statement.

Scope of Licence/Use	Criteria to Apply
Ownership Data Defined and Adequate	• In principle all Intellectual Property rights in the data such as copyrights and database rights, should belong to you.
Limitation of Liability Licensor Acceptable	•
Insurance Requirements Licensor Defined and Adequate	•
Non-Solicitation Acceptable	•
Payment term Defined and Acceptable (See Licence Fee)	•
Tax Provision Defined, Acceptable and Adequate	• If necessary, discuss tax implications with advisors.
Force Majeure Defined and Acceptable	•
Compliance with Applicable Laws Defined	•
Publicity Defined and Acceptable	•
Termination by Licensee Reasonable/Rights and Effects (Obligations) Clear	•
Termination by Licensor Reasonable/Rights and Effects (Obligations) Clear	•
Survival of Appropriate Post-Term Covenants Defined	•
Governing Law Defined and Acceptable	•
Dispute Resolution Defined and Acceptable	• If and where possible, mediation clauses should be part of the agreement.
Notices	•
Export Control and Rights Provisions Defined and Acceptable	•
Most Favoured Terms Clause Defined and Adequate	•

6 Software support and maintenance agreement[1]

THIS AGREEMENT is made on the [ ] day of [ ]

BETWEEN

(1)   (*licensor*) whose [registered office *or* principal place of business] is at (*address*) and whose facsimile ('fax') number is (*number*) ('the Licensor')

(2)   (*licensee*) whose [registered office *or* principal place of business] is at (*address*) and whose facsimile ('fax') number is (*number*) ('the Licensee')

RECITALS

A.   The Licensor has developed and owns, or has licensed from third parties, certain computer software applications and has granted to the Licensee a non-exclusive licence to use such programs and their associated documentation under an agreement dated (*date*) ('the Agreement')

B.   The Licensor has agreed to provide to the Licensee certain services in respect of the support and maintenance of the computer software applications, and the computer hardware equipment upon which such applications are installed, on the terms and conditions set out in this Agreement.

NOW IT IS AGREED as follows:

1.   DEFINITIONS

In this Agreement, unless inconsistent with the context or otherwise specified the following definitions will apply:

1.1   **'Basic Enhancements'** means changes or additions to the Licensed Programs, including any Error Corrections, which are logical improvements to the Licensed Programs. Basic Enhancements include only those improvements that are generally made available at no additional cost to Licensor's customers that purchase annual Maintenance.

1.2   **'Commencement Date'** means the date from which support and maintenance services shall begin for each element of the Supported Software.

1.3   **'Documentation'** means the operating manuals, user instructions, technical literature and all other related materials in eye-readable form supplied to the Licensee by the Licensor for aiding the use and application of the Supported Software.

1.4   **'Equipment'** means such computer equipment on which the Supported Software is installed and in operational use.

1.5   **'Error'** means any failure of the Licensed Programs to substantially conform to the specifications included in the Documentation.

1.6   **'Error Correction'** means a software modification or addition that, when made or added to the Licensed Programs, establishes material conformity to the specifications in the Documentation.

1.7   **'the Licensed Program Materials'** means the Licensed Programs, the Documentation, and the Media.

1.8   **'the Licensed Programs'** means the systems, applications and computer programs of the Licensor specified in SCHEDULE A, and all releases and versions thereof.

1.9   **'the Location'** means the Licensee's premises where the Equipment is to be installed as specified in SCHEDULE D.

1.10   **'Maintenance Charge'** means the fee for Maintenance Services to be provided under this Agreement and specified in SCHEDULE C.

1.11   **'Maintenance Services'** means the maintenance services to be provided by the Licensor including analysis, coding, testing, and release of corrections to software faults. Maintenance shall be within reasonable limits, as determined by the Licensor, and does not include requests for basic product training or technical consulting.

1.12   **'Major Enhancements'** means changes or additions to the Licensed Programs, other than an Error Correction or Basic Enhancement, that (i) contain significant new features; (ii) may be priced and offered separately as optional additions to the Licensed Programs; and (iii) are not made available to customers that purchase annual Maintenance Services from the Licensor without separate charge.

1.13   **'the Media'** means the media on which the Licensed Programs and the Documentation are recorded or printed, as provided to the Licensee by the Licensor and specified in SCHEDULE E.

1.14   **'the Normal Support Hours'** means from Monday through to Friday and from 09.00 to 17.30 (excluding national holidays).

1.15   **'Specification'** means the specification of the Licensed Programs describing the facilities and functions thereof, a copy of which is annexed to this Agreement as SCHEDULE A.

1.16   **'Supported Software'** means the Licensed Programs together with any releases or enhancements of software that have been made generally available to the Licensee during the preceding two years.

1.17   **'Support Fee'** means the fee for the Support Services to be provided under this Agreement and specified in SCHEDULE C.

1.18   **'Support'** means support services to be provided by the Licensor in respect of the Licensed Programs and available for the continuance of this Agreement.

1.19   **'Training'** means the programme of training of the Licensee's employees specified in SCHEDULE G.

1.20   **'Use the Licensed Program Materials'** means to Use the Licensed Programs, to read and possess the Documentation in conjunction with the use of the Licensed Programs and to possess the Media.

1.21   **'Use the Licensed Programs'** means to read all or any part of the Licensed Programs from magnetic or other storage media and to load the Licensed Programs on the Equipment for the storage and running of the Licensed Programs.

2. SERVICES TO BE PROVIDED

2.1   The Licensor hereby agrees to:

2.1.1   provide the Support to the Licensee;

2.1.2   provide the Maintenance Services for the Licensee;

2.1.3   provide training and operating manuals to the Licensee, if appropriate;

2.1.4   provide the other services hereinafter described upon the terms and conditions contained in this Agreement.[1]

3. TERM

The Support and the Maintenance Services shall commence on the Commencement Date and shall remain in force from year to year thereafter, unless and until terminated in accordance with any of the provisions of CLAUSE 15 or any other clause of this Agreement.[2]

4. PAYMENT

4.1   The Support Fee shall be paid by the Licensee on the Commencement Date as provided in SCHEDULE C.

4.2   The Licensee shall pay the Maintenance Charge (being non-refundable) periodically in advance in the manner as specified in SCHEDULE C. NO support shall be provided until payment has been received by the Licensor.

4.3   Any charges payable by the Licensee under this Agreement in addition to the Support Fee and Maintenance Charge shall be paid within 30 days after the receipt by the Licensee of the Licensor's invoice.

4.4   The Support Fee and Maintenance Charge and other charges payable under this Agreement are exclusive of VAT, which shall be payable by the Licensee at the rate and in the same manner for the time being prescribed by law against submission of a valid tax invoice.

4.5   The Licensor shall have the right to charge interest on overdue invoices at the rate of 4% per annum above the base rate of (specify bank), calculated from the date when payment of the invoice becomes due for payment up to and including the date of actual payment, whether before or after judgment.

4.6   The Licensor shall be entitled at any time, and from time to time, to increase the Maintenance Charge to accord with any change in the Licensor's standard scale of charges by giving to the client not less than 90 days' prior written notice.

5.   RISK

Risk in the Media shall pass to the Licensee on delivery.[3] If any part of the Media shall thereafter be lost, destroyed or damaged the Licensor shall promptly replace the same (embodying the relevant part of the Licensed Programs or Documentation) at no cost. The Licensor shall not make any further or additional charge for such replacement.

6.   SUPPORT

6.1   During the continuance of this Agreement, the Licensor shall provide the Licensee with all or any of the following Support Services:

   6.1.1   Hotline Support. For an urgent problem, the Licensee can telephone or fax the Licensor's Hotline which is available during the Normal Support Hours. An urgent problem is degradation or failure of the System, defective Software distribution media, or Software performance inconsistent with documentation. Problems which do not delay or inhibit system operation will be handled by written reports.

   6.1.2   On-site Support will be provided by the Licensor if specified in the Schedule and where appropriate in the event that telephone Support does not resolve a Software problem.

   6.1.3   Modem Support. The Licensor shall, where specified in the Schedule, supply on loan a modem for on-line problem resolution.

   6.1.4   Out-of-Hours Support shall, where specified in the Schedule, be provided by the Licensor.

   6.1.5   Correction of critical errors or assistance to overcome specific Software problems. The Licensor may, in its sole discretion, correct errors by 'patch' or by new version.

   6.1.6   Information on availability of new versions of Software.

6.1.7   Consultancy advice on Software development, enhancements and modifications, together with estimates for the same.

6.2   The Licensee shall supply in writing to the Licensor a detailed description of any fault requiring support services in CLAUSE 6.1 and the circumstances in which it arose, and shall submit sufficient material and information to enable the Licensor's support staff to duplicate the problem.

6.3   When appropriate, the Licensor will endeavour to give an estimate of how long a problem may take to resolve. The Licensor will keep the Licensee informed of the progress of problem resolution. The Licensor's support staff will attempt to solve a problem immediately, or as soon thereafter as possible and the response times shall be either:

6.3.1   basic service: between Monday to Friday from 09.00 to 17.30 (excluding national holidays) the Licensor shall use its reasonable endeavours to respond within [10] hours of receipt of a request; or

6.3.2   quick service: between Monday to [Saturday] from 09.00 to 17.30 (excluding national holidays) the Licensor shall use its reasonable endeavours to respond within [4] hours of receipt of a request.

7.   MAINTENANCE

During the continuance of this Agreement the Licensor shall provide the Licensee with the following maintenance services:

7.1   Error Correction

7.1.1   If the Licensee shall discover that a current release fails to perform in accordance with the Documentation, then the Licensee shall, within fourteen days after such discovery, notify the Licensor in writing of the defect or error in question and provide the Licensor (so far as the Licensee is able) with a documented example of such defect or error.

7.1.2   The Licensor shall thereupon use its reasonable endeavours to correct promptly such defect or error. Forthwith upon such correction being completed, the Licensor shall deliver to the Licensee the corrected version of the object code of the current release in machine readable form, together with the appropriate amendments (if any) to the Documentation, specifying the nature of the correction and providing instructions for the proper use of the corrected version of the current release. The Licensor shall provide the Licensee with all assistance reasonably required by the Licensee to enable the Licensee to implement the use of the corrected version of the current release.

7.1.3   The foregoing error correction service shall not include service in respect of:

7.1.3.1   defects or errors resulting from any modifications of the current release made by any person other than the Licensor;[4]

7.1.3.2   any version of the Licensed Programs other than the current release or the immediate current release;

7.1.3.3   incorrect use of the current release or operator error;

7.1.3.4   any fault in the Equipment or in any programs used in conjunction with the current release;

7.1.3.5   defects or errors caused by the use of the current release on or with equipment (other than the Equipment) or programs not supplied by or approved in writing by the Licensor, provided that for this purpose any programs designated for use with the current release in the Specification shall be deemed to have the written approval of the Licensor;

7.1.4   The Licensor shall make an additional charge in accordance with its standard scale of charges for the time being in force for any services provided by the Licensor:

7.1.4.1   at the request of the Licensee, but which do not qualify under the aforesaid error correction service by virtue of any of the exclusions referred to in CLAUSE 7.1.3 above; or

7.1.4.2   at the request of the Licensee but which the Licensor finds are not necessary. For the avoidance of doubt nothing in this paragraph shall impose any obligation on the Licensor to provide services in respect of any of the exclusions referred to in CLAUSE 7.1.3.

7.2   Releases

7.2.1   The Licensor shall promptly notify the Licensee of any improved version of the Licensed Programs that the Licensor shall from time to time make.

7.2.2   Upon receipt of such notification, the Licensor shall deliver to the Licensee as soon as reasonably practicable (having regard to the number of other users requiring the new release) the object code of the new release in machine-readable form together with the Documentation.

7.2.3   If required by the Licensee, the Licensor shall provide training for the Licensee's staff in the use of the new release at the Licensor's standard scale of charges for the time being in force as soon as reasonably practicable after the delivery of any new release.

7.2.4   The new release shall thereby become the current release and the provisions of this Agreement shall apply accordingly.

7.3   Advice

The Licensor will provide the Licensee with such technical advice by telephone, telex, facsimile transmission or mail (including electronic mail), as shall be necessary to resolve the Licensee's difficulties and queries in using the current release.

7.4   Changes in law

The Licensor will from time to time make such modifications to the current release as shall ensure that the current release conforms to any change of legislation or new legal requirements which affect the application of any function or facility described in the Documentation. The Licensor shall promptly notify the Licensee in writing of all such changes and new requirements and shall implement the modifications to the current release (and all consequential amendments to the Documentation which may be necessary to enable proper use of such modifications) as soon as reasonably practicable thereafter.

8.   EXCLUDED SUPPORT AND MAINTENANCE

8.1   The Licensor shall be under no obligation to provide Support and Maintenance in respect of:

8.1.1   problems resulting from any modifications or customisation of the Licensed Program Materials or the Equipment not authorised in writing by the Licensor. For the avoidance of doubt, modifications to the Licensed Program Materials shall include but not be limited to changes to the logical or physical database schema for the Licensed Program Materials, changes to the disk layout and configuration, and hand-modified changes to the data within the database;

8.1.2   any software other than the Licensed Program Materials;

8.1.3   incorrect or unauthorised use of the Licensed Program Materials or operator error where these are defined as use or operation not in accordance with the Documentation;

8.1.4   any fault in the Equipment;

8.1.5   any programs used in conjunction with the Licensed Program Materials;

8.1.6   use of the elements of the Licensed Program Materials in any combination other than those specified in the Documentation;

8.1.7   use of the Licensed Program Materials with computer hardware, operating systems or other supporting software other those specified in the Documentation; and

8.1.8   the Licensee's failure to install and use upon the Equipment in substitution for the previous release and new release of the Licensed Programs within [7] days of receipt of the same.

8.2 The Licensor shall upon request by the Licensee provide Support and Maintenance notwithstanding that the fault results from any of the circumstances described in CLAUSE 8.1 above. Any time spent by the Licensor investigating such faults will be chargeable at the Licensor's then current rates. The Licensor shall invoice such charges at its discretion and such shall be paid within 30 days of the date of said invoice.

8.3 The Licensor reserves the right to discontinue the Support and the Maintenance for any prior version of the Supported Software if a superseding version has been available to the Licensee.

8.4 The Licensor shall not be obliged to make modifications or provide support in relation to the Licensee's computer hardware, operating system software, or third party application software or any data feeds or external data.

9. WARRANTY

9.1 The Licensor warrants to the Licensee that all services supplied under this Agreement will be carried out with reasonable care and skill by personnel whose qualifications and experience will be appropriate for the tasks to which they are allocated.

9.2 The Licensee acknowledges that it is the responsibility of the Licensee to ensure that the facilities and functions described in the Specification meet its requirements.

9.3 Except as expressly provided in this Agreement, no warranty, condition, undertaking or term, express or implied, statutory or otherwise, as to the satisfactory quality, fitness for purpose, or ability to achieve a particular result, of the Licensed Program Materials is given or assumed by the Licensor, and all such warranties, conditions, undertakings and terms are hereby excluded.

9.4 The Licensee hereby agrees that its sole remedy in respect of any non-conformance with any warranty in this Agreement is that the Licensor will remedy such non-conformance (either by itself or through a third party) and if, in the Licensor's reasonable opinion, it is unable to remedy such non-conformance, the Licensor will refund the [Support Fee or Maintenance Charge] for the year in which the services, the subject of such claim, were supplied, if paid, whereupon this Agreement shall immediately terminate.

9.5 The Licensor does not warrant that all Errors can and will be corrected. The Licensor shall use its reasonable endeavours to correct errors in the Licensed Programs, so long as the Errors are repeatable by the Licensor, or to provide a software patch; or to bypass around such Error.

9.6 The Licensee must promptly notify the Licensor of any non-conformance to the above warranties in order to benefit from the remedy stated above, and in any event within three months.

10. LIABILITY[5]

10.1 [The Licensor shall during the term of this Agreement, maintain employer's liability, third party liability, product liability and professional negligence insurance cover in respect of its liabilities arising out of or connected with this Agreement, such cover to be to a minimum value of one million pounds and with an insurance company of repute. The Licensor shall on request supply copies of the relevant certificates of insurance to the Licensee as evidence that such policies remain in force. The Licensor undertakes to use reasonable commercial efforts to pursue claims under such insurance policies.]

10.2 The Licensor shall indemnify the Licensee for personal injury or death caused by the negligence of its employees in connection with the performance of their duties hereunder or by defects in any product supplied pursuant to this Agreement.

10.3 The Licensor will indemnify the Licensee for direct damage to tangible property caused by the negligence of its employees in connection with the performance of their duties under this agreement or by defects in any product supplied pursuant to this Agreement. The Licensor's total liability under this clause shall be limited to £500,000 for any one event or series of connected events.

10.4 Save in respect of claims for death or personal injury arising from the Licensor's negligence, in no event will the Licensor be liable for any damages resulting from loss of data or use, lost profits, loss of anticipated savings, nor for any damages that are an indirect or secondary consequence of any act or omission of the Licensor, whether such damages were reasonably foreseeable or actually foreseen.

10.5 Except as provided above in the case of personal injury, death and damage to tangible property, the Licensor's maximum liability to the Licensee under this Agreement or otherwise for any cause whatsoever (whether in the form of the additional cost of remedial services or otherwise) will be for direct costs and damages only and will be limited to the greater of:

10.5.1 the sum for which the Licensor carries comprehensive insurance cover pursuant to CLAUSE 10.1 above; or

10.5.2 a sum equivalent to the price paid to the Licensor for the products or services that are the subject of the Licensee's claim, plus damages limited to 25% of the same amount for any additional costs directly, reasonably and necessarily incurred by the Licensee in obtaining alternative products and/or services.

10.6 The parties hereby acknowledge and agree that the limitations contained in this CLAUSE 10 are reasonable in light of all the circumstances.

10.7 The Licensee's statutory rights as a consumer (if any) are not affected. All liability that is not expressly assumed in this Agreement is hereby excluded. These limitations will apply regardless of the form of action, whether under statute, in contract or tort, including negligence, or any other form of action. For the purposes of this clause, the 'Licensor' includes its employees, sub-contractors and suppliers who shall all have the benefit of the limits and exclusions of liability set out above in terms of the Contracts (Rights of Third Parties) Act 1999. Nothing in this Agreement shall exclude or limit liability for fraudulent misrepresentation.

11. LICENSEE'S WARRANTY

11.1 The Licensee warrants that it has not relied on any oral representation made by the Licensor or upon any descriptions, illustrations or specifications contained in any catalogues and publicity material produced by the Licensor which are only intended to convey a general idea of the products and services mentioned therein. The Licensee has however relied upon the descriptions, illustrations, functions, specifications contained in the user manual and software specification in SCHEDULE A.

11.2 The Licensee warrants that it shall comply in all material respects with all applicable laws, regulations and codes of conduct (whether statutory or otherwise) of the United Kingdom, and that all licences, permissions and consents required for carrying on its business have been obtained and are in full force and effect.

12. LICENSEE'S OBLIGATIONS

12.1 The Licensee shall:

12.1.1 operate the software, maintain data and the database in accordance with the user manual and operator manual;

12.1.2 by arrangement, grant access to premises and/or systems at all times for support and maintenance;

12.1.3 make hardware accessible to the Licensor's support staff, and when required enable logons/passwords required for such support staff (who will have their own logons);

12.1.4 permit the Licensor to install the current version of software from time-to-time; when upgrades or fixes occur, to provide a reasonable level of assistance in implementation and testing;

12.1.5 provide notice of intention to change hardware or operating system or data-feeds.

12.1.6 The Licensee shall provide the Licensor with reasonable direct and remote access to the Licensee's equipment and the Software, and shall provide such reasonable assistance as the Licensor may request, including, but not limited to, providing sample output and other diagnostic information.

13. CONFIDENTIAL INFORMATION

13.1 The Licensee undertakes to treat as confidential and keep secret the payment terms of this Agreement and all information contained or embodied in the Licensed Program Materials and the Specification and all documentation and/or information conveyed to the Licensee in respect of the software (hereinafter collectively referred to as 'the Information').

13.2 The Licensee shall not, without the prior written consent of the Licensor divulge, any part of the Information to any person except:

13.2.1 the Licensee's own employees and then only to those employees who need to know the same;

13.2.2 the Licensee's auditors, HM Inspector of Taxes, HM Customs and Excise and any other persons or bodies having a right, duty or obligation to know the business of the Licensee, and then only in pursuance of such right, duty or obligation;

13.2.3 any person who is for the time being appointed by the Licensee to maintain any equipment on which the Licensed Programs are for the time being used (in accordance with the terms of the Licence) and then only to the extent necessary to enable such person to properly maintain such equipment.

13.3 The Licensee undertakes to ensure that persons and bodies mentioned in CLAUSE 13.2 are made aware, prior to the disclosure of any part of the Information, that the same is confidential, and that they owe a duty of confidence to the Licensor. The Licensee shall indemnify the Licensor against any loss or damage which the Licensor may sustain or incur as a result of the Licensee failing to comply with such undertaking.

13.4 The Licensee shall promptly notify the Licensor if it becomes aware of any breach of confidence by any person to whom the Licensee divulges all or any part of the Information and shall give the Licensor all reasonable assistance in connection with any proceedings which the Licensor may institute against such person for breach of confidence.

13.5 The foregoing obligations as to confidentiality shall remain in full force and effect notwithstanding any termination of the Licence or this Agreement.

14. SECURITY AND CONTROL

The Licensee shall during the continuance of the Licence:

14.1 effect and maintain adequate security measures to safeguard the Licensed Program Materials from access or use by any unauthorised person;

14.2 retain the Licensed Program Materials and all copies thereof under the Licensee's effective control;

14.3   maintain a full and accurate record of the Licensee's copying and disclosure of the Licensed Program Materials and shall produce such record to the Licensor on request from time to time;

14.4   comply with all reasonable instructions of the Licensor with regard to the use of the Licensed Program Materials, including, without limitation, the implementation of upgrades to the Licensed Programs, third party software, specified operating system and computer hardware which the Licensor may provide from time to time.

15.   TERMINATION

15.1   The Licensee may terminate this Agreement at any time by giving at least 90 days' prior written notice to the Licensor.

15.2   The Licensor may terminate this Agreement forthwith on giving notice in writing to the Licensee if:

15.2.1   the Licensee commits any serious breach of any term of this Agreement and (in the case of a breach capable of being remedied) shall have failed, within 30 days after the receipt of a request in writing from the Licensor so to do, to remedy the breach (such request to contain a warning of the Licensor's intention to terminate); or

15.2.2   the Licensee permanently discontinues the use of the Licensed Program Materials.

15.3   Forthwith upon the termination of this Agreement, any licence made between the Licensor and the Licensee, and relating to any software or other materials subject to the Support and the Maintenance supplied under this Agreement, shall terminate in the manner provided in any such licence agreement.

15.4   Any termination of this Agreement (howsoever occasioned) shall not affect any accrued rights or liabilities of either party, nor shall it effect the coming into force or the continuance in force of any provision hereof which is expressly or by implication intended to come onto or continue in force on or after such termination.

15.5   If the Licensor terminates this Agreement pursuant to CLAUSE 15.2, then the Licensee shall not be entitled to any refund of the [Support Fee and the Maintenance Charge] or any part thereof that has been paid.

16.   ALTERATIONS

The Licensee hereby undertakes not to alter or modify the whole or any part of the Licensed

Program Materials in any way whatsoever, nor to permit the whole or any part of the Licensed

Programs to be combined with, or become incorporated in, any other program.[5]

17. TRAINING

17.1   The Licensor undertakes to provide training in the use of the Licensed Programs for the staff of the Licensee as set out in SCHEDULE G.

17.2   Any additional training required by the Licensee shall be provided by the Licensor in accordance with its standard scale of charges from time to time in force.

18. DOCUMENTATION

The Licensor shall provide the Licensee with [2] copies of a set of the Documentation containing sufficient information to enable proper use of all the facilities and functions set out in the Specification. If the Licensee requires further copies of the Documentation, then these may be obtained under licence from the Licensor in accordance with its standard scale of charges from time to time in force.

19. LICENSEE'S CONFIDENTIAL INFORMATION

19.1   The Licensor shall be entitled to identify the Licensee as a licensee of the Program Materials in the Licensor's publicity materials, subject to the Licensee's prior written approval on each publicity document.

19.2   Subject to CLAUSE 19.1 above, the Licensor shall treat as confidential all information supplied by the Licensee under this Agreement which is designated as confidential by the Licensee, or which is by its nature clearly confidential, provided that this Clause shall not extend to any information which was rightfully in the possession of the Licensor prior to the commencement of the negotiations leading to this Agreement, or which is already public knowledge or becomes so at a future date (otherwise than as a result of a breach of this Clause). The Licensor shall not divulge any confidential information to any person except to its own employees, and then only to those employees who need to know the same. The Licensor shall ensure that its employees are aware of and comply with the provisions of this Clause. The foregoing obligations shall survive any termination of the Licence or this Agreement.

20. DATA PROTECTION

The parties hereby undertake to comply with the provisions of the Data Protection Act 1998 and any related legislation insofar as the same relates to the provisions and obligations of this Agreement.[6]

21. REMOTE ACCESS

If the Licensor has remote dial-up or modem access to any part of the Licensee's Equipment in the course of performing its obligations under this Licence the following provisions of this CLAUSE 21 shall apply additionally. The Licensor:

21.1 will (a) only use a remote access method approved by the Licensee (such approval not to be unreasonably withheld or delayed); (b) provide the Licensee with the name of each individual who will have remote access to the Licensee's Equipment and the phone number at which the individual may be reached during dial-in; (c) ensure that any computer used by its personnel to remotely access the Licensee's Equipment will not simultaneously access the Internet or any other third party network while logged on to the Licensee's Equipment;

21.2 further warrants and agrees that its personnel will not remotely access the Licensee's Equipment from a networked computer unless the network is protected from all third party networks by a firewall that is maintained by a 7 × 24 administrative staff. Said firewall must be certified by the International Computer Security Association (ICSA) (or an equivalent certification as determined by the Licensee) if the connection to the Licensee's network is an ongoing connection such as frame relay or T1 line;

21.3 will restrict remote access by the Licensor to only the Licensee's test and/or training systems and nothing in this Clause shall entitle the Licensor to have access to the Licensee's live production copy of the Licensed Programs unless the parties have expressly agreed in writing that such access is to take place and the Licensee has given written confirmation of the date on which such access was implemented. The Licensor shall report in writing when such access takes places detailing all activities and actions taken during such access.

22. INTERPRETATION

In this Agreement unless the context otherwise requires:

22.1 words importing any gender include every gender;

22.2 words importing the singular number include the plural number and vice versa;

22.3 words importing persons include firms, companies and corporations and vice versa;

22.4 references to numbered clauses and Schedules are references to the relevant clause in or Schedule to this Agreement;

22.5 reference in any Schedule to this Agreement to numbered paragraphs relate to the numbered paragraphs of that Schedule;

22.6 the headings to the clauses, Schedules and paragraphs of this Agreement will not affect the interpretation;

22.7 any reference to an enactment includes reference to that enactment as amended or replaced from time to time and to any subordinate legislation or byelaw made under that enactment;

22.8 any obligation on any party not to do or omit to do anything is to include an obligation not to allow that thing to be done or omitted to be done respectively;

22.9 any party who agrees to do something will be deemed to fulfil that obligation if that party procures that it is done.

22.10 In the case of conflict or ambiguity between any provision contained in the body of this Agreement and any provision contained in any Schedule, the provision in the body of this Agreement shall take precedence.

23. AGENCY, PARTNERSHIP

This Agreement shall not constitute or imply any partnership, joint venture, agency, fiduciary relationship or other relationship between the parties other than the contractual relationship expressly provided for in this Agreement.

24. AMENDMENTS

This Agreement may not be released, discharged, supplemented, interpreted, amended, varied or modified in any manner except by an instrument in writing signed by a duly authorised officer or representative of each of the parties to this agreement.

25. ANNOUNCEMENTS

No party shall issue or make any public announcement or disclose any information regarding this Agreement, unless prior written consent has been obtained from the other party.

26. ASSIGNMENT

26.1 This Agreement is personal to the parties and, subject to CLAUSE 25.2 below, neither this Agreement nor any rights, licenses or obligations under this agreement, may be assigned by either party, without the prior written approval of the other party.

26.2 Notwithstanding the foregoing, either party may assign this Agreement to any acquirer of all, or of substantially all, of such party's equity securities, assets or business relating to the subject matter of this Agreement, or to any entity controlled by, that controls, or is under common control with, a party hereto. Any attempted assignment in violation of this clause will be void and without effect.[7]

27. ENTIRE AGREEMENT

This Agreement supersedes all prior agreements, arrangements and undertakings between the parties and constitutes the entire agreement between the parties relating to the subject matter of this agreement. However, the obligations of the parties under any pre-existing non-disclosure agreement shall remain in full force and effect insofar as there is no conflict between the same. The parties confirm that they have not entered into this Agreement on the basis of any representation that is not expressly incorporated into this Agreement.

28. FORCE MAJEURE[8]

Neither party shall have any liability under or be deemed to be in breach of this Agreement for any delays or failures in performance of this Agreement which result from circumstances beyond the reasonable control of that party. If such circumstances continue for a continuous period of more than [6 months], either party may terminate this Agreement by written notice to the other party.

29. NOTICES

29.1 All notices hereunder shall be in writing.

29.2 Notices shall be deemed to have been duly given:

29.2.1 when delivered, if delivered by courier or other messenger (including registered mail) during normal business hours of the recipient; or

29.2.2 when sent, if transmitted by fax or e-mail and a successful transmission report or return receipt is generated; or

29.2.3 on the fifth business day following mailing, if mailed by national ordinary mail, postage pre-paid; or

29.2.4 on the tenth business day following mailing, if mailed by airmail, postage pre-paid,

in each case addressed to the most recent address, e-mail address, or facsimile number notified to the other party.

30. SCHEDULES

The provisions of SCHEDULE[S] (A–G) to this Agreement shall form part of this Agreement as if set out here.

31. SEVERANCE

If any provision of this Agreement is prohibited by law or judged by a court to be unlawful, void or unenforceable, the provision shall, to the extent required, be severed from this Agreement and rendered ineffective as far as possible without modifying the remaining provisions of this Agreement, and shall not in any way affect any other circumstances of or the validity or enforcement of this Agreement.

32. SUCCESSORS AND ASSIGNEES

32.1   This Agreement shall be binding upon, and enure to the benefit of, the parties and their respective successors and permitted assignees, and references to a party in this Agreement shall include its successors and permitted assignees.

32.2   In this Agreement references to a party include references to a person:

32.2.1   who for the time being is entitled (by assignment, novation or otherwise) to that party's rights under this Agreement (or any interest in those rights); or

32.2.2   who, as administrator, liquidator or otherwise, is entitled to exercise those rights; and in particular those references include a person to whom those rights (or any interest in those rights) are transferred or pass as a result of a merger, division, reconstruction or other reorganisation involving that party. For this purpose, references to a party's rights under this Agreement include any similar rights to which another person becomes entitled as a result of a novation of this Agreement.

33. WAIVER

No delay, neglect or forbearance on the part of either party in enforcing against the other party any term or condition of this Agreement shall either be or be deemed to be a waiver or in any way prejudice any right of that party under this Agreement. No right, power or remedy herein conferred upon or reserved for either party is exclusive of any other right, power or remedy available to that party.

34. COUNTERPARTS

This Agreement may be executed in any number of counterparts or duplicates, each of which shall be an original, and such counterparts or duplicates shall together constitute one and the same Agreement.

35. TIME IS OF THE ESSENCE

Time shall be of the essence in this Agreement as regards any time, date or period mentioned in this Agreement or subsequently substituted as a time, date or period by agreement in writing between the parties.

36. SUBCONTRACTING

With the prior written consent of the Licensor (such consent not to be unreasonably withheld or delayed) the Licensee may perform any or all of its obligations under this Agreement through agents or sub-contractors, provided that the Licensee shall remain liable for such performance and shall indemnify the Licensor against any loss or damage suffered by the Licensor arising from any act or omission of such agents or sub-contractors.

37. LANGUAGE

This Agreement is made only in the English language. If there is any conflict in the meaning between the English language version of this Agreement and any version or translation of this Agreement in any other language, the English language version shall prevail.

38. COSTS AND EXPENSES

Each party shall bear its own legal costs and other costs and expenses arising in connection with the drafting, negotiation, execution and registration (if applicable) of this Agreement.

39. SET-OFF

Where either party has incurred any liability to the other party, whether under this Agreement or otherwise, and whether such liability is liquidated or unliquidated, each party may set off the amount of such liability against any sum that would otherwise be due to the other party under this Agreement.

40. THIRD PARTIES[9]

The parties confirm their intent (except as provided in CLAUSE 10.7 not to confer any rights on any third parties by virtue of this Agreement and accordingly the Contracts (Rights of Third Parties) Act 1999 shall not apply to this Agreement.

41. PROPER LAWAND JURISDICTION[10]

41.1   This Agreement and all matters arising from it and any dispute resolutions referred to below shall be governed by and construed in accordance with English Law notwithstanding the conflict of law provisions and other mandatory legal provisions save that:

41.1.1   The Licensor shall have the right to sue to recover its fees in any jurisdiction in which the Licensee is operating or has assets, and

41.1.2   The Licensor shall have the right to sue for breach of its intellectual property rights and other proprietary information and trade secrets ('IPR') (whether in connection with this Agreement or otherwise) in any country where it believes that infringement or a breach of this Agreement relating to its IPR might be taking place. For the avoidance of doubt, the place of performance of this Agreement is agreed by the parties to be England.

41.2   Each party recognises that the other party's business relies upon the protection of its IPR and that in the event of a breach or threatened breach of IPR, the other party will be caused irreparable damage and such other party may therefore be entitled to injunctive or other equitable relief in order to prevent a breach or threatened breach of its IPR.

41.3   With respect to all other disputes which are not IPR related pursuant to CLAUSES 40.1 and 40.2 above and its special rules, the following procedures in CLAUSES 40.3 to 40.5 shall apply. Where there is a dispute, the aggrieved party shall notify the other party in writing of the nature of the dispute with as much detail as possible about the deficient performance of the other party. A representative from senior management ('representatives') of each of the parties shall meet in person or communicate by telephone within five business days of the date of the written notification in order to reach an agreement about the nature of the deficiency and the corrective action to be taken by the respective parties. The representatives shall produce a report about the nature of the dispute in detail to their respective boards and if no agreement is reached on corrective action, then the chief executives of each party shall meet in person or by telephone, to facilitate an agreement within five business days of a written notice by one to the other. If the dispute cannot be resolved at board level within a further five business days, or if the agreed upon completion dates in any written plan of corrective action are exceeded, either party may seek its legal remedies as provided below.

41.4   If the parties cannot resolve a dispute in accordance with the procedure in CLAUSE 40.3 above, then they shall with the assistance of the Centre for Alternative Dispute Solution, seek to resolve the dispute or difference amicably by using an Alternative Dispute Resolution ('ADR') procedure acceptable to both parties before pursuing any other remedies available to them. If either party fails or refuses to agree to or participate in the ADR procedure or if in any event the dispute or difference is not resolved to the satisfaction of both parties within [90] days after it has arisen, the matter shall be settled in accordance with the procedure below.

41.5   If the parties cannot resolve the dispute by the procedure set out above, the parties shall irrevocably submit to the exclusive jurisdiction of the Courts of England and Wales for the purposes of hearing and determining any dispute arising out of this Agreement.

41.6   [While the dispute resolution procedure above is in progress and any party has an obligation to make a payment to another party or to allow a credit in respect of such payment, the sum relating to the matter in dispute shall be paid into an interest bearing deposit account to be held in the names of the relevant parties at a clearing bank and such payment shall be a good discharge of the parties' payment obligations under this Agreement. Following resolution of the dispute, whether by mediation or legal proceedings, the sum held in such account shall be payable as determined in accordance with the mediation or legal proceedings, and the interest accrued shall be allocated between the parties pro rata according to the split of the principal sum as between the parties.]

AS WITNESS etc

SCHEDULE A

THE SOFTWARE SPECIFICATION

This is software that provides facilities to: *eg enable the secure management of HR records, staff expenses and pension administration.*

SCHEDULE B

THE EQUIPMENT

I. HARDWARE

Any IBM compatible PC with a minimum specification equal or better than:

*   *Intel PIII 500 MHz processor*

*   *512 MByte RAM*

*   *Three 10 GByte 10,000 r.p.m. hard disks controlled by an Ultra Wide SCCI controller manufactured by Adaptec or other approved manufacturer*

*   *100 MBit Ethernet adapter manufactured by 3Com or other approved manufactured.*

2. OPERATING SYSTEM

[Microsoft Windows NT version 4 service pack 5 and such other subsequent version or service pack of Microsoft Windows or Sun Solaris Intel or Linux as may be specified by the Licensor for new versions of the software.]

3. THIRD PARTY SOFTWARE

Supplier   Name   Version

SCHEDULE C

ANNUAL SUPPORT AND MAINTENANCE FEES:

FOR FIRST L2 MONTHS

On signature   £

On delivery

AFTER FIRST 12 MONTHS

At start of each period   £ [   ]   [% of total fees of licenses purchased]

TRAINING:

Subject to SCHEDULE H:

On invoice £ [   ] per day

SCHEDULE D

LOCATION

[   ]

[Or, such other premises in the London area as may be used by the Licensee.]

SCHEDULE E

STORAGE MEDIA

[CD-ROM]

SCHEDULE F

LOCATIONS/COUNTRIES

Not applicable.

SCHEDULE G

TRAINING AND SET-UP

The Licensor will at no additional cost to the Licensee provide up to [   ] day's training and in connection with the first installation only.

Training will thereafter be provided (for multiple users) at the rate specified in SCHEDULE C.

The Licensor will also provide one person on site for the first five days to assist users, set-up data and integrate software to data feeds.

(signatures of (or on behalf of) the parties)

1 This Agreement is intended to provide software support and maintenance and is supplemental to the Software Licence Agreement in PRECEDENT 4.
   Escrow is usually the subject of separate contracts and is therefore not included in this agreement. For a range of escrow agreements see PRECEDENT 26.
2 The term of this agreement needs to be carefully considered. The licensee will want support and maintenance for as long as it needs it. The licensor may want to terminate support and maintenance if the licensee does not take up new releases of the licensor software.

3   If there is a considerable time lapse between delivery and subsequent acceptance of the software, risk can be stipulated to pass on acceptance.

4   Generally, the right to make changes in a program protected by copyright law is an exclusive right of the copyright owner. However the Copyright (Computer Programs) Regulations 1992, SI 1992/3233 allow maintenance to the extent of error correction.

Under English law, reverse engineering or de-compilation had previously been regarded as an infringement of copyright. However, the Copyright (Computer Programs) Regulations 1992, as a result of the European Directive on the Legal Protection of Computer Programs (Council Directive 91/250, OJ L122 17/05/1991, p 42), now allows a lawful licensee to analyse the underlying code, copy and translate the program and investigate the functioning of the program in order to evaluate and understand its ideas and principles. The consent of the copyright holder is not required so long as the right is exercised only for the purpose of achieving inter-operability of an independently created program with the licensed software, subject to a number of conditions. This is an implied right that may not be excluded by licensing arrangements within the European Union.

5   For a recent judicial view on limitation clauses in computer contracts see *Watford Electronics Ltd v Sanderson CFL Ltd* [2001] EWCA Civ 317, [2001] 1 All ER (Comm) 696, CA. Chadwick LJ held at [55]:

'Where experienced businessmen representing substantial companies of equal bargaining power negotiate an agreement ... [t]hey should ... be taken to be the best judge of the commercial fairness of the agreement which they have made ... The court should not assume that either is likely to commit his company to an agreement which he thinks is unfair, or which he thinks includes unreasonable terms. Unless satisfied that one party has, in effect, taken unfair advantage of the other, or that a term is so unreasonable that it cannot properly have been understood or considered, the court should not interfere.'

6   United Kingdom law requires any business which processes data about living individuals to be notified with the Data Protection Office. Under the Data Protection Act 1998, s 1(1) (the Act) data is defined as information which:

1   is being processed by means of equipment operating automatically in response to instructions given for that purpose;

2   is recorded with the intention that it should be processed by means of such equipment;

3   is recorded as part of a relevant filing system or with the intention that it should form part of a relevant filing system; and

4   does not fall within paragraph (a), (b) or (c) but forms part of an accessible record as defined in section 68 of the Act. Accessible records are health records, educational records and accessible public records defined in SCHEDULE 12 to the Act.

7   Many standard software provider agreements prohibit assignment of the licence agreement except with the express written permission of the provider, except where the assignee is an associate of the Licensee or the assignment is a result of re-construction or amalgamation.

8   This force majeure clause is short and general. It may be appropriate to insert a more detailed force majeure clause such as:

'Notwithstanding anything else contained in this Agreement, neither party shall be liable for any delay in performing its obligations hereunder if such delay is caused by circumstances beyond its reasonable control (including without limitation any delay caused by any act or omission of the other party) provided however that any delay by a sub-contractor or supplier of the party so delaying shall not relieve the party from liability for delay except where such delay is beyond the reasonable control of the sub-contractor or supplier concerned. Subject to the party so delaying promptly notifying the other party in writing of the reasons for the delay (and the likely duration of the delay), the performance of such party's obligations shall be suspended during the period that the said circumstances persist and such party shall be granted an extension of time for performance equal to the period of the delay. Save where such delay is caused by the act or omission of the other party (in which event the rights, remedies and liabilities of the parties shall be those conferred and imposed by the other terms of this Agreement and by law):

•   any costs arising from such delay shall be borne by the party incurring the same;
•   either party may, if such delay continues for more than 10 weeks,

terminate this Agreement forthwith giving notice in writing to the other by reason of such termination save that the Licensee shall pay the Licensor a reasonable sum in respect of any work carried out by it prior to such termination and for that purpose the

Licensor may deduct such sum from any amounts previously paid by the Licensee under this Agreement (the balance (if any) of which shall be refunded to the Licensee whether paid by way of deposit or otherwise).'

9   Before the Contracts (Rights of Third Parties) Act 1999 (the Act) it was the case that a person who was not a party to a contract (a third party) could not enforce any right under the contract. Similarly, a contract could not impose any obligations or liabilities on a third party.

However the Act attempts to draw a balance between the freedom of the parties to vary a contract and the interests of the third party. The Act means that a contractual clause benefiting a third party (eg the promisee's subsidiary company or sub-contractor or employee) will be straightforwardly enforceable by that third party if:

- the contract expressly provides that he may; or
- where a term in the contract purports to confer a benefit on him (unless on a proper construction of the contract it appears that the parties did not intend the term to be enforceable by the third party).

It is therefore prudent to include a clause to the effect of excluding the provisions of the Act. By doing so it ensures that any rights of third parties are not deemed to be enforceable by them. This is particularly the case where the parties are companies and may have subsidiaries or conversely parent companies.

10 In this Agreement it is felt appropriate to use an escalating dispute solutions clause (sometimes called an alternative dispute resolution clause) because during the period of the Agreement any dispute between the parties may be better settled in private and without recourse to litigation (except as reserved by the clause in relation to breach of IPR).

It may be felt in some circumstances an arbitration clause could be more appropriate or the parties may wish to simply indicate that they will resort to litigation in the courts.

An example of another governing law and dispute settlement clause is:

'Any dispute which may arise between the parties concerning this Agreement shall be determined as follows:

(1)   If the dispute shall be of a technical nature relating to the functions or capabilities of the Licensed Program Materials or any similar or related matter then such a dispute shall be referred for final settlement to an expert nominated jointly by the parties or failing such nomination within Fourteen (14) days after either party's request to the other therefore nominated at the request of either party by the President for the time being of the British Computer Society. Such expert shall be deemed to act as an expert and not as an arbitrator. His decision shall (in the absence of clerical or manifest error) be final and binding on the parties and whose costs shall be borne between the parties in equal shares unless he determines that the conduct of either party is such that such party should bear all of such fees.

(2)   In any other case the dispute shall be determined by the High Court of Justice in England and the parties hereby submit to the exclusive jurisdiction of that Court for such purposes.'

7 Memorandum of understanding in relation to negotiation of a formal joint venture and licensing agreement[1]

This Memorandum of Understanding ('MOU') is made this [ ] of [ ]

Between

ISP plc whose principal place of business is at [ ] ('ISP') and

Agency Limited whose registered office is at [ ] ('Agency').

Together ISP and Agency shall be referred to below as 'the Parties' and individually as 'a Party' or 'each Party').

BACKGROUND

A. ISP is an ISP and the operator of portal and other Internet related services.[2]

B. Agency is a marketing and advertising company.[3]

C. The Parties wish to work together to exploit via ISP portals certain intellectual property rights created and owned by Agency.[4]

NOW THEREFORE IT IS HEREBY AGREED AS FOLLOWS:

1. INTRODUCTION

1.1 **Joint Venture:** This MOU records in outline the basic principles that the Parties have provisionally agreed, subject to contract, for ISP and Agency to finalise their participation in a venture ('the Joint Venture') in order to exploit in an agreed market certain intellectual property owned by Agency ('the Agency Intellectual Property') and as described in greater detail in the Schedule attached.

1.2 **Negotiation of Formal Agreements:** During the term of this MOU the parties will negotiate in good faith formal agreements with each other and with third parties, ('the Formal Agreements') in time for signature by [ ]. It is envisaged that the principal agreement will be a licence agreement ('the Licence Agreement') whereby Agency licenses the Agency Intellectual Property to ISP for exploitation on a ISP portal subject to expense and revenue-sharing arrangements between the Parties.[5]

1.3 **Supercession:** The Formal Agreements once duly approved and executed shall supersede this MOU.[6]

1.4 **Attendance at Meetings:** The Parties will make themselves available on reasonable notice for meetings when negotiations concerning the Formal Agreements shall take place.

2. SUBJECT MATTER

2.1 **Basic principles:** The basic principles to be included in the Formal Agreements include the provisions specified in this CLAUSE 2 and the SCHEDULE along with such other matters as may be agreed in order to conclude the Formal Agreements.[7]

2.2 **Licence from Agency to the Joint Venture:** Agency will retain ownership in the Agency Intellectual Property whether created by Agency before or after the date of this Agreement. [The parties envisage that Agency will grant to the Joint Venture exclusive rights to exploit the Agency Intellectual Property.][8]

3. UNDERTAKING NOT TO NEGOTIATE WITH OTHERS

3.1 Each Party undertakes that until [ ][9] it shall not (without the prior written permission of the other Parties) enter or seek to enter into negotiations or discussions with another person or entity for participation in a joint venture or the granting of a licence covering broadly the same subject matter as that described in this MOU.

3.2 Each corporate entity which is a Party undertakes that until [ ][10] it shall not (without the prior written permission of the other Parties) enter or seek to enter into negotiations or discussions with another person or entity for the acquisition of shares in that Party.

4. CONFIDENTIALITY

4.1 **Confidentiality:** Each party undertakes that for a period of [three][11] years from the date of disclosure it will treat the other party's information marked 'confidential' or which from its very nature is obviously confidential (including all material relating to or constituting the Agency Intellectual Property) with the same degree of care as it employs with regard to its own confidential information of a like nature and in any event in accordance with best current commercial security practices.

4.2 **No intentional disclosure:** Neither party will intentionally disclose the other's confidential information to third parties other than those of its employee's, consultants and sub-contractors who need to have such information for the purposes of this Agreement, and shall ensure that such recipients shall be bound by the same confidentiality obligations as are set out in this clause.

4.3 **Exclusions:** This undertaking does not extend to information which was already known to one party prior to disclosure by the other, which is or becomes public knowledge, or which is disclosed by one party to a third party without any obligations of confidentiality.

5. PUBLICITY

Neither party shall make any public disclosures regarding this MOU or the subject matter hereof without the prior written consent of the other.

6. NON-BINDING MOU[12]

6.1 Unless and until the Formal Agreements are approved and executed between the Parties then CLAUSES 1 and 2 and the SCHEDULE of this MOU are not intended to and shall not create any legal obligations between the Parties and there is no legal obligation on either party to enter into the transactions anticipated therein. All negotiations and correspondence regarding clauses 1 and 2 and the Schedule shall be subject to contract.

6.2 CLAUSES 3 to 14 inclusive are intended to be legally binding and to create obligations between the Parties with immediate effect.

7. EXPENSES

Each Party shall be responsible for its own costs in relation to all matters arising out of this MOU.

8. TERM

This MOU shall continue in force until [   ][13] or until signature of the Formal Agreements (if sooner) or such other date as the Parties may otherwise agree.

9. IMMEDIATE TERMINATION FOR BREACH

Either party may terminate this MOU by notice in writing with immediate effect if the other party is in material breach of any of the terms of this MOU and such breach remains unremedied fourteen days after receipt of notice from the terminating party that the other party is in breach.

10. IMMEDIATE TERMINATION FOR CREDIT REASONS

Either party shall have the right to terminate this MOU with immediate effect on notice in writing if liquidation or similar proceedings are filed by or against the other party or if any action is taken by or against the other party under any law the purpose or effect of which is or may be to relieve such party in any manner from its debts or to extend the time of payment thereof or the other party makes an assignment for the benefit of creditors or makes any conveyance of any of its property which in the opinion of the terminating party may be to the detriment of that party's creditors or if a receiver or trustee or similar official is appointed with authority to take possession of the other party's property or any part thereof.

11. FORCE MAJEURE[14]

Neither party shall have any liability under or be deemed to be in breach of this Agreement for any delays or failures in performance of this Agreement which result from circumstances beyond the reasonable control of that party. If such circumstances continue for a continuous period of more than [6 months], either party may terminate this Agreement by written notice to the other party.

12. MISCELLANEOUS

12.1 **Assignment:**

    12.1.1   This Agreement is personal to the parties and, subject to CLAUSE 12.1.2 below, neither this Agreement nor any rights, licenses or obligations under this Agreement, may be assigned by either party without the prior written approval of the other party.

    12.1.2   Notwithstanding the foregoing, either party may assign this Agreement to any acquirer of all or of substantially all of such party's equity securities, assets or business relating to the subject matter of this Agreement or to any entity controlled by, that controls, or is under common control with a party to this Agreement. Any attempted assignment in violation of this clause will be void and without effect.

12.2 **Entire agreement:** This MOU embodies the entire understanding and agreement between the parties in connection with the subject matter of this MOU and neither party is relying on any representations, promises, terms, conditions or obligations oral or written express or implied other than those contained herein. Neither party seeks to exclude liability for fraudulent or grossly negligent misrepresentation.

12.3 **Waiver:** No delay, neglect or forbearance on the part of either party in enforcing against the other party any term or condition of this Agreement shall either be or be deemed to be a waiver or in any way prejudice any right of that party under this Agreement. No right, power or remedy in this Agreement conferred upon or reserved for either party is exclusive of any other right, power or remedy available to that party.

12.4 **Amendment:** This Agreement may not be released, discharged, supplemented, interpreted, amended, varied or modified in any manner except by an instrument in writing signed by a duly authorised officer or representative of each of the parties hereto.

12.5 **Headings:** The clause headings in this MOU are for reference purposes only and are not intended to be taken into account when interpreting the clauses.

13. NOTICES

13.1   All notices hereunder shall be in writing.

13.2   Notices shall be deemed to have been duly given:

  13.2.1   when delivered, if delivered by courier or other messenger (including registered mail) during normal business hours of the recipient; or

  13.2.2   when sent, if transmitted by fax or e-mail and a successful transmission report or return receipt is generated; or

  13.3.3   on the fifth business day following mailing, if mailed by national ordinary mail, postage pre-paid; or

  13.3.4   on the tenth business day following mailing, if mailed by airmail, postage pre- paid,

in each case addressed to the most recent address, e-mail address, or facsimile number notified to the other party.

14. PROPER LAW AND JURISDICTION[15]

14.1   This Agreement and all matters arising from it and any dispute resolutions referred to below shall be governed by and construed in accordance with English Law notwithstanding the conflict of law provisions and other mandatory legal provisions save that:

14.2   Each party recognises that the other party's business relies upon the protection of its IPR and that in the event of a breach or threatened breach of IPR, the other party will be caused irreparable damage and such other party may therefore be entitled to injunctive or other equitable relief in order to prevent a breach or threatened breach of its IPR.

14.3   With respect to all other disputes which are not IPR related pursuant to CLAUSES 14.1 and 14.2 above and its special rules the following procedures in CLAUSES 14.3 to 14.6 shall apply. Where there is a dispute the aggrieved party shall notify the other party in writing of the nature of the dispute with as much detail as possible about the deficient performance of the other party. A representative from senior management ('representatives') of each of the parties shall meet in person or communicate by telephone within five business days of the date of the written notification in order to reach an agreement about the nature of the deficiency and the corrective action to be taken by the respective parties. The representatives shall produce a report about the nature of the dispute in detail to their respective boards and if no agreement is reached on corrective action, then the chief executives of each party shall meet in person or by telephone, to facilitate an agreement within five business days of a written notice by one to the other. If the dispute cannot be resolved at board level within a further five business days, or if the agreed upon completion dates in any written plan of corrective action are exceeded, either party may seek its legal remedies as provided below.

14.4   If the parties cannot resolve a dispute in accordance with the procedure in CLAUSE 14.3 above, then they shall with the assistance of the Centre for Alternative Dispute Solution, seek to resolve the dispute or difference amicably by using an Alternative Dispute Resolution ('ADR') procedure acceptable to both parties before pursuing any other remedies available to them. If either party fails or refuses to agree to or participate in the ADR procedure or if in any event the dispute or difference is not resolved to the satisfaction of both parties within [90] days after it has arisen, the matter shall be settled in accordance with the procedure below.

14.5   If the parties cannot resolve the dispute by the procedure set out above, the parties shall irrevocably submit to the exclusive jurisdiction of the Courts of England and Wales for the purposes of hearing and determining any dispute arising out of this Agreement.

In Witness whereof the Parties have signed this MOU the day and year first above written

Signed for and on behalf of ISP plc [   ]

by [   ]

Signed for and on behalf of Agency Limited [   ]

by [   ]

SCHEDULE

[   ]

1   This Memorandum of Understanding might be used for a situation where two parties (or more) are looking to share their respective proprietary rights and form a 'partnership' or joint venture for the purposes of exploiting those rights.

Much of the Memorandum of Understanding would be applicable to any situation where two (or more) parties are looking to create a technology transfer relationship that needs to establish, quickly, ground rules for the transaction without necessarily having in place all of the legal documentation.

Some lawyers express concern at having a Memorandum of Understanding which is signed by both parties but non-binding, on the basis that it is of no real legal value. This particular precedent is binding in part and non-binding in others.

2   Here insert the description or function of the first party.

3   Here insert the description or function of the second party.

4   Here insert the reasons for the parties executing the MOU.

5 This clause describes the intentions of the parties.
6 This clause indicates that when the Formal Agreements, as defined in the MOU are executed, they will supersede this MOU.
7 This clause recites what terms and conditions of this MOU shall be expanded upon in the Formal Agreements.
8 This clause describes the grant of rights which in this instance is exclusive, but could be non-exclusive or
   more detailed in its description.
9 Here insert the date by which the parties intend the Formal Agreements to have been executed, or the term of the MOU to have expired.
10 Here insert the date by which the parties intend the Formal Agreements to have been executed, or the term of the MOU to have expired.
11 Here insert the number of years during which confidentiality is expected to be maintained.
12 This clause indicates that CLAUSES 1 and 2 of the MOU and the Schedule are not binding until the Formal Agreements have been signed, but the rest of the MOU is binding. In this way, until such time as the Formal Agreements are in place, or the MOU has expired, there is at least some certainty between the parties as to what the terms and conditions of their relationship are and how disputes will be settled.
13 Here insert the term of the MOU.
14 This force majeure clause is short and general. It may be appropriate to insert a more detailed force majeure clause such as:
   'Notwithstanding anything else contained in this Agreement, neither party shall be liable for any delay in performing its obligations hereunder if such delay is caused by circumstances beyond its reasonable control (including without limitation any delay caused by any act or omission of the other party) provided however that any delay by a sub-contractor or supplier of the party so delaying shall not relieve the party from liability for delay except where such delay is beyond the reasonable control of the sub-contractor or supplier concerned. Subject to the party so delaying promptly notifying the other party in writing of the reasons for the delay (and the likely duration of the delay), the performance of such party's obligations shall be suspended during the period that the said circumstances persist and such party shall be granted an extension of time for performance equal to the period of the delay. Save where such delay is caused by the act or omission of the other party (in which event the rights, remedies and liabilities of the parties shall be those conferred and imposed by the other terms of this Agreement and by law):
   • any costs arising from such delay shall be borne by the party incurring the same;
   • either party may, if such delay continues for more than 10 weeks,
   terminate this Agreement forthwith giving notice in writing to the other by reason of such termination.'
15 In this MOU it is felt appropriate to use an escalating dispute solutions clause (sometimes called an alternative dispute resolution clause) because during the period of the MOU any dispute between the parties may be better settled in private and without recourse to litigation (except as reserved by the clause in relation to breach of IPR).
   It may be felt in some circumstances an arbitration clause could be more appropriate or the parties may wish simply to indicate that they will resort to litigation in the courts.
   An example of another form of dispute settlement clause is:
   'Any dispute which may arise between the parties concerning this Agreement shall be determined as follows:
   (1) If the dispute shall be of a technical nature relating to the functions or capabilities of the Licensed Program Materials or any similar or related matter then such a dispute shall be referred for final settlement to an expert nominated jointly by the parties or failing such nomination within Fourteen (14) days after either party's request to the other therefore nominated at the request of either party by the President for the time being of the British Computer Society. Such expert shall be deemed to act as an expert and not as an arbitrator. His decision shall (in the absence of clerical or manifest error) be final and binding on the parties and his costs shall be borne between the parties in equal shares unless he determines that the conduct of either party is such that such party should bear all of such fees.
   (2) In any other case the dispute shall be determined by the High Court of Justice in England and the parties hereby submit to the exclusive jurisdiction of that Court for such purposes.'

8 Agreement for software development and licensing[1]

THIS AGREEMENT is made the [ ] day of [ ]

BETWEEN:

(1)   (*customer*) whose [registered office *or* principal place of business] is at (*address*) and whose facsimile ('fax') number is (*number*) ('the Customer') and

(2)   (*developer*) whose [registered office or principal place of business] is at (*address*) and whose facsimile ('fax') number is (*number*) ('the Developer')

WHEREAS

The Developer has agreed to develop (*specify description or function of software to be developed*) for the Customer and to provide other services in accordance with the terms and conditions of this

Agreement.

NOW IT IS AGREED as follows:

1. DEFINITIONS

1.1   **'Acceptance Date'** means the date on which the New Software is accepted (or deemed to be accepted) by Customer pursuant to CLAUSE 6.3.

1.2   **'Acceptance Tests'** means the tests specified in this Agreement and/ or such other tests as may be agreed in writing between the Customer and the Developer.

1.3   **'Additional Services'** means any additional services requested by the Customer to be provided by the Developer as set out in SCHEDULE 5.

1.4   **'Change Request'** means a request for a change made by the Customer or the Developer.

1.5   **'Confidential Information'** shall include, but not necessarily be limited to, all information which is not publicly known including the business, finances, technology (including without limitation the

Source Software, the New Software and the Documentation) trade secrets, and any other commercially sensitive information of either party regardless of its nature.

1.6 **'Customer Group'** shall be the Customer, Customer's parent company holding a majority interest in Customer, and such parent company's majority owned subsidiaries.

1.7 **'Development Services'** the software development, procurement, consulting and computer programming services required to produce the New Software.

1.8 **'Documentation'** means the documentation set out in PART 2 OF SCHEDULE 1.

1.9 **'Implementation Plan'** means the timing and sequence of events agreed between Customer and Developer for the performance of this Agreement, as set out in SCHEDULE 2.

1.10 **'Intellectual Property Rights'** means all copyright and other intellectual property rights, howsoever arising and in whatever media, whether or not registered, including (without limitation) patents, trademarks, service marks, trade names, registered design and any applications for the protection or registration of these rights and all renewals and extensions thereof throughout the world.

1.11 **'Licence'** means the licence granted by the Developer to the Customer pursuant to CLAUSE 10.

1.12 **'Payment Schedule'** means the payment schedule set out in SCHEDULE 3.

1.13 **'Planned Acceptance Date'** means the date specified in the Implementation Plan on which the New Software is intended to be accepted by the Customer in accordance with this Agreement.

1.14 **'Price'** means the fixed, all inclusive price for the provision of the New Software, the Licence and the Documentation.

1.15 **'Project'** means the development, delivery and testing of the New Software.

1.16 **'Rates'** means the rates set out in SCHEDULE 3.

1.17 **'New Software'** means the software being developed or customised by the Developer for the Customer, preliminary details of which are set out in the Specification, including any enhancements and modifications made.

1.18 **'Source Software'** means the software, details of which are set out in SCHEDULE 4, being the software owned by Customer upon which the New Software is to be developed in accordance with this Agreement.

1.19 **'Specified Equipment'** means the configuration of computer or computers, including operating systems, on which the New Software is to function as specified in PART 3 OF SCHEDULE 1.

1.20 **'Specification'** means the specification of the New Software set out in PART 1 OF SCHEDULE 1.

1.21 **'System'** means collectively the Specified Equipment and the New Software.

1.22 **'Warranty Period'** means the period of [two] months after the Acceptance Date.

2. THE PROJECT

2.1 The Developer shall provide the Customer with Development Services for the purpose of creating the New Software as detailed in the Specification; install and test the New Software on the Specified Equipment; provide the Documentation and carry out any Additional Services agreed by the parties.

2.2 The Developer shall carry out the obligations set out in CLAUSE 2.1 in accordance with the Implementation Plan.

2.3 The Developer shall supply to the Customer the object and source code of the New Software when requested by the Customer.

2.4 The Developer shall license the New Software to the Customer in accordance with CLAUSE 10.

2.5 Where the Customer requires the Developer to provide training, support and maintenance in relation to the New Software, both parties shall enter into a separate support and maintenance agreement, the terms of which shall be agreed between the parties.

3. PERSONNEL

The Developer shall ensure that all of its personnel engaged in the Project:

3.1 have the necessary skills, expertise and diligence to undertake such work and will conform to the professional standards generally observed in the computer industry for similar services.

3.2 comply with the provisions in this Agreement relating to Confidential Information.

4. THE CUSTOMER'S OBLIGATIONS

Customer shall:

4.1 deliver the Source Software to the Developer in a form suitable for the Developer to carry out the Development Work;

4.2 make available to the Developer, free of charge, such computer facilities (including but not limited to unhindered access to the Specified Equipment), office and secretarial services as are necessary to enable the Developer to carry out its obligations under this Agreement;

4.3 ensure that its employees and other independent contractors co-operate reasonably with the Developer and its employees in carrying out the Project;

4.4 promptly furnish the Developer with such information and documents as it may reasonably request for the proper performance of its obligations under this Agreement; and

4.5 ensure that its representative is available as reasonably required by the Developer.

5. CHANGE CONTROL

5.1 If either party identifies a requirement for a change, a Change Request will be sent to the other party detailing the change requirements. If sent by the Developer, the Change Request shall state the effect such a change shall have on the New Software, the Implementation Plan and the Price. If sent by the Customer, the receipt of the Change Request by the Developer will constitute a request to the Developer to state in writing the effect such a change shall have on the New Software, the Implementation Plan and the Price. The Developer shall use all reasonable endeavours to supply the necessary details within [ten] working days from receipt of the Change Request or such other period as may be agreed.

5.2 Where a change to the Price is required, the rates used as the basis for the additional cost for the Change Request shall be the Rates as detailed in SCHEDULE 3. The parties will then decide whether or not to implement the change. If the change is implemented, the amended New Software, Implementation Plan or Price shall then become the New Software, Implementation Plan and Price for the purpose of this Agreement.

5.3 The Developer shall not implement any changes unless instructed to do so by the Customer.

6. ACCEPTANCETESTS AND LIQUIDATED DAMAGES

6.1 The Acceptance Tests shall be agreed by the parties in accordance with the Implementation Plan.[2]

6.2 The Developer shall use its reasonable endeavours to ensure that the New Software is ready for acceptance testing by the Planned Acceptance Date. In any event, the Developer shall give to the Customer [five] working days' prior notice in writing of the date when it will be ready to commence the Acceptance Tests. Unless otherwise agreed, the Acceptance Tests shall take place on the [sixth] working day after such notice has been given.

6.3 The Customer shall accept the New Software immediately after the New Software has passed the Acceptance Tests.

6.4 If the New Software fails to pass the Acceptance Tests, repeat tests shall be carried out until the earlier of the following occurs:

6.4.1 the New Software passes the Acceptance Tests;

6.4.2 the Acceptance Tests have been repeated three times; or

6.4.3   a 30 day period from the Planned Acceptance Date has expired.

6.5   If at any time the Customer shall commence live running of the whole or any part of the New Software (other than in the Acceptance Tests) then the Customer shall be deemed to have accepted the New Software.

6.6   If the New Software has not been accepted by the Customer on or after the occurrence of the events specified in CLAUSFS 6.4.2 OR 6.4.3, then the Customer shall be entitled, without prejudice to any other rights or remedies it may have under this Agreement or at law, to terminate forthwith this Agreement by written notice upon the Developer and, notwithstanding the liquidated damages in CLAUSE 6.7 below, shall be entitled to damages or compensation for material breach.

6.7   If the New Software is not ready for acceptance testing by the Planned Acceptance Date in accordance with CLAUSE 6.2 above then, save where such failure results from the default by the Customer of its obligations under this Agreement, the Developer shall pay to the Customer by way of liquidated damages the sum of £[   ] per day commencing on the day after the Planned Acceptance Date and expiring on the Acceptance Date subject to a maximum of £[   ]. Such payment shall be without prejudice to the Developer's obligation to complete the New Software as soon after the Planned Acceptance Date as shall be reasonably possible.

6.8   For the avoidance of doubt time shall be of the essence.

7.   REPRESENTATIVES AND PROGRESS MEETINGS

7.1   Each party shall nominate in writing upon the signing of this Agreement, the person who will act as its representative for the purposes of this Agreement and who will be responsible for providing any information which may be required by the other party to perform its obligations under this Agreement.

7.2   The parties shall procure that their respective representatives will meet at least [once a month] between the date of this Agreement and the Planned Acceptance Date to discuss and minute the progress of the Project.

8.   WARRANTIES

8.1   The Developer warrants that:

8.1.1   it is entitled to enter into this Agreement and that it is entitled to grant the Licence in accordance with this Agreement;

8.1.2   the New Software shall:

8.1.2.1   perform substantially in accordance with the Specification on the Specified Equipment, minor interruptions and errors excluded;

8.1.2.2   be date compliant and neither the performance nor functionality of the New Software is affected by dates prior to, during and after the year 2000; and

8.1.2.3   support the introduction of the Euro currency unit.

8.1.3   the Documentation will provide users with adequate instructions to enable them effectively to operate and use the System;

8.1.4   the development of the New Software will be carried out in a professional manner conforming to best industry practices.

8.2   The Developer shall not be liable under CLAUSE 8.1.2 if a failure to meet the warranties set out therein is caused by:

8.2.1   software other than the New Software running on the Specified Equipment; or

8.2.2   modifications or customisation made by or on behalf of the Customer to the New Software, without the authorisation of the Developer.

8.3   If the Developer receives a written notice from the Customer identifying a breach of the warranties set out in CLAUSE 8.1, or otherwise becomes aware of its failure to comply with the warranties set out in CLAUSE 8.1, then the Developer shall, at its own expense, promptly remedy such breach or failure provided that the Developer shall have no liability or obligations under the warranties unless is shall have received written notice of the defect or error within the Warranty Period.

9. UNDERTAKINGS

9.1   The Developer shall:[3]

9.1.1   observe and obey all directions and regulations as may from time to time be reasonably given to or imposed on the Developer by or on behalf of the Customer for the purposes of this Agreement;

9.1.2   not either during nor after the end of the engagement under this Agreement create any product all or part of which relies directly or indirectly on any idea, style, production method, gimmick, character or other information relating to the Customer or the Source Software, of which the Developer may become aware as a result of the engagement under this Agreement, regardless of whether such material is confidential or not;

9.1.3   hold the Source Software strictly in accordance with the provisions of CLAUSE 11.1 and, on completion of the Project, return to the Customer the Source Software, all related materials and documentation and any Confidential Information belonging to the Customer and all copies of the whole or any part thereof or, if requested by the Customer, shall destroy the same and certify in writing to the Customer that it has been destroyed;

9.1.4　not incur unauthorised expenditure or costs on behalf of the Customer without the Customer's written consent in advance;

9.1.5　ensure that itself and its servants, agents and subcontractors take all reasonable precautions to ensure that no known viruses for which detection and antidote software is generally available are coded or introduced into the New Software.

9.2　If the Developer wishes to use material (in any medium) owned by third parties as part of the New Software, he shall (having first obtained the Customer's prior written agreement), obtain from those third parties such written assignments, releases, waivers, permissions and licences as necessary to permit such use, and to enable the Customer to exploit any program containing that material in the New Software in all present and future media. The Developer shall deliver copies of any documentation relevant to third party clearances to the Customer upon request.

10.　LICENCE

10.1　On payment in full of the Price, the Developer grants to the Customer (and to all members of the Customer Group who agree to the terms of this Licence) a non-exclusive, perpetual, non-transferable right to use the New Software and the Documentation on any processor owned or controlled by the Customer or a member of the Customer Group.[4]

10.2　The Customer may not disclose or make available the New Software to any entity other than members of the Customer Group who have agreed to these licence terms nor permit others to use it except the Customer's employees and agents who may use it only on the Customer's behalf within the limits of the application licence and who are deemed to have agreed to such terms.

11.　PROPRIETARY RIGHTS[5]

11.1　The Intellectual Property Rights in the Source Software (including the source and object code) together with any related materials or documentation are and shall remain the property of the Customer. The Developer shall notify the Customer immediately if the Developer becomes aware of any unauthorised use of the whole or any part of the Source Software by any person.

11.2　The Intellectual Property Rights in the New Software (including the source and object code) and the Documentation shall be and remain vested in the Developer apart from any elements which do not form part of the generic functionality of the New Software and which implement visual features or layouts created at the specific request of the Customer. All Intellectual Property Rights in such distinctive customer features (including the source and object code) shall be and remain vested in the Customer.

11.3 The Developer will indemnify the Customer on demand against all costs, claims, demands, expenses and liabilities of whatsoever nature arising out of or in connection with any claim that the use or possession of the New Software infringes the Intellectual Property Rights of any third party subject to the following conditions:

11.3.1 The Customer shall promptly notify the Developer in writing of any allegations of infringement of which it is aware and shall not make any admissions without the Developer's prior written consent;

11.3.2 The Customer, at the Developer's request and expense, shall allow the Developer to conduct and/or settle all negotiations and litigation resulting from any such claim subject to the Developer taking over such conduct within [ten] working days after being notified of the claim and providing that the Developer diligently pursues the settlement of any such claim; and

11.3.3 The Customer shall, at the request of the Developer, afford all reasonable assistance with such negotiations or litigation, and shall be reimbursed by the Developer on demand for all expenses incurred in doing so.

11.4 If the Customer's use or possession of the New Software or any part of the New Software in accordance with this Agreement, is held by a court of competent jurisdiction to constitute an infringement of a third party's Intellectual Property Rights, then the Developer shall promptly and at its own expense:

11.4.1 procure for the Customer the right to continue using and possessing the New Software or the infringing part; or

11.4.2 modify or replace the New Software (or part thereof) without detracting from the overall performance of the New Software, so as to avoid the infringement.

11.5 If the remedies set out in CLAUSE 11.4 above are not in the Developer's opinion reasonably available, then the Customer shall return the New Software which is the subject of the intellectual property claim and the Developer shall refund to the Customer the corresponding portion of the Price, as normally depreciated, whereupon this Agreement shall immediately terminate.

12. CHARGES AND EXPENSES

12.1 In consideration of the Developer carrying out the Project, the Customer shall pay to the Developer the Price which shall be invoiced to the Customer in the specified proportions set out in SCHEDULE 3 and subject to the terms set out in CLAUSE 13.

12.2 In consideration of any Additional Services, the Customer shall pay to the Developer the amounts invoiced by the Developer to the Customer based on the Rates set out in PART 2 OF SCHEDULE 3.

12.3 The Customer shall also pay or procure the payment to the Developer of all reasonable travelling and other out-of-pocket expenses incurred in the course of the Project subject to a maximum amount of £[   ] per day excluding all travel costs.

13. TERMS OF PAYMENT

13.1 Payment of sums due by the Customer to the Developer shall be made within [30 (thirty)] days of the receipt of an invoice from the Developer. All payments under this Agreement shall be made in [Pounds Sterling].

13.2 With effect from the beginning of each year commencing on the Acceptance Date, the Developer may increase the Rates in effect during the previous year provided that not less than [ten] working days prior written notice has been given to the Customer by the Developer.

[13.3 A one-off bonus of £[   ] shall be payable by the Customer to the Developer in the event that the Developer completes [Phases 1 and 2 (as specified in SCHEDULE 2 to this Agreement) in accordance with the Specification and within the timeframes specified in SCHEDULE 2.]

14. LIABILITY AND INSURANCE[6]

14.1 The Developer shall, during the term of this Agreement, maintain employer's liability, third party liability, product liability and professional negligence insurance cover in respect of its liabilities arising out of or connected with this Agreement, such cover to be to a minimum value of [ONE MILLION POUNDS] and with an insurance company of repute. The Developer shall on request supply copies of the relevant certificates of insurance to the Customer as evidence that such policies remain in force. The Developer undertakes to use reasonable commercial efforts to pursue claims under such insurance policies.

14.2 The Developer shall indemnify the Customer for personal injury or death caused by the negligence of its employees in connection with the performance of their duties under this Agreement or by defects in any product supplied pursuant to this Agreement.

14.3 The Developer will indemnify the Customer for direct damage to tangible property caused by the negligence of its employees in connection with the performance of their duties under this Agreement or by defects in any product supplied pursuant to this Agreement. The Developer's total liability under this clause shall be limited to [£500,000] for any one event or series of connected events.

14.4 Save in respect of claims for death or personal injury arising from the Developer's negligence, in no event will the Developer be liable for any damages resulting from loss of data or use, lost profits, loss of anticipated savings, nor for any damages that are an indirect or secondary consequence of any act or omission of the Developer whether such damages were reasonably foreseeable or actually foreseen.

14.5 Except as provided above in the case of personal injury, death and damage to tangible property, the Developer's maximum liability to the Customer under this Agreement or otherwise for any cause whatsoever (whether in the form of the additional cost of remedial services or otherwise) will be for direct costs and damages only and will be limited to the greater of:

14.5.1 the sum for which the Developer carries comprehensive insurance cover pursuant to CLAUSE 14.1 above; or

14.5.2 a sum equivalent to the price paid to the Developer for the products or services that are the subject of the Customer's claim, plus damages limited to 25% of the same amount for any additional costs directly, reasonably and necessarily incurred by the Customer in obtaining alternative products and/or services.

14.6 The parties hereby acknowledge and agree that the limitations contained in this CLAUSE 14 are reasonable in light of all the circumstances.

14.7 The Customer's statutory rights as a consumer (if any) are not affected. All liability that is not expressly assumed in this Agreement is hereby excluded. These limitations will apply regardless of the form of action, whether under statute, in contract or tort including negligence or any other form of action. For the purposes of this Clause, the 'Developer' includes its employees, sub-contractors and suppliers who shall all have the benefit of the limits and exclusions of liability set out above in terms of the Contracts (Rights of Third Parties) Act 1999. Nothing in this Agreement shall exclude or limit liability for fraudulent misrepresentation.

15. TERMINATION

15.1 This Agreement shall continue until completion of the Project unless either party gives to the other not less than [90] days prior written notice of termination or unless the Agreement is terminated in accordance with any of the provisions of this CLAUSE 15 or any other clause of this Agreement.

15.2 Either party shall be entitled to terminate this Agreement forthwith at any time by written notice to the other party if:

15.2.1 the other party commits a breach of any of the terms of this Agreement (and if the breach is capable of remedy) fails to remedy the breach within [30] days after receipt of notice in writing to do so; or

15.2.2 the other party becomes subject to an administration order; a receiver or administrative receiver or similar is appointed over, or an encumbrancer takes possession of any of the other party's property or assets; the other party enters into an arrangement or composition with its creditors, ceases or threatens to cease to carry on business, becomes insolvent, or ceases to be able to pay its debts as they fall due.

15.3 Forthwith upon the termination of this Agreement, the Developer shall return to the Customer the Source Software, all related materials and documentation and any Confidential Information belonging to the Customer and all copies of the whole or any part thereof or, if requested by the Customer, shall destroy the same and certify in writing to the Customer that it has been destroyed.

15.4 Any termination of the Licence or this Agreement (howsoever occasioned) shall not affect any accrued rights or liabilities of either party nor shall it effect the coming into force or the continuance in force of any provision hereof which is expressly or by implication intended to come into or continue in force on or after such termination.

16. CONFIDENTIALITY

16.1 Both during this Agreement and after its termination, the parties shall treat as confidential (and shall procure that its personnel and each of them treat as confidential) and shall not (and shall procure that their personnel and each of them does not) other than in the proper provision of the services required to fulfil the Project, use or disclose to any person, firm or company, any Confidential Information belonging to the other party or its clients, suppliers or customers, nor permit its use or disclosure. In particular, both parties shall maintain any source code provided by the other party under maximum security conditions.

16.2 The provisions of CLAUSE 16.1 shall not apply where Confidential Information is divulged to:

16.2.1 either parties' own employees and then only to those employees who need to know the same;

16.2.2 either parties' auditors, HM Inspector of Taxes, HM Customs and Excise, a court of competent jurisdiction, governmental body or applicable regulatory authority and any other persons or bodies having a right, duty or obligation to know the business of the other party and then only in pursuance of such right, duty or obligation.

16.3 Both parties undertake to ensure that persons and bodies referred to in CLAUSE 16.2 are made aware prior to the disclosure of any part of the Confidential Information that the same is confidential and that they owe a duty of confidence to the other party.

16.4 Each party to this Agreement shall promptly notify the other party if it becomes aware of any breach of confidence by any person to whom it divulges all or any part of the Confidential Information and shall give the other party all reasonable assistance in connection with any proceedings which the other party may institute against such person for breach of confidence.

16.5 The provisions of this clause shall survive the termination of this Agreement but the restrictions contained in CLAUSE 16.1 shall cease to apply to any information which may come into the public domain otherwise than through unauthorised disclosure.

16.6   Nothing in this CLAUSE 16 shall prevent the Developer from exploiting any inventions or software that it develops during the term of this Agreement.

17.   DATA PROTECTION

The parties hereby undertake to comply with the provisions of the Data Protection Act 1998 and any related legislation insofar as the same relates to the provisions and obligations of this Agreement.[7]

18.   INTERPRETATION

18.1   In this Agreement unless the context otherwise requires:

18.1.1   words importing any gender include every gender;

18.1.2   words importing the singular number include the plural number and vice versa;

18.1.3   words importing persons include firms, companies and corporations and vice versa;

18.1.4   references to numbered clauses and Schedules are references to the relevant clause in or Schedule to this Agreement;

18.1.5   reference in any Schedule to this Agreement to numbered paragraphs relate to the numbered paragraphs of that Schedule;

18.1.6   the headings to the clauses, Schedules and paragraphs of this Agreement will not affect the interpretation;

18.1.7   any reference to an enactment includes reference to that enactment as amended or replaced from time to time and to any subordinate legislation or byelaw made under that enactment;

18.1.8   any obligation on any party not to do or omit to do anything is to include an obligation not to allow that thing to be done or omitted to be done;

18.1.9   any party who agrees to do something will be deemed to fulfil that obligation if that party procures that it is done.

18.2   In the case of conflict or ambiguity between any provision contained in the body of this Agreement and any provision contained in any Schedule, the provision in the body of this Agreement shall take precedence.

19.   AGENCY, PARTNERSHIP

This Agreement shall not constitute or imply any partnership, joint venture, agency, fiduciary relationship or other relationship between the parties other than the contractual relationship expressly provided for in this Agreement.

20. AMENDMENTS

This Agreement may not be released, discharged, supplemented, interpreted, amended, varied or modified in any manner except by an instrument in writing signed by a duly authorised officer or representative of each of the parties hereto.

21. ANNOUNCEMENTS

No party shall issue or make any public announcement or disclose any information regarding this Agreement unless prior written consent has been obtained from the other party.

22. ASSIGNMENT

22.1   This Agreement is personal to the parties and, subject to CLAUSE 22.2 below, neither this Agreement nor any rights, licenses or obligations under this Agreement, may be assigned by either party without the prior written approval of the other party.

22.2   Notwithstanding the foregoing, either party may assign this Agreement to any acquirer of all or of substantially all of such party's equity securities, assets or business relating to the subject matter of this Agreement or to any entity controlled by, that controls, or is under common control with a party to this Agreement. Any attempted assignment in violation of this clause will be void and without effect.

23. ENTIRE AGREEMENT

This Agreement supersedes all prior agreements, arrangements and undertakings between the parties and constitutes the entire agreement between the parties relating to the subject matter of this Agreement. However the obligations of the parties under any pre-existing non-disclosure agreement shall remain in full force and effect insofar as there is no conflict between the same. The parties confirm that they have not entered into this Agreement on the basis of any representation that is not expressly incorporated into this Agreement.

24. FORCE MAJEURE[8]

Neither party shall have any liability under or be deemed to be in breach of this Agreement for any delays or failures in performance of this Agreement which result from circumstances beyond the reasonable control of that party. If such circumstances continue for a continuous period of more than [6 months], either party may terminate this Agreement by written notice to the other party.

25. NOTICES

25.1   All notices hereunder shall be in writing.

25.2   Notices shall be deemed to have been duly given:

25.2.1   when delivered, if delivered by courier or other messenger (including registered mail) during normal business hours of the recipient; or

25.2.2   when sent, if transmitted by fax or e-mail and a successful transmission report or return receipt is generated; or

25.2.3   on the fifth business day following mailing, if mailed by national ordinary mail, postage pre-paid; or

25.2.4   on the tenth business day following mailing, if mailed by airmail, postage pre-paid,

in each case addressed to the most recent address, e-mail address, or facsimile number notified to the other party.

26. SCHEDULES

The provisions of SCHEDULE[S] (*A–E*) to this Agreement shall form part of this Agreement as if set out here.[9]

27. SEVERANCE

If any provision of this Agreement is prohibited by law or judged by a court to be unlawful, void or unenforceable, the provision shall, to the extent required, be severed from this Agreement and rendered ineffective as far as possible without modifying the remaining provisions of this Agreement, and shall not in any way affect any other circumstances of or the validity or enforcement of this Agreement.

28. SUCCESSORS AND ASSIGNEES

28.1   This Agreement shall be binding upon, and enure to the benefit of, the parties and their respective successors and permitted assignees, and references to a party in this Agreement shall include its successors and permitted assignees.

28.2   In this Agreement references to a party include references to a person:

28.2.1   who for the time being is entitled (by assignment, novation or otherwise) to that party's rights under this Agreement (or any interest in those rights); or

28.2.2   who, as administrator, liquidator or otherwise, is entitled to exercise those rights;

and in particular those references include a person to whom those rights (or any interest in those rights) are transferred or pass as a result of a merger, division, reconstruction or other reorganisation involving that party. For this purpose, references to a party's rights under this Agreement include any similar rights to which another person becomes entitled as a result of a novation of this Agreement.

29. WAIVER

No delay, neglect or forbearance on the part of either party in enforcing against the other party any term or condition of this Agreement shall either be or be deemed to be a waiver or in any way prejudice any right of that party under this Agreement. No right, power or remedy in this Agreement conferred upon or reserved for either party is exclusive of any other right, power or remedy available to that party.

30. COUNTERPARTS

This Agreement may be executed in any number of counterparts or duplicates, each of which shall be an original, and such counterparts or duplicates shall together constitute one and the same agreement.

31. TIME IS OF THE ESSENCE

Time shall be of the essence in this Agreement as regards any time, date or period mentioned in this Agreement or subsequently substituted as a time, date or period by agreement in writing between the parties.

32. SUBCONTRACTING

With the prior written consent of the Customer (such consent not to be unreasonably withheld or delayed) the Developer may perform any or all of its obligations under this Agreement through agents or sub-contractors, provided that the Developer shall remain liable for such performance and shall indemnify the Customer against any loss or damage suffered by the Customer arising from any act or omission of such agents or sub-contractors.

33. LANGUAGE

This Agreement is made only in the English language. If there is any conflict in the meaning between the English language version of this Agreement and any version or translation of this Agreement in any other language, the English language version shall prevail.

34. COSTS AND EXPENSES

Each party shall bear its own legal costs and other costs and expenses arising in connection with the drafting, negotiation, execution and registration (if applicable) of this Agreement.

35. SET-OFF

Where either party has incurred any liability to the other party, whether under this Agreement or otherwise, and whether such liability is liquidated or unliquidated, each party may set off the amount of such liability against any sum that would otherwise be due to the other party under this Agreement.

36. THIRD PARTIES[10]

The parties confirm their intent (subject to CLAUSE 14.7) not to confer any rights on any third parties by virtue of this Agreement and accordingly the Contracts (Rights of Third Parties) Act 1999 shall not apply to this Agreement.

37. PROPER LAW AND JURISDICTION[11]

37.1 This Agreement and all matters arising from it and any dispute resolutions referred to below shall be governed by and construed in accordance with English Law notwithstanding the conflict of law provisions and other mandatory legal provisions save that:

37.1.1 the Customer shall have the right to sue to recover its fees in any jurisdiction in which the Developer is operating or has assets, and

37.1.2 the Customer shall have the right to sue for breach of its intellectual property rights and other proprietary information and trade secrets ('IPR') (whether in connection with this Agreement or otherwise) in any country where it believes that infringement or a breach of this Agreement relating to its IPR might be taking place. For the avoidance of doubt, the place of performance of this Agreement is agreed by the parties to be England.

37.2 Each party recognises that the other party's business relies upon the protection of its IPR and that in the event of a breach or threatened breach of IPR, the other party will be caused irreparable damage and such other party may therefore be entitled to injunctive or other equitable relief in order to prevent a breach or threatened breach of its IPR.

37.3 With respect to all other disputes which are not IPR related pursuant to CLAUSES 37.1 and 37.2 above and its special rules the following procedures in CLAUSES 37.3 to 37.5 shall apply. Where there is a dispute the aggrieved party shall notify the other party in writing of the nature of the dispute with as much detail as possible about the deficient performance of the other party. A representative from senior management ('representatives') of each of the parties shall meet in person or communicate by telephone within five business days of the date of the written notification in order to reach an agreement about the nature of the deficiency and the corrective action to be taken by the respective parties. The representatives shall produce a report about the nature of the dispute in detail to their respective boards and if no agreement is reached on corrective action, then the chief executives of each party shall meet in person or by telephone, to facilitate an agreement within five business days of a written notice by one to the other. If the dispute cannot be resolved at board level within a further five business days, or if the agreed upon completion dates in any written plan of corrective action are exceeded, either party may seek its legal remedies as provided below.

37.4 If the parties cannot resolve a dispute in accordance with the procedure in CLAUSE 37.3 above, then they shall with the assistance of the Centre for Alternative Dispute Solution, seek to resolve the dispute or difference amicably by using an Alternative Dispute Resolution ('ADR') procedure acceptable to both parties before pursuing any other remedies available to them. If either party fails or refuses to agree to or participate in the ADR procedure or if in any event the dispute or difference is not resolved to the satisfaction of both parties within [90] days after it has arisen, the matter shall be settled in accordance with the procedure below.

37.5 If the parties cannot resolve the dispute by the procedure set out above, the parties shall irrevocably submit to the exclusive jurisdiction of the Courts of England and Wales for the purposes of hearing and determining any dispute arising out of this Agreement.

37.6 [While the dispute resolution procedure above is in progress and any party has an obligation to make a payment to another party or to allow a credit in respect of such payment, the sum relating to the matter in dispute shall be paid into an interest bearing deposit account to be held in the names of the relevant parties at a clearing bank and such payment shall be a good discharge of the parties' payment obligations under this Agreement. Following resolution of the dispute, whether by mediation or legal proceedings, the sum held in such account shall be payable as determined in accordance with the mediation or legal proceedings, and the interest accrued shall be allocated between the parties pro rata according to the split of the principal sum as between the parties.]

AS WITNESS etc

SCHEDULE A

NEW SOFTWARE SPECIFICATION

PART I

Specification

PART 2

Documentation

PART 3

Specified equipment

Customer's Hardware

Customer's Operating System

PART 4

Licence Restrictions

Site	Number of Concurrent Users	Number of Designated Servers

SCHEDULE B

IMPLEMENTATION PLAN

SCHEDULE C

PAYMENT SCHEDULE

PART I

The Price

The Price shall be [£] and shall be payable in the following instalments:

Stage	Rate	Event of Payment
Initiation	£	on signature of the Agreement
Stage One	£	on successful testing cf PARTS 1-4 OF SCHEDULE 2
Stage Two	£	on successful testing cf PARTS 5 AND 6 OF SCHEDULE 2
Stage Three	£	on successful testing cf PARTS 7-9 OF SCHEDULE 2
Stage Four	£	on Acceptance Date

PART 2

Additional Services – Fee [% of list price]

SCHEDULE D

SOURCE SOFTWARE SPECIFICATION

SCHEDULE E

ADDITIONAL SERVICES

(signatures of (or on behalf of) the parties)

1 This agreement is intended to apply to the engagement by the customer of a software developer to develop an application for the customer and in doing so to licence the use of it and to provide ongoing support.

In this instance the software is licensed to the customer and not assigned but proprietary rights in customer specific data and features continue to be owned by the customer.

2 The acceptance test is a key element of a software licence agreement in a major software transaction. Software providers often use installation tests as the acceptance standard. Whatever type of subjective or objective acceptance test is negotiated, customers should be careful to also negotiate the consequences of an acceptance test failure and to include these consequences in the parties' contract.

3 These undertakings by the developer are specific warranties as to the developer's obligations.

4 It is essential for both parties that the contract spells out the licence terms in respect of both the application developed for the customer as well as the underlying technology of the developer which is a part of the application as well as third party tools and databases.

5 This clause is a combination of a reservation of intellectual property rights to the developer as well as an indemnity in favour of the customer for any infringement by the developer of third party rights as a result of the development and licence of the application.

6 Since *St Albans City and District Council v International Computers Ltd* [1996] 4 All ER 481, CA, it has become clear that where a Customer suffers loss as a result of faulty software and no terms and conditions vary the implied terms of merchantability or fitness for purpose, then any attempt by the supplier to limit its liability for such loss below what is deemed to be a reasonable figure (perhaps such a figure being linked to the suppliers' insurance cover for such losses) will be unavailable or even void as an unfair contract term. As a consequence Customers are more likely now to demand that any limit of liability in favour of the Supplier for losses other than indirect should be linked to a reasonable sum of at least £1,000,000 (the usual minimum limit for which insurance cover would be granted under a suitable policy).

However, in *Watford Electronics Ltd v Sanderson CFL Ltd* [2001] EWCA Civ 31 7, [2001] 1 All ER (Comm) 696, CA, it was held that provisions in a contract for the supply of computer software that both excluded the supplier liability for indirect loss, as well as limiting the damages recoverable to the amount paid by the customer under the contract, satisfied the reasonable test under the Unfair Contract Terms Act 1977, S 11. On appeal the court decided that the contract had been negotiated between experienced businessmen of equal bargaining power and skill and as such, the supplier limitation clause was reasonable.

As to limitation of liability generally see Paragraph 89 [2619] ante.

7 The UK law requires any business which processes data about living individuals to be notified with the Data Protection Office. Under the Data Protection Act 1998, S l(1) (the Act) data is defined as information which:

(a) is being processed by means of equipment operating automatically in response to instructions given for that purpose;

(b) is recorded with the intention that it should be processed by means of such equipment;

(c) is recorded as part of a relevant filing system or with the intention that it should form part of a relevant filing system; and

(d) does not fall within paragraph (a), (b) or (c) but forms part of an accessible record as defined in section 68 of the Act. Accessible records are health records, educational records and accessible public records defined in SCHEDULE 12 to the Act. 8 This force majeure clause is short and general. It may be appropriate to insert a more detailed force majeure clause such as:

'Notwithstanding anything else contained in this Agreement, neither party shall be liable for any delay in performing its obligations hereunder if such delay is caused by circumstances beyond its reasonable control (including without limitation any delay caused by any act or omission of the other party) provided however that any delay by a sub-contractor or supplier of the party so delaying shall not relieve the party from liability for delay except where such delay is beyond the reasonable control of the sub-contractor or supplier concerned. Subject to the party so delaying promptly notifying the other party in writing of the reasons for the delay (and the likely duration of the delay), the performance of such party's obligations shall be suspended during the period that the said circumstances persist and such party shall be granted an extension of time for performance equal to the period of the delay. Save where such delay is caused by the act or omission of the other party (in which event the rights, remedies and liabilities of the parties shall be those conferred and imposed by the other terms of this Agreement and by law):
- any costs arising from such delay shall be borne by the party incurring the same;
- either party may, if such delay continues for more than 10 weeks,

terminate this Agreement forthwith giving notice in writing to the other by reason of such termination save that the Customer shall pay the Developer a reasonable sum in respect of any work carried out by it prior to such termination and for that purpose the Customer may deduct such sum from any amounts previously paid by the Customer under this Agreement (the balance (if any) of which shall be refunded to the Customer whether paid by way of deposit or otherwise).'

9 As many contracts are varied or amended during their life cycle it is important that all Schedules are agreed to and signed or initialled by the parties so that there can be no dispute as to the totality of the contract and its contents.

10 Before the Contracts (Rights of Third Parties) Act 1999 (the Act) it was the case that a person who was not a party to a contract (a third party) could not enforce any right under the contract. Similarly, a contract could not impose any obligations or liabilities on a third party. However the Act attempts to draw a balance between the freedom of the parties to vary a contract and the interests of the third party. The Act means that a contractual clause benefiting a third party (eg the promisee's subsidiary company or sub-contractor or employee) will be straightforwardly enforceable by that third party if: the contract expressly provides that he may; or where a term in the contract purports to confer a benefit on him (unless on a proper construction of the contract it appears that the parties did not intend the term to be enforceable by the third party.) It is therefore prudent to include a clause to the effect of excluding the provisions of the Act. By doing so it ensures that any rights of third parties are not deemed to be enforceable by them. This is particularly the case where the parties are companies and may have subsidiaries or conversely parent companies.

11 An example of another governing law and dispute settlement clause is:

'Any dispute which may arise between the parties concerning this Agreement shall be determined as follows:

(1) If the dispute shall be of a technical nature relating to the functions or capabilities of the Licensed Program Materials or any similar or related matter then such a dispute shall be referred for final settlement to an expert nominated jointly by the parties or failing such nomination within Fourteen (14) days after either party's request to the other therefore nominated at the request of either party by the President for the time being of the British Computer Society. Such expert shall be deemed to act as an expert and not as an arbitrator. His decision shall (in the absence of clerical or manifest error) be final and binding on the parties in equal shares unless he determines that the conduct of either party is such that such party should bear all of such fees.

(2) In any other case the dispute shall be determined by the High Court of Justice in England and the parties hereby submit to the exclusive jurisdiction of that Court for such purposes.'

9 Demo licence[1]

PLEASE READ THIS DOCUMENT CAREFULLY BEFORE PROCEEDING. THIS AGREEMENT LICENSES USE OF THE DEMO SOFTWARE TO YOU AND CONTAINS WARRANTY AND LIABILITY DISCLAIMERS. BY [SELECTING THE 'DOWNLOAD' BUTTON] [OPENING THE SHRINK-WRAP PACKAGING FOR THIS PRODUCT] [SIGNING THIS AGREEMENT OR LOADING THE SAME ON TO YOUR SYSTEM],[2] YOU ARE CONFIRMING YOUR ACCEPTANCE OF THE DEMO SOFTWARE AND AGREEING TO BECOME BOUND BY THE TERMS OF THIS AGREEMENT.

'The Demo Software' means the software program covered by this Agreement, and all related documentation and all related updates supplied by us to you.

This Agreement allows you to use the Demo Software on a computer for evaluation only. You may distribute the Demo Software provided that, (a) you do not gain financial or other benefit in return, and (b) this Demo Licence accompanies the same.[3]

You may make one back-up copy of the Demo Software. You must reproduce on any such copy all copyright notices and any other proprietary legends found on the original.

You may not decompile, reverse engineer, disassemble, or otherwise tamper with the Demo Software unless allowed by law. You may not modify, sell, rent, transfer, resell for profit, distribute or create derivative works based upon the Demo Software or any part of it.

We retain ownership of the Demo Software.

The Demo Software is provided to you free of charge, and on an 'AS IS' basis, without any technical support or warranty of any kind from us including, without limitation, a warranty of satisfactory quality, fitness for a particular purpose and non-infringement. Your rights as a consumer are not affected.

WE AND OUR SUPPLIERS SHALL NOT BE LIABLE (DEATH OR PERSONAL INJURY EXCEPTED) FOR ANY INDIRECT, SPECIAL, INCIDENTAL OR CONSEQUENTIAL DAMAGES (NOR FOR ANY DAMAGES FOR LOSS OF BUSINESS, LOSS OF PROFITS, LOSS OF ANTICIPATED SAVINGS OR THE LIKE), WHETHER BASED ON BREACH OF CONTRACT, TORT (INCLUDING NEGLIGENCE), PRODUCT LIABILITY OR OTHERWISE, EVEN IF WE OR OUR SUPPLIERS HAVE BEEN ADVISED OF THE

POSSIBILITY OF SUCH DAMAGES. The limited warranty and limited liability set forth above are fundamental elements of the basis of the bargain between us and you. You agree that we would not be able to provide the Demo Software on an economic basis without such limitation.[4]

This Agreement is made under English law and the parties submit to the jurisdiction of the courts of England and Wales.

All questions concerning this Agreement shall be directed to:

© 2001 [   ] – All rights reserved.

1 This licence is primarily intended for downloadable demonstration or evaluation software from a computer games publisher's/developer's web site. Because the game is being provided free and because it is for demonstration only the licensor seeks to limit its liability as much as possible, and may indeed be able to do so more successfully than where there is consideration being paid by the licensee.
2 The intention is to enforce the licence terms on a click-wrap basis and the 'actions' in the squared brackets could all be applicable or not, as the case may be.
3 The intention is to make the restrictions in the licence as minimal as possible but without denying statutory consumer rights.
4 Although liability for loss suffered as a result of death or personal injury is not excluded, virtually every other liability is and the licensor seeks to validate these limitations of liability on the basis that without such limitations it would not be economically liable to make the demonstration software downloadable on a free basis.

10 Computer games development agreement[1]

THIS AGREEMENT is made the [ ] day of [ ]

BETWEEN:

(1) (*Publisher*) whose [registered office or principal place of business] is at (*address*) and whose facsimile ('fax') number is (*number*) ('the Games Publisher')

(2) (*Developer*) whose [registered office or principal place of business] is at (*address*) and whose facsimile ('fax') number is (*number*) ('the Developer')

RECITALS:[2]

A. The Games Publisher is in the business of developing, publishing and distributing interactive entertainment software products.

B. The Developer designs and develops interactive entertainment software products.

C. The Games Publisher desires to publish and distribute interactive entertainment software products designed and developed by the Developer on the terms and conditions set forth in this Agreement.

NOW IT IS AGREED as follows:

1. DEFINITIONS

In this Agreement, unless the context otherwise requires, the following expressions have the following meanings:

1.1 **'Acceptance Tests'** means tests designed to determine whether the Deliverables meet the criteria specified in the Design Documents, including but not limited to: (i) such performance and reliability demonstrations and tests as the Games Publisher determines, in its sole discretion, to be necessary in order to determine whether any Design Error exists with respect to any Deliverable; (ii) tests to determine whether the Deliverables can be compiled from source code into executable object code form and review of the source code to determine whether all portions of the source code have been delivered; and (iii) review of all related documentation to determine whether the Developer has delivered all such materials as are necessary to install, use, support, maintain and modify the Deliverables, or any portion thereof.

1.2 **'Agreement'** means this agreement, together with all schedules and exhibits hereto, as they may be amended from time to time in accordance with the terms hereof.

1.3 **'Alpha Version'** means the first complete version of the Title which is suitable for internal testing [by the Developer]. The Alpha Version shall (i) conform to the approved Final Design Specifications and any approved revisions thereto; (ii) include 100% of the text; (iii) contain sample multimedia content and structure which is capable of being navigated; and (iv) run on all target platforms. It will not include the title screen or demonstration mode. It is expected to undergo further tests and revision for design timing and elimination of Design Errors and bugs. The Developer shall deliver to the Games Publisher object code and source code of the Alpha Version together with any proprietary development tools and associated documentation used by the Developer to develop the Alpha Version.[3]

1.4 **'Beta Version'** means the version of the Title which is suitable for external (platform compatibility) testing plus the inclusion of the title screen and demonstration mode. The Beta version shall (i) conform to the Final Design Specifications with any approved revisions thereto, (ii) include all components of the Final Product, including software modules and 100% of the audio, text, graphics, etc; (iii) run on all targeted platforms and (iv) have been tested initially by the Developer, to its best capability, to identify and correct all Designer Errors and bugs.

1.5 **'Deliverables'** means the development work product to be performed by the Developer and delivered to the Games Publisher under the terms of this Agreement and set forth more fully in the Design and Development Plan, including, without limitation, the Alpha Version, the Beta Version, the Gold Master, the Final Design Specifications and object code and [source code],1 and related Technical Specifications.

1.6 **'Delivery Date'** means the respective dates set forth in the Design and Development Plan by which the Design Documents or Deliverables, as the case may be, are to be delivered to the Games Publisher by the Developer.

1.7 **'Derivative Works'** means (i) any port or re-development of a Title for any platform; (ii) any sequel of any Title developed for any platform; or (iii) any On Line version of any Title.

1.8 **'Design and Development Plan'** means the milestone schedule and development plan set forth as SCHEDULE A, as amended from time to time by the Relationship Managers in accordance with this Agreement.

1.9 **'Design Error'** means (i) any failure of a Deliverable to meet any applicable specification in the Final Design Specification and/or to meet any written representations made by the Developer; (ii) any failure of a Deliverable to interface properly with any related operating system software or related hardware design referenced in the Design and Development Plan or Final Design Specification and/or as may be otherwise mutually agreed upon by the parties; (iii) any malfunction or defect, or any inability of a Deliverable to perform repeatedly, without interruption, and in compliance with the performance characteristics described in the Final Design Specification; (iv) any misspelled or factually incorrect text in any Deliverable; and/or (v) any audio-visual display or programmer signature which in the opinion of the Games Publisher is offensive or inappropriate or could adversely affect the name or reputation or goodwill of the Games Publisher or the sale of the Title into markets for which it is intended.

1.10 **'Design Documents'** means the Design and Development Plan and the Final Design Specifications.

1.11 **'Final Design Specifications'** means the design specifications prepared by the Developer and accepted by the Games Publisher which shall contain all product elements, an overview structure user interface, level descriptions, layout and inventory of all art and audio assets, and details of the technical aspects of implementation.

1.12 **'Gold Master'** means the Beta Version of the Title that has successfully passed Acceptance Tests and is ready for duplication for commercial distribution.

1.13 **'Manual'** means the document describing the operation and functions of the Title and continuing instructions for using the Title in a manner suitable for the intended use of the Title.

1.14 **'Milestone Payment'** means the amount set forth in the Design and Development Plan to be paid to the Developer upon the approval of a Design Document or acceptance of a Deliverable, as the case may be, in accordance with the terms of this Agreement.

1.15 **'On Line Version'** means a version of a Title that allows consumers to play a Title via any proprietary or Internet based on-line service, regardless of the infrastructure over which such game-play takes place.

1.16 **'Prototype'** means a version of the Title which conforms to the preliminary design specifications for the Title, defines basic tasks and which shall demonstrate the key elements of the final product. The Prototype must include sufficient data, text and materials to illustrate functionality, variety and repeatability and clearly demonstrate the look and feel of the final product.

1.17 **'Relationship Manager'** means the respective persons appointed by the Games Publisher and the Developer pursuant to CLAUSE 2.1 to serve as the representative of each such party for the purpose of this Agreement.

1.18 **'Technical Specifications'** means all documents associated with the creation, design and development of the Title, including but not limited to materials identifying any and all licensors of any authoring system, applications or tools used by the Developer in developing the Title, licensing information related to any developer kit licensed by the Developer in connection with the development of the Title, files describing the control structure and all functions of the Title which can be maintained and modified at an object code level, and any and all source files (including without limitation, uncompiled code, graphics and audio source files), custom programs, utilities, tools, make files, file layouts, instructions, control logic, flow charts, internal documentation, designs, drawings, prints, technical data, and such other documentation as is necessary to install, use, support, recreate, revise, modify or enhance the Title or any portion thereof.

1.19 **'Title'** means the product tentatively entitled [ ] to be delivered as a Deliverable in accordance with the Design Documents and the terms of this Agreement, and described more fully in SCHEDULE B hereto, including all Modifications (as defined in CLAUSE 6.1) of the Title.

2. CO-OPERATION OF PARTIES

2.1 **Relationship Managers** Upon execution of this Agreement, the Games Publisher and Developer will each designate one Relationship Manager and shall promptly confirm to the other party in writing the identity and location of such person.

2.2 **Responsibilities of Relationship Managers** The Games Publisher and Developer Relationship Managers shall be responsible for the following activities:

2.2.1 representing the Games Publisher and Developer, respectively, in matters relating to performance under this Agreement;

2.2.2 submitting and receiving the Design Documents and Deliverables and other materials and documents required to be delivered under this Agreement;

2.2.3 proposing and developing modifications to the Design and Development Plan;

2.2.4 proposing and developing any modifications to the Final Design Specifications;

2.2.5 arranging any meetings to be held between the parties;

2.2.6 if necessary, selecting mutually acceptable independent contractors or agents to carry out research and accumulate footage for the Title;

2.2.7 maintaining, for record-keeping purposes, a log book containing summaries of all material communications and deliveries between the two Relationship Managers; and

2.2.8 implementing appropriate practices and procedures to assure the security of the items delivered under this Agreement.

3. DESIGN AND DEVELOPMENT OF THE TITLE

3.1 **Developer's Services** The Developer agrees to perform such services as are necessary to develop the Title in accordance with the Design Documents and for the platforms and/or operating systems indicated in SCHEDULE A. The Developer acknowledges that the Games Publisher may, from time to time, amend the Design Documents in the light of commercial or creative considerations or as reasonably necessary to ensure adequate performance of, and end user satisfaction with, the Deliverables and the Title, as determined in the Games Publisher's discretion.

3.2 **Games Publisher's right to review work in progress** The Games Publisher shall be entitled, but not obligated, to conduct periodic on-site reviews (including reviews of the Developer's facilities), upon reasonable notice and during normal business hours, of the development work being performed under the terms of this Agreement. The Games Publisher may request, in its sole discretion, and the Developer shall provide the prompt delivery to the Games Publisher of copies of all work in progress.

3.3 **Games Publisher materials and assistance to Developer** The Games Publisher shall provide the Developer with such materials and assistance in furtherance of the Developer's service obligations as the Games Publisher deems necessary for the development of the Title pursuant to this Agreement.[5]

3.4 **Licensed Product** The parties acknowledge that the Developer may incorporate in the Deliverables for use in the Title various materials from third parties ('Licensed Product'). The Developer shall not incorporate such material into the Deliverables for use in the Title unless it shall have obtained prior written permission from the owner of such material and appropriate releases from persons or entities portrayed in such materials in content and form substantially as indicated at SCHEDULE C, or in such other form as has been deemed reasonably acceptable to the Games Publisher, for the Games Publisher to use such material in and in connection with the Title to the full extent contemplated herein. Along with the submission of each Deliverable containing such Licensed Product, the Developer shall deliver written releases to the Games Publisher for such Licensed Product. The Games Publisher shall have the right to review such written statements of permission to ensure their acceptability. All costs associated with licenses to and delivery of Licensed Product and other materials that the Developer and/or its employee or agent has prepared for use in the Title, as set forth herein, shall be borne by the Developer.

3.5 **Consultants** In addition to the Licensed Product, the Developer may incorporate in the Deliverables for use in the Title materials that have been prepared by persons or entities other than the Developer and/or its regular employees. The Developer shall be entitled to engage the services of such consultants or independent contractors in the development of the Deliverables; provided, however, that all such consultants or independent contractors are required to execute and do execute a consulting or independent contractor's agreement, in content and form substantially as indicated at SCHEDULE D, or in such other form as has been deemed reasonably acceptable to the Games Publisher, irrevocably assigning all right, title and interest therein to the Developer or its assignee. Such consultants shall not be engaged by the Developer without the prior approval of the Games Publisher, and all costs associated with the engagement of such consultants and the delivery of any materials prepared by them, as set forth herein, shall be borne by the Developer.

4. DELIVERY AND ACCEPTANCE OF DELIVERABLES

4.1 **Approval of Design Documents**

4.1.1 [The Developer will submit a preliminary design specification for the Title to the Games Publisher for the Games Publisher's approval which shall include a general description of the Title, the Title elements, mechanics, storyboards to illustrate use, art and audio/video requirements. The Developer shall promptly make such modifications to the preliminary design specification as are requested (if any) and resubmit the revised preliminary design specification to the Games Publisher for approval. This process shall continue until written approval by the Games Publisher of the preliminary design specification. Once approved, the preliminary design specification shall become the Final Design Specification], or [the Developer has, prior to the date hereof, delivered to the Games Publisher, a Prototype for the Title, together with Technical Specifications, which Deliverables shall together constitute the Final Design specification].[6]

4.1.2 In the event that the Games Publisher determines, at any time prior to acceptance of the Gold Master, that the Final Design Specification is incomplete, the parties shall in good faith collaborate with each other to finalise such specifications in order to ensure 100% functionality, provided that final decisions relating to completion of functionality components shall remain within the Games Publisher's sole discretion.

4.2 **Delivery** The Developer agrees to reasonably test each Deliverable prior to delivery to the Games Publisher. The Developer will develop and deliver to the Games Publisher the Deliverables, including the Prototype, Alpha Version, Beta Version and Gold Master of the Title, in accordance with the Milestone Schedule and will demonstrate as a material part of each delivery that the relevant deliverable is complete, and satisfies the applicable portion of the Design Documents. Delivery shall occur when the Games Publisher's Relationship Manager (or his or her delegate) receives a Deliverable from the Developer accompanied by a written statement listing the items delivered, a report of any bugs found during the Developer's tests and a note of the Developer's time spent testing such Deliverable, and stating that such Deliverable is ready for the Games Publisher's Acceptance Testing.[7]

4.3   **Failure to deliver the Title** If the Developer fails to deliver any Deliverable within 10 days of the applicable date set forth in the Design and Development Plan (and such delivery failure is not due to a breach by the Games Publisher of its obligations hereunder), then the Games Publisher may at any time thereafter be entitled to terminate this Agreement in accordance with the provisions of CLAUSE 8.1.2.

4.4   **Acceptance of the Deliverables**

4.4.1   Following receipt of each Deliverable, the Games Publisher shall, as appropriate, perform Acceptance Tests on such Deliverables. The Games Publisher shall use its reasonable efforts to complete such Acceptance Tests within 10 working days of the delivery of each Deliverable and in the case of the Alpha Version, 45 working days and in the case of the Beta Version, 30 working days (the 'Test Period'). Upon completion of such Acceptance Tests, the Games Publisher shall deliver to the Developer a written statement of acceptance, conditional acceptance or rejection. For each day after the Test Period that the Games Publisher has not delivered to the Developer such a written statement, the re-Delivery Date for such Deliverable shall be extended by one day.

4.4.2   If a Deliverable successfully completes the Acceptance Test, the Games Publisher shall deliver to the Developer a written statement of acceptance.

4.4.3   If all or any portion of a Deliverable does not successfully complete the Acceptance Tests, the Games Publisher shall deliver to the Developer a written notice of conditional acceptance or rejection, specifying the nature of each and every deficiency. The Developer shall promptly take such action as may be required to correct such deficiency, at no additional charge, and shall redeliver such Deliverable to the Games Publisher for further testing. The resubmitted Deliverable under this clause shall be deemed to have been approved as resubmitted unless a written request for modifications thereto shall have been received by the Developer within 10 working days after the resubmitted Deliverable has been received by the Games Publisher. This procedure shall continue until such time as the Games Publisher has delivered to Developer a written statement of acceptance by the Games Publisher. If the Developer fails to correct the same error after three successive test passes, the Developer shall be in breach of this Agreement and the Games Publisher may terminate this Agreement under CLAUSE 8.1.

4.5   **Additional Testing** The Developer acknowledges that, in addition to the Acceptance Testing to be conducted pursuant to this CLAUSE 4, the Games Publisher may conduct (i) user testing to determine 'user friendliness' and potential design defects affecting the marketability of the Title and (ii) quality assurance testing on hardware configurations other than those referenced in the Design and Development Plan.

4.6   **Good Faith** The parties shall act in good faith in connection with the delivery and acceptance procedures outlined in this CLAUSE 4.

4.7   **Developer's precautions against surreptitious Code** The Developer will use best efforts and take all precautions required by prudence to prevent the inclusion of a 'Self-Help Code' not approved in advance by the Games Publisher or 'Unauthorised Code' in the Title, or any individual unit thereof, developed by the Developer pursuant to this Agreement. 'Self-Help Code' shall mean any back-door, time-bomb, drop-dead device, or other software routine designed to disable a computer program automatically with the passage of time or under the positive control of a person other than a licensee of the program. 'Self-Help Code' does not include software routines in a computer program, if any, designed to permit the Games Publisher (or other person acting by authority of the Games Publisher) to obtain access to a licensee's computer system(s) (eg remote access via a modem) for purposes of maintenance or technical support. 'Unauthorised Code' shall mean any virus, Trojan horse, worm, or other software routines or hardware components designed to permit unauthorised access; to disable, erase, or otherwise harm software, hardware or data; or to perform any other such actions. The term 'Unauthorised Code' does not include Self-Help Code. The Developer will defend, indemnify and hold harmless and indemnify the Games Publisher against any claims, damages, losses and expenses (including reasonable attorneys' fees) arising from any alleged presence of Unauthorised Code or Self-Help Code not approved in writing in advance by the Games Publisher.

4.8   **Developer's continuing obligations**

   4.8.1   **Warranty Period** During the one-year period following initial release of the Title (the 'Warranty Period'), the Developer shall, at no charge to the Games Publisher, within 30 days of its receipt of notice of a Design Error, defect or bug, furnish such materials and services and make whatever revisions as are necessary to correct any such Design Error, defect or bug and, upon completion, promptly redeliver the corrected master disk to the Games Publisher. If the Developer fails to make the required corrections within said 30-day period, the Games Publisher, at its option, may take such corrective steps as it deems necessary and the reasonable costs associated therewith may be offset against any of the Games Publisher's payment obligations to the Developer hereunder.

   4.8.2   **Ongoing Support** Following expiration of the applicable Warranty Period and during the Term of this Agreement, the Developer agrees to continue to provide Design Error and ongoing support services to the Games Publisher. In the event that the Games Publisher decides to upload the Title for on-line distribution, the Online Version, the Developer shall assist the Games Publisher in uploading the Title and updating the on-line components as the Games Publisher deems necessary or advisable. The Games Publisher shall reimburse the Developer, on a time and materials basis, for actual cost and expenses incurred by the Developer in rendering such services.

4.9 **Source Code** Within three days of the successful completion of Acceptance Testing with respect to each Deliverable and the Gold Master, to the extent to which it has not already done so, the Developer shall deliver to the Games Publisher one copy of the source code, object code and Technical Specifications for the Title, as it exists as of that date. During the term of this Agreement, the Developer shall provide to the Games Publisher any updated source code, object code and Technical Specifications within ten days after completion of any Modifications or revisions to the Title or any New version.[8]

4.10 **Assurance of Services** The Developer shall ensure that those individuals herein identified as 'Key Personnel' shall devote their primary time and best efforts while working for the Developer to the performance of the Developer's obligations under this Agreement, until the Developer has completed those obligations. For purposes of this Agreement, Key Personnel shall be:

[Fill in names and titles]

and other personnel designated in writing for this project by the Developer and approved by the Games Publisher. The identity of Key Personnel may be changed upon written notice given in advance by the Developer, with the approval of the Games Publisher, which shall not be unreasonably withheld.

4.11 **Key Development Personnel**[9] *[Named employee]* shall be personally, directly and extensively employed in the performance of the Developer's obligations in this Agreement. In the event that *[named employee]* leaves the employment of the Developer, and a replacement of comparable experience and expertise is not hired within ninety (90) days, the Games Publisher shall be entitled to terminate this Agreement in accordance with the provisions of CLAUSE 8.1.1.

5. COMPENSATION

5.1 **Development Fee** In consideration of all rights granted or relinquished by the Developer and for the services provided by the Developer hereunder, the Games Publisher agrees to pay the Developer a design and development fee of £ [   ] (the 'Development Fee') which shall be recouped against royalties. The Development Fee shall be payable upon delivery and acceptance (in accordance with CLAUSE 4 above) of each Deliverable, in an amount equal to the Milestone Payment for such Deliverable as set forth in the Design and Development Plan. [The Developer shall use the Development Fee solely to fund development of the Deliverables and not for the purpose of paying dividends or making loans, or to fund development of any other project.[10]]

5.2 **Royalties**

5.2.1 After recoupment of the Development Fee and any other offsets, the Games Publisher shall pay the Developer a royalty equal to [   ] % of Net Receipts, less a reasonable reserve for returns, for sales (which shall include licences) of the Title by the Games Publisher (including, without limitation, sales by or through the Games Publisher's distributors and value-added resellers). No Royalty shall be payable on samples of the Title that are given away free for promotional, publicity or demonstration purposes, are given or sold to the Developer or are remaindered or sold at or below cost and no royalty shall be payable hereunder until such time as the Games Publisher has recouped all amounts recoupable by the Games Publisher under CLAUSE 5.1 hereof.

5.2.2   As used herein, 'Net Receipts' shall mean the actual amount received by the Games Publisher from the sale, lease or license of the Title, or from the sub-license of rights with respect to the Title, (exclusive of sales, use, excise and other taxes, packing, insurance, shipping and similar charges reimbursed by customers), less: (i) the amount of any credits or refunds for returns, taking into account any reserves previously established by the Games Publisher; (ii) any credits, discounts, rebates, and promotional allowances to customers; and (iii) the amount of any sales or use taxes required to be paid or withheld by the Games Publisher with respect to the payments due to the Developer.

5.2.3   For purposes of calculating royalties from sales of the Title in combination with one or more other articles ('bundling'), 'Net Receipts' shall be calculated as set forth in CLAUSE 5.2.2 provided however, that the actual amount received by Games Publisher for such sale of a Title shall be determined by multiplying the amount actually received by the Games Publisher for the bundle by the ratio represented by the suggested retail price of the Title divided by the sum of the suggested retail price of all products included in the bundle.

5.2.4   For purposes of calculating royalties from sales to original equipment manufacturers ('OEMs') for bundling purposes, 'Net Receipts' shall mean the Games Publisher's gross receipts from OEM sales, less (i) direct costs associated with OEM sales including, without limitation, manufacturing and replication costs (ie discs, component parts and manuals) and the allocated cost of incremental technical support; (ii) related marketing costs and expenses (ie CO-promotions with OEMs, advertising, market development funds and promotional allowances); (iii) sales commissions and/or distribution fees to third parties; (iv) direct costs associated with foreign sales (including, without limitation, localisation expenses and shipping; (v) returns, credits, discounts, taxes and (vi) a reasonable reserve against future returns.

5.2.5   In the event that the Games Publisher makes the Title available for downloading via on-line distribution services, the Developer shall be entitled to a royalty equal to [   ] % of the Games Publisher's Net Receipts attributable to fees paid by members of the on-line service for downloading. For purposes of calculating royalties from on-line use of the Title, 'Net Receipts' shall mean actual cash receipts by the Games Publisher, from fees paid by members of any on-line service provider based on use of the Title, which fees are directly attributable to downloading of the Title, [including the Games Publisher's receipts for connection and/or time charges, but excluding communications surcharges, hook-up fees, on-line membership fees, or on-line service standard subscription fees and amounts collected for taxes or duties, or goods or services purchased].

5.3 **Accrual and payment of royalties** The Games Publisher shall render accounting statements to the Developer (i) in February for the preceding period 1 April to 30 September, and (ii) in August for the preceding period 1 October to 31 March. If for any royalty period the current period total activity in the Developer's account for the Title is less than £100, then the Games Publisher may defer the rendering of a statement and payment until such royalty period as the cumulative activity since the last statement exceeds such amount. The Games Publisher shall keep accurate books of account and records covering all transactions relating to this Agreement at its principal place of business for a period of two years after making any royalty payment reflected in such records.

5.4 **No obligation to distribute** The Games Publisher shall have no obligation whatsoever to manufacture, sell and/or distribute the Title and makes no guarantee or representation as to the amount, if any, of its Net Receipts for the Title or the selling price at which the Title will be licensed or sold.[11]

5.5 **Equipment** The Games Publisher shall pay the Developer £[ ] to enable the Developer to acquire capital equipment subject to the mutual agreement of the Developer and the Games Publisher. The Developer shall execute such documents and take such action as the Games Publisher may reasonably request to perfect its security interest in the capital equipment.[12]

6. MODIFICATIONS/NEW VERSIONS/NEW EDITIONS

6.1 **Modifications** The Games Publisher may, from time to time in its sole discretion, elect to prepare enhanced versions of the Title that execute on the same operating platform(s) as such Title, that may include, without limitation, improvements, enhancements, modifications or alterations thereto to ensure adequate performance ('Modifications'). For a period of 18 months from the acceptance of the Gold Master of the Title by the Games Publisher, the Developer agrees to provide such services as the Games Publisher may in its sole discretion request in connection with Modifications to the Title. In full consideration for the performance of such services and the delivery of any materials necessary therefor, the Games Publisher shall reimburse the Developer for the cost of the personnel time and materials required, and any such compensation shall constitute additional recoupable payments. Prior to the Games Publisher's engaging the Developer for such services, the Developer shall submit a detailed written estimate of the personnel time (broken down by category of personnel), hourly rate of each person who the Developer proposes to perform such Modifications, materials cost required to implement such Modifications and a proposed production schedule for its implementation (it being understood that any such estimate shall reflect an average rate for personnel time of no greater than £50 per hour). The Games Publisher may also elect itself to perform or engage a third party to perform such Modification and may deduct the percentage of royalty that must be paid or the expense of such services from the royalties accruing to the Developer. In the event that the Developer does render services hereunder, its services and submissions shall be subject to a delivery schedule and approval standards to be agreed upon by the parties in advance of the Developer's rendering such services.

6.2 **New Versions and New Editions** In addition to the foregoing, the Games Publisher may, from time to time in its sole discretion, elect to (i) convert the Title for operation in a different operating platform or to localise the Title to a language other than English ('New Versions') or (ii) produce new editions of the Title which contain updated text or other data ('New Editions'). The Developer agrees to provide such services as the Games Publisher may, in its sole discretion, request in connection with such New Versions and/or New Editions. In full consideration for the performance of such services and the delivery of any materials necessary, the Games Publisher shall compensate the Developer for the cost of the personnel time and materials required therefor, and any such compensation shall be a recoupable payment against royalties for such New Version and/or New Edition. Prior to the Games Publisher's engaging the Developer for such services, the Developer shall submit a detailed written estimate of the personnel time (broken down by category of personnel), hourly rate of each person who the Developer proposes to perform such services, materials cost required to implement such services, and a proposed production schedule for the implementation of such services (it being understood that any such estimate shall reflect an average rate for personnel time of no greater that £50 per hour). In the event that the Developer renders services for New Versions and/or New Editions hereunder, its services and submissions shall be subject to a delivery schedule and approval standards to be agreed upon by the parties in advance of the Developer's rendering such services.

6.3 **Developer royalties** The Developer shall be entitled to the royalties set forth in CLAUSE 5.2 only for the Title and for those New Versions and/or New Editions for which it renders services under CLAUSE 6.2 to the Games Publisher's reasonable satisfaction. On New Versions and/or New Editions for which the Developer has not rendered services under CLAUSE 6.2 or has not rendered services to the Games Publisher's reasonable satisfaction, the Developer shall be entitled to a royalty of [ ] % of Net Receipts. Except as otherwise set forth herein, all payments to the Developer shall be based on the provisions of this CLAUSE 6. Any development fees or similar payments made to the Developer on a New Version and/or New Edition pursuant to CLAUSE 6.2 may be recouped against royalties payable to the Developer hereunder. Notwithstanding the foregoing, in no event shall the Developer be entitled to royalties for any New Version and/or New Edition for which it has not rendered services wherein the editorial content is not the same or substantially the same as the editorial content of the Title or source code of such New Version and/or New Edition is not the same or substantially the same as the source code of the Title.

6.4 **Translation and localisation of Title** If the Games Publisher requests that the Developer prepares New Versions of a Title and the implementation of such services is agreed by the Games Publisher, the Developer shall incorporate translated text and voice files of a Title procured by the Games Publisher at its cost and expense.

6.5 **Additional platforms** During the term of this Agreement the Developer will have the right at first option, ahead of any other third party developer, to develop all Derivative Works. Any Derivative Work to be developed by the Developer will be subject to all of the terms and conditions of this Agreement, and implemented through amendments to the Design Documents, and will be considered a separate Title hereunder; provided, however that with respect to Derivative Works designed for platforms other than personal computers, and with respect to On Line Versions, the parties will negotiate in good faith to determine the applicable royalty rate for such Derivative Work. If the Games Publisher and the Developer are not able to reach agreement on the amendments to the Design Documents and, if applicable the royalty rate under which the developer would develop a Derivative Work, then the Games Publisher will thereafter be free to enter into an agreement with any other party or parties to develop the planned Derivative Works on terms not less favourable to the Games Publisher than the Developer's last offer. In the event that the Developer does not elect to develop the Title for any such additional platforms, the Developer shall deliver to the Games Publisher whatever materials are reasonably required by the Games Publisher to develop the title for the additional platform, including, without limitation, source code and development tools, and shall co-operate with any third party developer engaged by the Games Publisher. In such event the Developer will be entitled to receive a royalty to be mutually agreed in good faith by the parties.

7. PROPRIETARY RIGHTS; LICENCE OF RIGHTS

7.1 **Games Publisher ownership** The Games Publisher shall own all right, title and interest in and to the Title and the Deliverables, and all additions to, deletions from, alterations of or revisions in, and each part thereof, including all Modifications and New Versions and all tools and work in progress with respect thereto, all hardware, software or other materials provided to the Developer by or at the expense of the Games Publisher, and all other materials developed or furnished by the Developer in connection with the services provided hereunder (collectively, for purposes of this Agreement, the 'Properties').

7.2 **Exclusive rights** As between the Developer and Games Publisher, the Games Publisher has the exclusive rights throughout the Universe to the Properties, including, but not limited to, publishing, reproduction or use of the Properties in all formats and media, including computerised versions, now known or later developed and in all languages and by all media now known or later developed, broadcasting by radio, making audio and video recordings and other mechanical or electronic renditions, making derivative works, customised versions, translations and other versions, showing by motion picture, cable, satellite, electrical transmission or by television, and otherwise utilising the Properties and material based on the Properties.

7.3 **Work and services** Without limiting the foregoing, the Developer hereby acknowledges that the Developer's work and services hereunder and all results thereof, including the Properties, are works done which have been specially ordered or commissioned by the Games Publisher and the Games Publisher shall own all right, title and interest therein throughout the Universe. The Games Publisher shall be considered the author of the Properties for purposes of copyright and shall own all the rights in and to the copyright of the Properties, and, as between the Developer and Games Publisher, only the Games Publisher shall have the right to obtain a copyright registration on the same which the Games Publisher may do in its name, its trade name or the name of its nominee(s). Accordingly, among other things, the Games Publisher is the author and owner of the Deliverables and shall have the sole and exclusive rights to do and authorise any and all of the acts of a copyright holder with respect to the Deliverables and any derivatives thereof, and to secure any and all renewals and extensions of such copyrights. The Developer retains no right to use the Deliverables and agrees not to challenge the validity of the Games Publisher's ownership in the Deliverables.[13]

7.4 **Proprietary rights** If the Properties or any portion thereof is determined not to be included as commissioned work in CLAUSE 7.3 the Developer hereby forthwith irrevocably assigns, transfers, releases and conveys to the Games Publisher in perpetuity throughout the universe, from the moment of its creation, all right, title and interest of the Developer in and to the Properties, as well as all intellectual property rights embodied in or pertaining to any of the foregoing and the complete right to exploit or otherwise use the Properties and all so-called auxiliary and subsidiary rights in any form of medium, expression or technology now known or hereafter known, created, devised or developed (including but not limited to free, pay, toll, advertising, subscription, radio, television devices, theatrical, audio visual cassettes, cartridges and disks), free and clear of any and all rights and claims by the Developer or any other third party. Accordingly, among other things, the Games Publisher shall have the sole and exclusive right to do and authorise any and all of the acts of the copyright holder, including, without limitation, to copyright in its name, as the owner thereof, the Properties and any derivatives thereof and to secure any and all renewals and extensions of such copyrights. In addition, the Developer shall, upon the Games Publisher's request, enter into any further assignments, waivers or licences of the Properties or Intellectual Property Rights related to the Deliverables as the Games Publisher deems necessary or appropriate, and hereby appoints the Games Publisher as its attorney for the purpose of executing such assignments, waivers or licences for and in the name of the Developer.

7.5   **Moral rights** The Developer hereby waives any and all claims that the Developer may now or hereafter have in any jurisdiction to so-called 'moral rights' with respect to the results of the Developer's work and services hereunder.

8.   TERMINATION

8.1   **Termination** This Agreement may be terminated in accordance with any of the following provisions:

8.1.1   the Games Publisher may terminate this Agreement at any time upon five days' prior written notice to the Developer in the event that the Games Publisher determines to cancel development of the Title for any reason in its sole discretion;

8.1.2   either party may terminate this Agreement at any time where the other party is in material breach of its obligations under this Agreement, and such party fails to cure such breach within 30 days after written notice thereof is given by the non-breaching party; or

8.1.3   either party may, at its option, immediately terminate this Agreement if a receiver is appointed for the other party or its property; the other party becomes insolvent or unable to pay its debts as they mature, or makes an assignment for the benefit of its creditors; the other party seeks relief or if proceedings are commenced against the other party or on its behalf under any bankruptcy insolvency or debtor's relief law, and such proceedings have not been vacated or set aside within 60 days from the date of commencement thereof; or if the other party is liquidated or dissolved.

8.2   **Events upon termination** In the event of the termination of this Agreement in accordance with any of the provisions of CLAUSE 8.1 hereof, the parties agree to the following:

8.2.1   Upon termination of this Agreement by the Games Publisher in accordance with CLAUSE 8.1.1 or by Developer in accordance with any provision of CLAUSE 8:

8.2.1.1   the Developer shall immediately deliver to the Games Publisher all work products of any nature whatsoever generated by the Developer in connection with the performance of this Agreement;

8.2.1.2   the Developer shall be entitled to receive, and Games Publisher shall be obligated to make, payment of any Milestone Payment on any Deliverable for which the Games Publisher has delivered a written notice of acceptance; and

8.2.1.3   the Games Publisher shall be obligated to compensate the Developer for the value of the services [on a time and materials basis at the Developer's most favourable rates] performed by the Developer in contemplation of receiving the next Milestone Payment and for which the Developer has not, as of the date of such termination, received a Milestone Payment pursuant to the terms of CLAUSE 4. The Developer shall submit to the Games Publisher a detailed invoice (which shall not be binding upon the Games Publisher) of the value of such services, provided, however, that approval of such invoice shall not be unreasonably withheld or: the Games Publisher shall be obligated to compensate the Developer for services performed by the Developer in contemplation of receiving the next Milestone Payment and for which the Developer has not, as of the date of such termination, received a Milestone Payment pursuant to the terms of CLAUSE 4. The payment to the Developer shall be determined by multiplying the next Milestone Payment by the ratio represented by the number of days between acceptance of the last Deliverable by the Games Publisher and the date of termination of the Agreement divided by the number of days between acceptance of the last Deliverable by the Games Publisher and the Delivery Date for the next Deliverable. In no event shall the value of such services be greater than the next scheduled Milestone Payment for the services being performed.

8.2.2   Upon termination of this Agreement by the Games Publisher in accordance with clauses 8.1.2 or 8.1.3:

8.2.2.1   the Developer shall immediately deliver to Games Publisher all work product of any nature whatsoever generated by the Developer in connection with the performance of this Agreement; and

8.2.2.2   in addition to any and all rights and remedies of the Games Publisher in law or at equity, the Games Publisher shall be entitled to offset its damages in completing development of the Titles against any Milestone Payment not paid to the Developer prior to termination on any Deliverable for which the Games Publisher has delivered a written notice of acceptance.

8.2.3   Upon termination of this Agreement by either party in accordance with CLAUSE 8.1 above, the Developer shall immediately return to the Games Publisher all equipment, instruments, diskettes, handbooks, documents, photographs, images, video and materials of any kind, and all copies thereof, that were provided to the Developer by the Games Publisher in connection with this Agreement.

8.3   Any termination of this Agreement (howsoever occasioned) shall not affect any accrued liabilities of either party nor shall it affect the coming into force or the continuance in force of any provision hereof which is expressly or by implication intended to come into or continue in force on or after such termination.

9.   WARRANTIES AND REPRESENTATION

9.1   **Developer's representations and warranties** The Developer warrants and represents that:

9.1.1   the Developer possesses full power and authority to enter into this Agreement and to fulfil its obligations hereunder and that it is financially and technically competent to perform its obligations hereunder, and agrees that any change in such status shall be immediately communicated in writing to the Games Publisher, and that performance of the terms of this Agreement and of the Developer's obligations hereunder shall not breach Developer's memorandum of association, articles of association, constitution charter or bylaw or any separate agreement by which the Developer is bound;

9.1.2   except to the extent developed by the Games Publisher or its employees, the Deliverables and all portions thereof shall be developed solely by the Developer through the use of Developer employees or through the services of consultants pursuant to the provisions of CLAUSE 3.6 hereof, and have otherwise irrevocably assigned all rights in the product of their services to the Developer or its assignee;

9.1.3   the work provided to the Games Publisher by the Developer will be its original work (except for material in the public domain or as to which permission has been obtained from the copyright owner as provided in CLAUSE 3.5 for use in connection with the Title developed hereunder in form as set forth in SCHEDULE C);

9.1.4   the Design Documents and Deliverables will not contain any libellous or otherwise unlawful material or infringe any statutory or common law copyright, trademark, patent or otherwise infringe any personal or proprietary right of any person or entity;

9.1.5   the performance of the Title shall conform to the specifications set forth in SCHEDULE A, shall operate in accordance with the Design Documents and with commonly accepted standards for the operation of computer software, and shall be free of errors and defects; and

9.1.6   the Title does not contain any Self Help Code, Unauthorised Code, or other software routines or hardware components designed to permit unauthorised access, to disable, erase, or otherwise harm software, hardware, data, or to perform any other such actions.

9.2   **Insurance** The Developer agrees to maintain, at its own expense, liability insurance providing adequate protection for itself and the Games Publisher against any claims of products or professional services liability with coverage in an amount not less than £1,000,000. Within 30 days of the effective date of this Agreement, the Developer shall submit to the Games Publisher a fully paid policy or certificate of insurance noting the Games Publisher's interest thereon as beneficiary.

9.3   **Games Publisher's representations and warranties** The Games Publisher warrants and represents that it has all necessary rights and authority to execute and deliver this Agreement and perform its obligations hereunder, and nothing contained in this Agreement or in the performance of this Agreement will place the Games Publisher in breach of any other contract or obligation.

9.4   **Limitation on liabilities** Neither party shall be liable to the other party for any incidental, consequential, special, or punitive damages or lost or imputed profits or royalties arising out of this agreement or its termination, whether for breach of warranty or any obligation arising therefrom or otherwise, whether liability is asserted in contract or tort (including negligence and strict product liability) and irrespective of whether the party has advised or has been advised of the possibility of any such loss or damage. Each party hereby waives any claims that these exclusions deprive such party of an adequate remedy.

10.   INDEMNIFICATION

10.1   **Indemnification by the Developer** The Developer shall indemnify, and hold the Games Publisher and its successors, assigns, agents, officers, directors and employees, harmless from and against any and all liabilities, obligations, losses, claims, damage, cost, charges or other expenses of every kind and character (including but not limited to reasonable attorneys' fees and court costs) which arise out of or result from any breach or alleged breach of any representation or warranty by the Developer or arising out of the Developer's failure to obtain releases or permissions from third parties required in connection with the Design Documents and/or Deliverables. The Games Publisher shall have the right to withhold its reasonable estimate of the total damages and expenses from sums otherwise payable to the Developer pursuant to this or any other agreement between the Developer and Games Publisher or any other affiliated, subsidiary, or parent companies of the Games Publisher, and to apply such sums to payment of such damages and expenses. The Games Publisher shall have the sole right to control the defence of any such claim and shall consult with Developer prior to settlement thereof. The Developer agrees to provide reasonable assistance to the Games Publisher at the Games Publisher's expense, in the defence of same.

10.2 **Premises** If the Developer, its agents or employees, shall be required by the terms of this Agreement to perform, or does perform, work on the premises of the Games Publisher, the Developer agrees to indemnify and hold harmless the Games Publisher, its officers, employees, agents and invitees from and against all claims, liabilities, losses, injuries and damages of every nature arising out of or in connection with the performance of such work.

10.3 **No remedy exclusive** The rights of indemnification of the Games Publisher and its successors, assigns, officers, directors and employees shall not be limited to the provisions of this Article, and the provisions of this Article shall be in addition to, and shall not be exclusive of any other rights or remedies which may accrue to the Games Publisher and its successors, assigns, officers, directors and employees.

11. CONFIDENTIALITY

11.1 Both during this Agreement and after its termination, the parties shall treat as confidential (and shall procure that its personnel and each of them treat as confidential) and shall not (and shall procure that their personnel and each of them does not) other than in the proper performance of this Agreement, use or disclose to any person, firm or company, any Confidential Information belonging to the other party or its clients, suppliers or customers, nor permit its use or disclosure. In particular, both parties shall maintain any source code provided by the other party under maximum security conditions.

11.2 The provisions of CLAUSE 11.1 shall not apply where Confidential Information is divulged to:

11.2.1 either parties' own employees and then only to those employees who need to know the same;

11.2.2 either parties' auditors, HM Inspector of Taxes, HM Customs and Excise, a court of competent jurisdiction, governmental body or applicable regulatory authority and any other persons or bodies having a right, duty or obligation to know the business of the other party and then only in pursuance of such right, duty or obligation.

11.3 Both parties undertake to ensure that persons and bodies referred to in CLAUSE 11.2 are made aware prior to the disclosure of any part of the Confidential Information that the same is confidential and that they owe a duty of confidence to the other party.

11.4 Each party to this Agreement shall promptly notify the other party if it becomes aware of any breach of confidence by any person to whom it divulges all or any part of the Confidential Information and shall give the other party all reasonable assistance in connection with any proceedings which the other party may institute against such person for breach of confidence.

11.5 The provisions of this clause shall survive the termination of this Agreement but the restrictions contained in CLAUSE 11.1 shall cease to apply to any information which may come into the public domain otherwise than through unauthorised disclosure.

11.6 Nothing in this CLAUSE 11 shall prevent the Developer from exploiting any inventions or software that it develops during the term of this Agreement.

12. MARKETING AND ADVERTISING

12.1 **Control of marketing and distribution** All aspects of the distribution and marketing of the Title will be in the Games Publisher's sole control, including but not limited to determining the methods of marketing, pricing, packaging, labelling and identification, protection, advertising, terms and conditions of sale or license, collection of customers' names and warranty or user registration procedures.

12.2 **Marketing efforts** Upon the Games Publisher's Acceptance of the Gold Master, the Games Publisher warrants that it will make a diligent good faith effort to market the resulting Title. The Games Publisher makes no representation or warranty, however, that the Title will be successfully marketed or that any minimum level of sales or licensing will be achieved.14 Nothing in this Agreement will prevent the Games Publisher from marketing any other work, whether similar or dissimilar to the Title, and nothing herein will require the Games Publisher to devote the same or similar efforts to marketing the Title as it devotes to other works.

12.3 **Publicity involving Developer** The Games Publisher agrees to place the name of the Developer on the package in which the Title is distributed, and the Games Publisher agrees to credit the Developer as developer in the software and documentation of the Title; provided in both cases that such placement and credits are permitted by all relevant third-party licensors who have approval rights with respect to the Title; and provided further that the location and size of such placements and credits are in compliance with the software and packaging guidelines adopted by such third-party licensors. The Games Publisher will also have the right to use and publish and permit others to use and publish the Developer's name in connection with the marketing of the Title. If the Games Publisher reasonably requests that the Developer participate in certain aspects of the marketing and promotion of the Title, the Developer will co-operate with such reasonable requests provided that the Games Publisher will pay any reasonable out-of-pocket expenses incurred by the Developer in providing such co-operation. The Games Publisher will consult with the Developer in connection with, and the Developer will have the right reasonably to approve in a timely fashion, all corporate information concerning the Developer that is not furnished by the Developer.

13. DATA PROTECTION

The parties hereby undertake to comply with the provisions of the Data Protection Act 1998 and any related legislation insofar as the same relates to the provisions and obligations of this Agreement.[15]

14. INTERPRETATION

14.1   In this Agreement unless the context otherwise requires:

14.1.1   words importing any gender include every gender;

14.1.2   words importing the singular number include the plural number and vice versa;

14.1.3   words importing persons include firms, companies and corporations and vice versa;

14.1.4   references to numbered clauses and schedules are references to the relevant clause in or schedule to this Agreement;

14.1.5   reference in any schedule to this Agreement to numbered paragraphs relate to the numbered paragraphs of that schedule;

14.1.6   the headings to the clauses, schedules and paragraphs of this Agreement will not affect the interpretation;

14.1.7   any reference to an enactment includes reference to that enactment as amended or replaced from time to time and to any subordinate legislation or byelaw made under that enactment;

14.1.8   any obligation on any party not to do or omit to do anything is to include an obligation not to allow that thing to be done or omitted to be done;

14.1.9   any party who agrees to do something will be deemed to fulfil that obligation if that party procures that it is done.

15. AGENCY, PARTNERSHIP

This Agreement shall not constitute or imply any partnership, joint venture, agency, fiduciary relationship or other relationship between the parties other than the contractual relationship expressly provided for in this Agreement.

16. AMENDMENTS

This Agreement may not be released, discharged, supplemented, interpreted, amended, varied or modified in any manner except by an instrument in writing signed by a duly authorised officer or representative of each of the parties hereto.

17. ANNOUNCEMENTS

No party shall issue or make any public announcement or disclose any information regarding this Agreement unless prior written consent has been obtained from the other party.

18. ASSIGNMENT

18.1   This Agreement is personal to the parties and, subject to CLAUSE 22.2 below, neither this Agreement nor any rights, licenses or obligations under this Agreement, may be assigned by either party without the prior written approval of the other party.

18.2   Notwithstanding the foregoing, either party may assign this Agreement to any acquirer of all or of substantially all of such party's equity securities, assets or business relating to the subject matter of this Agreement or to any entity controlled by, that controls, or is under common control with a party to this Agreement. Any attempted assignment in violation of this clause will be void and without effect.

18.3   The Developer may assign or pledge its right to receive royalty payments hereunder.

19. ENTIRE AGREEMENT

This Agreement supersedes all prior agreements, arrangements and undertakings between the parties and constitutes the entire agreement between the parties relating to the subject matter of this Agreement. However the obligations of the parties under any pre-existing non-disclosure agreement shall remain in full force and effect insofar as there is no conflict between the same. The parties confirm that they have not entered into this Agreement on the basis of any representation that is not expressly incorporated into this Agreement.

20. FORCE MAJEURE[16]

Neither party shall have any liability under or be deemed to be in breach of this Agreement for any delays or failures in performance of this Agreement which result from circumstances beyond the reasonable control of that party. If such circumstances continue for a continuous period of more than [6 months], either party may terminate this Agreement by written notice to the other party.

21. NOTICES

21.1   Any notice to be given under this Agreement shall be in writing and shall be sent by first class mail or air mail, or by fax (confirmed by first class mail or air mail), to the address of the relevant party set out at the head of this Agreement or such other address as that party may from time to time notify to the other party in accordance with this CLAUSE 21.1.

21.2 Notices sent as above shall be deemed to have been received three working days after the day of posting (in the case of inland first class mail), or seven working days after the date of posting (in the case of air mail), or on the next working day after transmission (in the case of fax messages, but only if a transmission report is generated by the sender's fax machine recording a message from the recipient's fax machine, confirming that the fax was sent to the number indicated above and confirming that all pages were successfully transmitted).

21.3 In proving the giving of a notice it shall be sufficient to prove that the notice was left, or that the envelope containing the notice was properly addressed and posted, or that the applicable means of telecommunication was addressed and despatched and despatch of the transmission was confirmed and/or acknowledged as the case may be.

22. SCHEDULES

The provisions of SCHEDULE[S] (*A-E*) to this Agreement shall form part of this Agreement as if set out here.

23. SEVERANCE

If any provision of this Agreement is prohibited by law or judged by a court to be unlawful, void or unenforceable, -the provision shall, to the extent required, be severed from this Agreement and rendered ineffective as far as possible without modifying the remaining provisions of this Agreement, and shall not in any way affect any other circumstances of or the validity or enforcement of this Agreement.

24. SUCCESSORS AND ASSIGNEES

24.1 This Agreement shall be binding upon, and ensure to the benefit of, the parties and their respective successors and permitted assignees, and references to a party in this Agreement shall include its successors and permitted assignees.

24.2 In this Agreement references to a party include references to a person:

24.2.1 who for the time being is entitled (by assignment, novation or otherwise) to that party's rights under this Agreement (or any interest in those rights); or

24.2.2 who, as administrator, liquidator or otherwise, is entitled to exercise those rights;

and in particular those references include a person to whom those rights (or any interest in those rights) are transferred or pass as a result of a merger, division, reconstruction or other reorganisation involving that party. For this purpose, references to a party's rights under this Agreement include any similar rights to which another person becomes entitled as a result of a novation of this Agreement.

25. WAIVER

No delay, neglect or forbearance on the part of either party in enforcing against the other party any term or condition of this Agreement shall either be or be deemed to be a waiver or in any way prejudice any right of that party under this Agreement. No right, power or remedy in this Agreement conferred upon or reserved for either party is exclusive of any other right, power or remedy available to that party.

26. COUNTERPARTS

This Agreement may be executed in any number of counterparts or duplicates, each of which shall be an original, and such counterparts or duplicates shall together constitute one and the same agreement.

27. TIME IS OF THE ESSENCE

Time shall be of the essence in this Agreement as regards any time, date or period mentioned in this Agreement or subsequently substituted as a time, date or period by agreement in writing between the parties.

28. SUBCONTRACTING

With the prior written consent of the Games Publisher (such consent not to be unreasonably withheld or delayed) the Developer may perform any or all of its obligations under this Agreement through agents or sub-contractors, provided that the Developer shall remain liable for such performance and shall indemnify the Games Publisher against any loss or damage suffered by the Games Publisher arising from any act or omission of such agents or sub-contractors.

29. LANGUAGE

This Agreement is made only in the English language. If there is any conflict in the meaning between the English language version of this Agreement and any version or translation of this Agreement in any other language, the English language version shall prevail.

30. COSTS AND EXPENSES

Each party shall bear its own legal costs and other costs and expenses arising in connection with the drafting, negotiation, execution and registration (if applicable) of this Agreement.

31. SET-OFF

Where either party has incurred any liability to the other party, whether under this Agreement or otherwise, and whether such liability is liquidated or unliquidated, each party may set off the amount of such liability against any sum that would otherwise be due to the other party under this Agreement.

32. THIRD PARTIES[17]

[The parties confirm their intent not to confer any rights on any third parties by virtue of this Agreement and accordingly the Contracts (Rights of Third Parties) Act 1999 shall not apply to this Agreement.]

Or

[The parties recognise that this Agreement is intended to benefit and shall so benefit (insert name of third party) for the purposes of the Contracts (Rights of Third Parties) Act 1999 and, subject to that, the parties confirm their intent not to confer any rights on any other third parties by virtue of this Agreement.]

33. SURVIVAL

On any termination of this Agreement, clauses 6, 7, 8, 9, 10 and 11 shall remain in full force and effect.

34. PROPER LAW AND JURISDICTION[18]

34.1   This Agreement and all matters arising from it and any dispute resolutions referred to below shall be governed by and construed in accordance with English Law notwithstanding the conflict of law provisions and other mandatory legal provisions save that:

34.1.1   the Publisher shall have the right to sue to recover its fees in any jurisdiction in which the Developer is operating or has assets, and

34.1.2   the Publisher shall have the right to sue for breach of its intellectual property rights and other proprietary information and trade secrets ('IPR') (whether in connection with this Agreement or otherwise) in any country where it believes that infringement or a breach of this Agreement relating to its IPR might be taking place. For the avoidance of doubt, the place of performance of this Agreement is agreed by the parties to be England.

34.2   Each party recognises that the other party's business relies upon the protection of its IPR and that in the event of a breach or threatened breach of IPR, the other party will be caused irreparable damage and such other party may therefore be entitled to injunctive or other equitable relief in order to prevent a breach or threatened breach of its IPR.

34.3   With respect to all other disputes which are not IPR related pursuant to clauses 34.1 and 34.2 above and its special rules the following procedures in clauses 34.3 to 34.5 shall apply. Where there is a dispute the aggrieved party shall notify the other party in writing of the nature of the dispute with as much detail as possible about the deficient performance of the other party. A representative from senior management ('representatives') of each of the parties shall meet in person or communicate by telephone within five business days of the date of the written notification in order to reach an agreement about the nature of the deficiency and the corrective action to be taken by the respective parties. The representatives shall produce a report about the nature of the dispute in detail to their respective boards and if no agreement is reached on corrective action, then the chief executives of each party shall meet in person or by telephone, to facilitate an agreement within five business days of a written notice by one to the other. If the dispute cannot be resolved at board level within a further five business days, or if the agreed upon completion dates in any written plan of corrective action are exceeded, either party may seek its legal remedies as provided below.

34.4   If the parties cannot resolve a dispute in accordance with the procedure in CLAUSE 34.3 above, then they shall with the assistance of the Centre for Alternative Dispute Solution, seek to resolve the dispute or difference amicably by using an Alternative Dispute Resolution ('ADR') procedure acceptable to both parties before pursuing any other remedies available to them. If either party fails or refuses to agree to or participate in the ADR procedure or if in any event the dispute or difference is not resolved to the satisfaction of both parties within [90] days after it has arisen, the matter shall be settled in accordance with the procedure below.

34.5   If the parties cannot resolve the dispute by the procedure set out above, the parties shall irrevocably submit to the exclusive jurisdiction of the Courts of England and Wales for the purposes of hearing and determining any dispute arising out of this Agreement.

34.6   [While the dispute resolution procedure above is in progress and any party has an obligation to make a payment to another party or to allow a credit in respect of such payment, the sum relating to the matter in dispute shall be paid into an interest bearing deposit account to be held in the names of the relevant parties at a clearing bank and such payment shall be a good discharge of the parties' payment obligations under this Agreement. Following resolution of the dispute, whether by mediation or legal proceedings, the sum held in such account shall be payable as determined in accordance with the mediation or legal proceedings, and the interest accrued shall be allocated between the parties pro rata according to the split of the principal sum as between the parties.]

AS WITNESS etc

SCHEDULE A

DESIGN AND DEVELOPMENT PLAN

MILESTONE SCHEDULE

MILESTONE I   PRELIMINARY DESIGN SPECIFICATION

The Preliminary Design Specification shall include a general description of the product, product

elements, technical strategy, overview flowchart, storyboards to illustrate product play, art, audio/video, and licensing requirements and a preliminary budget.

Delivery Date [   ]

Payment [   ]

MILESTONE 2   PROTOTYPE AND FINAL DESIGN SPECIFICATIONS

The Final Design Specification shall include a finalised flowchart, the grounds for each individual screen and the final description of all product elements including: product overview, product structure (user interface, screen descriptions/layouts and inventory of all art and audio assets) and product flow. Inventories of all art and audio necessary to complete the product and a finalised art style shall be included along with storyboards for all key product graphic elements. The Final Design Specification details the technical aspects of the implementation (including codes for video, speed, fonts, graphic depth and other pieces of the interface screen design) with risks and alternatives and a final budget and schedule.

The Title Design Specifications will include: High concept; Feature overview; Description of installation process; Description of filing operations and save and load options; Feature map, including description of relationship to other features; For each major feature, the Goal of feature; User interface description; Musical content, if any; and Sound effect content.

The Design Specification will also include descriptions of the following: Programming language and proprietary and commercial development tools utilised including version numbers; Video driver technology; Sound driver technology; Mouse driver technology; CD driver technology; CD file map description and configuration; Memory map description and configuration.

Delivery Date [   ]

Payment [   ]

MILESTONE 3   DEMO I

Demo 1 will be based on the prototype and will be a running demo appropriate for marketing purposes.

MILESTONE 4   ROUGHLY PLAYABLE

The roughly playable product shall be based on the Final Design Specifications and shall demonstrate the navigation and interfaces to be used and the unique features of the product as they will appear on the delivery platforms. The roughly playable product will include sample demonstrations of all product elements, including music and sound effects, if applicable, response to user controller buttons, and a fully functioned user interface. The roughly playable product must demonstrate key elements of the final product. The roughly playable product must include sufficient data show variety and repeatability, must include sample media, must clearly demonstrate the look and feel and user navigation of the final product, and must run on all targeted platforms.

Delivery Date [   ]

Payment [   ]

MILESTONE 5   ALPHA VERSION COMPLETED

Delivery Date [   ]

Payment [   ]

MILESTONE 6   DEMO 2

Demo 2 will be based on the Alpha Version and will be a running demo incorporating any new components and/or design changes in the Alpha Version. Demo 2 will reflect all components of the product and will illustrate full functionality of the product. Demo 2 will be used for review purposes.

MILESTONE 7   BETA VERSION COMPLETED

Delivery Date [   ]

Payment [   ]

MILESTONE 8   DEMO 3

Demo 3 will be based on the Beta Version and will be a running demo incorporating any new components and/or design changes in the Beta Version. Demo 3 will reflect all components of the product and will demonstrate full functionality of the product. Demo 3 will be used for [   ] purposes.

MILESTONE 9   PACKAGING AND COLLATERAL REQUIREMENTS

The Developer shall deliver the following for incorporation into packaging and other materials collateral to the product: EPS versions of Developer logos, screen shots, tips and techniques for troubleshooting, installation instructions, guidance in navigating the system, notes, and photos and other assets in digital form. The Developer shall also review all packaging and other materials collateral to the product to the extent requested by the Games Publisher.

Delivery Date [   ]

Payment [   ]

MILESTONE 10   RIGHTS CLEARANCES

All rights clearances completed and evidenced by fully executed licence agreements.

Delivery Date [   ]

Payment [   ]

MILESTONE 11   GOLD MASTER AND DOCUMENTATION

The final version of the Title means the ROM files in the form of a duplicable program (a 'Gold Master'), on EPROMs or other suitable medium as specified by the Games Publisher, suitable for manufacture without any modifications. All development work and corrections to the Beta Version will be incorporated into the Gold Master. The Documentation shall also be provided.

Delivery Date [   ]

Payment [   ]

SCHEDULE B

DESCRIPTION OF THE TITLE

[*FILL IN*]

DESCRIPTION OF TITLE SPECIFICATIONS

OPERATING SYSTEM SPECIFICATIONS

The Title should be compatible with the following minimum configuration for the applicable operating system. The Title should take advantage wherever possible of any capabilities exceeding those described below.

PC Minimum Requirements: [   ]

Macintosh Minimum Requirements: [   ]

TITLE REQUIREMENTS

The Title should include application which, within reason, detects hardware capabilities of the machine and installs all required software and drivers on CD.

The Installer should also be able to perform de-install, removing all files installed on hard drive by original install process.

The Title should require no more than [   ] of hard drive space when installed in minimum configuration. The User should be allowed to specify the installation directory.

SCHEDULE C

FORM OF PERMISSION FORM

Description of Material [   ]

Owner [   ]

1.   ('Developer') wants to incorporate the above Material in a work tentatively titled [   ] (the 'Work') to be copyrighted and published by Games Publisher, its grantees and licensees (the 'Publisher'), and I want the Publisher to incorporate the above described Material in the Work and as set forth below.

2.   I, the undersigned, hereby grant to the Developer and Publisher throughout the universe, the perpetual and irrevocable right and permission to use and edit the above Material, as desired, for any and all editions of the Work in any and all languages, formats and media now known or hereafter known. Such right shall include, without limitation, the right to:

(a)   modify, or have modified the Material (including making derivative works of), to combine the Material or portions thereof with such other material (animation, video, sound, software, etc) as the Publisher and/or Developer selects to create the Work, and to put the material into digital electronic form;

(b)   to reproduce and manufacture, or have reproduced and manufactured, the Work containing the Material and/or any derivative works of the Work;

(c)   to market, distribute, sub-license, lease and rent, directly or indirectly to end users, products containing the Material; and (d) to grant sub-licenses to sub-distributors or value-added resellers to undertake the activities authorised above. The Publisher shall own all right, title and interest, including the copyright, in and to the Work, including, without limitation, electronic rights thereto, and may use, re-use, license, transfer or dispose of them, without limitation, for any and all purposes, in any and all languages formats and media now known or hereafter known, including, without limitation, print publications, electronic versions and audio and video recordings.

3.   [The Publisher shall list the following credit if it uses the above [ ] Material: [ ] Developer shall pay me the amount of £ [ ] in full consideration of the grant I make under this Agreement].

4.   I warrant and represent that I have full right and power to enter into this Agreement; that the Material is original; that the Material does not contain any libellous or otherwise unlawful material or violate any copyright, trademark, patent or other intellectual property right; and that the Material will not violate any personal or proprietary right of any person or entity.

5.   I agree to indemnify and hold the Publisher and its officers, representatives, agents, employees, assignees, grantees and licensees, harmless from and against all claims, losses, costs, expenses, settlements, demands and liabilities of every kind, including reasonable attorneys' fees and expenses, arising out of or incurred by reason of the use of the above Material as set forth above, or the inaccuracy, alleged or actual breach of any representation, warranty, covenant, agreement, or undertaking I have made herein.

Date [ ]

[OWNER]   [Developer]

By [ ]   By [ ]

Name [ ]   Name [ ]

Title [ ]   Title [ ]

Address [ ]   Address [ ]

FORM OF STANDARD APPEARANCE OR PERFORMANCE RELEASE (WITH ORIGINAL MUSIC)

1.   The Games Publisher, its grantees and licensees (the 'Publisher') wants to record my name, likeness, voice and/or original musical compositions and performances on multimedia, electronic, audio, video or film formats or on other media (the 'Recordings') for various uses in its sole discretion.

2.   I want the Publisher to make such Recordings and use them as set forth below, and I shall provide services to the Publisher in order to enable the Publisher to make such Recordings (the 'Services') .

3.   I, the undersigned, hereby grant to the Publisher, it successors, assigns, assignees, grantees and licensees, permission to make the Recordings and edit them as desired. The Publisher shall own all right, title and interest, including the copyright, in the Recordings, and may use, re-use, license, transfer or dispose of them, without limitation, for any purposes, in any language and media now known or hereafter developed, including in print publications and audio and video recordings and electronic uses; provided, however, that notwithstanding and subject to the foregoing, I shall retain the copyright in my original musical composition. My name, voice, likeness, picture and biographical data,

may be used to publicise, promote and advertise a work or other materials containing the Recordings, and in any materials that derive from, supplement or relate to such work or Recordings.

4.   I agree to indemnify and hold the Publisher and its officers, representatives, agents, employees, assignees, grantees and licensees, harmless from and against all claims, losses, costs, expenses, settlements, demands and liabilities of every kind, including reasonable attorneys' fees and expenses, arising out of or incurred by reason of the use of the above material cr my provision of Services, or the inaccuracy, alleged or actual breach of any representation, warranty, covenant, agreement, or undertaking I have made herein.

5.   I warrant that I own all rights to any musical compositions provided or performed by me for use in the Recordings. I further warrant that the use of my name, likeness, voice, musical composition and/ or other material provided by me will not violate the rights of any person or entity and will not cause the Publisher to incur any liability for payment to any person or entity. I represent and warrant that the grant and other provisions of this Release are not in conflict with and do not violate any commitment, agreement, obligation or understanding that I now have or will in the future have with any other person or entity.

6.   I hereby release the Publisher, its agents, employees, licensees, directors, officers, assigns and anyone using the Recordings or other material supplied by me from any and all claims, losses, demands, damages, liability, costs and expenses including reasonable attorneys' fees and expenses which I now have or may hereafter have by reason of the use of my name, likeness, voice, musical composition or performance or materials in connection with the Recording, or the inaccuracy, alleged breach or actual breach of any representation, warranty or undertaking I have made herein or in the Recording, or any loss, damage or injury to me that may be sustained by me or my property incurred during the performance of Services hereunder.

NAME [   ]

SIGNATURE [   ]

TITLE [   ]

ADDRESS [   ]

DATE [   ]

TELEPHONE [   ]

I represent that I am a parent (guardian) of the minor who signed the above Release and I hereby agree that we shall both be bound thereby.

Signature of Parent or Guardian [   ]

Name [   ]

Address (if different) [   ]

SCHEDULE D

FORM OF SUB-CONTRACTOR AGREEMENT

Dear [   ]

This Letter Agreement sets forth the terms of your agreement with [DEVELOPER] (the 'Developer') to perform services and/or create materials in connection with a work tentatively entitled (the 'Work') to be copyrighted and published by the Games Publisher (the 'Publisher').

1   **Materials** You agree to provide the following services (the 'Services') and the following materials (the 'Materials') for inclusion in the Work:

2   **Delivery** You agree to perform the Services and deliver the Materials to the Developer on or before [   ], in content and form satisfactory to the Developer. Time is of the essence in connection with your performance hereunder. If you fail to perform the Services or deliver the Materials, or any portion thereof, in accordance with the above date or such later deadline as the Developer may in its discretion fix in writing, the Developer may terminate this Agreement without any further obligation to you.

3   **Compensation** As full compensation for all Services performed and Materials provided by you hereunder, the Developer will pay to you £ [   ]. You acknowledge that the Developer bears the responsibility for making such payments and you will not look to or make any claim against the Publisher in connection therewith. Any claim by you against the Developer will not affect the Publisher's rights to or ownership of the Materials. You will be responsible for your own travel and out-of-pocket expenses incurred in connection with the Services and the delivery of the Materials, and you acknowledge that you are not authorised to incur any expenses on behalf of the Developer or Publisher without their prior written consent.

4   **Proprietary rights** You acknowledge and agree that the Services performed and the Materials provided hereunder have been specially ordered or commissioned as a work made for use as a contribution or supplement to the Work and that the Publisher shall own all right, title and interest thereto. You further acknowledge that the Publisher shall be considered the author of the Materials for purposes of copyright, shall own all rights in and to the copyright of the Materials and shall have the right to register and renew the copyright in its name or the name of its nominee(s). To the extent that the Materials do not forthwith automatically vest in the Publisher, you hereby forthwith irrevocably grant, assign and transfer all of your right, title and interest in and to the Materials to the Publisher. Without limiting the foregoing, you hereby waive any and all claims that you may now or hereafter have in any jurisdiction to so-called 'moral rights' or rights of 'adroit moral' in connection with the Materials.

5   **Advertising/promotion** You authorise the use of your name, biographical material and likeness in connection with the Work and

the advertising and promotion thereof, but the Publisher no obligation to acknowledge your contribution to the Work.

6   **Confidentiality** You shall treat all information provided to you in connection with this Letter Agreement, and the Services performed and the Materials created hereunder, as proprietary and confidential, whether or not so identified, and shall not disclose the whole, or any part thereof, to any third parties, without the prior written consent of the Developer.

7   **Editing/approvals** You acknowledge and agree that the Services performed and the Materials prepared hereunder shall be in form and content satisfactory to the Developer, and the Developer and Publisher have the right to edit, change, add to or delete from the Materials. You understand that the Developer will withhold final approval and acceptance of the Materials until the Publisher approves and accepts the Materials. In the event that the Publisher does not approve and accept the Materials, or any portion thereof, the Developer may either (i) request you to revise such Materials, at your own expense, and deliver such revised Materials to the Developer in accordance with delivery dates determined by the Developer, or (ii) terminate this Letter Agreement without any obligation to you. If the Developer terminates this Letter Agreement prior to the completion of the Services and Materials, the Developer's sole obligation will be to pay you, pro rata, the amount due for the Services acceptably performed and the Materials approved and accepted by the Publisher.

8.   **Independent contractor** You hereby acknowledge that you are an independent contractor and not an employee of the Developer or the Publisher. You understand and agree that you are not entitled to any benefits provided to any employee of the Developer or of the Publisher. You acknowledge that it is your sole responsibility to report as income any compensation received hereunder and to make requisite tax filings and payments to the appropriate tax authority.

9.   **Compliance** You agree that you will personally be responsible for compliance with all laws, regulations and orders in connection with taxes, unemployment insurance, social security, worker's compensation, disability or like matters.

10.   **Warranties and representations** You warrant and represent that you have full right and power to enter into this Letter Agreement; that the Materials will be original; that the Materials will not contain any libellous or otherwise unlawful material or violate any copyright, trademark, patent or other intellectual property right; and that the Materials will not violate any personal or proprietary right of any person or entity. You will defend any claim of breach of warranty and, if it is determined that you breached the warranties set forth herein, you will indemnify the Developer and the Publisher for any loss they may suffer as a result of such breach. You acknowledge that the warranties and representations herein shall survive the termination of this Agreement.

11.   **Entire understanding** This Letter Agreement sets forth the entire agreement and understanding between you and the Developer, and

supersedes any prior agreements or understanding, whether oral or in writing. This Letter Agreement may not be modified except in writing signed by both parties. This Letter Agreement and the rights and obligations of the parties shall be governed and construed under the laws of England as if executed and fully performed therein. You may not assign or delegate your duties hereunder and any such purported assignment shall be void.

[DEVELOPER]

BY [   ]

Name [   ]

Title [   ]

Agreed and accepted this

[   ] dayof [   ] [   ]

[NAME]

BY [   ]

Title [   ]

Address [   ]

1 This Agreement is intended to be used between a computer games publisher and its developer. Computer games developers on occasions may have part developed a game and need a publisher to commercialise it and take it to market. On other occasions the developer may have nothing more than a concept and needs a publisher to fund completion of the game. On other occasions publishers outsource game development in that they already have the rights to a game or the idea for a game but do not have the capacity to develop 'in-house'.

2 It is important to accurately recite the relationship between the parties and their reasons for entering into the agreement.

3 This heavily favours the Games Publisher. The Developer does not need to hand over these materials to enable Acceptance Tests to be performed.

4 Some Developers may not wish to reveal this to the Games Publisher.

5 Not only may the Games Publisher provide the Developer with information and materials, but may also provide computer equipment and third party development tools. It may be advisable where equipment is being 'loaned' by the Games Publisher that a formal agreement is entered into recognising that that equipment is being loaned and is returned on termination.

6 This clause recognises that the Developer may either be developing the game from scratch or may have already produced a prototype.

7 This favours the Games Publisher and adds extra pressure on the Developer.

8 Some developers may not wish to hand over source code, in which case that source code may have to be escrowed with an escrow agency such as the National Computing Centre.

9 This may not be relevant to certain situations, but if there is an outstanding designer which the Games Publisher heavily relies on, it becomes very important.

10 This is highly restrictive on the Developer, and a Games Publisher may use this provision in the case of new or young developers if there is a perceived cashflow problem which could jeopardise the development of the Game.

11 Likely that a Developer would find this clause unacceptable unless suitable wording is added to the effect that a prolonged period of non-use or non-exploitation, or lack of sales, means the Developer can take the work product to another Publisher.

12 The Developer may have great ideas for a Game, but not the facilities to complete the necessary work, in such cases, the Games Publisher may loan money to buy the equipment, or may even loan the equipment itself.

13 Depending on the bargaining position of the Developer, it may resist this clause and grant a long licence of rights as an alternative.

14 A more powerful Developer will be able to insist on minimum sales levels.

15 The UK law requires any business which processes data about living individuals to be notified with the Data Protection Office. Under the Data Protection Act 1998, S l(1) (the Act) data is defined as information which:

(a) is being processed by means of equipment operating automatically in response to instructions given for that purpose;

(b) is recorded with the intention that it should be processed by means of such equipment;

(c) is recorded as part of a relevant filing system or with the intention that it should form part of a relevant filing system; and

(d) does not fall within paragraph (a), (b) or (c) but forms part of an accessible record as defined in section 68 of the Act. Accessible records are health records, educational records and accessible public records defined in SCHEDULE 12 to the Act.

16 This force majeure clause is short and general. It may be appropriate to insert a more detailed force majeure clause such as:

'Notwithstanding anything else contained in this Agreement, neither party shall be liable for any delay in performing its obligations hereunder if such delay is caused by circumstances beyond its reasonable control (including without limitation any delay caused by any act or omission of the other party) provided however that any delay by a sub-contractor or supplier of the party so delaying shall not relieve the party from liability for delay except where such delay is beyond the reasonable control of the sub-contractor or supplier concerned. Subject to the party so delaying promptly notifying the other party in writing of the reasons for the delay (and the likely duration of the delay), the performance of such party's obligations shall be suspended during the period that the said circumstances persist and such party shall be granted an extension of time for performance equal to the period of the delay. Save where such delay is caused by the act or omission of the other party (in which event the rights, remedies and liabilities of the parties shall be those conferred and imposed by the other terms of this Agreement and by law):

Any costs arising from such delay shall be borne by the party incurring the same; either party may, if such delay continues for more than 10 weeks, terminate this Agreement forthwith giving notice in writing to the other by reason of such termination.'

17 Before the Contracts (Rights of Third Parties) Act 1999 (the Act) it was the case that a person who was not a party to a contract (a third party) could not enforce any right under the contract. Similarly, a contract could not impose any obligations or liabilities on a third party.

However the Act attempts to draw a balance between the freedom of the parties to vary a contract and the interests of the third party. The Act means that a contractual clause benefiting a third party (eg the promisee's subsidiary company or sub-contractor or employee) will be straightforwardly enforceable by that third party if:

• the contract expressly provides that he may; or

• where a term in the contract purports to confer a benefit on him (unless on a proper construction of the contract it appears that the parties did not intend the term to be enforceable by the third party.)

It is therefore prudent to include a clause to the effect of excluding the provisions of the Act. By doing so it ensures that any rights of third parties are not deemed to be enforceable by them. This is particularly the case where the parties are companies and may have subsidiaries or conversely parent companies.

18 In this Agreement it is felt appropriate to use an escalating dispute solutions clause (sometimes called an alternative dispute resolution clause) because during the period of the Agreement any dispute between the parties may be better settled in private and without recourse to litigation (except as reserved by the clause in relation to breach of IPR).

It may be felt in some circumstances an arbitration clause could be more appropriate or the parties may wish to simply indicate that they will resort to litigation in the courts.

An example of another governing law and dispute settlement clause is:

'Any dispute which may arise between the parties concerning this Agreement shall be determined as follows:

(1) If the dispute shall be of a technical nature relating to the functions or capabilities of the Licensed Program Materials or any similar or related matter then such a dispute shall be referred for final settlement to an expert nominated jointly by the parties or failing such nomination within Fourteen (14) days after either party's request to the other therefore nominated at the request of either party by the President for the time being of the British Computer Society. Such expert shall

be deemed to act as an expert and not as an arbitrator. His decision shall (in the absence of clerical or manifest error) be final and binding on the parties and whose costs shall be borne between the parties in equal shares unless he determines that the conduct of either party is such that such party should bear all of such fees.

(2)   In any other case the dispute shall be determined by the High Court of Justice in England and the parties hereby submit to the exclusive jurisdiction of that Court for such purposes.'

11 Heads of Agreement[1] for software distribution

Date [   ]

Parties [   ]

RECITALS[2]

A. The Supplier creates, develops and markets the software defined in PART 1 OF THE FIRST SCHEDULE ('the Software').

B. The Distributor is in the business of marketing, distributing and supporting Software products for use on the equipment specified in PART 2 OF THE FIRST SCHEDULE ('the Equipment') and wishes to acquire rights from the Supplier to licence and sub-licence the Software for use on the Equipment.

C. The Supplier proposes extending the market for the Software by granting to the Distributor the right for the Distributor to licence, sub-licence, market, distribute and support the same in [   ] ('the Territory') in accordance with the terms and conditions hereinafter contained.

NOW IT IS HEREBY AGREED as follows:

1. GRANT

The Supplier grants to the Distributor a non-exclusive right to sub-licence the Software in accordance with the provisions of the FOURTH SCHEDULE and generally to market, distribute and support the Software under the Supplier's trade mark and/or the agreed trade mark of the Distributor in the Territory for use on the Equipment during the term.

2. TERM

This Agreement is for a period of [   ] years commencing on the [   ] day of [   ] [   ] and thereafter from year to year unless and until terminated by either party giving to the other not less than three months' prior written notice subject always to prior termination as hereinafter specified.

3. TECHNICAL INFORMATION

3.1   The Supplier will deliver [*insert details*] ('the Distributor') to the Distributor.

3.2   The Supplier will keep the Distributor informed of any changes, additions or modifications to the Deliverables.

3.3   The Distributor shall on copies made of all the Deliverables reproduce the copyright symbol, legend, trade mark or other items as stipulated by the Supplier.

4. TRAINING

The Supplier will provide the training on the terms set out in the FIFTH SCHEDULE.

5. COMMERCIAL AND TECHNICAL ASSISTANCE

In addition to training provided for in CLAUSE 4 above, the Supplier undertakes from time to time at the request of the Distributor to render such further commercial and technical assistance as may be required at the cost and expense of the Distributor.

6. ORDERING OF SOFTWARE

6.1   The Distributor agrees to order from the Supplier a minimum number of copies of the Software specified in the Second SCHEDULE.

6.2   [*Insert other terms for ordering.*]

7. DELIVERY OF SOFTWARE

[*Insert method for delivery of Software.*]

8. RISK

Risk in the media on which Software is delivered shall pass on delivery of the Software.

9. PAYMENT

The Supplier shall upon dispatch invoice the Distributor for the Licence Fees payable in respect of each copy of the Software ordered as specified in the SECOND SCHEDULE and invoices shall be due and payable within fourteen days after date of invoice.

10. LICENCE TO END USERS[3]

The Distributor shall ensure that prior to delivery of the Software to an End User, such End User enters into the Supplier's standard Software Licence Agreement accompanying each copy of the Software the terms and conditions of which are contained in the FOURTH SCHEDULE.

11. LICENCE TO THE DISTRIBUTOR

11.1 This Agreement shall operate as a Licence for the Distributor to use the Software on the Equipment for demonstration testing, support and such other purposes connected with this Agreement.

11.2 The Distributor shall not modify, amend, add to or in any way alter any Software supplied to it without the supplier prior written consent, except as provided by article 6 of the EU Software Directive (Council Directive 91/250/EEC, article 6).[4]

12. ENHANCEMENTS AND MODIFICATIONS

Supplier will notify the Distributor of any enhancement or modification to the Software and reserves the right to introduce any substitute Software which will fulfil the same function as that which it replaces.

13. SOFTWARE SUPPORT

13.1 The Distributor shall maintain a sufficient and effective call control to deal with faults etc.

13.2 The Supplier shall provide backup support when reasonably required on the terms the FIFTH SCHEDULE.

13.3 The Distributor's obligations for support include the following.

14. UNDERTAKINGS BY THE DISTRIBUTOR

[Insert standard obligations of the Distributor for its duties under the Agreement.]

15. LIABILITY

[Agree limits of respective parties liability and establish that Distributor has suitable product liability insurance.]

16. FORCE MAJEURE

Delays or defaults resulting from events of force majeure shall not frustrate the contract.

17. WARRANTY

The Supplier does not warrant that the Software is error free but warrants the media on which the Software is embodied or supplied for 90 days from date of delivery, provided the Distributor and End User have used the Software in accordance with the User Manuals.

18. INTELLECTUAL PROPERTY RIGHTS.

All rights are reserved to the Supplier and Distributor is obligated to notify Supplier of any infringements of which it is aware of Suppliers intellectual property rights.

19. CONFIDENTIAL INFORMATION

The parties agree that all information supplied with them unless agreed otherwise, shall remain confidential and shall be marked accordingly.

20. TERMINATION

This Agreement and Licence shall terminate upon due notice, upon the receivership or bankruptcy of either party and upon any breach of obligations by the Distributor.

21. CHANGES IN THE DISTRIBUTOR

Where there is any material change in the Distributor and its structure, the Supplier has the right to terminate.

22. RELATIONSHIP OF DISTRIBUTOR TO SUPPLIER

The relationship between the parties is that of Distributor and Principal and not one of agency or joint venture.

23. WAIVER

Failure or neglect by the Supplier to enforce any prior breach shall not be deemed to be a waiver of the Supplier's subsequent rights.

24. ASSIGNMENT

This Agreement may not be transferred by the Distributor without the prior written consent of the Supplier.

25. SUCCESSORS AND ASSIGNEES

Successors and Assignees shall be bound equally.

26. NOTICES

Any notices to be given under this Agreement shall be in writing and are deemed to be effectively delivered if by hand when delivered or if by post within 48 hours of posting or if by fax or e-mail when dispatched to the correct address of the addressee.

27. ANNOUNCEMENTS

Any announcements concerning the Agreement shall be subject to the approval of both parties.

28. ENTIRE AGREEMENT

This Agreement shall be the entire Agreement and all previous communications, whether oral or written, and any prior representation shall be excepted.

29. AMENDMENTS

Amendments to the Agreement must be in writing and signed by both parties.

30. INTERPRETATION

[Not applicable.]

31. SEVERABILITY

If any clause is found to be invalid then it should be deemed struck from the Agreement and the rest of the Agreement shall remain binding.

32. COUNTERPARTS

The Agreement may be signed in counterparts.

33. LANGUAGE

The governing language of the Agreement shall be English.

34. COSTS AND EXPENSES

Each party shall meet its own expenses in negotiating the Agreement.

35. SET-OFF

Each party may set-off from its payments any amount owed to it by the other party.

36. THIRD PARTIES

Save as expressly provided, third parties shall not have rights under the Agreement.

37. LAW AND DISPUTES

In the event of a dispute if it is of a technical nature it should be settled by ADR and English law will apply.

Signature clause

SCHEDULE 1

To be attached

SCHEDULE 2

To be attached

SCHEDULE 3

To be attached

SCHEDULE 4

To be attached

SCHEDULE 5

To be attached

1 This document is intended to be a short form Heads of Agreement for software distribution with a view to the parties subsequently entering into a full form Software Distribution Agreement as per PRECEDENT 11.
2 Ensure that the recitals accurately define or describe the intentions of the parties to the Agreement.
3 Please insert the intended Software Licence Agreement into the Fourth Schedule.

4   This refers to the right for the End User or Licensee to reverse analyse where it is necessary to do so, for the purposes of interoperability or error correction. The Supplier may wish to include wording to ensure that before reverse analysing, the Distributor must first approach the Supplier to request interoperability data or demand error correction.

12 Software distribution agreement[1]

THIS AGREEMENT is made the [ ] day of [ ] [ ]

BETWEEN

1.   [ ] LIMITED a Company incorporated in England and Wales and having its Registered Office at [ ] ('the Supplier' which shall include all or any of its subsidiaries, agents, successors or assigns)

AND

2.   [ ] LIMITED a Company incorporated in England and Wales and having its Registered Office at [ ] ('the Distributor').

WHEREAS:

A.   The Supplier is engaged in creating, developing and/or marketing the software identified in PART I OF THE First Schedule hereto, including documentation and manuals therefore ('the Software').

B.   The Distributor is engaged in the business of [selling, licensing, sub-licensing, marketing, distributing and supporting the equipment specified in PART II OF THE First Schedule hereto ('the Equipment')] and wishes to acquire from the Supplier the right to licence or sub-licence the Software [for use on the Equipment].

C   The Supplier proposes extending the market for the Software by granting to the Distributor the right for the Distributor to licence, sub-licence, market, distribute and support the same in [ ] ('the Territory') in accordance with the terms and subject to the conditions herein contained.

NOW IT IS HEREBY AGREED as follows:

1. GRANT[2]

The Supplier hereby grants to the Distributor and the Distributor hereby accepts a [non-] exclusive right to sub-licence the Software in accordance with the provisions of the Fourth Schedule hereto and generally to sub-licence, market, distribute and support the Software [under the Supplier's trade mark] in the Territory [for use on the Equipment] during the continuance of this Agreement.

2. TERM

The Licence shall commence on [ ] ('the Commencement Date') and shall continue [for a period of *(insert number of years)* [and]] from year to year thereafter until or unless terminated in accordance with any of the provisions of CLAUSE 20 or any other clause of this Agreement.

3. TECHNICAL INFORMATION

3.1   The Supplier shall furnish the Distributor with one reproducible copy of all written information which the Supplier deems necessary for the Distributor to use in marketing, distributing, sub-licensing and supporting the Software within the Territory, including but not limited to the information contained in the THIRD SCHEDULE hereto.

3.2   The Supplier shall keep the Distributor informed of any changes, additions or modifications to such information that has an affect on operation, cost or performance of the Software.

3.3   The Distributor shall, on all copies made of such information, faithfully reproduce the copyright symbol, legerd or clause or, in the absence of same, insert the copyright symbol of the Supplier.

4. [TRAINING³

4.1   The Supplier will train at such cost (if any) as will be notified to the Distributor and at a place to be nominated by the Supplier, key demonstrator, technical and sales personnel of the Distributor.

4.2   The Supplier shall permit two persons (unless otherwise agreed by the Supplier) from each such category of personnel to engage in the training programme.

4.3   The Supplier shall for all enhanced or new software brought out by the Supplier and included in this Agreement provide a similar training programme.

4.4   The Distributor may request the Supplier to make available additional training facilities at the Distributor's expense.]

5. [COMMERCIAL AND TECHNICAL ASSISTANCE⁴

In addition to training provided for in CLAUSE 4 above, the Supplier undertakes from time to time during the continuance of this Agreement, at the request of the Distributor, to render to the Distributor adequate commercial and technical assistance in connection with distribution and marketing of the Software. The cost of such assistance will be agreed in advance between the parties.]

6. ORDERING OF SOFTWARE

6.1   [The Distributor agrees to order from the Supplier the minimum number of copies of the Software specified in the SECOND SCHEDULE.]⁵

6.2   Orders for copies of the Software shall be communicated in writing, to the Supplier at the above address or at such other address as the Supplier may from time to time notify to the Distributor. All orders shall (as far as possible) contain the names and addresses of the proposed End Users in order that the Supplier may accurately allocate a particular serialisation number for each End User.

6.3   [Orders shall not be binding on the Supplier unless and until accepted by the Supplier in writing.]

6.4   The Supplier will use all reasonable endeavours to fulfil accepted orders for Software with all reasonable despatch but shall not be liable in any way for any loss of trade profit or any other loss occurring to the Distributor in the event of delivery being frustrated or delayed.

6.5   [In the event that the Distributor fails to order and pay for the minimum number of copies of Software specified in the SECOND SCHEDULE, the Supplier shall be entitled to charge the Distributor for the value of the same, and, at its option, terminate this Agreement without liability.⁶]

7.   DELIVERY OF SOFTWARE

7.1   The Supplier will despatch copies of the Software ordered pursuant to CLAUSE 6 to the Distributor by post or by such other carrier as the Supplier may in its absolute discretion choose, to the Distributor's above address or to such other address as the Distributor shall from time to time notify to the Supplier as its delivery address within the Territory.

7.2   Carriage charges for delivery of Software to the Distributor shall be borne by the Distributor.

7.3   If at any time the Distributor is in default in the performance or observance of any of its obligations under this Agreement the Supplier shall be entitled, for so long as such default continues (but without prejudice to any of its other rights under this Agreement), to withhold delivery of Software to the Distributor notwithstanding that orders for Software have been accepted by the Supplier.

8.   RISK

Risk in the media on which the Software is delivered shall pass to the Distributor on delivery. If any part of the media shall thereafter be lost, destroyed or damaged the Supplier shall promptly replace the same (embodying the relevant part of the Software) subject to the Distributor paying the cost of such replacement.

9.   PAYMENT

9.1   The Supplier shall upon despatch, invoice the Distributor for the Licence Fees payable in respect of each copy of Software ordered by the Distributor as specified in the SECOND SCHEDULE hereto as the same may be amended from time to time by the Supplier by giving to the Distributor not less than thirty (30) days' prior notice thereof.

9.2 Any charges payable by the Distributor under this Agreement shall be paid within [30] days after the receipt by the Distributor of the Supplier's invoice therefor.

9.3 The Licence Fees and other charges payable under this Agreement are exclusive of any applicable VAT and other sales tax which shall be payable by the Distributor at the rate and in the manner prescribed by law against submission of a valid tax invoice.

9.4 The Supplier shall have the right to charge interest on overdue invoices at the rate of [4%] per annum above the base rate of (*insert name of bank*) Bank Plc, calculated from the date when payment of the invoice becomes due for payment up to and including the date of actual payment whether before or after judgment.

9.5 In the event of non-payment, the Supplier shall have the right to revoke the Distributor's Licence and its authority to sub-licence. The Supplier may re-possess any copies of the Software for which payment has not been received by the Supplier and any documentation, data, records or information relating thereto. For such purpose the Supplier or any one or more of its agents or authorised representatives shall be entitled at any time and without notice to enter upon any premises in which the same are or are reasonably believed by the Supplier, to be kept, stored or used.

9.6 Notwithstanding the foregoing, the Supplier may, in its sole discretion, invoice any End User directly for any licence fees payable in respect of Software supplied by or on behalf of the Distributor if the Distributor has failed to collect such monies from the End User or is otherwise in default of this Agreement.

10. LICENCE TO END USERS[7]

The Distributor shall ensure that prior to delivery of the Software to an End User, such End User enters into the Software Licence Agreement accompanying each copy of the Software, the terms and conditions of which are contained in the Fourth Schedule hereto as the same be amended from time to time by or with the prior written consent of the Supplier.

11. LICENCE TO THE DISTRIBUTOR

11.1 This Agreement shall operate as a licence for the Distributor to use the Software on the Equipment for demonstration, testing, support and such other purposes directly connected with this Agreement. This right shall subsist for so long as this Agreement remains in effect or until or unless otherwise revoked.

11.2 The Distributor shall not modify, amend, add to or in any way alter any Software supplied to it under this Agreement without the Supplier's prior written consent.

12. ENHANCEMENTS AND MODIFICATIONS

The Supplier will notify the Distributor of any enhancement or modification to the Software which affects its operation, performance or cost. The Supplier reserves the right to introduce any substitute Software which will fulfil the same function as that which it replaces.

13. SOFTWARE SUPPORT

13.1 During the continuance and (unless otherwise required by the Supplier) after the termination of this Agreement (for whatever reason) the Distributor shall maintain an efficient and effective call control to deal with fault calls relating to the Software and an efficient and effective support staff, sufficiently widespread through the Territory to respond properly to such calls. This facility shall apply to End Users supplied by the Distributor under this Agreement and to End Users supplied with the Software (whether before or after the commencement of this Agreement) by others PROVIDED ALWAYS that such End Users use the Software on the Equipment.

13.2 The Supplier shall provide back up support for the Distributor when reasonably required and upon the terms and for the charges specified in the Fifth Schedule hereto as the same may be amended from time to time by the Supplier upon giving to the Distributor thirty (30) days' prior written notice.

13.3 Without prejudice to the generality of the Distributor's obligations as expressed in CLAUSE 13.1 above the Distributor shall provide all such End Users with the following support services:

13.3.1 proper training for the End Users' operators in the use of the Software;

13.3.2 prompt receipt, analysis and reporting of reported faults in the operation of the Software;

13.3.3 prompt replacement of the master copy of any corrupted or damaged Software (such replacement being obtained from the Supplier);

13.3.4 technical information and advice on the use of the Software.

14. UNDERTAKINGS BY THE DISTRIBUTOR

The Distributor undertakes and agrees with the Supplier that it will at all times during the continuance in force of this Agreement and where applicable, following termination hereof observe and perform the terms and conditions set out in this Agreement and in particular:

14.1 will use at all times best endeavours to promote and extend the market for the Software to all potential licensees in the Territory and work diligently to obtain orders therefore;

14.2 will at its own expense provide advertising and publicity for the Software as extensive as the advertising and publicity provided by the Distributor for other goods of similar type to the Software which it distributes;

14.3 will not without the previous consent in writing of the Supplier be concerned or interested either directly or indirectly in the production, importation, sale, licensing or advertisement of any software which is so like or similar to the Software as to be capable of restricting, competing or otherwise interfering with or which might otherwise restrict or interfere with the market for the Software;

14.4 will, in all correspondence and other dealings relating directly or indirectly to the licensing or other transaction relating to the Software, clearly indicate that it is acting as a Distributor and not as author or developer of the Software;

14.5 will not incur any liability on behalf of the Supplier or in any way pledge or purport to pledge the Supplier's credit or purport to make any contract binding upon the Supplier;

14.6 will not alter, obscure, remove, conceal or otherwise interfere with any eye-readable or machine-readable marking on the Software or its packaging which refers to the Supplier as author or developer of the Software or otherwise refers to the Supplier's copyright or other intellectual property rights in the Software;

14.7 will permit any duly authorised representative of the Supplier upon reasonable prior notice to enter into any of its premises where any Software or any materials relating thereto are stored for the purpose of ascertaining that the provisions of this Agreement are being complied with by the Distributor;

14.8 will immediately bring to the attention of the Supplier any improper or wrongful use of the Supplier's trade marks, emblems, designs, models or other similar industrial, intellectual or commercial property rights which come to the notice of the Distributor and will in the performance of its duties under this Agreement use every effort to safeguard the property rights and interests of the Supplier take all steps required by the Supplier to defend such rights;

14.9 will promptly bring to the attention of the Supplier any information received by the Distributor which is likely to be of interest use or benefit to the Supplier in relation to the marketing and/or support of the Software;

14.10 will keep full, proper and up-to-date books of account and records showing clearly all enquiries transactions, proceedings and fault calls relating to the Software and its distributorship generally and will allow a duly authorised representative of the Supplier to have access to the said books and records and take such copies thereof as such representative may require; and

14.11 will from time to time on request by the Supplier, supply to the Supplier reports, returns and other information relating to the distributorship.

15. LIABILITY

15.1 The Distributor shall during the term of this Agreement maintain employer's liability, third party liability, product liability and professional negligence insurance cover in respect of its liabilities arising out of or connected with this Agreement, such cover to be to a minimum value of [ONE MILLION POUNDS] and with an insurance company of repute. The Distributor shall on request supply copies of the relevant certificates of insurance to the Supplier as evidence that such policies remain in force. The Distributor undertakes to use reasonable commercial efforts to pursue claims under such insurance policies.

15.2 The Distributor shall indemnify the Supplier for personal injury or death caused by the negligence of its employees in connection with the performance of their duties hereunder or by defects in any product supplied pursuant to this Agreement.

15.3 The Distributor will indemnify the Supplier for direct damage to tangible property caused by the negligence of its employees in connection with the performance of their duties hereunder or by defects in any product supplied pursuant to this Agreement. The Distributor's total liability under this clause shall be limited to [£500,000] for any one event or series of connected events.

15.4 Save in respect of claims for death or personal injury arising from the Supplier's negligence, in no event will the Supplier be liable for any damages resulting from loss of data or use, lost profits, loss of anticipated savings, nor for any damages that are an indirect or secondary consequence of any act or omission of the Supplier whether such damages were reasonably foreseeable or actually foreseen.

15.5 Except as provided above in the case of personal injury, death and damage to tangible property, the Supplier's maximum liability to the Distributor under this Agreement or otherwise for any cause whatsoever (whether in the form of the additional cost of remedial services or otherwise) will be for direct costs and damages only and will be limited to a sum equivalent to the price paid to the Supplier for the products or services that are the subject of the Distributor's claim, plus damages limited to 25% of the same amount for any additional costs directly, reasonably and necessarily incurred by the Distributor in obtaining alternative products and/or services.

15.6 The parties hereby acknowledge and agree that the limitations contained in this CLAUSE 15 are reasonable in light of all the circumstances.

15.7 The Distributor's statutory rights as a consumer (if any) are not affected. All liability that is not expressly assumed in this Agreement is hereby excluded. These limitations will apply regardless of the form of action, whether under statute, in contract or tort including negligence or any other form of action. For the purposes of this clause, the 'Distributor' includes its employees, sub-contractors and suppliers who shall all have the benefit of the limits and exclusions of liability set out above in terms of the Contracts (Rights of Third Parties) Act

1999. Nothing in this Agreement shall exclude or limit liability for fraudulent misrepresentation.

16. FORCE MAJEURE

Neither party shall have any liability under or be deemed to be in breach of this Agreement for any delays or failures in performance of this Agreement which result from circumstances beyond the reasonable control of that party. If such circumstances continue for a continuous period of more than [6 months], either party may terminate this Agreement by written notice to the other party.[8]

17. WARRANTY

17.1   The Supplier warrants that in providing its obligations hereunder it will attain standards of care and skills as high as any currently available in the software industry and that all personnel will have qualifications and experience appropriate for the tasks to which they are allocated.

17.2   The Supplier shall ensure that itself and its servants, agents and subcontractors take all reasonable precautions to ensure that no known viruses for which detection and antidote software is generally available are coded or introduced into the Software.

17.3   The Supplier warrants that neither the performance nor functionality of the Software is affected by dates prior to, during and after the year 2000.

17.4   The Supplier warrants that regardless of whether or not or when the United Kingdom becomes a participating country in the process commonly known as European Monetary Union, the Software:

17.4.1   is capable of performing all functions set out in its specification for any number of currencies and for any common currency adopted by members of the European Union ('the Euro');

17.4.2   will comply with all legal requirements now and hereafter applicable to the Euro in any jurisdiction including but not limited to the rules on conversion, triangulation and rounding set out in Council Regulation 1103/97 and any subsequent or similar regulation or law;

17.4.3   is capable of accepting displaying and printing and will incorporate in all relevant screen layouts all symbols and codes adopted by any government or any other European Union body in relation to the Euro or any other currency;

17.4.4   does and will comply with all laws and regulations applicable in the United Kingdom (including those applicable to the introduction of the Euro) or any country of the European Union.

17.5   If the Supplier receives written notice from the Distributor after delivery of any breach of the said warranties then the Supplier shall at its own expense and within [4] weeks after receiving such notice use all reasonable endeavours to remedy the defect or error in question.

17.6   When notifying a defect or error the Distributor shall (so far as it is able) provide the Supplier with a documented example of such defect or error.

17.7   The said warranties above shall be subject to the Distributor complying with its obligations under the terms of this Agreement and shall also be subject to the limits and exclusions of liability set out in CLAUSE 15 above. In particular, the said warranties shall not apply to the extent that any defect in the Software arose or was exacerbated as a result of:

17.7.1   incorrect use, operation or corruption of the Software;

17.7.2   any unauthorised modification or alteration of the Software;

17.7.3   use of the Software with other software or on equipment with which it is incompatible.

17.8   To the extent permitted by applicable law, the Supplier:

17.8.1   disclaims all other warranties with respect to the Software, either express or implied, including but not limited to any implied warranties relating to quality, fitness for any particular purpose or ability to achieve a particular result;

17.8.2   makes no warranty that the Software are error free or that its use will be uninterrupted and the Distributor acknowledges and agrees that the existence of such errors shall not constitute a breach of this Agreement;

17.8.3   does not give any warranty in respect of third party products. The Supplier will pass on to the Distributor the benefit of any third party warranty supplied by a third party manufacturer or supplier.

18.   COPYRIGHTS, PATENTS, TRADE MARKS AND INTELLECTUAL PROPERTY RIGHTS

18.1   The Distributor acknowledges that any and all of the copyrights, trade marks and other intellectual property rights used or embodied in or in connection with the Software including all documentation and manuals relating thereto is and shall remain the property of the Supplier or the Licensor (if not the Supplier) specified in the Licence in the FOURTH SCHEDULE (the 'Licensor') and the Distributor shall not during or at any time after the expiry of or termination of this Agreement in any way question or dispute the ownership or any such rights by the Supplier or the Licensor.

18.2   The Distributor also acknowledges that such trade marks, copyrights and other rights belonging to the Supplier or the Licensor are only used by the Distributor with the consent of the Supplier and during continuation of this Agreement. Upon expiry or termination hereof the Distributor shall forthwith discontinue such use, without receipt of compensation for such discontinuation, provided however that the Distributor may continue to use such trade names as previously agreed for the period following termination hereof for the purpose only of continuing the measure of support of the Software required to be provided by the Distributor hereunder unless the Supplier shall advise the Distributor that such right has been revoked.

18.3 The Distributor shall not during or after the expiry or termination of this Agreement, without the prior written consent of the Supplier, use or adopt any name, trade name, trading style or commercial designation used by the Supplier or Licensor.

18.4 The Supplier shall defend at its own expense any claim brought against the Distributor alleging that the Software infringes the Intellectual Property Rights of a third party ('Intellectual Property Claim') and the Supplier shall pay all costs and damages awarded or agreed to in settlement of an Intellectual Property Claim provided that the Distributor:

18.4.1 furnishes the Supplier with prompt written notice of the Intellectual Property Claim;

18.4.2 provides the Supplier with reasonable assistance in respect of the Intellectual Property Claim;

18.4.3 gives to the Supplier the sole authority to defend or settle the Intellectual Property Claim.

18.5 If, in the Supplier's reasonable opinion, the Software is or may become the subject of an Intellectual Property Claim then the Supplier shall either:

18.5.1 obtain for the Distributor the right to continue using the Software which is the subject of the Intellectual Property Claim; or

18.5.2 replace or modify the Software which is the subject of the Intellectual Property Claim so they become non-infringing.

18.6 If the remedies set out in CLAUSE 18.5 above are not in the Supplier's opinion reasonably available, then the Distributor shall return the Software which is the subject of the Intellectual Property Claim and the Supplier shall refund to the Distributor the corresponding portion of the Licence Fee, as normally depreciated, whereupon this Agreement shall immediately terminate.

18.7 The Supplier shall have no liability for any Intellectual Property Claim resulting from the use of the Software in combination with any equipment or programs not supplied or approved by the Supplier or any modification of any item of the Software by a party other than the Supplier or its authorised agent.

19. CONFIDENTIAL INFORMATION

19.1 Both parties to this Agreement undertake, except as provided below, to treat as confidential and keep secret all information marked 'confidential' or which may reasonably be supposed to be confidential, including, without limitation, information contained or embodied in the Software and other information supplied by the Supplier or Distributor (in this Agreement collectively referred to as 'the Information') with the same degree of care as it employs with regard to its own confidential information of a like nature and in any event in accordance with best current commercial security practices, provided that, this clause shall not extend to any information which was rightfully in the possession of either party prior to the commencement of the negotiations leading to this Agreement or which is already public knowledge or becomes so at a future date (otherwise than as a result of a breach of this clause).

19.2 Neither party shall without the prior written consent of the other party divulge any part of the other party's Information to any person except:

19.2.1 to their own employees and then only to those employees who need to know the same;

19.2.2 to either parties' auditors, HM Inspector of Taxes, HM Customs and Excise, a court of competent jurisdiction, governmental body or applicable regulatory authority and any other persons or bodies having a right duty or obligation to know the business of the other party and then only in pursuance of such right duty or obligation;

19.2.3 any person who is for the time being appointed by either party to maintain the Equipment on which the Software are for the time being used (in accordance with the terms of the Licence) and then only to the extent necessary to enable such person to properly maintain the Equipment.

19.3 Both parties undertake to ensure that persons and bodies referred to in CLAUSE 19.2 are made aware prior to the disclosure of any part of the Information that the same is confidential and that they owe a duty of confidence to the other party.

19.4 Each party to this Agreement shall promptly notify the other party if it becomes aware of any breach of confidence by any person to whom it divulges all or any part of the Information and shall give the other party all reasonable assistance in connection with any proceedings which the other party may institute against such person for breach of confidence.

19.5 The foregoing obligations as to confidentiality shall remain in full force and effect notwithstanding any termination of this Agreement.

The Supplier has imparted and may from time to time impart to the Distributor certain confidential information relating to the Software, successor or enhanced software or other Supplier software or marketing or support thereof (including specifications therefore). The Distributor hereby agrees that it will be as such confidential information solely for the purposes of this Agreement and that it shall not disclose, whether directly or indirectly, to any third party such information other than is required to carry out the purposes of this Agreement. In the event of such disclosure the Distributor will obtain from such third parties duly binding agreements to maintain in confidence the information to be disclosed to the same extent at least as the Distributor is so bound hereunder.

The Distributor further agrees that upon expiry or termination of this Agreement it shall not itself or through any subsidiary or agent or otherwise, sell, sub-license, market, distribute or otherwise deal with any of the Software (in whole or in part) or have any software developed upon any confidential information supplied to it by the Supplier, or in any way pursuant to this Agreement.

20. TERMINATION OR EXPIRY

20.1 Notwithstanding any provisions herein contained this Agreement may be terminated forthwith by either party by notice in writing from the party not at fault if any of the following events shall occur, namely:

20.1.1 if the other party shall commit any act of bankruptcy, shall have a receiving order made against it, shall make or negotiate for any composition or arrangement with or assignment for the benefit of its creditors or if the other party being a body corporate, shall present a petition or have a petition presented by a creditor for its winding up or shall enter into any liquidation (other than for the purpose of reconstruction or amalgamation), shall call any meeting of its creditors, shall have a receiver of all or any of its undertakings or assets appointed, or shall cease to carry on business;

20.1.2 if the other party shall at any time be in default under this Agreement and shall fail to remedy such default within thirty (30) days from receipt of notice in writing from the first party specifying such default;

20.1.3 if either party is by any case (other than a cause directly attributable to the other party) prevented from performing its obligations hereunder for a period of three (3) months or for a total period of six (6) months in any period of twelve (12) consecutive months.

If any such event referred to in this sub-clause shall occur, termination shall become effective forthwith or on the date set forth in such notice.

20.2 The expiry or termination of this Agreement shall be without prejudice to the rights of the parties accrued up to the date of such expiry or termination.

20.3 Upon expiry or termination (for whatever reason) of this Agreement, the Distributor shall return or destroy (as the Supplier shall instruct) no later than fourteen (14) days thereafter, all Software documentation, technical information and any other data supplied to the Distributor during the continuance of this Agreement and all and any copies made of the whole or any part of the same and the Distributor shall furnish the Supplier with a certificate, certifying that the same has been done, except such supporting software, information and data which the Supplier will require to continue to support the Software beyond the date of expiry or termination where the Supplier permits the Distributor so to do.

21. CHANGES IN THE DISTRIBUTOR

Unless otherwise agreed between the parties, the Distributor shall not, without first advising the Supplier, permit or suffer:

21.1   where the Distributor is a body corporate:

    21.1.1   a controlling interest in the Distributor to pass to any person(s) other than those having a controlling interest at the date hereof whether by reason of purchase of shares or otherwise;

    21.1.2   a change to take place in the Board of Directors;

    21.1.3   the Distributor to undergo any reorganisation or have any part of its business transferred to a subsidiary or associated company of the Distributor;

    21.1.4   the name of the Distributor to be changed;

21.2   where the Distributor is a partnership:

    21.2.1   any change in the partnership name or constitution;

    21.2.2   any partner to retire, resign or otherwise leave the partnership;

    21.2.3   any new partner to be added to the partnership;

In each and every such case, the Supplier shall have the option to terminate this Agreement without liability before any one or more of the above events shall occur subject to its right to claim compensation attributable to such enforced termination.

22. RELATIONSHIP OF THE DISTRIBUTOR TO THE SUPPLIER

It is agreed and understood that the Distributor is not the agent or representative of the Supplier and has no authority or power to bind or contract in the name of or to create any liability against the Supplier in any way or for any purpose. It is understood that the Distributor is an independent contractor with non-exclusive rights confirmed by this Agreement to sub-license, market, distribute and support the Software on its own accord and responsibility in the Territory.

23. WAIVER

No delay, neglect or forbearance on the part of either party in enforcing against the other party any term or condition of this Agreement shall either be or be deemed to be a waiver or in any way prejudice any right of that party under this Agreement. No right, power or remedy in this Agreement conferred upon or reserved for either party is exclusive of any other right, power or remedy available to that party.

24. ASSIGNMENT

This Agreement shall not be assigned by the Distributor whether voluntarily or involuntarily or by operation of law, in whole or in part, to any party without the prior written consent of the Supplier. No such assignment by the Distributor howsoever occurring shall relieve the assignor of its obligations hereunder.

25. SUCCESSORS AND ASSIGNEES

25.1 This Agreement shall be binding upon, and enure to the benefit of, the parties and their respective successors and permitted assignees, and references to a party in this Agreement shall include its successors and permitted assignees.

25.2 In this Agreement references to a party include references to a person:

25.2.1 who for the time being is entitled (by assignment, novation or otherwise) to that party's rights under this Agreement (or any interest in those rights); or

25.2.2 who, as administrator, liquidator or otherwise, is entitled to exercise those rights;

and in particular those references include a person to whom those rights (or any interest in those rights) are transferred or pass as a result of a merger, division, reconstruction or other reorganisation involving that party. For this purpose, references to a party's rights under this Agreement include any similar rights to which another person becomes entitled as a result of a novation of this Agreement.

26. NOTICES

26.1 All notices hereunder shall be in writing.

26.2 Notices shall be deemed to have been duly given:

26.2.1 when delivered, if delivered by courier or other messenger (including registered mail) during normal business hours of the recipient; or

26.2.2 when sent, if transmitted by fax cr e-mail and a successful transmission report or return receipt is generated; or

26.2.3   on the fifth business day following mailing, if mailed by national ordinary mail, postage pre-paid; or

26.2.4   on the tenth business day following mailing, if mailed by airmail, postage pre-paid

in each case addressed to the most recent address, e-mail address, or facsimile number notified to the other party.

27. ANNOUNCEMENTS

No party shall issue or make any public announcement or disclose any information regarding this Agreement unless prior written consent has been obtained from the other party.

28. ENTIRE AGREEMENT

This Agreement supersedes all prior agreements, arrangements and undertakings between the parties and constitutes the entire agreement between the parties relating to the subject matter of this Agreement. However the obligations of the parties under any pre-existing non-disclosure agreement shall remain in full force and effect insofar as there is no conflict between the same. The parties confirm that they have not entered into this Agreement on the basis of any representation that is not expressly incorporated into this Agreement.

29. AMENDMENTS

This Agreement may not be released, discharged, supplemented, interpreted, amended, varied or modified in any manner except by an instrument in writing signed by a duly authorised officer or representative of each of the hereto.

30. INTERPRETATION

30.1   In this Agreement unless the context otherwise requires:

30.1.1   words importing any gender include every gender;

30.1.2   words importing the singular number include the plural number and vice versa;

30.1.3   words importing persons include firms, companies and corporations and vice versa;

30.1.4   references to numbered clauses and Schedules are references to the relevant clause in or Schedule to this Agreement;

30.1.5   reference in any Schedule to this Agreement to numbered paragraphs relate to the numbered paragraphs of that Schedule;

30.1.6   the headings to the clauses, Schedules and paragraphs of this Agreement will not affect the interpretation;

30.1.7   any reference to an enactment includes reference to that enactment as amended or replaced from time to time and to any subordinate legislation or byelaw made under that enactment;

30.1.8   any obligation on any party not to do or omit to do anything is to include an obligation not to allow that thing to be done or omitted to be done;

30.1.9   any party who agrees to do something will be deemed to fulfil that obligation if that party procures that it is done.

30.2   In the case of conflict or ambiguity between any provision contained in the body of this Agreement and any provision contained in any Schedule, the provision in the body of this Agreement shall take precedence.

31. SEVERABILITY

If any provision of this Agreement is prohibited by law or judged by a court to be unlawful, void or unenforceable, the provision shall, to the extent required, be severed from this Agreement and rendered ineffective as far as possible without modifying the remaining provisions of this Agreement, and shall not in any way affect any other circumstances of or the validity or enforcement of this Agreement.

32. COUNTERPARTS

This Agreement may be executed in any number of counterparts or duplicates, each of which shall be an original, and such counterparts or duplicates shall together constitute one and the same Agreement.

33. LANGUAGE

This Agreement is made only in the English language. If there is any conflict in the meaning between the English language version of this Agreement and any version or translation of this Agreement in any other language, the English language version shall prevail.

34. COSTS AND EXPENSES

Each party shall bear its own legal costs and other costs and expenses arising in connection with the drafting, negotiation, execution and registration (if applicable) of this Agreement.

35. SET-OFF

Where either party has incurred any liability to the other party, whether under this Agreement or otherwise, and whether such liability is liquidated or unliquidated, each party may set off the amount of such liability against any sum that would otherwise be due to the other party under this Agreement.

36. THIRD PARTIES[9]

Subject to CLAUSE 15.7 above, a person who is not a party to this Agreement has no right under the Contracts (Rights of Third Parties) Act 1999 to enforce any term of this Agreement but this does not affect any right or remedy of a third party which exists or is available apart from such Act.

37. PROPER LAW AND JURISDICTION[10]

37.1 This Agreement and all matters arising from it and any dispute resolutions referred to below shall be governed by and construed in accordance with English Law notwithstanding the conflict of law provisions and other mandatory legal provisions save that:

37.1.1 the Supplier shall have the right to sue to recover its fees in any jurisdiction in which the Distributor is operating or has assets, and

37.1.2 the Supplier shall have the right to sue for breach of its intellectual property rights and other proprietary information and trade secrets ('IPR') (whether in connection with this Agreement or otherwise) in any country where it believes that infringement or a breach of this Agreement relating to its IPR might be taking place. For the avoidance of doubt, the place of performance of this Agreement is agreed by the parties to be England.

37.2 Each party recognises that the other party's business relies upon the protection of its IPR and that in the event of a breach or threatened breach of IPR, the other party will be caused irreparable damage and such other party may therefore be entitled to injunctive or other equitable relief in order to prevent a breach or threatened breach of its IPR.

37.3 With respect to all other disputes which are not IPR related pursuant to CLAUSES 37.1 and 37.2 above and its special rules the following procedures in CLAUSES 37.3 to 37.6 shall apply. Where there is a dispute the aggrieved party shall notify the other party in writing of the nature of the dispute with as much detail as possible about the deficient performance of the other party. A representative from senior management ('representatives') of each of the parties shall meet in person or communicate by telephone within five business days of the date of the written notification in order to reach an agreement about the nature of the deficiency and the corrective action to be taken by the respective parties. The representatives shall produce a report about the nature of the dispute in detail to their respective boards and if no agreement is reached on corrective action, then the chief executives of each party shall meet in person or by telephone, to facilitate an agreement within five business days of a written notice by one to the other. If the dispute cannot be resolved at board level within a further five business days, or if the agreed upon completion dates in any written plan of corrective action are exceeded, either party may seek its legal remedies as provided below.

37.4　If the parties cannot resolve a dispute in accordance with the procedure in CLAUSE 37.3 above, then they shall with the assistance of the Centre for Alternative Dispute Solution, seek to resolve the dispute or difference amicably by using an Alternative Dispute Resolution ('ADR') procedure acceptable to both parties before pursuing any other remedies available to them. If either party fails or refuses to agree to or participate in the ADR procedure or if in any event the dispute or difference is not resolved to the satisfaction of both parties within [90] days after it has arisen, the matter shall be settled in accordance with the procedure below.

37.5　If the parties cannot resolve .the dispute by the procedure set out above, the parties shall irrevocably submit to the exclusive jurisdiction of the Courts of England and Wales for the purposes of hearing and determining any dispute arising out of this Agreement.

37.6　[Wile the dispute resolution procedure above is in progress and any party has an obligation to make a payment to another party or to allow a credit in respect of such payment, the sum relating to the matter in dispute shall be paid into an interest bearing deposit account to be held in the names of the relevant parties at a clearing bank and such payment shall be a good discharge of the parties' payment obligations under this Agreement. Following resolution of the dispute, whether by mediation or legal proceedings, the sum held in such account shall be payable as determined in accordance with the mediation or legal proceedings, and the interest accrued shall be allocated between the parties pro rata according to the split of the principal sum as between the parties.]

SIGNED for and on behalf of the Supplier [　]

by [　]

in the presence of: [　]

SIGNED for and on behalf of [　]

the Distributor by [　]

in the presence of: [　]

THE FIRST SCHEDULE

PART I

The Software hereinbefore referred to

THE FIRST SCHEDULE

PART II

The Equipment hereinbefore referred to

THE SECOND SCHEDULE AS AT

Type and Minimum No of copies of Software	Licence Fee per copy of Software payable by the Distributor to the Supplier

Valid until Further Notice from the Supplier

THE THIRD SCHEDULE

TECHNICAL INFORMATION

THE FOURTH SCHEDULE

SOFTWARE LICENCE

THE FIFTH SCHEDULE

THE SUPPLIER'S SUPPORT TERMS AND CHARGES TO THE DISTRIBUTOR

1   This Agreement is intended to be used for the distribution of software on a non-exclusive basis with a right to sub-license. This Agreement is an expanded version of the Heads of Agreement for the software distribution in PRECEDENT 10.

2   Although the agreement is intended to be non-exclusive if the parties agree to exclusivity, this may be difficult to enforce within member states of the European Union where usually exclusivity would have to be across the whole European Union or alternatively non-exclusivity would have to be granted.

3   If training is part and parcel of the obligations of the Supplier, then this clause will need including and amending as necessary.

4   If additional assistance is part and parcel of the obligations of the Supplier, then this clause may be appropriate or may need amendment as necessary.

5   Some Suppliers demand an initial guaranteed order from the Distributor as a form of down payment or goodwill gesture.

6   This sub-clause further reinforces the down payment concept in CLAUSE 6.1.1.

7   If the software is to be provided on an End User licensed as is, then the Supplier may wish to ensure that its own Standard Software Licence terms are imposed and the parties may wish to use a shrink-wrap style agreement, or even a more full form End User Licence Agreement in the FOURTH SCHEDULE.

8   Note: Suppliers may find this clause is too permissive -potentially leaving a Distributor with the right to delay payment or otherwise fail to perform in a wide range of circumstances. A more specific clause is as follows:

'Notwithstanding anything else contained in this Agreement, neither party shall be liable for any delay in performing its obligations hereunder if such delay is caused by circumstances beyond its reasonable control (including without limitation any delay caused by any act or omission of the other party) provided however that any delay by a sub-contractor or supplier of the party so delaying shall not relieve the party from liability for delay except where such delay is beyond the reasonable control of the sub-contractor or supplier concerned. Subject to the party so delaying promptly notifying the other party in writing of the reasons for the delay (and the likely duration of the delay), the performance of such party's obligations shall be suspended during the period that the said circumstances persist and such party shall be granted an extension of time for performance equal to the period of the delay. Save where such delay is caused by the act or omission of the other party (in which event the rights, remedies and liabilities of the parties shall be those conferred and imposed by the other terms of this Agreement and by law):

Any costs arising from such delay shall be borne by the party incurring the same; either party may, if such delay continues for more than 10 weeks, terminate this Agreement forthwith giving notice in writing to the other by reason of such termination.'

9 Before the Contracts (Rights of Third Parties) Act 1999 (the Act) it was the case that a person who was not a party to a contract (a third party) could not enforce any right under the contract. Similarly, a contract could not impose any obligations or liabilities on a third party. However the Act attempts to draw a balance between the freedom of the parties to vary a contract and the interests of the third party. The Act means that a contractual clause benefiting a third party (eg the promisee's subsidiary company or sub-contractor or employee) will be straightforwardly enforceable by that third party if: the contract expressly provides that he may; or where a term in the contract purports to confer a benefit on him (unless on a proper construction of the contract it appears that the parties did not intend the term to be enforceable by the third party.) It is therefore prudent to include a clause to the effect of excluding the provisions of the Act. By doing so it ensures that any rights of third parties are not deemed to be enforceable by them. This is particularly the case where the parties are companies and may have subsidiaries or conversely parent companies.

10 An example of another governing law and dispute settlement clause is:

'Any dispute which may arise between the parties concerning this Agreement shall be determined as follows:

(1) If the dispute shall be of a technical nature relating to the functions or capabilities of the Licensed Program Materials or any similar or related matter then such a dispute shall be referred for final settlement to an expert nominated jointly by the parties or failing such nomination within Fourteen (14) days after either party's request to the other therefore nominated at the request of either party by the President for the time being of the British Computer Society. Such expert shall be deemed to act as an expert and not as an arbitrator. His decision shall (in the absence of clerical or manifest error) be final and binding on the parties in equal shares unless he determines that the conduct of either party is such that such party should bear all of such fees.

(2) In any other case the dispute shall be determined by the High Court of Justice in England and the parties hereby submit to the exclusive jurisdiction of that Court for such purposes.'

13 Multimedia product licence and distribution agreement

THIS AGREEMENT is made the [   ] day of [   ] [   ]

BETWEEN:

1.   [   ] ('the Company') and

2.   [   ] ('the Distributor').

RECITALS

A.   The Company is the manufacturer and producer of various computer products used in the field of multimedia interactive training.

B.   The Company has agreed to appoint the Distributor as its non-exclusive Distributor in the Territory (as hereinafter defined) for certain of its products on the terms and conditions hereinafter contained.

OPERATIVE PROVISIONS:

1. DEFINITIONS[1]

In this Agreement unless the context requires otherwise the following expressions shall have the following meanings:

1.1   **'Courseware Products':** those of the Products which are by their nature related to training course content and material and including methodology.

1.2   **'Hardware Products':** those of the Products which are computer hardware.

1.3   **'Initial Order':** the Distributor's initial order for the Products as set out in SCHEDULE 4.

1.4   **'Intellectual Property Rights':** patents, trade marks, service marks, registered designs, applications for any of the foregoing, copyright, database, sui generis rights, moral rights, know-how, confidential information, trade or business names and any other similar protected rights in any country.

1.5 **'Invoice Price':** in relation to the purchase of any of the Products, the amount invoiced by the Company to the Distributor excluding VAT and any other taxes, duties or levies and any transport and insurance charges included in such invoice.

1.6 **'Products':** the Hardware Products, Software Products and Courseware Products and product training described in SCHEDULE 1 and such other products as the parties may agree in writing from time to time.

1.7 **'Product Documentation':** the operating manuals and other literature accompanying the Products for use by end-users.

1.8 **'Software Products':** those of the Products which are computer software.

1.9 **'Territory':** those Countries listed in SCHEDULE 5.

1.10 **'Year':** any period of 12 months commencing on the date hereof or any anniversary of the date hereof.

2. APPOINTMENT

2.1 The Company hereby appoints the Distributor and the Distributor hereby agrees to act as the non-exclusive Distributor of the Company for the resale of the Products in the Territory.

2.2 The Distributor shall perform its obligations hereunder in accordance with all reasonable instructions which the Company may give the Distributor from time to time.

2.3 The Distributor shall not be entitled to assign any of its rights or obligations under this Agreement but shall be entitled to appoint sub-distributors to perform such obligations in the Territory provided that prior approval of the Company is sought, which approval shall not be unreasonably withheld, and provided further that the Distributor shall at all times remain responsible for the performance and obligations of its sub-distributors and shall procure that they be bound to the same extent of confidentiality as the Distributor.[2]

2.4 The Distributor shall not be entitled to any priority of supply of the Products over the Company's other customers but the Distributor will be entitled to an allocation of production and delivery not worse than in sequence of delivery of orders to the Company.

2.5 The Distributor represents and warrants to the Company that it has the ability and experience to carry out the obligations assumed by it under this Agreement.

3. DURATION

This Agreement shall commence on the date hereof for an initial period of three (3) years and shall continue thereafter for successive periods of three (3) years unless and until terminated by either party giving to the other not less than one (1) year's written notice expiring on the last day of the said initial period or at any time thereafter but shall be subject to earlier termination as hereinafter provided.

4. SALE AND PURCHASE OF THE PRODUCTS

4.1   The provisions of SCHEDULE 2 shall apply forthwith.

4.2   If there shall be any inconsistency between the provisions of SCHEDULE 2 and the other provisions of this Agreement then the latter shall prevail.

4.3   On the execution of this Agreement the Distributor shall deliver a banker's draft to the Company in payment of fifty per cent (50%) of the Initial Order, the value of which is indicated in SCHEDULE 4, the balance of fifty per cent (50%) to be payable on receipt of the Products the subject of the Initial Order.[3]

5. TRAINING

5.1   The Company shall provide training in the use, installation and maintenance of the Products for the Distributor's personnel in the manner specified in SCHEDULE 3.

5.2   Any additional training required by the Distributor shall be provided by the Company in accordance with its standard scale of charges in force from time to time (subject to the provisions of SCHEDULE 2 CLAUSE 2.1).

5.3   The Distributor shall offer training in the use of the Products to all its customers and shall use its reasonable endeavours to persuade them to complete training courses in accordance with the Company's minimum recommendations from time to time.

6. DISTRIBUTOR'S OBLIGATIONS

The Distributor shall:

6.1   use its best endeavours to promote and extend the sale of the Products throughout the Territory;

6.2   promptly inform the Company of any facts or opinions of which the Distributor becomes aware which are likely to be relevant to the commercial exploitation of the Products in the Territory and which are either advantageous or disadvantageous to the interests of the Company;

6.3   at all times conduct its business in a manner which will reflect favourably on the Products and on the good name and reputation of the Company;

6.4   not by itself or with others participate in any illegal, deceptive, misleading or unethical practices which may be detrimental to the Products, the Company or the public interest;

6.5   [not during the continuance of this Agreement (whether alone or jointly and whether directly or indirectly) be concerned or interested in the manufacture, marketing, distribution or sale of any products which are similar to or competitive with any of the Products or which perform the same or similar functions;][1]

6.6   if any dispute shall arise between the Distributor and any of its customers in respect of the Products (or their installation or maintenance) promptly inform the Company and comply with all reasonable directions of the Company in relation thereto;

6.7   at all times employ a sufficient number of full-time technical support and sales staff having sufficient training and expertise properly to display, demonstrate, sell and instruct customers in the installation and use of the Products and capable of addressing customer enquiries and needs regarding the Products;

6.8   at all times maintain adequate demonstration facilities for the Products;

6.9   supply to the Company such reports, returns and other information relating to orders and projected orders for the Products as the Company may from time to time reasonably require;

6.10   provide the Company with quarterly stock reports showing the Distributor's stock of each of the Products at the beginning and end of each quarter and the movement of stocks during the quarter;

6.11   provide the Company with such financial information relating to the Distributor's business dealing with the Products as may be necessary for the Company to establish and maintain a credit limit for the Distributor from time to time;

6.12   not make any promises or representations or give any warranties or guarantees in respect of the Products except such as are consistent with those which accompany the Products or as expressly authorised by the Company in writing;

6.13   use the Company's trade marks and trade names relating to the Products only in the registered or agreed style in connection with the marketing and sale of the Products and not use such trade marks or trade names in connection with any other products or services as a part of the corporate or any trade name of the Distributor;

6.14   except with the Company's prior consent not alter, obscure, remove, interfere with or add to any of the trade marks, trade names, markings or notices affixed to or contained in the Products or the Product Documentation at the time at which they are delivered to the Distributor;

6.15   except with the Company's prior consent not alter or interfere with the Products or the Product Documentation;

6.16   keep sufficient copies of the Products to satisfy customer demand for demonstration purposes;

6.17   be responsible for the proper installation of the Products save where installation can readily and easily be undertaken by the customer in accordance with the instructions set out in the Product Documentation and the customer indicates that he wishes to undertake installation himself;

6.18 offer maintenance contracts in respect of the Hardware Products to its customers on commercially reasonable terms and shall undertake its obligations thereunder to the standards generally observed in the industry;

6.19 not offer or undertake any maintenance services in respect of the Software Products that it does not have the expertise to do;

6.20 provide an efficient after sales service in respect of the Products;

6.21 observe all applicable laws and regulations in respect of and obtain all necessary licences, consents and permissions required for the storage, marketing and sale of the Products in the Territory;

6.22 provide the Company with all information necessary to enable the Company to ensure that the Products comply with local laws and regulations and promptly advise the Company of any change or proposed change thereto;

6.23 co-operate with the Company in the recall of any of the Products for safety checks or modifications;

6.24 not at any time represent itself as agent of the Company; and

6.25 permit the Company and its authorised agents at all reasonable times to enter any of the Distributor's premises used for the storage of the Products or maintenance of records relating to the Distributor for the purpose of ascertaining that the Distributor is complying with its obligations under this Agreement.

7. COMPANY'S OBLIGATIONS

7.1 The Company shall:

7.1.1 provide the Distributor with such marketing and technical assistance that the Company is able to provide to assist the Distributor with the promotion of the Products;

7.1.2 endeavour to respond as soon as possible to all technical queries raised by the Distributor or its customers concerning the use or application of the Products;

7.1.3 provide the Distributor with adequate quantities of instruction manuals, technical and promotional literature and other information relating to the Products;

7.1.4 subject to the Distributor complying with its obligations under CLAUSE 6.22 ensure that the Products comply with local laws and regulations relating to their sale and use in the Territory;

7.1.5 give reasonable advance written notice of any significant change to any of the Products or of the Company's intention to discontinue selling any of the Products to the Distributor;

7.1.6   offer to the Distributor for inclusion in the Products any product of the Company which can reasonably be regarded as a replacement for or successor to any Product which the Company discontinues selling pursuant to CLAUSE 10.2;

7.1.7   provide the Distributor promptly with all information and assistance necessary to enable the Distributor properly to perform its obligations hereunder in respect of any modified or enhanced versions of the Products;

7.1.8   endeavour upon request by the Distributor to make available to the Distributor any of the Products developed by the Company for third parties provided that royalty terms can be agreed between the Company and the Distributor in accordance with SCHEDULE 6;

7.1.9   where the Distributor so requests to provide the Distributor promptly with the services of Software Products and Courseware Products support personnel for the purposes of modifying and customising Courseware Products sold by the Distributor at the Company's agreed charge out rate from time to time in force;

7.1.10   pay the Distributor a royalty for Courseware Products developed by the Distributor and sold by the Company outside the Territory in accordance with PART 2 OF SCHEDULE 6.

7.2   The Company will not seek to use Courseware Products developed by the Distributor for any customer of the Distributor inside the Territory without the express prior approval of the Distributor which approval shall be subject to the provisions of PART 2 OF SCHEDULE 6.

7.3   The terms of CLAUSES 7.1.10 and 7.2 above will endure for a period of twenty-one (21) years after the termination of this Agreement including in circumstances where the Distributor is found to have repudiated this Agreement.

7.4   Subject to satisfactory terms being agreed the Company will grant to the Distributor a non-exclusive manufacturing licence throughout the Territory on a royalty basis in respect of the [Alpha Video Interface Processor] and any other Hardware Products developed by the Company during the duration of this Agreement.

8. INTELLECTUAL PROPERTY RIGHTS

8.1   All Intellectual Property Rights in or relating to the Products and the Product Documentation are and shall remain the property of the Company or its licensors.

8.2   The Distributor shall:

8.2.1   not cause or knowingly permit anything which may damage or endanger any of the Intellectual Property Rights or assist others to do so;

8.2.2   notify the Company immediately if the Distributor becomes aware of any illegal or unauthorised use of any of the Products or the Product Documentation or any of the Intellectual Property Rights therein or relating thereto and assist the Company (at the Company's expense) in taking all steps necessary to defend the Company's rights therein;

8.2.3   affix such notices to the Products or their packaging or advertising associated therewith or the Product Documentation as the Company may legally or statutorily be required so to do;

8.2.4   indemnify the Company for any liability incurred to third parties for any use by the Distributor and its customers of the Products or the Product Documentation or any of the Intellectual Property Rights therein or relating thereto otherwise than in accordance with this Agreement; and

8.2.5   acknowledge that any goodwill or reputation for the Product generated by this Agreement will belong to the Company and upon termination of this Agreement for whatever reason the Distributor shall not be entitled to claim recompense or compensation for such enhanced goodwill or reputation. The provisions of this clause shall survive the termination of this Agreement.

9. CONFIDENTIALITY

9.1   Neither party shall use or divulge or communicate to any person (other than those whose province it is to know the same or as permitted or contemplated by this Agreement or with the written authority of the other party or as may be required by law):

9.1.1   any confidential information concerning the products customers, business, accounts, finance or contractual arrangements or other dealings, transactions or affairs of the other party and its subsidiaries which may come to the first party's knowledge during the continuance of this Agreement; or

9.1.2   any of the terms of this Agreement and each party shall use its best endeavours to prevent the unauthorised publication or disclosure of any such information or documents and to ensure that any person to whom such information or documents are disclosed by such party is aware that the same is confidential to the other party.

9.2   Each party shall ensure that its employees are aware of and comply with the confidentiality and non-disclosure provisions contained in this clause and shall indemnify the other party against loss or damage which the other may sustain or incur as a result of any breach of confidence by any such party's employee.[5]

9.3   If either party becomes aware of any breach of confidence by any of its employees it shall promptly notify the other party and give the other party all reasonable assistance in connection with any proceedings which the other party may institute against any such employees.

9.4   The provisions of this clause shall survive the termination of this Agreement but the restrictions contained in CLAUSE 9.1 shall cease to apply to any information which may come into the public domain otherwise than through unauthorised disclosure by the receiving party or its employees.

10. RESERVATION OF RIGHTS

The Company reserves the right:

10.1   to make modifications or additions to the Products or the Product Documentation or the packaging or finish thereof in any way whatsoever as the Company may in its discretion determine;

10.2   to discontinue selling any of the Products to the Distributor; and

10.3   to require the Distributor not to use or to cease to use any advertising or promotional materials in respect of the Products which the Company considers not to be in the Company's best interests.

11. THE TERRITORY[6]

11.1   [The Company shall have no liability to the Distributor in the event that any of the Company's distributors appointed in other territories import any of the Products into the Territory for sale therein.

11.2   The Distributor shall not advertise or maintain stocks of the Products outside the Territory or otherwise actively solicit orders for the Products from persons who are situated outside the Territory but the Distributor shall not be prohibited from fulfilling any unsolicited orders actually placed by such persons.]

12. LEGAL RELATIONSHIP

12.1   During the continuance of this Agreement the Distributor shall be entitled to refer to itself as Authorised Distributor of the Company but such description shall be in accordance with the Company's policies in effect from time to time and before using such title (whether on the Distributor's business stationery, advertising material or elsewhere) the Distributor shall submit to the Company proof prints and such other details as the Company may require and the Company may in its discretion grant or withhold permission for such proposed use.

12.2   The relationship of the parties is that of seller and buyer and nothing in this Agreement shall render the Distributor a partner or agent of the Company. The Distributor is an independent contractor buying and selling in its own name and at its own risk. The Distributor shall not bind or purport to bind the Company to any obligation nor expose the Company to any liability nor pledge or purport to pledge the Company's credit.

12.3 The Company shall not use the name of the Distributor in any promotional or other material and shall not without the express written consent of the Distributor make reference to any relationship between the Company and the Distributor.

13. TERMINATION

13.1 Notwithstanding anything else contained herein, this Agreement may be terminated:

13.1.1 by the Company forthwith on giving notice in writing to the Distributor if:

13.1.1.1 the Distributor shall (or shall threaten to) sell, assign, part with or cease to carry on its business or that part of its business relating to the distribution of the Products; or

13.1.1.2 the control (as defined for the purposes of the Income and Corporation Taxes Act 1988, section 416) of the Distributor shall be transferred to any person or persons other than the person or persons in control of the Distributor at the date hereof (but the Company shall only be entitled to terminate within the period of sixty (60) days after the Company shall have been notified in writing of the change in control);

13.2 by either party forthwith on giving notice in writing to the other if:

13.2.1 the other party commits any material or persistent breach of any term of this Agreement and (in the case of a breach capable of being remedied) shall have failed, within thirty (30) days after the receipt of a request in writing from the other party so to do, to remedy the breach (such request to contain a warning of such party's intention to terminate);

13.2.2 diplomatic relations between the respective countries of the parties make the continuance of this Agreement unduly difficult;[7]

13.2.3 the other party shall have been unable to perform its obligations hereunder for a period of ninety (90) consecutive days or for periods aggregating one hundred and eighty (180) days in any Year (but the party entitled to terminate may only terminate within the period of sixty (60) days after the expiration of the said consecutive period or Year); or

13.2.4 the other party shall have a receiver or administrative receiver appointed of it or over any part of its undertaking or assets or shall pass a resolution for winding-up (otherwise than for the purpose of a bona fide scheme of solvent amalgamation or reconstruction) or a court of competent jurisdiction shall make an order to that effect or if the other party shall enter into any voluntary arrangement with its creditors or shall become subject to an administration order.

13.3 The Distributor shall not be entitled to any compensation (whether for loss of distribution rights, goodwill or otherwise) as a result of the termination of this Agreement in accordance with its terms.

13.4 Each delivery of a consignment of the Products shall be regarded as a separate contract of sale and no one default in a delivery shall be cause for terminating this agreement but persistent default shall fall within the terms of CLAUSE 13.2.1.

14. EFFECT OF TERMINATION[8]

14.1 On the termination of this Agreement all rights and obligations of the parties under this Agreement shall automatically terminate except for such rights of action as shall have accrued prior to such termination and any obligations which expressly or by implication are intended to come into or continue in force on or after such termination;

14.2 the Distributor shall be entitled to sell any of its stocks of the Products which have been fully paid for and which are required to fulfil any unperformed contracts of the Distributor outstanding at the date of termination (and to the extent and for that purpose the provisions of this Agreement shall continue in effect);

14.3 the Distributor shall immediately eliminate from all its literature, business stationery, publications, notices and advertisements all references to it being authorised distributor of the Company;

14.4 the Distributor shall at its own expense forthwith return to the Company or otherwise dispose of as the Company may instruct all technical and promotional materials and other documents and papers whatsoever sent to the Distributor and relating to the Products or the business of the Company (other than correspondence between the parties and all property of the Company being in each case in the Distributor's possession or under its control);

14.5 the Distributor shall cause the Software Products and Courseware Products held for demonstration purposes to be erased from all computers of or under the control of the Distributor and shall certify to the Company that the same has been done;

14.6 all orders for undelivered Products shall be automatically cancelled;

14.7 all outstanding unpaid invoices in respect of the Products shall become immediately payable in place of the payment terms previously agreed between the parties;

14.8 the Company shall forthwith pay to the Distributor any amount standing to the credit of the Distributor's account with the Company (less any moneys then owed by the Distributor to the Company);

14.9 the Company shall be entitled to repossess any of the Products which have not been paid for against cancellation of the relevant invoices (and so that the Distributor hereby irrevocably licenses the Company, its employees and agents to enter any of the premises of the Distributor for such purpose); and

14.10 the Company shall purchase all or any unsold Products in the possession or under the control of the Distributor which have been paid for by the Distributor (and which are not required to fulfil any unperformed contracts of the Distributor outstanding at the date of termination) at the Invoice Price (or, if lower, the written down value of the Products appearing in the accounting records of the Distributor at the date of termination) subject to the Company paying all necessary VAT and other taxes duties or levies and paying the cost of and arranging transport and insurance. The Distributor shall give the Company all necessary assistance and co-operation for the purpose of giving effect to the provisions of this sub-clause and of delivering the Products to the Company.

15. LIABILITY

15.1 The Company warrants to the Distributor that the Products sold to the Distributor hereunder will comply with their published specifications and will be of satisfactory quality.

15.2 If the Company shall be in breach of the warranty set out in CLAUSE 15.1 its liability shall be limited to replacing the Products concerning (at the Company's risk and expense) or at its option refunding the price paid by the Distributor (subject to the Distributor returning the defective Products to the Company at the Company's risk and expense) or (if an abatement of the price is agreed with the Distributor) refunding to the Distributor the appropriate part of the price paid.

15.3 The Company shall have no liability to the Distributor under CLAUSES 15.1 and 15.2 above:

15.3.1 for any damage to or defects in any of the Products caused by fair wear and tear, improper use, maintenance or repair, negligent handling, failure to observe the instructions accompanying the Products or any alterations thereto;

15.3.2 unless in the case of any damage to or defect in the Products which would have been apparent on reasonable visual inspection the Distributor notifies the Company of the same in writing within fourteen (14) days after the date of delivery thereof or in the case of any damage to defects in the Products which would not have been apparent on reasonable visual inspection the Distributor notifies the Company of the same in writing fourteen (14) days after the defect becomes apparent to the Distributor and if no such notification as aforesaid is given the Distributor shall not be entitled to reject the Products concerning and shall be obliged to pay the price therefor in full.

15.4 Notwithstanding anything else contained in this Agreement but subject to CLAUSE 15.5 below the Company shall not be liable to the Distributor for loss of profits or contracts or other indirect or consequential loss or damage whether arising from negligence, breach of contract or any other cause of action out of the subject matter of this agreement.

15.5 The Company does not exclude liability for death or personal injury caused by the Company's negligence.

15.6 Except as expressly provided in this Agreement no warranty, condition, undertaking, or term, express or implied, statutory or otherwise, as to the condition, quality, performance, merchantability, durability or fitness for purpose of the Products is given or assumed by the Company and all such warranties, conditions, undertakings and terms are hereby excluded.

16. INDEMNITIES

16.1 The Company shall indemnify the Distributor and keep the Distributor fully and effectively indemnified against any and all losses, claims, damages, costs, charges, expenses, liabilities, demands, proceedings and actions which the Distributor may sustain or incur or which may be brought or established against it by any person and which in any case arise out of or in relation to or by reason of:

16.1.1 any claim or allegation that any of the Products infringes any intellectual property rights of any third party;

16.1.2 any claim that the Products do not comply with local laws and regulations relating to their sale and use in the Territory and which are not due to the Distributor's negligence, recklessness or wilful misconduct or any breach of its obligations under this Agreement.

16.2 The Distributor shall indemnify the Company and keep the Company fully and effectively indemnified against any and all losses, claims, damages, costs, charges, expenses, liabilities, demands, proceedings and actions which the Company may sustain or incur or which may be brought or established against it by any person and which in any case arise out of or in relation to or by reason of:

16.2.1 the negligence, recklessness or wilful misconduct of the Distributor in the performance of any of its obligations in connection with the installation and maintenance of the Products;

16.2.2 any unauthorised action or omission of the Distributor or its employees;

16.2.3 the manner in which the Distributor markets and sells the Products (unless authorised by the Company);

16.2.4 the independent supply by the Distributor of any products or services for use in conjunction with or in relation to the Products; or

16.2.5 any breach or alleged breach of any applicable laws or regulations relating to the storage, marketing or sale by the Distributor of the Products in the Territory.

16.3 If any claim is made against either party for which indemnification is sought under this clause, the indemnified party shall consult with the other and, subject to being secured to its reasonable satisfaction, shall co-operate with the other in relation to any reasonable request made by the other in respect of such claim.

17. INTERPRETATION

17.1 In this Agreement unless the context otherwise requires:

17.1.1 words importing any gender include every gender;

17.1.2 words importing the singular number include the plural number and vice versa;

17.1.3 words importing persons include firms, companies and corporations and vice versa;

17.1.4 references to numbered clauses and Schedules are references to the relevant clause in or Schedule to this Agreement;

17.1.5 reference in any Schedule to this Agreement to numbered paragraphs relate to the numbered paragraphs of that Schedule;

17.1.6 the headings to the clauses, Schedules and paragraphs of this Agreement will not affect the interpretation;

17.1.7 reference to an enactment includes reference to that enactment as amended or replaced from time to time and to any subordinate legislation or byelaw made under that enactment;

17.1.8 any obligation on any party not to do or omit to do anything is to include an obligation not to allow that thing to be done or omitted to be done;

17.1.9 any party who agrees to do something will be deemed to fulfil that obligation if that party procures that is done.

17.2 In the case of conflict or ambiguity between any provision contained in the body of this Agreement and any provision contained in any Schedule, the provision in the body of this Agreement shall take precedence.

18. AGENCY, PARTNERSHIP

This Agreement shall not constitute or imply any partnership, joint venture, agency, fiduciary relationship or other relationship between the parties other than the contractual relationship expressly provided for in this Agreement.

19. AMENDMENTS

This Agreement may not be released, discharged, supplemented, interpreted, amended, varied or modified in any manner except by an instrument in writing signed by a duly authorised officer or representative of each of the parties hereto.

20. ANNOUNCEMENTS

No party shall issue or make any public announcement or disclose any information regarding this Agreement unless prior written consent has been obtained from the other party.

21. ASSIGNMENT

21.1   This Agreement is personal to the parties and, subject to CLAUSE 21.2 below, neither this Agreement nor any rights, licenses or obligations under this Agreement, may be assigned by either party without the prior written approval of the other party.

21.2   Notwithstanding the foregoing, either party may assign this Agreement to any acquirer of all or of substantially all of such party's equity securities, assets or business relating to the subject matter of this Agreement or to any entity controlled by, that controls, or is under common control with a party to this Agreement. Any attempted assignment in violation of this clause will be void and without effect.

22. ENTIRE AGREEMENT

This Agreement supersedes all prior agreements, arrangements and undertakings between the parties and constitutes the entire agreement between the parties relating to the subject matter of this Agreement. However the obligations of the parties under any pre-existing non-disclosure agreement shall remain in full force and effect insofar as there is no conflict between the same. The parties confirm that they have not entered into this Agreement on the basis of any representation that is not expressly incorporated into this Agreement.

23. FORCE MAJEURE[9]

Neither party shall have any liability under or be deemed to be in breach of this Agreement for any delays or failures in performance of this Agreement which result from circumstances beyond the reasonable control of that party. If such circumstances continue for a continuous period of more than [6 months], either party may terminate this Agreement by written notice to the other party.

24. NOTICES

24.1   All notices hereunder shall be in writing.

24.2   Notices shall be deemed to have been duly given:

24.2.1 when delivered, if delivered by courier or other messenger (including registered mail) during normal business hours of the recipient; or

24.2.2 when sent, if transmitted by fax or e-mail and a successful transmission report or return receipt is generated; or

24.2.3 on the fifth business day following mailing, if mailed by national ordinary mail, postage pre-paid; or

24.2.4 on the tenth business day following mailing, if mailed by airmail, postage pre-paid,

in each case addressed to the most recent address, e-mail address, or facsimile number notified to the other party.

25. SCHEDULES[10]

The provisions of SCHEDULE[S] 1 TO 7 to this Agreement shall form part of this Agreement as if set out here.

26. SEVERANCE

If any provision of this Agreement is prohibited by law or judged by a court to be unlawful, void or unenforceable, the provision shall, to the extent required, be severed from this Agreement and rendered ineffective as far as possible without modifying the remaining provisions of this Agreement, and shall not in any way affect any other circumstances of or the validity or enforcement of this Agreement.

27. SUCCESSORS AND ASSIGNEES

27.1 This Agreement shall be binding upon, and enure to the benefit of, the parties and their respective successors and permitted assignees, and references to a party in this Agreement shall include its successors and permitted assignees.

27.2 In this Agreement references to a party include references to a person:

27.2.1 who for the time being is entitled (by assignment, novation or otherwise) to that party's rights under this Agreement (or any interest in those rights); or

27.2.2 who, as administrator, liquidator or otherwise, is entitled to exercise those rights;

and in particular those references include a person to whom those rights (or any interest in those rights) are transferred or pass as a result of a merger, division, reconstruction or other reorganisation involving that party. For this purpose, references to a party's rights under this Agreement include any similar rights to which another person becomes entitled as a result of a novation of this Agreement.

28. WAIVER

No delay, neglect or forbearance on the part of either party in enforcing against the other party any term or condition of this Agreement shall either be or be deemed to be a waiver or in any way prejudice any right of that party under this Agreement. No right, power or remedy in this Agreement conferred upon or reserved for either party is exclusive of any other right, power or remedy available to that party.

29. COUNTERPARTS

This Agreement may be executed in any number of counterparts or duplicates, each of which shall be an original, and such counterparts or duplicates shall together constitute one and the same agreement.

30. TIME IS OF THE ESSENCE

Time shall be of the essence in this Agreement as regards any time, date or period mentioned in this Agreement or subsequently substituted as a time, date or period by agreement in writing between the parties.

31. LANGUAGE

This Agreement is made only in the English language. If there is any conflict in the meaning between the English language version of this Agreement and any version or translation of this Agreement in any other language, the English language version shall prevail.

32. COSTS AND EXPENSES

Each party shall bear its own legal costs and other costs and expenses arising in connection with the drafting, negotiation, execution and registration (if applicable) of this Agreement.

33. SET-OFF

Where either party has incurred any liability to the other party, whether under this Agreement or otherwise, and whether such liability is liquidated or unliquidated, each party may set off the amount of such liability against any sum that would otherwise be due to the other party under this Agreement.

34. THIRD PARTIES[11]

[The parties confirm their intent not to confer any rights on any third parties by virtue of this Agreement and accordingly the Contracts (Rights of Third Parties) Act 1999 shall not apply to this Agreement.]

[The parties recognise that this Agreement is intended to benefit and shall so benefit (insert name of third party) for the purposes of the Contracts (Rights of Third Parties) Act 1999 and, subject to that, the parties confirm their intent not to confer any rights on any other third parties by virtue of this Agreement.]

35. PROPER LAW AND JURISDICTION[12]

35.1   This Agreement and all matters arising from it and any dispute resolutions referred to below shall be governed by and construed in accordance with English Law notwithstanding the conflict of law provisions and other mandatory legal provisions save that:

    35.1.1   the Company shall have the right to sue to recover its fees in any jurisdiction in which the Developer is operating or has assets; and

    35.1.2   the Company shall have the right to sue for breach of its intellectual property rights and other proprietary information and trade secrets ('IPR') (whether in connection with this Agreement or otherwise) in any country where it believes that infringement or a breach of this Agreement relating to its IPR might be taking place. For the avoidance of doubt, the place of performance of this Agreement is agreed by the parties to be England.

35.2   Each party recognises that the other party's business relies upon the protection of its IPR and that in the event of a breach or threatened breach of IPR, the other party will be caused irreparable damage and such other party may therefore be entitled to injunctive or other equitable relief in order to prevent a breach or threatened breach of its IPR.

35.3   With respect to all other disputes which are not IPR related pursuant to CLAUSES 35.1 and 35.2 above and its special rules the following procedures in CLAUSES 35.3 to 35.6 shall apply. Where there is a dispute the aggrieved party shall notify the other party in writing of the nature of the dispute with as much detail as possible about the deficient performance of the other party. A representative from senior management ('representatives') of each of the parties shall meet in person or communicate by telephone within five business days of the date of the written notification in order to reach an agreement about the nature of the deficiency and the corrective action to be taken by the respective parties. The representatives shall produce a report about the nature of the dispute in detail to their respective boards and if no agreement is reached on corrective action, then the chief executives of each party shall meet in person or by telephone, to facilitate an agreement within five business days of a written notice by one to the other. If the dispute cannot be resolved at board level within a further five business days, or if the agreed upon completion dates in any written plan of corrective action are exceeded, either party may seek its legal remedies as provided below.

35.4 If the parties cannot resolve a dispute in accordance with the procedure in CLAUSE 35.3 above, then they shall with the assistance of the Centre for Alternative Dispute Solution, seek to resolve the dispute or difference amicably by using an Alternative Dispute Resolution ('ADR') procedure acceptable to both parties before pursuing any other remedies available to them. If either party fails or refuses to agree to or participate in the ADR procedure or if in any event the dispute or difference is not resolved to the satisfaction of both parties within [90] days after it has arisen, the matter shall be settled in accordance with the procedure below.

35.5 If the parties cannot resolve the dispute by the procedure set out above, the parties shall irrevocably submit to the exclusive jurisdiction of the Courts of England and Wales for the purposes of hearing and determining any dispute arising out of this Agreement.

35.6 While the dispute resolution procedure above is in progress and any party has an obligation to make a payment to another party or to allow a credit in respect of such payment, the sum relating to the matter in dispute shall be paid into an interest bearing deposit account to be held in the names of the relevant parties at a clearing bank and such payment shall be a good discharge of the parties' payment obligations under this Agreement. Following resolution of the dispute, whether by mediation or legal proceedings, the sum held in such account shall be payable as determined in accordance with the mediation or legal proceedings, and the interest accrued shall be allocated between the parties pro rata according to the split of the principal sum as between the parties.

AS WITNESS the hands of the authorised signatories of the parties the day and year first before written.

SCHEDULE 1

PRODUCTS

SCHEDULE 2

SALES TERMS

1. ORDERS

1.1 Each order for the Products submitted by the Distributor to the Company shall be in writing and shall stipulate the type and quality of the Products ordered and the requested delivery date and delivery destination.

1.2 The Distributor may cancel any order whether or not accepted or reduce the quantity of any of the Products ordered by submitting to the Company a written notice which specifically refers to the relevant order, stipulates the changes and is actually received by the Company not less than fourteen (14) days prior to the requested delivery date or, if later, the estimated delivery date notified to the Distributor pursuant to PARAGRAPH 3.2 below.

1.3   The Distributor shall be responsible for ensuring the accuracy of its orders.

2.   PRICE AND PAYMENT

2.1   Subject as hereinafter provided the price for each of the Products to be paid by the Distributor shall be the lower of the Company's price list as per SCHEDULE 7 as from time to time amended by agreement between the parties and the lowest price at which the Company sells any of the Products to its customers or other distributors.

2.2   All prices for the Products are exclusive of VAT or other applicable sales taxes which shall be paid by the Distributor at the appropriate rate.

2.3   Payment for the Products shall be no later than thirty (30) days after despatch of the Products or completion of services unless otherwise agree.

2.4   The Company may sue for the price of the Products notwithstanding that property has passed to the Distributor.

2.5   Payment for the Products shall be made in pounds sterling and by Bank transfer to such Bank account as the Company shall notify in writing to the Distributor from time to time.

2.6   If payment for any of the Products is not received by the due date then (without prejudice to the Company's other rights and remedies) the Company shall be entitled to:

2.6.1   suspend all further deliveries of the Products until payment is received; and

2.6.2   charge the Distributor interest on the unpaid sum on a day to day basis (as well after as before Judgment) from the due date to the date of payment (both dates inclusive) at the rate of four per cent (4%) above the Base Rate of Barclays Bank PLC from time to time in force.

2.7   The Company reserves the right to suspend deliveries of the Products while the aggregate amount of outstanding unpaid invoices exceeds the Company's credit limit for the Distributor from time to time as notified to the Distributor in writing.

3.   DELIVERIES

3.1   The Company shall use all reasonable endeavours to meet the delivery dates requested by the Distributor but time of delivery shall not be of the essence and the Company shall have no liability to the Distributor if it fails to meet any requested or estimated date for delivery.

3.2 If the Company is unable to meet any requested delivery date it shall as soon as practicable notify the Distributor of its estimated date for delivery.

3.3 Appropriation of the Products to any order of the Distributor shall occur when the Products are delivered to the Distributor.

3.4 Delivery of the Products will be ex the Company's premises at the [ ], or such other premises as the Company shall notify the Distributor from time to time ('the delivery point').

3.5 The Company shall bear the expense of putting the Products in the possession of the carrier at the delivery point but the Distributor shall pay all other costs of transport and insurance.

3.6 If requested in the Distributor's order the Company shall arrange (as agent for the Distributor) transport and insurance of the Products to the destination designated in the Distributor's order and shall obtain and promptly deliver to the Distributor the documents (if any) necessary for the Distributor or the Distributor's customer (as the case may be) to obtain possession of the Products. The Distributor shall reimburse the Company for all costs incurred by the company in respect of the foregoing and all applicable provisions of this Schedule shall apply mutatis mutandis to the payment of such cost as they shall apply to the payment of the price for the Products.

3.7 The Company reserves the right to make partial deliveries of any consignment of the Products ordered but unless otherwise agreed no delivery of the whole or any part of a consignment shall be made before the delivery date requested by the Distributor.

3.8 The Company will pack the Products suitable for delivery to the destinations requested by the Distributor and each consignment shall be accompanied by a delivery note in such form as may be agreed between the parties.

3.9 The Distributor shall be responsible for obtaining prior to delivery all necessary licenses, certificates of origin and other documents for the importation of the Products into the Territory and for paying all applicable import duties and other levies.

3.10 The Distributor shall notify the Company within fourteen (14) days after delivery of any consignment of the Products of any shortage in the quantity ordered. The Company shall make good any such shortage as soon as reasonably practicable after written notice is received from the Distributor in compliance with this paragraph but otherwise the Company shall have no liability to make good such shortage.

4. RISK AND PROPERTY

4.1 Risk in each consignment of the Products shall pass to the Distributor at the delivery point upon placement of that consignment into the carrier's possession by the Company.

4.2   Property in any consignment of the Product shall not pass to the Distributor until payment in full and in cleared funds has been received by the Company in respect of the price for that consignment and for all other consignments of the Products for which payment is then due.

SCHEDULE 3

TRAINING

SCHEDULE 4

INITIAL ORDER

SCHEDULE 5

TERRITORIES

SCHEDULE 6

ROYALTY PAYMENTS

PART I

The Distributor shall pay the Company a royalty on any of the Company's Courseware Products or third party courseware sold by or incorporated into a course requested by the Distributor. The amount of royalty will be agreed between the parties on a Courseware Products by Courseware Products basis but will at least cover the royalty payable by the Company to any third party in respect of third party courseware products.

For the avoidance of doubt in this Agreement reference to 'third party courseware' means software and accompanying documentation developed by the Company at the request of third party customers in which the Company acknowledges that copyright remains with the commissioning third party customer but in respect of which the third party customer will allow the Company to re-use the same either unmodified or modified for retail sale to the Distributor.

Courseware Products developed by the Company at the request of the Distributor as a result of the Distributor's own request will be licensed to the Company by the Distributor on a royalty basis for use in the United Kingdom.

The parties acknowledge that the enforceability of this Schedule is dependent upon mutual trust and an 'open book policy' and both parties will make available to each other such information as will be necessary for the parties to be sure that they are respectively complying with the true intent of this Agreement.

PART 2

The Company shall pay the Distributor a royalty on any Courseware Products developed by the Distributor on its own behalf or on behalf of any customer of the Distributor. The amount of the royalty will be agreed between the parties on a Courseware Products by Courseware Products basis but will at least cover the royalty payable by the Distributor to any third party in respect of third party courseware products.

SCHEDULE 7

PRICES

SIGNED by the authorised signatory [   ]

for and on behalf of [   ] LIMITED [   ]

SIGNED by the authorised signatory [   ]

for and on behalf of [   ]

1   This Agreement is intended to cover the licensing and distribution on a non-exclusive basis of multimedia products used in the interactive education and training sector. It is anticipated that the deliverables will consist of hardware as well as software and in this particular Agreement, some of the deliverables are specifically defined as 'Courseware' which is intended to mean the specific application software that relates to training courses and course material.

2   It is often advisable to indicate whether a distributor has the right to sub-distribute. If sub-distribution is allowed, then the distributor should remain liable for the performance of its sub-distributors. It may be considered worthwhile ensuring that any sub-distributors are bound by sub-distribution terms that are the same or similar as those in this Agreement.

3   This Agreement was used in a situation where the company was based in the United Kingdom but the distributor was based in a third world country and payment was requested to be by bankers draft. It could as equally have been dealt with by a letter of credit or other form of guaranteed bank payment.

4   This clause is of value to the Company, but may be difficult for a distributor to accept.

5   It may be advisable to ask the distributor to ensure that all employees and others to whom confidential information may be revealed specifically sign a confidentiality agreement direct with the Company and if this is felt advisable then the form of confidentiality letter to be signed should be included as a Schedule.

6   Care needs to be taken when the Company agrees contractually to protect the distributor's territory. It may be anti-competitive to contractually agree to ensure that the Company will now allow other distributors to enter the Territory.

7   This Agreement was used in a situation where the Company was British, but the Distributor was based in a country which had strained diplomatic relationships with Britain and it was felt that rather than use the force majeure clause to deal with suspension of the contract in the event that diplomatic relations or governmental intervention caused 'frustration of the contract', it was better to make this a cause for a right to terminate in the Termination Clause.

8   Many distribution agreements fail to detail the consequences of termination and it is wise to consider what the rights and obligations of the parties are at and beyond termination.

9   This force majeure clause is short and general. It may be appropriate to insert a more detailed force majeure clause such as:
    'Notwithstanding anything else contained in this Agreement, neither party shall be liable for any delay in performing its obligations hereunder if such delay is caused by circumstances beyond its reasonable control (including without limitation any delay caused by any act or omission of the other party) provided however that any delay by a sub-contractor or supplier of the party so delaying shall not relieve the party from liability for delay except where such delay is beyond the reasonable control of the sub-

contractor or supplier concerned. Subject to the party so delaying promptly notifying the other party in writing of the reasons for the delay (and the likely duration of the delay), the performance of such party's obligations shall be suspended during the period that the said circumstances persist and such party shall be granted an extension of time for performance equal to the period of the delay. Save where such delay is caused by the act or omission of the other party (in which event the rights, remedies and liabilities of the parties shall be those conferred and imposed by the other terms of this Agreement and by law):

- any costs arising from such delay shall be borne by the party incurring the same;
- either party may, if such delay continues for more than 10 weeks, terminate this Agreement forthwith giving notice in writing to the other by reason of such termination.'

10 As many contracts are varied or amended during their life cycle it is important that all Schedules are agreed to and signed or initialled by the parties so that there can be no dispute as to the totality of the contract and its contents.

11 Before the Contracts (Rights of Third Parties) Act 1999 (the Act) it was the case that a person who was not a party to a contract (a third party) could not enforce any right under the contract. Similarly, a contract could not impose any obligations or liabilities on a third party.

However the new Act attempts to draw a balance between the freedom of the parties to vary a contract and the interests of the third party. The Act means that a contractual clause limiting or excluding one's liability to a third party (eg the promisee's subsidiary company or sub-contractor or employee) will be straightforwardly enforceable by that third party if:

- the contract expressly provides that he may; or
- where a term in the contract purports to confer a benefit on him (unless on a proper construction of the contract it appears that the parties did not intend the term to be enforceable by the third party).

It is therefore prudent to include a clause to the effect of excluding the provisions of the Act. By doing so it ensures that any rights of third parties are not deemed to be enforceable by them. This is particularly the case where the parties are companies and may have subsidiaries or conversely parent companies.

12 In this MOU it is felt appropriate to use an escalating dispute solutions clause (sometimes called an alternative dispute resolution clause) because during the period of the MOU any dispute between the parties may be better settled in private and without recourse to litigation (except as reserved by the clause in relation to breach of IPR).

It may be felt in some circumstances an arbitration clause could be more appropriate or the parties may wish to simply indicate that they will resort to litigation in the courts.

An example of another governing law and dispute settlement clause is:

'Any dispute which may arise between the parties concerning this Agreement shall be determined as follows:

(1) If the dispute shall be of a technical nature relating to the functions or capabilities of the Licensed Program Materials or any similar or related matter then such a dispute shall be referred for final settlement to an expert nominated jointly by the parties or failing such nomination within Fourteen (14) days after either party's request to the other therefore nominated at the request of either party by the President for the time being of the British Computer Society. Such expert shall be deemed to act as an expert and not as an arbitrator. His decision shall (in the absence of clerical or manifest error) be final and binding on the parties in equal shares unless he determines that the conduct of either party is such that such party should bear all of such fees.

(2) In any other case the dispute shall be determined by the High Court of Justice in England and the parties hereby submit to the exclusive jurisdiction of that Court for such purposes.'

14 Joint software development agreement

DATED [ ]

(1)   THE SOFTWARE OWNER

(2)   THE DEVELOPER

JOINT SOFTWARE DEVELOPMENT AGREEMENT[1]

THIS AGREEMENT is made the [ ] day of [ ] [ ]

BETWEEN

1.   [ ] LIMITED incorporated in [ ] and having its registered office at
        [ ] (the 'Software Owner' which expression shall be deemed to include
        its subsidiaries, agents, successors and assigns)

AND

2.   [ ] LIMITED incorporated in [ ] and having its registered office at
        [ ] (the 'Developer' which expression shall be deemed to include its
        subsidiaries, agents, successors and assigns)

WHEREAS:

A.   The Developer wishes to develop and market certain computer software
        intended to [insert description or function], the outline specification for
        which is contained in SCHEDULE A hereto (the 'Software').

B.   The Developer requires to use existing software owned by the
        Software Owner known as [insert name of software product] specified
        in SCHEDULE A (the 'Source Software') and requires the Software
        Owner's support and co-operation for the purpose of developing the
        Software, the parties hereto have agreed to enter into this joint
        development upon the terms and subject to the conditions of this
        Agreement.

NOW THEREFORE IT IS HEREBY AGREED as follows:

1.   DEFINITIONS

In this Agreement, the following words and expressions shall have the
following meanings:

'**the Software**' shall have the meaning ascribed to it in Recital A above including any operator manuals relating thereto, to be developed by the Developer with the assistance and co-operation of the Software Owner in accordance with this Agreement and shall include any enhancements and modifications made thereto.

'**the Source Software**' shall have the meaning ascribed to it in Recital B being the software owned by the Software Owner upon which the Software to be developed in accordance with this Agreement shall be based.

'**the Equipment**' means the computer hardware equipment specified in SCHEDULE A upon which the Software is to operate when developed.

'**the Specification**' means the detailed specification document for development of the Software prepared by the Developer with the co-operation of the Software Owner and based upon the outline specification contained in SCHEDULE A.

'**the SAD**' means the Software Acceptance Document agreed between the Software Owner and the Developer as the acceptance tests to be passed by the Software.

'**the Development Work**' means the development required to produce the Software based upon the Specification.

'**the Development Timetable**' means the timetable forming SCHEDULE B to this Agreement, upon which development of the Software is proposed to take place (including the regular meetings to be held and the time to be spent by each party) as the same may be amended from time to time by mutual agreement between the parties.

'**the Distribution Agreement**' means the distribution agreement entered into between the parties dated [ ].

'**Acceptance**' or '**Accepted**' means acceptance by both parties of the Software which has successfully passed the agreed acceptance tests specified and approved in the SAD.

2. DELIVERY OF SOURCE SOFTWARE

Upon execution of this Agreement and receipt by the Software Owner of the sum of £ [ ] from the Developer as payment for the licence and right to modify the Source Software, the Software Owner shall deliver to the Developer the Source Software in a form suitable for the parties to carry out the Development Work. The Source Software is received, held and used by the Developer strictly in accordance with the provisions of this Agreement.

3. PREPARATION AND APPROVAL OF DOCUMENTS

3.1   The Developer and the Software Owner shall prepare the specification, the SAD and the Development Timetable.

3.2   The parties shall raise any amendments or recommendations to any of the above documents in writing or at a meeting to be held between the parties. All meetings shall be minuted. The party proposing the amendment shall amend the appropriate document accordingly and deliver the amended document to the other party for approval.

3.3 Upon approval of the documents by both parties the Developer shall commence the Development Work with the assistance and co-operation of the Software Owner in accordance with the Development Timetable.

4. TESTING AND ACCEPTANCE OF THE SOFTWARE

4.1 Upon completion of the Development Work or at any appropriate stage thereof as the case may be, the parties shall run the agreed acceptance tests specified in the SAD.

4.2 Upon passing the agreed acceptance tests to the satisfaction of both parties, the Software or that part of it (the 'module'), if not the whole, shall be deemed Accepted for marketing in terms of the Distribution Agreement and the Developer shall with the assistance of the Software Owner, prepare the necessary manuals sufficient to enable a reasonably skilled operator to install and use the Software on the Equipment.

4.3 In the event that the Software or any 'module' fails to pass the tests prescribed in the SAD, the parties shall make such adjustments or modifications as may be necessary to enable the Software to be retested.

4.4 In the event that the parties fail to complete the development in timely fashion or in the event that the Software repeatedly fails to pass Acceptance testing, either party shall be entitled to terminate this Agreement by reason of such failure in which event the sum specified in CLAUSE 2 shall be forfeit to the Software Owner in addition to payment to the Software Owner of any and all costs and expenses incurred by the Software Owner in co-operating with the Developer in this development unless the parties mutually agree to extend the completion date of the development or as the case may be, allow further modifications and retesting.

5. MEETINGS AND CHANGE CONTROL COMMITTEE

5.1 The Developer and the Software Owner undertake to hold regular meetings at such times and venues as shall be agreed between the parties. Such meeting shall be attended by a minimum of one nominated person representing each of the parties who shall, unless otherwise agreed, comprise the Change Control Committee.

5.2 Any proposed change, amendment or alteration to the Specification, SAD or Development Timetable following their approval or to the development shall be submitted to the Change Control Committee. Any such change, amendment or alteration submitted shall specify any effect the same shall have on price, marketing and timescale of the development.

5.3   Any such change, amendment or alteration requires the written approval of both parties prior to implementation.

5.4   Any enhancement or modification to the Software proposed by either party at any time shall require the written approval of both parties.

6.   COST OF DEVELOPMENT

Subject to the provisions of CLAUSE 2 and CLAUSE 7, the cost relating to development of the Software shall be shared between the parties in the same proportion as the royalties specified in the Distribution Agreement. Any additional contribution required to be given by the Software Owner beyond that specified in the Development Timetable shall be charged on a time and materials basis or as otherwise agreed between the parties.

7.   PAYMENT UPON ACCEPTANCE

7.1   Upon Acceptance of the Software, the Developer shall pay to the Software Owner the sum of £ [   ] as payment for the licence to reproduce unlimited copies of the Source Software or that part of it which is required to market the Software under the Distribution Agreement.

7.2   Where the payment of any sum due or invoice or any part thereof is not made, the Software Owner, without prejudice to its other rights hereunder or in law, shall be entitled to charge interest (as well before as after judgment) on the outstanding amount at the rate of [   ] per cent per annum above the [Bank] base rate for the time being in force from the due date or the date of invoice until the outstanding sum is paid.

7.3   In addition to the above, should the Developer fail to make any payment when due under this Agreement the Software Owner shall at the Software Owner's absolute discretion be entitled to terminate this Agreement and the Distribution Agreement without prejudice to any other rights or remedies which may be available to the Software Owner in accordance with these terms and conditions, this Agreement, at law or otherwise.

8.   SOFTWARE SUPPORT

In the event that the Developer requires the Software Owner to assist in the support of the Software following completion, the same shall be performed by the Software Owner upon its acceptance in writing of the same and upon the terms and conditions to be agreed between the parties or specified in the Distribution Agreement.

9. COPYRIGHT, PATENTS, TRADEMARKS AND INTELLECTUAL PROPERTY RIGHTS

9.1   The Developer acknowledges that any and all of the trademarks, trade names, copyrights, patents and other intellectual property rights created, developed, embodied in or in connection with the Source Software or any enhancement or other software provided by the Software Owner shall be and remain the sole property of the Software Owner. The Developer shall not during or at any time after the completion, expiry or termination of this Agreement in any way question or dispute the ownership by the Software Owner of any such rights.

9.2   The parties agree that they shall jointly own the copyright in and to the Software developed hereunder including any enhancements and modifications made thereto other than that part of it which is owned by the Software Owner and is specified in CLAUSE 9.19.1 above.

10. OBLIGATIONS AND WARRANTIES

10.1   The Software Owner shall:

10.1.1   make available to the Developer, free of charge, such computer facilities (including but not limited to unhindered access to the Equipment), office and secretarial services as are necessary to enable the Developer to carry out its obligations under this Agreement;

10.1.2   ensure that its employees and other independent contractors co-operate reasonably with the Developer and its employees in carrying out the Development Work;

10.2   promptly furnish the Developer with such information and documents as it may reasonably request for the proper performance of its obligations under this Agreement.

10.3   The Developer warrants that:

10.3.1   it is entitled to enter into this Agreement and that it is entitled to grant the Licence in accordance with this Agreement;

10.3.2   the Development Work shall:

10.3.2.1   perform substantially in accordance with the Specification on the Equipment, minor interruptions and errors excluded;

10.3.2.2   be date compliant and neither the performance nor functionality of the Development Work is affected by dates prior to, during and after the year 2000; and

10.3.2.3   support the introduction of the Euro currency unit.

10.3.3   the manuals (referred to in CLAUSE 4.2) will provide users with adequate instructions to enable them effectively to operate and use the Equipment;

      10.3.4   the development of the Development Work will be carried out in a professional manner conforming to best industry practices.

10.4   The Developer shall not be liable under CLAUSE 10.2.2 if a failure to meet the warranties set out therein is caused by:

      10.4.1   software other than the Development Work running on the Equipment; or

      10.4.2   modifications or customisation made by or on behalf of the Customer to the Development Work, without the authorisation of the Developer.

10.5   If the Developer receives a written notice from the Customer identifying a breach of the warranties set out in CLAUSE 10.2, or otherwise becomes aware of its failure to comply with the warranties set out in CLAUSE 10.2, then the Developer shall, at its own expense, promptly remedy such breach or failure provided that the Developer shall have no liability or obligations under the warranties unless it shall have received written notice of the defect or error within fourteen (14) days of such defect or error being discovered.

11. TERMINATION

11.1   Notwithstanding anything else contained herein, this Agreement may be terminated:

      11.1.1   by the Software Owner forthwith on giving notice in writing to the Developer if:

            11.1.1.1   the Developer shall (or shall threaten to) sell, assign, part with or cease to carry on its business or that part of its business relating to the distribution of the Products; or

            11.1.1.2   the control (as defined for the purposes of the Income and Corporation Taxes Act 1988, section 416) of the Developer shall be transferred to any person or persons other than the person or persons in control of the Developer at the date hereof (but the Software Owner shall only be entitled to terminate within the period of sixty (60) days after the Software Owner shall have been notified in writing of the change in control);

11.2   by either party forthwith on giving notice in writing to the other if:

      11.2.1   the other party commits any material or persistent breach of any term of this Agreement and (in the case of a breach capable of being remedied) shall have failed, within thirty (30) days after the receipt of a request in writing from the other party so to do, to remedy the breach (such request to contain a warning of such party's intention to terminate);

11.2.2 the other party shall have been unable to perform its obligations hereunder for a period of ninety (90) consecutive days or for periods aggregating one hundred and eighty (180) days in any year (but the party entitled to terminate may only terminate within the period of sixty (60) days after the expiration of the said consecutive period or year); or

11.2.3 the other party shall have a receiver or administrative receiver appointed of it or over any part of its undertaking or assets or shall pass a resolution for winding-up (otherwise than for the purpose of a bona fide scheme of solvent amalgamation or reconstruction) or a court of competent jurisdiction shall make an order to that effect or if the other party shall enter into any voluntary arrangement with its creditors or shall become subject to an administration order.

12. LIABILITY

12.1 Notwithstanding anything else contained in this Agreement but subject to CLAUSE 12.2 below the Software Owner shall not be liable to the Developer for loss of profits or contracts or other indirect or consequential loss or damage whether arising from negligence, breach of contract or any other cause of action out of the subject matter of this Agreement.

12.2 The Software Owner does not exclude liability for death or personal injury caused by the Software Owner's negligence.

12.3 Except as expressly provided in this Agreement no warranty, condition, undertaking, or term, express or implied, statutory or otherwise, as to the condition, quality, performance, merchantability, durability or fitness for purpose of the Source Software is given or assumed by the Software Owner and all such warranties, conditions, undertakings and terms are hereby excluded.

13. INDEMNITIES

13.1 The Software Owner shall indemnify the Developer and keep the Developer fully and effectively indemnified against any and all losses, claims, damages, costs, charges, expenses, liabilities, demands, proceedings and actions which the Developer may sustain or incur or which may be brought or established against it by any person and which in any case arise out of or in relation to or by reason of any claim or allegation that any of the Source Software infringes any intellectual property rights of any third party;

13.2 The Developer shall indemnify the Software Owner and keep the Software Owner fully and effectively indemnified against any and all losses, claims, damages, costs, charges, expenses, liabilities, demands, proceedings and actions which the Software Owner may sustain or incur or which may be brought or established against it by any person and which in any case arise out of or in relation to or by reason of:

13.2.1   the negligence, recklessness or wilful misconduct of the Developer in the performance of any of its obligations in connection with the source software;

13.2.2   any unauthorised action or omission of the Developer or its employees;

13.2.3   any breach or alleged breach of any applicable laws or regulations relating to the use of the Source Software by the Developer.

13.3   If any claim is made against either party for which indemnification is sought under this CLAUSE, the indemnified party shall consult with the other and, subject to being secured to its reasonable satisfaction, shall co-operate with the other in relation to any reasonable request made by the other in respect of such claim.

14. AGENCY, PARTNERSHIP

This Agreement shall not constitute or imply any partnership, joint venture, agency, fiduciary relationship or other relationship between the parties other than the contractual relationship expressly provided for in this Agreement.

15. AMENDMENTS

This Agreement may not be released, discharged, supplemented, interpreted, amended, varied or modified in any manner except by an instrument in writing signed by a duly authorised officer or representative of each of the parties hereto.

16. ANNOUNCEMENTS

No party shall issue or make any public announcement or disclose any information regarding this Agreement unless prior written consent has been obtained from the other party.

17. ASSIGNMENT

17.1   This Agreement is personal to the parties and, subject to CLAUSE 17.2 below, neither this Agreement nor any rights, licenses or obligations under this Agreement, may be assigned by either party without the prior written approval of the other party.

17.2   Notwithstanding the foregoing, either party may assign this Agreement to any acquirer of all or of substantially all of such party's equity securities, assets or business relating to the subject matter of this Agreement or to any entity controlled by, that controls, or is under common control with a party to this Agreement. Any attempted assignment in violation of this CLAUSE will be void and without effect.

18. ENTIRE AGREEMENT

This Agreement supersedes all prior agreements, arrangements and undertakings between the parties and constitutes the entire agreement between the parties relating to the subject matter of this Agreement. However the obligations of the parties under any pre-existing non-disclosure agreement shall remain in full force and effect insofar as there is no conflict between the same. The parties confirm that they have not entered into this Agreement on the basis of any representation that is not expressly incorporated into this Agreement.

19. FORCE MAJEURE[2]

Neither party shall have any liability under or be deemed to be in breach of this Agreement for any delays or failures in performance of this Agreement which result from circumstances beyond the reasonable control of that party. If such circumstances continue for a continuous period of more than [6 months], either party may terminate this Agreement by written notice to the other party.

20. NOTICES

20.1   All notices hereunder shall be in writing.

20.2   Notices shall be deemed to have been duly given:

    20.2.1   when delivered, if delivered by courier or other messenger (including registered mail) during normal business hours of the recipient; or

    20.2.2   when sent, if transmitted by fax or e-mail and a successful transmission report or return receipt is generated; or

    20.2.3   on the fifth business day following mailing, if mailed by national ordinary mail, postage pre-paid; or

    20.2.4   on the tenth business day following mailing, if mailed by airmail, postage pre-paid,

in each case addressed to the most recent address, e-mail address, or facsimile number notified to the other party.

21. SCHEDULES[3]

The provisions of SCHEDULE[S] (A *to B)* to this Agreement shall form part of this Agreement as if set out here.[8]

22. SEVERANCE

If any provision of this Agreement is prohibited by law or judged by a court to be unlawful, void or unenforceable, the provision shall, to the extent required, be severed from this Agreement and rendered ineffective as far as possible without modifying the remaining provisions of this Agreement, and shall not in any way affect any other circumstances of or the validity or enforcement of this Agreement.

23. SUCCESSORS AND ASSIGNEES

23.1 This Agreement shall be binding upon, and enure to the benefit of, the parties and their respective successors and permitted assignees, and references to a party in this Agreement shall include its successors and permitted assignees.

23.2 In this Agreement references to a party include references to a person:

23.2.1 who for the time being is entitled (by assignment, novation or otherwise) to that party's rights under this Agreement (or any interest in those rights); or

23.2.2 who, as administrator, liquidator or otherwise, is entitled to exercise those rights;

and in particular those references include a person to whom those rights (or any interest in those rights) are transferred or pass as a result of a merger, division, reconstruction or other reorganisation involving .that party. For this purpose, references to a party's rights under this Agreement include any similar rights to which another person becomes entitled as a result of a novation of this Agreement.

24. WAIVER

No delay, neglect or forbearance on the part of either party in enforcing against the other party any term or condition of this Agreement shall either be or be deemed to be a waiver or in any way prejudice any right of that party under this Agreement. No right, power or remedy in this Agreement conferred upon or reserved for either party is exclusive of any other right, power or remedy available to that party.

25. COUNTERPARTS

This Agreement may be executed in any number of counterparts or duplicates, each of which shall be an original, and such counterparts or duplicates shall together constitute one and the same agreement.

26. TIME IS OF THE ESSENCE

Time shall be of the essence in this Agreement as regards any time, date or period mentioned in this Agreement or subsequently substituted as a time, date or period by agreement in writing between the parties.

27. LANGUAGE

This Agreement is made only in the English language. If there is any conflict in the meaning between the English language version of this Agreement and any version or translation of this Agreement in any other language, the English language version shall prevail.

28. COSTS AND EXPENSES

Each party shall bear its own legal costs and other costs and expenses arising in connection with the drafting, negotiation, execution and registration (if applicable) of this Agreement.

29. SET-OFF

Where either party has incurred any liability to the other party, whether under this Agreement or otherwise, and whether such liability is liquidated or unliquidated, each party may set off the amount of such liability against any sum that would otherwise be due to the other party under this Agreement.

30. THIRD PARTIES[4]

[The parties confirm their intent not to confer any rights on any third parties by virtue of this Agreement and accordingly the Contracts (Rights of Third Parties) Act 1999 shall not apply to this Agreement.]

Or

[The parties recognise that this Agreement is intended to benefit and shall so benefit (insert name of third party) for the purposes of the Contracts (Rights of Third Parties) Act 1999 and, subject to that, the parties confirm their intent not to confer any rights on any other third parties by virtue of this Agreement.]

31. PROPER LAW AND JURISDICTION[5]

31.1   This Agreement and all matters arising from it and any dispute resolutions referred to below shall be governed by and construed in accordance with English Law notwithstanding the conflict of law provisions and other mandatory legal provisions save that:

31.1.1   either party shall have the right to sue to recover its fees or expenses in any jurisdiction in which the Developer is operating or has assets, and

31.1.2   either party shall have the right to sue for breach of its intellectual property rights and other proprietary information and trade secrets ('IPR') (whether in connection with this Agreement or otherwise) in any country where it believes that infringement or a breach of this Agreement relating to its IPR might be taking place. For the avoidance of doubt, the place of performance of this Agreement is agreed by the parties to be England.

31.2 Each party recognises that the other party's business relies upon the protection of its IPR and that in the event of a breach or threatened breach of IPR, the other party will be caused irreparable damage and such other party may therefore be entitled to injunctive or other equitable relief in order to prevent a breach or threatened breach of its IPR.

31.3 With respect to all other disputes which are not IPR related pursuant to CLAUSES 30.1 and 30.2 above and its special rules the following procedures in CLAUSES 30.3 to 30.5 shall apply. Where there is a dispute the aggrieved party shall notify the other party in writing of the nature of the dispute with as much detail as possible about the deficient performance of the other party. A representative from senior management ('representatives') of each of the parties shall meet in person or communicate by telephone within five business days of the date of the written notification in order to reach an agreement about the nature of the deficiency and the corrective action to be taken by the respective parties. The representatives shall produce a report about the nature of the dispute in detail to their respective boards and if no agreement is reached on corrective action, then the chief executives of each party shall meet in person or by telephone, to facilitate an agreement within five business days of a written notice by one to the other. If the dispute cannot be resolved at board level within a further five business days, or if the agreed upon completion dates in any written plan of corrective action are exceeded, either party may seek its legal remedies as provided below.

31.4 If the parties cannot resolve a dispute in accordance with the procedure in CLAUSE 30.3 above, then they shall with the assistance of the Centre for Alternative Dispute Solution, seek to resolve the dispute or difference amicably by using an Alternative Dispute Resolution ('ADR') procedure acceptable to both parties before pursuing any other remedies available to them. If either party fails or refuses to agree to or participate in the ADR procedure or if in any event the dispute or difference is not resolved to the satisfaction of both parties within [90] days after it has arisen, the matter shall be settled in accordance with the procedure below.

31.5 If the parties cannot resolve the dispute by the procedure set out above, the parties shall irrevocably submit to the exclusive jurisdiction of the Courts of England and Wales for the purposes of hearing and determining any dispute arising out of this Agreement.

31.6 [While the dispute resolution procedure above is in progress and any party has an obligation to make a payment to another party or to allow a credit in respect of such payment, the sum relating to the matter in dispute shall be paid into an interest bearing deposit account to be held in the names of the relevant parties at a clearing bank and such payment shall be a good discharge of the parties' payment obligations under this Agreement. Following resolution of the dispute, whether by mediation or legal proceedings, the sum held in such account shall be payable as determined in accordance with the mediation or legal proceedings, and the interest accrued shall be allocated between the parties pro rata according to the split of the principal sum as between the parties.]

IN WITNESS whereof

SIGNED for and on behalf of the

Software Owner

by: [   ]

in the presence of: [   ]

SIGNED for and on behalf of the

Developer

by: [   ]

in the presence of: [   ]

SCHEDULE A

OUTLINE SPECIFICATION FOR DEVELOPMENT OF THE SOFTWARE

SCHEDULE B

DEVELOPMENT TIMETABLE

1 This agreement is intended to be supplemented by a Distribution Agreement as in PRECEDENT 11.
2 This force majeure CLAUSE is short and general. It may be appropriate to insert a more detailed force majeure CLAUSE such as:
   'Notwithstanding anything else contained in this Agreement, neither party shall be liable for any delay in performing its obligations hereunder if such delay is caused by circumstances beyond its reasonable control (including without limitation any delay caused by any act or omission of the other party) provided however that any delay by a sub-contractor or supplier of the party so delaying shall not relieve the party from liability for delay except where such delay is beyond the reasonable control of the sub-contractor or supplier concerned. Subject to the party so delaying promptly notifying the other party in writing of the reasons for the delay (and the likely duration of the delay), the performance of such party's obligations shall be suspended during the period that the said circumstances persist and such party shall be granted an extension of time for performance equal to the period of the delay. Save where such delay is caused by the act or omission of the other party (in which event the rights, remedies and liabilities of the parties shall be those conferred and imposed by the other terms of this Agreement and by law):
   • any costs arising from such delay shall be borne by the party incurring the same;
   • either party may, if such delay continues for more than 10 weeks, terminate this Agreement forthwith giving notice in writing to the other by reason of such termination.'
3 As many contracts are varied or amended during their life cycle it is important that all Schedules are agreed to and signed or initialled by the parties so that there can be no dispute as to the totality of the contract and its contents.
4 Before the Contracts (Rights of Third Parties) Act 1999 (the Act) it was the case that a person who was not a party to a contract (a third party) could not enforce any right

under the contract. Similarly, a contract could not impose any obligations or liabilities on a third party.

However the Act attempts to draw a balance between the freedom of the parties to vary a contract and the interests of the third party. The Act means that a contractual CLAUSE benefiting a third party (eg the promisee's subsidiary company or sub-contractor or employee) will be straightforwardly enforceable by that third party if:

- the contract expressly provides that he may; or
- where a term in the contract purports to confer a benefit on him (unless on a proper construction of the contract it appears that the parties did not intend the term to be enforceable by the third party.) It is therefore prudent to include a CLAUSE to the effect of excluding the provisions of the Act. By doing so it ensures that any rights of third parties are not deemed to be enforceable by them. This is particularly the case where the parties are companies and may have subsidiaries or conversely parent companies.

5   In this Agreement it is felt appropriate to use an escalating dispute solutions CLAUSE (sometimes called an alternative dispute resolution CLAUSE) because during the period of the MOU any dispute between the parties may be better settled in private and without recourse to litigation (except as reserved by the CLAUSE in relation to breach of IPR).

It may be felt in some circumstances an arbitration CLAUSE could be more appropriate or the parties may wish to simply indicate that they will resort to litigation in the courts.

An example of another governing law and dispute settlement CLAUSE is:

'Any dispute which may arise between the parties concerning this Agreement shall be determined as follows:

(1)   If the dispute shall be of a technical nature relating to the functions or capabilities of the Licensed Program Materials or any similar or related matter then such a dispute shall be referred for final settlement to an expert nominated jointly by the parties or failing such nomination within Fourteen (14) days after either party's request to the other therefore nominated at the request of either party by the President for the time being of the British Computer Society. Such expert shall be deemed to act as an expert and not as an arbitrator. His decision shall (in the absence of clerical or manifest error) be final and binding on the parties and whose costs shall be borne between the parties in equal shares unless he determines that the conduct of either party is such that such party should bear all of such fees.

(2)   In any other case the dispute shall be determined by the High Court of Justice in England and the parties hereby submit to the exclusive jurisdiction of that Court for such purposes.'

15 Reciprocal software licence agreement

DATED [ ]

(1) THE SOFTWARE OWNER

(2) THE DEVELOPER

RECIPROCAL SOFTWARE LICENCE AGREEMENT[1]

THIS AGREEMENT is made the [ ] day of [ ] [ ]

BETWEEN

[ ] LIMITED a company incorporated in [ ] and having its registered office at [ ] (hereinafter referred to as the 'Software Owner' which expression shall be deemed to include its subsidiaries, agents, successors and assigns)

AND

[ ] LIMITED a company incorporated in [ ] and having its registered office at [ ] (the 'Developer').

WHEREAS:

A. By a Joint Software Development Agreement dated [ ] between the Software Owner and the Developer (the 'Development Agreement'), the parties developed certain software programs (the 'Software') using existing software owned by the Software Owner (the 'Source Software') and the copyrights of each of the parties were preserved and/or shared in terms of CLAUSE 9 OF THE DEVELOPMENT AGREEMENT.

B. By a Distribution Agreement entered into between the parties dated [ ] between the Software Owner and the Developer was granted the right to distribute the Software as therein granted.

C. The Software Owner and the Developer now wish to develop their own respective markets using the Source Software and the Software including all modifications, variations and enhancements made thereto, hereinafter collectively referred to as the 'Licensed Programs', which requires the grant from each party to the other of the right to use the other party's proprietary rights in the Licensed Programs.

NOW THEREFORE THE PARTIES AGREE as follows:

1.   RECIPROCAL GRANT

The Software Owner hereby grants to the Developer and the Developer hereby grants to the Software Owner the non-exclusive, non-transferable, royalty-free, worldwide right to reproduce, enhance, vary, modify, convert, distribute, market and support those parts of the Licensed Programs owned by the other but subject always to the provisions of CLAUSE 3 below.

2.   SOURCE CODE, OBJECT CODE AND DATA EXCHANGE

For the purposes of CLAUSE 1 above, each party shall upon execution of this Agreement or forthwith on a date mutually agreed between the parties exchange source codes, object codes and all data (written or otherwise) required by the receiving party to properly and commercially exploit the rights granted in CLAUSE 1 above.

3.   COPYRIGHT, PROPRIETARY AND CONFIDENTIAL INFORMATION[2]

3.1   The respective copyrights, proprietary and confidential information belonging to the parties and relating to the Licensed Programs shall not be affected by this Agreement and the provisions of clauses [ ] of the Development Agreement and clauses [ ] of the Distribution Agreement shall continue to apply notwithstanding that those agreements shall have been being superseded by this Agreement.

3.2   Each party agrees to acknowledge the copyright interest of the other in the Licensed Programs by displaying the appropriate legends therein and thereon.

4.   LIABILITY

Neither party shall be liable to the other for any loss or damage suffered by the other in exercise of their reciprocal rights hereunder.

5.   TERMINATION

5.1   Notwithstanding anything else contained herein, this Agreement may be terminated:

5.1.1   by the Software Owner forthwith on giving notice in writing to the Developer if:

5.1.1.1   the Developer shall (or shall threaten to) sell, assign, part with or cease to carry on its business or that part of its business relating to the distribution of the Products; or

5.1.1.2   the control (as defined for the purposes of the Income and Corporation Taxes Act 1988, section

416) of the Developer shall be transferred to any person or persons other than the person or persons in control of the Developer at the date hereof (but the Software Owner shall only be entitled to terminate within the period of sixty (60) days after the Software Owner shall have been notified in writing of the change in control);

5.2 by either party forthwith on giving notice in writing to the other if:

5.2.1 the other party commits any material or persistent breach of any term of this Agreement and (in the case of a breach capable of being remedied) shall have failed, within thirty (30) days after the receipt of a request in writing from the other party so to do, to remedy the breach (such request to contain a warning of such party's intention to terminate);

5.2.2 the other party shall have been unable to perform its obligations hereunder for a period of ninety (90) consecutive days or for periods aggregating one hundred and eighty (180) days in any Year (but the party entitled to terminate may only terminate within the period of sixty (60) days after the expiration of the said consecutive period or Year); or

5.2.3 the other party shall have a receiver or administrative receiver appointed of it or over any part of its undertaking or assets or shall pass a resolution for winding-up (otherwise than for the purpose of a bona fide scheme of solvent amalgamation or reconstruction) or a court of competent jurisdiction shall make an order to that effect or if the other party shall enter into any voluntary arrangement with its creditors or shall become subject to an administration order.

6. AGENCY, PARTNERSHIP

This Agreement shall not constitute or imply any partnership, joint venture, agency, fiduciary relationship or other relationship between the parties other than the contractual relationship expressly provided for in this Agreement.

7. AMENDMENTS

This Agreement may not be released, discharged, supplemented, interpreted, amended, varied or modified in any manner except by an instrument in writing signed by a duly authorised officer or representative of each of the parties hereto.

8. ANNOUNCEMENTS

No party shall issue or make any public announcement or disclose any information regarding this Agreement unless prior written consent has been obtained from the other party.

9. ASSIGNMENT

9.1   This Agreement is personal to the parties and, subject to CLAUSE 9.2 below, neither this Agreement nor any rights, licenses or obligations under this Agreement, may be assigned by either party without the prior written approval of the other party.

9.2   Notwithstanding the foregoing, either party may assign this Agreement to any acquirer of all or of substantially all of such party's equity securities, assets or business relating to the subject matter of this Agreement or to any entity controlled by, that controls, or is under common control with a party to this Agreement. Any attempted assignment in violation of this clause will be void and without effect.

10. ENTIRE AGREEMENT

This Agreement supersedes all prior agreements, arrangements and undertakings between the parties and constitutes the entire agreement between the parties relating to the subject matter of this Agreement. However the obligations of the parties under any pre-existing non-disclosure agreement shall remain in full force and effect insofar as there is no conflict between the same. The parties confirm that they have not entered into this Agreement on the basis of any representation that is not expressly incorporated into this Agreement.

11. FORCE MAJEURE[3]

Neither party shall have any liability under or be deemed to be in breach of this Agreement for any delays or failures in performance of this Agreement which result from circumstances beyond the reasonable control of that party. If such circumstances continue for a continuous period of more than [6 months], either party may terminate this Agreement by written notice to the other party.

12. NOTICES

12.1   All notices hereunder shall be in writing.

12.2   Notices shall be deemed to have been duly given:

12.2.1   when delivered, if delivered by courier or other messenger (including registered mail) during normal business hours of the recipient; or

12.2.2   when sent, if transmitted by fax or e-mail and a successful transmission report or return receipt is generated; or

12.2.3   on the fifth business day following mailing, if mailed by national ordinary mail, postage pre-paid; or

12.2.4   on the tenth business day following mailing, if mailed by airmail, postage pre-paid, in each case addressed to the most recent address, e-mail address, or facsimile number notified to the other party.

13.   SEVERANCE

If any provision of this Agreement is prohibited by law or judged by a court to be unlawful, void or unenforceable, the provision shall, to the extent required, be severed from this Agreement and rendered ineffective as far as possible without modifying the remaining provisions of this Agreement, and shall not in any way affect any other circumstances of or the validity or enforcement of this Agreement.

14.   SUCCESSORS AND ASSIGNEES

14.1   This Agreement shall be binding upon, and enure to the benefit of, the parties and their respective successors and permitted assignees, and references to a party in this Agreement shall include its successors and permitted assignees.

14.2   In this Agreement references to a party include references to a person:

14.2.1   who for the time being is entitled (by assignment, novation or otherwise) to that party's rights under this Agreement (or any interest in those rights); or

14.2.2   who, as administrator, liquidator or otherwise, is entitled to exercise those rights;

and in particular those references include a person to whom those rights (or any interest in those rights) are transferred or pass as a result of a merger, division, reconstruction or other reorganisation involving that party. For this purpose, references to a party's rights under this Agreement include any similar rights to which another person becomes entitled as a result of a novation of this Agreement.

15.   WAIVER

No delay, neglect or forbearance on the part of either party in enforcing against the other party any term or condition of this Agreement shall either be or be deemed to be a waiver or in any way prejudice any right of that party under this Agreement. No right, power or remedy in this Agreement conferred upon or reserved for either party is exclusive of any other right, power or remedy available to that party.

16.   COUNTERPARTS

This Agreement may be executed in any number of counterparts or duplicates, each of which shall be an original, and such counterparts or duplicates shall together constitute one and the same agreement.

17. TIME IS OF THE ESSENCE

Time shall be of the essence in this Agreement as regards any time, date or period mentioned in this Agreement or subsequently substituted as a time, date or period by agreement in writing between the parties.

18. LANGUAGE

This Agreement is made only in the English language. If there is any conflict in the meaning between the English language version of this Agreement and any version or translation of this Agreement in any other language, the English language version shall prevail.

19. COSTS AND EXPENSES

Each party shall bear its own legal costs and other costs and expenses arising in connection with the drafting, negotiation, execution and registration (if applicable) of this Agreement.

20. SET-OFF

Where either party has incurred any liability to the other party, whether under this Agreement or otherwise, and whether such liability is liquidated or unliquidated, each party may set off the amount of such liability against any sum that would otherwise be due to the other party under this Agreement.

21. THIRD PARTIES[4]

[The parties confirm their intent not to confer any rights on any third parties by virtue of this Agreement and accordingly the Contracts (Rights of Third Parties) Act 1999 shall not apply to this Agreement.]

Or

[The parties recognise that this Agreement is intended to benefit and shall so benefit (insert name of third party) for the purposes of the Contracts (Rights of Third Parties) Act 1999 and, subject to that, the parties confirm their intent not to confer any rights on any other third parties by virtue of this Agreement.]

22. PROPER LAW AND JURISDICTION[5]

22.1   This Agreement and all matters arising from it and any dispute resolutions referred to below shall be governed by and construed in accordance with English Law notwithstanding the conflict of law provisions and other mandatory legal provisions save that:

22.1.1 the Software Owner shall have the right to sue to recover its fees in any jurisdiction in which the Developer is operating or has assets, and

22.1.2 the Software Owner shall have the right to sue for breach of its intellectual property rights and other proprietary information and trade secrets ('IPR') (whether in connection with this Agreement or otherwise) in any country where it believes that infringement or a breach of this Agreement relating to its IPR might be taking place. For the avoidance of doubt, the place of performance of this Agreement is agreed by the parties to be England.

22.2 Each party recognises that the other party's business relies upon the protection of its IPR and that in the event of a breach or threatened breach of IPR, the other party will be caused irreparable damage and such other party may therefore be entitled to injunctive or other equitable relief in order to prevent a breach or threatened breach of its IPR.

22.2.1 With respect to all other disputes which are not IPR related pursuant to CLAUSES 22.1 and 22.2 above and its special rules the following procedures in CLAUSES 22.3 to 22.4 shall apply. Where there is a dispute the aggrieved party shall notify the other party in writing of the nature of the dispute with as much detail as possible about the deficient performance of the other party. A representative from senior management ('representatives') of each of the parties shall meet in person or communicate by telephone within five business days of the date of the written notification in order to reach an agreement about the nature of the deficiency and the corrective action to be taken by the respective parties. The representatives shall produce a report about the nature of the dispute in detail to their respective boards and if no agreement is reached on corrective action, then the chief executives of each party shall meet in person or by telephone, to facilitate an agreement within five business days of a written notice by one to the other. If the dispute cannot be resolved at board level within a further five business days, or if the agreed upon completion dates in any written plan of corrective action are exceeded, either party may seek its legal remedies as provided below.

22.3 If the parties cannot resolve a dispute in accordance with the procedure in CLAUSE 22.2.1 above, then they shall with the assistance of the Centre for Alternative Dispute Solution, seek to resolve the dispute or difference amicably by using an Alternative Dispute Resolution ('ADR') procedure acceptable to both parties before pursuing any other remedies available to them. If either party fails or refuses to agree to or participate in the ADR procedure or if in any event the dispute or difference is not resolved to the satisfaction of both parties within [90] days after it has arisen, the matter shall be settled in accordance with the procedure below.

22.4   If the parties cannot resolve the dispute by the procedure set out above, the parties shall irrevocably submit to the exclusive jurisdiction of the Courts of England and Wales for the purposes of hearing and determining any dispute arising out of this Agreement.

IN WITNESS whereof

SIGNED on behalf of

the Software Owner

By: [   ]

In the presence of: [   ]

Date: [   ]

SIGNED on behalf of

the Software Developer

By: [   ]

In the presence of: [   ]

Date: [   ]

1   This Agreement is supplemental to the joint Software Development Agreement at PRECEDENT 13 and the Distribution Agreement at PRECEDENT 11.
2   Please insert the clause numbers that are required from the Development Agreement and the Distribution Agreement.
3   This force majeure clause is short and general. It may be appropriate to insert a more detailed force majeure clause such as:
    'Notwithstanding anything else contained in this Agreement, neither party shall be liable for any delay in performing its obligations hereunder if such delay is caused by circumstances beyond its reasonable control (including without limitation any delay caused by any act or omission of the other party) provided however that any delay by a sub-contractor or supplier of the party so delaying shall not relieve the party from liability for delay except where such delay is beyond the reasonable control of the sub-contractor or supplier concerned. Subject to the party so delaying promptly notifying the other party in writing of the reasons for the delay (and the likely duration of the delay), the performance of such party's obligations shall be suspended during the period that the said circumstances persist and such party shall be granted an extension of time for performance equal to the period of the delay. Save where such delay is caused by the act or omission of the other party (in which event the rights, remedies and liabilities of the parties shall be those conferred and imposed by the other terms of this Agreement and by law):
    •   any costs arising from such delay shall be borne by the party incurring the same;
    •   either party may, if such delay continues for more than 10 weeks,
    terminate this Agreement forthwith giving notice in writing to the other by reason of such termination.'
4   Before the Contracts (Rights of Third Parties) Act 1999 (the Act) it was the case that a person who was not a party to a contract (a third party) could not enforce any right under the contract. Similarly, a contract could not impose any obligations or liabilities on a third party.
    However the Act attempts to draw a balance between the freedom of the parties to vary a contract and the interests of the third party. The Act means that a contractual clause benefiting a third party (eg the promisee's subsidiary company or sub-contractor or employee) will be straightforwardly enforceable by that third party if:
    •   the contract expressly provides that he may; or
    •   where a term in the contract purports to confer a benefit on him (unless on a proper construction of the contract it appears that the parties did not intend the term to be enforceable by the third party.)
    It is therefore prudent to include a clause to the effect of excluding the provisions of the Act. By doing so it ensures that any rights of third parties are not deemed to be

enforceable by them. This is particularly the case where the parties are companies and may have subsidiaries or conversely parent companies.

In this Agreement it is felt appropriate to use an escalating dispute solutions clause (sometimes called an alternative dispute resolution clause) because during the period of the Agreement any dispute between the parties may be better settled in private and without recourse to litigation (except as reserved by the clause in relation to breach of IPR).

It may be felt in some circumstances an arbitration clause could be more appropriate or the parties may wish to simply indicate that they will resort to litigation in the courts.

An example of another governing law and dispute settlement clause is:

'Any dispute which may arise between the parties concerning this Agreement shall be determined as follows:

(1) If the dispute shall be of a technical nature relating to the functions or capabilities of the Licensed Program Materials or any similar or related matter then such a dispute shall be referred for final settlement to an expert nominated jointly by the parties or failing such nomination within Fourteen (14) days after either party's request to the other therefore nominated at the request of either party by the President for the time being of the British Computer Society. Such expert shall be deemed to act as an expert and not as an arbitrator. His decision shall (in the absence of clerical or manifest error) be final and binding on the parties and whose costs shall be borne between the parties in equal shares unless he determines that the conduct of either party is such that such party should bear all of such fees.

(2) In any other case the dispute shall be determined by the High Court of Justice in England and the parties hereby submit to the exclusive jurisdiction of that Court for such purposes.'

16 Agreement for supply of hardware products[1]

THIS AGREEMENT is made the [ ] day of [ ]

BETWEEN:

(1) (*Supplier*) whose [registered office *or* principal place of business] is at (*address*) and whose facsimile ('fax') number is (*number*) ('the Supplier');

(2) (*Customer*) whose [registered office or principal place of business] is at (*address*) and whose facsimile ('fax') number is (*number*) ('the Customer').

RECITALS

A. The Supplier has developed and manufactured certain computer hardware equipment described in SCHEDULE A including spare parts and supply items.

B. The Supplier has agreed to provide and install the computer hardware equipment to the Customer on the terms and conditions set out in this Agreement

NOW IT IS AGREED as follows:

I. DEFINITIONS

In this Agreement, unless the context otherwise requires, the following expressions have the following meanings:

1.1 **'Business Day'** means a day other than a Saturday, Sunday or a public holiday;

1.2 **'Commencement Date'** means the date from which the supply of Equipment shall begin;

1.3 **'Commissioning Date'** means the date on which the Equipment is accepted by the Customer pursuant to CLAUSE 10 or one (1) month after operational use by the Customer of the Equipment has begun whichever shall be the earlier;

1.4   **'Delivery Date'** means the delivery date specified in SCHEDULE E or such extended date as may be granted pursuant to CLAUSE 29;

1.5   **'Documentation'** means the operating manuals, user instructions, technical literature and all other related materials in eye-readable form supplied to the Customer by the Supplier for aiding the use and application of the Equipment;

1.6   **'Equipment'** means such computer hardware equipment supplied by the Supplier to the Customer as described in SCHEDULE A and such additions and changes thereto as shall from time to time be agreed in writing between the parties;

1.7   **'Equipment price'** means that part of the Price payable in respect of the Equipment as specified in SCHEDULE A;

1.8   **'Location'** means the Customer's premises where the Equipment is to be installed as specified in SCHEDULE D;

1.9   **'Off-Loading Point'** means the Customer's off-loading point specified in SCHEDULE C;

1.10   **'Price'** means the price for the Equipment and the services to be provided hereunder as specified in SCHEDULE B.

2. PRODUCTS AND SERVICES TO BE PROVIDED

2.1   The Supplier hereby agrees during the continuance of this Agreement to:

2.1.1   sell the Equipment to the Customer free from encumbrances;

2.1.2   install the Equipment at the Location on the Delivery Date;[2]

2.1.3   provide the other services hereinafter described upon the terms and conditions hereinafter contained in this Agreement.

2.2   The Supplier reserves the right prior to delivery of the Equipment to substitute an alternative item of equipment for any item of equipment agreed to be supplied hereunder provided that such substitution will not materially affect the performance of such equipment and will not result in any increase in the Price.

2.3   Operating supplies such as tapes, disks packs, stationery, printing ribbons and similar accessories are not supplied as part of the Equipment.

3. PAYMENT

3.1   The Price shall be paid by the Customer as provided in SCHEDULE B.

3.2   The Price and any additional charges payable under this Agreement are in accordance with the Supplier's standard scale of charges in force on the date of this Agreement. [The Supplier shall be entitled at any time before the period of thirty (30) days immediately preceding the Delivery Date to vary the Price and any additional charges payable under this Agreement to accord with any change in the Supplier's standard scale of charges by giving the Customer not less than 90 days' prior written notice. This Agreement shall be deemed to be varied accordingly by such notice of variation unless the Customer shall within fourteen (14) days of the receipt of such notice terminate this Agreement by giving notice in writing to the Supplier in which event neither party shall have any liability to the other in respect of such termination.]

3.3   The Price and any additional charges payable under this Agreement are exclusive of any applicable VAT and other sales tax which shall be paid by the Customer at the rate and in the manner for the time being prescribed by law against submission of a valid tax invoice.

3.4   Any charges payable by the Customer under this Agreement in addition to the Price shall be paid on the Commissioning Date.

3.5   The Supplier shall have the right to charge interest on overdue invoices at rate of [4%] per annum above the base rate of (*specify bank*) Bank plc calculated from the date when payment of invoice becomes due for payment up to and including the date of actual payment whether before or after judgment.[3]

4.   DELIVERY AND INSTALLATION

4.1   The Supplier shall submit the Equipment to its standard works tests ('the Works Tests')[4] before delivery to the Customer. The Supplier shall promptly supply to the Customer on request copies of the specification of the Works Tests and a certificate that the Equipment has been passed the same.

4.2   The Customer or its authorised representative may attend the Works Tests. If the Works Tests are held in the presence of the Customer or its authorised representative the Supplier will charge the Customer its standard fee therefor. The Supplier shall give to the Customer at least seven (7) days' written notice of the date and time at which the Supplier proposes to carry out the Works Tests. In the event of any delay or failure by the Customer or its authorised representative in attending the Works Tests at such time the Supplier reserves the right to proceed with the Works Tests which will then be deemed to have been carried out in the presence of the Customer and the results thereof accepted by the Customer.

EITHER

4.3   [On the Delivery Date the Supplier shall deliver the Equipment to the Off-Loading Point but shall not be responsible for off-loading the Equipment or moving it to the Location which shall be undertaken by the Customer at its own expense.]

or

4.4

        [4.4.1   On the Delivery Date the Supplier shall deliver the Equipment to the Off-Loading Point and then move it to the Location.

4.4.2 The Supplier shall not carry out or be responsible for the removal of doors, widening of entrances or any other structural work of any description for the purpose of moving the Equipment from the Off-Loading Point to the Location which work shall be undertaken by the Customer at its own expense prior to delivery.[5]

4.4.3 The Customer shall be responsible for all reasonable costs incurred by the Supplier in providing special equipment personnel or works necessary to move the Equipment from the Off-Loading Point to the Location. Such costs shall be paid by the Customer in addition to the Price.]

EITHER

4.5 [Save for the special delivery costs referred to in SUB-CLAUSE 4.4.3 the Price includes the cost of delivery of the Equipment to the [Off-Loading Point] [the Location] by any method of transport selected by the Supplier.]

or

4.6 [The Price does not include the cost of transportation of the Equipment [from the Supplier's premises] [within the United Kingdom] or any other delivery costs which shall be paid by the Customer in addition to the Price.]

4.7 [All packing cases skid drums and other packaging materials used for delivery of the Equipment to the Location must be returned by the Customer to the Supplier in good condition and at the Customer's expense. The Supplier reserves the right to charge for any such cases and materials not so returned.]

4.8 The Supplier shall install the Equipment at the Location on the Delivery Date.

4.9 If in the reasonable opinion of the Supplier it is necessary to remove or otherwise disconnect any of the Customer's existing equipment at the Location in order to carry out the installation of the Equipment then the Customer shall permit and obtain all necessary consents for such removal and/or disconnection and shall give the Supplier all necessary assistance to enable such work to be carried out.

5. TITLE AND RISK

5.1 The title to the Equipment shall pass to the Customer on payment in full of the Price and any other sums which may then be due under this Agreement.

5.2 Risk in the Equipment shall pass to the Customer on delivery. If any part of the Equipment shall thereafter be lost, destroyed or damaged the Supplier shall promptly replace the same subject to the Customer paying the cost of such replacement. Accordingly the Customer shall be responsible for insuring the Equipment against all normal risks with effect from the time risk passes.

6. LOCATION PREPARATION

The Supplier shall supply to the Customer in reasonable time before delivery of the Equipment such information and assistance as may be necessary to enable the Customer to prepare the Location for the installation of the Equipment and to provide proper environmental and operational conditions for the efficient working and maintenance of the Equipment and for this purpose the Supplier will make available to the Customer free of charge the advice of a suitably qualified engineer. The Customer shall at its own expense prepare a Location and provide such environmental and operational conditions prior to delivery.

7. INFORMATION AND ACCESS

7.1   The Customer undertakes to provide the Supplier promptly with any information which the Supplier may reasonably require from time to time to enable the Supplier to proceed uninterruptedly with the performance of this Agreement.

7.2   The Customer shall for the purposes of this Agreement afford to the authorised personnel of the Supplier during normal working hours full and safe access to the Location and shall provide adequate free working space and such other facilities as may be necessary for the installation of the Equipment.

8. POST-DELIVERY TESTS

8.1   The Supplier shall within fourteen (14) days after the Equipment has been installed submit the Equipment to the Supplier's standard installation test ('the Installation Test')[6] to ensure that the Equipment and every part thereof is in full working order. The Supplier shall supply to the Customer copies of the specification and results of the Installation Tests.

8.2   If any part of the Equipment fails to pass the Installation Tests then if required by the Customer the Installation Tests shall be repeated on such part of the Equipment within a reasonable time thereafter.

8.3   The Customer or its authorised representative may attend the Installation Tests. The Supplier shall give the Customer at least three (3) days' written notice of the date and time at which the Supplier proposes to carry out the Installation Tests. In the event of any delay or failure by the Customer or its authorised representative in attending the Installation Tests at such time the Supplier reserves the right to proceed with the Installation Tests which will then be deemed to have been carried out in the presence of the Customer and the results thereof accepted by the Customer.

9. ACCEPTANCE

Once the Equipment and every part thereof has successfully passed the Installation Tests the Equipment shall be accepted by the Customer and the

Customer shall if required by the Supplier sign a commissioning certificate in the form annexed hereto acknowledging such acceptance.

10. TELECOMMUNICATIONS

10.1   In this Clause the expression 'Relevant Experience' means any part of the Equipment which is intended to be connected to any telecommunication system which is or is to be connected to a public telecommunication system.

10.2   The Supplier warrants to the Customer that at the date hereof the Relevant Equipment is approved by the Secretary of State for Trade and Industry for connection to the telecommunication systems specified in the instructions for use of the Relevant Equipment subject to the conditions set out therein but does not warrant the continuance of any such approval.

10.3   If after the date hereof the Secretary of State or any person to whom he has delegated his powers requires the Relevant Equipment or any part thereof to be modified as a condition of the continuance of any such approval the Supplier reserves the right to make such modifications at the Customer's expense.

10.4   If the Customer connects the relevant Equipment to any telecommunication system the Customer shall be responsible for obtaining the consent of the owner of that system (if necessary) to such connection and for complying with all conditions relating thereto.

10.5   The Customer undertakes to the Supplier that it will not make any modification to the Relevant Equipment without the prior written consent of the Supplier.

10.6   Where any data transmission speeds are given by the Supplier in relation to the Equipment such speeds are at all time subject to any conditions attached to the use of the relevant modem or telecommunication equipment at the speeds indicated and to the capability of such modem or other telecommunication equipment to achieve such speeds.

11. CUSTOMER'S DEFAULT

If the Supplier is prevented or delayed from performing its obligations under this Agreement by reason of any act or omission of the Customer (other than a delay by the Customer for which the Customer is excused under CLAUSE 30) then the Customer will pay to the Supplier all reasonable costs charges and losses sustained or incurred by the Supplier as a result (including without limitation the cost of storage and insurance of the Equipment). The Supplier shall promptly notify the Customer in writing of any claim which it may have under this Clause giving such particulars thereof as it is then able to provide.

12. CANCELLATION

12.1   If the Customer wishes to cancel this Agreement in respect of all or any part of the Equipment (other than for any breach of this Agreement by the Supplier as would entitle the Customer to terminate) then the Customer shall be entitled so to do at any time up to fourteen (14) days prior to the Delivery Date upon giving written notice to the Supplier and upon paying to the Supplier as agreed and liquidated cancellation charges:

    12.1.1   a sum equal to six per cent (6%) of the price of the equipment cancelled; and

    12.1.2   a sum equal to twelve per cent (12%) of such price reduced by one per cent (1%) in respect of each complete calendar month unexpired between the date of cancellation and the Delivery Date.

12.2   [The amount of the Customer's deposit paid under CLAUSE 3.1 if forfeited to the Supplier shall be deducted from the cancellation charges payable under SUB-CLAUSE 12.1.

12.3   Until the Supplier shall have received such payment the Customer's notice of termination shall be of no effect and the Supplier may treat this Agreement as subsisting.]

13. TERMINATION

13.1   The Customer may terminate this Agreement at any time by giving at least [30] days' prior written notice to the Supplier.

13.2   The Supplier may terminate this Agreement forthwith on giving notice in writing to the Customer if:

    13.2.1   the Customer commits any serious breach of any term of this Agreement and (in the case of a breach capable of being remedied) shall have failed, within [30] days after the receipt of a request in writing from the Supplier to do so, to remedy the breach (such request to contain a warning of the Supplier's intention to terminate);

    or

    13.2.2   the Customer fails to pay any sum due under the terms of this Agreement and such sum remains unpaid for fourteen (14) days after written notice from the Supplier that such sum has not been paid.

13.3   The Customer may terminate this Agreement forthwith on giving notice in writing to the Supplier if the Equipment is lost, stolen or destroyed or damaged beyond economic repair.

13.4   Any termination of this Agreement (howsoever occasioned) shall not affect any accrued rights or liabilities of either party nor shall it effect the coming into force or the continuance in force of any provision in this Agreement which is expressly or by implication intended to come into or continue in force on or after such termination.

14. WARRANTIES[7]

14.1.1 The Supplier warrants that the Equipment will be free from defects in material workmanship and installation for a period of twelve (12) months after the Commissioning Date ('the Warranty Period');

14.1.2 If the Supplier receives written notice from the Customer of any breach of the said warranty then the Supplier shall at its own expense and within a reasonable time after receiving such notice repair or at its opinion replace the Equipment or such parts of it as are defective or otherwise remedy such defect provided that the Supplier shall have no liability or obligations under the said warranty unless it shall have received written notice of the defect in question no later than the enquiry of the Warranty Period. The title to the Equipment or any defective parts shall revert to the Supplier upon the replacement of the Equipment or such defective parts;

14.1.3 The Supplier shall have no liability or obligations under the said warranty other than to remedy breaches thereof by the provision of materials and services within a reasonable time and without charge to the Customer. If the Supplier shall fail to comply with such obligations its liability for such failure shall be limited to a sum equal to the Price. The foregoing states the entire liability of the Supplier whether in contract or tort for defects in the Equipment notified to it after the Commissioning Date other than liability assumed under CLAUSE 21;

14.1.4 The said warranty is contingent upon the proper use of the Equipment by the Customer and does not cover any part of the Equipment which has been modified without the Supplier's prior written consent or which has been subjected to unusual physical or electrical stress or on which the original identification marks have been removed or altered. Nor will such warranty apply if repair or parts replacement is required as a result of causes other than ordinary use including without limitation accident hazard humidity control or other environmental conditions.

14.2 The Supplier does not give any warranty that the Equipment is fit for any particular purpose unless that purpose is specifically advised to the Supplier in writing by the Customer and the Supplier confirms in writing that the Equipment can fulfil that particular purpose.

14.3 The Supplier does not warrant that the Equipment will achieve any particular performance criteria unless:

14.3.1   the Supplier has specifically guaranteed such criteria in writing subject to specified tolerances in an agreed sum as liquid damages; and

14.3.2   the environmental conditions specified by the Supplier are maintained.

14.4   Except as expressly provided in this Agreement no warranty condition undertaking or term express or implied statutory or otherwise as to the condition quality performance merchantability durability or fitness for purpose of the Equipment is given or assumed by the Supplier and all such warranties conditions undertakings and terms are hereby excluded.

15. CUSTOMER'S WARRANTY

The Customer warrants that he has not relied on any oral representation made by the Supplier or upon any descriptions, illustrations or specifications contained in any catalogues and publicity material produced by the Supplier which are only intended to convey a general idea of the products and services mentioned therein.

16. TRAINING

16.1   The Supplier shall provide the Customer with two copies of a set of operating manuals containing sufficient information for the proper operation of the Equipment. If the Customer requires further copies of operating manuals then these will be provided by the Supplier in accordance with its standard scale of charges from time to time in force.

16.2   The Supplier undertakes to provide training in the use of the Equipment for the staff of the Customer as set out in SCHEDULE F.

16.3   Any additional training required by the Customer shall be provided by the Supplier in accordance with its standard scale of charges from time to time in force.

17. DOCUMENTATION

The Supplier shall provide the Customer with [2] copies of a set of the Documentation containing sufficient information to enable proper use of all the facilities and functions set out in the Specification. If the Customer requires further copies of the Documentation, then these may be obtained under licence from the Supplier in accordance with its standard scale of charges from time to time in force.

18. REMOVAL OF LABELS

The Customer shall not change, remove or obscure any labels, plates, insignia, lettering or other markings which are on the Equipment at the time of installation thereof.

19. MAINTENANCE

The parties undertake to enter into a maintenance agreement on the Commissioning Date in respect of the Equipment in the form of the draft annexed hereto.

20. INTELLECTUAL PROPERTY RIGHTS INDEMNITY

20.1 The Supplier will indemnify the Customer and keep the Customer fully and effectively indemnified against all costs, claims, demands, expenses and liabilities of whatsoever nature arising out of or in connection with any claim that the use or possession of the Equipment infringes the intellectual property rights (including without limitation any patent, copyright, registered design or trademark) of any third party subject to the following conditions:

20.1.1 the Customer shall promptly notify the Supplier in writing of any allegations of infringement of which it has notice and will not make any admission without the Supplier's prior written consent;

20.1.2 the Customer at the Supplier's request and expense shall allow the Supplier (subject to SUB-CLAUSE 20.1.3 below) to conduct and/or settle all negotiations and litigation resulting from any such claim;

20.1.3 [the conduct by the Supplier of any such negotiations or litigation shall be conditional upon the Supplier:

20.1.3.1 giving to the Customer such reasonable security as shall from time to time be required by the Customer to cover the amount ascertained or agreed or estimate as the case may be of any compensation, damages, expenses and costs for which the Customer may become liable; and

20.1.3.2 taking over such conduct within a reasonable time after being notified of the claim in question];

20.1.4 the Customer shall at the request of the Supplier afford all reasonable assistance with such negotiations or litigation and shall be reimbursed by the Supplier for any out of pocket expenses incurred in so doing.

20.2 The indemnity given under the sub-clause above will not apply to infringement arising out of the use of the Equipment or any part thereof in combination with any equipment and/or computer programs not supplied or approved by the Supplier for use with the Equipment.

20.3 If the Customer's use or possession of the Equipment is held by a Court of competent jurisdiction to constitute an infringement of a third party's intellectual property rights or if the Supplier is advised by legal counsel that such use or possession is likely to constitute such an infringement then the Supplier shall promptly and at its own expense:

20.3.1   procure for the Customer the right to continue using and possessing the Equipment; or

20.3.2   modify or replace the Equipment (without detracting from its overall performance) so as to avoid the infringement (infringement of the intellectual property rights of any third party);

20.3.3   if SUB-CLAUSE 20.3.1 OR 20.3.2 cannot be accomplished on reasonable terms remove the Equipment from the Location and refund the Price to the Customer.

The foregoing states the Supplier's entire liability to the Customer in respect of the infringement of the intellectual property rights of any third party.

21.   LIABILITY[8]

21.1   The Supplier shall indemnify the Customer and keep the Customer fully and effectively indemnified against any loss or damage to any property or injury to or death of any person caused by any negligent act or omission or wilful misconduct of the Supplier, its employees, agents or sub-contractors or by any defect in the design or workmanship of the Equipment.

21.2   The Customer shall indemnify the Supplier and keep the Supplier fully and effectively indemnified against any loss or damage to any property or injury to or death caused by any negligent act or omission or wilful misconduct of the Customer, its employees, agents or sub-contractors.

21.3   Except in respect of injury or death of any person (for which no limit applies) the respective liability of the Supplier and the Customer under SUB-CLAUSES 20.1 and 20.2 in respect of each event or series of connected events shall not exceed five hundred thousand pounds (£500,000.00).

21.4   Notwithstanding anything else contained in this Agreement the Supplier shall not be liable to the Customer for loss of profits or contacts or other indirect or consequential loss whether arising from negligence breach of contract or howsoever.

22.   DATA PROTECTION[9]

The parties hereby undertake to comply with the provisions of the Data Protection Act 1998 and any related legislation insofar as the same relates to the provisions and obligations of this Agreement.

23.   INTERPRETATION

23.1   In this Agreement unless the context otherwise requires:

23.1.1   words importing any gender include every gender;

23.1.2   words importing the singular number include the plural number and vice versa;

23.1.3   words importing persons include firms, companies and corporations and vice versa;

23.1.4   references to numbered clauses and Schedules are references to the relevant clause in or Schedule to this Agreement;

23.1.5   reference in any Schedule to this Agreement to numbered paragraphs relate to the numbered paragraphs of that Schedule;

23.1.6   the headings to the clauses, Schedules and paragraphs of this Agreement will not affect the interpretation;

23.1.7   any reference to an enactment includes reference to that enactment as amended or replaced from time to time and to any subordinate legislation or byelaw made under that enactment;

23.1.8   any obligation on any party not to do or omit to do anything is to include an obligation not to allow that thing to be done or omitted to be done;

23.1.9   any party who agrees to do something will be deemed to fulfil that obligation if that party procures that it is done.

23.2   In the case of conflict or ambiguity between any provision contained in the body of this Agreement and any provision contained in any Schedule, the provision in the body of this Agreement shall take precedence.

24. AGENCY, PARTNERSHIP

This Agreement shall not constitute or imply any partnership, joint venture, agency, fiduciary or other relationship between the parties other than the contractual relationship expressly provided for in this Agreement.

25. AMENDMENTS

This Agreement may not be released, discharged, supplemented, interpreted, amended, varied or modified in any manner except by an instrument in writing signed by a duly authorised officer or representative of each of the parties hereto.

26. ANNOUNCEMENTS

No party shall issue or make any public announcement or disclose any information regarding this Agreement unless prior written consent has been obtained from the other party.

27. ASSIGNMENT

27.1   This Agreement is personal to the parties and, subject to CLAUSE 27.2 below, neither this Agreement nor any rights, licenses or obligations under this Agreement, may be assigned by either party without the prior written approval of the other party.

27.2   Notwithstanding the foregoing, either party may assign this Agreement to any acquirer of all or of substantially all of such party's equity securities, assets or business relating to the subject matter of this Agreement or to any entity controlled by, that controls, or is under common control with a party to this Agreement. Any attempted assignment in violation of this clause will be void and without effect.

28. ENTIRE AGREEMENT

This Agreement supersedes all prior agreements, arrangements and undertakings between the parties and constitutes the entire agreement between the parties relating to the subject matter of this Agreement. However the obligations of the parties under any pre-existing non-disclosure agreement shall remain in full force and effect insofar as there is no conflict between the same. The parties confirm that they have not entered into this Agreement on the basis of any representation that is not expressly incorporated into this Agreement.

29. FORCE MAJEURE[10]

Neither party shall have any liability under or be deemed to be in breach of this Agreement for any delays or failures in performance of this Agreement which result from circumstances beyond the reasonable control of that party. If such circumstances continue for a continuous period of more than [6 months], either party may terminate this Agreement by written notice to the other party.

30. NOTICES

30.1   All notices hereunder shall be in writing.

30.2   Notices shall be deemed to have been duly given:

30.2.1   when delivered, if delivered by courier or other messenger (including registered mail) during normal business hours of the recipient; or

30.2.2   when sent, if transmitted by fax or e-mail and a successful transmission report or return receipt is generated; or

30.2.3   on the fifth business day following mailing, if mailed by national ordinary mail, postage pre-paid; or

30.2.4   on the tenth business day following mailing, if mailed by airmail, postage pre-paid, in each case addressed to the most recent address, e-mail address, or facsimile number notified to the other party.

31. SCHEDULES[11]

The provisions of SCHEDULE[S] (*A–G*) to this Agreement shall form part of this Agreement as if set out here.

32. SEVERANCE

If any provision of this Agreement is prohibited by law or judged by a court to be unlawful, void or unenforceable, the provision shall, to the extent required, be severed from this Agreement and rendered ineffective as far as possible without modifying the remaining provisions of this Agreement, and shall not in any way affect any other circumstances of or the validity or enforcement of this Agreement.

33. SUCCESSORS AND ASSIGNEES

33.1　This Agreement shall be binding upon, and ensure to the benefit of, the parties and their respective successors and permitted assignees, and references to a party in this Agreement shall include its successors and permitted assignees.

33.2　In this Agreement references to a party include references to a person:

33.2.1　who for the time being is entitled (by assignment, novation or otherwise) to that party's rights under this Agreement (or any interest in those rights); or

33.2.2　who, as administrator, liquidator or otherwise, is entitled to exercise those rights;

and in particular those references include a person to whom those rights (or any interest in those rights) are transferred or pass as a result of a merger, division, reconstruction or other reorganisation involving that party. For this purpose, references to a party's rights under this Agreement include any similar rights to which another person becomes entitled as a result of a novation of this Agreement.

34. WAIVER

No delay, neglect or forbearance on the part of either party in enforcing against the other party any term or condition of this Agreement shall either be or be deemed to be a waiver or in any way prejudice any right of that party under this Agreement. No right, power or remedy in this Agreement conferred upon or reserved for either party is exclusive of any other right, power or remedy available to that party.

35. COUNTERPARTS

This Agreement may be executed in any number of counterparts or duplicates, each of which shall be an original, and such counterparts or duplicates shall together constitute one and the same Agreement.

36. TIME IS OF THE ESSENCE

Time shall be of the essence in this Agreement as regards any time, date or period mentioned in this Agreement or subsequently substituted as a time, date or period by agreement in writing between the parties.

37. SUBCONTRACTING

With the prior written consent of the Customer (such consent not to be unreasonably withheld or delayed) the Supplier may perform any or all of its obligations under this Agreement through agents or sub-contractors, provided that the Supplier shall remain liable for such performance and shall indemnify the Customer against any loss or damage suffered by the Customer arising from any act or omission of such agents or sub-contractors.

38. LANGUAGE

This Agreement is made only in the English language. If there is any conflict in the meaning between the English language version of this Agreement and any version or translation of this Agreement in any other language, the English language version shall prevail.

39. COSTS AND EXPENSES

Each party shall bear its own legal costs and other costs and expenses arising in connection with the drafting, negotiation, execution and registration (if applicable) of this Agreement.

40. SET-OFF

Where either party has incurred any liability to the other party, whether under this Agreement or otherwise, and whether such liability is liquidated or unliquidated, each party may set off the amount of such liability against any sum that would otherwise be due to the other party under this Agreement.

41. THIRD PARTIES[12]

[The parties confirm their intent not to confer any rights on any third parties by virtue of this Agreement and accordingly the Contracts (Rights of Third Parties) Act 1999 shall not apply to this Agreement.]

Or

[The parties recognise that this Agreement is intended to benefit and shall so benefit (insert name of third party) for the purposes of the Contracts (Rights of Third Parties) Act 1999 and, subject to that, the parties confirm their intent not to confer any rights on any other third parties by virtue of this Agreement.]

42. PROPER LAW AND JURISDICTION[13]

42.1 This Agreement and all matters arising from it and any dispute resolutions referred to below shall be governed by and construed in accordance with English Law notwithstanding the conflict of law provisions and other mandatory legal provisions save that:

42.1.1 The Supplier shall have the right to sue to recover its fees in any jurisdiction in which the Customer is operating or has assets, and

42.1.2 The Supplier shall have the right to sue for breach of its intellectual property rights and other proprietary information and trade secrets ('IPR') (whether in connection with this Agreement or otherwise) in any country where it believes that infringement or a breach of this Agreement relating to its IPR might be taking place. For the avoidance of doubt, the place of performance of this Agreement is agreed by the parties to be England.

42.2 Each party recognises that the other party's business relies upon the protection of its IPR and that in the event of a breach or threatened breach of IPR, the other party will be caused irreparable damage and such other party may therefore be entitled to injunctive or other equitable relief in order to prevent a breach or threatened breach of its IPR.

42.3 With respect to all other disputes which are not IPR related pursuant to CLAUSES 42.1 and 42.2 above and its special rules the following procedures in CLAUSES 42.3 to 42.6 shall apply. Where there is a dispute the aggrieved party shall notify the other party in writing of the nature of the dispute with as much detail as possible about the deficient performance of the other party. A representative from senior management ('representative') of each of the parties shall meet in person or communicate by telephone within five business days of the date of the written notification in order to reach an agreement about the nature of the deficiency and the corrective action to be taken by the respective parties. The representatives shall produce a report about the nature of the dispute in detail to their respective boards and if no agreement is reached on corrective action, then the chief executives of each party shall meet in person or by telephone, to facilitate an agreement within five business days of a written notice by one to the other. If the dispute cannot be resolved at board level within a further five business days, or if the agreed upon completion dates in any written plan of corrective action are exceeded, either party may seek its legal remedies as provided below.

42.4 If the parties cannot resolve a dispute in accordance with the procedure in CLAUSE 42.3 above, then they shall with the assistance of the Centre for Alternative Dispute Solution, seek to resolve the dispute or difference amicably by using an Alternative Dispute Resolution ('ADR') procedure acceptable to both parties before pursuing any other remedies available to them. If either party fails or refuses to agree to or participate in the ADR procedure or if in any event the dispute or difference is not resolved to the satisfaction of both parties within [90] days after it has arisen, the matter shall be settled in accordance with the procedure below.

42.5 If the parties cannot resolve the dispute by the procedure set out above, the parties shall irrevocably submit to the exclusive jurisdiction of the Courts of England and Wales for the purposes of hearing and determining any dispute arising out of this Agreement.

42.6 [While the dispute resolution procedure above is in progress and any party has an obligation to make a payment to another party or to allow a credit in respect of such payment, the sum relating to the matter in dispute shall be paid into an interest bearing deposit account to be held in the names of the relevant parties at a clearing bank and such payment shall be a good discharge of the parties' payment obligations under this Agreement. Following resolution of the dispute, whether by mediation or legal proceedings, the sum held in such account shall be payable as determined in accordance with the mediation or legal proceedings, and the interest accrued shall be allocated between the parties pro rata according to the split of the principal sum as between the parties.]

SCHEDULE A

THE EQUIPMENT

SCHEDULE B

THE PRICE

Fifteen per cent (15%) upon the signing of this Agreement [(by way of a deposit)] [(by way of a part payment)] Balance upon the Commissioning Date

SCHEDULE C

THE OFF-LOADING POINT

SCHEDULE D

THE LOCATION

SCHEDULE E

THE DELIVERY DATE

SCHEDULE F

TRAINING

SCHEDULE G

SUB-CONTRACTS

COMMISSIONING CERTIFICATE

TO: COMPUTER COMPANY LIMITED

FROM: CUSTOMER LIMITED

Date:

Dear Sirs

We refer to the Agreement between our respective companies dated [ ] ('the Agreement') relating to the sale and installation of certain computer equipment ('the Equipment') and confirm the following:

1. We have today accepted the Equipment.

2. We have inspected the Equipment and confirm that the same confirms to the description contained in the Agreement and that the same has been installed and set up to our satisfaction at the Location (as defined in the Agreement).

3. The Equipment has passed the Installaticns Tests (as defined in the Agreement) the results of which are annexed hereto and signed by us for the purpose of identification.

SIGNED for and on behalf of

CUSTOMER LIMITED

By [ ]

Signature [ ]

Title [ ]

Witness [ ]

1 This agreement for the supply of computer hardware may be read in conjunction with the Hardware Maintenance Agreement at PRECEDENT 16.

2 It is assumed in this agreement that installation is part of the service. If it is not then several of the clauses will need amendment.

3 In certain jurisdictions excessive amounts of interest charged may be viewed as unreasonable, usury or a 'penalty' thus invalidating the provision.

4   The Work Tests are different from the Installation Tests. A prudent Customer will require such Installation Tests as they will prove that the Equipment functions in situ.

5   In practice this may not be necessary unless the Equipment is major mainframe!

6   The Customer may wish to add certain test criteria to ensure that the Equipment functions to the Customers requirements.

7   There has already been much discussion as to whether or not software is 'goods' for the purposes of implied warranties under the Sale of Goods Act 1979, s 14 and on the whole, the more mass market the software, the more it is likely to be seen as 'goods'. The more the software is delivered on an integration and commission basis the more likely it is that the software will be treated as 'services', thereby weakening the degree of implied warranties.

In general the more that a customer negotiates extended warranties into a contract the more the supplier will seek to limit the impact of those warranties under the Limitation of Liability Clauses.

8   Since *St Albans City and District Council v International Computers Ltd* [1996] 4 All ER 481, CA, it has become clear that where a Customer suffers loss as a result of faulty software and no terms and conditions vary the implied terms of merchantability or fitness for purpose, then any attempt by the supplier to limit its liability for such loss below what is deemed to be a reasonable figure (perhaps such a figure being linked to the suppliers' insurance cover for such losses) will be unavailable or even void as an unfair contract term. As a consequence Customers are more likely now to demand that any limit of liability in favour of the supplier for losses other than indirect should be linked to a reasonable sum of at least £1,000,000 (the usual minimum limit for which insurance cover would be granted under a suitable policy). As to limitation of liability generally see Paragraph 89 [2619] ante.

However, in *Watford Electronics Ltd v Sanderson CFL Ltd* [2001] EWCA Civ 317, [2001] 1 All ER (Comm) 696, CA, it was held that provisions in a contract for the supply of computer software that both excluded the supplier liability for indirect loss, as well as limiting the damages recoverable to the amount paid by the Customer under the contract, satisfied the reasonable test under the Unfair Contract Terms Act 1977, s 11.

On appeal the court decided that the contract had been negotiated between experienced businessmen of equal bargaining power and skill and as such, the supplier limitation clause was reasonable.

9   UK law requires any business which processes data about living individuals to be notified with the Office of the Information Commissioner. Under the Data Protection Act 1998, s 1(1) (the Act) data is defined as information which:

(a)   is being processed by means of equipment operating automatically in response to instructions given for that purpose;

(b)   is recorded with the intention that it should be processed by means of such equipment;

(c)   is recorded as part of a relevant filing system or with the intention that it should form part of a relevant filing system; and

(d)   does not fall within paragraph (a), (b) or (c) but forms part of an accessible record as defined in section 68 of the Act.

Accessible records are health records, educational records and accessible public records defined in SCHEDULE 12 to the Act.

10 This force majeure clause is short and general. It may be appropriate to insert a more detailed force majeure clause such as:

'Notwithstanding anything else contained in this Agreement, neither party shall be liable for any delay in performing its obligations hereunder if such delay is caused by circumstances beyond its reasonable control (including without limitation any delay caused by any act or omission of the other party) provided however that any delay by a sub-contractor or supplier of the party so delaying shall not relieve the party from liability for delay except where such delay is beyond the reasonable control of the sub-contractor or supplier concerned. Subject to the party so delaying promptly notifying the other party in writing of the reasons for the delay (and the likely duration of the delay), the performance of such party's obligations shall be suspended during the period that the said circumstances persist and such party shall be granted an extension of time for performance equal to the period of the delay. Save where such delay is caused by the act or omission of the other party (in which event the rights, remedies and liabilities of the parties shall be those conferred and imposed by the other terms of this Agreement and by law):

●   any costs arising from such delay shall be borne by the party incurring the same;

- either party may, if such delay continues for more than 10 weeks,
terminate this Agreement forthwith giving notice in writing to the other by reason of such termination.'

11 As many contracts are varied or amended during their life cycle it is important that all schedules are agreed to and signed or initialled by the parties so that there can be no dispute as to the totality of the contract and its contents.

12 Before the Contracts (Rights of Third Parties) Act 1999 (the Act) it was the case that a person who was not a party to a contract (a third party) could not enforce any right under the contract. Similarly, a contract could not impose any obligations or liabilities on a third party.

However, the Act attempts to draw a balance between the freedom of the parties to vary a contract and the interests of the third party. The Act means that a contractual clause benefiting a third party (eg the promisee's subsidiary company or sub-contractor or employee) will be straightforwardly enforceable by that third party if:

- the contract expressly provides that he may; or
- where a term in the contract purports to confer a benefit on him (unless on a proper construction of the contract it appears that the parties did not intend the term to be enforceable by the third party).

It is therefore prudent to include a clause to the effect of excluding the provisions of the Act. By doing so it ensures that any rights of third parties are not deemed to be enforceable by them. This is particularly the case where the parties are companies and may have subsidiaries or conversely parent companies.

13 An example of another dispute settlement clause is:

'Any dispute which may arise between the parties concerning this Agreement shall be determined as follows:

(1) If the dispute shall be of a technical nature relating to the functions or capabilities of the Licensed Program Materials or any similar or related matter then such a dispute shall be referred for final settlement to an expert nominated jointly by the parties or failing such nomination within Fourteen (14) days after either party's request to the other therefore nominated at the request of either party by the President for the time being of the British Computer Society. Such expert shall be deemed to act as an expert and not as an arbitrator. His decision shall (in the absence of clerical or manifest error) be final and binding on the parties and whose costs shall be borne between the parties in equal shares unless he determines that the conduct of either party is such that such party should bear all of such fees.

(2) In any other case the dispute shall be determined by the High Court of Justice in England and the parties hereby submit to the exclusive jurisdiction of that Court for such purposes.'

17 Hardware maintenance agreement[1]

THIS AGREEMENT is made the [　] day of [　]

BETWEEN

(1)   (*Supplier*) whose [registered office or principal place of business] is at (*address*) and whose facsimile ('fax') number is (*number*) ('the Supplier')

(2)   (*Customer*) whose [registered office or principal place of business] is at (*address*) and whose facsimile ('fax') number is (*number*) ('the Customer').

RECITALS

A.   The Supplier has developed and manufactured the computer hardware equipment described in SCHEDULE A including spare parts and supply items.

B.   The Supplier has agreed to provide to the Customer certain services in respect of the support and maintenance of the computer hardware equipment, on the terms and conditions set out in this Agreement.

NOW IT IS AGREED as follows:

1. DEFINITIONS

In this Agreement, unless inconsistent with the context or otherwise specified the following definitions will apply:

1.1   **'Commencement Date'** means the date from which support and maintenance services shall begin;

1.2   **'Documentation'** means the operating manuals, user instructions, technical literature and all other related materials in eye-readable form supplied to the Customer by the Supplier for aiding the use and application of the Equipment;

1.3   **'Equipment'** means such computer hardware equipment supplied by the Supplier to the Customer as described in SCHEDULE A and such additions and changes thereto as shall from time to time be agreed in writing between the parties;

1.4   **'the Location'** means the Customer's premises where the Equipment is to be installed as specified in SCHEDULE C;

1.5   **'Maintenance Charge'** means the fee for Maintenance Services to be provided under this Agreement and specified in SCHEDULE B;

1.6   **'Maintenance Services'** means the maintenance services to be provided by the Supplier pursuant to CLAUSE 5 including analysis, coding, testing and support. Maintenance shall be within reasonable limits, as determined by the Supplier, and does not include requests for basic product training or technical consulting;

1.7   **'Normal Support Hours'** means from Monday through to Friday and from 09.00 to 17.30 (excluding national holidays);

1.8   **'Specification'** means the specification of the Equipment describing the facilities and functions thereof, a copy of which is annexed to this Agreement as SCHEDULE A;

1.9   **'Training'** means the programme of training of the Customer's employees specified in SCHEDULE F;

1.10   **'Territory'** means the countries specified in SCHEDULE G which are within the scope of this Agreement.

2.   SERVICES TO BE PROVIDED

2.1   The Supplier hereby agrees during the continuance of this Agreement to:

2.1.1   provide the Maintenance Services for the Customer;

2.1.2   provide training and operating manuals to the Customer, if appropriate;

2.1.3   provide the other services hereinafter described upon the terms and conditions contained in this Agreement.

3.   TERM[2]

The Maintenance Services shall commence on the Commencement Date and shall remain in force from year to year thereafter, unless and until terminated in accordance with any of the provisions of CLAUSE 13 or any other clause of this Agreement.

4.   PAYMENT

4.1   In consideration of the Maintenance Services the Customer shall pay the Maintenance Charge (being non-refundable) periodically in advance in the manner as specified in SCHEDULE B.

4.2   Any charges payable by the Customer under this Agreement in addition to the Maintenance Charge shall be paid within 30 days after the receipt by the Customer of the Supplier's invoice.

4.3   The Maintenance Charge and other charges payable under this Agreement are exclusive of VAT, which shall be payable by the Customer at the rate and in the same manner for the time being prescribed by law against submission of a valid tax invoice.

4.4   The Supplier shall have the right to charge interest on overdue invoices at the rate of 4% per annum above the base rate of (specify bank) Bank plc, calculated from the date when payment of the invoice becomes due for payment up to and including the date of actual payment, whether before or after judgment.[3]

4.5   The Supplier shall be entitled at any time, and from time to time, to increase the Maintenance Charge to accord with any change in the Supplier's standard scale of charges by giving to the Customer not less than 90 days' prior written notice.

5.   MAINTENANCE

During the continuance of this Agreement the Supplier shall provide the Customer with the following maintenance services:

5.1   Preventative

The Supplier shall make visits to the Location every three (3) months to test the functions of the Equipment and make such adjustments as shall be necessary to keep the Equipment in good working order. Such visits shall be made during the Normal Support Hours by prior appointment with the Customer. If it is expedient in the opinion of the Supplier so to do such maintenance may be carried out at the time of the corrective maintenance.

5.2   Corrective

Upon receipt of notification from the Customer that the Equipment has failed or is malfunctioning the Supplier shall during Normal Support Hours make such repairs and adjustments to and replace such parts of the Equipment as may be necessary to restore the Equipment to its proper operating condition.

5.3   Emergency

In addition to the Maintenance Services set out in CLAUSES 5.1 and 5.2 the Supplier shall provide during the continuance of this Agreement an emergency corrective maintenance service outside Normal Support Hours as soon as practicable after the receipt of a request by the Customer therefore at the Supplier's standard scale of charges for such service for the time being in force. Such charges shall run from the first arrival of the Supplier's service engineer at the Location to his final departure there from.

5.4   Replacement

5.4.1   The Supplier reserves the right to replace the whole of the Equipment or any part or parts thereof which may be found to be faulty or in need of investigation.[4]

5.4.2   The Supplier in effecting any such replacement shall not remove the Equipment or any part or parts thereof until it is ready to move in equipment to replace it ('the Replacement Equipment').

5.4.3   If the Replacement Equipment is not equipment which is identical in all respects to that replaced the Supplier shall inform the Customer in writing at the time of replacement.

5.4.4   Within two (2) weeks of being informed of replacement of non-identical equipment the Customer shall have the right to request that the Replacement Equipment or any part or parts thereof be removed and either the original equipment be put back or other equipment identical to the original equipment be put in and the Supplier shall comply with such request forthwith.

5.4.5   The Replacement Equipment shall become the property of the owner of the Equipment. The Equipment or any part or parts thereof removed shall become the property of the Supplier provided always that the owner of the Equipment shall be the owner of equipment identical in value and performance to the Equipment.

5.4.6   The provisions of this Agreement shall apply to all replacements and renewals of any part or parts of the Equipment made by the Supplier during the continuance of this Agreement.

5.5   Advice

The Supplier will provide the Customer with such technical advice by telephone, telex, facsimile transmission or mail (including electronic mail), as shall be necessary to resolve the Customer's difficulties and queries in using the Equipment or Replacement Equipment.

6. EXCLUDED MAINTENANCE

6.1   The Supplier shall be under no obligation to provide Maintenance in respect of:

6.1.1   problems resulting from any modifications or customisation of the Equipment not authorised in writing by the Supplier;

6.1.2   any software;

6.1.3   incorrect or unauthorised use of the Equipment or operator error where these are defined as use or operation not in accordance with the Documentation;

6.1.4   any neglect or fault of the Customer or any third party;

6.1.5   failure or fluctuation of electric power, air conditioning, humidity control or other environmental conditions;

6.1.6   any fault in any attachments or associated equipment (whether or not supplied by the Supplier) which do not form part of the Equipment;

6.1.7   use of the Equipment with computer hardware, or operating systems other than those specified in the Documentation; and

6.1.8   act of God, fire, flood, war, act of violence or any other similar occurrence or in accordance with the provisions of CLAUSE 25.

6.2   The Supplier shall upon request by the Customer provide Maintenance notwithstanding that the fault results from any of the circumstances described in CLAUSE 6.1 above. Any time spent by the Supplier investigating such faults will be chargeable at the Supplier's then current rates. The Supplier shall invoice such charges at its discretion and such shall be paid within 30 days of the date of said invoice.

6.3   The Supplier shall not be obliged to provide Maintenance Services to any place other than at the Location (or such other location as the Supplier shall have approved in writing).

6.4   The Supplier shall not be obliged to make modifications or provide Maintenance Services in relation to the repair or renewal of cards, tapes, disk packs, printing ribbons or other consumable supplies.

6.5   The Supplier shall make an additional charge in accordance with its standard scale of charges for the time being in force for service visits made at the request of the Customer by reason of any fault in the Equipment due to causes not covered by the Maintenance Services.

7.   WARRANTY

7.1   The Supplier warrants to the Customer that all services supplied under this Agreement will be carried out with reasonable care and skill by personnel whose qualifications and experience will be appropriate for the tasks to which they are allocated.

7.2   The Customer acknowledges that it is the responsibility of the Customer to ensure that the facilities and functions described in the Specification meet its requirements.

7.3   Except as expressly provided in this Agreement, no warranty, condition, undertaking or term, express or implied, statutory or otherwise, as to the satisfactory quality, fitness for purpose, or ability to achieve a particular result, of the Equipment is given or assumed by the Supplier, and all such warranties, conditions, undertakings and terms are hereby excluded.

7.4   The Customer hereby agrees that its sole remedy in respect of any non-conformance with any warranty in this Agreement is that the Supplier will remedy such non-conformance (either by itself or through a third party) and if, in the Supplier's reasonable opinion, it is unable to remedy such non-conformance, the Supplier will refund the Maintenance Charge for the year in which the services, the subject of such claim, were supplied, if paid, whereupon this Agreement shall immediately terminate.

7.5   The Customer must promptly notify the Supplier of any non-conformance to the above warranties in order to benefit from the remedy stated above, and in any event within three months.

8. LIABILITY[5]

8.1 [The Supplier shall during the term of this Agreement, maintain employer's liability, third party liability, product liability and professional negligence insurance cover in respect of its liabilities arising out of or connected with this Agreement, such cover to be to a minimum value of one million pounds and with an insurance company of repute. The Supplier shall on request supply copies of the relevant certificates of insurance to the Customer as evidence that such policies remain in force. The Supplier undertakes to use reasonable commercial efforts to pursue claims under such insurance policies.]

8.2 The Supplier shall indemnify the Customer for personal injury or death caused by the negligence of its employees in connection with the performance of their duties hereunder or by defects in any product supplied pursuant to this Agreement.

8.3 The Supplier will indemnify the Customer for direct damage to tangible property caused by the negligence of its employees in connection with the performance of their duties under this agreement or by defects in any product supplied pursuant to this Agreement. The Supplier's total liability under this clause shall be limited to £500,000 for any one event or series of connected events.

8.4 Save in respect of claims for death or personal injury arising from the Supplier's negligence, in no event will the Supplier be liable for any damages resulting from loss of data or use, or loss of or spoiling of the Customer's programs or data, lost profits, loss of anticipated savings, breakdown of or fault in the Equipment nor for any damages that are an indirect or secondary consequence of any act or omission of the Supplier, whether such damages were reasonably foreseeable or actually foreseen.

8.5 Except as provided above in the case of personal injury, death and damage to tangible property, the Supplier's maximum liability to the Customer under this Agreement or otherwise for any cause whatsoever (whether in the form of the additional cost of remedial services or otherwise) will be for direct costs and damages only and will be limited to the greater of:

8.5.1 the sum for which the Supplier carries comprehensive insurance cover pursuant to CLAUSE 8.1 above; or

8.5.2 a sum equivalent to the price paid to the Supplier for the products or services that are the subject of the Customer's claim, plus damages limited to 25% of the same amount for any additional costs directly, reasonably and necessarily incurred by the Customer in obtaining alternative products and/or services.

8.6 The parties hereby acknowledge and agree that the limitations contained in this CLAUSE 8 are reasonable in light of all the circumstances.

8.7 The Customer's statutory rights as a consumer (if any) are not affected. All liability that is not expressly assumed in this Agreement is hereby excluded. These limitations will apply regardless of the form of action, whether under statute, in contract or tort, including negligence, or any other form of action. For the purposes of this clause, the 'Supplier' includes its employees, sub-contractors and suppliers who shall all have the benefit of the limits and exclusions of liability set out above in terms of the Contracts (Rights of Third Parties) Act 1999. Nothing in this Agreement shall exclude or limit liability for fraudulent misrepresentation.

9. CUSTOMER'S WARRANTY

9.1 The Customer warrants that it has not relied on any oral representation made by the Supplier or upon any descriptions, illustrations or specifications contained in any catalogues and publicity material produced by the Supplier which are only intended to convey a general idea of the products and services mentioned therein. The Customer has however relied upon the descriptions, illustrations, functions, specifications contained in the user manual and specification in SCHEDULE A.

9.2 The Customer warrants that it shall comply in all material respects with all applicable laws, regulations and codes of conduct (whether statutory or otherwise) of the United Kingdom, and that all licences, permissions and consents required for carrying on its business have been obtained and are in full force and effect.

10. CUSTOMER'S OBLIGATIONS

10.1 The Customer shall during the continuance of this Agreement:

10.1.1 keep and operate the Equipment in a proper and prudent manner in accordance with the user manual and operator manual;

10.1.2 ensure that proper environmental conditions as previously accepted by the Supplier are maintained for the Equipment and shall maintain in good condition the accommodation of the Equipment, the cables and fittings associated therewith and the electricity supply thereto;

10.1.3 ensure only competent trained employees (or persons under their supervision) are allowed to operate the Equipment;

10.1.4 not make any modification to the Equipment without the Supplier's prior written consent;

10.1.5 make hardware accessible to the Supplier's support staff, and when required enable logons/passwords required for such support staff (who will have their own logons);

10.1.6 ensure that external surfaces are kept clean and in good condition and shall carry out any minor maintenance recommended by the Supplier from time to time;

10.1.7 save as aforesaid not attempt to adjust, repair or maintain the Equipment and shall not request, permit or authorise anyone other than the Supplier to carry out any adjustments, repairs or maintenance of the Equipment;

10.1.8 provide notice of intention to change hardware or operating system or data-feeds or remove the Equipment from the Location;

10.1.9 not make any movement of the Equipment nor remove the Equipment from the Location without the Supplier's prior written consent;

10.1.10 not use in conjunction with the Equipment any necessary attachment or additional equipment other than that which has been supplied or approved in writing by the Supplier;

10.1.11 by arrangement, grant full and safe, direct or remote, access to premises and/or the Equipment at all times for Maintenance Services and shall provide such reasonable assistance as the Supplier may request, including, but not limited to, providing sample output and other diagnostic information;

10.1.12 promptly notify the Supplier if the Equipment needs maintenance or is not operating correctly;

10.1.13 at all times keep a record of the use of the Equipment in a form to be approved by the Supplier and at the Supplier's request provide the Supplier with copies of the entries and allow the Supplier to inspect such record at all reasonable time;

10.1.14 keep full security copies of the Customer's program databases and computer records in accordance with best computing practice.

11. CONFIDENTIAL INFORMATION

11.1 The Customer undertakes to treat as confidential and keep secret the payment terms of this Agreement and all information contained or embodied in the Equipment and the Specification and all documentation and/or information conveyed to the Customer pursuant to this Agreement (hereinafter collectively referred to as 'the Information').

11.2 The Customer shall not, without the prior written consent of the Supplier divulge, any part of the Information to any person except:

11.2.1 the Customer's own employees and then only to those employees who need to know the same;

11.2.2 the Customer's auditors, HM Inspector of Taxes, HM Customs and Excise and any other persons or bodies having a right, duty or obligation to know the business of the Customer, and then only in pursuance of such right, duty or obligation;

11.2.3 any person who is for the time being appointed by the Customer to maintain the Equipment (in accordance with the terms of the Licence) and then only to the extent necessary to enable such person to properly maintain such equipment.

11.3   The Customer undertakes to ensure that persons and bodies mentioned in CLAUSE 11.2 are made aware, prior to the disclosure of any part of the Information, that the same is confidential, and that they owe a duty of confidence to the Supplier. The Customer shall indemnify the Supplier against any loss or damage which the Supplier may sustain or incur as a result of the Customer failing to comply with such undertaking.

11.4   The Customer shall promptly notify the Supplier if it becomes aware of any breach of confidence by any person to whom the Customer divulges all or any part of the Information and shall give the Supplier all reasonable assistance in connection with any proceedings which the Supplier may institute against such person for breach of confidence.

11.5   The foregoing obligations as to confidentiality shall remain in full force and effect notwithstanding any termination of the Licence or this Agreement.

12.   SECURITY AND CONTROL

The Customer shall during the continuance of this Agreement:

12.1   effect and maintain adequate security measures to safeguard the Equipment from access or use by any unauthorised person;

12.2   retain the Equipment under the Customer's effective control;

12.3   comply with all reasonable instructions of the Supplier with regard to the use of the Equipment including, without limitation, the implementation of upgrades to the Equipment, third party software, specified operating system and computer hardware which the Supplier may provide from time to time.

13.   TERMINATION

13.1   The Customer may terminate this Agreement at any time by giving at least 90 days' prior written notice to the Supplier.

13.2   The Customer may terminate this Agreement forthwith on giving notice in writing to the Supplier if the Equipment is lost, stolen or destroyed or damaged beyond economic repair.

13.3   The Supplier may terminate this Agreement forthwith on giving notice in writing to the Customer if:

13.3.1   the Customer commits any serious breach of any term of this Agreement and (in the case of a breach capable of being remedied) shall have failed, within 30 days after the receipt of a request in writing from the Supplier so to do, to remedy the breach (such request to contain a warning of the Supplier's intention to terminate); or

13.3.2 the Customer fails to pay any sum due under the terms of this Agreement and such sum remains unpaid for fourteen (14) days after written notice from the Supplier that such sum has not been paid.

13.4 Any termination of this Agreement (howsoever occasioned) shall not affect any accrued rights or liabilities of either party, nor shall it effect the coming into force or the continuance in force of any provision hereof which is expressly or by implication intended to come onto or continue in force on or after such termination.

13.5 If the Supplier terminates this Agreement pursuant to CLAUSE 13.3, then the Customer shall not be entitled to any refund of the Maintenance Charge or any part thereof that has been paid.

14. ALTERATIONS

The Customer hereby undertakes not to alter or modify the whole or any part of the Equipment in any way whatsoever, nor to permit the whole or any part of the Equipment to be combined with, or become incorporated in, any other programs.[5]

15. TRAINING

15.1 The Supplier undertakes to provide training in the use of the Equipment for the staff of the Customer as set out in SCHEDULE F.

15.2 Any additional training required by the Customer shall be provided by the Supplier in accordance with its standard scale of charges from time to time in force.

16. DOCUMENTATION

The Supplier shall provide the Customer with [2] copies of a set of the Documentation containing sufficient information to enable proper use of all the facilities and functions set out in the Specification. If the Customer requires further copies of the Documentation, then these may be obtained under licence from the Supplier in accordance with its standard scale of charges from time to time in force.

17. CUSTOMER'S CONFIDENTIAL INFORMATION

17.1 The Supplier shall be entitled to identify the Customer as a licensee of the Equipment in the Supplier's publicity materials, subject to the Customer's prior written approval on each publicity document.

17.2 Subject to CLAUSE 17.1 above, the Supplier shall treat as confidential all information supplied by the Customer under this Agreement which is designated as confidential by the Customer, or which is by its nature clearly confidential, provided that this Clause shall not extend to any information which was rightfully in the possession of the Supplier prior to the commencement of the negotiations leading to this Agreement, or which is already public knowledge or becomes so at a future date (otherwise than as a result of a breach of this Clause). The Supplier shall not divulge any confidential information to any person except to its own employees, and then only to those employees who need to know the same. The Supplier shall ensure that its employees are aware of and comply with the provisions of this Clause. The foregoing obligations shall survive any termination of this Agreement.

18. DATA PROTECTION[6]

The parties hereby undertake to comply with the provisions of the Data Protection Act 1998 and any related legislation insofar as the same relates to the provisions and obligations of this Agreement.

19. INTERPRETATION

19.1   In this Agreement unless the context otherwise requires:

19.1.1   words importing any gender include every gender;

19.1.2   words importing the singular number include the plural number and vice versa;

19.1.3   words importing persons include firms, companies and corporations and vice versa;

19.1.4   references to numbered clauses and Schedules are references to the relevant clause in or Schedule to this Agreement;

19.1.5   reference in any Schedule to this Agreement to numbered paragraphs relate to the numbered paragraphs of that Schedule;

19.1.6   the headings to the clauses, Schedules and paragraphs of this Agreement will not affect the interpretation;

19.1.7   any reference to an enactment includes reference to that enactment as amended or replaced from time to time and to any subordinate legislation or byelaw made under that enactment;

19.1.8   any obligation on any party not to do or omit to do anything is to include an obligation not to allow that thing to be done or omitted to be done respectively;

19.1.9   any party who agrees to do something will be deemed to fulfil that obligation if that party procures that it is done.

19.2   In the case of conflict or ambiguity between any provision contained in the body of this Agreement and any provision contained in any Schedule, the provision in the body of this Agreement shall take precedence.

20. AGENCY, PARTNERSHIP

This Agreement shall not constitute or imply any partnership, joint venture, agency, fiduciary relationship or other relationship between the parties other than the contractual relationship expressly provided for in this Agreement.

21. AMENDMENTS

This Agreement may not be released, discharged, supplemented, interpreted, amended, varied or modified in any manner except by an instrument in writing signed by a duly authorised officer or representative of each of the parties hereto.

22. ANNOUNCEMENTS

No party shall issue or make any public announcement or disclose any information regarding this Agreement, unless prior written consent has been obtained from the other party.

23. ASSIGNMENT[7]

23.1   This Agreement is personal to the parties and, subject to CLAUSE 23.2 below, neither this Agreement nor any rights, licenses or obligations under this agreement, may be assigned by either party, without the prior written approval of the other party.

23.2   Notwithstanding the foregoing, either party may assign this Agreement to any acquirer of all, or of substantially all, of such party's equity securities, assets or business relating to the subject matter of this Agreement, or to any entity controlled by, that controls, or is under common control with, a party hereto. Any attempted assignment in violation of this clause will be void and without effect.

24. ENTIRE AGREEMENT

This Agreement supersedes all prior agreements, arrangements and undertakings between the parties and constitutes the entire agreement between the parties relating to the subject matter of this agreement. However, the obligations of the parties under any pre-existing non-disclosure agreement shall remain in full force and effect insofar as there is no conflict between the same. The parties confirm that they have not entered into this Agreement on the basis of any representation that is not expressly incorporated into this Agreement.

25. FORCE MAJEURE[8]

Neither party shall have any liability under or be deemed to be in breach of this Agreement for any delays or failures in performance of this Agreement which result from circumstances beyond the reasonable control of that party. If such circumstances continue for a continuous period of more than [6 months], either party may terminate this Agreement by written notice to the other party.

26. NOTICES

26.1   All notices hereunder shall be in writing.

26.2   Notices shall be deemed to have been duly given:

26.2.1   when delivered, if delivered by courier or other messenger (including registered mail) during normal business hours of the recipient; or

26.2.2   when sent, if transmitted by fax or e-mail and a successful transmission report or return receipt is generated; or

26.2.3   on the fifth business day following mailing, if mailed by national ordinary mail, postage pre-paid; or

26.2.4   on the tenth business day following mailing, if mailed by airmail, postage pre-paid in each case addressed to the most recent address, e-mail address, or facsimile number notified to the other party.

27. SCHEDULES

The provisions of SCHEDULE[S] (A–G) to this Agreement shall form part of this Agreement as if set out here.[9]

28. SEVERANCE

If any provision of this Agreement is prohibited by law or judged by a court to be unlawful, void or unenforceable, the provision shall, to the extent required, be severed from this Agreement and rendered ineffective as far as possible without modifying the remaining provisions of this Agreement, and shall not in any way affect any other circumstances of or the validity or enforcement of this Agreement.

29. SUCCESSORS AND ASSIGNEES

29.1   This Agreement shall be binding upon, and enure to the benefit of, the parties and their respective successors and permitted assignees, and references to a party in this Agreement shall include its successors and permitted assignees.

29.2   In this Agreement references to a party include references to a person:

29.2.1 who for the time being is entitled (by assignment, novation or otherwise) to that party's rights under this Agreement (or any interest in those rights); or

29.2.2 who, as administrator, liquidator or otherwise, is entitled to exercise those rights;

and in particular those references include a person to whom those rights (or any interest in those rights) are transferred or pass as a result of a merger, division, reconstruction or other reorganisation involving that party. For this purpose, references to a party's rights under this Agreement include any similar rights to which another person becomes entitled as a result of a novation of this Agreement.

30. WAIVER

No delay, neglect or forbearance on the part of either party in enforcing against the other party any term or condition of this Agreement shall either be or be deemed to be a waiver or in any way prejudice any right of that party under this Agreement. No right, power or remedy herein conferred upon or reserved for either party is exclusive of any other right, power or remedy available to that party.

31. COUNTERPARTS

This Agreement may be executed in any number of counterparts or duplicates, each of which shall be an original, and such counterparts or duplicates shall together constitute one and the same agreement.

32. TIME IS OF THE ESSENCE

Time shall be of the essence in this Agreement as regards any time, date or period mentioned in this Agreement or subsequently substituted as a time, date or period by agreement in writing between the parties.

33. SUBCONTRACTING

With the prior written consent of the Supplier such consent not to be unreasonably withheld or delayed the Customer may perform any or all of its obligations under this Agreement through agents or sub-contractors, provided that the Customer shall remain liable for such performance and shall indemnify the Supplier against any loss or damage suffered by the Supplier arising from any act or omission of such agents or sub-contractors.

34. LANGUAGE

This Agreement is made only in the English language. If there is any conflict in the meaning between the English language version of this Agreement and any version or translation of this Agreement in any other language, the English language version shall prevail.

35. COSTS AND EXPENSES

Each party shall bear its own legal costs and other costs and expenses arising in connection with the drafting, negotiation, execution and registration (if applicable) of this Agreement.

36. SET-OFF

Where either party has incurred any liability to the other party, whether under this Agreement or otherwise, and whether such liability is liquidated or unliquidated, each party may set off the amount of such liability against any sum that would otherwise be due to the other party under this Agreement.

37. THIRD PARTIES[10]

Subject to the provisions of CLAUSE 8.7 the parties confirm their intent not to confer any rights on any third parties by virtue of this Agreement and accordingly the Contracts (Rights of Third parties) Act 1999 shall not apply to this Agreement.

38. PROPER LAW AND JURISDICTION[11]

38.1 This Agreement and all matters arising from it and any dispute resolutions referred to below shall be governed by and construed in accordance with English Law notwithstanding the conflict of law provisions and other mandatory legal provisions save that:

38.1.1 The Supplier shall have the right to sue to recover its fees in any jurisdiction in which the Customer is operating or has assets, and

38.1.2 The Supplier shall have the right to sue for breach of its intellectual property rights and other proprietary information and trade secrets ('IPR') (whether in connection with this Agreement or otherwise) in any country where it believes that infringement or a breach of this Agreement relating to its IPR might be taking place. For the avoidance of doubt, the place of performance of this Agreement is agreed by the parties to be England.

38.2 Each party recognises that the other party's business relies upon the protection of its IPR and that in the event of a breach or threatened breach of IPR, the other party will be caused irreparable damage and such other party may therefore be entitled to injunctive or other equitable relief in order to prevent a breach or threatened breach of its IPR.

38.3 With respect to all other disputes which are not IPR related pursuant to CLAUSES 38.1 and 38.2 above and its special rules, the following procedures in CLAUSES 38.3 to 38.5 shall apply. Where there is a dispute, the aggrieved party shall notify the other party in writing of the nature of the dispute with as much detail as possible about the deficient performance of the other party. A representative from senior management ('representatives') of each of the parties shall meet in person or communicate by telephone within five business days of the date of the written notification in order to reach an agreement about the nature of the deficiency and the corrective action to be taken by the respective parties. The representatives shall produce a report about the nature of the dispute in detail to their respective boards and if no agreement is reached on corrective action, then the chief executives of each party shall meet in person or by telephone, to facilitate an agreement within five business days of a written notice by one to the other. If the dispute cannot be resolved at board level within a further five business days, or if the agreed upon completion dates in any written plan of corrective action are exceeded, either party may seek its legal remedies as provided below.

38.4 If the parties cannot resolve a dispute in accordance with the procedure in CLAUSE 38.3 above, then they shall with the assistance of the Centre for Alternative Dispute Solution, seek to resolve the dispute or difference amicably by using an Alternative Dispute Resolution ('ADR') procedure acceptable to both parties before pursuing any other remedies available to them. If either party fails or refuses to agree to or participate in the ADR procedure or if in any event the dispute or difference is not resolved to the satisfaction of both parties within [90] days after it has arisen, the matter shall be settled in accordance with the procedure below.

38.5 If the parties cannot resolve the dispute by the procedure set out above, the parties shall irrevocably submit to the exclusive jurisdiction of the Courts of England and Wales for the purposes of hearing and determining any dispute arising out of this Agreement.

AS WITNESS etc

SCHEDULE A

THE EQUIPMENT

SCHEDULE B

ANNUAL SUPPORT AND MAINTENANCE FEES:

FOR FIRST 12 MONTHS

On signature	£
On delivery	£

AFTER FIRST 12 MONTHS

At start of each period £ [   ] [% of total fees of licenses purchased]

TRAINING:

Subject to SCHEDULE F:

On invoice £ [   ] per day

SCHEDULE C

LOCATION

[   ]

[Or, such other premises in the London area as may be used by the Customer.]

SCHEDULE D

STORAGE MEDIA

SCHEDULE E

LOCATIONS/COUNTRIES

SCHEDULE F

TRAINING

SCHEDULE G

TERRITORY

1   This Agreement is intended to provide hardware support and maintenance and is supplemental to the Hardware Supply Agreement in PRECEDENT 15.
2   The term of this agreement needs to be carefully considered. The Customer will want support and maintenance for as long as it needs it.
3   In certain jurisdictions excessive amounts of interest charged may be viewed as unreasonable, usury or a 'penalty' thus invalidating the provision.
4   The Customer may want to add additional words to the effect that such replacement equipment should not cause any deterioration in performance of the hardware and/or software.
5   Since *St Albans City and District Council v International Computers Ltd* [1996] 4 All ER 481, CA, it has become clear that where a Customer suffers loss as a result of faulty software and no terms and conditions vary the implied terms of merchantability or fitness for purpose, then any attempt by the supplier to limit its liability for such loss below what is deemed to be a reasonable figure (perhaps such a figure being linked to the suppliers' insurance cover for such losses) will be unavailable or even void as an unfair contract term. As a consequence Customers are more likely now to demand that any

limit of liability in favour of the supplier for losses other than indirect should be linked to a reasonable sum of at least £1,000,000 (the usual limit for which insurance cover would be granted under a suitable policy). As to limitation of liability generally see Paragraph 89 [2619] ante.

However, in *Watford Electronics Ltd v Sanderson CFL Ltd* [2001] EWCA Civ 317, [2001] 1 All ER (Comm) 696, CA, it was held that provisions in a contract for the supply of computer software that both excluded the supplier liability for indirect loss, as well as limiting the damages recoverable to the amount paid by the customer under the contract, satisfied the reasonable test under the Unfair Contract Terms Act 1977, S 11. On appeal the court decided that the contract had been negotiated between experienced businessmen of equal bargaining power and skill and as such, the supplier limitation clause was reasonable.

6   UK law requires any business which processes data about living individuals to be notified with the Office of the Information Commissioner. Under the Data Protection Act 1998, s 1(1) (the Act) data is defined as information which:
   (a)   is being processed by means of equipment operating automatically in response to instructions given for that purpose;
   (b)   is recorded with the intention that it should be processed by means of such equipment;
   (c)   is recorded as part of a relevant filing system or with the intention that it should form part of a relevant filing system; and
   (d)   does not fall within paragraph (a), (b) or (c) but forms part of an accessible record as defined in section 68 of the Act. Accessible records are health records, educational records and accessible public records defined in SCHEDULE 12 to the Act.

7   Many standard hardware provider agreements prohibit assignment of the licence agreement except with the express written permission of the provider, except where the assignee is an associate of the Customer or the assignment is a result of reconstruction or amalgamation.

8   This force majeure clause is short and general. It may be appropriate to insert a more detailed force majeure clause such as:
   'Notwithstanding anything else contained in this Agreement, neither party shall be liable for any delay in performing its obligations hereunder if such delay is caused by circumstances beyond its reasonable control (including without limitation any delay caused by any act or omission of the other party) provided however that any delay by a sub-contractor or supplier of the party so delaying shall not relieve the party from liability for delay except where such delay is beyond the reasonable control of the sub-contractor or supplier concerned. Subject to the party so delaying promptly notifying the other party in writing of the reasons for the delay (and the likely duration of the delay), the performance of such party's obligations shall be suspended during the period that the said circumstances persist and such party shall be granted an extension of time for performance equal to the period of the delay. Save where such delay is caused by the act or omission of the other party (in which event the rights, remedies and liabilities of the parties shall be those conferred and imposed by the other terms of this agreement and by law):
   •   any costs arising from such delay shall be borne by the party incurring the same;
   •   either party may, if such delay continues for more than 10 weeks, terminate this Agreement forthwith giving notice in writing to the other by reason of such termination.'

9   As many contracts are varied or amended during their life cycle it is important that all schedules are agreed to and signed or initialled by the parties so that there can be no dispute as to the totality of the contract and its contents.

10   Before the Contracts (Rights of Third Parties) Act 1999 (the Act) it was the case that a person who was not a party to a contract (a third party) could not enforce any right under the contract. Similarly, a contract could not impose any obligations or liabilities on a third party.

   However the Act attempts to draw a balance between the freedom of the parties to vary a contract and the interests of the third party. The Act means that a contractual clause benefiting a third party (eg the promisee's subsidiary company or sub-contractor or employee) will be straightforwardly enforceable by that third party if:
   •   the contract expressly provides that he may; or
   •   where a term in the contract purports to confer a benefit on him (unless on a proper construction of the contract it appears that the parties did not intend the term to be enforceable by the third party).

It is therefore prudent to include a clause to the effect of excluding the provisions of the Act. By doing so it ensures that any rights of third parties are not deemed to be enforceable by them. This is particularly the case where the parties are companies and may have subsidiaries or conversely parent companies.

11 In this Agreement it is felt appropriate to use an escalating dispute solutions clause (sometimes called an alternative dispute resolution clause) because during the period of the Agreement any dispute between the parties may be better settled in private and without recourse to litigation (except as reserved by the clause in relation to breach of IPR).

It may be felt in some circumstances an arbitration clause could be more appropriate or the parties may wish to simply indicate that they will resort to litigation in the courts.

An example of another governing law and dispute settlement clause is:

'Any dispute which may arise between the parties concerning this Agreement shall be determined as follows:

(1) If the dispute shall be of a technical nature relating to the functions or capabilities of the Licensed Program Materials or any similar or related matter then such a dispute shall be referred for final settlement to an expert nominated jointly by the parties or failing such nomination within Fourteen (14) days after either party's request to the other therefore nominated at the request of either party by the President for the time being of the British Computer Society. Such expert shall be deemed to act as an expert and not as an arbitrator. His decision shall (in the absence of clerical or manifest error) be final and binding on the parties and whose costs shall be borne between the parties in equal shares unless he determines that the conduct of either party is such that such party should bear all of such fees.

(2) In any other case the dispute shall be determined by the High Court of Justice in England and the parties hereby submit to the exclusive jurisdiction of that Court for such purposes.'

18 Agreement for loan of hardware and software products[1]

THIS AGREEMENT is made the day of [ ] BETWEEN:

(1)   (*Supplier*) whose [registered office or principal place of business] is at (*address*) and whose facsimile ('fax') number is (*number*) ('the Supplier') and

(2)   (*Customer*) whose [registered office or principal place of business] is at (*address*) and whose facsimile ('fax') number is (*number*) ('the Customer')

RECITALS

1.   The Customer is [*insert a brief description of the Customer's business*]

2.   The Supplier [*is willing to lend a computer system, insert description*]

NOW IT IS AGREED as follows:

I.   DEFINITIONS

In this Agreement, unless the context otherwise requires, the following expressions have the following meanings:

1.1   **'Delivery Date'** means the delivery date specified in SCHEDULE E or such extended date as may be agreed by the Supplier;

1.2   **'Documentation'** means the operating manuals, user instructions, technical literature and all other related materials in eye-readable form supplied to the Customer by the Supplier for aiding the use and application of the Products;

1.3   **'Equipment'** means such computer hardware equipment as may be specified by the Supplier from time to time and is as presently listed in SCHEDULE A;

1.4   **'Intellectual Property Rights'** means all vested contingent and future intellectual property rights including but not limited to copyright, trade marks, service marks, design rights (whether registered or unregistered), patents, know-how, trade secrets, inventions, get-up, database rights and any applications for the protection or registration or these rights and all renewals and extensions thereof existing in any part of the world whether now known or in the future created to which the Supplier may be entitled;

1.5 **'Licence'** means the licence granted by the Supplier pursuant to CLAUSE 2;

1.6 **'Licence Fee'** means the fee for the Licence provided under this Agreement as specified in SCHEDULE B;

1.7 **'Licensed Program Materials'** means the Licensed Programs, the Program Documentation and the Media;

1.8 **'Licensed Programs'** means the systems, applications and computer programs of the Supplier specified in SCHEDULE A and all releases and versions thereof;

1.9 **'Loan Period'** means the period specified in SCHEDULE F;

1.10 **'Location'** means the computer room where the Products are to be installed and used as specified by the Customer from time to time as listed in SCHEDULE C;

1.11 **'Media'** means the media on which the Licensed Programs and the Program Documentation are recorded or printed as provided to the Customer by the Supplier specified in SCHEDULE D;

1.12 **'Products'** means the Licensed Program Materials and the Equipment;

1.13 **'Program Documentation'** means the operating manuals, user instructions, technical literature and all other related materials in eye-readable form supplied to the Customer by the Supplier for aiding the use and application of the Licensed Programs;

1.14 **'Specification'** means the specification of the Licensed Programs describing the facilities and functions thereof, a copy of which is annexed to this Agreement as SCHEDULE A;

1.15 **'Use the Licensed Program Materials'** means to read all or any part of the Licensed Programs from magnetic or other storage media, to load the Licensed Programs for the storage and running of the Licensed Programs, to read and possess the Program Documentation in con junction with the use of the Licensed Programs and to possess the Media.

2. GRANT OF LICENCE[2]

2.1 The Supplier hereby grants to the Customer a [royalty-free] non-exclusive non-transferable licence to Use the Licensed Program Materials on and in conjunction with the Equipment subject to the terms and conditions contained in this Agreement.

2.2 The Customer shall Use the Licensed Program Materials for processing its own data for its own internal business purposes only.

2.3 The Customer shall not without the prior written consent of the Supplier Use the Licensed Program Materials in any location except the Location.

2.4 The Licence shall not be deemed to extend to any programs or materials of the Supplier other than the Licensed Program Materials unless specifically agreed to in writing by the Supplier.

2.5 The Customer hereby acknowledges that it is licensed to Use the Licensed Program Materials only in accordance with the express terms of this Agreement and not further or otherwise.

2.6 The Customer shall keep adequate records showing the use and disposition of the Licensed Program Materials and any copies thereof, and shall make such records available to the Supplier on request.

2.7 At the end of the Loan Period, all copies of the Licensed Program Materials shall be returned to the Supplier or otherwise disposed of pursuant to the Supplier's written instructions.

3. DELIVERY AND INSTALLATION

On the Delivery Date the Supplier shall deliver the Products to the Customer and install the Licensed Programs on the Equipment at the Location. The Products so delivered shall consist of one copy of the object code of the Licensed Programs in machine-readable form only, on the Media.

4. RISK

Risk in the Media shall pass to the Customer on delivery. If any part of the Media shall thereafter be lost, destroyed or damaged the Supplier shall promptly replace the same (embodying the relevant part of the Licensed Programs or Program Documentation) subject to the Customer paying the cost of such replacement.

5. LOAN OF PRODUCTS

5.1 The Supplier agrees to lend to the Customer the Products to be delivered by the Supplier to the Customer at the Location on the Delivery Date.

5.2 The Products will be kept by the Customer during the Loan Period at the Location and will be used by the Customer solely for the purpose of preparing for and supporting the [insert what Customer will be using the system for].

5.3 The Customer agrees to abide by all applicable United States and United Kingdom export regulations and shall not export or re-export the Products.

5.4 The Customer may hold and enjoy quiet possession of the Products provided it is not in default of any of its obligations under these terms.

6. PAYMENT

6.1   The Loan Fee shall be paid by the Customer as provided in SCHEDULE B.[3]

6.2   The Loan Fee is exclusive of any applicable VAT and other sales tax which shall be payable by the Customer at the rate and in the manner prescribed by law against submission of a valid tax invoice.

6.3   Any charges payable by the Customer under this Agreement shall be paid within 30 days after the receipt by the Customer of the Supplier's invoice.

6.4   The Supplier shall have the right to charge interest on overdue invoices at rate of [4%] per annum above the base rate of *(specify bank)* Bank plc calculated from the date when payment of invoice becomes due for payment up to and including the date of actual payment whether before or after judgment.[4]

7. OBLIGATIONS OF THE SUPPLIER

The Supplier shall:

7.1   arrange and/or pay for the delivery to and installation of the Products at the Location at the beginning of the Loan Period;[5] and the de-installation of the Products and their return to the Supplier at the end of the Loan Period;

7.2   insure the Products at all times when they are not at the Location;

7.3   maintain the Products at [no cost] during the Loan Period.

8. OBLIGATIONS OF THE CUSTOMER

The Customer agrees:

8.1   to make prompt payment of the Loan Fee to the Supplier;

8.2   to inspect the Products on delivery and notify the Supplier immediately in writing of any defects in the Products;

8.3   to allow the Supplier or its duly authorised agent or representative upon reasonable notice during working hours to inspect the Products and any records, logbook, manual, or handbook forming part of the Products;

8.4   to use the Products in a skilful and proper manner and in accordance with any operating instructions issued for them and to ensure that the Products are operated and used by properly skilled and trained personnel, and indemnify the Supplier against any failure to do so;

8.5   to keep the Products at its own expense and at all times in good repair,[6] condition, and working order properly serviced and maintained;

8.6   to make no alteration, and not remove any existing components from the Products (unless in the ordinary course of repair and maintenance);[7]

8.7   to keep or procure to be kept throughout the Loan Period accurate and complete records of all use, maintenance, servicing and repairs carried out to the Products;

8.8   to insure the Products and keep the Products insured throughout the Loan Period, for their full replacement value against all risks on a comprehensive insurance policy;

8.9   to keep the Products in its own possession at the Location and in compliance with any policy of insurance affecting the Products;

8.10   not to transfer, sell, assign, sublicense, pledge, or otherwise dispose of, encumber or suffer a lien or encumbrance upon or against any interest in the Products;

8.11   to deliver up the Products serviced and maintained and in good repair and working order at the end of the Loan Period or upon earlier determination of this Agreement to such address as the Supplier shall notify to the Customer;[8]

8.12   to assume all risk of loss or damage to the Hardware Products upon delivery by Supplier to Customer and insure them against loss or damage at their list price in the case of hardware, or restoration price in the case of software;

8.13   to notify the Supplier in writing immediately on the loss of or damage to the Products;

8.14   to indemnify the Supplier against any loss or damage to the Products while in the possession of the Customer, ordinary wear and tear excepted;

8.15   to pay for all data communications costs arising out of use of the Products while at the Location;

8.16   that within one month of the return of the Products, the Customer shall provide the Supplier with a written report describing their experience of the Products, their opinion of the Products in relation to the applications undertaken, and any suggested enhancements;

8.17   to use the Products in any conformance or inter-operability testing activities, either internally or externally.

9.   EXTENDED LOAN PERIOD

The Customer shall have the option of extending the Loan Period for periods of one month at a time by giving to the Supplier one month's notice in writing. Such Extended Loan Period must be in respect of all the Products.

10.   COPYING

10.1   The Customer may make only so many copies of the Licensed Programs as are reasonably necessary for operational security and use.[9] Such copies and the media on which they are stored shall be the property of the Supplier and the Customer shall ensure that all such copies bear the Supplier's proprietary notice. The Licence shall apply to all such copies as it applies to the Licensed Programs.

10.2 No copies may be made of the Program Documentation without the prior written consent of the Supplier. The Supplier shall provide the Customer with [2] copies of the Program Documentation containing sufficient information to enable proper use of all the facilities and functions set out in the Specification. If the Customer requires further copies of the Program Documentation then these may be obtained under licence from the Supplier in accordance with its standard scale of charges from time to time in force.

11. PROPRIETARY RIGHTS

11.1 The Products and the Intellectual Property Rights are and shall remain the property of the Supplier.

11.2 The Customer shall notify the Supplier immediately if the Customer becomes aware of any unauthorised use of the whole or any part of the Licensed Program Materials by any person.

12. LIABILITY

12.1 The Supplier shall during the term of this Agreement maintain employer's liability, third party liability, product liability and professional negligence insurance cover in respect of its liabilities arising out of or connected with this Agreement, such cover to be to a minimum value of [ONE MILLION POUNDS] and with an insurance company of repute. The Supplier shall on request supply copies of the relevant certificates of insurance to the Customer as evidence that such policies remain in force. The Supplier undertakes to use reasonable commercial efforts to pursue claims under such insurance policies.

12.2 The Supplier shall indemnify the Customer for personal injury or death caused by the negligence of its employees in connection with the performance of their duties hereunder or by defects in any product supplied pursuant to this Agreement.

12.3 The Supplier will indemnify the Customer for direct damage to tangible property caused by the negligence of its employees in connection with the performance of their duties hereunder or by defects in any product supplied pursuant to this Agreement. The Supplier's total liability under this clause shall be limited to [£500,000] for any one event or series of connected events.

12.4 Save in respect of claims for death or personal injury arising from the Supplier's negligence, in no event will the Supplier be liable for any damages resulting from loss of data or use, lost profits, loss of anticipated savings, nor for any damages that are an indirect or secondary consequence of any act or omission of the Supplier whether such damages were reasonably foreseeable or actually foreseen.

12.5   Except as provided above in the case of personal injury, death and damage to tangible property, the Supplier's maximum liability to the Customer under this Agreement or otherwise for any cause whatsoever (whether in the form of the additional cost of remedial services or otherwise) will be for direct costs and damages only and will be limited to the greater of:

12.5.1   the sum for which the Supplier carries comprehensive insurance cover pursuant to CLAUSE 12.1 above; or

12.5.2   a sum equivalent to the price paid to the Supplier for the products or services that are the subject of the Customer's claim, plus damages limited to 25% of the same amount for any additional costs directly, reasonably and necessarily incurred by the Customer in obtaining alternative products and/or services.

12.6   The parties hereby acknowledge and agree that the limitations contained in this clause 12 are reasonable in light of all the circumstances.[10]

12.7   The Customer's statutory rights as a consumer (if any) are not affected. All liability that is not expressly assumed in this Agreement is hereby excluded. These limitations will apply regardless of the form of action, whether under statute, in contract or tort including negligence or any other form of action. For the purposes of this clause, the 'Supplier' includes its employees, sub-contractors and suppliers who shall all have the benefit of the limits and exclusions of liability set out above in terms of the Contracts (Rights of Third Parties) Act 1999. Nothing in this Agreement shall exclude or limit liability for fraudulent misrepresentation.

13.   CONFIDENTIAL INFORMATION

13.1   Both parties to this Agreement undertake, except as provided below, to treat as confidential and keep secret all information marked 'confidential' or which may reasonably be supposed to be confidential, including, without limitation, information contained or embodied in the Licensed Program Materials, the Specification and other information supplied by the Customer or Supplier (in this Agreement collectively referred to as 'the Information') with the same degree of care as it employs with regard to its own confidential information of a like nature and in any event in accordance with best current commercial security practices, provided that, this clause shall not extend to any information which was rightfully in the possession of either party prior to the commencement of the negotiations leading to this Agreement or which is already public knowledge or becomes so at a future date (otherwise than as a result of a breach of this clause).

13.2   Neither party shall without the prior written consent of the other party divulge any part of the other party's Information to any person except:

13.2.1 to their own employees and then only to those employees who need to know the same;

13.2.2 to either parties' auditors, HM Inspector of Taxes, HM Customs and Excise, a court of competent jurisdiction, governmental body or applicable regulatory authority and any other persons or bodies having a right duty or obligation to know the business of the other party and then only in pursuance of such right duty or obligation;

13.2.3 any person who is for the time being appointed by either party to maintain the Equipment on which the Licensed Programs are for the time being used (in accordance with the terms of the Licence) and then only to the extent necessary to enable such person to properly maintain the Equipment.

13.3 Both parties undertake to ensure that persons and bodies referred to in clause 13.2 are made aware prior to the disclosure of any part of the Information that the same is confidential and that they owe a duty of confidence to the other party.

13.4 Each party to this Agreement shall promptly notify the other party if it becomes aware of any breach of confidence by any person to whom it divulges all or any part of the Information and shall give the other party all reasonable assistance in connection with any proceedings which the other party may institute against such person for breach of confidence.

13.5 The foregoing obligations as to confidentiality shall remain in full force and effect notwithstanding any termination of the Licence or this Agreement.

14. TERMINATION

14.1 The Customer may terminate this Agreement at any time by giving at least [30] days' prior written notice to the Supplier.

14.2 The Supplier may terminate this Agreement forthwith on giving notice in writing to the Customer if:

14.2.1 the Customer commits any serious breach of any term of this Agreement and (in the case of a breach capable of being remedied) shall have failed, within [30] days after the receipt of a request in writing from the Supplier to do so, to remedy the breach (such request to contain a warning of the Supplier's intention to terminate); or

14.2.2 the Customer permanently discontinues the use of the Licensed Program Materials.

14.3 Any termination of this Agreement shall automatically terminate the Licence.

14.4 Forthwith upon the termination of the Agreement, the Customer shall return to the Supplier the Products and all copies of the whole or any part thereof or, if requested by the Supplier, shall destroy the same (in the case of the Licensed Programs by erasing them from the magnetic media on which they are stored) and certify in writing to the Supplier that they have been destroyed, PROVIDED THAT the Customer may extract and store any Customer data upon a separate media for continuity purposes.

14.5   Any termination of the Licence or this Agreement (howsoever occasioned) shall not affect any accrued rights or liabilities of either party nor shall it effect the coming into force or the continuance in force of any provision in this Agreement which is expressly or by implication intended to come into or continue in force on or after such termination.

15.   DATA PROTECTION[11]

The parties hereby undertake to comply with the provisions of the Data Protection Act 1998 and any related legislation insofar as the same relates to the provisions and obligations of this Agreement.

16.   INTERPRETATION

16.1   In this Agreement unless the context otherwise requires:

16.1.1   words importing any gender include every gender;

16.1.2   words importing the singular number include the plural number and vice versa;

16.1.3   words importing persons include firms, companies and corporations and vice versa;

16.1.4   references to numbered clauses and Schedules are references to the relevant clause in or Schedule to this Agreement;

16.1.5   reference in any Schedule to this Agreement to numbered paragraphs relate to the numbered paragraphs of that Schedule;

16.1.6   the headings to the clauses, Schedules and paragraphs of this Agreement will not affect the interpretation;

16.1.7   any reference to an enactment includes reference to that enactment as amended or replaced from time to time and to any subordinate legislation or byelaw made under that enactment;

16.1.8   any obligation on any party not to do or omit to do anything is to include an obligation not to allow that thing to be done or omitted to be done;

16.1.9   any party who agrees to do something will be deemed to fulfil that obligation if that party procures that it is done.

16.2   In the case of conflict or ambiguity between any provision contained in the body of this Agreement and any provision contained in any

Schedule, the provision in the body of this Agreement shall take precedence.

17. AGENCY, PARTNERSHIP

This Agreement shall not constitute or imply any partnership, joint venture, agency, fiduciary relationship or other relationship between the parties other than the contractual relationship expressly provided for in this Agreement.

18. AMENDMENTS

This Agreement may not be released, discharged, supplemented, interpreted, amended, varied or modified in any manner except by an instrument in writing signed by a duly authorised officer or representative of each of the parties hereto.

19. ANNOUNCEMENTS

No party shall issue or make any public announcement or disclose any information regarding this Agreement unless prior written consent has been obtained from the other party.

20. ASSIGNMENT

20.1 This Agreement is personal to the parties and, subject to clause 20.2 below, neither this Agreement nor any rights, licenses or obligations under this Agreement, may be assigned by either party without the prior written approval of the other party.

20.2 Notwithstanding the foregoing, either party may assign this Agreement to any acquirer of all or of substantially all of such party's equity securities, assets or business relating to the subject matter of this Agreement or to any entity controlled by, that controls, or is under common control with a party to this Agreement. Any attempted assignment in violation of this clause will be void and without effect.

21. WARRANTIES[12]

21.1 The Supplier agrees on request and at the cost and expense of the Customer to assign to the Customer the benefit of all express warranties granted in favour of the Supplier by the supplier of the Products or the manufacturer of them or any third party.

21.2 The Products are selected by the Customer and acquired by the Supplier at the request of the Customer solely for the purpose of hiring the Products to the Customer and save as above the Customer does not let or supply the Products with any representation concerning the condition performance or qualities of the Products or with or subject to any term, condition or warranty express or to be implied and all such representations, conditions or warranties whether relating to the capacity, age, quality, description, condition, leasing, possession, transportation or use of the Products or to the suitability or fitness of the Products for a particular or any purpose are excluded.

21.3 The Supplier does not warrant that the Products do not or that the Customer's use of the Products will not infringe any patents trademarks and registered designs, copyrights or confidential information or intellectual property rights owned or possessed by any third party and the Supplier shall not be liable to the Customer for any loss suffered by the Customer in any way by reason of any such infringement.

22. ENTIRE AGREEMENT

This Agreement supersedes all prior agreements, arrangements and undertakings between the parties and constitutes the entire agreement between the parties relating to the subject matter of this Agreement. However the obligations of the parties under any pre-existing non-disclosure agreement shall remain in full force and effect insofar as there is no conflict between the same. The parties confirm that they have not entered into this Agreement on the basis of any representation that is not expressly incorporated into this Agreement.

23. FORCE MAJEURE[13]

Neither party shall have any liability under or be deemed to be in breach of this Agreement for any delays or failures in performance of this Agreement which result from circumstances beyond the reasonable control of that party. If such circumstances continue for a continuous period of more than [6 months], either party may terminate this Agreement by written notice to the other party.

24. NOTICES

24.1 All notices hereunder shall be in writing.

24.2 Notices shall be deemed to have been duly given:

24.2.1 when delivered, if delivered by courier or other messenger (including registered mail) during normal business hours of the recipient; or

24.2.2 when sent, if transmitted by fax or e-mail and a successful transmission report or return receipt is generated; or

24.2.2 on the fifth business day following mailing, if mailed by national ordinary mail, postage pre-paid; or

24.2.3 on the tenth business day following mailing, if mailed by airmail, postage pre-paid in each case addressed to the most recent address, e-mail address, or facsimile number notified to the other party.

25. SCHEDULES[14]

The provisions of SCHEDULE[S] (*A–E*) to this Agreement shall form part of this Agreement as if set out here.

26. SEVERANCE

If any provision of this Agreement is prohibited by law or judged by a court to be unlawful, void or unenforceable, the provision shall, to the extent required, be severed from this Agreement and rendered ineffective as far as possible without modifying the remaining provisions of this Agreement, and shall not in any way affect any other circumstances of or the validity or enforcement of this Agreement.

27. SUCCESSORS AND ASSIGNEES

27.1   This Agreement shall be binding upon, and enure to the benefit of, the parties and their respective successors and permitted assignees, and references to a party in this Agreement shall include its successors and permitted assignees.

27.2   In this Agreement references to a party include references to a person:

27.2.1   who for the time being is entitled (by assignment, novation or otherwise) to that party's rights under this Agreement (or any interest in those rights); or

27.2.2   who, as administrator, liquidator or otherwise, is entitled to exercise those rights;

and in particular those references include a person to whom those rights (or any interest in those rights) are transferred or pass as a result of a merger, division, reconstruction or other reorganisation involving that party. For this purpose, references to a party's rights under this Agreement include any similar rights to which another person becomes entitled as a result of a novation of this Agreement.

28. WAIVER

No delay, neglect or forbearance on the part of either party in enforcing against the other party any term or condition of this Agreement shall either be or be deemed to be a waiver or in any way prejudice any right of that party under this Agreement. No right, power or remedy in this Agreement conferred upon or reserved for either party is exclusive of any other right, power or remedy available to that party.

29. COUNTERPARTS

This Agreement may be executed in any number of counterparts or duplicates, each of which shall be an original, and such counterparts or duplicates shall together constitute one and the same agreement.

30. TIME IS OF THE ESSENCE

Time shall be of the essence in this Agreement as regards any time, date or period mentioned in this Agreement or subsequently substituted as a time, date or period by agreement in writing between the parties.

31. SUBCONTRACTING

With the prior written consent of (*Supplier*) (such consent not to be unreasonably withheld or delayed) (*Customer*) may perform any or all of its obligations under this Agreement through agents or sub-contractors, provided that (*Customer*) shall remain liable for such performance and shall indemnify (*Supplier*) against any loss or damage suffered by (*Supplier*) arising from any act or omission of such agents or sub-contractors.

32. LANGUAGE

This Agreement is made only in the English language. If there is any conflict in the meaning between the English language version of this Agreement and any version or translation of this Agreement in any other language, the English language version shall prevail.

33. COSTS AND EXPENSES

Each party shall bear its own legal costs and other costs and expenses arising in connection with the drafting, negotiation, execution and registration (if applicable) of this Agreement.

34. SET-OFF

Where either party has incurred any liability to the other party, whether under this Agreement or otherwise, and whether such liability is liquidated or unliquidated, each party may set off the amount of such liability against any sum that would otherwise be due to the other party under this Agreement.

35. THIRD PARTIES[15]

Subject to CLAUSE 12.7 above, a person who is not a party to this Agreement has no right under the Contracts (Rights of Third Parties) Act 1999 to enforce any term of this Agreement but this does not affect any right or remedy of a third party which exists or is available apart from such Act.

36. PROPER LAW AND JURISDICTION[16]

36.1 This Agreement and all matters arising from it and any dispute resolutions referred to below shall be governed by and construed in accordance with English Law notwithstanding the conflict of law provisions and other mandatory legal provisions save that:

36.1.1   (*Supplier*) shall have the right to sue to recover its fees in any jurisdiction in which (*Customer*) is operating or has assets, and

36.1.2   (*Supplier*) shall have the right to sue for breach of its intellectual property rights and other proprietary information and trade secrets ('IPR') (whether in connection with this Agreement or otherwise) in any country where it believes that infringement or a breach of this Agreement relating to its IPR might be taking place. For the avoidance of doubt, the place of performance of this Agreement is agreed by the parties to be England.

36.2   Each party recognises that the other party's business relies upon the protection of its IPR and that in the event of a breach or threatened breach of IPR, the other party will be caused irreparable damage and such other party may therefore be entitled to injunctive or other equitable relief in order to prevent a breach or threatened breach of its IPR.

36.3   With respect to all other disputes which are not IPR related pursuant to CLAUSFS 36.1 and 36.2 above and its special rules the following procedures in CLAUSFS 36.3 TO 36.6 shall apply. Where there is a dispute the aggrieved party shall notify the other party in writing of the nature of the dispute with as much detail as possible about the deficient performance of the other party. A representative from senior management ('representatives') of each of the parties shall meet in person or communicate by telephone within five business days of the date of the written notification in order to reach an agreement about the nature of the deficiency and the corrective action to be taken by the respective parties. The representatives shall produce a report about the nature of the dispute in detail to their respective boards and if no agreement is reached on corrective action, then the chief executives of each party shall meet in person or by telephone, to facilitate an agreement within five business days of a written notice by one to the other. If the dispute cannot be resolved at board level within a further five business days, or if the agreed upon completion dates in any written plan of corrective action are exceeded, either party may seek its legal remedies as provided below.

36.4   If the parties cannot resolve a dispute in accordance with the procedure in CLAUSE 36.3 above, then they shall with the assistance of the Centre for Alternative Dispute Solution, seek to resolve the dispute or difference amicably by using an Alternative Dispute Resolution ('ADR') procedure acceptable to both parties before pursuing any other remedies available to them. If either party fails or refuses to agree to or participate in the ADR procedure or if in any event the dispute or difference is not resolved to the satisfaction of both parties within [90] days after it has arisen, the matter shall be settled in accordance with the procedure below.

36.5   If the parties cannot resolve the dispute by the procedure set out above, the parties shall irrevocably submit to the exclusive jurisdiction of the Courts of England and Wales for the purposes of hearing and determining any dispute arising out of this Agreement.

36.6 While the dispute resolution procedure above is in progress and any party has an obligation to make a payment to another party or to allow a credit in respect of such payment, the sum relating to the matter in dispute shall be paid into an interest bearing deposit account to be held in the names of the relevant parties at a clearing bank and such payment shall be a good discharge of the parties' payment obligations under this Agreement. Following resolution of the dispute, whether by mediation or legal proceedings, the sum held in such account shall be payable as determined in accordance with the mediation or legal proceedings, and the interest accrued shall be allocated between the parties pro rata according to the split of the principal sum as between the parties.

AS WITNESS etc

SCHEDULE A

EQUIPMENT

SCHEDULE B

FEES

SCHEDULE C

LOCATION

SCHEDULE D

STORAGE MEDIA

SCHEDULE E

DELIVERY DATE

1 This agreement is intended to be used in circumstances where hardware and/or software is to be loaned on a limited basis to the Customer. This might occur where a computer games publisher loans equipment to a games developer to enable development work to be completed, or where a Supplier loans equipment to a potential customer during a pilot project in order for the potential customer to trial new software.

2 As a general rule, rights not granted expressly or by implication in the grant clause are not conveyed by the licence agreement. Of course, rights are sometimes conveyed and restrictions are fairly often located in other sections of a licence agreement. Also, additional rights may be conveyed verbally after contract execution, implied through the parties' course of dealing with one another, or added to a contract in an addendum.

3 The amount(s) payable can be couched in various forms. For example, some software licence agreements require payment of a one-time, lump-sum licence fee. Others require annual or monthly licence fee payments. In development projects, payments may hinge on satisfaction of milestone requirements during the project. Some portion of a licence fee may be conditional upon acceptance. Countless payment schemes are used in different

situations and the scheme employed helps to dictate the amount(s) payable at one or more points in time.

4   In certain jurisdictions excessive amounts of interest charged may be viewed as unreasonable, usury or a 'penalty' thus invalidating the provision.

5   As a general rule, the licensor will not specify in the licence agreement a firm delivery date or deadline, and the licensee must negotiate for clarification and written commitments on this point if it is important to him.

6   The agreement can be adapted to provide that the Supplier meets the cost of maintenance and repairs.

7   Under English law reverse engineering or decompilation had previously been regarded as an infringement of copyright but the Copyright (Computer Programs) Regulations 1992, S1 1992/3233, as a result of the European Directive on the legal protection of computer programs, now allow a lawful licensee to analyse the underlying code, copy and translate the program and investigate the functioning of the program in order to evaluate and understand its ideas and principles without the need to obtain consent of the copyright holder. Such analysis is only for the purpose of achieving inter-operability of an independently created program with the licensed software subject to a number of conditions. This is an implied right that may not be excluded by licensing arrangements within the European Union.

8   The agreement can be drafted to make the Supplier or the Customer responsible for the safe return of the Products at the expiry of the Loan Period.

9   In the UK restrictions on back-up are now invalid as a result of the Copyright (Computer Programs) Regulations 1992, S1 1992/3233 resulting from the European Union Directive on the legal protection of computer programs; 91/250/EEC, OJ 1991 L122/42. The Regulations and the Directive are incorporated in an amendment to the Copyright Design and Patents Act 1988, s 50A, which state that a lawful acquirer, a licensee of the program, is permitted to carry out any form of copying which is necessary for the program to be used and in order to make a security back-up without having to obtain express consent. There is even a stated right that error correction will be permitted but this is only for the purpose of enabling the program to run correctly. It will not affect the requirement for maintenance and support contracts to be entered into.

10 Since *St Albans City and District Council v International Computers Ltd* [1996] 4 All ER 481, CA, it has become clear that where a Customer suffers loss as a result of faulty software and no terms and conditions vary the implied terms of merchantability or fitness for purpose, then any attempt by the supplier to limit its liability for such loss below what is deemed to be a reasonable figure (perhaps such a figure being linked to the suppliers' insurance cover for such losses) will be unavailable or even void as an unfair contract term. As a consequence Customers are more likely now to demand that any limit of liability in favour of the supplier for losses other than indirect should be linked to a reasonable sum of at least £1,000,000 (the usual minimum limit for which insurance cover would be granted under a suitable policy). As to limitation of liability generally see Paragraph 89 [2619] ante.

   However, in *Watford Electronics Ltd v Sanderson CFL Ltd* [2001] EWCA Civ 31 7, [2001] 1 All ER (Comm) 696, CA, it was held that provisions in a contract for the supply of computer software that both excluded the supplier liability for indirect loss, as well as limiting the damages recoverable to the amount paid by the customer under the contract, satisfied the reasonable test under the Unfair Contract Terms Act 1977, s 11. On appeal the court decided that the contract had been negotiated between experienced businessmen of equal bargaining power and skill and as such, the supplier limitation clause was reasonable.

11 UK law requires any business which processes data about living individuals to be notified with the Data Protection Office. Under the Data Protection Act 1998, s 1(1) (the Act) data is defined as information which:

   (a)   is being processed by means of equipment operating automatically in response to instructions given for that purpose;

   (b)   is recorded with the intention that it should be processed by means of such equipment;

   (c)   is recorded as part of a relevant filing system or with the intention that it should form part of a relevant filing system; and

   (d)   does not fall within paragraph (a), (b) or (c) but forms part of an accessible record as defined in section 68 of the Act.

   Accessible records are health records, educational records and accessible public records defined in SCHEDULE 12 to the Act.

12 There has already been much discussion as to whether or not software is 'goods' for the purposes of implied warranties under the Sale of Goods Act 1979, s 14 and on the whole, the more mass market the software, the more it is likely to be seen as 'goods'. The more the software is delivered on an integration and commission basis the more likely it is that the software will be treated as 'services', thereby weakening the degree of implied warranties.

In general the more that a customer negotiates extended warranties into a contract the more the supplier will seek to limit the impact of those warranties under the Limitation of Liability Clauses.

13 This force majeure clause is short and general. It may be appropriate to insert a more detailed force majeure clause such as:

'Notwithstanding anything else contained in this Agreement, neither party shall be liable for any delay in performing its obligations hereunder if such delay is caused by circumstances beyond its reasonable control (including without limitation any delay caused by any act or omission of the other party) provided however that any delay by a sub-contractor or supplier of the party so delaying shall not relieve the party from liability for delay except where such delay is beyond the reasonable control of the sub-contractor or supplier concerned. Subject to the party so delaying promptly notifying the other party in writing of the reasons for the delay (and the likely duration of the delay), the performance of such party's obligations shall be suspended during the period that the said circumstances persist and such party shall be granted an extension of time for performance equal to the period of the delay. Save where such delay is caused by the act or omission of the other party (in which event the rights, remedies and liabilities of the parties shall be those conferred and imposed by the other terms of this Agreement and by law):

• any costs arising from such delay shall be borne by the party incurring the same;
• either party may, if such delay continues for more than 10 weeks,

terminate this Agreement forthwith giving notice in writing to the other by reason of such termination save that the Customer shall pay the Supplier a reasonable sum in respect of any work carried out by it prior to such termination and for that purpose the Supplier may deduct such sum from any amounts previously paid by the Customer under this Agreement (the balance (if any) of which shall be refunded to the Customer whether paid by way of deposit or otherwise).'

14 As many contracts are varied or amended during their life cycle it is important that all schedules are agreed to and signed or initialled by the parties so that there can be no dispute as to the totality of the contract and its contents.

15 Before the Contracts (Rights of Third Parties) Act 1999 (the Act) it was the case that a person who was not a party to a contract (a third party) could not enforce any right under the contract. Similarly, a contract could not impose any obligations or liabilities on a third party.

However, the Act attempts to draw a balance between the freedom of the parties to vary a contract and the interests of the third party. The Act means that a contractual clause benefiting a third party (eg the promisee's subsidiary company or sub-contractor or employee) will be straightforwardly enforceable by that third party if:

• the contract expressly provides that he may; or
• where a term in the contract purports to confer a benefit on him (unless on a proper construction of the contract it appears that the parties did not intend the term to be enforceable by the third party).

It is therefore prudent to include a clause to the effect of excluding the provisions of the Act. By doing so it ensures that any rights of third parties are not deemed to be enforceable by them. This is particularly the case where the parties are companies and may have subsidiaries or conversely parent companies.

16 An example of another dispute settlement clause is:

'Any dispute which may arise between the parties concerning this Agreement shall be determined as follows:

(1) If the dispute shall be of a technical nature relating to the functions or capabilities of the Licensed Program Materials or any similar or related matter then such a dispute shall be referred for final settlement to an expert nominated jointly by the parties or failing such nomination within Fourteen (14) days after either party's request to the other therefore nominated at the request of either party by the President for the time being of the British Computer Society. Such expert shall be deemed to act as an expert and not as an arbitrator. His decision shall (in the absence of clerical or manifest error) be final and binding on the parties and whose

costs shall be borne between the parties in equal shares unless he determines that the conduct of either party is such that such party should bear all of such fees.

(2) In any other case the dispute shall be determined by the High Court of Justice in England and the parties hereby submit to the exclusive jurisdiction of that Court for such purposes.'

19 Invitation to tender[1]

1. LEGAL NOTICES

1.1 **Confidentiality** This document constitutes confidential and proprietary information of Customer Limited ('the Customer') and shall not be disclosed in whole or in part by the recipient to any third party, or to any employees of the recipient, other than those who have a need to know such information for the purpose of responding to this request, and shall not be duplicated or used by the recipient for any other purpose than to evaluate this document. If a recipient is designated the successful Supplier ('the Supplier') as a result of, or in connection with, the submission of this document, the Supplier will have the right to duplicate, use or disclose this document under the terms provided in the contract to be signed by the Customer and the Supplier. This restriction does not limit the Supplier's right to use similar information to that contained in this document if such information is obtained under proper authorisation from another source without restriction.[2]

1.2 **Reliance on information and due diligence** The Customer makes no representations of warranties as to the accuracy of the information contained or referred to in this document. The Supplier shall rely absolutely on its own professional competence in evaluating and verifying the information contained or referred to in this document. The recipient must take every opportunity to inspect and independently verify the information contained or referred to in this document or, subsequent to it, subject to comply with any agreed provisions as to confidentiality. The Customer reserves the right to supplement or amend the information contained or referred to in this document from time to time and undertakes to communicate any such amendment to the recipient.

1.3 **No legal effect** Nothing in this document shall impose upon the Customer an obligation to accept any response to this document. The Customer shall be under no liability to pay any of the recipient's costs involved in the preparation of a tender for the negotiation of any final contract. This document is not intended to have legal effect. Neither this document nor any accompanying information is intended to form a contract between the recipient and the Customer. In the event that the Customer intends to make an award to the Supplier, no contract or legal relationship shall take effect until the execution in writing of contracts between the Supplier and Customer. Such contracts shall be substantially in the form enclosed with this document, or as otherwise agreed between the Supplier and Customer. The commencement of negotiations does not signify a commitment on the part of the Customer to enter into a contract with the Supplier. If the Supplier and Customer cannot reach agreement on terms satisfactory to both parties, either party may terminate negotiations at any time.[3]

1.4 **Legal compliance** No acknowledgement, representation or warranty is given as to the conformity of any information contained or referred to in this document with the laws of any governing jurisdiction including, but not limited to, the agreements incorporated herein. The Supplier must seek independent legal advice on applicable laws and regulations before responding to this document.

2. INTRODUCTION[4]

2.1 **Purpose of this document** The Customer intends to outsource the provision of PC and network procurement and support services in the UK. This Request for Proposal sets out the Customer's preliminary requirements for desktop services within the UK. It is designed to provide a shortlist of Suppliers with an opportunity to submit proposals to supply these services in various ways.

2.2 **Initial objectives** The Customer's initial objectives in developing this document are as follows:

- to set out its possible requirements for desktop services in the UK;

- to describe its approach to the definition of services, service measurement, pricing principles, processes and procedures;

- to provide sufficient information to enable the Tenderer to present a proposal or range of alternative proposals to meet the Customer's requirements;

- to highlight areas where the Customer believes that further discussion with the Tenderer will be necessary;

- to establish the principals under which the services will be provided and the relationship developed;

- to further develop a long-term strategy on how desktop services should be delivered by the Supplier to the Customer.

3. GENERAL INSTRUCTIONS TO TENDERER

3.1 Proposal

3.1.1 The Tenderer is invited to respond to this document by submitting a detailed proposal which fully addresses all of the requirements set out here. This document contains requests for information, which require the Tenderer to make statements of compliance or non-compliance with the requirements.

3.1.2 Templates for responding to the request for information and supplying specific information are attached.

3.2 Response procedure

3.2.1 The Tenderer is invited to submit its Proposal to the Customer on or before noon on Friday [ ] day of [ ]. Six hard and two soft copies (in Microsoft Word) of the Proposal should be delivered to [ ].

3.2.2 The Tenderer shall adopt the following procedure in responding to this document:

- the Tenderer must acknowledge receipt of this document in writing to the Customer, together with an indication of its intention to submit a proposal;

- following an initial review of the document and as necessary, the Tenderer may request one meeting with the Customer to discuss the requirements further, to ask for clarification and to illicit more information about the Customer's requirements;

- following this meeting, the Tenderer may submit written requests to the Customer for clarification.

3.2.3 All communications and correspondence prior to submission of the Tenderer's proposal must be made through [named person] who will be at liberty to share any information provided to the Tenderer to other Tenderers.

3.3 Required format of proposal

3.3.1 The Tenderer must respond to all questions set out in this document including all the associated attachments.

3.3.2 Responses must reflect the same order as this document, and be referenced by the same paragraph numbers. [To assist with this response, templates are provided in hard and soft copy form.]

3.4 Summary of proposal evaluation criteria All proposals will be evaluated on the basis of the following criteria which are set out in descending order of importance to the Customer:

3.4.1 An assessment of the responses to the Customer's service quality requirements. The assessment will include, but is not limited to, the following:

- the capability of the Supplier from a service delivery perspective; eg experience in this area, proposal resources and organisation to be deployed for the benefit of the Customer;

- the Supplier's approach to service improvement, access to additional skills and monitoring of new developments in the desktop and network field;

- the approach proposed (if necessary) to transfer services from the current arrangements.

3.4.2 Comparison of the Tenderer's commercial proposal with those of other Tenderers.

3.4.3 The ability of the Tenderer to provide an innovative pricing solution.

3.4.4 Compliance with the Customer's proposed contract terms and conditions.

3.5 **Outline timetable** Below is an outline timetable:

Activity	Date to be completed
Request for proposal issued.	
Confirmation or receipt of RFP and indication of intention to bid.	
Proposal submitted to Customer.	
Bid evaluation and preferred Supplier selected, including reference visits.	
Contract negotiation and signature.	
Transition to provision of outsourced services.	

4. BUSINESS BACKGROUND

4.1 Customer Limited

4.2 [Here give full details of the company which will be the recipient of the services and alternative proposals.]

5. EXISTING DESKTOP AND NETWORK TECHNOLOGY

[Description of current desktop arrangements, including names of manufacturers, quantities, presence or absence of other third-party Suppliers, etc.]

6. CUSTOMER'S GENERAL DESKTOP STRATEGY

6.1 The Customer requires a desktop environment that:

- operates reliably to required levels and can be managed to those levels;

- responds flexibly and quickly to changing business needs;
- provides 'value for money' with costs that are understood and accepted by the
- Customer's business managers; and
- promotes maximum utilisation of the available technology.

6.2 **Existing user base** [Here give a description of existing types of users.]

6.3 **Overall aim** The overall aim is to provide delivery of desktop and network services measured in terms of the accessibility and availability of applications to the end user. Details of the infra structure and technical issues are of secondary interest to the Customer, who relies on the consultancy and other services to be provided by the Tenderer in order to obtain a technical architecture and overall service which maximises consistency, reliability, flexibility and adaptability to new technology.

7. SUMMARY OF MAJOR SERVICES

The Customer is looking for the provision of services in the following areas:

7.1 Audit of existing equipment and software licences.

7.2 Development of desktop and network strategy for the next five years.

7.3 Managing and developing commercial and technical relationships with Suppliers and monitoring their overall performance.

7.4 Routine and preventive maintenance.

7.5 Remedial maintenance and problem solving.

7.6 Helpdesk function.

8. GENERAL INFORMATION REQUIREMENTS

The Tenderer is requested to provide the following background information:

8.1 Company overview and business background, including details of corporate ownership and structure, plus financial results for the last three years.

8.2 Technical and managerial resources directly available to the subsidiary or division which will be providing the desktop services, together with details of alliances with third parties.

8.3 Details of all sub-contractors to be used in connection with the provision of the services, along with details of the relationship, eg formal/informal, length, whether specific to this contract or part of a long-term strategic partnership, and degree of dependence of the sub-contractor on the business of the Tenderer.

8.4 List of the due diligence tasks which the Supplier will wish to conduct, including a timetable, and an assessment of the impact on Customer resources.

8.5 Statement by the Tenderer confirming willingness to work with others, including details of how the relationships with other manufacturers and Suppliers will be managed.

8.6 Proposals by the Tenderer as to how it intends to improve the provision of services to the Customer.

8.7 Details of how the Tenderer will take on existing supply contracts entered into by the Customer.

9.　SERVICE ELEMENTS[5]

9.1 **Resource management** The Supplier will be responsible for providing all technical and managerial staff necessary to provide the services.

9.2 **Service window** The service window occupies the hours from 07.30 to 19.30 Monday to Friday on all business days unless otherwise specified. Service windows for specified services may be increased to 24 hours or decreased to normal business hours as will be specified by the Customer. [Alter as may be necessary.]

9.3 **Change management** [To be completed as necessary.]

9.4 **Requests for service** [To be completed as necessary.]

9.5 **Performance reporting** [To be completed as necessary.]

9.6 **Disaster and business continuity planning** [To be completed as necessary.]

9.7 **Security** [To be completed as necessary.]

9.8 **Asset management** [To be completed as necessary.]

10.　SERVICE MEASURES AND LEVELS[6]

10.1 The Customer requires that all services shall be provided to an agreed level of service. Service measures are therefore required to allow service levels to be identified.

10.2 Targets will be set for each service level and the Supplier will be expected to meet (or exceed) the target for each service.

10.3 The Customer will revise the specification of the required measures and items of service to be measured as and when required for the purpose of keeping the measurement regime effective and relevant to the changing nature of the services.

10.4 The Customer will also assess the quality of service provided by the Supplier to end users by inviting responses to quality surveys, which will be carried out at least twice a year.

10.5 The Supplier shall provide, on request, all data required by the Customer to support any analysis of service levels and any revision of service measures.

10.6 **Service charge adjustments** The objective of the service charge adjustment regime is to provide an incentive to the Supplier to maintain services at the agreed and contracted service levels. Service level deficiencies of a minor nature will be ignored but those that are excessive or persistent will involve increasing levels of service charge adjustment.

11. DETAILED INFORMATION REQUESTED

The Supplier shall provide the following:

11.1 A statement that the service definitions are understood.

11.2 Details of those services the Supplier is able to provide.

11.3 If appropriate, alternative service descriptions.

11.4 Acceptance of responsibility for transition to the new service, including mending all records etc.

11.5 Demonstration of competence and expertise in the transition process.

11.6 Details of how the service descriptions and inventories will be finalised prior to contract commencement.

11.7 Description of how the Supplier will deal with new hardware and software products being added to the inventory from time to time.

11.8 Details of how the Supplier sees the descriptions, measuring and pricing of services being developed throughout the life of the contract with a commitment that there will be no negative impact on service levels or increases in charges as a result.

11.9 Statement of acceptance of interface responsibilities with telecommunications service providers.

11.10 A statement that the Supplier is able to provide all services to the specified service levels during the service window. Any exceptions should be documented.

11.11 Details of how the Supplier will provide standby support outside the service window. Any reductions in the service levels should be stated.

11.12 Details of the resources provided and how they are managed, their technical skill levels and any contractors used.

11.13 Details of the manner in which the Supplier will identify, escalate and resolve issues and disputes that may arise while providing services.

11.14 An explanation of how the Supplier will provide a central point for reporting and liaising with the service support and users.

11.15 A commitment that the Supplier will work positively with other service providers to resolve problems.

11.16 A commitment to comply with any fault reporting system in use by the Customer.

11.17 A description of arrangements for floor walkers, including how they will fit into the support organisation and how they will liaise with users.

11.18 A commitment to comply with the Customer's changed management process.

11.19 A commitment to work with the Customer and other service providers to refine the changed management process.

11.20 A commitment to comply with the Customer's request for service procedures.

11.21 Details of how the Supplier proposes to monitor quality of service delivery, the performance measurement tools utilised, the data available and the type of report to be produced.

11.22 Examples of typical performance reports produced for other customers.

11.23 Details of any equipment upgrades required by the Supplier to the services made available to the current service provider.

11.24 An undertaking to adhere to health and safety policies.

11.25 An undertaking to ensure services remain available in the event of a disaster, together with details of the circumstances where this will not be possible.

11.26 Details of how the Supplier will meet with security requirements.

11.27 A statement of understanding and adherence to the service measures as required.

11.28 A statement confirming acceptance of the concept of a Service Charge Adjustment regime.

11.29 Proposals for performance acceptance criteria.

11.30 Statement as to whether or not the proposal includes an undertaking to take ownership of current Customer assets, together with a statement of proposed licensing arrangements in that eventuality.

11.31 The terms and conditions which the Supplier proposes should be incorporated in the contract for supply of services.

Note: The Customer reserves the right to award the contract on the basis of Customer terms and conditions.

12. RELATIONSHIP BETWEEN CUSTOMER AND SUPPLIER

12.1 **Account management** The Supplier will appoint an account manager to manage the overall relationship between Customer and Supplier.

12.2 **Service manager** The Supplier will provide a service manager who will be responsible for the delivery of all services. The Service manager must be immediately available during normal business hours, and contactable at all other times.

13.   HUMAN RESOURCES REQUIREMENTS

13.1   **Customer staff** Currently there are [   ] staff members dedicated to the provision of the services. Of these, [   ] are contractors and [   ] are employees of the Customer.

13.2   **TUPE** Suppliers are requested to submit a proposal on the basis that the Transfer of Undertakings (Protection of Employment) Regulations 1981 will not apply to the outsourcing of the provision of these services, and that if this approach is for any reason mistaken, the Customer will indemnify the Supplier in respect of TUPE claims arising during a period of one month after the contract commencement date, subject to precise wording to be agreed.

13.3   **Supplier staff** Supplier staff will be appropriately dressed for work in the City of London during normal working hours, readily identifiable at all times by means of badges showing name and company represented and must sign a confidentiality agreement and shared dealing declaration.

13.4   **Security** The Supplier will be responsible for vetting staff in their employ and for carrying out relevant security checks.

14.   AUDIT AND COMPLIANCE

14.1   Scope Audits will focus on compliance with:

- internal control standards;

- regulatory requirements relating to the insurance industry and all applicable legal requirements;

- contractual requirements, including in particular accuracy in billing;

- agreed service levels;

- the Pricing Principles.

14.2   **Internal audits** The Supplier will be subject to audits by the Customer's internal auditors.

14.3   **External audits** The Supplier may also be subject to periodic audits by the Customer's external auditors.

14.4   **Access** The Customer requires access to all external or internal auditors' reviews of the Supplier in relation to this contract.

15.   FINANCIAL INFORMATION AND REQUIREMENTS

15.1   **Open books philosophy** The Customer wishes to conduct the process of choosing its preferred desktop Supplier on an 'open books' basis,

485

in order to ensure a relevant comparison between all bidders. Each bidder is requested to supply the Customer with a full breakdown of the bidding and to share details of the relevant commercial opportunities which underpin the price. It is in the Customer's interest that its chosen Supplier makes a sustainable level of profit and that the Supplier discloses the prospective margins it will enjoy.

15.2 **Variable charges** The Customer is looking for a pricing regime based on agreed unit prices for discrete services or pieces of work, which enable overall charging levels to move up and down in line with business requirements. The Customer requires that the Supplier tenders on the basis of committed prices for the whole contract period.

15.3 **Procurement** Two options are being considered and the Supplier should submit proposals on the basis of both alternatives. In either case, Suppliers should set out the warranty implications for the Customer.

15.4 **Equipment purchase** The first approach is that the Supplier will purchase equipment on behalf of the Customer on a costs plus basis. Under this scenario asset ownership would be retained by the Customer. This approach is viewed as the easiest to implement.

15.5 **Rental approach** The Customer is also interested in exploring the possibility of introducing a pre-determined annual rental charge for its desktop equipment. Under this scenario the Supplier will be responsible for funding costs and asset residuals in return for an all in charge. This approach could be applied to new requirements and also to existing assets (subject to validation of the Customer's inventory records and valuation).

15.6 **Commitment to competitive pricing** The Supplier undertakes that its prices will be the best available in the industry for a contract of this size. It is intended that the competitiveness of the Supplier's prices will be tested through both internal and external benchmarking reviews. The Supplier must undertake that support and procurement services prices will be reduced if reviews indicate that the prices charged are substantially higher than comparable third-party prices.

15.7 **Price increases** It is expected that underlying contract prices will be driven down to reflect the opportunities arising from managing existing technology more effectively, the application of new technologies and increased staffing efficiencies. Overall, the Customer expects that decreases in technology prices will more than keep pace with increases in the complexity of its requirements, resulting in declining absolute support charges and falling capital commitments. In the case of procurement, the Customer anticipates that the mark-up added by Suppliers (or implicit in the period of rental charge) will be no greater than 5%.

15.8 **Assumptions for provision of price information** Assumptions to be used by bidders in preparing pricing information are as follows:

- the commencement date will be no later than [   ];

- separate bids are required for contract periods of 1, 2 and 3 years. The Supplier should indicate the extent to which the term of the contract will have an impact on the level of their service charges;

- for support, prices should reflect a flat profile of service requirements, a static inventory and constant volumes across that contract period;

- the impact of inflation during the life of the contract should be separately identified in the price;

- any staff transferred from the Customer should be compensated at their current overall remuneration levels;

- severance costs for any staff transferred will be the Supplier's responsibility following commencement of service. The Customer will be responsible for any severance costs arising in respect of staff not transferred to the Supplier, but these costs will be taken into account in reviewing bids;

- no Customer premises are assumed to transfer to the Supplier. A limited amount of space will be provided by the Customer for essential on-site staff and the Supplier should indicate their requirements in this respect;

- the proposed asset purchased and associated consideration payable to the Customer should be indicated separately, if relevant to the Supplier's bid;

- any other assumptions regarding, for example, meantime between failure of PCs, should be provided;

- all assumptions in relation to tax should be made clear.

15.9 **Billing** Invoices in respect of services will be issued to the Customer monthly in arrears and settled by the Customer within 30 days.

15.10 **Asset transfer provisions** If assets are to be transferred to the Supplier, this will be effected at net book value or other approximation of the fair market value, which will be determined by agreement.

16. LEGAL REQUIREMENTS AND CONTRACTUAL NEGOTIATIONS

16.1 **General requirements** This section addresses certain general legal requirements considered essential by the Customer. It does not constitute an exhaustive statement of contractual and legal requirements.

16.2 **Control of documentation** The Supplier must accept that control of all documentation (whether in draft or final form) relating to the provision of desktop and network services shall be with the Customer.

16.3 **Format** Any soft copy documentation, Schedules, annexes or exhibits shall be provided to the Customer on Microsoft Word for Windows 6.0 format and on 3.5 inch floppy disk.

16.4 **Supplier documentation** All responses to this request for proposal shall be made on the basis that the Supplier grants to the Customer, for the Customer's business use only, an unlimited, non-exclusive, royalty-free licence to use, adapt, alter or develop any material (of whatever type) provided to the Customer (on whatever material) in any way whatsoever.

16.5 **Warranties** The Customer expects the Supplier to warrant that:[8]

16.5.1 all equipment and software provided will be free from defects in workmanship and material and fit for use in the Customer's business. The Customer expects the Supplier to pass on the benefit of any other warranties from other Suppliers; and

16.5.2 all services will be provided by fully qualified and trained personnel observing best industry standards of care and skill.

16.6 **Insurance** The Supplier must, of course, have appropriate insurance cover for the usual risks, including employer's liability, third-party liability and professional negligence, to limits to be agreed further with the Customer.

16.7 **Liability** The Customer is a relatively small company whose business operations would be greatly affected by poor quality desktop services. It also has limited opportunities to obtain insurance cover at competitive rates for business interruption and other risks. The Customer will therefore be particularly interested in proposals which indicate a willingness on the part of the Supplier to accept realistic limits of liability for damage to property, loss of data and breach of contract.

1 There is no hard and fast template for an invitation to tender. The example given here is one used for an invitation to tender for the provision of desktop hardware and software.
2 This confidentiality clause may need to also reference any prior confidentiality agreement executed between the parties.
3 This document is indicated as not being binding upon the Customer who issued it, thereby not indicating in any way that the Customer is bound to accept the response of the Supplier.
4 CLAUSES 2.1 and 2.2 would need to be substantially amended to reflect the purposes and objectives of any invitation to tender.
5 SECTION 9 sets out the elements of service level required by the Customer.
6 SECTION 10 sets out the service level framework required by the Customer.
7 The Transfer of Undertakings (Protection of Employment) Regulations 1981, SI 1981/1794, as amended by the Trade Union Reform and Employment Rights Act 1993.
8 The warranties here may need to be expanded, depending upon the needs of the Customer.

20 IT services outsourcing agreement

THIS AGREEMENT is made the [ ] day of [ ]

BETWEEN:

(1) OUTSOURCER a company registered in England and Wales under company number whose registered office is at [ ] ('the Outsourcer'); and

(2) CLIENT the party whose details appear in PART I of the Schedule ('the Client').

RECITAL

A. The Client wishes to appoint the Outsourcer to provide certain [information technology,] [computer,] [management support and maintenance services], [administrative] and [business] services to the Client and the Outsourcer has agreed to provide such services on the terms of this Agreement.

B. By an agreement dated [ ], the Client has transferred to the Outsourcer certain [hardware], [premises] and [employees].[1]

OPERATIVE PROVISIONS

I. DEFINITIONS

1.1 In this Agreement (which expression includes the Recital, the Schedule and any Annexures hereto) the following words and phrases shall, unless the context otherwise requires, have the following meanings:

   1.1.1 **'Authorised Representatives'** means the persons respectively designated as such by the Client and Outsourcer as set out in PART II of the Schedule;

   1.1.2 **'Change Control Procedure'** means the procedure set out in CLAUSE 7;

   1.1.3 **'Change Request'** shall have the meaning ascribed to it in CLAUSE 7 hereof;

1.1.4   **'Change Order'** shall have the meaning ascribed to it in CLAUSE 7 hereof;

1.1.5   **'Client IT'** means any components of the Client's current IT infrastructure (including but not limited to cabling, hardware and software);

1.1.6   **'Dispute Resolution Procedure'** means the procedure set out in CLAUSE 25;

1.1.7   **'Effective Date'** means the date set out in PART III of the Schedule;

1.1.8   **'Implementation Plan'** means the implementation plan as set out in ANNEX B;

1.1.9   **'Intellectual Property'** means property in which intellectual property rights of whatever nature (including but not limited to patents, trade marks, service marks, design rights, database rights, know-how rights, goodwill, reputation, get-up, logos, devices, plans, models, data, diagrams, specifications, source and object code materials, data and processes, design rights, trade or business name rights, rights in confidential information, present contingent and future copyright, rights to sue for passing-off, plus applications or rights to apply for any of the foregoing) subsist;

1.1.10   **'Month'** means a calendar month and Monthly shall be construed accordingly;'

1.1.11   **'Premises'** means the premises occupied by the Client as set out in PART IV of the Schedule;

1.1.12   **'Required Service Level'** in respect of any Service in any period means the standard of performance referred to in CLAUSE 2.2 in the provision of that Service in the period in question;

1.1.13   **'Services'** means the services to be provided by the Outsourcer to the Client as set out in ANNEX A;

1.1.14   **'Services Charges'** means the charges levied by the Outsourcer for the Services in accordance with the tariffs, scales, charges, invoicing methods and terms of payment as set out in ANNEX C;

1.1.15   **'Service Credits'** means the credits which become payable to the Client by way of a reduction in the Service Charges where the Required Service Levels are not achieved as set out in ANNEX A;

1.1.16   **'Service Manager'** means the individual appointed by the Outsourcer and the Client pursuant to CLAUSE 8 hereof and as set out in PART V of the Schedule;

1.1.17   **'Third Party Provider'** means the provider of any of the third party products;

1.1.18   **'VAT'** means value added tax.

1.2   In the case of conflict or ambiguity between any provision contained in the body of this Agreement and any provision contained in any Schedule or Annex, the provision in the body of this Agreement shall take precedence.

2.   SUPPLY OF SERVICES

2.1   The Outsourcer will provide the Services[2] to the Client with effect from the Effective Date for the duration of this Agreement in accordance with the provisions of this Agreement.

2.2   The service levels to be obtained by the Outsourcer in supplying the Services to the Client shall be in accordance with the Service level statement set out in ANNEX A.

2.3   The Outsourcer agrees to provide the Services in accordance with the Implementation Plan, provided always that the Implementation Plan shall be amended to the extent reasonably necessary in order to reflect:

2.3.1   any breach of any obligations of the Client under this Agreement and/or negligence by it; and/or

2.3.2   any cause of delay which was beyond the reasonable control of the Outsourcer.

2.4   The Outsourcer shall keep records of the service levels achieved for the Services it is providing to the Client for each 3 Month period throughout this Agreement and provide copies of such records to the Client upon request.

2.5   In the event that the service levels[3] achieved by the Outsourcer falls short of the Required Service Level in any [3] Month period or the goals set out in the Implementation Plan are not achieved, the provisions of CLAUSE 6.2 shall apply.

2.6   [The Outsourcer shall ensure that fully up to date virus protection software shall be installed upon all computer systems to which Outsourcer requires access for the purpose of performing any Services and the Client agrees to pay for such installation. The Outsourcer shall ensure that all such virus protection software is used by the Outsourcer in accordance with manufacturer's instructions.]

3.   OUTSOURCER'S OBLIGATIONS[4]

3.1   The Outsourcer will provide the Services with reasonable skill and care in accordance with relevant industry best practice.

3.2   In the provision of the Services, the Outsourcer shall use personnel who possess a degree of skill and experience which is appropriate to the tasks to which they are allotted and who shall perform those tasks in a workmanlike and professional manner.

3.3   The Outsourcer shall comply with the Client's IT security, premises and health and safety policies as notified to it from time to time.

4. CLIENT'S OBLIGATIONS AND WARRANTIES[5]

4.1 The Client undertakes throughout the term of this Agreement to:

    4.1.1 enter into and maintain contracts directly with Third Party Providers and ensure that such contracts permit the Outsourcer to request resources from each Third Party Provider on behalf of the Client when required in order to carry out the Services;

    4.1.2 [keep in place current software maintenance agreements with the vendors of all supported software applications used by the Client to ensure adequate assistance from such vendors if required;]

    4.1.3 grant to the Outsourcer such access to and such facilities at the Premises as the Outsourcer may require from time to time in order to discharge its obligations hereunder;

    4.1.4 take all reasonable precautions to protect the health and safety of the Outsourcer's personnel, agents and subcontractors whilst at the Premises;

    4.1.5 provide the Outsourcer with all assistance, materials and accurate information for the purposes of enabling the Outsourcer to provide the Services;

    4.1.6 ensure that all personnel assigned by it to provide assistance to the Outsourcer shall have the requisite skill, qualification and experience to perform the tasks assigned to them.

4.2 The Client warrants that it is the owner of all the Client IT (including any machines, drawings, connectors, cables, parts or other items, computer room documents, manuals, tapes, disk media, items of furniture and other equipment which is the subject of Services to be provided by the Outsourcer), or is authorised by the owner thereof to make them available to the Outsourcer.

4.3 The Client warrants that the details of the existing hardware and software at the Premises and all current licences it holds for software provided to Outsourcer are complete and accurate.

4.4 The Client warrants that all data and other information provided by it shall not be obscene, defamatory or likely to result in any claim being made against the Outsourcer by any third party.

5. SERVICE CHARGES AND PAYMENTS

5.1 In consideration of the provision of the Services by the Outsourcer the Client shall pay to the Outsourcer the Service Charges without any set-off, counterclaim or other deduction whatsoever.

5.2 The Service Charge shall be invoiced to the Client monthly in arrears. Each invoice shall be paid by the Client within [30] days of the Client's receipt of such invoice.

5.3 Any additional Service Charges shall be invoiced by the Outsourcer to the Client monthly in arrears accompanied by any substantiating documentation which may be reasonably required by the Client.

5.4 All Service Charges and payments to be made by the Client under this Agreement are stated exclusive of VAT which shall additionally be paid by the Client where relevant at the rate and from time to time in the manner prescribed by law.

5.5 All Service Charges are [inclusive of expenses] [exclusive of the Outsourcer's reasonable expenses incurred in connection with the provision of the Services, which shall be payable by the Client in addition].

5.6 If the Client fails to make any payment (which is not the subject of a bona fide dispute)[6] due to the Outsourcer in full within [14 days] of the due date and has failed to give a reasonable written explanation for such failure to the Outsourcer, then, without prejudice to any other right or remedy, the Outsourcer shall be entitled to:

    5.6.1 suspend performance of any Services until all sums due to the Outsourcer have been paid in full (but only after having given written notice to the Client of its intention so to do);

    5.6.2 [charge the Client interest (both before and after any judgment) on any unpaid amount at the rate of 2% above the base rate of National Westminster Bank Plc, from time to time from the due date until the actual date of receipt of such amount by the Outsourcer; and/or]

    5.6.3 charge the Client for any costs incurred in obtaining (or attempting to obtain) payment of any unpaid amounts including, without limitation, reasonable legal fees and back charges.

5.7 The Outsourcer reserves the right, by giving notice to the Client at any time before performance of the relevant Services to increase the price of such Services to reflect any increase in the cost to the Outsourcer which is due to an act or omission of the Client including but not limited to any change in the date for the performance of Services or any delay caused by any instructions of the Client or failure by the Client to give the Outsourcer adequate information or instructions.

6. FAILURE TO MEET REQUIRED SERVICE LEVEL[7]

6.1 The Outsourcer shall provide Monthly service level reports to the Client in accordance with the Service Level statement set out in ANNEX A.

[6.2 If the Outsourcer fails to provide the Services in accordance with the Required Service Levels measured over any three Monthly period the Client shall be entitled to terminate this Agreement upon giving at least [ten] days notice to Outsourcer expiring not later than that end of the Month following the relevant three Month period.][8]

OR

[6.2   If the Outsourcer fails to provide the Services in accordance with the Required Service Levels measured over any three Monthly period the Client shall incur Service Credits as set out in ANNEX C. Such Service Credits shall be calculated monthly and applied as a deduction to any Service Charges payable pursuant to CLAUSE 5.]

6.3   The Outsourcer shall not be liable for any failure to achieve the Required Service Levels and the Client shall not incur Service Credits to the extent that such failure results from:

    6.3.1   a breach by the Client of any of its obligations under this Agreement;

    6.3.2   an event of force majeure falling within the scope of CLAUSE 13.

6.4   In the event that the parties are unable to agree upon the cause of the failure to reach the Required Service Level or the extent to which the Required Service Levels may be adjusted, the matter shall be reverted to an expert for determination in accordance with the Dispute Resolution Procedure.

7.   CHANGE CONTROL[9]

7.1   For the purposes of this Agreement a 'Change Request' is:

    7.1.1   a request to change (including to cease) any service or add new services to the Services; or

    7.1.2   a request to amend this Agreement or any document attached to it or referred to in this Agreement; or

    7.1.3   any proposal which causes or is likely to cause the Client to incur costs or charges outside the scope of the Service Charges.

    A Change Request shall become a 'Change Order' when the requirements of the Change Control Procedure have been satisfied and the Change Request is signed by the Authorised Representatives of both parties to signify their approval to the change.

7.2   Change Requests may be originated either by the Client or by the Outsourcer.

7.3   Where the Outsourcer originates a Change Request it shall provide, with the Change Request, details of the impact which the proposed change will have upon the Services; the Implementation Plan; the Required Service Levels; any systems or operations of the Client which communicate with, or are otherwise affected by the Services; the Service Charges; and the other terms of this Agreement.

7.4   Where the Client originates a Change Request, the Outsourcer shall provide the Client, within [21] days of receiving the Change Request, details of the impact which the proposed change will have upon the Services; the Implementation Plan; the Required Service Levels; any systems or operations of the Client which communicate with, or are otherwise affected by the Services; the Service Charges; and the other terms of this Agreement.

7.5   Save where otherwise stated herein, neither party shall be obliged to agree a Change Request originated by the other.

7.6   The costs of implementing a Change Order shall be borne as set out therein.

7.7   The Outsourcer shall be entitled to charge the Client for work undertaken by the Outsourcer in analysing the effect of any proposed Change Request. Where the Outsourcer wishes to make a charge for carrying out such analysis, it will first notify the Client in writing, in order to allow the Client to choose whether or not to authorise the Outsourcer to proceed with the analysis of the requested change.

7.8   The Outsourcer reserves the right at any time without notifying the Client to make changes to any Services which are necessary to comply with any applicable safety or other statutory requirement provided that such variation does not materially affect the quality or performance anticipated by the Client.

8.   CO-OPERATION BETWEEN THE PARTIES

8.1   Each party will appoint a Service Manager to deal with any Change Control Procedure. The first appointees are as set out in PART V of the Schedule. Neither party shall change its Service Managers without prior consultation with the other.

8.2   The Service Managers shall meet Monthly to review the performance of the Implementation Plan and the Services provided under this Agreement and any changes required.

9.   TERM OF THIS AGREEMENT

This Agreement shall commence on the Effective Date and shall, subject to prior termination provided for under this Agreement, continue for an initial period of [12 months] and thereafter indefinitely, unless terminated by either party upon giving three Months' prior written notice of termination of the Agreement, such notice to expire on, or at any time after, the expiration of the initial period of [12 months].

10.   ASSIGNMENTS AND SUCCESSORS

10.1   This Agreement is personal to the parties and, subject to CLAUSE 10.2 below, neither this Agreement nor any rights, licenses or obligations under this Agreement, may be assigned by either party without the prior written approval of the other party.

10.2   Notwithstanding the foregoing, either party may assign this Agreement to any acquirer of all or of substantially all of such party's equity securities, assets or business relating to the subject matter of this Agreement or to any entity controlled by, that controls, or is under common control with a party to this Agreement. Any attempted assignment in violation of this clause will be void and without effect.

10.3 This Agreement shall be binding upon, and enure to the benefit of, the parties and their respective successors and permitted assignees, and references to a party in this Agreement shall include its successors and permitted assignees.

10.4 In this Agreement references to a party include references to a person:

10.4.1 who for the time being is entitled (by assignment, novation or otherwise) to that party's rights under this Agreement (or any interest in those rights); or

10.4.2 who, as administrator, liquidator or otherwise, is entitled to exercise those rights;

10.4.3 and in particular those references include a person to whom those rights (or any interest in those rights) are transferred or pass as a result of a merger, division, reconstruction or other reorganisation involving that party. For this purpose, references90 a party's rights under this Agreement include any similar rights to which another person becomes entitled as a result of a novation of this Agreement.

11. INTELLECTUAL PROPERTY RIGHTS

11.1 In the absence of prior written agreement to the contrary, all Intellectual Property created by the Outsourcer or any employee, agent or sub-contractor of the Outsourcer in the course of performing the Services shall vest in the Outsourcer.[10]

11.2 Where, in connection with the provision of the Services, the Client uses any Intellectual Property which is owned by the Outsourcer, the Outsourcer shall grant to the Client, or shall procure that the Client is granted (without charge to the Client and for the benefit of the Client) an indefinite non-exclusive, royalty-free licence to use, adapt, maintain and support such Intellectual Property, which licence shall include the right for any person providing services to the Client to use, adapt, maintain and support such Intellectual Property for the benefit of the Client.

11.3 In the absence of prior written agreement to the contrary, all Intellectual Property in the Client IT and any other information, materials or assets supplied to the Outsourcer by the Client shall remain vested in the Client or its third party licensors. The Client shall grant or shall procure the grant of a licence to the Outsourcer to utilise the Client IT or such other information, materials or assets to the extent required for the provision of the Services.

11.4 Unless stated expressly in writing in this Agreement, neither party will acquire any ownership interest in or licence of the other's Intellectual Property by virtue of this Agreement.

11.5 The Client shall defend any claim (at the Client's expense) brought against the Outsourcer alleging that the use of the Client IT infringes the Intellectual Property of a third party including infringement of rights which arise as a result of storage or processing of any Client IT on the Outsourcer's systems and/or the provision of any information, materials or other assets to the Outsourcer by the Client ('IPR Claim'). Client shall pay all costs and damages awarded or agreed to in settlement of an IPR Claim provided that the Outsourcer:

11.5.1 furnishes the Client with prompt written notice of the IPR Claim;

11.5.2 provides the Client with reasonable assistance in respect of the IPR Claim;

11.5.3 gives to the Client the sole authority to defend or settle the IPR Claim.

11.6 The Outsourcer shall defend any claim (at the Outsourcer's expense) brought against the Client alleging that the provision of the Services or the use of any deliverables provided by the Outsourcer infringes the Intellectual Property of a third party ('IPR Claim'). The Outsourcer shall pay all costs and damages awarded or agreed to in settlement of an IPR Claim provided that the Client:

11.6.1 furnishes the Outsourcer with prompt written notice of the IPR Claim;

11.6.2 provides the Outsourcer with reasonable assistance in respect of the IPR Claim;

11.6.3 gives to the Outsourcer the sole authority to defend or settle the IPR Claim.

12. CONFIDENTIALITY

12.1 Both parties to this Agreement undertake, except as provided below, to treat as confidential and keep secret all information marked 'confidential' or which may reasonably be supposed to be confidential supplied by the Outsourcer or Client (in this Agreement collectively referred to as 'the Information') with the same degree of care as it employs with regard to its own confidential information of a like nature and in any event in accordance with best current commercial security practices, provided that, this clause shall not extend to any information which was rightfully in the possession of either party prior to the commencement of the negotiations leading to this Agreement or which is already public knowledge or becomes so at a future date (otherwise than as a result of a breach of this clause).

12.2 Neither party shall not without the prior written consent of the other party divulge any part of the other party's Information to any person except:

12.2.1 to their own employees, consultants or sub-contractors and then only to those employees, consultants or sub-contractors who need to know the Information for the purposes of this Agreement; and

12.2.2 to either parties' auditors, HM Inspector of Taxes, HM Customs and Excise, a court of competent jurisdiction, governmental body or applicable regulatory authority and any other persons or bodies having a right duty or obligation to know the business of the other party and then only in pursuance of such right duty or obligation.

12.3 Both parties undertake to ensure that persons and bodies referred to in CLAUSE 12.2 are made aware prior to the disclosure of any part of the Information that the same is confidential and that they owe a duty of confidence to the other party.

12.4 Each party to this Agreement shall promptly notify the other party if it becomes aware of any breach of confidence by any person to whom it divulges all or any part of the Information and shall give the other party all reasonable assistance in connection with any proceedings which the other party may institute against such person for breach of confidence.

12.5 The foregoing obligations as to confidentiality shall remain in full force and effect notwithstanding any termination of this Agreement.

12.6 Provided that it is not in breach of the confidentiality obligations set out above, the Outsourcer may refer to and publicise its involvement with the Client, but only with the Client's prior written approval in relation to each publication, which shall not be unreasonably withheld or delayed.

13. FORCE MAJEURE[11]

13.1 Neither party shall have any liability under or be deemed to be in breach of this Agreement for any delays or failures in performance of this Agreement which result from circumstances beyond the reasonable control of that party (an event of 'force majeure'). In the event that a force majeure event continues for a continuous period of more than [6 months], either party may terminate this Agreement by written notice to the other party.

13.2 [The Client shall be free to obtain substitute services from an alternative supplier during the continuance of the event of force majeure and shall be under no obligation to pay the Outsourcer for Services which have not been supplied by the Outsourcer because of the event of force majeure.]

14. COMPLIANCE WITH RELEVANT LAW

Both parties will comply with all applicable laws, rules and regulations in respect of all activities conducted under this Agreement.

15. OUTSOURCER'S EXCLUSION OF LIABILITY

15.1   The Outsourcer shall not be liable to the Client or be deemed to be in breach of its warranties or obligations under any provision in this Agreement:

   15.1.1   for any delay in performing or failure to perform the Outsourcer's obligations to the extent that such delay or failure was due to a failure by the Client to perform its obligations under this Agreement or if delay results from a failure by the Client to comply with reasonable requests by the Outsourcer for instructions, information or action required by it to perform its obligations within a reasonable time limit; or

   15.1.2   for the consequences of any acts or omissions of the Client, its employees or agents or any Third Party Provider or other third party suppliers or manufacturers engaged by or on behalf of the Client (other than third party sub-contractors or suppliers selected by the Outsourcer); or

   15.1.3   if the Client is in default of any of its payment obligations under this Agreement.

16. INDEMNITY, LIMITATION OF LIABILITY AND INSURANCE[12]

16.1   The Outsourcer shall, during the term of this Agreement, maintain employer's liability, third party liability, product liability and professional negligence insurance cover in respect of its liabilities arising out of or connected with this Agreement, such cover to be to a minimum value of [ONE MILLION POUNDS] and with an insurance company of repute. The Outsourcer shall on request supply copies of the relevant certificates of insurance to the Client as evidence that such policies remain in force. The Outsourcer undertakes to use reasonable commercial efforts to pursue claims under such insurance policies.

16.2   The Outsourcer shall indemnify the Client for personal injury or death caused by the negligence of its employees in connection with the performance of their duties hereunder or by the provision of the Services supplied pursuant to this Agreement.

16.3   The Outsourcer will indemnify the Client for direct damage to tangible property caused by the negligence of its employees in connection with the performance of their duties hereunder. Outsourcer's total liability under this clause shall be limited to [£500,000] for any one event or series of connected events.

16.4   Save in respect of claims for death or personal injury arising from the Outsourcer's negligence, in no event will the Outsourcer be liable for any damages resulting from loss of data or use, lost profits, loss of anticipated savings, nor for any damages that are an indirect or secondary consequence of any act or omission of the Outsourcer whether such damages were reasonably foreseeable or actually foreseen.

16.5   Except as provided above in the case of personal injury, death and damage to tangible property, the Outsourcer's maximum liability to the Client under this Agreement or otherwise for any cause whatsoever (whether in the form of the additional cost of remedial services or otherwise) will be for direct costs and damages only and will be limited to the greater of:

16.5.1   the sum for which the Outsourcer carries comprehensive insurance cover pursuant to CLAUSE 16.1 above; or

16.5.2   a sum equivalent to the price paid to the Outsourcer under this Agreement for the Services that are the subject of the Client's claim, plus damages limited to 25% of the same amount for any additional costs directly, reasonably and necessarily incurred by the Client in obtaining alternative services.

16.6   The parties hereby acknowledge and agree that the limitations contained in this CLAUSE 16 are reasonable in light of all the circumstances.

16.7   The Client's statutory rights as a consumer (if any) are not affected. All liability that is not expressly assumed in this Agreement is hereby excluded. These limitations will apply regardless of the form of action, whether under statute, in contract or tort including negligence or any other form of action. For the purposes of this Clause, 'Outsourcer' includes its employees, sub-contractors and suppliers who shall all have the benefit of the limits and exclusions of liability set out above in terms of the Contracts (Rights of Third Parties) Act 1999. Nothing in this Agreement shall exclude or limit liability for fraudulent misrepresentation.

17.   TERMINATION FOR CAUSE

17.1   Subject to the Dispute Resolution Procedure, this Agreement may be terminated for cause in the following circumstances:

17.1.1   by either the Client or Outsourcer with immediate effect from service on the other party of written notice if the other party is in breach of any material obligation under this Agreement and, if the breach is capable of remedy, that party has failed to remedy such breach within [30] days of receipt of notice so to do (or within 7 days of receipt of such notice in respect of breach of payment obligations by the Client);

17.1.2   by either party with immediate effect from the date of service on the other of written notice if a resolution is passed or an order is made for the winding up of the other (otherwise than for the purpose of solvent amalgamation or reconstruction) or the other becomes subject to an administration order or a receiver or administrative receiver is appointed over or an encumbrancer takes possession of any of the other's property;

17.1.3 by either party with immediate effect from the date of service on the other of written notice if the other party ceases or threatens to cease to carry on business in the United Kingdom;

17.1.4 [by the Client at any time on one Month's prior written notice expiring at any time either before or after the initial period of [12 Months] in the event that the Client notifies the Outsourcer in writing of substantial concerns about the performance of the Outsourcer and (in the sole opinion of the Client) the situation is not remedied within three Months of the date on which the Client first notifies such concerns to the Outsourcer.]

18. CONSEQUENCES OF TERMINATION[13]

18.1 If this Agreement is terminated in whole or in part for any reason the Outsourcer shall, subject to payment of its reasonable fees, co-operate fully with the Client to ensure an orderly migration of the Services or replacement services to the Client or, at the Client's request, a new service provider.

18.2 Forthwith on termination of this Agreement, the Outsourcer shall return to the Client all Client IT together with all other materials, assets and other information provided to the Outsourcer, or if requested by the Client, the Outsourcer shall destroy the same (in the case of any software erasing it from the magnetic media on which it is stored) and certify in writing to the Client that the same has been destroyed.

18.3 Any termination of this Agreement (howsoever occasioned) shall not affect any accrued rights or liabilities of either party nor shall it affect the coming into force or the continuance in force of any provision hereof which is expressly or by implication intended to come into or continue in force on or after termination.

19. DATA PROTECTION

19.1 The Outsourcer undertakes to the Client that it will comply with obligations equivalent to the obligations of a 'data controller' under the provisions of the seventh data protection principle as set out in the Data Protection Act 1998, Schedule 1.

19.2 In addition, the Outsourcer:

19.2.1 warrants that it has appropriate technical and organisational measures in place against unauthorised or unlawful processing of personal data and against accidental loss or destruction of, or damage to, personal data held or processed by it and that it has taken reasonable steps to ensure the reliability of any of its staff who have access to personal data processed in connected with this Agreement;

19.2.2 undertakes that it will act only on the instructions of the Client in relation to the processing of any personal data in connection with this Agreement; and

19.2.3 undertakes to allow the Client access to any relevant premises on reasonable notice to inspect its procedures described above.

19.3 The obligations set out in this Clause shall remain in force not withstanding termination of this Agreement.

20. WAIVER

No delay, neglect or forbearance on the part of either party in enforcing against the other party any term or condition of this Agreement shall either be or be deemed to be a waiver or in any way prejudice any right of that party under this Agreement. No right, power or remedy in this Agreement conferred upon or reserved for either party is exclusive of any other right, power or remedy available to that party.

21. CUMULATION OF REMEDIES

Subject to the specific limitations set out in this Agreement, no remedy conferred by any provision of this Agreement is intended to be exclusive of any other remedy except as expressly provided for in this Agreement and each and every remedy shall be cumulative and shall be in addition to every other remedy given thereunder or existing at law or in equity by statute or otherwise.

22. SEVERABILITY

If any provision of this Agreement is prohibited by law or judged by a court to be unlawful, void or unenforceable, the provision shall, to the extent required, be severed from this Agreement and rendered ineffective as far as possible without modifying the remaining provisions of this Agreement, and shall not in any way affect any other circumstances of or the validity or enforcement of this Agreement.

23. PARTNERSHIP OR AGENCY

This Agreement shall not constitute or imply any partnership, joint venture, agency, fiduciary relationship or other relationship between the parties other than the contractual relationship expressly provided for in this Agreement.

24. NOTICES

24.1 All notices hereunder shall be in writing.

24.2   Notices shall be deemed to have been duly given:

24.2.1   when delivered, if delivered by courier or other messenger (including registered mail) during normal business hours of the recipient; or

24.2.2   when sent, if transmitted by fax or e-mail and a successful transmission report or return receipt is generated; or

24.2.3   on the fifth business day following mailing, if mailed by national ordinary mail, postage pre-paid; or

24.2.4   on the tenth business day following mailing, if mailed by airmail, postage pre-paid in each case addressed to the most recent address, e-mail address, or facsimile number notified to the other party.

25. DISPUTE RESOLUTION PROCEDURE AND GOVERNING LAW

25.1   This Agreement and all matters arising from it and any dispute resolutions referred to below shall be governed by and construed in accordance with English Law notwithstanding the conflict of law provisions and other mandatory legal provisions save that:

25.1.1   Either party shall have the right to sue to recover its fees in any jurisdiction in which the other party is operating or has assets, and

25.1.2   Either party shall have the right to sue for breach of its Intellectual Property and other proprietary information and trade secrets (whether in connection with this Agreement or otherwise) in any country where it believes that infringement or a breach of this Agreement relating to its Intellectual Property might be taking place. For the avoidance of doubt, the place of performance of this Agreement is agreed by the parties to be England.

25.2   Each party recognises that the other party's business relies upon the protection of its Intellectual Property and that in the event of a breach or threatened breach of its Intellectual Property, the other party will be caused irreparable damage and such other party may therefore be entitled to injunctive or other equitable relief in order to prevent a breach or threatened breach of its Intellectual Property.

25.3   With respect to all other disputes which are not Intellectual Property related pursuant to CLAUSES 25.1 and 25.2 above and its special rules the following procedures in CLAUSES 25.3 to 25.5 shall apply. Where there is a dispute the aggrieved party shall notify the other party in writing of the nature of the dispute with as much detail as possible about the deficient performance of the other party. A representative from senior management ('representatives') of each of the parties shall meet in person or communicate by telephone within five business days of the date of the written notification in order to reach an agreement about the nature of the deficiency and the corrective action to be taken by the respective parties. The representatives shall produce a report about the nature of the dispute in detail to their respective boards and if no agreement is reached on corrective action, then the chief executives of each party shall meet in person or by telephone, to facilitate an agreement within five business days of a written notice by one to the other. If the dispute cannot be resolved at board level within a further five business days, or if the agreed upon completion dates in any written plan of corrective action are exceeded, either party may seek its legal remedies as provided below.

25.4   If the parties cannot resolve a dispute in accordance with the procedure in CLAUSE 25.3 above, then thhy shall with the assistance of the Centre for Alternative Dispute Solution, seek to resolve the dispute or difference amicably by using an Alternative Dispute Resolution ('ADR') procedure acceptable to both parties before pursuing any other remedies available to them. If either party fails or refuses to agree to or participate in the ADR procedure or if in any event the dispute or difference is not resolved to the satisfaction of both parties within [90] days after it has arisen, the matter shall be settled in accordance with the procedure below.

25.5   If the parties cannot resolve the dispute by the procedure set out above, the parties shall irrevocably submit to the exclusive jurisdiction of the Courts of England and Wales for the purposes of hearing and determining any dispute arising out of this Agreement.

25.6   [While the dispute resolution procedure above is in progress and any party has an obligation to make a payment to another party or to allow a credit in respect of such payment, the sum relating to the matter in dispute shall be paid into an interest bearing deposit account to be held in the names of the relevant parties at a clearing bank and such payment shall be a good discharge of the parties' payment obligations under this Agreement. Following resolution of the dispute, whether by mediation or legal proceedings, the sum held in such account shall be payable as determined in accordance with the mediation or legal proceedings, and the interest accrued shall be allocated between the parties pro rata according to the split of the principal sum as between the parties.]

26. NON POACHING OF STAFF

The Client covenants with the Outsourcer that it shall not either during the term of this Agreement within a period of 6 months thereafter directly or indirectly entice away or endeavour to entice away from the Outsourcer any person who has during the previous 12 months been employed by the Outsourcer to provide Services in connection with this Agreement.

27. THIRD PARTY RIGHTS[14]

Subject to CLAUSE 16.7 above, a person who is not a party to this Agreement has no right under the Contracts (Rights of Third Parties) Act 1999 to enforce any term of this Agreement but this does not affect any right or remedy of a third party which exists or is available apart from such Act.

28. INTERPRETATION

28.1 In this Agreement unless the context otherwise requires:

    28.1.1 words importing any gender include every gender;

    28.1.2 words importing the singular number include the plural number and vice versa;

    28.1.3 words importing persons include firms, companies and corporations and vice versa;

    28.1.4 references to numbered clauses, Schedules and annexes are references to the relevant clause in or Schedule or annex to this Agreement;

    28.1.5 reference in any Schedule or annex to this Agreement to numbered paragraphs relate to the numbered paragraphs of that Schedule or annex;

    28.1.6 the headings to the clauses. Schedules, annexes and paragraphs of this Agreement will not affect the interpretation;

    28.1.7 any reference to an enactment includes reference to that enactment as amended or replaced from time to time and to any subordinate legislation or byelaw made under that enactment;

    28.1.8 any obligation on any party not to do or omit to do anything is to include an obligation not to allow that thing to be done or omitted to be done;

    28.1.9 If any party who agrees to do something will be deemed to fulfil that obligation if that party procures that it is done.

29. AMENDMENTS

This Agreement may not be released, discharged, supplemented, interpreted, amended, varied or modified in any manner except by an instrument in writing signed by a duly authorised Officer or representative of each of the parties hereto.

30. ENTIRE AGREEMENT

This Agreement supersedes all prior agreements, arrangements and undertakings between the parties and constitutes the entire agreement between the parties relating to the subject matter of this Agreement. However the obligations of the parties under any pre-existing non-disclosure agreement shall remain in full force and effect insofar as there is no conflict between the same. The parties confirm that they have not entered into this Agreement on the basis of any representation that is not expressly incorporated into this Agreement.

31. COUNTERPARTS

This Agreement may be executed in any number of counterparts or duplicates, each of which shall be an original, and such counterparts or duplicates shall together constitute one and the same agreement.

32. TIME IS OF THE ESSENCE

[Time shall be of the essence in this Agreement as regards any time, date or period mentioned in this Agreement or subsequently substituted as a time, date or period by agreement in writing between the parties.]

33. SUBCONTRACTING

With the prior written consent of the Client (such consent not to be unreasonably withheld or delayed) the Outsourcer may perform any or all of its obligations under this Agreement through agents or sub-contractors, provided that the Outsourcer shall remain liable for such performance and shall indemnify the Client against any loss or damage suffered by the Client arising from any act or omission of such agents or sub-contractors.

34. LANGUAGE

This Agreement is made only in the English language. If there is any conflict in the meaning between the English language version of this Agreement and any version or translation of this Agreement in any other language, the English language version shall prevail.

35. COSTS AND EXPENSES

Each party shall bear its own legal costs and other costs and expenses arising in connection with the drafting, negotiation, execution and registration (if applicable) of this Agreement.

36. SET-OFF

Where either party has incurred any liability to the other party, whether under this Agreement or otherwise, and whether such liability is liquidated or unliquidated, each party may set off the amount of such liability against any sum that would otherwise be due to the other party under this Agreement.

37. REMOTE ACCESS CONTROL[15]

If the Outsourcer has remote dial-up or modem access to any part of the Client's equipment in the course of performing its obligations under this Agreement, the following provisions of this Clause shall apply additionally. The Outsourcer:

37.1 will (a) only use a remote access method approved by the Client (such approval not to be unreasonably withheld or delayed); (b) provide the Client with the name of each individual who will have remote access to the Client's equipment and the phone number at which the individual may be reached during dial-in; (c) ensure that any computer used by its personnel to remotely access the Client's equipment will not simultaneously access the Internet or any other third party network while logged on to the Client's equipment;

37.2 further warrants and agrees that its personnel will not remotely access the Client's equipment from a networked computer unless the network is protected from all third party networks by a firewall that is maintained by a 7x24 administrative staff. Said firewall must be certified by the International Computer Security Association (ICSA) (or an equivalent certification as determined by the Client) if the connection to the Client's network is an ongoing connection such as frame relay or T1 line;

37.3 will restrict remote access by the Outsourcer to only the Client's test and/or training systems and nothing in this Clause shall entitle the Outsourcer to have access to the Client's live production copy of any software unless the parties have expressly agreed in writing that such access is to take place and the Client has given written confirmation of the date on which such access was implemented. The Outsourcer shall report in writing when such access takes places detailing all activities and actions taken during such access;

37.4 will comply at all times with the Data Protection Act 1998 in relation to any processing of personal data as a data processor on behalf of the Client and will indemnify the Client for any liability that the Client incurs as a result of a breach of this warranty.

AS WITNESS the hands of the duly authorised representatives of the parties on the -date first appearing above.

SCHEDULE

PART I

CLIENT DETAILS

PART II

AUTHORISED REPRESENTATIVE

For Outsourcer: [   ]

For Client: [   ]

PART III

EFFECTIVE DATE

PART IV

PREMISES

PART V

SERVICE MANAGERS

For Outsourcer: [   ]

For Client: [   ]

ANNEX A

[OUTSOURCER SERVICE LEVEL DOCUMENT]

ANNEX B

[IMPLEMENTATION PLAN]

ANNEX C

[SERVICE CHARGES AND SERVICE CREDITS]

Signed by [   ]

For and on behalf of

OUTSOURCER

In the presence of

Signed by [   ]

For and on behalf of

CLIENT

In the presence of

1 This Agreement describes an arrangement whereby certain activities, perhaps of an in-house department, are transferred to a third party. Such a third party uses the assets and people who had previously worked within that service department for the purpose of providing the same facilities back to the Client. There should be detailed provisions for the Outsourcer to take over the Client's premises, hardware and employees which are normally dealt with in a separate agreement.

2 Services to be provided need to be precisely defined and may be based on the Client's existing service level agreement.

3 Performance standards for the Services should be established as these will be used to monitor the standard of Services provided every 3 months (or other such regular period).

4 It may be necessary to add a clause regarding acceptance of any software to be provided by the Outsourcer. Acceptance tests may be necessary during the initial transition phase as the Outsourcer may need to demonstrate that it has appropriate infrastructures in

place to provide the Services. Once the Services are running, acceptance procedures may become unnecessary. However, if an acceptance clause is required, the following could be used:

'1. Where the Outsourcer supplies any software to the Client, such software shall be subject to acceptance by the Client pursuant to this Clause.

2. The Outsourcer shall supply to the Client immediately after installation of any software, test data which in the reasonable opinion of the parties is suitable to test whether the software performs to the specification agreed between the parties. The Client shall not be entitled to object to such test data or expected results unless the Client can demonstrate to the Outsourcer that they are not suitable for testing the software as aforesaid, in which event the Outsourcer shall make any reasonable amendments to such test data and expected results as the Client may request. Subject to the receipt of such test data and expected results, the Client shall process such data, in the presence of the Outsourcer or its Authorised Representative, by way of acceptance testing within [7] days after such receipt at a time mutually convenient to both parties.

3. The Client shall accept the software immediately after the Outsourcer has demonstrated that the software has correctly processed the test data by achieving the expected results.

4. In the event of failure of the software to pass the tests referred to in CLAUSE 2 above the Outsourcer shall, and in any event not later than [3] days following notification of the relevant failure, at its own expense correct the errors in the software and notify the Client that it is ready to repeat the tests and such tests shall be repeated within [7] days after such notice at a time mutually convenient to both parties.

5. In the event of failure of the software to pass the repeat tests referred to in CLAUSE 3 above, the Client shall be entitled to terminate this Agreement pursuant to CLAUSE [   ] or, by notice to the Client, within [3] days require the Outsourcer to correct the errors in the software in which event the provisions of CLAUSE 4 shall, mutatis mutandis, apply.

Notwithstanding the above, installation of the software shall be deemed to be completed and the software shall be deemed to be accepted upon successful execution of the tests referred to above or when the software has been put into operational use, whichever is the earlier.'

5   Usually most of the Client's responsibilities relate to ensuring that all of their assets can be transferred to the Outsourcer. However, this is not dealt with here as it should be dealt with in a separate agreement.

6   According to the degree of reliance the Client places on the particular Outsourcer and the services it provides, the Outsourcer's right to suspend the Services may be particularly onerous for the Client. Therefore, it is essential to provide that the Services cannot be suspended where there is a bona fide dispute over payment.

7   Where the Outsourcer fails to provide the level of service required by the Client, most contracts allow for the Client to either claw back some of the fees or permit early termination of the contract.

8   If the Client decides to terminate the contract, finding a new contractor or taking the Services back in- house may take considerable time and effort. This clause states that the agreement will expire at the end of one month. Realistically it will take the Client much longer to either find a new contractor or take the Services in-house. Therefore, perhaps a longer notice period with the Outsourcer should be agreed whereby the Outsourcer continues to provide the Services until they can be transferred.

9   Depending on the length of the contract, it may become necessary for the Client to require changes in order to reflect changes in his business. Accordingly, the parties could agree a tariff which is to be applied once a change request is made and also a provision for reference to an independent expert in the event that the parties do not agree on the changes or the price for such a change. If the contract is to subsist for a long period of time, the Outsourcer's duties should include an obligation to upgrade the relevant systems over the course of the contract period. This is often referred to as 'technology refresh' and could be included in the description of the Services to be provided.

10 The Client may require ownership of all intellectual property rights in any software or other material created by the Outsourcer under this Agreement. If this is the case, CLAUSES 11.1 and 11.2 need to be amended accordingly.

11 This force majeure clause is short and general. It may be appropriate to insert a more detailed force majeure clause such as:

'Notwithstanding anything else contained in this Agreement, neither party shall be liable for any delay in performing its obligations hereunder if such delay is caused by circumstances beyond its reasonable control (including without limitation any delay caused by any act or omission of the other party) provided however that any delay by a sub-contractor or supplier of the party so delaying shall not relieve the party from liability for delay except where such delay is beyond the reasonable control of the sub-contractor or supplier concerned. Subject to the party so delaying promptly notifying the other party in writing of the reasons for the delay (and the likely duration of the delay), the performance of such party's obligations shall be suspended during the period that the said circumstances persist and such party shall be granted an extension of time for performance equal to the period of the delay. Save where such delay is caused by the act or omission of the other party (in which event the rights, remedies and liabilities of the parties shall be those conferred and imposed by the other terms of this Agreement and by law) any costs arising from such delay shall be borne by the party incurring the same.'

In general, the more a client negotiates extended warranties into a contract the more an outsourcer will seek to limit the impact of those warranties under the Limitation of Liability clauses.

Since *St Albans City and District Council v International Computers Ltd* [1996] 4 All ER 481, CA, it has become clear that where a client suffers loss as a result of faulty software, and no terms and conditions vary the implied terms of merchantability or fitness for purpose, then any attempt by the supplier to limit its liability for such loss below what is deemed to be a reasonable figure (perhaps such a figure being linked to the suppliers' insurance cover for such losses) will be unavailable or even void as an unfair contract term. As a consequence clients are more likely now to demand that any limit of liability in favour of the supplier for losses other than indirect should be linked to a reasonable sum of at least £1,000,000 (the usual minimum limit for which insurance cover would be granted under a suitable policy).

However, in *Watford Electronics Ltd v Sanderson CFL Ltd* [2001] EWCA Civ 317, [2001] 1 All ER (Comm) 696, CA, it was held that provisions in a contract for the supply of computer software that both excluded the supplier's liability for indirect loss, as well as limiting the damages recoverable to the amount paid by the customer under the contract, satisfied the reasonable test under the Unfair Contract Terms Act 1977, s 11. On appeal the court decided that the contract had been negotiated between experienced businessmen of equal bargaining power and skill and, as such, the supplier limitation clause was reasonable.

13 It may be that detailed provisions are needed here in order to migrate the Services to an alternative supplier or in-house in order to ensure the continuity of the Services. The licence granted by the Outsourcer to the Client in CLAUSE 11.2 should allow the Client to continue using any intellectual property created by the Outsourcer when the Services are transferred.

Before the Contracts (Rights of Third Parties) Act 1999 (the 'Act') it was the case that a person who was not a party to a contract (a 'third party') could not enforce any rights under the contract. Similarly, a contract could not impose any obligations or liabilities on a third party.

However, the Act attempts to draw a balance between the freedom of the parties to vary a contract and the interests of a third party. The Act provides that a contractual clause benefiting a third party (eg the promisee's subsidiary company or sub-contractor or employee) will be straightforwardly enforceable by that third party if:

• the contract expressly provides that he may; or
• a term in the contract purports to confer a benefit on him (unless on a proper construction of the contract it appears that the parties did not intend the term to be enforceable by the third party).

It is therefore prudent to include a clause to the effect of excluding the provisions of the Act. By doing so it ensures that any rights of third parties are not deemed to be enforceable by them. This is particularly the case where the parties are companies and may have subsidiaries or conversely parent companies.

15 Quite often Outsourcers need access to the Client's equipment or system remotely. If this is the case, this clause protects the Client's software, equipment and any data the Client holds under the Data Protection Act 1998. Without such a clause, it may be difficult to hold the Outsourcer responsible if the Client suffers loss as a result of damage to its software or equipment or is held liable for disclosure of its users' personal data to a third party who manages to gain access to the Client's systems through the remote dial in or modem access granted to the Outsourcer.

21 Agreement for website hosting[1]

This Web Hosting Services Agreement ('the Agreement') is made the [ ] day of [ ] [ ] BETWEEN

[ ] of [ ] ('the Company') and

[ ] of [ ] ('the Customer')[2]

WHEREBY the parties agree as follows:

WEB HOSTING SERVICES
Services:[3]
Limits:[4]
Maintenance:[5]

FEES[6]

IN WITNESS whereof Company and Customer have caused this Agreement to be executed by their respective duly authorised officers or representatives, effective as on the day and year first written.

Company [ ]	Customer [ ]
By [ ]	By [ ]
(Authorised Signature)	(Authorised Signature)
Name [ ]	Name [ ]
(Print Name)	(PrintName)
Title [ ]	Title [ ]

1. **Services** The Company agrees to provide to Customer the Web Hosting Services more particularly described above ('Web Hosting Services') on the terms described herein. The Company agrees to place the 'HomePage' created by the Company for the Customer in accordance with this Agreement on the computer server owned or operated by the Company and allow storage of information received by the Customer or from the general public on such server on a monthly basis subject

to the limits as more particularly described above and further agrees to provide on a monthly basis those maintenance services described above.

All Web Hosting Services under this Agreement shall be performed in accordance with the Company's standard procedures so long as such procedures do not conflict with the express terms of this Agreement. Nothing under this Agreement shall affect the Customer's statutory rights in particular but without limitation those under the Consumer Credit Act 1974 or the Data Protection Act 1998.

2. **Fees** The Customer agrees to pay to the Company the fees specified above for the Web Hosting Services ('Web Hosting Fees'). Web Hosting Fees are due upon execution of this Agreement unless otherwise provided above. Any additional fees shall be invoiced on a monthly basis and shall be paid within 30 days after the date of invoice.

3. **Taxes** All payments due hereunder are net of applicable taxes.

4. **Term** This Agreement shall be effective commencing on the date stated overleaf for a period of one year and thereafter from year to year subject to earlier termination as set forth in this section unless and until either party gives to the other not less than 30 days' notice in writing. Either party may terminate this Agreement without notice upon the other party's breach of any term, condition or obligation hereunder if such breach is not remedied (if remediable) (i) within 10 days from the date of written notice with regard of any monetary obligation, and (ii) within 30 days from the date of written notice with regard to any other breach.

5. **Customer responsibilities** In addition to the obligations of the Customer as otherwise specified in this Agreement, the Customer shall be solely responsible for the following:

   5.1 the accuracy and content of any information provided by the Customer to the Company[8]; and

   5.2 any information, programs and other information that the Customer receives as a result of the use of the Services, including without limitation, the entire responsibility of any losses of data, programs, breaches of security, viruses and disabling or harmful devices that the Customer may download or otherwise experience as a result of the Customer's use of the service.[9]

   5.3 The Customer shall notify the Company at least seven days in advance if it intends to change its business details or stop providing any of the goods or services being offered through the Company.

   5.4 The Customer agrees to use the Services in a manner consistent with any and all applicable laws and regulations.[10]

6. **Ownership** All materials, documentation, computer programs, inventions (whether or not patentable), pictures, audio, video, artistic works and all works of authorship, including all worldwide rights therein under patent, copyright, trade secret or other property right,

created or developed by Company while providing Web Hosting Services (collectively, 'Work Product') are owned by the Company. The Company shall not be liable to return any artwork or other material supplied by the Customer for the purposes of Web Hosting Services. Work Product shall not include the Confidential Information (defined below) of Customer. If ownership of all right, title and interest of the intellectual property rights in the Work Product shall not otherwise vest exclusively in the Company, the Customer hereby assigns to the Company and upon the future creation thereof automatically assigns to the Company without further consideration, the ownership of all Work Product.[11]

7. **Limited warranty** The Company warrants that for a period of 90 days from the date of first installation of the Customer's completed HomePage on the server described above, the coding of such HomePage shall be reasonably HTML-compliant. Notwithstanding the foregoing, the sole and exclusive remedy for a breach of the warranties contained in this CLAUSE 7 shall be that the Company shall replace the nonconforming coding to make such HomePage reasonably HTML-compliant. The Customer acknowledges that HTML is an industry standard that contains some ambiguous provisions and that does not completely address all issues associated with the coding of Homepages accessible via the World Wide Web. The Customer also acknowledges that HTML is a standard that will be amended from time to time and that not all 'browsers' used by third parties to access the World Wide Web implement HTML in the same way. Variations in HTML coding associated with ambiguities or revisions to the HTML standard or variations among World Wide Web browsers shall not be the basis for a claim of breach of the Company's warranties under this Agreement. The warranties described in this CLAUSE 7 are subject to the limitations of liability described below. Except as provided in this CLAUSE 7, the Company does not make any express or implied warranties with respect to the services or any products provided under this Agreement, including but not restricted to the implied warranties of merchantability and fitness for a particular purpose. Some jurisdictions do not allow the exclusion of implied warranties, so the above exclusion may not apply to the Customer.[12]

8. **Limitation of liability** In no event (death or personal injury excepted) will the Company be liable to the Customer for any indirect, incidental or consequential damages arising out of the Web Hosting Services or any products provided under this Agreement, even if the Company has been advised of the possibility of such damages. Some jurisdictions do not allow the limitation or exclusion of liability for incidental or consequential damages, so the above limitation or exclusion may not apply to Customer. The Company's liability to the Customer for actual damages for any cause whatsoever, regardless of the form of the action, will be strictly limited to 125% of the Fees paid for the prior 12 months.[13]

9. **Limitations of service** The Company does not guarantee that the Customer or any third parties will be able to access the HomePage created by the Company at any particular time. The Company access

services are provided on an 'as-is, as-available' basis. The Customer acknowledges that the need for routine maintenance and error correction may result in down time and that the Company cannot control the timing or volume of attempts to access the Company's server.

10. CONFIDENTIAL INFORMATION

10.1 Each party hereto:

10.1.1 shall use the same care and discretion, but in no event less than reasonable care and discretion, to prevent disclosure, publication or dissemination of the other party's Confidential Information (defined below) as it employs with similar information of its own; and

10.1.2 shall not use, reproduce, distribute, disclose or otherwise disseminate the Confidential Information except in connection with the performance of its obligations under this Agreement.

10.2 As used herein the term 'Confidential Information' means any and all data and information relating to the business of the disclosing party (i) of which the receiving party becomes aware as a consequence of or through this Agreement; (ii) which has value to the disclosing party and is not generally known by its competitors; (iii) which is treated by the disclosing party as confidential; and (iv) which has been reduced to tangible form and marked clearly and conspicuously with a legend identifying its confidential or proprietary nature, provided, however, that Confidential Information does not include any data or information which is already known to the receiving party, or which (1) has become generally known to the public through no wrongful act of the receiving party; (2) has been rightfully received by the receiving party from a third party without restriction on disclosure and without, to the knowledge of the receiving party, a breach of an obligation of confidentiality running directly or indirectly to the other party hereto; (3) has been disclosed pursuant to a requirement of a governmental agency or of law without similar restrictions or other protection against public disclosure, or is required to be disclosed by operation of law;[14] (4) is independently developed by the receiving party without use, directly or indirectly, of the Confidential Information received from the other party hereto; or (5) is furnished to a third party by the disclosing party hereunder without restrictions on the third party's right to disclose the information. Confidential Information may include, but is not limited to, information relating to the products, processes or financial affairs of the disclosing party.

11. **Data transmission** The Company may collect, hold, control, use and transmit data obtained from and about the Customer and visitors to the website in the course of providing the Web Hosting Services and the website. By signing the Web Hosting Services Agreement the Customer agrees to such data being so used and further agrees that it may be transmitted to others in accordance with the Company's registration under the Data Protection Act 1998.

12.   **Force majeure** Neither party shall have any liability under or be deemed to be in breach of this Agreement for any delays or failures in performance of this Agreement which result from circumstances beyond the reasonable control of that party. If such circumstances continue for a continuous period of more than 6 months, either party may terminate this

Agreement by written notice to the other party.[15]

13. GENERAL

13.1   Nothing in this Agreement is intended to or shall operate to create a partnership or joint venture of any kind between the parties, or to authorise either party to act as agent for the other, and neither party shall have authority to act in the name or on behalf of or otherwise to bind the other in any way (including but not limited to the making of any representation or warranty, the assumption of any obligation or liability and the exercise of any right or power).

13.2   In any action or proceeding to enforce rights under this Agreement, the prevailing party will be entitled to recover costs and legal fees.

13.3   All notices under this Agreement shall be in writing and shall be deemed given when personally delivered, when sent by confirmed fax, or three (3) days after being sent by pre-paid FIRST CLASS POST to the address of the party to be noticed as set forth herein or such other address as such party last provided to the other by written notice.

13.4   Neither party shall have any right or ability to assign, transfer, or sublicense any obligations or benefit under this Agreement without the written consent of the other (and any such attempt shall be void), except that a party may assign and transfer this Agreement and its rights and obligations hereunder to any third party who succeeds to substantially all its business or assets.

13.5   This Agreement is drawn up in the English language [except that some of the schedules may in whole or in part be drawn up in the [   ] language]. If this Agreement is translated into another language, the English language text shall in any event prevail.

13.6   If any portion of this Agreement is illegal or unenforceable, such portion(s) shall be limited to exclude from this Agreement to the minimum extent required and the balance of this Agreement shall remain in full force and effect and enforceable.

13.7   This Agreement supersedes all prior agreements, arrangements and undertakings between the parties and constitutes the entire agreement between the parties relating to the subject matter hereof and can only be modified or waived by a subsequent written agreement signed by both parties. However, the obligations of the parties under any pre-existing non-disclosure agreement shall remain in full force and effect insofar as there is no conflict between the same. The parties confirm that they have not entered into this Agreement on the basis of any representation that is not expressly incorporated into this Agreement.

13.8 The parties confirm their intent not to confer any rights on any third parties by virtue of this Agreement and accordingly the Contracts (Rights of Third Parties) Act 1999 shall not apply to this Agreement.

13.9 This Agreement shall be governed by and construed in accordance with the laws of England and Wales and the parties accept the non-exclusive jurisdiction of the English courts over any claim or matter arising under or in connection with this Agreement [or the legal relationships established by this Agreement].

1   This agreement is between the website owner and its ISP or other host. The larger ISPs are likely to insist on use of their own standard terms. Use this precedent to compare and where appropriate request amendments to such standard terms.

2   The Company is the host. The Customer is the website owner.

3   The description of the services which are the subject matter of the agreement may include reference to IP numbers. See CLAUSE 1 below for the contractual obligations with respect to the performance of services, and CLAUSE 9 for limitations on the availability of service. Where substantial e-commerce transactions are envisaged on the website, the service description and any limitations should be carefully drafted in detail and reviewed from a technical, legal and financial standpoint.

4   The host may wish to place limits on the traffic which it is undertaking to process at the agreed price.

5   Maintenance service specification should include response times and contact details.

6   This will list the amounts payable for the relevant period of each of the services. Where the host is in a different jurisdiction from the website owner, consider whether to specify the currency in which fees are payable. See CLAUSE 2 for payment terms.

7   Such notice will be adequate if the website owner owns and controls the domain name registration, since migration to another host will be relatively straightforward. Where the host owns or controls the domain name, and/or proprietary platform software on which the website sits and depends, consider much more extensive notice periods for non-renewal/cancellation. This is especially likely in those instances where the website is to be hosted by a party which has been involved in the design and development of the website.

8   The case law both in the United Kingdom and internationally so far suggests that hosts are able to avoid liability for content except where illegality has been specifically drawn to their attention, and this simple customer obligation does no more than reflect the common law position. However, concern about certain aspects of the development of the Internet has prompted some pressure groups to call for extending liability for content to hosts. The contractual position of both website owners and hosts should be kept under review.

9   This contract is silent as to the responsibilities of the parties for security. It is usual for website owners themselves to carry responsibility for appropriate firewalls, passwords and other security measures for their sites.

10 This CLAUSE commits the website owner to a substantial obligation: consumer (B to C) sites, in particular, may be subject to consumer law in jurisdictions all over the world, which may not be avoidable by means of website terms and conditions. The host's risk/liability for the actions and omissions of the website owner may not be great (but see NOTE 8 above) but it is inevitable that the host, with many and disparate parties doing business on its servers, will seek to allocate such risks of legal compliance to its customers.

11 See NOTE 7 above. The existence of substantial Work Product (as defined) may make it difficult to migrate to another host.

12 The clause only warrants HTML compliance. If your website uses other engines or languages as an integral part of the offering, consider extending the warranty to cover such other technology.

13 This *St Albans City and District Council v International Computers Ltd* ([1996] 4 All ER 481, CA)-proof clause may not be necessary for web hosting agreements; it may be sufficient after *Watford Electronics Ltd v Sanderson CFL Ltd* [2001] EWCA Civ 317, [2001] 1 All ER (Comm) 696, CA to identify a mutually acceptable limit such as the Fees paid under the agreement, and specify that both parties consider such a limit to be reasonable. For further discussion, see the notes to the software licence agreement.

14 Under the Anti-terrorism, Crime and Security Act 2001, ISPs are now obliged to retain and if requested make available traffic data to several United Kingdom government authorities. Provisions requiring a party to warn the other of any request for such data would be illegal; at the time of writing, Home Office guidelines on the retention of such data under the terms of this Act are yet to be published.

15 This is a widely-drawn force majeure clause which will favour the host. Consider whether to specify third parties (such as certain of the host's agents, suppliers, such as Network Providers, or sub-contractors) for exclusion from the operation of this clause.

22 Website software development, licensing and support agreement[1]

THIS AGREEMENT is made the [ ] day of [ ] [ ]

BETWEEN[2]

(1) (*Customer*) whose [registered office or principal place of business] is at (*address*) and whose facsimile ('fax') number is (*number*) ('the Customer'); and

(2) (*Developer*) whose [registered office or principal place of business] is at (*address*) and whose facsimile ('fax') number is (*number*) ('the Developer').

RECITALS

A.   The Customer wishes to establish a world wide website in relation to its business.

B.   The Developer has agreed to develop a world wide website for the Customer and in particular to develop certain software programs and applications for such website and to provide other services in accordance with the terms and conditions of this Agreement.

IT IS AGREED as follows:

I.   DEFINITIONS

1.1   **'Acceptance Date'** means the date on which the Software is accepted (or deemed to be accepted) by the Customer pursuant to CLAUSE 6.3;

1.2   **'Acceptance Tests'** means the tests designed to determine specified in the Agreement and for such other tests as may be agreed in writing between the Customer and Developer;

1.3   **'Additional Services'** means any additional services requested by the Customer to be provided by the Developer;

1.4   **'Change Request'** means a request for a change made by the Customer or Developer;

1.5 **'Customer Group'** is defined as the Customer, the Customer's parent company holding a majority interest in the Customer, and such parent company's majority owned subsidiaries;

1.6 **'Confidential Information'** shall include, but not necessarily be limited to, all information which is not publicly known including the business, finances, technology (including without limitation the Software and the Documentation) trade secrets, and any other commercially sensitive information of either party regardless of its nature;

1.7 **'Customer Representative'** means the person for the time being or from time to time duly appointed by the Customer and notified in writing to the Developer to act as the Customer's representative for the purpose of the Agreement;

1.8 **'Documentation'** means the documentation set out in SCHEDULE A;

1.9 **'Development Services'** means software development, procurement, consulting and computer programming services for the purpose of creating the Website Pages for use on the World Wide Web service of the Internet;

1.10 **'Distinctive Customer Features'** means any elements which do not form part of the generic functionality of the Software and which implement visual features or layouts created at the specific request of the Customer;

1.11 **'Implementation Plan'** means the timing and sequence of events agreed between the Customer and Developer for the performance of the Agreement, as set out in SCHEDULE B;

1.12 **'Intellectual Property Rights'** means all copyright and other intellectual property rights, howsoever arising and in whatever media, whether or not registered, including (without limitation) patents, trademarks, service marks, trade names, registered design and any applications for the protection or registration of these rights and all renewals and extensions thereof throughout the world;

1.13 **'Payment Schedule'** means the payment schedule set out in SCHEDULE C;

1.14 **'Planned Acceptance Date'** means the date specified in the Implementation Plan on which the Software is intended to be accepted by the Customer in accordance with this Agreement;

1.15 **'Price'** means the fixed, all inclusive price for the provision of the Software, the Licence and the Documentation;

1.16 **'Project'** means the development, delivery and testing of the Software;

1.17 **'Rates'** means the rates set out in SCHEDULE C;

1.18 **'Software'** means the software being developed or customised by the Developer to the specification of the Customer forming a major part of the website materials;

1.19 **'Specified Equipment'** means the configuration of computer or computers, including operating systems, on which the Software is to function as specified in SCHEDULE A;

1.20 **'Specification'** means the specification of the Software set out in SCHEDULE A;

1.21 **'Support Services'** means those services specified in SCHEDULE D;

1.22 **'System'** means collectively the Specified Equipment and the Software;

1.23 **'Warranty Period'** means the period of two (2) months after the Acceptance Date;

1.24 **'Website Pages'** means the World Wide Web site comprising all pages including graphics, audio-visual effects and other digital content as detailed in the Specification.

2. SERVICES TO BE PROVIDED

2.1 The Developer hereby agrees during the continuance of this Agreement to:

2.1.1 supply the Development Services to the Customer;

2.1.2 install and test the Software on the Specified Equipment;

2.1.3 provide the Documentation;

2.1.4 provide the Support Services and carry out any Additional Services agreed by the parties.

2.2 The Developer shall carry out the obligations set out in CLAUSE 2.1 in accordance with the Implementation Plan.

2.3 The Developer shall supply to the Customer the object and source code of the Software when requested by the Customer.

3. PERSONNEL

3.1 The Developer shall ensure that all of its personnel engaged in the Project:

3.1.1 have the necessary skills, expertise and diligence to undertake such work and will conform to the professional standards generally observed in the computer industry for similar services;

3.1.2 comply with the provisions in this Agreement relating to Confidential Information.

4. CUSTOMER'S OBLIGATIONS

4.1 The Customer shall:

4.1.1 make available to the Developer, free of charge, such computer facilities (including but not limited to unhindered access to the Specified Equipment), office and secretarial services as are necessary to enable the Developer to carry out its obligations under this Agreement;

4.1.2 ensure that its employees and other independent contractors co-operate reasonably with the Developer and its employees in carrying out the Project;

4.1.3 promptly furnish the Developer with such information and documents as it may reasonably request for the proper performance of its obligations under this Agreement; and

4.1.4 ensure that the Customer Representative is available as reasonably required by the Developer.

5. CHANGE CONTROL

5.1 If either party identifies a requirement for a change, a Change Request will be sent to the other party detailing the change requirements. If sent by the Developer, the Change Request shall state the effect such a change shall have on the Software, the Implementation Plan and the Price. If sent by the Customer, the receipt of the Change Request by the Developer will constitute a request to the Developer to state in writing the effect such a change shall have on the Software, the Implementation Plan and the Price. The Developer shall use all reasonable endeavours to supply the necessary details within 10 working days from receipt of the Change Request or such other period as may be agreed.

5.2 Where a change to the Price is required, the rates used as the basis for the additional cost for the Change Request shall be the Rates as detailed in SCHEDULE C. The parties will then decide whether or not to implement the change. If the change is implemented, the amended Software, Implementation Plan or Price shall then become the Software, Implementation Plan and Price for the purpose of this Agreement.

5.3 The Developer shall not implement any changes unless instructed to do so by the Customer Representative.

6. ACCEPTANCE TESTS

6.1 The Acceptance Tests shall be agreed by the parties in accordance with the Implementation Plan.

6.2 The Developer shall use its reasonable endeavours to ensure that the Software is ready for acceptance testing by the Planned Acceptance Date. In any event, Developer shall give to the Customer 5 working days' prior notice in writing of the date when it will be ready to commence the Acceptance Tests. Unless otherwise agreed, the Acceptance Tests shall take place on the sixth working day after such notice has been given.

6.3 The Customer shall accept the Software immediately after the Software has passed the Acceptance Tests.

6.4 If the Software fails to pass the Acceptance Tests, repeat tests shall be carried out until the earlier of the following occurs:

6.4.1 the Software passes the Acceptance Tests;

6.4.2 the Acceptance Tests have been repeated three times; or

6.4.3 a 30 day period from the Planned Acceptance Date has expired.

6.5 If the Software has not been accepted by the Customer on or after the occurrence of the events specified in CLAUSES 6.4.2 or 6.4.3 then the Customer may by written notice to the Developer terminate this Agreement and, upon any such termination, the Customer will promptly return to the Developer all Software, Documentation and other equipment or Confidential Information belonging to the Developer.

6.6 If at any time the Customer shall commence live running of the whole or any part of the Software (other than in the Acceptance Tests) then the Customer shall be deemed to have accepted the Software.

7. REPRESENTATIVES AND PROGRESS MEETINGS

7.1 Each party shall nominate in writing upon the signing of this Agreement, the person who will act as its representative for the purposes of this Agreement and who will be responsible for providing any information which may be required by the other party to perform its obligations under this Agreement.

7.2 The parties shall procure that their respective representatives will meet at least once a [month] between the date of this Agreement and the Planned Acceptance Date to discuss and minute the progress of the Project.

8. WARRANTIES[3]

8.1 The Developer warrants that:

8.1.1 it is entitled to enter into this Agreement and that it is entitled to grant the licence pursuant to CLAUSE 9 in accordance with this Agreement;

8.1.2 the Software shall:

8.1.2.1 perform substantially in accordance with the Specification on the Specified Equipment, minor interruptions and errors excluded;

8.1.2.2 be date compliant in accordance with the definition set out in SCHEDULE E; and

8.1.2.3 support the introduction of the Euro currency unit.

8.1.3 the Documentation and any training offered by the Developer with respect to the System will provide users with adequate instructions to enable them effectively to operate and use the System;

8.1.4 the Development Services will be carried out in a professional manner conforming to best industry practices.

8.2 The Developer shall not be liable under CLAUSE 8.1.2 if a failure to meet the warranties set out therein is caused by:

8.2.1 software other than the Software running on the Specified Equipment; or

8.2.2 modifications or customisation made by or on behalf of the Customer to the Software, without the authorisation of the Developer.

8.3 If the Developer receives a written notice from the Customer identifying a breach of the warranties set out in CLAUSE 8.1, or otherwise becomes aware of its failure to comply with the warranties set out in CLAUSE 8.1, then the Developer shall, at its own expense, promptly remedy such breach or failure provided that the Developer shall have no liability or obligations under the warranties unless it shall have received written notice of the defect or error within the Warranty Period.

8.4 To the extent permitted by applicable law, the Developer:

8.4.1 excludes all conditions, terms, representations (other than fraudulent or negligent representations) and warranties relating to the Software (and any new release) and the Documentation, either express or implied, that are not expressly stated herein, including but not limited to any implied warranties relating to quality, fitness for any particular purpose or ability to achieve a particular result;

8.4.2 makes no warranty that the Software is error free or that its use will be uninterrupted and the Customer acknowledges and agrees that the existence of such errors shall not constitute a breach of this Agreement;

8.4.3 does not give any warranty in respect of third party products. The Developer will pass on to the Customer the benefit of any third party warranty supplied by a third party manufacturer or supplier.

9. GRANT OF RIGHTS[4]

9.1 On payment in full of the Price, the Developer grants to the Customer (and to all members of the Customer Group who agree to the terms of this licence) a non-exclusive, non-transferable right to use the Software and the Documentation on any processor owned or controlled by the Customer or a member of the Customer Group. The Customer may not disclose or make available Software to any entity other than members of the Customer Group who have agreed to these licence terms nor permit others to use it except the Customer's employees and agents who may use it only on the Customer's behalf within the limits of the application licence and who are deemed to have agreed to such terms.

9.2   The Developer shall not be involved in the creation of an interactive website that uses tradenames, trademarks, colours, visual features or layouts that might result in such site being confused by Internet users with any site maintained by or for the benefit of the Customer and using the Software and Documentation.

10.   PROPRIETARY RIGHTS

10.1   The Intellectual Property Rights in the Software (including the source and object code) and the Documentation shall be and remain vested in the Developer apart from the Distinctive Customer Features. All Intellectual Property Rights in the Distinctive Customer Features (including the source and object code) and the Documentation shall be and remain vested in the Customer.

10.2   The Developer will indemnify the Customer on demand against all costs, claims, demands, expenses and liabilities of whatsoever nature arising out of or in connection with any claim that the use or possession of the Software infringes the intellectual property rights of any third party subject to the following conditions:

10.2.1   The Customer shall promptly notify the Developer in writing of any allegations of infringement of which it is aware and shall not make any admissions without the Developer's prior written consent;

10.2.2   The Customer, at the Developer's request and expense, shall allow the Developer to conduct and/or settle all negotiations and litigation resulting from any such claim subject to the Developer taking over such conduct within 10 working days after being notified of the claim and providing that the Developer diligently pursues the settlement of any such claim; and

10.2.3   The Customer shall, at the request of the Developer, afford all reasonable assistance with such negotiations or litigation, and shall be reimbursed by the Developer on demand for all expenses incurred in doing so.

10.3   If the Customer's use or possession of the Software or any part thereof in accordance with this Agreement, is held by a court of competent jurisdiction to constitute an infringement of a third party's intellectual property rights, then the Developer shall promptly and at its own expense:

10.3.1 procure for the Customer the right to continue using and possessing the Software or the infringing part; or

10.3.2 modify or replace the Software (or part thereof) without detracting from the overall performance of the Software, so as to avoid the infringement.

11. PAYMENT

11.1 The Price and the Rates shall be paid by the Customer as provided in SCHEDULE C.

11.2 The Price and other charges payable under this Agreement are exclusive of any applicable VAT and other sales tax which shall be payable by the Customer at the rate and in the manner prescribed by law against submission of a valid tax invoice.

11.3 Any charges payable by the Customer under this Agreement in addition to the Price shall be paid within [30] days after the receipt by the Customer of the Developer's invoice therefor.

11.4 The Developer shall have the right to charge interest on overdue invoices at the rate of [4%] per annum above the base rate of (*insert name of bank*) Bank plc, calculated from the date when payment of invoice becomes due for payment up to and including the date of actual payment whether before or after judgment.[5]

11.5 The Customer shall also pay or procure the payment to the Developer of all reasonable travelling and other out-of-pocket expenses incurred in the course of the Project subject to a maximum amount of £ [　] per day excluding all travel costs.

11.6 With effect from the beginning of each year commencing on the Acceptance Date, the Developer may increase the Rates in effect during the previous year provided that not less than 10 working days' prior written notice has been given to the Customer by the Developer.

11.7 A one-off bonus of £ [　] shall be payable by the Customer to the Developer in the event that the Developer [completes Phases 1 and 2 (as specified in SCHEDULE C to this Agreement) in accordance with the Specification and within the timeframes specified in SCHEDULE C].

12. LIABILITY

12.1 The Developer shall during the term of this Agreement maintain employer's liability, third party liability, product liability and professional negligence insurance cover in respect of its liabilities arising out of or connected with this Agreement, such cover to be to a minimum value of [ONE MILLION POUNDS] and with an insurance company of repute. The Developer shall on request supply copies of the relevant certificates of insurance to the Customer as evidence that such policies remain in force. The Developer undertakes to use reasonable commercial efforts to pursue claims under such insurance policies.

12.2   The Developer shall indemnify the Customer for personal injury or death caused by the negligence of its employees in connection with the performance of their duties hereunder or by defects in any product supplied pursuant to this Agreement.

12.3   The Developer will indemnify the Customer for direct damage to tangible property caused by the negligence of its employees in connection with the performance of their duties hereunder or by defects in any product supplied pursuant to this Agreement. The Customer's total liability under this clause shall be limited to [£500,000] for any one event or series of connected events.

12.4   Save in respect of claims for death or personal injury arising from the Developer's negligence, in no event will the Developer be liable for any damages resulting from loss of data or use, lost profits, loss of anticipated savings, nor for any damages that are an indirect or secondary consequence of any act or omission of the Developer whether such damages were reasonably foreseeable or actually foreseen.

12.5   Except as provided above in the case of personal injury, death and damage to tangible property, the Developer's maximum liability to the Customer under this Agreement or otherwise for any cause whatsoever (whether in the form of the additional cost of remedial services or otherwise) will be for direct costs and damages only and will be limited to the greater of:

   12.5.1   the sum for which the Licensor carries comprehensive insurance cover pursuant to CLAUSE 12.1 above; or

   12.5.2   a sum equivalent to the price paid to the Licensor for the products or services that are the subject of the Licensee's claim, plus damages limited to 25% of the same amount for any additional costs directly, reasonably and necessarily incurred by the Licensee in obtaining alternative products and/or services.

12.6   The parties hereby acknowledge and agree that the limitations contained in this CLAUSE 12 are reasonable in light of all the circumstances.[6]

12.7   The Customer's statutory rights as a consumer (if any) are not affected. All liability that is not expressly assumed in this Agreement is hereby excluded. These limitations will apply regardless of the form of action, whether under statute, in contract or tort including negligence or any other form of action. For the purposes of this clause, the 'Developer' includes its employees, sub-contractors and suppliers who shall all have the benefit of the limits and exclusions of liability set out above in terms of the Contracts (Rights of Third Parties) Act 1999.

13.   CONFIDENTIALITY

13.1   Both parties to this Agreement undertake, except as provided below, to treat as confidential and keep secret all information marked 'confidential' or which may reasonably be supposed to be confidential, including, without limitation, information contained or embodied in the Software, the Specification and other information supplied by the Customer or Developer (in this Agreement collectively referred to as 'the Information') with the same degree of care as it employs with regard to its own confidential information of a like nature and in any event in accordance with best current commercial security practices, provided that, this clause shall not extend to any information which was rightfully in the possession of either party prior to the commencement of the negotiations leading to this Agreement or which is already public knowledge or becomes so at a future date (otherwise than as a result of a breach of this clause).

13.2 Neither party shall without the prior written consent of the other party divulge any part of the other party's Information to any person except:

13.2.1 to their own employees and then only to those employees who need to know the same;

13.2.2 to either parties' auditors, HM Inspector of Taxes, HM Customs and Excise, a court of competent jurisdiction, governmental body or applicable regulatory authority and any other persons or bodies having a right, duty or obligation to know the business of the other party and then only in pursuance of such right, duty or obligation;

13.2.3 any person who is for the time being appointed by either party to maintain the Specified Equipment on which the Software is for the time being used (in accordance with the terms of the licence) and then only to the extent necessary to enable such person to properly maintain the Specified Equipment.

13.3 Both parties undertake to ensure that persons and bodies referred to in CLAUSE 13.2 are made aware prior to the disclosure of any part of the Information that the same is confidential and that they owe a duty of confidence to the other party.

13.4 Each party to this Agreement shall promptly notify the other party if it becomes aware of any breach of confidence by any person to whom it divulges all or any part of the Information and shall give the other party all reasonable assistance in connection with any proceedings which the other party may institute against such person for breach of confidence.

13.5 The foregoing obligations as to confidentiality shall remain in full force and effect notwithstanding any termination of the licence or this Agreement.

13.6 The provisions of this Clause shall survive the termination of this Agreement but the restrictions contained in this Clause shall cease to apply to any information which may come into the public domain otherwise than through unauthorised disclosure.

13.7 Nothing in this CLAUSE 13 shall prevent the Developer from exploiting any inventions or software that it develops during the source of this Agreement.

14. TERMINATION

14.1 The Customer may terminate this Agreement at any time by giving at least [30] days' prior written notice to the Developer.

14.2 The Developer may terminate this Agreement forthwith on giving notice in writing to the Customer if:

14.2.1 the Customer commits any serious breach of any term of this Agreement (and if the breach is capable of being remedied) shall have failed, within [30] days after receipt of a request in writing from the Developer to do so, to remedy the breach (such request to contain a warning of the Developer's intention to terminate); or

14.2.2 the Customer permanently discontinues use of the Software.

14.3 [Forthwith upon the termination of this Agreement, the Customer shall return to the Developer the Software and all copies of the whole or any part thereof or, if requested by the Developer, shall destroy the same (in the case of the Software by erasing them from the magnetic media on which they are stored) and certify in writing to the Developer that they have been destroyed. PROVIDED THAT the Developer may extract and store any Customer data upon a separate media for continuity purposes.][7]

14.4 Any termination of this Agreement (howsoever occasioned) shall not affect any accrued rights or liabilities of either party nor shall it effect the coming into force or the continuance in force of any provision in this Agreement which is expressly or by implication intended to come into or continue in force on or after such termination.

15. DATA PROTECTION[8]

The parties hereby undertake to comply with the provisions of the Data Protection Act 1998 and any related legislation insofar as the same relates to the provisions and obligations of this Agreement.

16. INTERPRETATION

16.1 In this Agreement unless the context otherwise requires:

16.1.1 words importing any gender include every gender;

16.1.2 words importing the singular number include the plural number and vice versa;

16.1.3 words importing persons include firms, companies and corporations and vice versa;

16.1.4 references to numbered clauses and Schedules are references to the relevant clause in or Schedule to this Agreement;

16.1.5 reference in any Schedule to this Agreement to numbered paragraphs relate to the numbered paragraphs of that Schedule;

16.1.6   the headings to the clauses, Schedules and paragraphs of this Agreement will not affect the interpretation;

16.1.7   any reference to an enactment includes reference to that enactment as amended or replaced from time to time and to any subordinate legislation or byelaw made under that enactment;

16.1.8   any obligation on any party not to do or omit to do anything is to include an obligation not to allow that thing to be done or omitted to be done;

16.1.9   any party who agrees to do something will be deemed to fulfil that obligation if that party procures that it is done.

16.2   In the case of conflict or ambiguity between any provision contained in the body of this Agreement and any provision contained in any Schedule, the provision in the body of this Agreement shall take precedence.

17. AGENCY, PARTNERSHIP

This Agreement shall not constitute or imply any partnership, joint venture, agency, fiduciary relationship or other relationship between the parties other than the contractual relationship expressly provided for in this Agreement.

18. AMENDMENTS

This Agreement may not be released, discharged, supplemented, interpreted, amended, varied or modified in any manner except by an instrument in writing signed by a duly authorised officer or representative of each of the parties hereto.

19. ANNOUNCEMENTS

No party shall issue or make any public announcement or disclose any information regarding this Agreement unless prior written consent has been obtained from the other party.

20. ASSIGNMENT

20.1   This Agreement is personal to the parties and, subject to CLAUSE 20.2 below, neither this Agreement nor any rights, licenses or obligations under this Agreement, may be assigned by either party without the prior written approval of the other party.

20.2   Notwithstanding the foregoing, either party may assign this Agreement to any acquirer of all or of substantially all of such party's equity securities, assets or business relating to the subject matter of this Agreement or to any entity controlled by, that controls, or is under common control with a party to this Agreement. Any attempted assignment in violation of this clause will be void and without effect.

21. ENTIRE AGREEMENT

This Agreement supersedes all prior agreements, arrangements and undertakings between the parties and constitutes the entire agreement between the parties relating to the subject matter of this Agreement. However the obligations of the parties under any pre-existing non-disclosure agreement shall remain in full force and effect insofar as there is no conflict between the same. The parties confirm that they have not entered into this Agreement on the basis of any representation that is not expressly incorporated into this Agreement.

22. FORCE MAJEURE[9]

Neither party shall have any liability under or be deemed to be in breach of this Agreement for any delays or failures in performance of this Agreement which result from circumstances beyond the reasonable control of that party. If such circumstances continue for a continuous period of more than [6 months], either party may terminate this Agreement by written notice to the other party.

23. NOTICES

23.1   All notices hereunder shall be in writing.

23.2   Notices shall be deemed to have been duly given:

23.2.1   when delivered, if delivered by courier or other messenger (including registered mail) during normal business hours of the recipient; or

23.2.2   when sent, if transmitted by fax or e-mail and a successful transmission report or return receipt is generated; or

23.2.3   on the fifth business day following mailing, if mailed by national ordinary mail, postage pre-paid; or

23.2.4   on the tenth business day following mailing, if mailed by airmail, postage pre-paid,

in each case addressed to the most recent address, e-mail address, or facsimile number notified to the other party.

24. SCHEDULES

The provisions of SCHEDULE[S] (A–D) to this Agreement shall form part of this Agreement as if set out here.[10]

25. SEVERANCE

If any provision of this Agreement is prohibited by law or judged by a court to be unlawful, void or unenforceable, the provision shall, to the extent required, be severed from this Agreement and rendered ineffective as far as possible without modifying the remaining provisions of this Agreement, and shall not in any way affect any other circumstances of or the validity or enforcement of this Agreement.

26. SUCCESSORS AND ASSIGNEES

26.1 This Agreement shall be binding upon, and enure to the benefit of, the parties and their respective successors and permitted assignees, and references to a party in this Agreement shall include its successors and permitted assignees.

26.2 In this Agreement references to a party include references to a person:

26.2.1 who for the time being is entitled (by assignment, novation or otherwise) to that party's rights under this Agreement (or any interest in those rights); or

26.2.2 who, as administrator, liquidator or otherwise, is entitled to exercise those rights;

and in particular those references include a person to whom those rights (or any interest in those rights) are transferred or pass as a result of a merger, division, reconstruction or other reorganisation involving that party. For this purpose, references to a party's rights under this Agreement include any similar rights to which another person becomes entitled as a result of a novation of this Agreement.

27. WAIVER

No delay, neglect or forbearance on the part of either party in enforcing against the other party any term or condition of this Agreement shall either be or be deemed to be a waiver or in any way prejudice any right of that party under this Agreement. No right, power or remedy in this Agreement conferred upon or reserved for either party is exclusive of any other right, power or remedy available to that party.

28. COUNTERPARTS

This Agreement may be executed in any number of counterparts or duplicates, each of which shall be an original, and such counterparts or duplicates shall together constitute one and the same Agreement.

29. TIME IS OF THE ESSENCE

Time shall be of the essence in this Agreement as regards any time, date or period mentioned in this Agreement or subsequently substituted as a time, date or period by agreement in writing between the parties.

30. SUBCONTRACTING

With the prior written consent of the Customer (such consent not to be unreasonably withheld or delayed) the Developer may perform any or all of its obligations under this Agreement through agents or sub-contractors, provided that the Developer shall remain liable for such performance and shall indemnify the Customer against any loss or damage suffered by the Customer arising from any act or omission of such agents or sub-contractors.

31. LANGUAGE

This Agreement is made only in the English language. If there is any conflict in the meaning between the English language version of this Agreement and any version or translation of this Agreement in any other language, the English language version shall prevail.

32. COSTS AND EXPENSES

Each party shall bear its own legal costs and other costs and expenses arising in connection with the drafting, negotiation, execution and registration (if applicable) of this Agreement.

33. SET-OFF

Where either party has incurred any liability to the other party, whether under this Agreement or otherwise, and whether such liability is liquidated or unliquidated, each party may set off the amount of such liability against any sum that would otherwise be due to the other party under this Agreement.

34. THIRD PARTIES[11]

Subject to CLAUSE 12.7 above, a person who is not a party to this Agreement has no right under the Contracts (Rights of Third Parties) Act 1999 to enforce any term of this Agreement but this does not affect any right or remedy of a third party which exists or is available apart from such Act.

35. PROPER LAW AND JURISDICTION[12]

35.1 This Agreement and all matters arising from it and any dispute resolutions referred to below shall be governed by and construed in accordance with English Law notwithstanding the conflict of law provisions and other mandatory legal provisions save that:

35.1.1 The Developer shall have the right to sue to recover its fees in any jurisdiction in which the Customer is operating or has assets, and

35.1.2 The Developer shall have the right to sue for breach of its intellectual property rights and other proprietary information and trade secrets ('IPR') (whether in connection with this Agreement or otherwise) in any country where it believes that infringement or a breach of this Agreement relating to its IPR might be taking place. For the avoidance of doubt, the place of performance of this Agreement is agreed by the parties to be England.

35.2   Each party recognises that the other party's business relies upon the protection of its IPR and that in the event of a breach or threatened breach of IPR, the other party will be caused irreparable damage and such other party may therefore be entitled to injunctive or other equitable relief in order to prevent a breach or threatened breach of its IPR.

35.3   With respect to all other disputes which are not IPR related pursuant to CLAUSES 35.1 and 35.2 above and its special rules the following procedures in CLAUSES 35.3 to 35.5 shall apply. Where there is a dispute the aggrieved party shall notify the other party in writing of the nature of the dispute with as much detail as possible about the deficient performance of the other party. A representative from senior management ('representatives') of each of the parties shall meet in person or communicate by telephone within five business days of the date of the written notification in order to reach an agreement about the nature of the deficiency and the corrective action to be taken by the respective parties. The representatives shall produce a report about the nature of the dispute in detail to their respective boards and if no agreement is reached on corrective action, then the chief executives of each party shall meet in person or by telephone, to facilitate an agreement within five business days of a written notice by one to the other. If the dispute cannot be resolved at board level within a further five business days, or if the agreed upon completion dates in any written plan of corrective action are exceeded, either party may seek its legal remedies as provided below.

35.4   If the parties cannot resolve a dispute in accordance with the procedure in CLAUSE 35.3 above, then they shall with the assistance of the Centre for Alternative Dispute Solution, seek to resolve the dispute or difference amicably by using an Alternative Dispute Resolution ('ADR') procedure acceptable to both parties before pursuing any other remedies available to them. If either party fails or refuses to agree to or participate in the ADR procedure or if in any event the dispute or difference is not resolved to the satisfaction of both parties within [90] days after it has arisen, the matter shall be settled in accordance with the procedure below.

35.5   If the parties cannot resolve the dispute by the procedure set out above, the parties shall irrevocably submit to the exclusive jurisdiction of the Courts of England and Wales for the purposes of hearing and determining any dispute arising out of this Agreement.

SCHEDULE A

SOFTWARE SPECIFICATION

SCHEDULE B

IMPLEMENTATION PLAN

SCHEDULE C

PAYMENT SCHEDULE

SCHEDULE D

SUPPORT SERVICES

1 This agreement is intended to be used where a Customer requires the development of a website which will incorporate customer-specific software applications and other requirements.

2 It is worthwhile considering as to whether the parties to the contract are the correct contracting parties. Many providers 'ring fence' their intellectual property rights by placing ownership of software and other assets into non-trading holding companies which may be situated offshore or in other jurisdictions separate from the jurisdiction in which the trading or supplying-provider company is actually based. If ownership of intellectual property rights and other assets are vested in such a manner, then the customer needs to be sure that the provider company with whom it is contracting is capable of making the guarantees and warranties in the agreement and is also in a position to control source code if it is placed in escrow. If the contracting provider's company is not the owner of the software then the customer may need to ask for some further assurances from the provider that the true owner of the software can provide the necessary escrow arrangements and performance warranties which only the true owner can give. In the case of small software developers, often the developer company is no more than the corporate embodiment of one or two essential programmers and the customer may want to contract not only with the developer company, but also with its director/shareholder programmers in order to obtain the maximum guarantees and warranties as to performance, quality and the like of the services being provided.

3 There has already been much discussion as to whether or not software is 'goods' for the purposes of implied warranties under the Sale of Goods Act 1979, s 14 and on the whole, the more mass market the software, the more it is likely to be seen as 'goods'. The more the software is delivered on an integration and commission basis the more likely it is that the software will be treated as 'services', thereby weakening the degree of implied warranties.

   In general the more that a customer negotiates extended warranties into a contract the more the supplier will seek to limit the impact of those warranties under the Limitation of Liability Clauses.

4 As a general rule, rights not granted expressly or by implication in the grant clause are not conveyed by the licence agreement. Of course, rights are sometimes conveyed and restrictions are often located in other sections of an agreement. Also, additional rights may be conveyed verbally after contract execution, implied through the parties' course of dealing with one another, or added to a contract in an addendum.

   Licensees are well advised to co-ordinate the life of their software grant and the life of their agreement in a manner that makes sense in the transaction in question.

5 In certain jurisdictions excessive amounts of interest charged may be viewed as unreasonable, usury or a 'penalty' thus invalidating the provision.

6 Since *St Albans City and District Council v International Computers Ltd* [1996] 4 All ER 481, CA, it has become clear that where a Customer suffers loss as a result of faulty software and no terms and conditions vary the implied terms of merchantability or fitness for purpose, then any attempt by the supplier to limit its liability for such loss below what is deemed to be a reasonable figure (perhaps such a figure being linked to the suppliers' insurance cover for such losses) will be unavailable or even void as an unfair contract term. As a consequence Customers are more likely now to demand that any limit of liability in favour of the supplier for losses other than indirect should be linked to a reasonable sum of at least £1,000,000 (the usual minimum limit for which insurance

cover would be granted under a suitable policy). As to limitation of liability generally see Paragraph 89 [2619] ante.

However in *Watford Electronics Ltd v Sanderson CFL Ltd* [2001] EWCA Civ 317, [2001] All ER (Comm) 696, CA, it was held that provisions in a contract for the supply of computer software that both excluded the supplier liability for indirect loss, as well as limiting the damages recoverable to the amount paid by the customer under the contract, satisfied the reasonable test under the Unfair Contract Terms Act 1977, s 11. On appeal the court decided that the contract had been negotiated between experienced businessmen of equal bargaining power and skill and as such, the supplier limitation clause was reasonable.

7 On expiry, the Customer should not be in the position where it does not own its website which it has paid the Developer to develop. At the very least it should have a perpetual licence to use the website for a nominal fee. In addition the Customer may well want to demand escrow of key source code to the website and its software. For examples of escrow agreements see the NCC Precedents at APPENDIX 26.

8 UK law requires any business which processes data about living individuals to be notified with the Office of the Information Commissioner. Under the Data Protection Act 1998, s 1(1) (the Act) data is defined as information which:

(a) is being processed by means of equipment operating automatically in response to instructions given for that purpose;

(b) is recorded with the intention that it should be processed by means of such equipment;

(c) is recorded as part of a relevant filing system or with the intention that it should form part of a relevant filing system; and

(d) does not fall within paragraph (a), (b) or (c) but forms part of an accessible record as defined in section 68 of the Act.

Accessible records are health records, educational records and accessible public records defined in SCHEDULE 12 to the Act.

9 This force majeure clause is short and general. It may be appropriate to insert a more detailed force majeure clause such as:

'Notwithstanding anything else contained in this Agreement, neither party shall be liable for any delay in performing its obligations hereunder if such delay is caused by circumstances beyond its reasonable control (including without limitation any delay caused by any act or omission of the other party) provided however that any delay by a sub-contractor or supplier of the party so delaying shall not relieve the party from liability for delay except where such delay is beyond the reasonable control of the sub-contractor or supplier concerned. Subject to the party so delaying promptly notifying the other party in writing of the reasons for the delay (and the likely duration of the delay), the performance of such party's obligations shall be suspended during the period that the said circumstances persist and such party shall be granted an extension of time for performance equal to the period of the delay. Save where such delay is caused by the act or omission of the other party (in which event the rights, remedies and liabilities of the parties shall be those conferred and imposed by the other terms of this Agreement and by law):

• any costs arising from such delay shall be borne by the party incurring the same;

• either party may, if such delay continues for more than 10 weeks, terminate this Agreement forthwith giving notice in writing to the other by reason of such termination.'

10 As many contracts are varied or amended during their life cycle it is important that all Schedules are agreed to and signed or initialled by the parties so that there can be no dispute as to the totality of the contract and its contents

11 Before the Contracts (Rights of Third Parties) Act 1999 (the Act) it was the case that a person who was not a party to a contract (a third party) could not enforce any right under the contract. Similarly, a contract could not impose any obligations or liabilities on a third party.

However the Act attempts to draw a balance between the freedom of the parties to vary a contract and the interests of the third party. The Act means that a contractual clause benefiting a third party (eg the promisee's subsidiary company or sub-contractor or employee) will be straightforwardly enforceable by that third party if:

• the contract expressly provides that he may; or

• where a term in the contract purports to confer a benefit on him (unless on a proper construction of the contract it appears that the parties did not intend the term to be enforceable by the third party).

It is therefore prudent to include a clause to the effect of excluding the provisions of the Act. By doing so it ensures that any rights of third parties are not deemed to be enforceable by them. This is particularly the case where the parties are companies and may have subsidiaries or conversely parent companies.

12 An example of another dispute settlement clause is:

'Any dispute which may arise between the parties concerning this Agreement shall be determined as follows:

(1) If the dispute shall be of a technical nature relating to the functions or capabilities of the Licensed Program Materials or any similar or related matter then such a dispute shall be referred for final settlement to an expert nominated jointly by the parties or failing such nomination within Fourteen (14) days after either party's request to the other therefore nominated at the request of either party by the President for the time being of the British Computer Society. Such expert shall be deemed to act as an expert and not as an arbitrator. His decision shall (in the absence of clerical or manifest error) be final and binding on the parties and whose costs shall be borne between the parties in equal shares unless he determines that the conduct of either party is such that such party should bear all of such fees.

(2) In any other case the dispute shall be determined by the High Court of Justice in England and the parties hereby submit to the exclusive jurisdiction of that Court for such purposes.'

23 Licence agreement for link between web sites

THIS AGREEMENT[1] is made the [ ] day of [ ] [ ]

BETWEEN:

(1) (*web site owner*) whose registered office is at (*address*) and whose facsimile ('fax') number is (*number*) ('the Owner')

(2) (*linker*) whose registered office is at (*address*) and whose facsimile ('fax') number is (*number*) ('the Linker').

RECITALS

A. The Owner owns a web site at the URL (*web site address*) ('Owner URL') comprising *inter alia* proprietary text and images [and offering [goods] [and] [services] for sale].[2]

B. The Linker owns a web site at the URL (*web site address*) ('Linker URL') and wishes to post on it a hypertext link to Owner Web Site.

C. The Owner has agreed to grant to the Linker a licence to post such a link on the terms and conditions set out in this Agreement.

NOW IT IS AGREED as follows:

I. DEFINITIONS

In this Agreement, unless the context otherwise requires, the following expressions have the following meanings:

1.1 **'Advertising revenue'**[3] means the aggregate amounts collected plus the fair market value of other compensation received by or on behalf of the Owner arising from the licence or sale of promotional, advertising, sponsorship or marketing services or rights directly related to the Owner Web Site;

1.2 **'Designated Page'** means the page that a User's web browser will generate as the result of requesting the following URL: [*home page URL*], (otherwise known as '[*Home*] Page' in the Linker Web Site), or any new URL with which the Linker replaces the above-stated URL Link in the Linker Web Site);

1.3   **'Effective Date'** means the date of this Agreement;

1.4   **'Impression'** means an occasion in which a User clicks on the Link, resulting in the Linked Page being generated on his web browser;

1.5   **'Link'** means the hypertext link to the Linked Page, in the form of a GIF Button detailed in SCHEDULE B;[4]

1.6   **'Linked Page'**[5] means the page on the Owner Web Site at URL: [*www. linkedpage.com*] that a User's web browser will generate as the result of clicking on the Link;

1.7   **'Linker Purchasers'** means Users making purchases [via the Owner Web Site] [from the Owner];[6]

1.8   **'Linker Web Site'** means the web pages on the World Wide Web site operated by or on behalf of the Linker and generated as a result of requesting the Linker URL;

1.9   **'Owner Web Site'** means the web pages on the World Wide Web site operated by or on behalf of the Owner and generated as a result of requesting the Owner URL, or any new URL with which the Owner replaces the above-stated URL;

1.10   **'Silent User Information'** means User Information not voluntarily provided by the User, including but not limited to, navigational information;[7]

1.11   **'Transaction Revenues'** means the aggregate amounts collected plus the fair market value of other compensation received by or on behalf of the Owner arising from the sale, licensing, distribution or provision of any information, good or service sold through the Owner web site;

1.12   **'User Information'** means (i) navigational information, including but not limited to usage of other hyperlinks within or available through Owner' site, (ii) transactional information, including but not limited to billing information, including products purchased and method of payment, and (iii) user's Internet address and/or other identifying information such as actual name or address;

1.13   **'User'** means a user accessing the Owner Web Site through the Link;

1.14   In this Agreement unless the context otherwise requires:

        1.14.1   words importing any gender include every gender;

        1.14.2   words importing the singular number include the plural number and vice versa;

        1.14.3   words importing persons include firms, companies and corporations and vice versa;

        1.14.4   references to numbered clauses and Schedules are references to the relevant clause in or Schedule to this Agreement;

        1.14.5   reference in any Schedule to this Agreement to numbered paragraphs relate to the numbered paragraphs of that Schedule;

1.14.6 the headings to the clauses, Schedules and paragraphs of this Agreement will not affect the interpretation;

1.14.7 any reference to an enactment includes reference to that enactment as amended or replaced from time to time and to any subordinate legislation or byelaw made under that enactment;

1.14.8 any reference to an English legal term for any action, remedy, method of judicial proceeding, legal document, legislation, legal status, court, official or any legal concept or thing shall, in respect of any jurisdiction other than England, be deemed to include a reference to what most nearly approximates in that jurisdiction to the English legal term; and

1.14.9 any obligation on any party not to do or omit to do anything is to include an obligation not to allow that thing to be done or omitted to be done.

2. LICENCE

The Owner hereby grants to the Linker a non-exclusive licence to (i) place the Link on the Designated Page and (ii) establish a link to the Linked Page. The foregoing licence shall be limited to the purposes of establishing the link as more fully described below.

3. LINK

3.1 The Linker agrees to incorporate the Link into the Linker Web Site in a prominent position on the Designated Page of the Linker Web Site.

OR

The Linker agrees to place the Link on the Designated Page of the Linker Web Site on a rotating basis with links to no more than [ ] other sites. Rotation will occur following each access to the Designated Page. The Linker will structure the rotation so that the Link appears on [ ] % of new visits to the Designated Page.[8]

3.2 The Link shall appear on the Designated Page such that it is visible to a user when loaded into and displayed by a web browser at 640 by 480 standard VGA resolution running so that the browser occupies the full screen of the VGA monitor. [The Link shall appear in the Designated Page such that the user will see the entire Link without scrolling.]

3.3 The Link provided by the Owner shall be [ ] pixels by [ ] pixels in size. [The Linker shall not include any HTML code in the file used to generate the Designated Page that will alter the size of the Link.] [The Linker may make stylistic and editorial changes to the format shown in SCHEDULE B, but will ensure that the relative size and prominence of the Link retains a reasonable equivalence to its size and prominence as depicted in SCHEDULE B.] The Owner agrees to provide the necessary graphic and textual material for the Link as a computer-readable file in a compatible file format.[9]

4. CONTROL OF WEB SITE CONTENT

4.1 [Both parties agree to notify each other of any significant changes to the content or structure of their web sites within [ ] days of the change. A party may terminate this Agreement on [ ] days' notice after any significant change to the other party's web site.] [The Linker agrees that all changes to the [Linker Web Site] [Designated Page] are subject to the prior review and approval of the Owner, and that failure to obtain such approval constitutes a material breach of this Agreement. The Owner agrees to conduct its review and give its approval in a reasonably timely manner.]

4.2 [The Linker agrees to provide initially only those hypertext links specified in SCHEDULE B. Subsequent links are subject to the prior approval of the Owner, which shall not be unreasonably withheld. Failure to obtain such approval shall constitute a material breach of this Agreement.]

4.3 [The Linker agrees that, for the term of this Agreement, it will not provide links from its site to entities whose product(s) [directly] compete with those of the Owner.]

5. [FRAMING

The Linker shall [not] be authorised to display the Linked Page within a frame of the Linker Web Site [provided that such frame shall in no way obscure any part of the Linked Page[10]].

6. REVENUE[11] AND PAYMENT

6.1 [The Owner hereby agrees to pay the Linker a monthly linking fee of £ [ ] for each month during the term of this Agreement.]

6.2 [The Owner hereby agrees to pay the Linker an annual licence fee of £ [ ] as consideration for the rights granted by the Linker to the Owner.]

6.3 [The Owner agrees to pay the Linker [ ] % of all Transaction Revenues received by the Owner.]

6.4 [The Owner agrees to pay the Linker [ ] % of all Advertising Revenues received by the Owner.]

OR

[The Owner agrees to pay the Linker [ ] % of the product of:

6.4.1 all Advertising Revenues; and

6.4.2 the quotient of the number of Impressions by Users to the Owner web site divided by the number of Impressions by all users of Party's X's web site.]

6.5 Within [thirty (30)] days following the close of each calendar quarter for so long as the Owner receives Transaction Revenue on which fees are payable pursuant to CLAUSES 6.1 to 6.4 hereof, the Owner shall pay the Linker all amounts due for such quarter and shall submit with payment a statement providing in reasonable detail the basis for such payment.

6.6 All fees are exclusive of any VAT or other taxes or duties levied on such sums and the Owner undertakes to pay and indemnify the Linker in respect of any such VAT or other taxes or duty properly chargeable to the Owner by the Linker.

6.7 The Linker shall have the right at its expense, on sixty (60) business days' written notice during normal business hours to inspect the site logs of the Owner Web Site and the directly relevant books and records of the Owner for the purpose of verifying the statements provided by the Owner pursuant to CLAUSE 6.5 above.[12] [Any such audit shall be performed by independent certified public accountants reasonably acceptable to the Owner.] [In the event that any shortfall in payment to the Linker is found exceeding [ten (10)] per cent of the total due to the Linker for the audited reporting period, the Owner shall reimburse the Linker for the reasonable fees of the accountants conducting the audit.

7. RECORDING[13]

[The Linker will electronically register and record each time a [web browser on the Internet] [a unique IP address] requests the Link. The Linker will report the recorded information to the Owner on a monthly basis. [The parties agree not to artificially inflate the number of reported requests through their own visits to the linked web page or other surreptitious means].]

OR

[The Linker will engage an independent third party to electronically monitor and record requests for the Link, and report the recorded information to the Linker on a monthly basis. To the extent possible, the Owner will direct the third party to employ measures that record web site visits by individual users, rather than automated or repeated accesses. The Owner agrees to co-operate with the third party to ensure that tracking software is installed and operational on the Linker web site. Linker agrees not to interfere with the operation of the tracking software.]

8. USER INFORMATION

8.1 [The parties agree that the Owner shall not collect and store any User Information not voluntarily provided by the User, including but not limited to, navigational information.]

8.2 [The parties agree that the Owner may collect, store and use any Silent User Information. If the Owner chooses to collect, store or use any Silent User Information, the Owner must clearly and prominently disclose this to User in that User's first visit through the Link and explain what information is collected, what information is stored and what information is used for what purposes. The Owner must also disclose whether the User can 'opt out' of any portion or all of the collection, storage or usage of Silent User Information and provide a simple method to do so.]

8.3   Information that is knowingly and voluntarily provided by the User to the Owner may be collected, stored and used for the Owner's own internal marketing or research efforts but only if the Owner prominently and adequately discloses to User the intended uses of the User Information prior to User's disclosure. This disclosure requirement can be satisfied by prominently placing the disclosure information on the registration screen, the ordering screen, or other such relevant screen.

8.4   [The Owner shall provide to the Linker monthly reports of User Information.]

8.5   [The Linker notwithstanding, the Owner may not disclose User Information of any kind to any third party without valid legal process and only in compliance with all applicable laws. In the event applicable law prevents the collection, processing use or disclosure of User Information, the provisions affected shall be construed so as to comply with such laws or regulations.]

OR

8.6   [The parties agree that the Agreement does not restrict the gathering, use, dissemination of information concerning users collected by either party during the term of the Agreement, [except as otherwise provided herein]. Each party is responsible for determining whether any such gathering, use, or dissemination it performs is consistent with applicable laws and regulations.]

8.7   The parties hereby undertake to comply with the provisions of the Data Protection Act 1998 and any related legislation insofar as the same relates to the provisions and obligations of this Agreement and the provisions of this CLAUSE 8 shall be construed as to so comply.

9.   FORCE MAJEURE

Neither party shall have any liability under or be deemed to be in breach of this Agreement for any delays or failures in performance of this Agreement which result from circumstances beyond the reasonable control of that party. If such circumstances continue for a continuous period of more than 6 months, either party may terminate this Agreement by written notice to the other party.[14]

10.   REPRESENTATIONS AND WARRANTIES

10.1   The Linker represents and warrants to the Owner that, as of the date of execution of this Agreement: (i) the Linker has duly registered the domain name of its web site with all applicable authorities; and (ii) the content and materials which the Linker has placed within the Linker's

Web Site does not and will not infringe upon or violate any copyright, patent, trademark or other proprietary right of a third party, or any applicable law, regulation or non-proprietary third-party right.[15]

10.2　The Owner represents and warrants to the Linker that: (i) the graphical representation of the Link does not infringe upon or violate any copyright, patent, trademark or other proprietary right of any third party or any applicable law, regulation or non-proprietary third-party right.

10.3　Each party hereby disclaims any representations or warranties, express or implied, regarding the subject matter of this agreement, including any implied warranties of quality, fitness for a particular purpose, non-infringement and implied warranties arising from course of dealing or course of performance.

11.　TERM/TERMINATION

11.1　This Agreement shall commence on the Effective Date and shall continue for [*insert number of years*] year(s) thereafter until or unless terminated in accordance with any of the provisions of this Clause or any other Clause of this Agreement.

11.2　Either party may terminate this Agreement if the other party commits any serious breach of any term of this Agreement and (in the case of a breach capable of being remedied) shall have failed, within [30] days after the receipt of a request in writing from the Licensor to do so, to remedy the breach (such request to contain a warning of the Licensor's intention to terminate).

11.3　Forthwith upon the termination of the Agreement the Linker shall remove the Link from the Designated Page.

11.4　SECTIONS [8.7, 9, 11, 12] shall survive termination of this Agreement.

12.　LIMITATION ON LIABILITY

12.1　Neither party nor their affiliates shall be liable or obligated under any section of this Agreement or under contract, negligence, strict liability or other legal or equitable theory for any special, incidental or consequential damages including without limitation damages for loss of profits and/or loss of data.

12.2　Nothing in this Agreement shall be so construed as to limit or exclude either party's liabilities in respect of death or personal injury howsoever caused.

13.　GENERAL

13.1　Nothing in this Agreement is intended to or shall operate to create a partnership or joint venture of any kind between the parties, or to authorise either party to act as agent for the other, and neither party shall have authority to act in the name or on behalf of or otherwise to bind the other in any way (including but not limited to the making of any representation or warranty, the assumption of any obligation or liability and the exercise of any right or power).

13.2 In any action or proceeding to enforce rights under this Agreement, the prevailing party will be entitled to recover costs and attorneys fees.

13.3 All notices under this Agreement shall be in writing and shall be deemed given when personally delivered, when sent by confirmed fax, or three (3) days after being sent by prepaid FIRST CLASS POST to the address of the party to be noticed as set forth herein or such other address as such party last provided to the other by written notice.

13.4 Neither party shall have any right or ability to assign, transfer, or sublicense any obligations or benefit under this Agreement without the written consent of the other (and any such attempt shall be void), except that a party may assign and transfer this Agreement and its rights and obligations hereunder to any third party who succeeds to substantially all its business or assets.

13.5 This Agreement is drawn up in the English language [except that some of the schedules may in whole or in part be drawn up in the [ ] language]. If this Agreement is translated into another language, the English language text shall in any event prevail.

13.6 If any portion of this Agreement is illegal or unenforceable, such portion(s) shall be limited to excluded from this Agreement to the minimum extent required and the balance of this Agreement shall remain in full force and effect and enforceable.

13.7 This Agreement supersedes all prior agreements, arrangements and undertakings between the parties and constitutes the entire agreement between the parties relating to the subject matter hereof and can only be modified or waived by a subsequent written agreement signed by both parties. However, the obligations of the parties under any pre-existing non-disclosure agreement shall remain in full force and effect insofar as there is no conflict between the same. The parties confirm that they have not entered into this Agreement on the basis of any representation that is not expressly incorporated into this Agreement.

13.8 The parties confirm their intent not to confer any rights on any third parties by virtue of this Agreement and accordingly the Contracts (Rights of Third Parties) Act 1999 shall not apply to this Agreement.

13.9 This Agreement shall be governed by and construed in accordance with the laws of England and Wales and the parties accept the non-exclusive jurisdiction of the English courts over any claim or matter arising under or in connection with this Agreement [or the legal relationships established by this Agreement].

ACCEPTED AND AGREED TO:

LINKER   OWNER

By [ ]   By [ ]

Title [   ]   Title [   ]

Date [   ]   Date [   ]

SCHEDULE A

LINK SPECIFICATIONS

'GIF-1'	Size (Pixels)	Place Example Here

SCHEDULE B

LINKER WEB SITE HYPERTEXT LINKS

Link   URL

1 The linker brings traffic to the owner which has value for the owner. The essence of a linking agreement is to specify the consideration payable for the traffic ('users') generated by the link. The value may be in terms of opportunities to sell or actual sales of goods or services to the user, or in terms of marketing exposure to the user. Many contracts reward the linker both for traffic (a payment per visitor/user) and for sales generated by the link (a commission on sales). By the use of cookies it is possible to tie a sale achieved on a subsequent visit to the original 'customer introduction' by the linker, and so sales commission may be payable on all subsequent sales to a visitor/user originally introduced by the link.

2 It may be worth specifying in detail the operational functions of the website: changes to a website during the term of a linking agreement may mean a change in the nature of the contract, and it will be useful to have a point of reference for the original contract. See also CLAUSE 4 regarding notification of changes to the content of the site.

3 An owner whose website attracts many visitors/users may be able to sell (or even to sell at a premium) advertising on its website: if a particular linker is generating a high proportion of the traffic to the owner's site, it may be appropriate to share such advertising revenues.

4 The owner will want to control the look and feel of the button by which the link is generated.

5 This must be specified and agreed. Leaving the linked page to the discretion of the linker may mean that an owner's valuable advertising is bypassed (see the *Shetland Times v Wills* [1997] FSR 604).

6 If an owner requires linker users to register their details, sales direct by mail or through a telesales call centre to the visitor/user can be tracked and included in the consideration package for the link.

7 The consumer data generated by visits to e-commerce and other websites is becoming increasingly valuable. Ownership of and the right to exploit, mine and otherwise process this data must be clarified in the linking agreement.

8 Where a link appears in rotation, owners should consider whether they wish to have a say in the other rotating links – are they appropriate? – are they competitors? See also CLAUSES 4.2 and 4.3.

9 This clause is designed to avoid manipulation of software coding so as to distort the agreed link.

10 The use of framing is an opportunity to stamp the linker's brand onto the owner's website content. In some instances, this is in the nature of the agreement; an owner may even provide a facility to brand the linked page with the linker's livery. In other cases, (particularly where a link is granted to generate marketing 'impressions') the owner may want and need to assert its brand and will want expressly to exclude any right of framing by the linker.

11 These are all ways in which consideration may be calculated and can be used in combination if required.

12 All agreements based on commission payments or royalties need to grant the 'sales generator' (in this instance, the linker) a right to inspect books and records.
13 How the data is collected is important: different counting methods may produce considerable variation in the consideration payable.
14 Linkers and owners should both consider whether the link is time-critical. Where traffic needs to be generated to coincide with a product launch or media event or other timely event, it may be important to have a more extensive and onerous force majeure clause.
15 Even though the linker enjoys the benefit of this indemnity, it should nevertheless also make sure to exclude in its own terms and conditions liability for the content of the websites to which it links.

24 Trans border data flow agreement

(1) EXPORTING COUNTRY[1]

(2) IMPORTING COUNTRY[2]

TRANS BORDER DATA FLOW AGREEMENT[3]

THIS AGREEMENT is made the [   ] day of [   ] [   ]

BETWEEN:

[   ] of [   ] ('the Data Exporter')

AND

[   ] of [   ][4] (the Data Importer')

BACKGROUND

The Data Exporter and the Data Importer wish to exchange Personal Data (defined below) between them and in order for the Data Exporter to be in compliance with the European Data Protection Directive, Council Directive 95/46/EC ('the Directive') the parties have agreed to enter into this Agreement and to be bound by the terms of the following clauses ('the Clauses') in order to adduce adequate safeguards with respect to the protection of privacy and fundamental rights and freedoms of individuals.

1. DEFINITIONS

For the purposes of these Clauses, the following terms shall have the following meanings:

1.1 **'Data Controller'** shall mean the natural or legal person, public authority, agency or any other body which alone or jointly with others determines the purposes and means of the processing of personal data; where no purposes and means of processing are determined by national or community laws or regulations, the controller or the specific [   ] for his nomination may be designated by national or community law;

1.2 **'Data Exporter'** shall mean the party to this contract as identified elsewhere herein which alone or jointly with others determines the purpose and means of the processing of personal data and which transfers such data to a country which does not provide protection for such data which the source country authorities deem adequate or equivalent;

1.3 **'Data Importer'** shall mean the party to this contract as identified elsewhere herein which agrees to receive Personal Data from the Data Exporter for further processing in accordance with the terms of this contract and who is not subject to a third country's system ensuring adequate protection;

1.4 **'Mandatory Data Protection Principles'** shall mean in relation to processing personal data, those principles set out in SCHEDULE 2;

1.5 **'Personal Data'** or **'personal data'** shall mean any information relating to an identified or identifiable natural person ('Data Subject'); an identifiable person[5] is one who can be identified, directly or indirectly, in particular by reference to an identification number or to one or more factors specific to his physical, physiological, mental, economic, cultural or social identity;

1.6 **'Processing'** or **'processing'** shall mean any operation or set of operations which is performed upon personal data, whether or not by automatic means, such as collection, recording, organisation, storage, adaptation or alteration, retrieval, consultation, use, disclosure by transmission, dissemination or otherwise making available, alignment or combination, blocking, erasure or destruction;

1.7 **'Processor'** shall mean a natural or legal person, public authority, agency or any other body which process personal data on behalf of the controller;

1.8 **'Sensitive Personal Data'** shall mean Personal Data revealing racial or ethnic origin, political opinions, religious or philosophical beliefs, trade union membership and the processing of data concerning one's health or sex life and as may be contained in the relevant definition in the Directive;

1.9 **'Supervisory Authority'** shall mean the public authority responsible for monitoring the application within its territory of the provisions adopted pursuant to the Directive.

2. DETAILS OF THE TRANSFER

The details of the transfer and in particular the categories of personal data and the purposes for which they are transferred, are specified in SCHEDULE 1 which forms an integral part of the Clauses.

3. THIRD PARTY BENEFICIARY CLAUSE[6]

The Data Subject can enforce this Clause, CLAUSES 4.2, 4.3 and 4.4, CLAUSES 5.1, 5.2, 5.3 and 6.5, CLAUSES 6.1 and 6.2 and CLAUSFS 8, 10 and 11 as a third-party beneficiary. The parties do not object to the Data Subject being represented by an association or other bodies if it so wishes and if permitted by national law.

4. OBLIGATIONS OF THE DATA EXPORTER[7]

The Data Exporter agrees and warrants:

4.1 that the processing, including the transfer itself, of the personal data by itself has been and, up to the moment of the transfer, will continue to be carried out in accordance with all the relevant provisions of the country in which the Data Exporter is established (and where applicable has been notified to the relevant Supervisory Authority of that country) and does not violate the relevant provisions of that country;

4.2 that if the transfer involves Sensitive Personal Data the Data Subject has been informed or will be informed before the transfer that his data could be transmitted to a third country not providing adequate protection;

4.3 to make available to the Data Subject a copy of the Clauses upon request;

4.4 to respond within a reasonable time and to the extent reasonably possible to enquiries from the Supervisory Authority on the processing of the relevant Personal Data by the Data Importer and to any enquiries from the Data Subject concerning the processing of his Personal Data by the Data Importer;

4.5 that where applicable, it has registered with the relevant Supervisory Authority, and, where required, has provided notice that it exports personal data and has received any licence or consent necessary to do so lawfully;

4.6 that any changes to the relevant provisions of applicable legislation of the country in which the Data Exporter is established, are notified to the Data Importer as soon as possible.

5. OBLIGATIONS OF THE DATA IMPORTER[8]

The Data Importer agrees and warrants:

5.1 that it has no reason to believe that applicable legislation prevents it from fulfilling its obligations under the Clause and that in the event of a change in that legislation which is likely to have a substantial adverse effect on the guarantees provided by the Clauses, it will notify the change to the Data Exporter and to the Supervisory Authority where the Data Exporter is established, in which case the Data Exporter is entitled to suspend the transfer of data and/or terminate this Agreement;

5.2 to process the Personal Data in accordance with the Mandatory Data Protection Principles;

5.3 to deal promptly and properly with all reasonable enquiries from the Data Exporter or the Data Subject relating to its processing of Personal Data and to co-operate with the relevant Supervisory Authority in the course of all its enquiries and abide (in so far as the law requires) by the advice of such Supervisory Authority with regard to the processing of the personal data;

5.4 at the reasonable request of the Data Exporter to submit its data processing facilities for audit which shall be carried out by the Data Exporter or an inspection body composed of independent members and in possession of the required professional qualifications, selected by the Data Exporter, where applicable, in agreement with the Supervisory Authority and in any event subject to such terms of confidentiality as the Data Importer may reasonably impose;

5.5 to make available to the Data Subject a copy of the Clauses upon request and indicate the office or officer that handles complaints;

5.6 to ensure that it has full legal authority in the country where the personal data will be processed to receive, store and process such data, to use it for the purpose(s) for which such data was collected and exported, as set out herein, and to give the warranties and fulfil the undertakings set out herein; and

5.7 that it will not disclose or transfer the personal data to a third party without ensuring that a trans border data flow agreement or similar agreement upon terms similar to those in this agreement is entered into between the Data Importer and such third party, and upon request from the Data Exporter will make available a true copy of such agreement to the Data Exporter. Where the Data Importer transfers personal data to the Data Exporter which the Data Importer has previously received from a third party, the Data Importer warrants that it has ascertained that such personal data is available for such transfer with the consent of the Data Subject.

6. LIABILITY

6.1 The parties agree that a Data Subject is entitled to bring an action before court against, and receive compensation from, the Data Exporter, the Data Importer or from both for any damage resulting from any act incompatible with the provisions referred to in CLAUSE 4.

6.2 The Data Exporter and the Data Importer agree that they will be jointly and severally liable for damage to the Data Subject resulting from any violation of those provisions referred to in CLAUSE 4.[9]

6.3 The Data Exporter and the Data Importer acknowledge that any liability incurred under this Agreement may be discharged provided that it is established that neither was responsible for any such violation.[10]

7. INDEMNITIES[11]

7.1 The Data Importer will immediately indemnify and hold harmless the Data Exporter from and against any costs, claims, liabilities, demands, damages, expenses or losses resulting from Data Importer's failure to fulfil any of its warranties or undertakings herein.

7.2 The Data Exporter will immediately indemnify and hold harmless the Data Importer from any costs, claims, liabilities, demands, damages, or judgments against the Data Importer in favour of a Data Subject as a consequence of the Data Exporter's failure to fulfil any of its warranties or undertakings herein.

8. DISPUTES

8.1 In the event of a dispute between a Data Subject and the parties which is not amicably resolved and where the Data Subject invokes the third-party beneficiary provision in CLAUSE3, the Data Subject may choose to resolve the dispute as follows:

8.1.1 to refer the dispute to mediation by an independent person or, where applicable, by the Supervisory Authority;

8.1.2 to refer the dispute to an arbitration body, if that party is established in a country which has ratified the New York Convention on enforcement of arbitration awards;

8.1.3 to refer the dispute to the courts in the country in which the Data Exporter is established.

8.2 In the event of a dispute under this Clause, the Data Exporter agrees to use reasonable efforts to defend the lawfulness of the Data Importer's processing of the Data Subject's personal data through available means of dispute resolution as applicable, provided for in the country having jurisdiction. Data Importer agrees to abide by the decision of the Supervisory Authority (or other authority having jurisdiction of the dispute) with respect to such processing as finally affirmed by the judicial authority to which appeal of such decision may be made, as if it were party to the proceedings. The Data Importer hereby authorises the Data Exporter to settle any such dispute without recourse to completion of all such formal dispute resolution formalities pursuant to advice of counsel that such settlement is warranted and reasonable in the circumstances. The Data Importer shall execute and deliver to the Data Exporter any further documents or instruments necessary under the laws of any relevant jurisdiction to give effect to the foregoing.

8.3 The parties agree that CLAUSES 8.1, 8.2 and 8.3 apply without prejudice to the Data Subject's substantive or procedural rights to seek remedies in accordance with other provisions of national or international law.

9. SUPERVISORY AUTHORITY

The parties agree to deposit a copy of this contract with the Supervisory Authority if it so requests or if such deposit is required under applicable law.

10.   TERMINATION

10.1   This Agreement shall remain in force for an indefinite period. It shall be terminable by agreement between the parties hereto at any time by one party sending thirty (30) days' notice in writing of termination to the other. It shall automatically be terminated in the event that Data Importer fails to fulfil its obligations under this Agreement, or if a notice is sent by the relevant Supervisory Authority in the country in which the Data Exporter is established to Data Exporter requesting revision or cancellation of this Agreement.

10.2   Upon termination of this Agreement, Data Importer shall immediately transfer the complete volume of personal data covered by this Agreement to Data Exporter and thereupon shall immediately delete the data from its own system and data media and shall deliver up a certificate certifying the same has been done.

10.3   The parties agree that the termination of the Agreement at any time, in any circumstances and for whatever reason does not exempt them from the obligations and/or conditions under the Agreement as regards the processing of the data transferred.[12]

11.   GENERAL

11.1   This Agreement shall be governed by the laws of the country in which the Data Exporter is established. Any dispute arising between Data Importer and Data Exporter out of this Agreement shall be subject to the jurisdiction of the courts of the country in which the Data Exporter is established.

11.2   Any provisions of this Agreement which are or become invalid shall not affect the validity of the remaining provisions. The parties hereto shall replace the invalid provision with a valid provision which comes as close as possible to achieving the commercial purpose of the invalid provision.

11.3   All notices which are required to be given hereunder shall be in writing and shall be sent to the address of the recipient set out in this Agreement or such other address as the recipient may designate by notice given in accordance with the provisions of this Clause. Any such notice may be delivered personally or by recorded mail and shall be deemed to have been served if by hand when delivered, if by recorded mail when delivered and acknowledged.

11.4   If any term of this Agreement shall require to be amended, added to or deleted by the law of the country of the Data Exporter, then such changes shall be incorporated in an Addendum to this Agreement signed by both parties and attached hereto and shall be deemed a part of this Agreement.

Signed for and on behalf of the Parties to this Agreement by their authorised signatories the day and year before written:

SIGNED for and on behalf of [   ]

the DATA EXPORTER

SIGNED for and on behalf of [   ]

the DATA IMPORTER

SCHEDULE I[13]

This Schedule forms part of the Clauses and must be completed and signed by the parties.[14]

DATA EXPORTER

The Data Exporter is (*please specify briefly your activities relevant to the transfer*):

....

....

....

DATA IMPORTER

The Data Importer is (*please specify briefly your activities relevant to the transfer*):

....

....

....

DATA SUBJECTS

The personal data transferred concern the following categories of Data Subjects (*please specify*):

....

....

....

PURPOSES OF THE TRANSFER

The transfer is necessary for the following purposes (*please specify*):

....

....

....

CATEGORIES OF DATA

The personal data transferred fall within the following categories of data (*please specify*):

....

....

....

SENSITIVE PERSONAL DATA (IF APPROPRIATE)

The personal data transferred fall within the following categories of sensitive personal data (*please specify*):

....

....

....

RECIPIENTS

The personal data transferred may be disclosed only to the following recipients or categories of recipients (*please specify*):

....

....

....

STORAGE LIMIT

The personal data transferred may be stored for no more than (please indicate): [ ] (*monthly/years*)

DATA EXPORTER	DATA IMPORTER
Name:	Name:
Authorised Signature:	Authorised Signature:

SCHEDULE 2

MANDATORY DATA PROTECTION PRINCIPLES

These Data Protection Principles shall apply subject to the mandatory requirements of the national legislation applicable to the Data Importer which do not go beyond what is necessary in a democratic society on the basis of one of the interests listed in Council Directive, 95/46/EC, article 13(1) that is, if they constitute a necessary measure to safeguard national security, defence, public security, the prevention, investigation, detection and prosecution of criminal offences or of breaches of ethics for the regulated professions, an important economic or financial interest of the country or the protection of the Data Subject or the rights and freedoms of others.

1. PURPOSE LIMITATION

Personal Data must be processed and subsequently used or further communicated only for the specific purposes in SCHEDULE 1 to the Clauses. Personal Data must not be kept longer than necessary for the purposes for which they are transferred.

2. RIGHTS OF ACCESS, RECTIFICATION, ERASURE AND BLOCKING OF DATA

As provided for in Council Directive, 95/46/EC, article 12, the Data Subject must have a right of access to all data relating to him that are processed and, as appropriate, the right to the rectification, erasure or blocking of certain data the processing of which does not comply with the principles set out in this Schedule, in particular because the data is incomplete or inaccurate. He should also be able to object to the processing of personal data relating to him on compelling legitimate grounds relating to his particular situations.

3. DATA QUALITY AND PROPORTIONALITY

Personal Data must be accurate and, where necessary, kept up to date. Personal Data must be adequate, relevant and not excessive in relation to the purposes for which they are transferred and further processed.

4. TRANSPARENCY

Data Subjects must be provided with information as to the purposes of the processing and the identity of the Data Controller in the third country and other information insofar as this is necessary to ensure fair processing, unless such information has already been given by the Data Exporter.

5. SECURITY AND CONFIDENTIALITY

Technical and organisational security measures must be taken by the Data Controller that are appropriate to the risks, such as unauthorised access, presented by the processing. Any person acting under the authority of the Data Controller, including a Processor, must not process the Personal Data except on instructions from the Data Controller.

6. RESTRICTIONS ON ONWARD TRANSFERS

Further transfers of personal data from the Data Importer to another Data Controller established in a third country not providing adequate protection or not covered by a Decision adopted by the Commission pursuant to Council Directive, 95/46/EC, article 25(6) (onward transfer) may take place only if either:

6.1   Data Subjects have, in the case of Sensitive Personal Data, given their unambiguous consent to the onward transfer or, in other cases, have been given the opportunity to object.

The minimum information to be provided to Data Subjects must contain in a language understandable to them:

6.1.1   the purposes of the onward transfer;

6.1.2   the identification of the Data Exporter established in the European Community;

6.1.3   the categories of further recipients of the personal data and the countries of destination; and

6.1.4   an explanation that, after the onward transfer, the personal data may be processed by a Data Controller established in a country where there is not an adequate level of protection of the privacy of individuals.

OR

6.2   The Data Exporter and the Data Importer agree to the adherence to the Clauses of another Data Controller which thereby becomes a party to the Clauses and assumes the same obligations as the Data Importer.

7. SPECIAL CATEGORIES OF DATA

Where data revealing racial or ethnic origin, political opinions, religious or philosophical beliefs or trade union memberships and data concerning health or sex life and data relating to offences, criminal convictions or security measures are processed, additional safeguards should be in place within the meaning of Council Directive, 95/46/EC, in particular, appropriate security measures such as strong encryption for transmission or such as keeping a record of access to sensitive data.

8. DIRECT MARKETING

Where personal data are processed for the purposes of direct marketing, effective procedures should exist allowing the Data Subject at any time to 'opt-out' from having his personal data used for such purposes.

9. AUTOMATED INDIVIDUAL DECISIONS

Data Subjects are entitled not to be subject to a decision which is based solely on automated processing of personal data, unless other measures are taken to safeguard the individual's legitimate interests as provided for in Council Directive, 95/46/EC, article 15(2). Where the purpose of the transfer is the taking of an automated decision as referred to in article 15 of the Directive, which produces legal effects concerning the individual or significantly affects him and which is based solely on automated processing of data intended to evaluate certain personal aspects relating to him, such as his performance at work, creditworthiness, reliability, conduct, etc, the individual should have the right to know the reasoning for this decision.

1   Here insert name of country of export, which will normally be the country of incorporation of the exporting entity.
2   Here insert name of country of import, which will normally be the country of incorporation of the importing entity.
3   This Agreement incorporates the model clauses set out in the EC Decision of 15 June 2001 on standard contractual clauses for the transfer of personal data to third countries under Council Directive 95/46/ EC(2001)/497/EC published in the Official Journal on 4 July 2001 (OJ L181/19). This Decision confirms that these clauses are to be used where a Data Controller in the European Union exports personal data to another Data Controller outside the European Economic Area and provided that the clauses are not amended, then the Agreement is valid in each member state.

    This Agreement does not need to be used where personal data is being exported between member states or to countries that are 'approved' by the European Commission, or where the recipient company is compliant with the United States Safe Harbor program. Approved countries that have adequate data protection laws in place are, Canada (subject to certain exemptions) Hungary and Switzerland. The Safe Harbor program benefits United States corporates who have self certified as being compliant with seven good data processing principles, but does not benefit companies in the banking and financial services sectors in the United States, nor in certain media sectors. Details of the Safe Harbor program are available at www.export.gov/safeharbor/.
4   Insert name and registered address of importing entity.
5   This definition might need to include natural as well as legal 'entity' for some member states.
6   Because this contract is usable in each member state, this clause has been drafted to provide an equivalent effect to the Contract (Rights of Third Parties) Act 1999, thus enabling an individual who is not a party of the contract to enforce its rights against either the Data Exportor or the Data Importer.
7   The model clauses place obligations on the Data Exporter (the Data Controller) that ensure that the Data Controller is compliant with the European Data Protection Directive and its own national laws that interpret or implement that Directive and, in particular, for the United Kingdom the Seventh and Eighth Principles of the Data Protection Act 1998.
8   These obligations are included in the model clauses to ensure that the Data Controller at all times maintains control over the Data Importer's data processing activities and at the same time seek to protect as much as possible, the confidentiality of the Data Importer's business as well as the security measures that it has in place in relation to its data processing activities.
9   This joint and severable liability may be unacceptable to a Data Importer.
10 The parties should consider the insurable risks as regards liability and indemnity.
11 Indemnities might not be important in an inter-group contract.
12 This clause is recommended by the European Commission and intends to bind the parties to adhering to data protection principles even after the contract has ended. In practice, if the Data Importer has returned the data, this provision may not apply.
13 The fact that this Appendix 1 has to be completed in some detail means that the Data Processing Agreements may not be used, on a 'framework' basis. It may need to be completed each and every time there are specifically different processing activities.
14 The parties may complete or specify, according to their national procedures, any additional necessary information to be contained in this Schedule.

25 Data processing agreement

(1)   DATA EXPORTER'S COUNTRY[1]

(2)   DATA IMPORTER'S COUNTRY[2]

DATA PROCESSING AGREEMENT

THIS AGREEMENT[3] is made the [   ] day of [   ] [   ] BETWEEN:

[   ] of [   ] ('the Data Exporter')

AND

[   ] of [   ][4] ('the Data Importer')

BACKGROUND

For the purposes of Article 26(2) of Council Directive 95/46/EC for the transfer of personal data to processors established in third countries which do not ensure an adequate level of data protection, the parties have agreed on the following contractual clauses ('the Clauses') in order to adduce adequate safeguards with respect to the protection of privacy and fundamental rights and freedom of individuals for the transfer by the Data Exporter to the Data Importer of the personal data specified in the Appendix.

The parties agree and warrant that the data transfer is solely for the provision of data processing services by the Data Importer to the Data Exporter.

I. DEFINITIONS

For the purposes of the Clauses:

1.1   **'personal data', 'special categories of data', 'process/processing', 'controller', 'processor', 'Data Subject', 'Supervisory Authority'** and **'technical and organisational measures'** shall have the same meaning as in Council Directive 95/46/EC of 24 October 1995 on the protection of individuals with regard to the processing of personal data and on the free movement of such data ('the Directive');

1.2   'the **Data Exporter**' who has been identified above, shall mean the controller who transfers the Personal Data;

1.3   'the **Data Importer**' who has been identified above, shall mean the processor who agrees to receive from the Data Exporter personal data intended for processing on his behalf after the transfer in accordance with his instructions and the terms of these Clauses and who is not subject to a third country's system ensuring adequate protection.

1.4   the **Applicable Data Protection Law** shall mean the legislation protecting the fundamental rights and freedoms of natural persons and, in particular, their right to privacy with respect to the processing of personal data applicable to a Data Exporter in the member state in which the Data Exporter is established.

2. DETAILS OF THE TRANSFER

The details of the transfer, and in particular the categories of personal data and the purposes for which they are transferred, are specified in the APPENDIX 1 which forms an integral part of these Clauses.

3. THIRD PARTY BENEFICIARY CLAUSE[5]

The Data Subjects can enforce against the Data Exporter this Clause and CLAUSES 4.2 to 4.8, CLAUSES 5.1 to 5.3 and 5.7, CLAUSES 6.1 and 6.2, CLAUSES 7, 8.2, 9, 10 and 11 as third party beneficiaries. The Data Subjects can enforce against the Data Exporter this Clause and CLAUSES 5.1 to 5.5 and 5.7, CLAUSES 6.1 and 6.2, CLAUSE 8.2 and CLAUSE 7, CLAUSES 9, 10 and 11, in cases where the Data Exporter has factually disappeared or has ceased to exist in law. The parties do not object to the Data Subjects being represented by an association or other bodies if they so wish and if permitted by national law.

4. OBLIGATIONS OF THE DATA EXPORTER[6]

The Data Exporter agrees and warrants:

4.1   that the processing including the transfer itself of the personal data by him has been and will continue to be carried out in accordance with the relevant provisions of the Applicable Data Protection Law (and, where applicable, has been notified to the relevant Authorities of that member state where the Data Exporter is established) and does not violate the relevant provisions of that state;

4.2   that he has instructed and throughout the duration of the personal data processing services will instruct the Data Importer to process the personal data transferred only on the Data Exporter's behalf and in accordance with the Applicable Data Protection Law and these Clauses;

4.3   that the Data Importer shall provide sufficient guarantees in respect of the technical and organisational security measures specified in ANNEX 2 to this contract;

4.4   that, after assessment of the requirements of the Applicable Data Protection Law, the security measures are appropriate to protect personal data against accidental or unlawful destruction or accidental loss, alteration, unauthorised disclosure or access, in particular where the process involves the transmission of data over a network, and against all other unlawful forms of processing, and that these measures ensure a level of security appropriate to the risks presented by the processing and the nature of the data to be protected having regard to the state of the art and the cost of their implementation;

4.5   that the Data Importer will ensure compliance with the security measures;

4.6   that, if the transfer involves special categories of data, the Data Subject has been informed or will be informed before the transfer that his data could be transmitted to a third country not providing adequate protection;

4.7   that the Data Exporter agrees to forward the notification received from the Data Importer, pursuant to CLAUSE 5.2 to the Data Protection Supervisory Authority if the Data Exporter decides to continue the transfer or to lift its suspension;

4.9   to make available to the Data Subjects upon request, a copy of these Clauses with the exception of APPENDIX 2 which shall be replaced by a summary description of the security measures.[7]

5.   OBLIGATIONS OF THE DATA IMPORTER[8]

The Data Importer agrees and warrants:

5.1   to process the Personal Data only on behalf of the Data Exporter and in accordance with his instructions and these Clauses and that in the event he could not provide such compliance for whatever reasons, he agrees to inform the Data Exporter of that, in which case the Data Exporter is entitled to suspend the transfer of data and/or terminate the contract;

5.2   that he has no reason to believe that the legislation applicable to him prevents him from fulfilling the instructions received from the Data Exporter and his obligations under the contract and that in the event a change in this legislation which is likely to have a substantial adverse effect on the warranties and obligations provided by the Clauses, he will promptly notify the change to the Data Exporter and to the Supervisory Authority where the Data Exporter is established, in which case the Data Exporter is entitled to suspend the transfer of data and/or terminate the contract;

5.3   that he has implemented the technical and organisational security measures specified in APPENDIX 2 before processing the personal data transferred;

5.4   that he shall promptly notify to the Data Exporter about:

5.4.1   any legally binding request for the disclosure of the personal data by a law enforcement authority, unless otherwise prohibited, such as a prohibition under criminal law, to preserve the confidentiality of a law enforcement investigation;

5.4.2   any accidental or unauthorised access; and

5.4.3   any request received directly from the Data Subjects without responding to that request, unless he has been otherwise authorised to do so;

5.5   to deal promptly and properly with all enquiries from the Data Exporter relating to his processing of the personal data subject to the transfer and to abide by the advice of the Supervisory Authority with regard to the processing of the data transferred;

5.6   at the request of the Data Exporter to submit the Data Importer's data processing facilities for audit of the processing activities covered by the Clauses which shall be carried out by the Data Exporter or an inspection body composed of independent members and in possession of the required professional qualifications bound by a duty of confidentiality, selected by the Data Exporter, where applicable, in agreement with the Supervisory Authority;

5.7   to make available to the Data Subject upon request a copy of the Clauses, with the exception of APPENDIX 2, which shall be replaced by a summary description of the security measures in those cases, where the Data Subject is unable to obtain a copy from the Data Exporter.

6. LIABILITY[9]

6.1   The parties agree that a Data Subject who has suffered damage as a result of any violation of the provisions referred to in CLAUSE 3, is entitled to receive compensation from the Data Exporter for the damage suffered.

6.2   If the Data Subject is not able to bring the action referred to in CLAUSE 6.1 above, arising out of a breach by the Data Importer of any of his obligations referred to in CLAUSE 3, against the Data Exporter because the Data Exporter has disappeared factually or has ceased to exist in law, or become insolvent, the Data Importer agrees that the Data Subject may issue a claim against the Data Importer as if he were the Data Exporter.

6.3   The parties agree that if one party is held liable for a violation of the Clauses committed by the other party, the latter will, to the extent to which it is liable, indemnify the first party for any costs, charges, damages, expenses or loss it has incurred. Indemnification is contingent upon:[10]

6.3.1   the Data Exporter promptly notifying the Data Importer of a claim; and

6.3.2   the Data Importer being given the possibility to co-operate with the Data Exporter in the defence and settlement of the claim.

7. MEDIATION AND JURISDICTION

7.1   The Data Importer agrees that if the Data Subject invokes against him third party beneficiary rights and/or claims compensation for damages under the Clauses, the Data Importer will accept the decision of the Data Subject:

7.1.1   to refer the dispute to mediation, by an independent person or, where applicable, by the Supervisory Authority;

7.1.2   to refer the dispute to the courts in the member state where the Data Exporter is established.

7.2   The Data Importer agrees that, by agreement with the Data Subject, the resolution of a specific dispute can be referred to an arbitration body if the Data Importer is established in a country which has ratified the New York Convention on enforcement of arbitration awards.

7.3   The parties agree that the available above options will not prejudice the Data Subject's substantive or procedural rights to seek remedies in accordance with other provisions of national or international law.

8. CO-OPERATION WITH SUPERVISORY AUTHORITIES[11]

8.1   The Data Exporter agrees to deposit a copy of this contract with the Supervisory Authority if it so requests or if such deposit is required under the Applicable Data Protection Law.

8.2   The parties agree that the Supervisory Authority has the right to audit the Data Importer with the same extension and conditions the Authority would have to audit the Data Exporter under the Applicable Data Protection Law.

9. GOVERNING LAW

The Clauses shall be governed by the law of the member state where the Data Exporter is established, namely [ ].

10. VARIATION OF THE CONTRACT

The parties undertake not to vary or modify the terms of the Clauses.

11. OBLIGATION AFTER THE TERMINATION OF THE CLAUSE

11.1 The parties agree that at the termination of the provision of data processing services, at the choice of the Data Exporter, the Data Importer shall return all personal data transferred and the copies thereof to the Data Exporter or shall destroy all personal data and certify to the Data Exporter that he has done so, unless legislation imposed upon the Data Importer prevents him from the devolution or destruction of whole or part of the personal data transferred. In that case, the Data Importer warrants that he shall guarantee the confidentiality of the personal data transferred and will not actively process the personal data transferred anymore.

11.2 The Data Importer warrants that upon request of the Data Exporter and/or of the Supervisory Authority, he shall submit his data processing facilities for audit of the mentioned referred to in CLAUSE 11.1.

ON BEHALF OF THE DATA EXPORTER

Name (written out in full) [   ]

Position [   ]

Address [   ]

Other information necessary in order for the contract to be binding (if any) [   ]

Signature [   ]

(stamp of organisation)

ON BEHALF OF THE DATA IMPORTER

Name (written out in full) [   ]

Position [   ]

Address [   ]

Other information necessary in order for the contract to be binding (if any) [   ]

Signature [   ]

(stamp of organisation)

APPENDIX 1[12]

This Appendix forms part of the Clauses and must be completed and subscribed by the parties.

(*The member states may complete or specify, according to their national procedures, any additional necessary information to be contained in this Appendix)

DATA EXPORTER

The Data Exporter is (*please specify briefly your activities relevant to the transfer*):

....

....

....

DATA IMPORTER

The Data Importer is (*please specify briefly your activities relevant to the transfer*):

....

....

....

DATA SUBJECTS

The Personal Data transferred concern the following categories of Data Subjects (*please specify*):

....

....

....

CATEGORIES OF DATA

The personal data transferred concern the following categories of data (*please specify*):

....

....

....

SPECIAL CATEGORIES OF DATA (IF APPROPRIATE)

The personal data transferred concern the following categories of sensitive data (*please specify*):

....

....

....

PROCESSING OPERATIONS

The personal data transferred will be subject tc the following basic processing activities (*please specify*):

DATA EXPORTER

DATA IMPORTER

Name:

Name:

Authorised
Signature:

Authorised
Signature:

APPENDIX 2

This Appendix forms part of the Clauses and must be completed and signed by the parties.

Description of the technical and organisational measures implemented by the Data Importer in accordance with CLAUSE 4.4 and CLAUSE 5.3 (or document/legislation attached):

....

....

....

1   Here insert name of country of export, which will normally be the country of incorporation of the exporting entity.
2   Here insert name of country of import, which will normally be the country of incorporation of the importing entity.
3   This Data Processing Agreement is drafted to accord with Commission Decision 2002/16/EC of 27 December 2001. This Decision amongst other things, states that the following clauses, if unaltered, will be valid in each member state. As the recital to this Agreement indicates, this contract is to be used where a data controller out sources the processing of personal data to an entity which is based outside the European Economic Area.
4   Insert name and registered address of importing entity.
5   Because this contract is useable in each member state, this clause has been drafted to provide an equivalent effect to the Contract (Rights of Third Parties) Act 1999, thus enabling an individual who is not a party of the contract to enforce its rights against either the data exporter or the data importer.
6   The model clauses place obligations on the data exporter (the data controller) that ensure that the data controller is compliant with the European Union Data Protection Directive and its own national laws that interpret or implement that Directive and in particular, for the United Kingdom the Seventh and Eighth Principles of the Data Protection Act 1998.
7   This sub-clause was included in the European Commission Decision because a number of businesses expressed concern that if a full disclosure of their security provisions had to be given to a third party, this might weaken their actual security. Therefore, where a data exporter has to disclose security provisions, they are allowed to do so on a summary description basis.
8   These obligations are included in the model clauses to ensure that the data controller at all times maintains control over the data importer's data processing activities and at the same time seeks to protect as much as possible, the confidentiality of the data importer's business as well as the security measures that it has in place in relation to its data processing activities.

9 This clause may cause some data importer's concern, because it gives rights of action against a data importer by a data subject, who may be in any part of the world but can bring an action in the jurisdiction where the data importer is established.

10 CLAUSE 6.3 is optional.

11 Here again, data importers may be concerned that by signing this agreement they are subjecting themselves to the control of a data protection authority that is not in their own country.

12 The fact that this Appendix 1 has to be completed in some detail means that the Data Processing Agreements may not be used on a 'framework' basis. It may need to be completed each and every time there are specifically different processing activities.

26   Software licence code

INTRODUCTION

This code has been prepared to prevent misunderstandings between software suppliers and users as to the restrictions on the use of software and charges. It is a code to provide guidance on good practice and as such is not a legal document and should not be treated as such. Software can be licensed in many different ways and this code may not be appropriate for all circumstances. The important point is that the spirit of the code should be followed. All such restrictions should be clearly highlighted and their effect explained. Furthermore any such restrictions should only be those which are legitimate, fair, reasonable and necessary to protect the intellectual property rights in the software and the supplier's revenue. This code explains how the software licence should be written and what information should be provided as part of the licence agreement. The responsibility of a software supplier is to charge increased licence fees and maintenance fees only where it is fair and reasonable to do so and they have legitimate grounds for so doing. For example, where a change in use of the software causes additional cost or where the user gets significant benefit from such a change in use. The responsibility of a user, aside from reading and understanding the licence, is to think ahead and consider how its business may change in the future and ensure that it is clear what the cost, if any, will be for the most likely business changes. This code is no substitute for expert advice and users are recommended to use expert advice whether from within their own organisation or externally.

1.   PLAIN ENGLISH

All software licences should be written in plain English, particularly the restrictions on the scope of use and any schedule or order form in which the software is listed. The 'acid test' is whether the licence is understandable to a user without any explanation from the supplier. Suppliers should seek to obtain 'crystal mark' approval from the Plain English Campaign.

2.   RESTRICTIONS ON LOCATION

Provided the software is being used within the EU or UK, the supplier's consent should not be required and there should be no charge to change the physical location of the use of the software (ie the location of the hardware on which the software is installed) provided that the user notifies the supplier of the change of location. Access by users located overseas should not be restricted.

3.   HARDWARE RESTRICTIONS

If the supplier's licence fee structure is based on size of hardware rather than number of users (see below), the supplier must explain in advance what the pricing structure is and how changes in hardware will result in increased licence fees. Unless the supplier has clearly explained to the user where additional fees are payable the supplier will have no right to charge an additional licence fee. Subject to the payment of any additional licence fee, in any event, consent of the supplier should not be required. All the user has to do is notify the supplier in advance of a change of hardware platform. Where the new hardware platform is not of a type generally recommended by the supplier any change to that platform would be at the user's risk. If a new hardware platform requires, for technical reasons, a different version of the software, again the supplier should explain what charge if any is payable for the supply of a different version of the software.

4.   USER RESTRICTIONS

Where the use of software is restricted to a number of users the supplier should make it clear whether that means concurrent users or named users. Concurrent users means any users may access the relevant system provided that at any time the number accessing the system/'logged on' does not exceed a specified number. Named users means only identified individual users (preferably by job title rather than name) may access the system up to a specified number. Where it is named users, restrictions (if any) on changing named users should reflect normal staff turnover in any organisation. As additional licence fees are payable for increases in the number of users, the supplier should inform the user of the thresholds for additional licence fees for an increased number of users. Furthermore, if the software is licensed on a concurrent user or named user basis the supplier cannot move to a different basis of user base pricing or otherwise unilaterally change the pricing structure without the consent of the licensee.

5.   PRICE STRUCTURE

Whether the price structure depends upon number of users (concurrent or named) or hardware sizing, the pricing structure should be clearly set out so that the user is aware at which point he will be liable to pay additional licence fees. The supplier should commit to the fact that, although prices within the structure may change, the structure itself will not change without the prior agreement of the user. Where licence fees are periodic the supplier should explain how licence fees vary over time. As a matter of practice the software supplier should provide a periodic licence fee and variation structure which does not permit the software supplier to make uninhibited variations to the periodic licence fees to the detriment of the customer.

6. EMPLOYEE RESTRICTIONS

Use of the software should not be limited to employees only, as many companies now 'employ' contractors who should be entitled to use the software for the benefit of the user. The user should of course be responsible for any breach of the licence which results from the activities of contractors and the provision of training. Given that many users are in fact in a group of companies, use by any employee/contractor of another member of a group should be permitted.

7. INTRAGROUP USE

Where the user is effectively a group of companies the software may be used by other members of the group of which the named customer is a member. A group relationship exists where the companies in the group are subsidiaries or holding companies of the others as defined in the Companies Act 1989.

8. INTRAGROUP ASSIGNMENT

The named customer should be entitled to assign the licence to any member of the group of companies of which it is a member.

9. OUTSOURCING

If a user outsources its IT services, the supplier must agree to the assignment of the licence to the outsourcing supplier unless the supplier has good grounds for refusing, for example the outsourcing supplier is a direct competitor of the software supplier or if the outsourcing supplier has in the past committed a serious infringement of the software supplier's intellectual property rights. In circumstances whereby the supplier is a competitor consent must not be unreasonably withheld.

10. TESTING

Where testing of the software is necessary on a separate platform (for example Millennium or EMU compliance) such testing shall be permitted subject to the software supplier being notified.

11. DISPOSALS

The user should be permitted on an interim basis (a period not exceeding 12 months) to use the software to provide an IT service to any business or company which was formerly part of its group which has been sold unless the purchaser is a direct competitor of the software supplier or has in the past committed a serious infringement of the software supplier's intellectual property rights. In circumstances whereby the supplier is a competitor, consent must not be unreasonably withheld.

12. MAINTENANCE

The continuation of a licence should not be dependent upon the continued payment for maintenance. Where maintenance is provided the supplier should explain in advance what the maintenance service is (eg whether new versions and upgrades are provided free of charge and what is meant by 'new version' and 'upgrade'), the structure of maintenance payments and how maintenance fees may vary over time. As a matter of practice the software supplier should, wherever possible, provide a maintenance fee and variation structure which does not permit the software supplier to make uninhibited variations to the maintenance fees.

13. INTEGRATION WORK

Where access to the supplier's source code is required for the purposes of integration work the supplier should either provide the source code or agree to do the integration work at a reasonable fee. In the event that a fee cannot be agreed, both parties will submit the amount of the fee to an independent expert for a decision.

14. AUTOMATIC RENEWAL

Where a licence agreement is automatically renewed at the end of a licence period (unless notice to terminate is given in advance by a user) the renewal term should not be greater than one year for the user so that a user is not inadvertently locked into a further long-term contract.

15. TERM AND TERMINATION

Given that substantial sums are paid for the right to use the software, minor breaches of the software licence should not permit the software supplier to terminate the licence. Only breaches which represent serious infringements of the software supplier's intellectual property rights or non-payment of licence fees which are undisputed should justify termination of the licence. If the licence agreement has a fixed term this should be clearly specified.

16. DISPUTES OVER CHARGES

In the event of a dispute over charges the parties will submit the dispute to an independent expert for a decision.

HAMMOND SUDDARDS 1998

Organisations that helped develop the Software Licensing Code: British Computer Society (BCS), National Computing Centre (NCC), Institute for the Management of Information Systems (IMIS), IBM Computer User Association (IBM CUA), UK Computer Measurement Group (UKCMG), Sema, IBM and Visual.

Reproduced with kind permission of *Computer Weekly*.

27 Escrow agreements

These are examples of NCC Group's standard escrow agreements which it will, upon request, tailor to suit the specific requirements of the parties. Its address is NCC Group plc, Escrow Solutions, Manchester Technology Centre, Oxford Road, Manchester, M1 7EF. Telephone 0161 209 5200; Fax 0161 209 5118 email: escrow@nccgroup.com.

Further details and sample agreements offered by NCC Group plc are available from its website at www.nccgroup.com

Development
Single Licensee
Software Escrow Agreement

Date

Owner   [Ownername]

Agreement Number   [Agreement#]

Notice: The parties to this Agreement are obliged to inform NCC Escrow of any changes to the Package or in their circumstances (including change of name, registered office, contact details or change of owner of the intellectual property in the Package).

Version: 07/05

27 ● Appendix ● Precedents

Escrow Agreement Dated:

Between:

(1)   [Ownername] whose registered office is at [Owneraddress] (CRN: [Ownercrn]) (**"Owner"**);

(2)   [Licenseename] whose registered office is at [Licenseeaddress] (CRN: [Licenseecrn]) (**"Licensee"**); and

(3)   NCC ESCROW INTERNATIONAL LIMITED a company registered in England whose registered office is at Manchester Technology Centre, Oxford Road, Manchester M1 7EF, ENGLAND (CRN: 3081952) (**"NCC Escrow"**).

Background:

(A)   The Owner has granted or has agreed to grant a licence to the Licensee for the Package that the Owner is developing to the Licensee's specification pursuant to the Development Agreement.

(B)   Certain technical information and/or documentation relating to the software package is the confidential information and intellectual property of the Owner or a third party.

(C)   The Owner acknowledges that in certain circumstances, such information and/or documentation would be required by the Licensee in order to give continued effect to the Licensee's rights under the Development Agreement.

(D)   The parties therefore agree that such information and/or documentation should be placed with a trusted third party, NCC Escrow, so that such information and/or documentation can be released to the Licensee should certain circumstances arise.

Agreement:

In consideration of the mutual undertakings and obligations contained in this Agreement, the parties agree that:

1   **Definitions and Interpretation**

1.1   In this Agreement the following terms shall have the following meanings:

"Agreement" means the terms and conditions of this escrow agreement set out below, including the schedules hereto.

"Confidential Information" means all technical and/or commercial information not in the public domain and which is designated in writing as confidential by any party together with all other information of any party which may reasonably be regarded as confidential information.

"Development Agreement" means the agreement between the Owner and the Licensee relating to the development of the Package.

"Full Verification" means the tests and processes forming NCC Escrow's Full Verification service and/or such other tests and processes as may be agreed between the parties for the verification of the Material.

"Independent Expert" means a suitably qualified and independent solicitor or barrister.

"Integrity Testing" means those tests and processes forming NCC Escrow's Integrity Testing service, in so far as they can be applied to the Material.

"Integrity Plus Testing" means those tests and processes forming NCC Escrow's Integrity Plus Testing service, in so far as they can be applied to the Material.

Intellectual Property Rights" mean any copyright, patents, design patents, registered designs, design rights, utility models, trademarks, service marks, trade secrets, know how, database rights, moral rights, confidential information, trade or business names, domain names, and any other rights of a similar nature including industrial and proprietary rights and other similar protected rights in any country or jurisdiction together with all registrations, applications to register and rights to apply for registration of any of the aforementioned rights and any licences of or in respect of such rights.

"Licence" means the licence granted or to be granted to the Licensee pursuant to the Development Agreement for the use of the Package by the Licensee.

"Material" means the Source Code of the Package and such other material and documentation (including updates and upgrades thereto and new versions thereof) as are necessary to be delivered or deposited to comply with clause 2 of this Agreement.

"Order Form" means the order form setting out the details of the order placed with NCC Escrow for setting up this Agreement.

"Package" means the software package together with any updates and upgrades thereto and new versions thereof being developed pursuant to the Development Agreement details of which are set out in schedule 1.

"Release Purposes" means the purposes of understanding, maintaining, modifying and correcting the Package exclusively for and on behalf of the Licensee together with such other purposes (if any) as are permitted under the Development Agreement or the Licence.

"**Source Code**" means the computer programming code of the Package in human readable form.

"**Third Party Material**" means Source Code which is not the confidential information and intellectual property of the Owner or the Licensee.

1.2 This Agreement shall be interpreted in accordance with the following:

1.2.1 headings are for ease of reference only and shall not be taken into consideration in the interpretation of this Agreement;

1.2.2 all references to clauses and schedules are references to clauses and schedules of this Agreement; and

1.2.3 all references to a party or parties are references to a party or parties to this Agreement.

2 **Owner's Duties and Warranties**

2.1 The Owner shall:

2.1.1 deliver a copy of the Material to NCC Escrow within 30 days of the date of this Agreement;

2.1.2 deliver a copy of each part of the Material to NCC Escrow that has passed acceptance tests in accordance with the terms of the Development Agreement within 7 days of passing such tests;

2.1.3 deliver a complete copy of the Material to NCC Escrow within 7 days of acceptance of the Package by the Licensee in accordance with the terms of the Development Agreement;

2.1.4 during development of the Material under the Development Agreement, deliver to NCC Escrow a replacement copy of the Material every 3 months (beginning on the date of the first delivery of Material to NCC Escrow);

2.1.5 after completion of development of the Material under the Development Agreement:

2.1.5.1 deliver a further copy of the Material to NCC Escrow each time that there is a change to the Package;

2.1.5.2 deliver to NCC Escrow a replacement copy of the Material within 30 days after the anniversary of the last delivery of the Material to ensure that the integrity of the Material media is maintained;

2.1.6 ensure that each copy of the Material deposited with NCC Escrow comprises the Source Code of the latest version of the Package:

2.1.6.1 under development, if deposited during development of the Material; or

2.1.6.2 used by the Licensee, if deposited after completion of development of the Material;

2.1.7 deliver a replacement copy of the Material to NCC Escrow within 14 days of a notice given to it by NCC Escrow under the provisions of clause 4.1.3;

2.1.8 deliver with each deposit of the Material the following information:

2.1.8.1 details of the deposit including the full name of the Package (i.e. the original name as set out under schedule 1 together with any new names given to the Package by the Owner), version details, media type, backup command/software used, compression used, archive hardware and operating system details; and

2.1.8.2 password/encryption details required to access the Material;

2.1.9 deliver with each deposit of the Material the following technical information (where applicable):

2.1.9.1 documentation describing the procedures for building, compiling and installing the software, including names and versions of the development tools;

2.1.9.2 software design information (e.g. module names and functionality); and

2.1.9.3 name and contact details of employees with knowledge of how to maintain and support the Material; and

2.1.10 if required by the Licensee, deposit a backup copy of the object code of any third party software package required to access, install, build or compile or otherwise use the Material.

2.2 The Owner warrants to both NCC Escrow and the Licensee at the time of each deposit of the Material with NCC Escrow that:

2.2.1 other than any third party object code referred to in clause 2.1.10 or any Third Party

Material, it owns the Intellectual Property Rights in the Material;

2.2.2 in respect of any Third Party Material, it has been granted valid and ongoing rights under licence by the third party owner(s) thereof to deal with such Third Party Material in the manner anticipated under this Agreement and that the Owner has the express authority of such third party owner(s) to deposit the Third Party Material under this Agreement as evidenced by a signed letter of authorisation in the form required by NCC Escrow;

2.2.3 in entering into this Agreement and performing its obligations under it, it is not in breach of any of its ongoing express or implied obligations to any third party(s);

2.2.4 the Material deposited under clause 2.1 contains all information in human-readable form (except for any third party object code deposited pursuant to clause 2.1.10) and is on suitable media to enable a reasonably skilled programmer or analyst to develop (where the deposit was made prior to completion of development of the Package), understand, maintain, modify and correct the Package; and

2.2.5 in respect of any third party object code that the Owner, at its option, or, at the request of the Licensee, deposits with NCC Escrow in conjunction with the Material pursuant to clause 2.1.10, it has the full right and authority to do so.

3 **Licensee's Responsibilities and Undertakings**

3.1 The Licensee shall notify NCC Escrow of:

3.1.1 final completion and acceptance of the Package in accordance with the terms of the Development Agreement; and thereafter

3.1.2 any change to the Package that necessitates a replacement deposit of the Material.

3.2 In the event that the Material is released under clause 6 prior to acceptance of the Material by the Licensee in accordance with the Development Agreement, the Licensee shall use the Material only for the purpose of developing and completing the Package as contemplated by the Development Agreement and for the Release Purposes.

3.3 In the event that the Material is released under clause 6 after completion of the development and acceptance of the Material by the Licensee in accordance with the Development Agreement, the Licensee shall use the Material only for the Release Purposes.

3.4 In the event that the Material is released under clause 6, whether before or after completion and acceptance of the Package, the Licensee shall:

3.4.1 keep the Material confidential at all times;

3.4.2 not disclose the Material to any person save such of the Licensee's employees or contractors who need to know the same in order to use the Material for the purposes for which the Licensee is allowed to use the Material. In the event that Material is disclosed to its employees or contractors, the Licensee shall ensure that they are bound by the same confidentiality obligations as are contained in this clause 3.4;

3.4.3 hold all media containing the Material in a safe and secure environment when not in use; and

3.4.4 forthwith destroy the Material should the Licensee cease to have rights to the Package under the Development Agreement or the Licence.

3.5 In the event that the Material is released under clause 6, it shall be the responsibility of the Licensee to obtain the necessary licences to utilise the object code of any third party material deposited by the Owner pursuant to clause 2.1.10.

4 **NCC Escrow's Duties**

4.1 NCC Escrow shall:

4.1.1 at all times during the term of this Agreement, retain the latest deposit of the Material in a safe and secure environment;

4.1.2 inform the Owner and the Licensee of the receipt of any deposit of the Material by sending to both parties a copy of the Integrity Testing report, Integrity Plus Testing report or Full Verification report (as the case may be) generated from the testing processes carried out under clause 10; and

4.1.3 notify the Owner and the Licensee if it becomes aware at any time during the term of this Agreement that the copy of the Material held by it has been lost, damaged or destroyed so that a replacement may be obtained.

4.2 In the event of failure by the Owner to deposit any Material with NCC Escrow, NCC Escrow shall not be responsible for procuring such deposit and may, at its sole discretion, notify the Licensee of the Owner's failure to deposit any Material.

4.3 NCC Escrow may appoint agents, contractors or sub-contractors as it deems fit to carry out the Integrity Testing and the Full Verification processes. NCC Escrow shall ensure that any such agents, contractors and sub-contractors are bound by the same confidentiality obligations as are contained in clause 8.

4.4   NCC Escrow has the right to make such copies of the Material as may be necessary solely for the purposes of this Agreement.

5   Payment

5.1   The parties shall pay NCC Escrow's standard fees and charges as published from time to time or as otherwise agreed, in the proportions set out in schedule 2. NCC Escrow's fees as published are exclusive of value added tax.

5.2   NCC Escrow shall be entitled to review and vary its standard fees and charges for its services under this Agreement from time to time but no more than once a year and only upon 45 days written notice to the parties.

5.3   All invoices are payable within 30 days from the date of invoice. NCC Escrow reserves the right to charge interest in respect of the late payment of any sum due under this Agreement (both before and after judgement) at the rate of 2% per annum over the prevailing base rate of HSBC Bank Plc accruing on a daily basis from the due date therefor until full payment.

6   Release Events

6.1   Subject to: (i) the remaining provisions of this clause 6 and (ii) the receipt by NCC Escrow of its release fee and any other fees and interest (if any) outstanding under this Agreement, NCC Escrow will release the Material to a duly authorised officer of the Licensee if any of the following events (**"Release Event(s)"**) occur:

6.1.1   if the Owner is a company:

6.1.1.1   an order is made for the winding up of the Owner, the Owner passes a resolution for winding up (other than for the purposes of a solvent reconstruction or amalgamation) or a liquidator of the Owner is appointed; or

6.1.1.2   an order is made for the appointment of an administrator of the Owner or an administrator of the Owner is appointed; or

6.1.1.3   the Owner enters into a compromise or arrangement with creditors; or

6.1.1.4   the Owner has a receiver, administrative receiver or manager appointed over all or any part of its assets or undertaking; or

6.1.1.5   the Owner is dissolved; or

6.1.2   if the Owner is an individual:

6.1.2.1   the Owner enters into a compromise or arrangement with creditors; or

6.1.2.2   the Owner is declared bankrupt; or

6.1.2.3   the Owner dies; or

6.1.3   if the Owner is a partnership:

6.1.3.1   any of the partners in the Owner are declared bankrupt or enter into a compromise or arrangement with creditors; or

6.1.3.2   the Owner is wound up or dissolved; or

6.1.3.3   the Owner enters into a compromise or arrangement with creditors; or

6.1.3.4   a partnership administration order is made in respect of the Owner; or

6.1.4   any similar or analogous proceedings or event to those in clauses 6.1.1 to 6.1.3 above occurs in respect of the Owner within any jurisdiction outside England; or

6.1.5   the Owner ceases to carry on its business or the part of its business which relates to the Package; or

6.1.6   the Owner assigns its rights to the Intellectual Property Rights in the Material to a third party (**"Assignee"**) and the Assignee fails, within 60 days of all parties' knowledge of such assignment, to continue escrow protection for the benefit of the Licensee by failing to enter into either:

6.1.6.1   a novation agreement with the Licensee and NCC Escrow for the assumption of the Owner's rights and obligations under this Agreement by the Assignee; or

6.1.6.2   a new escrow agreement with the Licensee for the Package which offers the Licensee substantially similar protection to that provided by this Agreement without significantly increasing the overall cost to the Licensee,

provided that if the Assignee offers to enter into a novation or new escrow agreement within 60 days of all parties' knowledge of the assignment and the Licensee fails to accept

© NCC Group 1984 - 2007   SLDEV

the Assignee's offer within 30 days of such offer being notified to the Licensee, there shall be no Release Event under this clause; or

6.1.7   the Owner or, where relevant, its agent, parent, subsidiary or associated company is in material breach of its obligations as to development, support, maintenance or modification of the Package under the Development Agreement, the Licence or any maintenance agreement entered into in connection with the Package and has failed to remedy such default notified by the Licensee to the Owner within a reasonable period.

6.2   The Licensee must notify NCC Escrow of the Release Event specified in clause 6.1 by delivering to NCC Escrow a statutory or notarised declaration (**"Declaration"**) made by an officer of the Licensee declaring that such Release Event has occurred, setting out the facts and circumstances of the Release Event, that the Development Agreement or the Licence and any maintenance agreement, if relevant, for the Package was still valid and effective up to the occurrence of such Release Event and exhibiting such documentary evidence in support of the Declaration as NCC Escrow shall reasonably require.

6.3   Upon receipt of a Declaration from the Licensee claiming that a Release Event has occurred:

6.3.1   NCC Escrow shall submit a copy of the Declaration to the Owner by courier or other form of guaranteed delivery; and

6.3.2   unless within 14 days after the date of despatch of the Declaration by NCC Escrow, NCC Escrow receives a counter-notice signed by a duly authorised officer of the Owner stating that in their view no such Release Event has occurred or, if appropriate, that the event or circumstance giving rise to the Release Event has been rectified as shown by documentation in support thereof,

NCC Escrow will release the Material to the Licensee for its use for the Release Purposes.

6.4   Upon receipt of the counter-notice from the Owner under clause 6.3.2, NCC Escrow shall send a copy of the counter-notice and any supporting evidence to the Licensee by courier or other form of guaranteed delivery.

6.5   Upon receipt by the Licensee of the counter-notice from NCC Escrow or, in any event, within 90 days of despatch of the counter-notice by NCC Escrow, the Licensee may give notice to NCC Escrow that they wish to invoke the dispute resolution procedure under clause 7.

6.6   If, within 90 days of despatch of the counter-notice by NCC Escrow to the Licensee, NCC Escrow has not been informed by the Licensee that they wish the dispute resolution procedure under clause 7 to apply, the Declaration submitted by the Licensee will be deemed to be no longer valid and the Licensee shall be deemed to have waived their right to release of the Material for the particular reason or event specified in the original Declaration.

6.7   For the avoidance of doubt, where a Release Event has occurred under clauses 6.1.1 to 6.1.5, a subsequent assignment of the Intellectual Property Rights in the Material shall not prejudice the Licensee's right to release of the Material and its use for the Release Purposes.

7   **Disputes**

7.1   NCC Escrow shall notify the Owner of the Licensee's request for dispute resolution. Unless the Owner or the Licensee objects, NCC Escrow's Chief Executive Officer for the time being will appoint an Independent Expert to resolve the dispute. If the Owner or the Licensee objects to this appointment, they shall endeavour to appoint a mutually acceptable Independent Expert within 7 days of registering their objection. If they fail to appoint an Independent Expert within this 7 day period, NCC Escrow shall request that the President of The Law Society appoints an Independent Expert to resolve the dispute. Any appointment of an Independent Expert under this clause shall be binding upon the parties.

7.2   Within 5 working days of the appointment of the Independent Expert, the Owner and the Licensee shall each provide full written submissions to the Independent Expert together with all relevant documentary evidence in their possession in support of their claim.

7.3   The Independent Expert shall be requested to give a decision on the matter within 14 days of the date of referral or as soon as practicable thereafter and to send a copy of that decision to the Owner, Licensee and NCC Escrow. The Independent Expert's decision shall be final and binding on all parties and shall not be subject to appeal to a court in legal proceedings except in the case of manifest error.

7.4   If the Independent Expert's decision is in favour of the Licensee, NCC Escrow is hereby authorised to release and deliver the Material to the Licensee within 5 working days of the decision being notified by the Independent Expert to the parties.

7.5   The parties hereby agree that the costs and expenses of the Independent Expert shall be borne by the party against whom the decision of the Independent Expert is given.

8   **Confidentiality**

8.1   The Material shall remain at all times the confidential and intellectual property of its owner.

8.2   In the event that NCC Escrow releases the Material to the Licensee, the Licensee shall be permitted to use the Material only in accordance with clause 3.

8.3   NCC Escrow agrees to keep all Confidential Information relating to the Material and/or the Package that comes into its possession or to its knowledge under this Agreement in strictest confidence and secrecy. NCC Escrow further agrees not to make use of such information and/or documentation other than for the purposes of this Agreement and, unless the parties should agree otherwise in writing, will not disclose or release it other than in accordance with the terms of this Agreement.

9   Intellectual Property Rights

9.1   The release of the Material to the Licensee will not act as an assignment of any Intellectual Property Rights that the Owner or any third party possesses in the Material.

9.2   The Intellectual Property Rights in the Integrity Testing report and any Integrity Testing Plus or Full Verification report shall remain vested in NCC Escrow. The Owner and the Licensee shall each be granted a non-exclusive right and licence to use such report for the purposes of this Agreement and their own internal purposes only.

10   Integrity Testing and Full Verification

10.1   NCC Escrow shall bear no obligation or responsibility to any party to this Agreement or person, firm, company or entity whatsoever to determine the existence, relevance, completeness, accuracy, operation, effectiveness, functionality or any other aspect of the Material received by NCC Escrow under this Agreement.

10.2   As soon as practicable after the Material has been deposited with NCC Escrow, NCC Escrow shall apply its Integrity Testing processes to the Material.

10.3   Any party to this Agreement shall be entitled to require NCC Escrow to apply its Integrity Plus Testing processes to the Material or to carry out a Full Verification. Subject to clause 10.4, NCC Escrow's prevailing fees and charges for the Integrity Plus Testing or Full Verification processes and all reasonable expenses incurred by NCC Escrow in carrying out the Integrity Plus Testing or Full Verification processes shall be payable by the requesting party.

10.4   If the Material fails to satisfy NCC Escrow's Full Verification tests as a result of being defective or incomplete in content, NCC Escrow's fees, charges and expenses in relation to the Integrity Plus Testing or Full Verification tests shall be paid by the Owner.

10.5   Should the Material deposited fail to satisfy NCC Escrow's Integrity Testing, Integrity Plus Testing or Full Verification tests under clauses 10.2 or 10.3, the Owner shall, within 14 days of the receipt of the notice of test failure from NCC Escrow, deposit such new, corrected or revised Material as shall be necessary to ensure its compliance with its warranties and obligations in clause 2. If the Owner fails to make such deposit of the new, corrected or revised Material, NCC Escrow will issue a report to the Licensee detailing the problem with the Material as revealed by the relevant tests.

11   NCC Escrow's Liability

11.1   Nothing in this clause 11 excludes or limits the liability of NCC Escrow for fraudulent misrepresentation or for death or personal injury caused by NCC Escrow's negligence. Save as aforesaid the following provisions set out the entire financial liability of NCC Escrow (including any liability for the acts or omissions of its employees, agents and sub-contractors) to the other parties:

11.1.1   NCC Escrow shall not be liable for any loss or damage caused to either the Owner or the Licensee either jointly or severally except to the extent that such loss or damage is caused by the negligent acts or omissions of or a breach of any contractual duty by NCC Escrow, its employees, agents or sub-contractors and in such event NCC Escrow's total liability in respect of all claims arising under or by virtue of this Agreement or in connection with the performance or contemplated performance of this Agreement, shall not exceed the sum of £1,000,000 (one million UK pounds); and

11.1.2   NCC Escrow shall not be liable to the Owner or the Licensee for any indirect or consequential loss or damage whether for loss of profit, loss of business, depletion of goodwill or otherwise whatsoever or howsoever caused which arise out of or in connection with this Agreement even if such loss was reasonably foreseeable or NCC Escrow had been advised of the possibility of incurring the same by the Owner, the Licensee or any third party.

11.2   NCC Escrow shall not be liable in any way to the Owner or the Licensee for acting in accordance with the terms of this Agreement and specifically (without limitation) for acting upon any notice, written request, waiver, consent, receipt, statutory declaration or any other document furnished to it pursuant to and in accordance with this Agreement.

11.3   NCC Escrow shall not be required to make any investigation into and shall be entitled in good faith without incurring any liability to the Owner or the Licensee to assume (without requesting evidence thereof) the validity, authenticity, veracity and due and authorised execution of any documents, written requests, waivers, consents, receipts, statutory declarations or notices received by it in respect of this Agreement.

27 • Appendix • Precedents

12 Indemnity

12.1 Save for any claim falling within the provisions of clause 11.1.1, the Owner and the Licensee jointly and severally agree at all times to indemnify and hold harmless NCC Escrow in respect of all of its legal and all other costs, fees and expenses incurred directly or indirectly as a result of being brought into or otherwise becoming involved in any form of dispute resolution proceedings or any litigation of any kind between the Owner and the Licensee in relation to this Agreement to the extent that this Agreement does not otherwise provide for reimbursement of such costs.

12.2 The Owner shall assume all liability and shall at all times indemnify and hold harmless NCC Escrow and its officers, agents, sub-contractors and employees from and against any and all liability, loss, damages, costs, legal costs, professional and other expenses and any other liabilities of whatever nature, awarded against or agreed to be paid or otherwise suffered, incurred or sustained by NCC Escrow, whether direct, indirect or consequential as a result of or in connection with any claim by any third party(s) for alleged or actual infringement of Intellectual Property Rights arising out of or in connection with all and any acts or omissions of NCC Escrow in respect of the Material as contemplated under this Agreement.

13 Term and Termination

13.1 This Agreement shall continue until terminated in accordance with this clause 13.

13.2 If the Owner or the Licensee, as the case may be, fails to pay an invoice addressed to it for services under this Agreement within 30 days of its issue, NCC Escrow reserves the right to give that party written notice to pay the outstanding invoice within 30 days. If the Licensee has not paid its invoice by the expiry of the 30 day notice period, this Agreement will automatically immediately terminate. If the Owner has not paid its invoice by the expiry of the 30 day notice period, NCC Escrow will give the Licensee a period of 15 days to pay the Owner's invoice. If the Owner's invoice has not been paid by the expiry of the 15 day optional payment period given to the Licensee, this Agreement will automatically immediately terminate. Any amounts owed by the Owner but paid by the Licensee will be recoverable by the Licensee direct from the Owner as a debt and, if requested, NCC Escrow shall provide appropriate documentation to assist in such recovery.

13.3 Upon termination under the provisions of clause 13.2, for 30 days from the date of termination NCC Escrow will make the Material available for collection by the Owner or its agents from the premises of NCC Escrow during office hours. After such 30 day period NCC Escrow will destroy the Material.

13.4 Notwithstanding any other provision of this clause 13, NCC Escrow may terminate this Agreement by giving 30 days written notice to the Owner and the Licensee. In that event, the Owner and the Licensee shall appoint a mutually acceptable new custodian on similar terms and conditions to those contained herein. If a new custodian is not appointed within 14 days of delivery of such notice, the Owner or the Licensee shall be entitled to request the President for the time being of the British Computer Society (or successor body) to appoint a suitable new custodian upon such terms and conditions as he/she shall require. Such appointment shall be final and binding on the Owner and the Licensee. If NCC Escrow is notified of the new custodian within the notice period, NCC Escrow will forthwith deliver the Material to the new custodian. If NCC Escrow is not notified of the new custodian within the notice period, NCC Escrow will return the Material to the Owner.

13.5 The Licensee may terminate this Agreement at any time by giving written notice to NCC Escrow. Upon such termination, NCC Escrow will return the Material to the Owner.

13.6 If NCC Escrow discovers that a Release Event has occurred and the Licensee has failed to exercise its right to claim for release of the Material under clause 6.2, NCC Escrow shall have the right to terminate this Agreement upon 30 days written notice to the Owner and the Licensee. The Licensee shall have the option of applying for release in accordance with clause 6 during this notice period, but if it fails to do so, upon the expiry of this notice period, this Agreement shall automatically terminate and, unless otherwise instructed by the Owner or the Assignee prior to expiry of the notice period, NCC Escrow shall destroy the Material.

13.7 If the Intellectual Property Rights in the Material have been assigned to a third party and the proviso in clause 6.1.6 applies such that there has been no Release Event under that clause, NCC Escrow shall be entitled to terminate this Agreement immediately by written notice to the Owner and the Licensee and upon such termination, unless otherwise instructed by the Owner or the Assignee, NCC Escrow shall destroy the Material.

13.8 If the Development Agreement and the Licence (if any) has expired or has been lawfully terminated, then the Licensee shall give notice to NCC Escrow within 14 days thereof to terminate this Agreement, failing which, the Owner shall be entitled to give written notice to NCC Escrow to terminate this Agreement. Upon receipt of such a notice from the Owner, NCC Escrow shall notify the Licensee of the Owner's notice to terminate. Unless within 14 days of NCC Escrow giving such notice to the Licensee, NCC Escrow receives a counter-notice signed by a duly authorised officer of the Licensee disputing the termination of the Development and Licence, then the Licensee shall be deemed to have consented to such termination and this Agreement shall immediately automatically terminate. Any disputes arising under this clause shall be dealt with in accordance with the dispute resolution procedure in clause 7. Upon termination under this clause, NCC

SLDEV

Escrow shall return the Material to the Owner.

13.9 Subject to clause 13.8, the Owner may only terminate this Agreement with the written consent of the Licensee.

13.10 This Agreement shall automatically immediately terminate upon release of the Material to the Licensee in accordance with clause 6.

13.11 If this Agreement is superseded and replaced by a new agreement in respect of the Material, this Agreement shall, upon the coming into force of the new agreement, automatically terminate. The relevant party or parties shall request NCC Escrow to either transfer the Material to the new agreement or ask the owner under the new agreement to deposit new material. If new material is deposited, upon its receipt, NCC Escrow shall, unless otherwise instructed, destroy the Material.

13.12 The provisions of clauses 1, 3.2, 3.3, 3.4, 3.5, 5, 8, 9, 10.1, 11, 12, 13.12 to 13.14 (inclusive) and 14 shall continue in full force after termination of this Agreement.

13.13 On and after termination of this Agreement, the Owner and/or the Licensee (as appropriate) shall remain liable to NCC Escrow for payment in full of any fees and interest which have become due but which have not been paid as at the date of termination.

13.14 The termination of this Agreement, however arising, shall be without prejudice to the rights accrued to the parties prior to termination.

14 General

14.1 A party shall notify the other parties to this Agreement, within 30 days of its occurrence, of any of the following:

14.1.1 a change of its name, registered office, contact address or other contact details; and

14.1.2 any material change in its circumstances that may affect the validity or operation of this Agreement.

14.2 Within 14 days of any assignment or transfer by the Owner of any part of its Intellectual Property Rights in the Material, the Owner shall notify:

14.2.1 NCC Escrow and the Licensee of such assignment and the identity of the Assignee; and

14.2.2 the Assignee of the provisions of clause 6.1.6.

14.3 The formation, existence, construction, performance, validity and all other aspects of this Agreement shall be governed by and construed in accordance with the laws of England and the parties submit to the exclusive jurisdiction of the English courts.

14.4 This Agreement, together with the Order Form and any relevant NCC Escrow standard terms and conditions represent the whole agreement relating to the escrow arrangements between NCC Escrow and the other parties for the Package and shall supersede all prior agreements, discussions, arrangements, representations, negotiations and undertakings. In the event of any conflict between any of these documents, the terms of this Agreement shall prevail.

14.5 Unless the provisions of this Agreement otherwise provide, any notice or other communication required or permitted to be given or made in writing hereunder shall be validly given or made if delivered by hand or courier or if despatched by first class recorded delivery (airmail if overseas) addressed to the address specified for the parties in this Agreement (or such other address as may be notified to the parties from time to time) or if sent by facsimile message to such facsimile number as has been notified to the parties from time to time and shall be deemed to have been received:

(i) if delivered by hand or courier, at the time of delivery;

(ii) if sent by first class recorded delivery (airmail if overseas), 2 business days after posting (6 days if sent by airmail);

(iii) if sent by facsimile, at the time of completion of the transmission of the facsimile with facsimile machine confirmation of transmission to the correct facsimile number of all pages of the notice.

14.6 The Owner and the Licensee shall not assign, transfer or subcontract this Agreement or any rights or obligations thereunder without the prior written consent of the other parties.

14.7 NCC Escrow shall be entitled to transfer or assign this Agreement upon written notice to both the Owner and the Licensee.

14.8 This Agreement shall be binding upon and survive for the benefit of the successors in title and permitted assigns of the parties.

14.9 If any provision of this Agreement is declared too broad in any respect to permit enforcement to its full extent, the parties agree that such provision shall be enforced to the maximum extent permitted by law and that such provision shall be deemed to be varied accordingly. If any provision of this Agreement is found by any court, tribunal or administrative body of competent

SLDEV

jurisdiction to be wholly or partly illegal, invalid, void or unenforceable, it shall, to the extent of such illegality, invalidity or unenforceability, be deemed severable and the remaining part of the provision and the rest of the provisions of this Agreement shall continue in full force and effect.

14.10   Save as expressly provided in this Agreement, no amendment or variation of this Agreement shall be effective unless in writing and signed by a duly authorised representative of each of the parties to it.

14.11   The parties shall not be liable to each other or be deemed to be in breach of this Agreement by reason of any delay in performing, or failure to perform, any of their obligations under this Agreement if the delay or failure was for a reason beyond that party's reasonable control (including, without limitation, fire, flood, explosion, epidemic, riot, civil commotion, any strike, lockout or other industrial action, act of God, war or warlike hostilities or threat of war, terrorist activities, accidental or malicious damage, or any prohibition or restriction by any governments or other legal authority which affects this Agreement and which is not in force on the date of this Agreement). A party claiming to be unable to perform its obligations under this Agreement (either on time or at all) in any of the circumstances set out above must notify the other parties of the nature and extent of the circumstances in question as soon as practicable. If such circumstances continue for more than six months, any of the other parties shall be entitled to terminate this Agreement by giving one month's notice in writing.

14.12   No waiver by any party of any breach of any provisions of this Agreement shall be deemed to be a waiver of any subsequent or other breach and, subject to clause 6.6, no failure to exercise or delay in exercising any right or remedy under this Agreement shall constitute a waiver thereof.

14.13   This Agreement is not intended to create any right under the Contracts (Rights of Third Parties) Act 1999 which is enforceable by any person who is not a party to this Agreement and the rights of any third party under the said act are hereby expressly excluded.

14.14   This Agreement may be executed in any number of counterparts and by different parties in separate counterparts. Each counterpart when so executed shall be deemed to be an original and all of which together shall constitute one and the same agreement.

Signed for and on behalf of [Ownername]

Name: .... | ....

Position: .... | (Authorised Signatory)

Signed for and on behalf of [Licenseename]

Name: .... | ....

Position: .... | (Authorised Signatory)

Signed for and on behalf of NCC ESCROW INTERNATIONAL LIMITED

Name: .... | ....

Position: .... | (Authorised Signatory)

SLDEV

Schedule 1

The Package

The software package known as [SoftwareName] or any other name(s) as may be given to it by the Owner from time to time.

Schedule 2

NCC Escrow's Fees

	DESCRIPTION	OWNER	LICENSEE
1	Annual Fee (payable on completion of this Agreement and in advance of each anniversary thereafter)	[OwnerAnnual]	[Licensee Annual]
2	Scheduled Update Fee (2nd and subsequent scheduled deposits n any one year, payable on completion of this Agreement and in advance of each anniversary thereafter – NB. a minimum of 3 are required during development of the Material in accordance with clause 2.1.4).	[OwnerSched]	[Licensee Sched]
3	Unscheduled Update Fee (per unscheduled deposit)	[OwnerUnsched]	[Licensee Unsched]
4	Release Fee (plus NCC Escrow's reasonable expenses)	Nil	100%

Additional fees will be payable to NCC Escrow by the Licensee (unless otherwise agreed between the parties) for the following where applicable:

- Storage Fee for deposits in excess of 1 cubic foot;
- Any novation or replacement of this Agreement at the request of the Owner or the Licensee;
- Integrity Testing Fee for deposits consisting of more than 5 med a items.

Escrow Secure - Single Licensee
Software Escrow Agreement

Date
Owner   [Ownername]
Agreement Number   [Agreement#]

Notice: The parties to this Agreement are obliged to inform NCC Escrow of any changes to the Package or in their circumstances (including change of name, registered office, contact details or change of owner of the intellectual property in the Package).

Version: 03/07

ESSL

Escrow Agreement Dated:

Between:

(1)   [Ownername] whose registered office is at [Owneraddress] (CRN: [Ownercrn]) (**"Owner"**);

(2)   [Licenseename] whose registered office is at [Licenseeaddress] (CRN: [Licenseecrn]) (**"Licensee"**); and

(3)   NCC ESCROW INTERNATIONAL LIMITED a company registered in England whose registered office is at Manchester Technology Centre, Oxford Road, Manchester M1 7EF, ENGLAND (CRN: 3081952) (**"NCC Escrow"**).

Background:

(A)   The Licensee has been granted a licence to use the Package which comprises computer programs.

(B)   Certain technical information and/or documentation relating to the software package is the confidential information and intellectual property of the Owner or a third party.

(C)   The Owner acknowledges that in certain circumstances, such information and/or documentation would be required by the Licensee in order for it to continue to exercise its rights under the Licence Agreement.

(D)   The parties therefore agree that such information and/or documentation should be placed with a trusted third party, NCC Escrow, so that such information and/or documentation can be released to the Licensee should certain circumstances arise.

Agreement:

In consideration of the mutual undertakings and obligations contained in this Agreement, the parties agree that:

1   **Definitions and Interpretation**

         1.1   In this Agreement the following terms shall have the following meanings:

                  "Agreement" means the terms and conditions of this escrow agreement set out below, including the schedules hereto.

                  "Confidential Information" means all technical and/or commercial information not in the public domain and which is designated in writing as confidential by any party together with all other information of any party which may reasonably be regarded as confidential information.

                  "Full Verification" means the tests and processes forming NCC Escrow's Full Verification service and/or such other tests and processes as may be agreed between the parties for the verification of the Material.

                  "Independent Expert" means a suitably qualified and independent solicitor or barrister.

                  "Integrity Testing" means those tests and processes forming NCC Escrow's Integrity Testing service, in so far as they can be applied to the Material.

                  "Intellectual Property Rights" mean any copyright, patents, design patents, registered designs, design rights, utility models, trademarks, service marks, trade secrets, know how, database rights, moral rights, confidential information, trade or business names, domain names, and any other rights of a similar nature including industrial and proprietary rights and other similar protected rights in any country or jurisdiction together with all registrations, applications to register and rights to apply for registration of any of the aforementioned rights and any licences of or in respect of such rights.

                  "Licence Agreement" means the agreement under which the Licensee was granted a licence to use the Package.

                  "Material" means the Source Code of the Package and such other material and documentation (including updates and upgrades thereto and new versions thereof) as are necessary to be delivered or deposited to comply with clause 2 of this Agreement.

                  "Order Form" means the order form setting out the details of the order placed with NCC Escrow for setting up this Agreement.

                  "Package" means the software package together with any updates and upgrades thereto and new versions thereof licensed to the Licensee under the Licence Agreement details of which are set out in schedule 1.

                  "Release Purposes" means the purposes of understanding, maintaining, modifying and correcting the Package exclusively for and on behalf of the Licensee together with such other purposes (if any) as are permitted under the Licence Agreement.

                  "Source Code" means the computer programming code of the Package in human readable form.

                  "Third Party Material" means Source Code which is not the confidential information and

© NCC Group 1984 - 2007

ESSL

intellectual property of the Owner or the Licensee.

1.2 This Agreement shall be interpreted in accordance with the following:

 1.2.1 headings are for ease of reference only and shall not be taken into consideration in the interpretation of this Agreement;

 1.2.2 all references to clauses and schedules are references to clauses and schedules of this Agreement; and

 1.2.3 all references to a party or parties are references to a party or parties to this Agreement.

2 Owner's Duties and Warranties

2.1 The Owner shall:

 2.1.1 arrange for NCC Escrow to carry out a Full Verification of the Material within 30 days of the date of this Agreement and shall make the Material available for the Full Verification and subsequent deposit;

 2.1.2 arrange for NCC Escrow to carry out further Full Verifications in accordance with clause 4.1.2 and shall on each occasion make the Material available to NCC Escrow for the Full Verification and subsequent deposit;

 2.1.3 deliver a further copy of the Material to NCC Escrow each time that there is a change to the Package;

 2.1.4 ensure that each copy of the Material deposited with NCC Escrow comprises the Source Code of the latest version of the Package used by the Licensee;

 2.1.5 deliver to NCC Escrow a replacement copy of the Material within 30 days after the anniversary of the last delivery of the Material to ensure that the integrity of the Material media is maintained;

 2.1.6 deliver a replacement copy of the Material to NCC Escrow within 14 days of a notice given to it by NCC Escrow under the provisions of clause 4.1.5;

 2.1.7 deliver with each deposit of the Material the following information:

  2.1.7.1 details of the deposit including the full name of the Package (i.e. the original name as set out under schedule 1 together with any new names given to the Package by the Owner), version details, media type, backup command/software used, compression used, archive hardware and operating system details; and

  2.1.7.2 password/encryption details required to access the Material;

 2.1.8 deliver with each deposit of the Material the following technical information (where applicable):

  2.1.8.1 documentation describing the procedures for building, compiling and installing the software, including names and versions of the development tools;

  2.1.8.2 software design information (e.g. module names and functionality); and

  2.1.8.3 name and contact details of employees with knowledge of how to maintain and support the Material; and

 2.1.9 if required by the Licensee, deposit a backup copy of the object code of any third party software package required to access, install, build or compile or otherwise use the Material.

2.2 The Owner warrants to both NCC Escrow and the Licensee at the time of each deposit of the Material with NCC Escrow that:

 2.2.1 other than any third party object code referred to in clause 2.1.9 or any Third Party Material, it owns the Intellectual Property Rights in the Material;

 2.2.2 in respect of any Third Party Material, it has been granted valid and ongoing rights under licence by the third party owner(s) thereof to deal with such Third Party Material in the manner anticipated under this Agreement and that the Owner has the express authority of such third party owner(s) to deposit the Third Party Material under this Agreement as evidenced by a signed letter of authorisation in the form required by NCC Escrow;

 2.2.3 in entering into this Agreement and performing its obligations under it, it is not in breach of any of its ongoing express or implied obligations to any third party(s);

2.2.4   the Material deposited under clause 2.1 contains all information in human-readable form (except for any third party object code deposited pursuant to clause 2.1.9) and is on suitable media to enable a reasonably skilled programmer or analyst to understand, maintain, modify and correct the Package; and

2.2.5   in respect of any third party object code that the Owner, at its option, or, at the request of the Licensee, deposits with NCC Escrow in conjunction with the Material pursuant to clause 2.1.9, it has the full right and authority to do so.

3   Licensee's Responsibilities and Undertakings

3.1   The Licensee shall notify NCC Escrow of any change to the Package that necessitates a replacement deposit of the Material.

3.2   In the event that the Material is released under clause 6 the Licensee shall:

3.2.1   keep the Material confidential at all times;

3.2.2   use the Material only for the Release Purposes;

3.2.3   not disclose the Material to any person save such of the Licensee's employees or contractors who need to know the same for the Release Purposes. In the event that Material is disclosed to its employees or contractors, the Licensee shall ensure that they are bound by the same confidentiality obligations as are contained in this clause 3.2;

3.2.4   hold all media containing the Material in a safe and secure environment when not in use; and

3.2.5   forthwith destroy the Material should the Licensee cease to be entitled to use the Package under the terms of the Licence Agreement.

3.3   In the event that the Material is released under clause 6, it shall be the responsibility of the Licensee to obtain the necessary licences to utilise the object code of any third party material deposited by the Owner pursuant to clause 2.1.9.

4   NCC Escrow's Duties

4.1   NCC Escrow shall:

4.1.1   carry out a Full Verification of the Material in accordance with Clause 2.1.1;

4.1.2   carry out a Full Verification of the most recent version of the Material within 30 days of each anniversary of the date of this Agreement unless the Owner notifies NCC Escrow in writing before such anniversary that another version of the Package is to be issued shortly thereafter, in which case the Full Verification shall be delayed until such time as the new version is available;

4.1.3   at all times during the term of this Agreement, retain the latest deposit of the Material in a safe and secure environment;

4.1.4   inform the Owner and the Licensee of the receipt of any deposit of the Material by sending to both parties a copy of the Integrity Testing report or Full Verification report (as the case may be) generated from the testing processes carried out under clause 10; and

4.1.5   notify the Owner and the Licensee if it becomes aware at any time during the term of this Agreement that the copy of the Material held by it has been lost, damaged or destroyed so that a replacement may be obtained.

4.2   In the event of failure by the Owner to deposit any Material with NCC Escrow, NCC Escrow shall not be responsible for procuring such deposit and may, at its sole discretion, notify the Licensee of the Owner's failure to deposit any Material.

4.3   NCC Escrow may appoint agents, contractors or sub-contractors as it deems fit to carry out the Integrity Testing and the Full Verification processes. NCC Escrow shall ensure that any such agents, contractors and sub-contractors are bound by the same confidentiality obligations as are contained in clause 8.

4.4   NCC Escrow has the right to make such copies of the Material as may be necessary solely for the purposes of this Agreement.

5   Payment

5.1   The parties shall pay NCC Escrow's standard fees and charges as published from time to time or as otherwise agreed, in the proportions set out in schedule 2. NCC Escrow's fees as published are exclusive of value added tax.

27 ● Appendix ● Precedents

5.2 NCC Escrow shall be entitled to review and vary its standard fees and charges for its services under this Agreement from time to time but no more than once a year and only upon 45 days written notice to the parties.

5.3 All invoices are payable within 30 days from the date of invoice. NCC Escrow reserves the right to charge interest in respect of the late payment of any sum due under this Agreement (both before and after judgement) at the rate of 2% per annum over the prevailing base rate of HSBC Bank Plc accruing on a daily basis from the due date therefor until full payment.

6   Release Events

6.1 Subject to: (i) the remaining provisions of this clause 6 and (ii) the receipt by NCC Escrow of its release fee and any other fees and interest (if any) outstanding under this Agreement, NCC Escrow will release the Material to a duly authorised officer of the Licensee if any of the following events (**"Release Event(s)"**) occur:

6.1.1 if the Owner is a company:

6.1.1.1 an order is made for the winding up of the Owner, the Owner passes a resolution for winding up (other than for the purposes of a solvent reconstruction or amalgamation) or a liquidator of the Owner is appointed; or

6.1.1.2 an order is made for the appointment of an administrator of the Owner or an administrator of the Owner is appointed; or

6.1.1.3 the Owner enters into a compromise or arrangement with creditors; or

6.1.1.4 the Owner has a receiver, administrative receiver or manager appointed over all or any part of its assets or undertaking; or

6.1.1.5 the Owner is dissolved; or

6.1.2 if the Owner is an individual:

6.1.2.1 the Owner enters into a compromise or arrangement with creditors; or

6.1.2.2 the Owner is declared bankrupt; or

6.1.2.3 the Owner dies; or

6.1.3 if the Owner is a partnership:

6.1.3.1 any of the partners in the Owner are declared bankrupt or enter into a compromise or arrangement with creditors; or

6.1.3.2 the Owner is wound up or dissolved; or

6.1.3.3 the Owner enters into a compromise or arrangement with creditors; or

6.1.3.4 a partnership administration order is made in respect of the Owner; or

6.1.4 any similar or analogous proceedings or event to those in clauses 6.1.1 to 6.1.3 above occurs in respect of the Owner within any jurisdiction outside England; or

6.1.5 the Owner ceases to carry on its business or the part of its business which relates to the Package; or

6.1.6 the Owner assigns its rights to the Intellectual Property Rights in the Material to a third party (**"Assignee"**) and the Assignee fails, within 60 days of all parties' knowledge of such assignment, to continue escrow protection for the benefit of the Licensee by failing to enter into either:

6.1.6.1 a novation agreement with the Licensee and NCC Escrow for the assumption of the Owner's rights and obligations under this Agreement by the Assignee; or

6.1.6.2 a new escrow agreement with the Licensee for the Package which offers the Licensee substantially similar protection to that provided by this Agreement without significantly increasing the overall cost to the Licensee,

provided that if the Assignee offers to enter into a novation or new escrow agreement within 60 days of all parties' knowledge of the assignment and the Licensee fails to accept the Assignee's offer within 30 days of such offer being notified to the Licensee, there shall be no Release Event under this clause; or

6.1.7 the Owner or, where relevant, its agent, parent, subsidiary or associated company is in material breach of its obligations as to maintenance or modification of the Package under the Licence Agreement or any maintenance agreement entered into in connection with the Package and has failed to remedy such default notified by the Licensee to the Owner within a reasonable period.

© NCC Group 1984 - 2007

ESSL

6.2   The Licensee must notify NCC Escrow of the Release Event specified in clause 6.1 by delivering to NCC Escrow a statutory or notarised declaration ("**Declaration**") made by an officer of the Licensee declaring that such Release Event has occurred, setting out the facts and circumstances of the Release Event, that the Licence Agreement and any maintenance agreement, if relevant, for the Package was still valid and effective up to the occurrence of such Release Event and exhibiting such documentary evidence in support of the Declaration as NCC Escrow shall reasonably require.

6.3   Upon receipt of a Declaration from the Licensee claiming that a Release Event has occurred:

6.3.1   NCC Escrow shall submit a copy of the Declaration to the Owner by courier or other form of guaranteed delivery; and

6.3.2   unless within 14 days after the date of despatch of the Declaration by NCC Escrow, NCC Escrow receives a counter-notice signed by a duly authorised officer of the Owner stating that in their view no such Release Event has occurred or, if appropriate, that the event or circumstance giving rise to the Release Event has been rectified as shown by documentation in support thereof,

NCC Escrow will release the Material to the Licensee for its use for the Release Purposes.

6.4   Upon receipt of the counter-notice from the Owner under clause 6.3.2, NCC Escrow shall send a copy of the counter-notice and any supporting evidence to the Licensee by courier or other form of guaranteed delivery.

6.5   Upon receipt by the Licensee of the counter-notice from NCC Escrow or, in any event, within 90 days of despatch of the counter-notice by NCC Escrow, the Licensee may give notice to NCC Escrow that they wish to invoke the dispute resolution procedure under clause 7.

6.6   If, within 90 days of despatch of the counter-notice by NCC Escrow to the Licensee, NCC Escrow has not been informed by the Licensee that they wish the dispute resolution procedure under clause 7 to apply, the Declaration submitted by the Licensee will be deemed to be no longer valid and the Licensee shall be deemed to have waived their right to release of the Material for the particular reason or event specified in the original Declaration.

6.7   For the avoidance of doubt, where a Release Event has occurred under clauses 6.1.1 to 6.1.5, a subsequent assignment of the Intellectual Property Rights in the Material shall not prejudice the Licensee's right to release of the Material and its use for the Release Purposes.

7   Disputes

7.1   NCC Escrow shall notify the Owner of the Licensee's request for dispute resolution. Unless the Owner or the Licensee objects, NCC Escrow's Chief Executive Officer for the time being will appoint an Independent Expert to resolve the dispute. If the Owner or the Licensee objects to this appointment, they shall endeavour to appoint a mutually acceptable Independent Expert within 7 days of registering their objection. If they fail to appoint an Independent Expert within this 7 day period, NCC Escrow shall request that the President of The Law Society appoints an Independent Expert to resolve the dispute. Any appointment of an Independent Expert under this clause shall be binding upon the parties.

7.2   Within 5 working days of the appointment of the Independent Expert, the Owner and the Licensee shall each provide full written submissions to the Independent Expert together with all relevant documentary evidence in their possession in support of their claim.

7.3   The Independent Expert shall be requested to give a decision on the matter within 14 days of the date of referral or as soon as practicable thereafter and to send a copy of that decision to the Owner, Licensee and NCC Escrow. The Independent Expert's decision shall be final and binding on all parties and shall not be subject to appeal to a court in legal proceedings except in the case of manifest error.

7.4   If the Independent Expert's decision is in favour of the Licensee, NCC Escrow is hereby authorised to release and deliver the Material to the Licensee within 5 working days of the decision being notified by the Independent Expert to the parties.

7.5   The parties hereby agree that the costs and expenses of the Independent Expert shall be borne by the party against whom the decision of the Independent Expert is given.

ESSL

8 Confidentiality

8.1 The Material shall remain at all times the confidential and intellectual property of its owner.

8.2 In the event that NCC Escrow releases the Material to the Licensee, the Licensee shall be permitted to use the Material only for the Release Purposes.

8.3 NCC Escrow agrees to keep all Confidential Information relating to the Material and/or the Package that comes into its possession or to its knowledge under this Agreement in strictest confidence and secrecy. NCC Escrow further agrees not to make use of such information and/or documentation other than for the purposes of this Agreement and, unless the parties should agree otherwise in writing, will not disclose or release it other than in accordance with the terms of this Agreement.

9 Intellectual Property Rights

9.1 The release of the Material to the Licensee will not act as an assignment of any Intellectual Property Rights that the Owner or any third party possesses in the Material.

9.2 The Intellectual Property Rights in the Integrity Testing report and any Full Verification report shall remain vested in NCC Escrow. The Owner and the Licensee shall each be granted a non-exclusive right and licence to use such report for the purposes of this Agreement and their own internal purposes only.

10 Integrity Testing and Full Verification

10.1 NCC Escrow shall bear no obligation or responsibility to any party to this Agreement or person, firm, company or entity whatsoever to determine the existence, relevance, completeness, accuracy, operation, effectiveness, functionality or any other aspect of the Material received by NCC Escrow under this Agreement.

10.2 As soon as practicable after the Material has been deposited with NCC Escrow, NCC Escrow shall apply its Integrity Testing processes to the Material or carry out a Full Verification if applicable pursuant to clause 4.1.1 or 4.1.2.

10.3 Without prejudice to any of the foregoing provisions, any party to this Agreement shall be entitled to require NCC Escrow to carry out a Full Verification at any time during the term of this Agreement. Subject to clause 10.4, NCC Escrow's prevailing fees and charges for the Full Verification processes and all reasonable expenses incurred by NCC Escrow in carrying out the Full Verification processes shall be payable by the requesting party.

10.4 If the Material fails to satisfy NCC Escrow's Full Verification tests as a result of being defective or incomplete in content, NCC Escrow's fees, charges and expenses in relation to the Full Verification tests shall be paid by the Owner.

10.5 Should the Material deposited fail to satisfy NCC Escrow's Integrity Testing or Full Verification tests under clauses 10.2 or 10.3, the Owner shall, within 14 days of the receipt of the notice of test failure from NCC Escrow, deposit such new, corrected or revised Material as shall be necessary to ensure its compliance with its warranties and obligations in clause 2. If the Owner fails to make such deposit of the new, corrected or revised Material, NCC Escrow will issue a report to the Licensee detailing the problem with the Material as revealed by the relevant tests.

11 NCC Escrow's Liability

11.1 Nothing in this clause 11 excludes or limits the liability of NCC Escrow for fraudulent misrepresentation or for death or personal injury caused by NCC Escrow's negligence. Save as aforesaid the following provisions set out the entire financial liability of NCC Escrow (including any liability for the acts or omissions of its employees, agents and sub-contractors) to the other parties:

11.1.1 NCC Escrow shall not be liable for any loss or damage caused to either the Owner or the Licensee either jointly or severally except to the extent that such loss or damage is caused by the negligent acts or omissions of or a breach of any contractual duty by NCC Escrow, its employees, agents or sub-contractors and in such event NCC Escrow's total liability in respect of all claims arising under or by virtue of this Agreement or in connection with the performance or contemplated performance of this Agreement, shall not exceed the sum of £1,000,000 (one million UK pounds); and

11.1.2 NCC Escrow shall not be liable to the Owner or the Licensee for any indirect or consequential loss or damage whether for loss of profit, loss of business, depletion of goodwill or otherwise whatsoever or howsoever caused which arise out of or in connection with this Agreement even if such loss was reasonably foreseeable or NCC Escrow had been advised of the possibility of incurring the same by the Owner, the Licensee or any third party.

11.2 NCC Escrow shall not be liable in any way to the Owner or the Licensee for acting in accordance with the terms of this Agreement and specifically (without limitation) for acting upon any notice, written request, waiver, consent, receipt, statutory declaration or any other document furnished to it pursuant to and in accordance with this Agreement.

11.3 NCC Escrow shall not be required to make any investigation into and shall be entitled in good faith without incurring any liability to the Owner or the Licensee to assume (without requesting evidence thereof) the validity, authenticity, veracity and due and authorised execution of any documents, written requests, waivers, consents, receipts, statutory declarations or notices received by it in respect of this Agreement.

12 Indemnity

12.1 Save for any claim falling within the provisions of clause 11.1.1, the Owner and the Licensee jointly and severally agree at all times to indemnify and hold harmless NCC Escrow in respect of all of its legal and all other costs, fees and expenses incurred directly or indirectly as a result of being brought into or otherwise becoming involved in any form of dispute resolution proceedings or any litigation of any kind between the Owner and the Licensee in relation to this Agreement to the extent that this Agreement does not otherwise provide for reimbursement of such costs.

12.2 The Owner shall assume all liability and shall at all times indemnify and hold harmless NCC Escrow and its officers, agents, sub-contractors and employees from and against any and all liability, loss, damages, costs, legal costs, professional and other expenses and any other liabilities of whatever nature, awarded against or agreed to be paid or otherwise suffered, incurred or sustained by NCC Escrow, whether direct, indirect or consequential as a result of or in connection with any claim by any third party(s) for alleged or actual infringement of Intellectual Property Rights arising out of or in connection with all and any acts or omissions of NCC Escrow in respect of the Material as contemplated under this Agreement.

13 Term and Termination

13.1 This Agreement shall continue until terminated in accordance with this clause 13.

13.2 If the Owner or the Licensee, as the case may be, fails to pay an invoice addressed to it for services under this Agreement within 30 days of its issue, NCC Escrow reserves the right to give that party written notice to pay the outstanding invoice within 30 days. If the Licensee has not paid its invoice by the expiry of the 30 day notice period, this Agreement will automatically immediately terminate. If the Owner has not paid its invoice by the expiry of the 30 day notice period, NCC Escrow will give the Licensee a period of 15 days to pay the Owner's invoice. If the Owner's invoice has not been paid by the expiry of the 15 day optional payment period given to the Licensee, this Agreement will automatically immediately terminate. Any amounts owed by the Owner but paid by the Licensee will be recoverable by the Licensee direct from the Owner as a debt and, if requested, NCC Escrow shall provide appropriate documentation to assist in such recovery.

13.3 Upon termination under the provisions of clause 13.2, for 30 days from the date of termination NCC Escrow will make the Material available for collection by the Owner or its agents from the premises of NCC Escrow during office hours. After such 30 day period NCC Escrow will destroy the Material.

13.4 Notwithstanding any other provision of this clause 13, NCC Escrow may terminate this Agreement by giving 30 days written notice to the Owner and the Licensee. In that event, the Owner and the Licensee shall appoint a mutually acceptable new custodian on similar terms and conditions to those contained herein. If a new custodian is not appointed within 14 days of delivery of such notice, the Owner or the Licensee shall be entitled to request the President for the time being of the British Computer Society (or successor body) to appoint a suitable new custodian upon such terms and conditions as he/she shall require. Such appointment shall be final and binding on the Owner and the Licensee. If NCC Escrow is notified of the new custodian within the notice period, NCC Escrow will forthwith deliver the Material to the new custodian. If NCC Escrow is not notified of the new custodian within the notice period, NCC Escrow will return the Material to the Owner.

13.5 The Licensee may terminate this Agreement at any time by giving written notice to NCC Escrow. Upon such termination, NCC Escrow will return the Material to the Owner.

13.6 If NCC Escrow discovers that a Release Event has occurred and the Licensee has failed to exercise its right to claim for release of the Material under clause 6.2, NCC Escrow shall have the right to terminate this Agreement upon 30 days written notice to the Owner and the Licensee. The Licensee shall have the option of applying for release in accordance with clause 6 during this notice period, but if it fails to do so, upon the expiry of this notice period, this Agreement shall automatically terminate and, unless otherwise instructed by the Owner or the Assignee prior to expiry of the notice period, NCC Escrow shall destroy the Material.

13.7 If the Intellectual Property Rights in the Material have been assigned to a third party and the proviso in clause 6.1.6 applies such that there has been no Release Event under that clause, NCC Escrow shall be entitled to terminate this Agreement immediately by written notice to the Owner and the Licensee and upon such termination, unless otherwise instructed by the Owner or the Assignee, NCC Escrow shall destroy the Material.

13.8 If the Licence Agreement has expired or has been lawfully terminated, then the Licensee shall give notice to NCC Escrow within 14 days thereof to terminate this Agreement, failing which, the Owner shall be entitled to give written notice to NCC Escrow to terminate this Agreement. Upon receipt of such a notice from the Owner, NCC Escrow shall notify the Licensee of the Owner's notice to terminate. Unless within 14 days of NCC Escrow giving such notice to the Licensee, NCC Escrow receives a counter-notice signed by a duly authorised officer of the Licensee disputing the termination of the Licence Agreement, then the Licensee shall be deemed to have consented to such termination and this Agreement shall immediately automatically terminate. Any disputes arising under this clause shall be dealt with in accordance with the dispute resolution procedure in clause 7. Upon termination under this clause, NCC Escrow shall return the Material to the Owner.

13.9 Subject to clause 13.8, the Owner may only terminate this Agreement with the written consent of the Licensee.

13.10 This Agreement shall automatically immediately terminate upon release of the Material to the Licensee in accordance with clause 6.

13.11 If this Agreement is superseded and replaced by a new agreement in respect of the Material, this Agreement shall, upon the coming into force of the new agreement, automatically terminate. The relevant party or parties shall request NCC Escrow to either transfer the Material to the new agreement or ask the owner under the new agreement to deposit new material. If new material is deposited, upon its receipt, NCC Escrow shall, unless otherwise instructed, destroy the Material.

13.12 The provisions of clauses 1, 3.2, 3.3, 5, 8, 9, 10.1, 11, 12, 13.12 to 13.14 (inclusive) and 14 shall continue in full force after termination of this Agreement.

13.13 On and after termination of this Agreement, the Owner and/or the Licensee (as appropriate) shall remain liable to NCC Escrow for payment in full of any fees and interest which have become due but which have not been paid as at the date of termination.

13.14 The termination of this Agreement, however arising, shall be without prejudice to the rights accrued to the parties prior to termination.

14 General

14.1 A party shall notify the other parties to this Agreement, within 30 days of its occurrence, of any of the following:

14.1.1 a change of its name, registered office, contact address or other contact details; and

14.1.2 any material change in its circumstances that may affect the validity or operation of this Agreement.

14.2 Within 14 days of any assignment or transfer by the Owner of any part of its Intellectual Property Rights in the Material, the Owner shall notify:

14.2.1 NCC Escrow and the Licensee of such assignment and the identity of the Assignee; and

14.2.2 the Assignee of the provisions of clause 6.1.6.

14.3 The formation, existence, construction, performance, validity and all other aspects of this Agreement shall be governed by and construed in accordance with the laws of England and the parties submit to the exclusive jurisdiction of the English courts.

14.4 This Agreement, together with the Order Form and any relevant NCC Escrow standard terms and conditions represent the whole agreement relating to the escrow arrangements between NCC Escrow and the other parties for the Package and shall supersede all prior agreements, discussions, arrangements, representations, negotiations and undertakings. In the event of any conflict between any of these documents, the terms of this Agreement shall prevail.

14.5   Unless the provisions of this Agreement otherwise provide, any notice or other communication required or permitted to be given or made in writing hereunder shall be validly given or made if delivered by hand or courier or if despatched by first class recorded delivery (airmail if overseas) addressed to the address specified for the parties in this Agreement (or such other address as may be notified to the parties from time to time) or if sent by facsimile message to such facsimile number as has been notified to the parties from time to time and shall be deemed to have been received:

(i)   if delivered by hand or courier, at the time of delivery;

(ii)   if sent by first class recorded delivery (airmail if overseas), 2 business days after posting (6 days if sent by airmail);

(iii)   if sent by facsimile, at the time of completion of the transmission of the facsimile with facsimile machine confirmation of transmission to the correct facsimile number of all pages of the notice.

14.6   The Owner and the Licensee shall not assign, transfer or subcontract this Agreement or any rights or obligations hereunder without the prior written consent of the other parties.

14.7   NCC Escrow shall be entitled to transfer or assign this Agreement upon written notice to both the Owner and the Licensee.

14.8   This Agreement shall be binding upon and survive for the benefit of the successors in title and permitted assigns of the parties.

14.9   If any provision of this Agreement is declared too broad in any respect to permit enforcement to its full extent, the parties agree that such provision shall be enforced to the maximum extent permitted by law and that such provision shall be deemed to be varied accordingly. If any provision of this Agreement is found by any court, tribunal or administrative body of competent jurisdiction to be wholly or partly illegal, invalid, void or unenforceable, it shall, to the extent of such illegality, invalidity or unenforceability, be deemed severable and the remaining part of the provision and the rest of the provisions of this Agreement shall continue in full force and effect.

14.10   Save as expressly provided in this Agreement, no amendment or variation of this Agreement shall be effective unless in writing and signed by a duly authorised representative of each of the parties to it.

14.11   The parties shall not be liable to each other or be deemed to be in breach of this Agreement by reason of any delay in performing, or failure to perform, any of their obligations under this Agreement if the delay or failure was for a reason beyond that party's reasonable control (including, without limitation, fire, flood, explosion, epidemic, riot, civil commotion, any strike, lockout or other industrial action, act of God, war or warlike hostilities or threat of war, terrorist activities, accidental or malicious damage, or any prohibition or restriction by any governments or other legal authority which affects this Agreement and which is not in force on the date of this Agreement). A party claiming to be unable to perform its obligations under this Agreement (either on time or at all) in any of the circumstances set out above must notify the other parties of the nature and extent of the circumstances in question as soon as practicable. If such circumstances continue for more than six months, any of the other parties shall be entitled to terminate this Agreement by giving one month's notice in writing.

14.12   No waiver by any party of any breach of any provisions of this Agreement shall be deemed to be a waiver of any subsequent or other breach and, subject to clause 6.6, no failure to exercise or delay in exercising any right or remedy under this Agreement shall constitute a waiver thereof.

14.13   This Agreement is not intended to create any right under the Contracts (Rights of Third Parties) Act 1999 which is enforceable by any person who is not a party to this Agreement and the rights of any third party under the said act are hereby expressly excluded.

ESSL

14.14 This Agreement may be executed in any number of counterparts and by different parties in separate counterparts. Each counterpart when so executed shall be deemed to be an original and all of which together shall constitute one and the same agreement.

Signed for and on behalf of [Ownername]

Name: .... |..

Position: .... | (Authorised Signatory)

Signed for and on behalf of [Licenseename]

Name: .... |..

Position: .... | (Authorised Signatory)

Signed for and on behalf of NCC ESCROW INTERNATIONAL LIMITED

Name: .... |..

Position: .... | (Authorised Signatory)

ESSL

Schedule 1

The Package

The software package known as [SoftwareName] or any other name(s) as may be given to it by the Owner from time to time.

Schedule 2

NCC Escrow's Fees

	DESCRIPTION	OWNER	LICENSEE
1	Annual Fee (payable on completion of this Agreement and in advance of each anniversary thereafter)		
2	Escrow Secure Annual Fee (plus NCC Escrow's reasonable travel and subsistence expenses). Payable on the carrying out of the Full Verification pursuant to clause 4.1.2. **10% discount on Escrow Secure Fee**		
3	Scheduled Update Fee (2nd and subsequent scheduled deposits in any one year, payable on completion of this Agreement and in advance of each anniversary thereafter) **Free update for deposits that undergo Full Verification**		
4	Unscheduled Update Fee (per unscheduled deposit)		
5	Release Fee (plus NCC Escrow's reasonable expenses)	Nil	100%

Additional fees will be payable to NCC Escrow by the Licensee (unless otherwise agreed between the parties) for the following where applicable:

- Storage Fee for deposits in excess of 1 cubic foot;
- Any novation or replacement of this Agreement at the request of the Owner or the Licensee;
- Integrity Testing Fee for deposits consisting of more than 5 media items.

ncc group
assure · secure · advise

Holding Agreement
(Owner Deposits)

Date
Owner   [Ownername]
Agreement Number [Agreement#]

Notice: The Owner is obliged to inform NCC Escrow of any changes in its circumstances (including change of name, registered office, contact details or change of owner of the intellectual property in the Material).

Version: 07/05   1

HAOD

Agreement Dated:

Between:

(1)   [Ownername] whose registered office is at [Owneraddress] (CRN: [Ownercrn]) (**"Owner"**); and

(2)   NCC ESCROW INTERNATIONAL LIMITED a company registered in England whose registered office is at Manchester Technology Centre, Oxford Road, Manchester M᾽ 7EF, ENGLAND (CRN: 3081952) (**"NCC Escrow"**).

Background:

The Owner wishes to deposit the Material with NCC Escrow for NCC Escrow to hold on the terms and conditions set out in this Agreement.

Agreement:

In consideration of the mutual undertakings and obligations contained in this Agreement, the parties agree that:

1   Definitions and Interpretation

1.1   In this Agreement the following terms shall have the following meanings:

"Agreement" means the terms and conditions of this agreement set out below, including the schedules hereto.

"Confidential Information" means all technical and/or commercial information not in the public domain and which is designated in writing as confidential by any party together with all other information of any party which may reasonably be regarded as confidential information.

"Full Verification" means the tests and processes forming NCC Escrow's Full Verification service and/or such other tests and processes as may be agreed between the parties for the verification of the Material.

"Integrity Testing" means those tests and processes forming NCC Escrow's Integrity Testing service, in so far as they can be applied to the Material.

"Intellectual Property Rights" mean any copyright, patents, design patents, registered designs, design rights, utility models, trademarks, service marks, trade secrets, know how, database rights, moral rights, confidential information, trade or business names, domain names, and any other rights of a similar nature including industrial and proprietary rights and other similar protected rights in any country or jurisdiction together with all registrations, applications to register and rights to apply for registration of any of the aforementioned rights and any licences of or in respect of such rights.

"Material" means the material and documentation described in schedule 1 together with any updates and upgrades thereto and new versions thereof.

"Order Form" means the order form setting out the details of the order placed with NCC Escrow for setting up this Agreement.

1.2   This Agreement shall be interpreted in accordance with the following:

1.2.1   headings are for ease of reference only and shall not be taken into consideration in the interpretation of this Agreement;

1.2.2   all references to clauses and schedules are references to clauses and schedules of this Agreement; and

1.2.3   all references to a party or parties are references to a party or parties to this Agreement.

2   Owner's Duties and Warranties

2.1   The Owner is responsible for delivering the Material to NCC Escrow.

2.2   The Owner may make further deposits of Material as and when necessary.

2.3   The Owner shall deliver with each deposit of the Material the following information:

2.3.1   details of the deposit including its full name (i.e. the original name as set out under schedule 1 together with any new names given to the Material by the Owner), version details, media type, backup command/software used, compression used, archive hardware and operating system details; and

2.3.2   password/encryption details required to access the Material.

2.4   The Owner warrants to NCC Escrow at the time of each deposit of the Material with NCC Escrow that:

2.4.1   it owns the Intellectual Property Rights in the Material; and

2.4.2   in entering into this Agreement and performing its obligations under it, it is not in breach of any of its ongoing express or implied obligations to any third party(s).

3   NCC Escrow's Duties

27 • Appendix • Precedents

3.1   NCC Escrow shall:

    3.1.1   at all times during the term of this Agreement, retain the latest deposit of the Material in a safe and secure environment;

    3.1.2   confirm to the Owner receipt of any deposit of the Material by sending to the Owner a copy of the Integrity Testing report or Full Verification report (as the case may be) generated from the testing processes carried out under clause 8; and

    3.1.3   notify the Owner if it becomes aware at any time during the term of this Agreement that the copy of the Material held by it has been lost, damaged or destroyed so that a replacement may be obtained.

3.2   NCC Escrow may appoint agents, contractors or sub-contractors as it deems fit to carry out the Integrity Testing and the Full Verification processes. NCC Escrow shall ensure that any such agents, contractors and sub-contractors are bound by the same confidentiality obligations as are contained in clause 6.

3.3   NCC Escrow has the right to make such copies of the Material as may be necessary solely for the purposes of this Agreement.

4   Payment

4.1   The Owner shall pay NCC Escrow's standard fees and charges as set out in schedule 2 at the rates published from time to time or as otherwise agreed. NCC Escrow's fees as published are exclusive of value added tax.

4.2   NCC Escrow shall be entitled to review and vary its standard fees and charges for its services under this Agreement from time to time but no more than once a year and only upon 45 days written notice to the Owner.

4.3   All invoices are payable within 30 days from the date of invoice. NCC Escrow reserves the right to charge interest in respect of the late payment of any sum due under this Agreement (both before and after judgement) at the rate of 2% per annum over the prevailing base rate of HSBC Bank Plc accruing on a daily basis from the due date therefor until full payment.

5   Release

5.1   Subject to the receipt by NCC Escrow of: (i) its release fee and any other fees outstanding under this Agreement and (ii) a written request signed by a duly authorised officer of the Owner, NCC Escrow will release the Material to the Owner.

5.2   The Owner may re-deposit the Material at any time after release provided that this Agreement has not been terminated in accordance with clause 11 and the Owner has continued to pay the relevant fees.

6   Confidentiality

6.1   The Material shall remain at all times the confidential and intellectual property of the Owner.

6.2   NCC Escrow agrees to keep all Confidential Information relating to the Material that comes into its possession or to its knowledge under this Agreement in strictest confidence and secrecy. NCC Escrow further agrees not to make use of such information and/or documentation other than for the purposes of this Agreement and, unless the Owner should agree otherwise in writing, will not disclose or release it other than in accordance with the terms of this Agreement.

7   Intellectual Property Rights

The Intellectual Property Rights in the Integrity Testing report and any Full Verification report shall remain vested in NCC Escrow. The Owner shall be granted a non-exclusive right and licence to use such report for the purposes of this Agreement and its own internal purposes only.

8   Integrity Testing and Full Verification

8.1   NCC Escrow shall bear no obligation or responsibility to the Owner or any other person, firm, company or entity whatsoever to determine the existence, relevance, completeness, accuracy, operation, effectiveness, functionality or any other aspect of the Material received by NCC Escrow under this Agreement.

8.2   As soon as practicable after the Material has been deposited with NCC Escrow, NCC Escrow shall apply its Integrity Testing processes to the Material.

8.3   The Owner shall be entitled to require NCC Escrow to carry out a Full Verification. NCC Escrow's prevailing fees and charges for the Full Verification processes and all reasonable expenses incurred by NCC Escrow in carrying out the Full Verification processes shall be payable by the Owner.

9   NCC Escrow's Liability

9.1   Nothing in this clause 9 excludes or limits the liability of NCC Escrow for fraudulent misrepresentation or for death or personal injury caused by NCC Escrow's negligence. Save as aforesaid the following

HAOD

provisions set out the entire financial liability of NCC Escrow (including any liability for the acts or omissions of its employees, agents and sub-contractors) to the Owner:

9.1.1   NCC Escrow shall not be liable for any loss or damage caused to the Owner except to the extent that such loss or damage is caused by the negligent acts or omissions of or a breach of any contractual duty by NCC Escrow, its employees, agents or sub-contractors and in such event NCC Escrow's total liability in respect of all claims arising under or by virtue of this Agreement or in connection with the performance or contemplated performance of this Agreement, shall not exceed the sum of £1,000,000 (one million UK pounds); and

9.1.2   NCC Escrow shall not be liable to the Owner for any indirect or consequential loss or damage whether for loss of profit, loss of business, depletion of goodwill or otherwise whatsoever or howsoever caused which arise out of or in connection with this Agreement even if such loss was reasonably foreseeable or NCC Escrow had been advised of the possibility of incurring the same by the Owner or any third party.

9.2   NCC Escrow shall not be liable in any way to the Owner for acting in accordance with the terms of this Agreement and specifically (without limitation) for acting upon any notice, written request, waiver, consent, receipt, statutory declaration or any other document furnished to it pursuant to and in accordance with this Agreement.

9.3   NCC Escrow shall not be required to make any investigation into and shall be entitled in good faith without incurring any liability to the Owner to assume (without requesting evidence thereof) the validity, authenticity, veracity and due and authorised execution of any documents, written requests, waivers, consents, receipts, statutory declarations or notices received by it in respect of this Agreement.

10   Indemnity

The Owner shall assume all liability and shall at all times indemnify and hold harmless NCC Escrow and its officers, agents, sub-contractors and employees from and against any and all liability, loss, damages, costs, legal costs, professional and other expenses and any other liabilities of whatever nature, awarded against or agreed to be paid or otherwise suffered, incurred or sustained by NCC Escrow, whether direct, indirect or consequential as a result of or in connection with any claim by any third party(s) for alleged or actual infringement of Intellectual Property Rights arising out of or in connection with all and any acts or omissions of NCC Escrow in respect of the Material as contemplated under this Agreement.

11   Term and Termination

11.1   This Agreement shall continue until terminated in accordance with this clause 11.

11.2   If the Owner fails to pay an invoice addressed to it for services under this Agreement within 30 days of its issue, NCC Escrow reserves the right to give the Owner written notice to pay the outstanding invoice within 30 days. If the Owner has not paid its invoice by the expiry of the 30 day notice period, this Agreement will automatically immediately terminate.

11.3   The Owner may terminate this Agreement at any time by giving written notice to NCC Escrow.

11.4   Upon termination under the provisions of clause 11.2 or 11.3, for 30 days from the date of termination, NCC Escrow will make the Material available for collection by the Owner or its agents from the premises of NCC Escrow during office hours. After such 30 day period NCC Escrow will destroy the Material.

11.5   Notwithstanding any other provision of this clause 11, NCC Escrow may terminate this Agreement by giving 30 days written notice to the Owner.

11.6   Upon termination under the provisions of clause 11.5, NCC Escrow will return the Material to the Owner.

11.7   The provisions of clauses 1, 4, 6, 7, 8.1, 9, 10, 11.7 to 11.9 (inclusive) and 12 shall continue in full force after termination of this Agreement.

11.8   On and after termination of this Agreement, the Owner shall remain liable to NCC Escrow for payment in full of any fees and interest which have become due but which have not been paid as at the date of termination.

11.9   The termination of this Agreement, however arising, shall be without prejudice to the rights accrued to the parties prior to termination.

12   General

12.1   A party shall notify the other party to this Agreement, within 30 days of its occurrence, of any of the following:

12.1.1   a change of its name, registered office, contact address or other contact details; and

12.1.2   any material change in its circumstances that may affect the validity or operation of this Agreement.

599

HAOD

12.2   The formation, existence, construction, performance, validity and all other aspects of this Agreement shall be governed by and construed in accordance with the laws of England and the parties submit to the exclusive jurisdiction of the English courts.

12.3   This Agreement, together with the Order Form and any relevant NCC Escrow standard terms and conditions represent the whole agreement relating to the escrow arrangements between NCC Escrow and the Owner in respect of the Material and shall supersede all prior agreements, discussions, arrangements, representations, negotiations and undertakings. In the event of any conflict between any of these documents, the terms of this Agreement shall prevail.

12.4   Unless the provisions of this Agreement otherwise provide, any notice or other communication required or permitted to be given or made in writing hereunder shall be validly given or made if delivered by hand or courier or if despatched by first class recorded delivery (airmail if overseas) addressed to the address specified for the parties in this Agreement (or such other address as may be notified to the parties from time to time) or if sent by facsimile message to such facsimile number as has been notified to the parties from time to time and shall be deemed to have been received:

   (i)   if delivered by hand or courier, at the time of delivery;

   (ii)   if sent by first class recorded delivery (airmail if overseas), 2 business days after posting (6 days if sent by airmail);

   (iii)   if sent by facsimile, at the time of completion of the transmission of the facsimile with facsimile machine confirmation of transmission to the correct facsimile number of all pages of the notice.

12.5   The Owner shall not assign, transfer or subcontract this Agreement or any rights or obligations thereunder without the prior written consent of NCC Escrow.

12.6   NCC Escrow shall be entitled to transfer or assign this Agreement upon written notice to the Owner.

12.7   This Agreement shall be binding upon and survive for the benefit of the successors in title and permitted assigns of the parties.

12.8   If any provision of this Agreement is declared too broad in any respect to permit enforcement to its full extent, the parties agree that such provision shall be enforced to the maximum extent permitted by law and that such provision shall be deemed to be varied accordingly. If any provision of this Agreement is found by any court, tribunal or administrative body of competent jurisdiction to be wholly or partly illegal, invalid, void or unenforceable, it shall, to the extent of such illegality, invalidity or unenforceability, be deemed severable and the remaining part of the provision and the rest of the provisions of this Agreement shall continue in full force and effect.

12.9   Save as expressly provided in this Agreement, no amendment or variation of this Agreement shall be effective unless in writing and signed by a duly authorised representative of each of the parties to it.

12.10   The parties shall not be liable to each other or be deemed to be in breach of this Agreement by reason of any delay in performing, or failure to perform, any of their obligations under this Agreement if the delay or failure was for a reason beyond that party's reasonable control (including, without limitation, fire, flood, explosion, epidemic, riot, civil commotion, any strike, lockout or other industrial action, act of God, war or warlike hostilities or threat of war, terrorist activities, accidental or malicious damage, or any prohibition or restriction by any governments or other legal authority which affects this Agreement and which is not in force on the date of this Agreement). A party claiming to be unable to perform its obligations under this Agreement (either on time or at all) in any of the circumstances set out above must notify the other parties of the nature and extent of the circumstances in question as soon as practicable. If such circumstances continue for more than six months, any of the other parties shall be entitled to terminate this Agreement by giving one month's notice in writing.

12.11   No waiver by any party of any breach of any provisions of this Agreement shall be deemed to be a waiver of any subsequent or other breach and no failure to exercise or delay in exercising any right or remedy under this Agreement shall constitute a waiver thereof.

12.12   This Agreement is not intended to create any right under the Contracts (Rights of Third Parties) Act 1999 which is enforceable by any person who is not a party to this Agreement and the rights of any third party under the said act are hereby expressly excluded.

12.13   This Agreement may be executed in any number of counterparts and by different parties in separate counterparts. Each counterpart when so executed shall be deemed to be an original and all of which together shall constitute one and the same agreement.

HAOD

Signed for and on behalf of [Ownername]

Name: ....   ¦ ....

Position: ....   ¦   (Authorised Signatory)

Signed for and on behalf of NCC ESCROW INTERNATIONAL LIMITED

Name: ....   ¦ ....

Position: ....   ¦   (Authorised Signatory)

27 • Appendix • Precedents

Schedule 1

The Material

The material known as [SoftwareName] or any other name(s) as may be given to it by the Owner from time to time.

Schedule 2

NCC Escrow's Fees

	DESCRIPTION
1	Annual Fee (payable on completion of this Agreement and in advance of each anniversary thereafter)
2	Scheduled Update Fee (2nd and subsequent scheduled deposits in any one year, payable on completion of this Agreement and in advance of each anniversary thereafter)
3	Unscheduled Update Fee (per unscheduled deposit)
4	Release Fee (plus NCC Escrow's reasonable expenses)

Additional fees will be payable to NCC Escrow by the Owner for the following where applicable:

- Storage Fee for deposits in excess of 1 cubic foot;
- Any novation or replacement of this Agreement at the request of the Owner;
- Integrity Testing Fee for deposits consisting of more than 5 media items.

Information Escrow Agreement

Date

Owner [Ownername]

Agreement Number [Agreement#]

Notice: The parties to this Agreement are obliged to inform NCC Escrow of any changes to the Material or in their circumstances (including change of name, registered office, contact details or change of owner of the intellectual property in the Material).

Version: 07/05

Escrow Agreement Dated:

Between:

(1)   [Ownername] whose registered office is at [Owneraddress] (CRN: [Ownercrn]) (**"Owner"**);

(2)   [Licenseename] whose registered office is at [Licenseeaddress] (CRN: [Licenseecrn]) (**"Customer"**); and

(3)   NCC ESCROW INTERNATIONAL LIMITED a company registered in England whose registered office is at Manchester Technology Centre, Oxford Road, Manchester M1 7EF, ENGLAND (CRN: 3081952) (**"NCC Escrow"**).

Background:

(A)   Certain technical information and/or documentation is the confidential information and intellectual property of the Owner.

(B)   The Owner acknowledges that in certain circumstances, such information and/or documentation would be required by the Customer in order for it to continue to use or otherwise enjoy the benefit of a certain product or products.

(C)   To provide assurance to the Customer that the Customer can obtain access to the information and/documentation, the parties have agreed that such information and/or documentation should be placed with a trusted third party, NCC Escrow, so that it can be released to the Customer should certain circumstances arise.

Agreement:

In consideration of the mutual undertakings and obligations contained in this Agreement, the parties agree that:

1   **Definitions and Interpretation**

        1.1   In this Agreement the following terms shall have the following meanings:

                "Agreement" means the terms and conditions of this escrow agreement set out below, including the schedules hereto.

                "Confidential Information" means all technical and/or commercial information not in the public domain and which is designated in writing as confidential by any party together with all other information of any party which may reasonably be regarded as confidential information.

                "Independent Expert" means a suitably qualified and independent solicitor or barrister.

                "Integrity Plus Testing" means those tests forming NCC Escrow's Integrity Plus Testing service, in so far as they can be applied to the Material.

                "Integrity Testing" means those tests and processes forming NCC Escrow's Integrity Testing service, in so far as they can be applied to the Material.

                "Intellectual Property Rights" mean any copyright, patents, design patents, registered designs, design rights, utility models, trademarks, service marks, trade secrets, know how, database rights, moral rights, confidential information, trade or business names, domain names, and any other rights of a similar nature including industrial and proprietary rights and other similar protected rights in any country or jurisdiction together with all registrations, applications to register and rights to apply for registration of any of the aforementioned rights and any licences of or in respect of such rights.

                "User Rights" means the Customer's rights to use or otherwise enjoy the benefit of the Product(s) (whether or not such rights have been granted to the Customer by the Owner in any form of agreement).

                "Material" means the technical information and documentation which relates to the Product(s) and which is described in schedule 1, together with any updates and upgrades thereto and new versions thereof.

                "Order Form" means the order form setting out the details of the order placed with NCC Escrow for setting up this Agreement.

                "Product(s)" means any product or products which the Owner has a right to use or otherwise enjoy the benefit of and/or which are being or are to be designed, created, manufactured or constructed for the Customer by the Owner.

                "Release Purposes" means only those purposes which will enable the Customer to continue to fully exercise the User Rights.

        1.2   This Agreement shall be interpreted in accordance with the following:

                1.2.1   headings are for ease of reference only and shall not be taken into consideration in the interpretation of this Agreement;

                1.2.2   all references to clauses and schedules are references to clauses and schedules of this Agreement; and

                1.2.3   all references to a party or parties are references to a party or parties to this Agreement.

Version: 07/05   2
Agreement Number: [Agreement#]

2 Owner's Duties and Warranties

2.1 The Owner shall:

2.1.1 deliver a copy of the Material to NCC Escrow within 30 days of the date of this Agreement;

2.1.2 deliver a further copy of the Material to NCC Escrow each time that there is a change to the Material;

2.1.3 ensure that each copy of the Material deposited with NCC Escrow is the latest version of the Material;

2.1.4 where the media upon which the Material is stored is electronically-readable, deliver to NCC Escrow a replacement copy of the Material within 30 days after the anniversary of the last delivery of the Material to ensure that the integrity of the Material media is maintained;

2.1.5 deliver a replacement copy of the Material to NCC Escrow within 14 days of a notice given to it by NCC Escrow under the provisions of clause 4.1.3;

2.1.6 deliver with each deposit of the Material the following information:

2.1.6.1 the overall name of the Material (its original name as set out under schedule 1 together with any new names given to the Material by the Owner) and, where appropriate, a more detailed description;

2.1.6.2 version details, media type, backup command/software used, compression used, archive hardware and operating system details; and

2.1.6.3 password/encryption details required to access the Material.

2.2 The Owner warrants to both NCC Escrow and the Customer at the time of each deposit of the Material with NCC Escrow that:

2.2.1 it owns the Intellectual Property Rights in the Material;

2.2.2 in entering into this Agreement and performing its obligations under it, it is not in breach of any of its ongoing express or implied obligations to any third party(s); and

2.2.3 the Material is the latest version of the Material.

3 Customer's Responsibilities and Undertakings

3.1 The Customer shall notify NCC Escrow of any changes to the Material and/or the Product(s) that necessitates a replacement deposit of the Material.

3.2 In the event that the Material is released under clause 5, the Customer shall:

3.2.1 keep the Material confidential at all times;

3.2.2 use the Material only for the Release Purposes;

3.2.3 not disclose the Material to any person save such of the Customer's employees or contractors who need to know the same in order to use the Material exclusively on behalf of the Customer for the Release Purposes. In the event that Material is disclosed to its employees or contractors, the Customer shall ensure that they are bound by the same confidentiality obligations as are contained in this clause 3.2;

3.2.4 hold all media containing the Material in a safe and secure environment when not in use; and

3.2.5 forthwith destroy the Material should the Customer cease to be entitled to exercise the User Rights.

4 NCC Escrow's Duties

4.1 NCC Escrow shall:

4.1.1 at all times during the term of this Agreement retain the latest deposit of the Material in a safe and secure environment;

4.1.2 inform the Owner and the Customer of the receipt of any deposit of the Material by sending to both parties a copy of the Integrity Testing report or Integrity Plus Testing report (as the case may be) generated from the testing processes carried out under clause 10; and

4.1.3 notify the Owner and the Customer if it becomes aware at any time during the term of this Agreement that the copy of the Material held by it has been lost, damaged or destroyed so that a replacement may be obtained.

4.2 In the event of failure by the Owner to deposit any Material with NCC Escrow, NCC Escrow shall not be responsible for procuring such deposit and may, at its sole discretion, notify the Customer of the Owner's failure to deposit any Material.

27 ● Appendix ● Precedents

© NCC Group 1984 - 2007

4.3 NCC Escrow may appoint agents, contractors or sub-contractors as it deems fit to carry out the Integrity Testing and the Integrity Plus Testing processes. NCC Escrow shall ensure that any such agents, contractors and sub-contractors are bound by the same confidentiality obligations as are contained in clause 8.

4.4 NCC Escrow has the right to make such copies of the Material as may be necessary solely for the purposes of this Agreement.

5 Payment

5.1 The parties shall pay NCC Escrow's standard fees and charges as published from time to time or as otherwise agreed, in the proportions set out in schedule 2. NCC Escrow's fees as published are exclusive of value added tax.

5.2 NCC Escrow shall be entitled to review and vary its standard fees and charges for its services under this Agreement from time to time but no more than once a year and only upon 45 days written notice to the parties.

5.3 All invoices are payable within 30 days from the date of invoice. NCC Escrow reserves the right to charge interest in respect of the late payment of any sum due under this Agreement (both before and after judgement) at the rate of 2% per annum over the prevailing base rate of HSBC Bank Plc accruing on a daily basis from the due date therefor until full payment.

6 Release Events

6.1 Subject to: (i) the remaining provisions of this clause 6 and (ii) the receipt by NCC Escrow of its release fee and any other fees and interest (if any) outstanding under this Agreement, NCC Escrow will release the Material to a duly authorised officer of the Customer if any of the following events (**"Release Event(s)"**) occur:

6.1.1 if the Owner is a company:

6.1.1.1 an order is made for the winding up of the Owner, the Owner passes a resolution for winding up (other than for the purposes of a solvent reconstruction or amalgamation) or a liquidator of the Owner is appointed; or

6.1.1.2 an order is made for the appointment of an administrator of the Owner or an administrator of the Owner is appointed; or

6.1.1.3 the Owner enters into a compromise or arrangement with creditors; or

6.1.1.4 the Owner has a receiver, administrative receiver or manager appointed over all or any part of its assets or undertaking; or

6.1.1.5 the Owner is dissolved; or

6.1.2 if the Owner is an individual:

6.1.2.1 the Owner enters into a compromise or arrangement with creditors; or

6.1.2.2 the Owner is declared bankrupt; or

6.1.2.3 the Owner dies; or

6.1.3 if the Owner is a partnership:

6.1.3.1 any of the partners in the Owner are declared bankrupt or enter into a compromise or arrangement with creditors; or

6.1.3.2 the Owner is wound up or dissolved; or

6.1.3.3 the Owner enters into a compromise or arrangement with creditors; or

6.1.3.4 a partnership administration order is made in respect of the Owner; or

6.1.4 any similar or analogous proceedings or event to those in clauses 6.1.1 to 6.1.3 above occurs in respect of the Owner within any jurisdiction outside England; or

6.1.5 the Owner ceases to carry on its business or the part of its business which relates to the Product(s); or

6.1.6 the Owner assigns its rights to the Intellectual Property Rights in the Material to a third party (**"Assignee"**) and the Assignee fails, within 60 days of all parties' knowledge of such assignment, to continue escrow protection for the benefit of the Customer by failing to enter into either:

6.1.6.1 a novation agreement with the Customer and NCC Escrow for the assumption of the Owner's rights and obligations under this Agreement by the Assignee; or

6.1.6.2 a new escrow agreement with the Customer for the Material which offers the Customer substantially similar protection to that provided by this Agreement without significantly increasing the overall cost to the Customer,

provided that if the Assignee offers to enter into a novation or new escrow agreement within 60 days of all parties' knowledge of the assignment and the Customer fails to accept the Assignee's offer within 30 days of such offer being notified to the Customer, there shall be no Release Event under this clause; or

6.1.7   the Owner is in material breach of its obligations under any agreement with the Customer relating to the Product(s)and has failed to remedy such default notified by the Customer to the Owner within a reasonable period.

6.2   The Customer must notify NCC Escrow of the Release Event specified in clause 6.1 by delivering to NCC Escrow a statutory or notarised declaration (**"Declaration"**) made by an officer of the Customer declaring that such Release Event has occurred, setting out the facts and circumstances of the Release Event, that the User Rights and any agreement with the Owner relating to the Product(s) were still valid and effective up to the occurrence of such Release Event and exhibiting such documentary evidence in support of the Declaration as NCC Escrow shall reasonably require.

6.3   Upon receipt of a Declaration from the Customer claiming that a Release Event has occurred:

6.3.1   NCC Escrow shall submit a copy of the Declaration to the Owner by courier or other form of guaranteed delivery; and

6.3.2   unless within 14 days after the date of despatch of the Declaration by NCC Escrow, NCC Escrow receives a counter-notice signed by a duly authorised officer of the Owner stating that in their view no such Release Event has occurred, or, if appropriate, that the event or circumstance giving rise to the Release Event has been rectified as shown by documentation in support thereof,

NCC Escrow will release the Material to the Customer for its use for the Release Purposes.

6.4   Upon receipt of the counter-notice from the Owner under clause 6.3.2, NCC Escrow shall send a copy of the counter-notice and any supporting evidence to the Customer by courier or other form of guaranteed delivery.

6.5   Upon receipt by the Customer of the counter-notice from NCC Escrow or, in any event, within 90 days of despatch of the counter-notice by NCC Escrow, the Customer may give notice to NCC Escrow that they wish to invoke the dispute resolution procedure under clause 7.

6.6   If, within 90 days of despatch of the counter-notice by NCC Escrow to the Customer, NCC Escrow has not been informed by the Customer that they wish the dispute resolution procedure under clause 7 to apply, the Declaration submitted by the Customer will be deemed to be no longer valid and the Customer shall be deemed to have waived their right to release of the Material for the particular reason or event specified in the original Declaration.

6.7   For the avoidance of doubt, where a Release Event has occurred under clauses 6.1.1 to 6.1.5, a subsequent assignment of the Intellectual Property Rights in the Material shall not prejudice the Customer's right to release of the Material and its use for the Release Purposes.

7   Disputes

7.1   NCC Escrow shall notify the Owner of the Customer's request for dispute resolution. Unless the Owner or the Customer objects, NCC Escrow's Chief Executive Officer for the time being will appoint an Independent Expert to resolve the dispute. If the Owner or the Customer objects to this appointment, they shall endeavour to appoint a mutually acceptable Independent Expert within 7 days of registering their objection. If they fail to appoint an Independent Expert within this 7 day period, NCC Escrow shall request that the President of The Law Society appoints an Independent Expert to resolve the dispute. Any appointment of an Independent Expert under this clause shall be binding upon the parties.

7.2   Within 5 working days of the appointment of the Independent Expert, the Owner and the Customer shall each provide full written submissions to the Independent Expert together with all relevant documentary evidence in their possession in support of their claim.

7.3   The Independent Expert shall be requested to give a decision on the matter within 14 days of the date of referral or as soon as practicable thereafter and to send a copy of that decision to the Owner, Customer and NCC Escrow. The Independent Expert's decision shall be final and binding on all parties and shall not be subject to appeal to a court in legal proceedings except in the case of manifest error.

7.4   If the Independent Expert's decision is in favour of the Customer, NCC Escrow is hereby authorised to release and deliver the Material to the Customer within 5 working days of the decision being notified by the Independent Expert to the parties.

7.5   The parties hereby agree that the costs and expenses of the Independent Expert shall be borne by the party against whom the decision of the Independent Expert is given.

8   Confidentiality

8.1   The Material shall remain at all times the confidential and intellectual property of the Owner.

8.2   In the event that NCC Escrow releases the Material to the Customer, the Customer shall be

IEA

permitted to use the Material only for the Release Purposes.

8.3 NCC Escrow agrees to keep all Confidential Information relating to the Material that comes into its possession or to its knowledge under this Agreement in strictest confidence and secrecy. NCC Escrow further agrees not to make use of such information and/or documentation other than for the purposes of this Agreement and, unless the parties should agree otherwise in writing, will not disclose or release it other than in accordance with the terms of this Agreement.

9 Intellectual Property Rights

9.1 The release of the Material to the Customer will not act as an assignment of any Intellectual Property Rights that the Owner possesses in the Material.

9.2 The Intellectual Property Rights in the Integrity Testing report and any Integrity Plus Testing report shall remain vested in NCC Escrow. The Owner and the Customer shall each be granted a non-exclusive right and licence to use such report for the purposes of this Agreement and their own internal purposes only.

10 Integrity Testing and Integrity Plus Testing

10.1 NCC Escrow shall bear no obligation or responsibility to any party to this Agreement or person, firm, company or entity whatsoever to determine the existence, relevance, completeness, accuracy, operation, effectiveness, functionality or any other aspect of the Material received by NCC Escrow under this Agreement.

10.2 As soon as practicable after the Material has been deposited with NCC Escrow, NCC Escrow shall apply its Integrity Testing processes to the Material.

10.3 Any party to this Agreement shall be entitled to require NCC Escrow to apply its Integrity Plus Testing processes to the Material. Subject to clause 10.4, NCC Escrow's prevailing fees and charges for the Integrity Plus Testing processes and all reasonable expenses incurred by NCC Escrow in carrying out the Integrity Plus Testing processes shall be payable by the requesting party.

10.4 If the Material fails to satisfy NCC Escrow's Integrity Plus Testing processes as a result of being defective or incomplete in content, NCC Escrow's fees charges and expenses in relation to the Integrity Plus Testing processes shall be paid by the Owner.

10.5 Should the Material deposited fail to satisfy NCC Escrow's Integrity Testing or Integrity Plus Testing processes under clauses 10.2 or 10.3, the Owner shall within 14 days of the receipt of the notice of test failure from NCC Escrow, deposit such new, corrected or revised Material as shall be necessary to ensure its compliance with its warranties and obligations in clause 2. If the Owner fails to make such deposit of the new, corrected or revised Material, NCC Escrow will issue a report to the Customer detailing the problem with the Material as revealed by the relevant tests.

11 NCC Escrow's Liability

11.1 Nothing in this clause 11 excludes or limits the liability of NCC Escrow for fraudulent misrepresentation or for death or personal injury caused by NCC Escrow's negligence. Save as aforesaid the following provisions set out the entire financial liability of NCC Escrow (including any liability for the acts or omissions of its employees, agents and sub-contractors) to the other parties:

11.1.1 NCC Escrow shall not be liable for any loss or damage caused to either the Owner or the Customer either jointly or severally except to the extent that such loss or damage is caused by the negligent acts or omissions of or a breach of any contractual duty by NCC Escrow, its employees, agents or sub-contractors and in such event NCC Escrow's total liability in respect of all claims arising under or by virtue of this Agreement or in connection with the performance or contemplated performance of this Agreement, shall not exceed the sum of £1,000,000 (one million UK pounds); and

11.1.2 NCC Escrow shall not be liable to the Owner or the Customer for any indirect or consequential loss or damage whether for loss of profit, loss of business, depletion of goodwill or otherwise whatsoever or howsoever caused which arise out of or in connection with this Agreement even if such loss was reasonably foreseeable or NCC Escrow had been advised of the possibility of incurring the same by the Owner, the Customer or any third party.

11.2 NCC Escrow shall not be liable in any way to the Owner or the Customer for acting in accordance with the terms of this Agreement and specifically (without limitation) for acting upon any notice, written request, waiver, consent, receipt, statutory declaration or any other document furnished to it pursuant to and in accordance with this Agreement.

11.3 NCC Escrow shall not be required to make any investigation into and shall be entitled in good faith without incurring any liability to the Owner or the Customer to assume (without requesting evidence thereof) the validity, authenticity, veracity and due and authorised execution of any documents, written requests, waivers, consents, receipts, statutory declarations or notices received by it in respect of this Agreement.

© NCC Group 1984 - 2007

12 Indemnity

12.1 Save for any claim falling within the provisions of clause 11.1.1, the Owner and the Customer jointly and severally agree at all times to indemnify and hold harmless NCC Escrow in respect of all of its legal and all other costs, fees and expenses incurred directly or indirectly as a result of being brought into or otherwise becoming involved in any form of dispute resolution proceedings or any litigation of any kind between the Owner and the Customer in relation to this Agreement to the extent that this Agreement does not otherwise provide for reimbursement of such costs.

12.2 The Owner shall assume all liability and shall at all times indemnify and hold harmless NCC Escrow and its officers, agents, sub-contractors and employees from and against any and all liability, loss, damages, costs, legal costs, professional and other expenses and any other liabilities of whatever nature, awarded against or agreed to be paid or otherwise suffered, incurred or sustained by NCC Escrow, whether direct, indirect or consequential as a result of or in connection with any claim by any third party(s) for alleged or actual infringement of Intellectual Property Rights arising out of or in connection with all and any acts or omissions of NCC Escrow in respect of the Material as contemplated under this Agreement.

13 Term and Termination

13.1 This Agreement shall continue until terminated in accordance with this clause 13.

13.2 If the Owner or the Customer, as the case may be, fails to pay an invoice addressed to it for services under this Agreement within 30 days of its issue, NCC Escrow reserves the right to give that party written notice to pay the outstanding invoice within 30 days. If the Customer has not paid its invoice by the expiry of the 30 day notice period, this Agreement will automatically immediately terminate. If the Owner has not paid its invoice by the expiry of the 30 day notice period, NCC Escrow will give the Customer a period of 15 days to pay the Owner's invoice. If the Owner's invoice has not been paid by the expiry of the 15 day optional payment period given to the Customer, this Agreement will automatically immediately terminate. Any amounts owed by the Owner but paid by the Customer will be recoverable by the Customer direct from the Owner as a debt and, if requested, NCC Escrow shall provide appropriate documentation to assist in such recovery.

13.3 Upon termination under the provisions of clause 13.2, for 30 days from the date of termination NCC Escrow will make the Material available for collection by the Owner or its agents from the premises of NCC Escrow during office hours. After such 30 day period NCC Escrow will destroy the Material.

13.4 Notwithstanding any other provision of this clause 13, NCC Escrow may terminate this Agreement by giving 30 days written notice to the Owner and the Customer. In that event the Owner and the Customer shall appoint a mutually acceptable new custodian on similar terms and conditions to those contained herein. If a new custodian is not appointed within 14 days of delivery of such notice, the Owner or the Customer shall be entitled to request the President for the time being of the British Computer Society (or successor body) to appoint a suitable new custodian upon such terms and conditions as he/she shall require. Such appointment shall be final and binding on the Owner and the Customer. If NCC Escrow is notified of the new custodian within the notice period, NCC Escrow will forthwith deliver the Material to the new custodian. If NCC Escrow is not notified of the new custodian within the notice period, NCC Escrow will return the Material to the Owner.

13.5 The Customer may terminate this Agreement at any time by giving written notice to NCC Escrow. Upon such termination, NCC Escrow will return the Material to the Owner.

13.6 If NCC Escrow discovers that a Release Event has occurred and the Customer has failed to exercise its right to claim for release of the Material under clause 6.2, NCC Escrow shall have the right to terminate this Agreement upon 30 days written notice to the Owner and the Customer. The Customer shall have the option of applying for release in accordance with clause 6 during this notice period, but if it fails to do so, upon the expiry of this notice period, this Agreement shall automatically terminate and, unless otherwise instructed by the Owner or the Assignee prior to expiry of the notice period, NCC Escrow shall destroy the Material.

13.7 If the Intellectual Property Rights in the Material have been assigned to a third party and the proviso in clause 6.1.6 applies such that there has been no Release Event under that clause, NCC Escrow shall be entitled to terminate this Agreement immediately by written notice to the Owner and the Customer and upon such termination, unless otherwise instructed by the Owner or the Assignee, NCC Escrow shall destroy the Material.

13.8 If the User Rights have expired or have been lawfully terminated, then the Customer shall give notice to NCC Escrow within 14 days thereof to terminate this Agreement, failing which, the Owner shall be entitled to give written notice to NCC Escrow to terminate this Agreement. Upon receipt of such a notice from the Owner, NCC Escrow shall notify the Customer of the Owner's notice to terminate. Unless within 14 days of NCC Escrow giving such notice to the Customer, NCC Escrow receives a counter-notice signed by a duly authorised officer of the Customer disputing the termination of the User Rights, then the Customer shall be deemed to have consented to such termination and this Agreement shall immediately automatically terminate. Any disputes arising under this clause shall be dealt with in accordance with the dispute resolution procedure in clause 7. Upon termination under this clause, NCC Escrow shall return the Material to the Owner.

13.9 Subject to clause 13.8, the Owner may only terminate this Agreement with the written consent of the Customer.

13.10 This Agreement shall automatically immediately terminate upon release of the Material to the Customer in accordance with clause 6.

13.11 If this Agreement is superseded and replaced by a new agreement in respect of the Material, this Agreement shall, upon the coming into force of the new agreement, automatically terminate. The relevant party or parties shall request NCC Escrow to either transfer the Material to the new agreement or ask the owner under the new agreement to deposit new material. If new material is deposited, upon its receipt, NCC Escrow shall, unless otherwise instructed, destroy the Material.

13.12 The provisions of clauses 1, 3.2, 3.3, 5, 8, 9, 10.1, 11, 12, 13.12 to 13.14 (inclusive) and 14 shall continue in full force after termination of this Agreement.

13.13 On and after termination of this Agreement, the Owner and/or the Customer (as appropriate) shall remain liable to NCC Escrow for payment in full of any fees and interest which have become due but which have not been paid as at the date of termination.

13.14 The termination of this Agreement, however arising, shall be without prejudice to the rights accrued to the parties prior to termination.

14 **General**

14.1 A party shall notify the other parties to this Agreement, within 30 days of its occurrence, of any of the following:

14.1.1 a change of its name, registered office, contact address or other contact details; and

14.1.2 any material change in its circumstances that may affect the validity or operation of this Agreement.

14.2 Within 14 days of any assignment or transfer by the Owner of any part of its Intellectual Property Rights in the Material, the Owner shall notify:

14.2.1 NCC Escrow and the Customer of such assignment and the identity of the Assignee; and

14.2.2 the Assignee of the provisions of clause 6.1.6.

14.3 The formation, existence, construction, performance, validity and all other aspects of this Agreement shall be governed by and construed in accordance with the laws of England and the parties submit to the exclusive jurisdiction of the English courts.

14.4 This Agreement, together with the Order Form and any relevant NCC Escrow standard terms and conditions represent the whole agreement relating to the escrow arrangements between NCC Escrow and the other parties for the Material and shall supersede all prior agreements, discussions, arrangements, representations, negotiations and undertakings. In the event of any conflict between any of these documents, the terms of this Agreement shall prevail.

14.5 Unless the provisions of this Agreement otherwise provide, any notice or other communication required or permitted to be given or made in writing hereunder shall be validly given or made if delivered by hand or courier or if despatched by first class recorded delivery (airmail if overseas) addressed to the address specified for the parties in this Agreement (or such other address as may be notified to the parties from time to time) or if sent by facsimile message to such facsimile number as has been notified to the parties from time to time and shall be deemed to have been received:

(i) if delivered by hand or courier, at the time of delivery;

(ii) if sent by first class recorded delivery (airmail if overseas), 2 business days after posting (6 days if sent by airmail);

(iii) if sent by facsimile, at the time of completion of the transmission of the facsimile with facsimile machine confirmation of transmission to the correct facsimile number of all pages of the notice.

14.6 The Owner and the Customer shall not assign, transfer or subcontract this Agreement or any rights or obligations thereunder without the prior written consent of the other parties.

14.7 NCC Escrow shall be entitled to transfer or assign this Agreement upon written notice to both the Owner and the Customer.

14.8 This Agreement shall be binding upon and survive for the benefit of the successors in title and permitted assigns of the parties.

14.9 If any provision of this Agreement is declared too broad in any respect to permit enforcement to its full extent, the parties agree that such provision shall be enforced to the maximum extent permitted by law and that such provision shall be deemed to be varied accordingly. If any

IEA

provision of this Agreement is found by any court, tribunal or administrative body of competent jurisdiction to be wholly or partly illegal, invalid, void or unenforceable, it shall, to the extent of such illegality, invalidity or unenforceability, be deemed severable and the remaining part of the provision and the rest of the provisions of this Agreement shall continue in full force and effect.

14.10 Save as expressly provided in this Agreement, no amendment or variation of this Agreement shall be effective unless in writing and signed by a duly authorised representative of each of the parties to it.

14.11 The parties shall not be liable to each other or be deemed to be in breach of this Agreement by reason of any delay in performing, or failure to perform, any of their obligations under this Agreement if the delay or failure was for a reason beyond that party's reasonable control (including, without limitation, fire, flood, explosion, epidemic, riot, civil commotion, any strike, lockout or other industrial action, act of God, war or warlike hostilities or threat of war, terrorist activities, accidental or malicious damage, or any prohibition or restriction by any governments or other legal authority which affects this Agreement and which is not in force on the date of this Agreement). A party claiming to be unable to perform its obligations under this Agreement (either on time or at all) in any of the circumstances set out above must notify the other parties of the nature and extent of the circumstances in question as soon as practicable. If such circumstances continue for more than six months, any of the other parties shall be entitled to terminate this Agreement by giving one month's notice in writing.

14.12 No waiver by any party of any breach of any provisions of this Agreement shall be deemed to be a waiver of any subsequent or other breach and, subject to clause 6.6, no failure to exercise or delay in exercising any right or remedy under this Agreement shall constitute a waiver thereof.

14.13 This Agreement is not intended to create any right under the Contracts (Rights of Third Parties) Act 1999 which is enforceable by any person who is not a party to this Agreement and the rights of any third party under the said act are hereby expressly excluded.

14.14 This Agreement may be executed in any number of counterparts and by different parties in separate counterparts. Each counterpart when so executed shall be deemed to be an original and all of which together shall constitute one and the same agreement.

Signed for and on behalf of [Ownername]

Name: .... | ....

Position: .... | (Authorised Signatory)

Signed for and on behalf of [Licenseename]

Name: .... | ....

Position: .... | (Authorised Signatory)

Signed for and on behalf of NCC ESCROW INTERNATIONAL LIMITED

Name: .... | ....

Position: .... | (Authorised Signatory)

27 • Appendix • Precedents

IEA

Schedule 1

The Material

Overall name of the Material: [   ]

Detailed description (where applicable):

Schedule 2

NCC Escrow's Fees

	DESCRIPTION	OWNER	CUSTOMER
1	Annual Fee (payable on completion of this Agreement and in advance of each anniversary thereafter)	[OwnerAnnual]	[LicenseeAnnual]
2	Scheduled Update Fee (2nd and subsequent scheduled deposits in any one year, payable on completion of this Agreement and in advance of each anniversary thereafter)	[OwnerSched]	[LicenseeSched]
3	Unscheduled Update Fee (per unscheduled deposit)	[OwnerUnsched]	[LicenseeUnsched]
4	Release Fee (plus NCC Escrow's reasonable expenses)	NIL	100%

Additional fees will be payable to NCC Escrow by the Customer (unless otherwise agreed between the parties) for the following where applicable:

- Storage Fee for deposits in excess of 1 cubic foot;
- Any novation or replacement of this Agreement at the request of the Owner or the Customer;
- Integrity Testing Fee for deposits consisting of more than 5 media items.

Multi Licensee
Software Escrow Agreement

Date
Owner   [Ownername]
Agreement Number [Agreement#]

Notice: The parties to this Agreement are obliged to inform NCC Escrow of any changes to the Package or in their circumstances (including change of name, registered office, contact details or change of owner of the intellectual property in the Package).

Version: 07/05

27 ● Appendix ● Precedents

Escrow Agreement Dated:

Between:

(1) [Ownername] whose registered office is at [Owneraddress] (CRN: [Ownercrn]) (**"Owner"**); and

(2) NCC ESCROW INTERNATIONAL LIMITED a company registered in England whose registered office is at Manchester Technology Centre, Oxford Road, Manchester M1 7EF, ENGLAND (CRN: 3081952) (**"NCC Escrow"**).

Background:

(A) The Licensee has been granted a licence to use the Package which comprises computer programs.

(B) Certain technical information and/or documentation relating to the software package is the confidential information and intellectual property of the Owner or a third party.

(C) The Owner acknowledges that in certain circumstances, such information and/or documentation would be required by the Licensee in order for it to continue to exercise its rights under the Licence Agreement.

(D) The parties therefore agree that such information and/or documentation should be placed with a trusted third party, NCC Escrow, so that such information and/or documentation can be released to the Licensee should certain circumstances arise.

Agreement:

In consideration of the mutual undertakings and obligations contained in this Agreement, the parties agree that:

1 **Definitions and Interpretation**

1.1 In this Agreement the following terms shall have the following meanings:

"Agreement" means the terms and conditions of this escrow agreement set out below, including the schedules and appendix hereto.

"Confidential Information" means all technical and/or commercial information not in the public domain and which is designated in writing as confidential by any party together with all other information of any party which may reasonably be regarded as confidential information.

"Confirmation Agreement" means an agreement in the form set out in appendix 1 to be signed by a party wishing to be a party to this Agreement as a Licensee and, accordingly, to take the benefit of and be bound by the terms and conditions of this Agreement.

"Full Verification" means the tests and processes forming NCC Escrow's Full Verification service and/or such other tests and processes as may be agreed between the parties for the verification of the Material.

"Independent Expert" means a suitably qualified and independent solicitor or barrister.

"Integrity Testing" means those tests and processes forming NCC Escrow's Integrity Testing service, in so far as they can be applied to the Material.

"Intellectual Property Rights" mean any copyright, patents, design patents, registered designs, design rights, utility models, trademarks, service marks, trade secrets, know how, database rights, moral rights, confidential information, trade or business names, domain names, and any other rights of a similar nature including industrial and proprietary rights and other similar protected rights in any country or jurisdiction together with all registrations, applications to register and rights to apply for registration of any of the aforementioned rights and any licences of or in respect of such rights.

"Licence Agreement" means the agreement under which a Licensee was granted a licence to use the Package.

"Licensee" means any person, firm, company or other entity:

1.1.1 to whom a licence to use the Package has been granted;

1.1.2 whom the Owner has approved for registration under this Agreement; and

1.1.3 who has agreed to be bound by the terms and conditions of this Agreement by executing a completed Confirmation Agreement, forwarded the same to NCC Escrow and the receipt and registration of which has been acknowledged by NCC Escrow in writing to the Licensee;

and references in this Agreement to the Licensee shall be to the relevant Licensee or Licensees given the context in which such reference is made.

"Material" means the Source Code of the Package and such other material and documentation (including updates and upgrades thereto and new versions thereof) as are necessary to be delivered or deposited to comply with clause 2 of this Agreement.

"Order Form" means an order form setting out the details of the order placed with NCC Escrow for setting up this Agreement and/or the registration of a Licensee under this Agreement.

"**Package**" means the software package together with any updates and upgrades thereto and new versions thereof licensed to the Licensee under the Licence Agreement details of which are set out in schedule 1.

"**Release Purposes**" means the purposes of understanding, maintaining, modifying and correcting the Package exclusively for and on behalf of the Licensee together with such other purposes (if any) as are permitted under the Licence Agreement.

"**Source Code**" means the computer programming code of the Package in human readable form.

"**Third Party Material**" means Source Code which is not the confidential information and intellectual property of the Owner or the Licensee.

1.2 This Agreement shall be interpreted in accordance with the following:

1.2.1 headings are for ease of reference only and shall not be taken into consideration in the interpretation of this Agreement;

1.2.2 all references to clauses and schedules are references to clauses and schedules of this Agreement; and

1.2.3 all references to a party or parties are references to a party or parties to this Agreement.

2 **Owner's Duties and Warranties**

2.1 The Owner shall:

2.1.1 deliver a copy of the Material to NCC Escrow within 30 days of the date of this Agreement;

2.1.2 deliver a further copy of the Material to NCC Escrow each time that there is a change to the Package;

2.1.3 ensure that each copy of the Material deposited with NCC Escrow comprises the Source Code of the latest version of the Package used by the Licensee;

2.1.4 deliver to NCC Escrow a replacement copy of the Material within 30 days after the anniversary of the last delivery of the Material to ensure that the integrity of the Material media is maintained;

2.1.5 deliver a replacement copy of the Material to NCC Escrow within 14 days of a notice given to it by NCC Escrow under the provisions of clause 4.1.4;

2.1.6 deliver with each deposit of the Material the following information:

2.1.6.1 details of the deposit including the full name of the Package (i.e. the original name as set out under schedule 1 together with any new names given to the Package by the Owner), version details, media type, backup command/software used, compression used, archive hardware and operating system details; and

2.1.6.2 password/encryption details required to access the Material;

2.1.7 deliver with each deposit of the Material the following technical information (where applicable):

2.1.7.1 documentation describing the procedures for building, compiling and installing the software, including names and versions of the development tools;

2.1.7.2 software design information (e.g. module names and functionality); and

2.1.7.3 name and contact details of employees with knowledge of how to maintain and support the Material; and

2.1.8 if required by a Licensee, deposit a backup copy of the object code of any third party software package required to access, install, build or compile or otherwise use the Material.

2.2 The Owner warrants to both NCC Escrow and the Licensee at the time of each deposit of the Material with NCC Escrow that:

2.2.1 other than any third party object code referred to in clause 2.1.8 or any Third Party Material, it owns the Intellectual Property Rights in the Material;

2.2.2 in respect of any Third Party Material, it has been granted valid and ongoing rights under licence by the third party owner(s) thereof to deal with such Third Party Material in the manner anticipated under this Agreement and that the Owner has the express authority of such third party owner(s) to deposit the Third Party Material under this Agreement as evidenced by a signed letter of authorisation in the form required by NCC Escrow;

2.2.3 in entering into this Agreement and performing its obligations under it, it is not in breach of any of its ongoing express or implied obligations to any third party(s);

2.2.4 the Material deposited under clause 2.1 contains all information in human-readable form (except for any third party object code deposited pursuant to clause 2.1.8) and is on suitable media to enable a reasonably skilled programmer or analyst to understand, maintain, modify and correct the Package; and

2.2.5   in respect of any third party object code that the Owner, at its option, or, at the request of the Licensee, deposits with NCC Escrow in conjunction with the Material pursuant to clause 2.1.8, it has the full right and authority to do so.

3   Licensee's Responsibilities and Undertakings

3.1   The Licensee shall notify NCC Escrow of any change to the Package that necessitates a replacement deposit of the Material.

3.2   In the event that the Material is released under clause 6, the Licensee shall:

3.2.1   keep the Material confidential at all times;

3.2.2   use the Material only for the Release Purposes;

3.2.3   not disclose the Material to any person save such of the Licensee's employees or contractors who need to know the same for the Release Purposes. In the event that Material is disclosed to its employees or contractors, the Licensee shall ensure that they are bound by the same confidentiality obligations as are contained in this clause 3.2;

3.2.4   hold all media containing the Material in a safe and secure environment when not in use; and

3.2.5   forthwith destroy the Material should the Licensee cease to be entitled to use the Package under the terms of the Licence Agreement.

3.3   In the event that the Material is released under clause 6, it shall be the responsibility of the Licensee to obtain the necessary licences to utilise the object code of any third party material deposited by the Owner pursuant to clause 2.1.8.

4   NCC Escrow's Duties

4.1   NCC Escrow shall:

4.1.1   at all times during the term of this Agreement, retain the latest deposit of the Material in a safe and secure environment;

4.1.2   notify the Owner and the relevant Licensee of the acceptance of any Confirmation Agreement;

4.1.3   inform the Owner and the Licensee of the receipt of any deposit of the Material by sending to both parties a copy of the Integrity Testing report or Full Verification report (as the case may be) generated from the testing processes carried out under clause 10; and

4.1.4   notify the Owner and the Licensee if it becomes aware at any time during the term of this Agreement that the copy of the Material held by it has been lost, damaged or destroyed so that a replacement may be obtained.

4.2   In the event of failure by the Owner to deposit any Material with NCC Escrow, NCC Escrow shall not be responsible for procuring such deposit and may, at its sole discretion, notify the Licensee of the Owner's failure to deposit any Material.

4.3   NCC Escrow may appoint agents, contractors or sub-contractors as it deems fit to carry out the Integrity Testing and the Full Verification processes. NCC Escrow shall ensure that any such agents, contractors and sub-contractors are bound by the same confidentiality obligations as are contained in clause 8.

4.4   NCC Escrow has the right to make such copies of the Material as may be necessary solely for the purposes of this Agreement.

5   Payment

5.1   The parties shall pay NCC Escrow's standard fees and charges as published from time to time or as otherwise agreed, in the proportions set out in schedule 2. NCC Escrow's fees as published are exclusive of value added tax.

5.2   NCC Escrow shall be entitled to review and vary its standard fees and charges for its services under this Agreement from time to time but no more than once a year and only upon 45 days written notice to the parties.

5.3   All invoices are payable within 30 days from the date of invoice. NCC Escrow reserves the right to charge interest in respect of the late payment of any sum due under this Agreement (both before and after judgement) at the rate of 2% per annum over the prevailing base rate of HSBC Bank Plc accruing on a daily basis from the due date therefor until full payment.

6   Release Events

6.1   Subject to: (i) the remaining provisions of this clause 6 and (ii) the receipt by NCC Escrow of its release

ML

fee and any other fees and interest (if any) outstanding under this Agreement, NCC Escrow will release the Material to a duly authorised officer of the Licensee if any of the following events (**"Release Event(s)"**) occur:

6.1.1 if the Owner is a company:

6.1.1.1 an order is made for the winding up of the Owner, the Owner passes a resolution for winding up (other than for the purposes of a solvent reconstruction or amalgamation) or a liquidator of the Owner is appointed; or

6.1.1.2 an order is made for the appointment of an administrator of the Owner or an administrator of the Owner is appointed or

6.1.1.3 the Owner enters into a compromise or arrangement with creditors; or

6.1.1.4 the Owner has a receiver, administrative receiver or manager appointed over all or any part of its assets or undertaking; or

6.1.1.5 the Owner is dissolved; or

6.1.2 if the Owner is an individual:

6.1.2.1 the Owner enters into a compromise or arrangement with creditors; or

6.1.2.2 the Owner is declared bankrupt; or

6.1.2.3 the Owner dies; or

6.1.3 if the Owner is a partnership:

6.1.3.1 any of the partners in the Owner are declared bankrupt or enter into a compromise or arrangement with creditors; or

6.1.3.2 the Owner is wound up or dissolved; or

6.1.3.3 the Owner enters into a compromise or arrangement with creditors; or

6.1.3.4 a partnership administration order is made in respect of the Owner; or

6.1.4 any similar or analogous proceedings or event to those in clauses 6.1.1 to 6.1.3 above occurs in respect of the Owner within any jurisdiction outside England; or

6.1.5 the Owner ceases to carry on its business or the part of its business which relates to the Package; or

6.1.6 the Owner assigns its rights to the Intellectual Property Rights in the Material to a third party (**"Assignee"**) and the Assignee fails, within 60 days of all parties knowledge of such assignment, to continue escrow protection for the benefit of the Licensee(s) by failing to enter into either:

6.1.6.1 a novation agreement with NCC Escrow for the assumption of the Owner's rights and obligations under this Agreement by the Assignee; or

6.1.6.2 a new escrow agreement for the Package which offers the Licensee(s) substantially similar protection to that provided by this Agreement without significantly increasing the overall cost to the Licensee(s),

provided that if the Assignee signs a novation or new escrow agreement within 60 days of all parties' knowledge of the assignment and a Licensee fails to consent to the novation or fails to register to or sign the new agreement within 30 days of the Licensee being notified of the signature of the novation or the new agreement by the Assignee, there shall be no Release Event under this clause in respect of that Licensee; or

6.1.7 the Owner or, where relevant, its agent, parent, subsidiary or associated company, is in material breach of its obligations as to maintenance or modification of the Package under the Licence Agreement or any maintenance agreement entered into in connection with the Package and has failed to remedy such default notified by the Licensee to the Owner within a reasonable period.

6.2 The Licensee must notify NCC Escrow of the Release Event specified in clause 6.1 by delivering to NCC Escrow a statutory or notarised declaration (**"Declaration"**) made by an officer of the Licensee declaring that such Release Event has occurred, setting out the facts and circumstances of the Release Event, that the Licence Agreement and any maintenance agreement, if relevant, for the Package was still valid and effective up to the occurrence of such Release Event and exhibiting such documentary evidence in support of the Declaration as NCC Escrow shall reasonably require.

6.3 Upon receipt of a Declaration from the Licensee claiming that a Release Event has occurred:

6.3.1 NCC Escrow shall submit a copy of the Declaration to the Owner by courier or other form of guaranteed delivery; and

6.3.2 unless within 14 days after the date of despatch of the Declaration by NCC Escrow, NCC

© NCC Group 1984 - 2007   ML

Escrow receives a counter-notice signed by a duly authorised officer of the Owner stating that in their view no such Release Event has occurred or, if appropriate, that the event or circumstance giving rise to the Release Event has been rectified as shown by documentation in support thereof,

NCC Escrow will release the Material to the Licensee for its use for the Release Purposes.

6.4 Upon receipt of the counter-notice from the Owner under clause 6.3.2, NCC Escrow shall send a copy of the counter-notice and any supporting evidence to the Licensee by courier or other form of guaranteed delivery.

6.5 Upon receipt by the Licensee of the counter-notice from NCC Escrow or, in any event, within 90 days of despatch of the counter-notice by NCC Escrow, the Licensee may give notice to NCC Escrow that they wish to invoke the dispute resolution procedure under clause 7.

6.6 If, within 90 days of despatch of the counter-notice by NCC Escrow to the Licensee, NCC Escrow has not been informed by the Licensee that they wish the dispute resolution procedure under clause 7 to apply, the Declaration submitted by the Licensee will be deemed to be no longer valid and the Licensee shall be deemed to have waived their right to release of the Material for the particular reason or event specified in the original Declaration.

6.7 For the avoidance of doubt, where a Release Event has occurred under clauses 6.1.1 to 6.1.5, a subsequent assignment of the Intellectual Property Rights in the Material shall not prejudice the Licensee's right to release of the Material and its use for the Release Purposes.

7 Disputes

7.1 NCC Escrow shall notify the Owner of the Licensee's request for dispute resolution. Unless the Owner or the Licensee objects, NCC Escrow's Chief Executive Officer for the time being will appoint an Independent Expert to resolve the dispute. If the Owner or the Licensee objects to this appointment, they shall endeavour to appoint a mutually acceptable Independent Expert within 7 days of registering their objection. If they fail to appoint an Independent Expert within this 7 day period, NCC Escrow shall request that the President of The Law Society appoints an Independent Expert to resolve the dispute. Any appointment of an Independent Expert under this clause shall be binding upon the parties.

7.2 Within 5 working days of the appointment of the Independent Expert, the Owner and the Licensee shall each provide full written submissions to the Independent Expert together with all relevant documentary evidence in their possession in support of their claim.

7.3 The Independent Expert shall be requested to give a decision on the matter within 14 days of the date of referral or as soon as practicable thereafter and to send a copy of that decision to the Owner, Licensee and NCC Escrow. The Independent Expert's decision shall be final and binding on all parties and shall not be subject to appeal to a court in legal proceedings except in the case of manifest error.

7.4 If the Independent Expert's decision is in favour of the Licensee, NCC Escrow is hereby authorised to release and deliver the Material to the Licensee within 5 working days of the decision being notified by the Independent Expert to the parties.

7.5 The parties hereby agree that the costs and expenses of the Independent Expert shall be borne by the party against whom the decision of the Independent Expert is given.

8 Confidentiality

8.1 The Material shall remain at all times the confidential and intellectual property of its owner.

8.2 In the event that NCC Escrow releases the Material to the Licensee, the Licensee shall be permitted to use the Material only for the Release Purposes.

8.3 NCC Escrow agrees to keep all Confidential Information relating to the Material and/or the Package that comes into its possession or to its knowledge under this Agreement in strictest confidence and secrecy. NCC Escrow further agrees not to make use of such information and/or documentation other than for the purposes of this Agreement and, unless the parties should agree otherwise in writing, will not disclose or release it other than in accordance with the terms of this Agreement.

8.4 Any request by a Licensee under clause 10.3 for a Full Verification shall not be disclosed to the other Licensees.

9 Intellectual Property Rights

9.1 The release of the Material to the Licensee will not act as an assignment of any Intellectual Property Rights that the Owner or any third party possesses in the Material.

9.2 The Intellectual Property Rights in the Integrity Testing report and any Full Verification report shall remain vested in NCC Escrow. The Owner and the Licensee shall each be granted a non-exclusive right and licence to use the Integrity Testing report for the purposes of this Agreement and their own internal purposes only. The Owner and the party who commissioned the Full Verification shall each be granted a non-exclusive right and licence to use the Full Verification report for the purposes of this Agreement and their own internal purposes only.

ML

10   **Integrity Testing and Full Verification**

10.1   NCC Escrow shall bear no obligation or responsibility to any party to this Agreement or person, firm, company or entity whatsoever to determine the existence, relevance, completeness, accuracy, operation, effectiveness, functionality or any other aspect of the Material received by NCC Escrow under this Agreement.

10.2   As soon as practicable after the Material has been deposited with NCC Escrow, NCC Escrow shall apply its Integrity Testing processes to the Material.

10.3   Any party to this Agreement shall be entitled to require NCC Escrow to carry out a Full Verification. Subject to clause 10.4, NCC Escrow's prevailing fees and charges for the Full Verification processes and all reasonable expenses incurred by NCC Escrow in carrying out the Full Verification processes shall be payable by the requesting party.

10.4   If the Material fails to satisfy NCC Escrow's Full Verification tests as a result of being defective or incomplete in content, NCC Escrow's fees, charges and expenses in relation to the Full Verification tests shall be paid by the Owner.

10.5   Should the Material deposited fail to satisfy NCC Escrow's Integrity Testing or Full Verification tests under clauses 10.2 or 10.3, the Owner shall, within 14 days of the receipt of the notice of test failure from NCC Escrow, deposit such new, corrected or revised Material as shall be necessary to ensure its compliance with its warranties and obligations in clause 2. If the Owner fails to make such deposit of the new, corrected or revised Material, NCC Escrow will issue a report to the Licensee detailing the problem with the Material as revealed by the relevant tests.

11   **NCC Escrow's Liability**

11.1   Nothing in this clause 11 excludes or limits the liability of NCC Escrow for fraudulent misrepresentation or for death or personal injury caused by NCC Escrow's negligence. Save as aforesaid the following provisions set out the entire financial liability of NCC Escrow (including any liability for the acts or omissions of its employees, agents and sub-contractors) to the other parties:

11.1.1   NCC Escrow shall not be liable for any loss or damage caused to either the Owner or the Licensee either jointly or severally except to the extent that such loss or damage is caused by the negligent acts or omissions of or a breach of any contractual duty by NCC Escrow, its employees, agents or sub-contractors and in such event NCC Escrow's total liability in respect of all claims arising under or by virtue of this Agreement or in connection with the performance or contemplated performance of this Agreement, shall not exceed the sum of £1,000,000 (one million UK pounds); and

11.1.2   NCC Escrow shall not be liable to the Owner or the Licensee for any indirect or consequential loss or damage whether for loss of profit, loss of business, depletion of goodwill or otherwise whatsoever or howsoever caused which arise out of or in connection with this Agreement even if such loss was reasonably foreseeable or NCC Escrow had been advised of the possibility of incurring the same by the Owner, the Licensee or any third party.

11.2   NCC Escrow shall not be liable in any way to the Owner or the Licensee for acting in accordance with the terms of this Agreement and specifically (without limitation) for acting upon any notice, written request, waiver, consent, receipt, statutory declaration or any other document furnished to it pursuant to and in accordance with this Agreement.

11.3   NCC Escrow shall not be required to make any investigation into and shall be entitled in good faith without incurring any liability to the Owner or the Licensee to assume (without requesting evidence thereof) the validity, authenticity, veracity and due and authorised execution of any documents, written requests, waivers, consents, receipts, statutory declarations or notices received by it in respect of this Agreement.

12   **Indemnity**

12.1   Save for any claim falling within the provisions of clause 11.1.1, the Owner and the Licensee involved in the dispute or litigation jointly and severally agree at all times to indemnify and hold harmless NCC Escrow in respect of all of its legal and all other costs, fees and expenses incurred directly or indirectly as a result of being brought into or otherwise becoming involved in any form of dispute resolution proceedings or any litigation of any kind between the Owner and the Licensee in relation to this Agreement to the extent that this Agreement does not otherwise provide for reimbursement of such costs.

12.2   The Owner shall assume all liability and shall at all times indemnify and hold harmless NCC Escrow and its officers, agents, sub-contractors and employees from and against any and all liability, loss, damages, costs, legal costs, professional and other expenses and any other liabilities of whatever nature, awarded against or agreed to be paid or otherwise suffered, incurred or sustained by NCC Escrow, whether direct, indirect or consequential as a result of or in connection with any claim by any third party(s) for alleged or actual infringement of Intellectual Property Rights arising out of or in connection with all and any acts or omissions of NCC Escrow in respect of the Material as contemplated under this Agreement.

13 Term and Termination

13.1 This Agreement shall continue until terminated in accordance with this clause 13.

13.2 If the Owner or the Licensee, as the case may be, fails to pay an invoice addressed to it for services under this Agreement within 30 days of its issue, NCC Escrow reserves the right to give that party written notice to pay the outstanding invoice within 30 days. If the Licensee has not paid its invoice by the expiry of the 30 day notice period, this Agreement will automatically immediately terminate in respect of the Licensee. If the Owner has not paid its invoice by the expiry of the 30 day notice period, NCC Escrow will give the Licensee(s) a period of 30 days to pay the Owner's invoice. If the Owner's invoice has not been paid by the expiry of the 30 day optional payment period given to the Licensee(s), this Agreement will automatically immediately terminate in respect of the relevant Licensee(s) or in its entirety (as appropriate). Any amounts owed by the Owner but paid by the Licensee(s) will be recoverable by the Licensee(s) direct from the Owner as a debt and, if requested, NCC Escrow shall provide appropriate documentation to assist in such recovery.

13.3 Upon termination of this Agreement in its entirety under the provisions of clause 13.2, for 30 days from the date of termination NCC Escrow will make the Material available for collection by the Owner or its agents from the premises of NCC Escrow during office hours. After such 30 day period NCC Escrow will destroy the Material.

13.4 Notwithstanding any other provision of this clause 13, NCC Escrow may terminate this Agreement by giving 30 days written notice to the Owner and the Licensee(s). In the event that it is terminated in its entirety, the Owner and the Licensee(s) shall appoint a mutually acceptable new custodian on similar terms and conditions to those contained herein. If a new custodian is not appointed within 14 days of delivery of such notice, the Owner or the Licensee(s) shall be entitled to request the President for the time being of the British Computer Society (or successor body) to appoint a suitable new custodian upon such terms and conditions as he/she shall require. Such appointment shall be final and binding on the Owner and the Licensee(s). If NCC Escrow is notified of the new custodian within the notice period, NCC Escrow will forthwith deliver the Material to the new custodian. If NCC Escrow is not notified of the new custodian within the notice period and this Agreement has been terminated in its entirety, NCC Escrow will return the Material to the Owner.

13.5 The Licensee may terminate this Agreement in respect of itself only at any time by giving written notice to NCC Escrow.

13.6 If NCC Escrow discovers that a Release Event has occurred and the Licensee(s) have failed to exercise their right to claim for release of the Material under clause 6.2, NCC Escrow shall have the right to terminate this Agreement in its entirety, upon 30 days written notice to the Owner and the Licensee(s). The Licensee(s) shall have the option of applying for release in accordance with clause 6 during this notice period, but if they fail to do so, upon the expiry of this notice period, this Agreement shall automatically terminate in its entirety. Where this Agreement is terminated in its entirety under this clause, unless instructed otherwise by the Owner or the Assignee prior to expiry of the notice period, NCC Escrow shall destroy the Material.

13.7 If the Intellectual Property Rights in the Material have been assigned to a third party and the proviso in clause 6.1.6 applies such that there has been no Release Event under that clause, NCC Escrow shall be entitled to terminate this Agreement immediately by written notice to the Owner and the Licensee(s) and upon such termination, unless otherwise instructed by the Owner or the Assignee, NCC Escrow shall destroy the Material.

13.8 If the Licence Agreement with a Licensee has expired or has been lawfully terminated, then the Licensee shall give notice to NCC Escrow within 14 days thereof to terminate its interest under this Agreement, failing which, the Owner shall be entitled to give written notice to NCC Escrow to terminate the relevant Licensee's interests under this Agreement. Upon receipt of such a notice from the Owner, NCC Escrow shall notify the Licensee of the Owner's notice to terminate. Unless within 14 days of NCC Escrow giving such notice to the Licensee, NCC Escrow receives a counter-notice signed by a duly authorised officer of the Licensee disputing the termination of the Licence Agreement, then the Licensee shall be deemed to have consented to such termination and the Licensee's rights under this Agreement shall immediately automatically terminate. Any disputes arising under this clause shall be dealt with in accordance with the dispute resolution procedure in clause 7. Upon termination of the entire agreement under this clause, NCC Escrow shall return the Material to the Owner.

13.9 Subject to clause 13.8, the Owner may only terminate the interests of any Licensee under this Agreement with the written consent of that Licensee.

13.10 The Owner may only terminate this Agreement in its entirety with the written consent of all Licensees.

13.11 This Agreement shall automatically immediately terminate in respect of a Licensee upon release of the Material to that Licensee in accordance with clause 6.

13.12 If this Agreement is superseded and replaced by a new agreement in respect of the Material, this Agreement shall, upon the coming into force of the new agreement in respect of a Licensee, automatically terminate in respect of that Licensee. When this Agreement has been terminated in respect of all Licensees who are registered under it, it shall immediately terminate in its entirety. The relevant party or parties shall request NCC Escrow to either transfer the Material to the new

ML

agreement or ask the owner under the new agreement to deposit new material. If new material is deposited, upon its receipt, NCC Escrow shall, unless otherwise instructed, destroy the Material.

13.13 The termination of this Agreement in respect of a Licensee shall be without prejudice to the continuation of this Agreement in respect of any other Licensees.

13.14 If any terminations of Licensees' interests under this Agreement result in there being no Licensees registered under this Agreement, unless otherwise instructed by the Owner, this Agreement will continue and the Material will be retained by NCC Escrow pending registration of other Licensees.

13.15 The provisions of clauses 1, 3.2, 3.3, 5, 8, 9, 10.1, 11, 12, 13.15 to 13.17 (inclusive) and 14 shall continue in full force after termination of this Agreement.

13.16 On and after termination of this Agreement, the Owner and/or the Licensee(s) (as appropriate) shall remain liable to NCC Escrow for payment in full of any fees and interest which have become due but which have not been paid as at the date of termination.

13.17 The termination of this Agreement, however arising, shall be without prejudice to the rights accrued to the parties prior to termination.

14 **General**

14.1 The Owner and the Licensee(s) shall notify NCC Escrow, within 30 days of its occurrence, of any of the following:

14.1.1 a change of its name, registered office, contact address or other contact details; and

14.1.2 any material change in its circumstances that may affect the validity or operation of this Agreement.

14.2 Within 14 days of any assignment or transfer by the Owner of any part of its Intellectual Property Rights in the Material, the Owner shall notify:

14.2.1 NCC Escrow and the Licensee(s) of such assignment and the identity of the Assignee; and

14.2.2 the Assignee of the provisions of clause 6.1.6.

14.3 The formation, existence, construction, performance, validity and all other aspects of this Agreement shall be governed by and construed in accordance with the laws of England and the parties submit to the exclusive jurisdiction of the English courts.

14.4 This Agreement together with, in respect of each Licensee, their Confirmation Agreement, their Order Form and any relevant NCC Escrow standard terms and conditions represent the whole agreement relating to the escrow arrangements between NCC Escrow, the Owner and that Licensee for the Package and shall supersede all prior agreements, discussions, arrangements, representations, negotiations and undertakings. In the event of any conflict between any of these documents, the terms of this Agreement shall prevail.

14.5 Unless the provisions of this Agreement otherwise provide, any notice or other communication required or permitted to be given or made hereunder shall be validly given or made if delivered by hand or courier or if despatched by first class recorded delivery (airmail if overseas) addressed to the address specified for the parties in this Agreement or their Confirmation Agreement (or such other address as may be notified to the parties from time to time) or if sent by facsimile message to such facsimile number as has been notified to the parties from time to time and shall be deemed to have been received:

(i) if delivered by hand or courier, at the time of delivery;

(ii) if sent by first class recorded delivery (airmail if overseas), 2 business days after posting (6 days if sent by airmail);

(iii) if sent by facsimile, at the time of completion of the transmission of the facsimile with facsimile machine confirmation of transmission to the correct facsimile number of all pages of the notice.

14.6 The Owner shall not assign, transfer or subcontract this Agreement or any rights or obligations hereunder without the prior written consent of NCC Escrow and all the Licensees. A Licensee shall not assign, transfer or subcontract its rights under this Agreement without the Owner and NCC Escrow's prior written consent.

14.7 NCC Escrow shall be entitled to transfer or assign this Agreement upon written notice to both the Owner and all the Licensees.

14.8 This Agreement shall be binding upon and survive for the benefit of the successors in title and permitted assigns of the parties.

14.9 If any provision of this Agreement is declared too broad in any respect to permit enforcement to its full extent, the parties agree that such provision shall be enforced to the maximum extent permitted by law and that such provision shall be deemed to be varied accordingly. If any provision of this Agreement is found by any court, tribunal or administrative body of competent jurisdiction to be wholly or partly illegal, invalid, void, or unenforceable, it shall, to the extent of such illegality, invalidity

ML

or unenforceability, be deemed severable and the remaining part of the provision and the rest of the provisions of this Agreement shall continue in full force and effect.

14.10   Save as expressly provided in this Agreement, no amendment or variation of this Agreement shall be effective unless in writing and signed by a duly authorised representative of each of the parties to it.

14.11   The parties shall not be liable to each other or be deemed to be in breach of this Agreement by reason of any delay in performing, or failure to perform, any of their obligations under this Agreement if the delay or failure was for a reason beyond that party's reasonable control (including, without limitation, fire, flood, explosion, epidemic, riot, civil commotion, any strike, lockout or other industrial action, act of God, war or warlike hostilities or threat of war, terrorist activities, accidental or malicious damage, or any prohibition or restriction by any governments or other legal authority which affects this Agreement and which is not in force on the date of this Agreement). A party claiming to be unable to perform its obligations under this Agreement (either on time or at all) in any of the circumstances set out above must notify the other parties of the nature and extent of the circumstances in question as soon as practicable. If such circumstances continue for more than six months, any of the other parties shall be entitled to terminate this Agreement by giving one month's notice in writing.

14.12   No waiver by any party of any breach of any provisions of this Agreement shall be deemed to be a waiver of any subsequent or other breach and, subject to clause 6.6, no failure to exercise or delay in exercising any right or remedy under this Agreement shall constitute a waiver thereof.

14.13   This Agreement is not intended to create any right under the Contracts (Rights of Third Parties) Act 1999 which is enforceable by any person who is not a party to this Agreement and the rights of any third party under the said act are hereby expressly excluded.

14.14   This Agreement may be executed in any number of counterparts and by different parties in separate counterparts. Each counterpart when so executed shall be deemed to be an original and all of which together shall constitute one and the same agreement.

Signed for and on behalf of [Ownername]

Name: .... | ....

Position: .... |

                                                                           (Authorised Signatory)

Signed for and on behalf of NCC ESCROW INTERNATIONAL LIMITED

Name: .... | ....

Position: .... |

                                                                           (Authorised Signatory)

ML

Schedule 1

The Package

The software package known as [SoftwareName] or any other name(s) cs may be given to it by the Owner from time to time.

Schedule 2

NCC Escrow's Fees

	DESCRIPTION	OWNER	LICENSEE
1	Annual Fee (per Licensee, payable on registration and in advance of each anniversary thereafter)	[Owner Annual]	[Licensee Annual]
2	Minimum Annual Fee (payable in arrears in the event that there are fewer than two Licensees registered on any anniversary of this Agreement; if the Agreement is terminated prior to its anniversary, the fee will be pro-rated for the period prior to termination; if one Licensee is registered on the Agreement's anniversary or on the date of its termination, the fee will be reduced by 50%).	100%	Nil
3	Scheduled Update Fee (2nd and subsequent scheduled deposits in any one year, payable on completion of this Agreement and in advance of each anniversary thereafter)	100%	Nil
4	Unscheduled Update Fee (per unscheduled deposit)	100%	Nil
5	Release Fee (plus NCC Escrow's reasonable expenses)	Nil	100%

Additional fees will be payable to NCC Escrow by the Owner (unless otherwise agreed between the parties) for the following where applicable:

- Storage Fee for deposits in excess of 1 cubic foot;
- Integrity Testing Fee for deposits consisting of more than 5 media items.

Additional fees for any novation or replacement of this Agreement at the request of the Owner or the Licensee shall be paid by the Owner or the new owner of the Package (as appropriate) (unless otherwise agreed between the parties).

ML

Appendix 1

Confirmation Agreement

NOTE: A COPY OF THIS CONFIRMATION AGREEMENT MUST BE DULY SIGNED BY AN AUTHORISED SIGNATORY AND RETURNED TO NCC ESCROW BEFORE A LICENSEE CAN CLAIM PROTECTION UNDER THE ESCROW AGREEMENT.

Agreement between:

(1)   [Ownername] whose registered office is at [Owneraddress] (CRN: [Ownercrn]) (**"Owner"**);

(2)   NCC ESCROW INTERNATIONAL LIMITED a company registered in England whose registered office is at Manchester Technology Centre, Oxford Road, Manchester M1 7EF, ENGLAND (CRN: 3081952) (**"NCC Escrow"**); and

(3)   Licensee's Name: ....

        whose registered office is at

        ....

        ....

        ....

        ....

        (Company Registration Number:...) (**"Licensee"**);

Agreement:

1   This confirmation agreement (**"Confirmation Agreement"**) is supplemental to the terms and conditions of escrow agreement number [Agreement#] dated _____ (**"Escrow Agreement"**) between the Owner and NCC Escrow.

2   This Confirmation Agreement and the Escrow Agreement together shall form a binding agreement between the Owner, NCC Escrow and the Licensee in accordance with the terms of the Escrow Agreement.

3   The Licensee hereby agrees to take the benefit of, agrees and undertakes to perform its obligations under and be bound by the terms and conditions of the Escrow Agreement as though they were a party to the Escrow Agreement and named therein as a Licensee.

4   This Confirmation Agreement shall take effect when NCC Escrow has:

        (i)   received written approval from the Owner of the Licensee's application to join the Escrow Agreement;

        (ii)   acknowledged in writing to the Licensee that it has received a copy of this Confirmation Agreement completed and duly executed; and

        (iii)   registered the Licensee as a party to the Escrow Agreement.

Signed for and on behalf of [Licenseename]

Name: .... | ....

Position: .... | (Authorised Signatory)

Date: .... |

Signed for and on behalf of NCC ESCROW INTERNATIONAL LIMITED

Name: .... | ....

Position: .... | (Authorised Signatory)

Date: .... |

Single Licensee
Software Escrow Agreement

Date
Owner   [Ownername]
Agreement Number   [Agreement#]

> **Notice:** The parties to this Agreement are obliged to inform NCC Escrow of any changes to the Package or in their circumstances (including change of name, registered office, contact details or change of owner of the intellectual property in the Package).

Version: 07/05

27 ● Appendix ● Precedents

SL

Escrow Agreement Dated:

Between:

(1)   [Ownername] whose registered office is at [Owneraddress] (CRN: [Ownercrn]) (**"Owner"**);

(2)   [Licenseename] whose registered office is at [Licenseeaddress] (CRN: [Licenseecrn]) (**"Licensee"**); and

(3)   NCC ESCROW INTERNATIONAL LIMITED a company registered in England whose registered office is at Manchester Technology Centre, Oxford Road, Manchester M1 7EF, ENGLAND (CRN: 3081952) (**"NCC Escrow"**).

Background:

(A)   The Licensee has been granted a licence to use the Package which comprises computer programs.

(B)   Certain technical information and/or documentation relating to the software package is the confidential information and intellectual property of the Owner or a third party.

(C)   The Owner acknowledges that in certain circumstances, such information and/or documentation would be required by the Licensee in order for it to continue to exercise its rights under the Licence Agreement.

(D)   The parties therefore agree that such information and/or documentation should be placed with a trusted third party, NCC Escrow, so that such information and/or documentation can be released to the Licensee should certain circumstances arise.

Agreement:

In consideration of the mutual undertakings and obligations contained in this Agreement, the parties agree that:

1   **Definitions and Interpretation**

         1.1   In this Agreement the following terms shall have the following meanings:

                   "Agreement" means the terms and conditions of this escrow agreement set out below, including the schedules hereto.

                   "Confidential Information" means all technical and/or commercial information not in the public domain and which is designated in writing as confidential by any party together with all other information of any party which may reasonably be regarded as confidential information.

                   "Full Verification" means the tests and processes forming NCC Escrow's Full Verification service and/or such other tests and processes as may be agreed between the parties for the verification of the Material.

                   "Independent Expert" means a suitably qualified and independent solicitor or barrister.

                   "Integrity Testing" means those tests and processes forming NCC Escrow's Integrity Testing service, in so far as they can be applied to the Material.

                   "Intellectual Property Rights" mean any copyright, patents, design patents, registered designs, design rights, utility models, trademarks, service marks, trade secrets, know how, database rights, moral rights, confidential information, trade or business names, domain names, and any other rights of a similar nature including industrial and proprietary rights and other similar protected rights in any country or jurisdiction together with all registrations, applications to register and rights to apply for registration of any of the aforementioned rights and any licences of or in respect of such rights.

                   "Licence Agreement" means the agreement under which the Licensee was granted a licence to use the Package.

                   "Material" means the Source Code of the Package and such other material and documentation (including updates and upgrades thereto and new versions thereof) as are necessary to be delivered or deposited to comply with clause 2 of this Agreement.

                   "Order Form" means the order form setting out the details of the order placed with NCC Escrow for setting up this Agreement.

                   "Package" means the software package together with any updates and upgrades thereto and new versions thereof licensed to the Licensee under the Licence Agreement details of which are set out in schedule 1.

                   "Release Purposes" means the purposes of understanding, maintaining, modifying and correcting the Package exclusively for and on behalf of the Licensee together with such other purposes (if any) as are permitted under the Licence Agreement.

                   "Source Code" means the computer programming code of the Package in human readable form.

                   "Third Party Material" means Source Code which is not the confidential information and

SL

1.2   intellectual property of the Owner or the Licensee.

1.2   This Agreement shall be interpreted in accordance with the following:

    1.2.1   headings are for ease of reference only and shall not be taken into consideration in the interpretation of this Agreement;

    1.2.2   all references to clauses and schedules are references to clauses and schedules of this Agreement; and

    1.2.3   all references to a party or parties are references to a party or parties to this Agreement.

2   Owner's Duties and Warranties

2.1   The Owner shall:

    2.1.1   deliver a copy of the Material to NCC Escrow within 30 days of the date of this Agreement;

    2.1.2   deliver a further copy of the Material to NCC Escrow each time that there is a change to the Package;

    2.1.3   ensure that each copy of the Material deposited with NCC Escrow comprises the Source Code of the latest version of the Package used by the Licensee;

    2.1.4   deliver to NCC Escrow a replacement copy of the Material within 30 days after the anniversary of the last delivery of the Material to ensure that the integrity of the Material media is maintained;

    2.1.5   deliver a replacement copy of the Material to NCC Escrow within 14 days of a notice given to it by NCC Escrow under the provisions of clause 4.1.3;

    2.1.6   deliver with each deposit of the Material the following information:

        2.1.6.1 details of the deposit including the full name of the Package (i.e. the original name as set out under schedule 1 together with any new names given to the Package by the Owner), version details, media type, backup command/software used, compression used, archive hardware and operating system details; and

        2.1.6.2 password/encryption details required to access the Material;

    2.1.7   deliver with each deposit of the Material the following technical information (where applicable):

        2.1.7.1 documentation describing the procedures for building, compiling and installing the software, including names and versions of the development tools;

        2.1.7.2 software design information (e.g. module names and functionality); and

        2.1.7.3 name and contact details of employees with knowledge of how to maintain and support the Material; and

    2.1.8   if required by the Licensee, deposit a backup copy of the object code of any third party software package required to access, install, build or compile or otherwise use the Material.

2.2   The Owner warrants to both NCC Escrow and the Licensee at the time of each deposit of the Material with NCC Escrow that:

    2.2.1   other than any third party object code referred to in clause 2.1.8 or any Third Party Material, it owns the Intellectual Property Rights in the Material;

    2.2.2   in respect of any Third Party Material, it has been granted valid and ongoing rights under licence by the third party owner(s) thereof to deal with such Third Party Material in the manner anticipated under this Agreement and that the Owner has the express authority of such third party owner(s) to deposit the Third Party Material under this Agreement as evidenced by a signed letter of authorisation in the form required by NCC Escrow;

    2.2.3   in entering into this Agreement and performing its obligations under it, it is not in breach of any of its ongoing express or implied obligations to any third party(s);

    2.2.4   the Material deposited under clause 2.1 contains all information in human-readable form (except for any third party object code deposited pursuant to clause 2.1.8) and is on suitable media to enable a reasonably skilled programmer or analyst to understand, maintain, modify and correct the Package; and

    2.2.5   in respect of any third party object code that the Owner, at its option, or, at the request of the Licensee, deposits with NCC Escrow in conjunction with the Material pursuant to clause 2.1.8, it has the full right and authority to do so.

3   Licensee's Responsibilities and Undertakings

627

27 ● Appendix ● Precedents

3.1 The Licensee shall notify NCC Escrow of any change to the Package that necessitates a replacement deposit of the Material.

3.2 In the event that the Material is released under clause 6, the Licensee shall:

3.2.1 keep the Material confidential at all times;

3.2.2 use the Material only for the Release Purposes;

3.2.3 not disclose the Material to any person save such of the Licensee's employees or contractors who need to know the same for the Release Purposes. In the event that Material is disclosed to its employees or contractors, the Licensee shall ensure that they are bound by the same confidentiality obligations as are contained in this clause 3.2;

3.2.4 hold all media containing the Material in a safe and secure environment when not in use; and

3.2.5 forthwith destroy the Material should the Licensee cease to be entitled to use the Package under the terms of the Licence Agreement.

3.3 In the event that the Material is released under clause 6, it shall be the responsibility of the Licensee to obtain the necessary licences to utilise the object code of any third party material deposited by the Owner pursuant to clause 2.1.8.

4 NCC Escrow's Duties

4.1 NCC Escrow shall:

4.1.1 at all times during the term of this Agreement, retain the latest deposit of the Material in a safe and secure environment;

4.1.2 inform the Owner and the Licensee of the receipt of any deposit of the Material by sending to both parties a copy of the Integrity Testing report or Full Verification report (as the case may be) generated from the testing processes carried out under clause 10; and

4.1.3 notify the Owner and the Licensee if it becomes aware at any time during the term of this Agreement that the copy of the Material held by it has been lost, damaged or destroyed so that a replacement may be obtained.

4.2 In the event of failure by the Owner to deposit any Material with NCC Escrow, NCC Escrow shall not be responsible for procuring such deposit and may, at its sole discretion, notify the Licensee of the Owner's failure to deposit any Material.

4.3 NCC Escrow may appoint agents, contractors or sub-contractors as it deems fit to carry out the Integrity Testing and the Full Verification processes. NCC Escrow shall ensure that any such agents, contractors and sub-contractors are bound by the same confidentiality obligations as are contained in clause 8.

4.4 NCC Escrow has the right to make such copies of the Material as may be necessary solely for the purposes of this Agreement.

5 Payment

5.1 The parties shall pay NCC Escrow's standard fees and charges as published from time to time or as otherwise agreed, in the proportions set out in schedule 2. NCC Escrow's fees as published are exclusive of value added tax.

5.2 NCC Escrow shall be entitled to review and vary its standard fees and charges for its services under this Agreement from time to time but no more than once a year and only upon 45 days written notice to the parties.

5.3 All invoices are payable within 30 days from the date of invoice. NCC Escrow reserves the right to charge interest in respect of the late payment of any sum due under this Agreement (both before and after judgement) at the rate of 2% per annum over the prevailing base rate of HSBC Bank Plc accruing on a daily basis from the due date therefor until full payment.

6 Release Events

6.1 Subject to: (i) the remaining provisions of this clause 6 and (ii) the receipt by NCC Escrow of its release fee and any other fees and interest (if any) outstanding under this Agreement, NCC Escrow will release the Material to a duly authorised officer of the Licensee if any of the following events (**"Release Event(s)"**) occur:

6.1.1 if the Owner is a company:

6.1.1.1 an order is made for the winding up of the Owner, the Owner passes a resolution for winding up (other than for the purposes of a solvent reconstruction or amalgamation) or a liquidator of the Owner is appointed; or

6.1.1.2 an order is made for the appointment of an administrator of the Owner or an

SL

administrator of the Owner is appointed; or

6.1.1.3 the Owner enters into a compromise or arrangement with creditors; or

6.1.1.4 the Owner has a receiver, administrative receiver or manager appointed over all or any part of its assets or undertaking; or

6.1.1.5 the Owner is dissolved; or

6.1.2 if the Owner is an individual:

6.1.2.1 the Owner enters into a compromise or arrangement with creditors; or

6.1.2.2 the Owner is declared bankrupt; or

6.1.2.3 the Owner dies; or

6.1.3 if the Owner is a partnership:

6.1.3.1 any of the partners in the Owner are declared bankrupt or enter into a compromise or arrangement with creditors; or

6.1.3.2 the Owner is wound up or dissolved; or

6.1.3.3 the Owner enters into a compromise or arrangement with creditors; or

6.1.3.4 a partnership administration order is made in respect of the Owner; or

6.1.4 any similar or analogous proceedings or event to those in clauses 6.1.1 to 6.1.3 above occurs in respect of the Owner within any jurisdiction outside England; or

6.1.5 the Owner ceases to carry on its business or the part of its business which relates to the Package; or

6.1.6 the Owner assigns its rights to the Intellectual Property Rights in the Material to a third party (**"Assignee"**) and the Assignee fails, within 60 days of all parties' knowledge of such assignment, to continue escrow protection for the benefit of the Licensee by failing to enter into either:

6.1.6.1 a novation agreement with the Licensee and NCC Escrow for the assumption of the Owner's rights and obligations under this Agreement by the Assignee; or

6.1.6.2 a new escrow agreement with the Licensee for the Package which offers the Licensee substantially similar protection to that provided by this Agreement without significantly increasing the overall cost to the Licensee,

provided that if the Assignee offers to enter into a novation or new escrow agreement within 60 days of all parties' knowledge of the assignment and the Licensee fails to accept the Assignee's offer within 30 days of such offer being notified to the Licensee, there shall be no Release Event under this clause; or

6.1.7 the Owner or, where relevant, its agent, parent, subsidiary or associated company is in material breach of its obligations as to maintenance or modification of the Package under the Licence Agreement or any maintenance agreement entered into in connection with the Package and has failed to remedy such default notified by the Licensee to the Owner within a reasonable period.

6.2 The Licensee must notify NCC Escrow of the Release Event specified in clause 6.1 by delivering to NCC Escrow a statutory or notarised declaration (**"Declaration"**) made by an officer of the Licensee declaring that such Release Event has occurred, setting out the facts and circumstances of the Release Event, that the Licence Agreement and any maintenance agreement, if relevant, for the Package was still valid and effective up to the occurrence of such Release Event and exhibiting such documentary evidence in support of the Declaration as NCC Escrow shall reasonably require.

6.3 Upon receipt of a Declaration from the Licensee claiming that a Release Event has occurred:

6.3.1 NCC Escrow shall submit a copy of the Declaration to the Owner by courier or other form of guaranteed delivery; and

6.3.2 unless within 14 days after the date of despatch of the Declaration by NCC Escrow, NCC Escrow receives a counter-notice signed by a duly authorised officer of the Owner stating that in their view no such Release Event has occurred or, if appropriate, that the event or circumstance giving rise to the Release Event has been rectified as shown by documentation in support thereof,

NCC Escrow will release the Material to the Licensee for its use for the Release Purposes.

6.4 Upon receipt of the counter-notice from the Owner under clause 6.3.2, NCC Escrow shall send a copy of the counter-notice and any supporting evidence to the Licensee by courier or other form of guaranteed delivery.

629

6.5   Upon receipt by the Licensee of the counter-notice from NCC Escrow or, in any event, within 90 days of despatch of the counter-notice by NCC Escrow, the Licensee may give notice to NCC Escrow that they wish to invoke the dispute resolution procedure under clause 7.

6.6   If, within 90 days of despatch of the counter-notice by NCC Escrow to the Licensee, NCC Escrow has not been informed by the Licensee that they wish the dispute resolution procedure under clause 7 to apply, the Declaration submitted by the Licensee will be deemed to be no longer valid and the Licensee shall be deemed to have waived their right to release of the Material for the particular reason or event specified in the original Declaration.

6.7   For the avoidance of doubt, where a Release Event has occurred under clauses 6.1.1 to 6.1.5, a subsequent assignment of the Intellectual Property Rights in the Material shall not prejudice the Licensee's right to release of the Material and its use for the Release Purposes.

7   Disputes

7.1   NCC Escrow shall notify the Owner of the Licensee's request for dispute resolution. Unless the Owner or the Licensee objects, NCC Escrow's Chief Executive Officer for the time being will appoint an Independent Expert to resolve the dispute. If the Owner or the Licensee objects to this appointment, they shall endeavour to appoint a mutually acceptable Independent Expert within 7 days of registering their objection. If they fail to appoint an Independent Expert within this 7 day period, NCC Escrow shall request that the President of The Law Society appoints an Independent Expert to resolve the dispute. Any appointment of an Independent Expert under this clause shall be binding upon the parties.

7.2   Within 5 working days of the appointment of the Independent Expert, the Owner and the Licensee shall each provide full written submissions to the Independent Expert together with all relevant documentary evidence in their possession in support of their claim.

7.3   The Independent Expert shall be requested to give a decision on the matter within 14 days of the date of referral or as soon as practicable thereafter and to send a copy of that decision to the Owner, Licensee and NCC Escrow. The Independent Expert's decision shall be final and binding on all parties and shall not be subject to appeal to a court in legal proceedings except in the case of manifest error.

7.4   If the Independent Expert's decision is in favour of the Licensee, NCC Escrow is hereby authorised to release and deliver the Material to the Licensee within 5 working days of the decision being notified by the Independent Expert to the parties.

7.5   The parties hereby agree that the costs and expenses of the Independent Expert shall be borne by the party against whom the decision of the Independent Expert is given.

8   Confidentiality

8.1   The Material shall remain at all times the confidential and intellectual property of its owner.

8.2   In the event that NCC Escrow releases the Material to the Licensee, the Licensee shall be permitted to use the Material only for the Release Purposes.

8.3   NCC Escrow agrees to keep all Confidential Information relating to the Material and/or the Package that comes into its possession or to its knowledge under this Agreement in strictest confidence and secrecy. NCC Escrow further agrees not to make use of such information and/or documentation other than for the purposes of this Agreement and, unless the parties should agree otherwise in writing, will not disclose or release it other than in accordance with the terms of this Agreement.

9   Intellectual Property Rights

9.1   The release of the Material to the Licensee will not act as an assignment of any Intellectual Property Rights that the Owner or any third party possesses in the Material.

9.2   The Intellectual Property Rights in the Integrity Testing report and any Full Verification report shall remain vested in NCC Escrow. The Owner and the Licensee shall each be granted a non-exclusive right and licence to use such report for the purposes of this Agreement and their own internal purposes only.

10   Integrity Testing and Full Verification

10.1   NCC Escrow shall bear no obligation or responsibility to any party to this Agreement or person, firm, company or entity whatsoever to determine the existence, relevance, completeness, accuracy, operation, effectiveness, functionality or any other aspect of the Material received by NCC Escrow under this Agreement.

10.2   As soon as practicable after the Material has been deposited with NCC Escrow, NCC Escrow shall apply its Integrity Testing processes to the Material.

10.3   Any party to this Agreement shall be entitled to require NCC Escrow to carry out a Full Verification. Subject to clause 10.4, NCC Escrow's prevailing fees and charges for the Full Verification

SL

processes and all reasonable expenses incurred by NCC Escrow in carrying out the Full Verification processes shall be payable by the requesting party.

10.4   If the Material fails to satisfy NCC Escrow's Full Verification tests as a result of being defective or incomplete in content, NCC Escrow's fees, charges and expenses in relation to the Full Verification tests shall be paid by the Owner.

10.5   Should the Material deposited fail to satisfy NCC Escrow's Integrity Testing or Full Verification tests under clauses 10.2 or 10.3, the Owner shall, within 14 days of the receipt of the notice of test failure from NCC Escrow, deposit such new, corrected or revised Material as shall be necessary to ensure its compliance with its warranties and obligations in clause 2. If the Owner fails to make such deposit of the new, corrected or revised Material, NCC Escrow will issue a report to the Licensee detailing the problem with the Material as revealed by the relevant tests.

11   NCC Escrow's Liability

11.1   Nothing in this clause 11 excludes or limits the liability of NCC Escrow for fraudulent misrepresentation or for death or personal injury caused by NCC Escrow's negligence. Save as aforesaid the following provisions set out the entire financial liability of NCC Escrow (including any liability for the acts or omissions of its employees, agents and sub-contractors) to the other parties:

11.1.1   NCC Escrow shall not be liable for any loss or damage caused to either the Owner or the Licensee either jointly or severally except to the extent that such loss or damage is caused by the negligent acts or omissions of or a breach of any contractual duty by NCC Escrow, its employees, agents or sub-contractors and in such event NCC Escrow's total liability in respect of all claims arising under or by virtue of this Agreement or in connection with the performance or contemplated performance of this Agreement, shall not exceed the sum of £1,000,000 (one million UK pounds); and

11.1.2   NCC Escrow shall not be liable to the Owner or the Licensee for any indirect or consequential loss or damage whether for loss of profit, loss of business, depletion of goodwill or otherwise whatsoever or howsoever caused which arise out of or in connection with this Agreement even if such loss was reasonably foreseeable or NCC Escrow had been advised of the possibility of incurring the same by the Owner, the Licensee or any third party.

11.2   NCC Escrow shall not be liable in any way to the Owner or the Licensee for acting in accordance with the terms of this Agreement and specifically (without limitation) for acting upon any notice, written request, waiver, consent, receipt, statutory declaration or any other document furnished to it pursuant to and in accordance with this Agreement.

11.3   NCC Escrow shall not be required to make any investigation into and shall be entitled in good faith without incurring any liability to the Owner or the Licensee to assume (without requesting evidence thereof) the validity, authenticity, veracity and due and authorised execution of any documents, written requests, waivers, consents, receipts, statutory declarations or notices received by it in respect of this Agreement.

12   Indemnity

12.1   Save for any claim falling within the provisions of clause 11.1.1, the Owner and the Licensee jointly and severally agree at all times to indemnify and hold harmless NCC Escrow in respect of all of its legal and all other costs, fees and expenses incurred directly or indirectly as a result of being brought into or otherwise becoming involved in any form of dispute resolution proceedings or any litigation of any kind between the Owner and the Licensee in relation to this Agreement to the extent that this Agreement does not otherwise provide for reimbursement of such costs.

12.2   The Owner shall assume all liability and shall at all times indemnify and hold harmless NCC Escrow and its officers, agents, sub-contractors and employees from and against any and all liability, loss, damages, costs, legal costs, professional and other expenses and any other liabilities of whatever nature, awarded against or agreed to be paid or otherwise suffered, incurred or sustained by NCC Escrow, whether direct, indirect or consequential as a result of or in connection with any claim by any third party(s) for alleged or actual infringement of Intellectual Property Rights arising out of or in connection with all and any acts or omissions of NCC Escrow in respect of the Material as contemplated under this Agreement.

13   Term and Termination

13.1   This Agreement shall continue until terminated in accordance with this clause 13.

13.2   If the Owner or the Licensee, as the case may be, fails to pay an invoice addressed to it for services under this Agreement within 30 days of its issue, NCC Escrow reserves the right to give that party written notice to pay the outstanding invoice within 30 days. If the Licensee has not paid its invoice by the expiry of the 30 day notice period, this Agreement will automatically immediately terminate. If the Owner has not paid its invoice by the expiry of the 30 day notice period, NCC Escrow will give the Licensee a period of 15 days to pay the Owner's invoice. If the Owner's invoice has not been paid by the expiry of the 15 day optional payment period given to the

Licensee, this Agreement will automatically immediately terminate. Any amounts owed by the Owner but paid by the Licensee will be recoverable by the Licensee direct from the Owner as a debt and, if requested, NCC Escrow shall provide appropriate documentation to assist in such recovery.

13.3 Upon termination under the provisions of clause 13.2, for 30 days from the date of termination NCC Escrow will make the Material available for collection by the Owner or its agents from the premises of NCC Escrow during office hours. After such 30 day period NCC Escrow will destroy the Material.

13.4 Notwithstanding any other provision of this clause 13, NCC Escrow may terminate this Agreement by giving 30 days written notice to the Owner and the Licensee. In that event, the Owner and the Licensee shall appoint a mutually acceptable new custodian on similar terms and conditions to those contained herein. If a new custodian is not appointed within 14 days of delivery of such notice, the Owner or the Licensee shall be entitled to request the President for the time being of the British Computer Society (or successor body) to appoint a suitable new custodian upon such terms and conditions as he/she shall require. Such appointment shall be final and binding on the Owner and the Licensee. If NCC Escrow is notified of the new custodian within the notice period, NCC Escrow will forthwith deliver the Material to the new custodian. If NCC Escrow is not notified of the new custodian within the notice period, NCC Escrow will return the Material to the Owner.

13.5 The Licensee may terminate this Agreement at any time by giving written notice to NCC Escrow. Upon such termination, NCC Escrow will return the Material to the Owner.

13.6 If NCC Escrow discovers that a Release Event has occurred and the Licensee has failed to exercise its right to claim for release of the Material under clause 6.2, NCC Escrow shall have the right to terminate this Agreement upon 30 days written notice to the Owner and the Licensee. The Licensee shall have the option of applying for release in accordance with clause 6 during this notice period, but if it fails to do so, upon the expiry of this notice period, this Agreement shall automatically terminate and, unless otherwise instructed by the Owner or the Assignee prior to expiry of the notice period, NCC Escrow shall destroy the Material.

13.7 If the Intellectual Property Rights in the Material have been assigned to a third party and the proviso in clause 6.1.6 applies such that there has been no Release Event under that clause, NCC Escrow shall be entitled to terminate this Agreement immediately by written notice to the Owner and the Licensee and upon such termination, unless otherwise instructed by the Owner or the Assignee, NCC Escrow shall destroy the Material.

13.8 If the Licence Agreement has expired or has been lawfully terminated, then the Licensee shall give notice to NCC Escrow within 14 days thereof to terminate this Agreement, failing which, the Owner shall be entitled to give written notice to NCC Escrow to terminate this Agreement. Upon receipt of such a notice from the Owner, NCC Escrow shall notify the Licensee of the Owner's notice to terminate. Unless within 14 days of NCC Escrow giving such notice to the Licensee, NCC Escrow receives a counter-notice signed by a duly authorised officer of the Licensee disputing the termination of the Licence Agreement, then the Licensee shall be deemed to have consented to such termination and this Agreement shall immediately automatically terminate. Any disputes arising under this clause shall be dealt with in accordance with the dispute resolution procedure in clause 7. Upon termination under this clause, NCC Escrow shall return the Material to the Owner.

13.9 Subject to clause 13.8, the Owner may only terminate this Agreement with the written consent of the Licensee.

13.10 This Agreement shall automatically immediately terminate upon release of the Material to the Licensee in accordance with clause 6.

13.11 If this Agreement is superseded and replaced by a new agreement in respect of the Material, this Agreement shall, upon the coming into force of the new agreement, automatically terminate. The relevant party or parties shall request NCC Escrow to either transfer the Material to the new agreement or ask the owner under the new agreement to deposit new material. If new material is deposited, upon its receipt, NCC Escrow shall, unless otherwise instructed, destroy the Material.

13.12 The provisions of clauses 1, 3.2, 3.3, 5, 8, 9, 10.1, 11, 12, 13.12 to 13.14 (inclusive) and 14 shall continue in full force after termination of this Agreement.

13.13 On and after termination of this Agreement, the Owner and/or the Licensee (as appropriate) shall remain liable to NCC Escrow for payment in full of any fees and interest which have become due but which have not been paid as at the date of termination.

13.14 The termination of this Agreement, however arising, shall be without prejudice to the rights accrued to the parties prior to termination.

14 **General**

14.1 A party shall notify the other parties to this Agreement, within 30 days of its occurrence, of any of the following:

SL

14.1.1   a change of its name, registered office, contact address or other contact details; and

14.1.2   any material change in its circumstances that may affect the validity or operation of this Agreement.

14.2   Within 14 days of any assignment or transfer by the Owner of any part of its Intellectual Property Rights in the Material, the Owner shall notify:

14.2.1   NCC Escrow and the Licensee of such assignment and the identity of the Assignee; and

14.2.2   the Assignee of the provisions of clause 6.1.6.

14.3   The formation, existence, construction, performance, validity and all other aspects of this Agreement shall be governed by and construed in accordance with the laws of England and the parties submit to the exclusive jurisdiction of the English courts.

14.4   This Agreement, together with the Order Form and any relevant NCC Escrow standard terms and conditions represent the whole agreement relating to the escrow arrangements between NCC Escrow and the other parties for the Package and shall supersede all prior agreements, discussions, arrangements, representations, negotiations and undertakings. In the event of any conflict between any of these documents, the terms of this Agreement shall prevail.

14.5   Unless the provisions of this Agreement otherwise provide, any notice or other communication required or permitted to be given or made in writing hereunder shall be validly given or made if delivered by hand or courier or if despatched by first class recorded delivery (airmail if overseas) addressed to the address specified for the parties in this Agreement (or such other address as may be notified to the parties from time to time) or if sent by facsimile message to such facsimile number as has been notified to the parties from time to time and shall be deemed to have been received:

(i)   if delivered by hand or courier, at the time of delivery;

(ii)   if sent by first class recorded delivery (airmail if overseas), 2 business days after posting (6 days if sent by airmail);

(iii)   if sent by facsimile, at the time of completion of the transmission of the facsimile with facsimile machine confirmation of transmission to the correct facsimile number of all pages of the notice.

14.6   The Owner and the Licensee shall not assign, transfer or subcontract this Agreement or any rights or obligations thereunder without the prior written consent of the other parties.

14.7   NCC Escrow shall be entitled to transfer or assign this Agreement upon written notice to both the Owner and the Licensee.

14.8   This Agreement shall be binding upon and survive for the benefit of the successors in title and permitted assigns of the parties.

14.9   If any provision of this Agreement is declared too broad in any respect to permit enforcement to its full extent, the parties agree that such provision shall be enforced to the maximum extent permitted by law and that such provision shall be deemed to be varied accordingly. If any provision of this Agreement is found by any court, tribunal or administrative authority of competent jurisdiction to be wholly or partly illegal, invalid, void or unenforceable, it shall, to the extent of such illegality, invalidity or unenforceability, be deemed severable and the remaining part of the provision and the rest of the provisions of this Agreement shall continue in full force and effect.

14.10 Save as expressly provided in this Agreement, no amendment or variation of this Agreement shall be effective unless in writing and signed by a duly authorised representative of each of the parties to it.

14.11 The parties shall not be liable to each other or be deemed to be in breach of this Agreement by reason of any delay in performing, or failure to perform, any of their obligations under this Agreement if the delay or failure was for a reason beyond that party's reasonable control (including, without limitation, fire, flood, explosion, epidemic, riot, civil commotion, any strike, lockout or other industrial action, act of God, war or warlike hostilities or threat of war, terrorist activities, accidental or malicious damage, or any prohibition or restriction by any governments or other legal authority which affects this Agreement and which is not in force on the date of this Agreement).   A party claiming to be unable to perform its obligations under this Agreement (either on time or at all) in any of the circumstances set out above must notify the other parties of the nature and extent of the circumstances in question as soon as practicable.   If such circumstances continue for more than six months, any of the other parties shall be entitled to terminate this Agreement by giving one month's notice in writing.

27 • Appendix • Precedents

14.12 No waiver by any party of any breach of any provisions of this Agreement shall be deemed to be a waiver of any subsequent or other breach and, subject to clause 6.6, no failure to exercise or delay in exercising any right or remedy under this Agreement shall constitute a waiver thereof.

14.13 This Agreement is not intended to create any right under the Contracts (Rights of Third Parties) Act 1999 which is enforceable by any person who is not a party to this Agreement and the rights of any third party under the said act are hereby expressly excluded.

14.14 This Agreement may be executed in any number of counterparts and by different parties in separate counterparts. Each counterpart when so executed shall be deemed to be an original and all of which together shall constitute one and the same agreement.

Signed for and on behalf of [Ownername]

Name: .... ¦ ....

Position: .... ¦ (Authorised Signatory)

Signed for and on behalf of [Licenseename]

Name: .... ¦ ....

Position: .... ¦ (Authorised Signatory)

Signed for and on behalf of NCC ESCROW INTERNATIONAL LIMITED

Name: .... ¦ ....

Position: .... ¦ (Authorised Signatory)

SL

Schedule 1

The Package

The software package known as [SoftwareName] or any other name(s) as may be given to it by the Owner from time to time.

Schedule 2

NCC Escrow's Fees

	DESCRIPTION	OWNER	LICENSEE
1	Annual Fee (payable on completion of this Agreement and in advance of each anniversary thereafter)	[OwnerAnnual]	[LicenseeAnnual]
2	Scheduled Update Fee (2nd and subsequent scheduled deposits in cny one year, payable on completion of this Agreement and in advance of each anniversary thereafter)	[OwnerSched]	[LicenseeSched]
3	Unscheduled Update Fee (per unscheduled deposit)	[OwnerUnsched]	[LicenseeUnsched]
4	Release Fee (plus NCC Escrow's reasonable expenses)	Nil	100%

Additional fees will be payable to NCC Escrow by the Licensee (unless otherwise agreed between the parties) for the following where applicable:

- Storage Fee for deposits in excess of 1 cubic foot;
- Any novation or replacement of this Agreement at the request of the Owner or the Licensee;
- Integrity Testing Fee for deposits consisting of more than 5 medic items.

ncc group
assure · secure · advise

Single Licensee
Website and Software
Escrow Agreement

Date
Owner   [Ownername]
Agreement Number   [Agreement#]

Notice: The parties to this Agreement are obliged to inform NCC Escrow of any changes to the Material or in their circumstances (including change of name, registered office, contact details or change of owner of the intellectual property in the Material).

Version: 07/05

SLWEBSOFT

Escrow Agreement Dated:

Between:

(1)   [Ownername] whose registered office is at [Owneraddress] (CRN: [Ownercrn]) (**"Owner"**);

(2)   [Licenseename] whose registered office is at [Licenseeaddress] (CRN: [Licenseecrn]) (**"Licensee"**); and

(3)   NCC ESCROW INTERNATIONAL LIMITED a company registered in England whose registered office is at Manchester Technology Centre, Oxford Road, Manchester M1 7EF, ENGLAND (CRN: 3081952) (**"NCC Escrow"**).

Background:

(A)   The Licensee has been granted a licence or right to use a website comprising web pages and a software package used through the website that the Owner has agreed to develop and/or maintain on the Licensee's behalf and to the Licensee's specification.

(B)   Certain technical information and/or documentation relating to the website is the confidential information and intellectual property of the Owner or a third party.

(C)   The Owner acknowledges that in certain circumstances, such information and/or documentation would be required by the Licensee in order for it to continue to exercise its rights under the Licence.

(D)   The parties therefore agree that such information and/or documentation should be placed with a trusted third party, NCC Escrow, so that such information and/or documentation can be released to the Licensee should certain circumstances arise.

Agreement:

In consideration of the mutual undertakings and obligations contained in this Agreement, the parties agree that:

1   **Definitions and Interpretation**

1.1   In this Agreement the following terms shall have the following meanings:

"Agreement" means the terms and conditions of this escrow agreement set out below, including the schedules hereto.

"Confidential Information" means all technical and/or commercial information not in the public domain and which is designated in writing as confidential by any party together with all other information of any party which may reasonably be regarded as confidential information.

"Development Agreement" means the agreement between the Owner and the Licensee relating to the development of the Website and the Package.

"Full Verification" means the tests and processes forming NCC Escrow's Full Verification service and/or such other tests and processes as may be agreed between the parties for the verification of the Material.

"Independent Expert" means a suitably qualified and independent solicitor or barrister.

"Integrity Testing" means those tests and processes forming NCC Escrow's Integrity Testing service, in so far as they can be applied to the Material.

"Intellectual Property Rights" mean any copyright, patents, design patents, registered designs, design rights, utility models, trademarks, service marks, trade secrets, know how, database rights, moral rights, confidential information, trade or business names, domain names, and any other rights of a similar nature including industrial and proprietary rights and other similar protected rights in any country or jurisdiction together with all registrations, applications to register and rights to apply for registration of any of the aforementioned rights and any licences of or in respect of such rights.

"Licence" means the licence or rights to use the Website and the Package granted to the Licensee pursuant to the Development Agreement.

"Material" means the Source Code of the Website and the Package and such other material and documentation (including updates and upgrades thereto and new versions thereof) as are necessary to be delivered or deposited to comply with clause 2 of this Agreement.

"Order Form" means the order form setting out the details of the order placed with NCC Escrow for setting up this Agreement.

"Package" means the software package together with any updates and upgrades thereto and new versions thereof licensed to the Licensee under the Licence details of which are set out in schedule 1.

"Release Purposes" means the purposes of understanding, maintaining, modifying and correcting the Website and/or Package exclusively for and on behalf of the Licensee together with such other purposes (if any) as are permitted under the Licence.

"Source Code" means the computer programming code of the Website and the Package in human readable form.

"Third Party Material" means Source Code which is not the confidential information and intellectual property of the Owner or the Licensee.

"Website" means the website referred to in Schedule 1.

1.2   This Agreement shall be interpreted in accordance with the following:

    1.2.1   headings are for ease of reference only and shall not be taken into consideration in the interpretation of this Agreement;

    1.2.2   all references to clauses and schedules are references to clauses and schedules of this Agreement; and

    1.2.3   all references to a party or parties are references to a party or parties to this Agreement.

2   Owner's Duties and Warranties

2.1   The Owner shall:

    2.1.1   deliver a copy of the Material to NCC Escrow within 30 days of the date of this Agreement;

    2.1.2   deliver a further copy of the Material to NCC Escrow each time that there is a change to the Package and/or the Website;

    2.1.3   deliver a further copy of the Material to NCC Escrow every three months from the date of the first delivery of the Material;

    2.1.4   ensure that each copy of the Material deposited with NCC Escrow comprises the Source Code of the latest version of the Package and Website used by the Licensee;

    2.1.5   deliver a replacement copy of the Material to NCC Escrow within 14 days of a notice given to it by NCC Escrow under the provisions of clause 4.1.3;

    2.1.6   deliver with each deposit of the Material the following information:

       2.1.6.1   details of the deposit including the full name of the Website and the Package (i.e. the original name as set out under schedule 1 together with any new names given to the Website and the Package by the Owner), version details, media type, backup command/software used, compression used, archive hardware and operating system details; and

       2.1.6.2   password/encryption details required to access the Material;

    2.1.7   deliver with each deposit of the Material the following technical information (where applicable):

       2.1.7.1   website or gateway uniform resource locator (URL);

       2.1.7.2   documentation describing the procedures for building, compiling and installing the software, rebuilding the web server and installing the Website including names and versions of the development tools and web browsers;

       2.1.7.3   documentation describing the procedures for maintaining the Website including names and versions of required web tools;

       2.1.7.4   access details required for web server administration, Website administration and secure shell administration;

       2.1.7.5   website design information (e.g. module names, architecture and functionality); and

       2.1.7.6   name and contact details of employees with knowledge of how to maintain and support the Material and contact details of remote host;

    2.1.8   if required by the Licensee, deposit a backup copy of the object code of any third party software package required to access, install, build or compile or otherwise use the Material.

2.2   The Owner warrants to both NCC Escrow and the Licensee at the time of each deposit of the Material with NCC Escrow that:

    2.2.1   other than any third party object code referred to in clause 2.1.8 or any Third Party Material, it owns the Intellectual Property Rights in the Material;

    2.2.2   in respect of any Third Party Material, it has been granted valid and ongoing rights under licence by the third party owner(s) thereof to deal with such Third Party Material in the manner anticipated under this Agreement and that the Owner has the express authority of such third party owner(s) to deposit the Third Party Material under this Agreement as evidenced by a signed letter of authorisation in the form required by NCC Escrow;

    2.2.3   in entering into this Agreement and performing its obligations under it, it is not in breach of

SLWEBSOFT

any of its ongoing express or implied obligations to any third party(s);

2.2.4 the Material deposited under clause 2.1 contains all information in human-readable form (except for any third party object code deposited pursuant to clause 2.1.8) and is on suitable media to enable a reasonably skilled programmer or analyst to understand, maintain, modify and correct the Website and the Package; and

2.2.5 in respect of any third party object code that the Owner, at its option, or, at the request of the Licensee, deposits with NCC Escrow in conjunction with the Material pursuant to clause 2.1.8, it has the full right and authority to do so.

3 Licensee's Responsibilities and Undertakings

3.1 The Licensee shall notify NCC Escrow of any change to the Website and/or Package that necessitates a replacement deposit of the Material.

3.2 In the event that the Material is released under clause 6, the Licensee shall:

3.2.1 keep the Material confidential at all times;

3.2.2 use the Material only for the Release Purposes;

3.2.3 not disclose the Material to any person save such of the Licensee's employees or contractors who need to know the same for the Release Purposes. In the event that Material is disclosed to its employees or contractors, the Licensee shall ensure that they are bound by the same confidentiality obligations as are contained in this clause 3.2;

3.2.4 hold all media containing the Material in a safe and secure environment when not in use; and

3.2.5 forthwith destroy the Material should the Licensee cease to be entitled to use the Package under the terms of the Licence.

3.3 In the event that the Material is released under clause 6, it shall be the responsibility of the Licensee to obtain the necessary licences to utilise the object code of any third party material deposited by the Owner pursuant to clause 2.1.8.

4 NCC Escrow's Duties

4.1 NCC Escrow shall:

4.1.1 at all times during the term of this Agreement, retain the latest deposit of the Material in a safe and secure environment;

4.1.2 inform the Owner and the Licensee of the receipt of any deposit of the Material by sending to both parties a copy of the Integrity Testing report or Full Verification report (as the case may be) generated from the testing processes carried out under clause 10; and

4.1.3 notify the Owner and the Licensee if it becomes aware at any time during the term of this Agreement that the copy of the Material held by it has been lost, damaged or destroyed so that a replacement may be obtained.

4.2 In the event of failure by the Owner to deposit any Material with NCC Escrow, NCC Escrow shall not be responsible for procuring such deposit and may, at its sole discretion, notify the Licensee of the Owner's failure to deposit any Material.

4.3 NCC Escrow may appoint agents, contractors or sub-contractors as it deems fit to carry out the Integrity Testing and the Full Verification processes. NCC Escrow shall ensure that any such agents, contractors and sub-contractors are bound by the same confidentiality obligations as are contained in clause 8.

4.4 NCC Escrow has the right to make such copies of the Material as may be necessary solely for the purposes of this Agreement.

5 Payment

5.1 The parties shall pay NCC Escrow's standard fees and charges as published from time to time or as otherwise agreed, in the proportions set out in schedule 2. NCC Escrow's fees as published are exclusive of value added tax.

5.2 NCC Escrow shall be entitled to review and vary its standard fees and charges for its services under this Agreement from time to time but no more than once a year and only upon 45 days written notice to the parties.

5.3 All invoices are payable within 30 days from the date of invoice. NCC Escrow reserves the right to charge interest in respect of the late payment of any sum due under this Agreement (both before and after judgement) at the rate of 2% per annum over the prevailing base rate of HSBC Bank Plc accruing on a daily basis from the due date therefor until full payment.

6 Release Events

6.1 Subject to: (i) the remaining provisions of this clause 6 and (ii) the receipt by NCC Escrow of its release fee and any other fees and interest (if any) outstanding under this Agreement, NCC Escrow will release the Material to a duly authorised officer of the Licensee if any of the following events (**"Release Event(s)"**) occur:

6.1.1 if the Owner is a company:

6.1.1.1 an order is made for the winding up of the Owner, the Owner passes a resolution for winding up (other than for the purposes of a solvent reconstruction or amalgamation) or a liquidator of the Owner is appointed; or

6.1.1.2 an order is made for the appointment of an administrator of the Owner or an administrator of the Owner is appointed; or

6.1.1.3 the Owner enters into a compromise or arrangement with creditors; or

6.1.1.4 the Owner has a receiver, administrative receiver or manager appointed over all or any part of its assets or undertaking; or

6.1.1.5 the Owner is dissolved; or

6.1.2 if the Owner is an individual:

6.1.2.1 the Owner enters into a compromise or arrangement with creditors; or

6.1.2.2 the Owner is declared bankrupt; or

6.1.2.3 the Owner dies; or

6.1.3 if the Owner is a partnership:

6.1.3.1 any of the partners in the Owner are declared bankrupt or enter into a compromise or arrangement with creditors; or

6.1.3.2 the Owner is wound up or dissolved; or

6.1.3.3 the Owner enters into a compromise or arrangement with creditors; or

6.1.3.4 a partnership administration order is made in respect of the Owner; or

6.1.4 any similar or analogous proceedings or event to those in clauses 6.1.1 to 6.1.3 above occurs in respect of the Owner within any jurisdiction outside England; or

6.1.5 the Owner ceases to carry on its business or the part of its business which relates to the Website and/or the Package; or

6.1.6 the Owner assigns its rights to the Intellectual Property Rights in the Material to a third party (**"Assignee"**) and the Assignee fails, within 60 days of all parties' knowledge of such assignment, to continue escrow protection for the benefit of the Licensee by failing to enter into either:

6.1.6.1 a novation agreement with the Licensee and NCC Escrow for the assumption of the Owner's rights and obligations under this Agreement by the Assignee; or

6.1.6.2 a new escrow agreement with the Licensee for the Website and the Package which offers the Licensee substantially similar protection to that provided by this Agreement without significantly increasing the overall cost to the Licensee,

provided that if the Assignee offers to enter into a novation or new escrow agreement within 60 days of all parties' knowledge of the assignment and the Licensee fails to accept the Assignee's offer within 30 days of such offer being notified to the Licensee, there shall be no Release Event under this clause; or

6.1.7 the Owner or, where relevant, its agent, parent, subsidiary or associated company is in material breach of its obligations as to maintenance or modification of the Website and/or the Package under the Development Agreement, the Licence or any maintenance agreement entered into in connection with the Website and/ or the Package and has failed to remedy such default notified by the Licensee to the Owner within a reasonable period.

6.2 The Licensee must notify NCC Escrow of the Release Event specified in clause 6.1 by delivering to NCC Escrow a statutory or notarised declaration (**"Declaration"**) made by an officer of the Licensee declaring that such Release Event has occurred, setting out the facts and circumstances of the Release Event, that the Development Agreement or the Licence and any maintenance agreement, if relevant, for the Website and/or the Package was still valid and effective up to the occurrence of such Release Event and exhibiting such documentary evidence in support of the Declaration as NCC Escrow shall reasonably require.

6.3 Upon receipt of a Declaration from the Licensee claiming that a Release Event has occurred:

6.3.1 NCC Escrow shall submit a copy of the Declaration to the Owner by courier or other form

SLWEBSOFT

of guaranteed delivery; and

6.3.2   unless within 14 days after the date of despatch of the Declaration by NCC Escrow, NCC Escrow receives a counter-notice signed by c duly authorised officer of the Owner stating that in their view no such Release Event has occurred or, if appropriate, that the event or circumstance giving rise to the Release Event has been rectified as shown by documentation in support thereof,

NCC Escrow will release the Material to the Licensee for its use for the Release Purposes.

6.4   Upon receipt of the counter-notice from the Owner under clause 6.3.2, NCC Escrow shall send a copy of the counter-notice and any supporting evidence to the Licensee by courier or other form of guaranteed delivery.

6.5   Upon receipt by the Licensee of the counter-notice from NCC Escrow or, in any event, within 90 days of despatch of the counter-notice by NCC Escrow, the Licensee may give notice to NCC Escrow that they wish to invoke the dispute resolution procedure under clause 7.

6.6   If, within 90 days of despatch of the counter-notice by NCC Escrow to the Licensee, NCC Escrow has not been informed by the Licensee that they wish the dispute resolution procedure under clause 7 to apply, the Declaration submitted by the Licensee will be deemed to be no longer valid and the Licensee shall be deemed to have waived their right to release of the Material for the particular reason or event specified in the original Declaration.

6.7   For the avoidance of doubt, where a Release Event has occurred under clauses 6.1.1 to 6.1.5, a subsequent assignment of the Intellectual Property Rights in the Material shall not prejudice the Licensee's right to release of the Material and its use for the Release Purposes.

7   Disputes

7.1   NCC Escrow shall notify the Owner of the Licensee's request for dispute resolution. Unless the Owner or the Licensee objects, NCC Escrow's Chief Executive Officer for the time being will appoint an Independent Expert to resolve the dispute. If the Owner or the Licensee objects to this appointment, they shall endeavour to appoint a mutually acceptable Independent Expert within 7 days of registering their objection. If they fail to appoint an Independent Expert within this 7 day period, NCC Escrow shall request that the President of The Law Society appoints an Independent Expert to resolve the dispute. Any appointment of an Independent Expert under this clause shall be binding upon the parties.

7.2   Within 5 working days of the appointment of the Independent Expert, the Owner and the Licensee shall each provide full written submissions to the Independent Expert together with all relevant documentary evidence in their possession in support of their claim.

7.3   The Independent Expert shall be requested to give a decision on the matter within 14 days of the date of referral or as soon as practicable thereafter and to send a copy of that decision to the Owner, Licensee and NCC Escrow. The Independent Expert's decision shall be final and binding on all parties and shall not be subject to appeal to a court in legal proceedings except in the case of manifest error.

7.4   If the Independent Expert's decision is in favour of the Licensee, NCC Escrow is hereby authorised to release and deliver the Material to the Licensee within 5 working days of the decision being notified by the Independent Expert to the parties.

7.5   The parties hereby agree that the costs and expenses of the Independent Expert shall be borne by the party against whom the decision of the Independent Expert is given.

8   Confidentiality

8.1   The Material shall remain at all times the confidential and intellectual property of its owner.

8.2   In the event that NCC Escrow releases the Material to the Licensee, the Licensee shall be permitted to use the Material only for the Release Purposes.

8.3   NCC Escrow agrees to keep all Confidential Information relating to the Material, the Website and/or the Package that comes into its possession or to its knowledge under this Agreement in strictest confidence and secrecy. NCC Escrow further agrees not to make use of such information and/or documentation other than for the purposes of this Agreement and, unless the parties should agree otherwise in writing, will not disclose or release it other than in accordance with the terms of this Agreement.

9   Intellectual Property Rights

9.1   The release of the Material to the Licensee will not act as an assignment of any Intellectual Property Rights that the Owner or any third party possesses in the Material.

9.2   The Intellectual Property Rights in the Integrity Testing report and any Full Verification report shall remain vested in NCC Escrow. The Owner and the Licensee shall each be granted a non-exclusive right and licence to use such report for the purposes of this Agreement and their own internal purposes only.

10   **Integrity Testing and Full Verification**

10.1   NCC Escrow shall bear no obligation or responsibility to any party to this Agreement or person, firm, company or entity whatsoever to determine the existence, relevance, completeness, accuracy, operation, effectiveness, functionality or any other aspect of the Material received by NCC Escrow under this Agreement.

10.2   As soon as practicable after the Material has been deposited with NCC Escrow, NCC Escrow shall apply its Integrity Testing processes to the Material.

10.3   Any party to this Agreement shall be entitled to require NCC Escrow to carry out a Full Verification. Subject to clause 10.4, NCC Escrow's prevailing fees and charges for the Full Verification processes and all reasonable expenses incurred by NCC Escrow in carrying out the Full Verification processes shall be payable by the requesting party.

10.4   If the Material fails to satisfy NCC Escrow's Full Verification tests as a result of being defective or incomplete in content, NCC Escrow's fees, charges and expenses in relation to the Full Verification tests shall be paid by the Owner.

10.5   Should the Material deposited fail to satisfy NCC Escrow's Integrity Testing or Full Verification tests under clauses 10.2 or 10.3, the Owner shall, within 14 days of the receipt of the notice of test failure from NCC Escrow, deposit such new, corrected or revised Material as shall be necessary to ensure its compliance with its warranties and obligations in clause 2. If the Owner fails to make such deposit of the new, corrected or revised Material, NCC Escrow will issue a report to the Licensee detailing the problem with the Material as revealed by the relevant tests.

11   **NCC Escrow's Liability**

11.1   Nothing in this clause 11 excludes or limits the liability of NCC Escrow for fraudulent misrepresentation or for death or personal injury caused by NCC Escrow's negligence. Save as aforesaid the following provisions set out the entire financial liability of NCC Escrow (including any liability for the acts or omissions of its employees, agents and sub-contractors) to the other parties:

11.1.1   NCC Escrow shall not be liable for any loss or damage caused to either the Owner or the Licensee either jointly or severally except to the extent that such loss or damage is caused by the negligent acts or omissions of or a breach of any contractual duty by NCC Escrow, its employees, agents or sub-contractors and in such event NCC Escrow's total liability in respect of all claims arising under or by virtue of this Agreement or in connection with the performance or contemplated performance of this Agreement, shall not exceed the sum of £1,000,000 (one million UK pounds); and

11.1.2   NCC Escrow shall not be liable to the Owner or the Licensee for any indirect or consequential loss or damage whether for loss of profit, loss of business, depletion of goodwill or otherwise whatsoever or howsoever caused which arise out of or in connection with this Agreement even if such loss was reasonably foreseeable or NCC Escrow had been advised of the possibility of incurring the same by the Owner, the Licensee or any third party.

11.2   NCC Escrow shall not be liable in any way to the Owner or the Licensee for acting in accordance with the terms of this Agreement and specifically (without limitation) for acting upon any notice, written request, waiver, consent, receipt, statutory declaration or any other document furnished to it pursuant to and in accordance with this Agreement.

11.3   NCC Escrow shall not be required to make any investigation into and shall be entitled in good faith without incurring any liability to the Owner or the Licensee to assume (without requesting evidence thereof) the validity, authenticity, veracity and due and authorised execution of any documents, written requests, waivers, consents, receipts, statutory declarations or notices received by it in respect of this Agreement.

12   **Indemnity**

12.1   Save for any claim falling within the provisions of clause 11.1.1, the Owner and the Licensee jointly and severally agree at all times to indemnify and hold harmless NCC Escrow in respect of all of its legal and all other costs, fees and expenses incurred directly or indirectly as a result of being brought into or otherwise becoming involved in any form of dispute resolution proceedings or any litigation of any kind between the Owner and the Licensee in relation to this Agreement to the extent that this Agreement does not otherwise provide for reimbursement of such costs.

12.2   The Owner shall assume all liability and shall at all times indemnify and hold harmless NCC Escrow and its officers, agents, sub-contractors and employees from and against any and all liability, loss, damages, costs, legal costs, professional and other expenses and any other liabilities of whatever nature, awarded against or agreed to be paid or otherwise suffered, incurred or sustained by NCC Escrow, whether direct, indirect or consequential as a result of or in connection with any claim by any third party(s) for alleged or actual infringement of Intellectual Property Rights arising

SLWEBSOFT

out of or in connection with all and any acts or omissions of NCC Escrow in respect of the Material as contemplated under this Agreement.

13   Term and Termination

13.1   This Agreement shall continue until terminated in accordance with this clause 13.

13.2   If the Owner or the Licensee, as the case may be, fails to pay an invoice addressed to it for services under this Agreement within 30 days of its issue, NCC Escrow reserves the right to give that party written notice to pay the outstanding invoice within 30 days. If the Licensee has not paid its invoice by the expiry of the 30 day notice period, this Agreement will automatically immediately terminate. If the Owner has not paid its invoice by the expiry of the 30 day notice period, NCC Escrow will give the Licensee a period of 15 days to pay the Owner's invoice. If the Owner's invoice has not been paid by the expiry of the 15 day optional payment period given to the Licensee, this Agreement will automatically immediately terminate. Any amounts owed by the Owner but paid by the Licensee will be recoverable by the Licensee direct from the Owner as a debt and, if requested, NCC Escrow shall provide appropriate documentation to assist in such recovery.

13.3   Upon termination under the provisions of clause 13.2, for 30 days from the date of termination NCC Escrow will make the Material available for collection by the Owner or its agents from the premises of NCC Escrow during office hours. After such 30 day period NCC Escrow will destroy the Material.

13.4   Notwithstanding any other provision of this clause 13, NCC Escrow may terminate this Agreement by giving 30 days written notice to the Owner and the Licensee. In that event, the Owner and the Licensee shall appoint a mutually acceptable new custodian on similar terms and conditions to those contained herein. If a new custodian is not appointed within 14 days of delivery of such notice, the Owner or the Licensee shall be entitled to request the President for the time being of the British Computer Society (or successor body) to appoint a suitable new custodian upon such terms and conditions as he/she shall require. Such appointment shall be final and binding on the Owner and the Licensee. If NCC Escrow is notified of the new custodian within the notice period, NCC Escrow will forthwith deliver the Material to the new custodian. If NCC Escrow is not notified of the new custodian within the notice period, NCC Escrow will return the Material to the Owner.

13.5   The Licensee may terminate this Agreement at any time by giving written notice to NCC Escrow. Upon such termination, NCC Escrow will return the Material to the Owner.

13.6   If NCC Escrow discovers that a Release Event has occurred and the Licensee has failed to exercise its right to claim for release of the Material under clause 6.2, NCC Escrow shall have the right to terminate this Agreement upon 30 days written notice to the Owner and the Licensee. The Licensee shall have the option of applying for release in accordance with clause 6 during this notice period, but if it fails to do so, upon the expiry of this notice period, this Agreement shall automatically terminate and, unless otherwise instructed by the Owner or the Assignee prior to expiry of the notice period, NCC Escrow shall destroy the Material.

13.7   If the Intellectual Property Rights in the Material have been assigned to a third party and the proviso in clause 6.1.6 applies such that there has been no Release Event under that clause, NCC Escrow shall be entitled to terminate this Agreement immediately by written notice to the Owner and the Licensee and upon such termination, unless otherwise instructed by the Owner or the Assignee, NCC Escrow shall destroy the Material.

13.8   If the Licence has expired or has been lawfully terminated, then the Licensee shall give notice to NCC Escrow within 14 days thereof to terminate this Agreement, failing which, the Owner shall be entitled to give written notice to NCC Escrow to terminate this Agreement. Upon receipt of such a notice from the Owner, NCC Escrow shall notify the Licensee of the Owner's notice to terminate. Unless within 14 days of NCC Escrow giving such notice to the Licensee, NCC Escrow receives a counter-notice signed by a duly authorised officer of the Licensee disputing the termination of the Licence, then the Licensee shall be deemed to have consented to such termination and this Agreement shall immediately automatically terminate. Any disputes arising under this clause shall be dealt with in accordance with the dispute resolution procedure in clause 7. Upon termination under this clause, NCC Escrow shall return the Material to the Owner.

13.9   Subject to clause 13.8, the Owner may only terminate this Agreement with the written consent of the Licensee.

13.10   This Agreement shall automatically immediately terminate upon release of the Material to the Licensee in accordance with clause 6.

13.11   If this Agreement is superseded and replaced by a new agreement in respect of the Material, this Agreement shall, upon the coming into force of the new agreement, automatically terminate. The relevant party or parties shall request NCC Escrow to either transfer the Material to the new agreement or ask the owner under the new agreement to deposit new material. If new material is deposited, upon its receipt, NCC Escrow shall, unless otherwise instructed, destroy the Material.

13.12   The provisions of clauses 1, 3.2, 3.3, 5, 8, 9, 10.1, 11, 12, 13.12 to 13.14 (inclusive) and 14 shall

643

SLWEBSOFT

continue in full force after termination of this Agreement.

13.13   On and after termination of this Agreement, the Owner and/or the Licensee (as appropriate) shall remain liable to NCC Escrow for payment in full of any fees and interest which have become due but which have not been paid as at the date of termination.

13.14   The termination of this Agreement, however arising, shall be without prejudice to the rights accrued to the parties prior to termination.

14   General

14.1   A party shall notify the other parties to this Agreement, within 30 days of its occurrence, of any of the following:

14.1.1   a change of its name, registered office, contact address or other contact details; and

14.1.2   any material change in its circumstances that may affect the validity or operation of this Agreement.

14.2   Within 14 days of any assignment or transfer by the Owner of any part of its Intellectual Property Rights in the Material, the Owner shall notify:

14.2.1   NCC Escrow and the Licensee of such assignment and the identity of the Assignee; and

14.2.2   the Assignee of the provisions of clause 6.1.6.

14.3   The formation, existence, construction, performance, validity and all other aspects of this Agreement shall be governed by and construed in accordance with the laws of England and the parties submit to the exclusive jurisdiction of the English courts.

14.4   This Agreement, together with the Order Form and any relevant NCC Escrow standard terms and conditions represent the whole agreement relating to the escrow arrangements between NCC Escrow and the other parties for the Website and the Package and shall supersede all prior agreements, discussions, arrangements, representations, negotiations and undertakings. In the event of any conflict between any of these documents, the terms of this Agreement shall prevail.

14.5   Unless the provisions of this Agreement otherwise provide, any notice or other communication required or permitted to be given or made in writing hereunder shall be validly given or made if delivered by hand or courier or if despatched by first class recorded delivery (airmail if overseas) addressed to the address specified for the parties in this Agreement (or such other address as may be notified to the parties from time to time) or if sent by facsimile message to such facsimile number as has been notified to the parties from time to time and shall be deemed to have been received:

(i)   if delivered by hand or courier, at the time of delivery;

(ii)   if sent by first class recorded delivery (airmail if overseas), 2 business days after posting (6 days if sent by airmail);

(iii)   if sent by facsimile, at the time of completion of the transmission of the facsimile with facsimile machine confirmation of transmission to the correct facsimile number of all pages of the notice.

14.6   The Owner and the Licensee shall not assign, transfer or subcontract this Agreement or any rights or obligations thereunder without the prior written consent of the other parties.

14.7   NCC Escrow shall be entitled to transfer or assign this Agreement upon written notice to both the Owner and the Licensee.

14.8   This Agreement shall be binding upon and survive for the benefit of the successors in title and permitted assigns of the parties.

14.9   If any provision of this Agreement is declared too broad in any respect to permit enforcement to its full extent, the parties agree that such provision shall be enforced to the maximum extent permitted by law and that such provision shall be deemed to be varied accordingly. If any provision of this Agreement is found by any court, tribunal or administrative body of competent jurisdiction to be wholly or partly illegal, invalid, void or unenforceable, it shall, to the extent of such illegality, invalidity or unenforceability, be deemed severable and the remaining part of the provision and the rest of the provisions of this Agreement shall continue in full force and effect.

14.10   Save as expressly provided in this Agreement, no amendment or variation of this Agreement shall be effective unless in writing and signed by a duly authorised representative of each of the parties to it.

14.11   The parties shall not be liable to each other or be deemed to be in breach of this Agreement by reason of any delay in performing, or failure to perform, any of their obligations under this Agreement if the delay or failure was for a reason beyond that party's reasonable control (including, without limitation, fire, flood, explosion, epidemic, riot, civil commotion, any strike, lockout or other industrial action, act of God, war or warlike hostilities or threat of war, terrorist activities, accidental or malicious damage, or any prohibition or restriction by any governments or other legal authority which affects this Agreement and which is not in force on the date of this Agreement). A party claiming to be unable to perform its obligations under this Agreement (either on time or at all) in any of the circumstances set out above must notify the other parties of the nature and extent of the circumstances in question as soon as practicable. If such circumstances continue for more than six months, any of the other parties shall be entitled to terminate this Agreement by giving one month's notice n writing.

14.12   No waiver by any party of any breach of any provisions of this Agreement shall be deemed to be a waiver of any subsequent or other breach and, subject to clause 6.6, no failure to exercise or delay in exercising any right or remedy under this Agreement shall constitute a waiver thereof.

14.13   This Agreement is not intended to create any right unde¯ the Contracts (Rights of Third Parties) Act 1999 which is enforceable by any person who is not a party to this Agreement and the rights of any third party under the said act are hereby expressly excluded.

14.14   This Agreement may be executed in any number of counterparts and by different parties in separate counterparts. Each counterpart when so executed shall be deemed to be an original and all of which together shall constitute one and the same agreement.

Signed for and on behalf of [Ownername]

Name: .... | ....

Position: .... | (Authorised Signatory)

Signed for and on behalf of [Licenseename]

Name: .... | ....

Position: .... | (Authorised Signatory)

Signed for and on behalf of NCC ESCROW INTERNATIONAL LIMITED

Name: .... | ....

Position: .... | (Authorised Signatory)

27 ● Appendix ● Precedents

Schedule 1

The Website and the Package

The website and the software package known as [SoftwareName] or any other name(s) as may be given to it by the Owner from time to time.

Schedule 2

NCC Escrow's Fees

	DESCRIPTION	OWNER	LICENSEE
1	Annual Fee (payable on completion of this Agreement and in advance of each anniversary thereafter)	[OwnerAnnual]	[LicenseeAnnual]
2	Scheduled Update Fee (2nd and subsequent scheduled deposits in any one year, payable on completion of this Agreement and in advance of each anniversary thereafter)	[OwnerSched]	[LicenseeSched]
3	Unscheduled Update Fee (per unscheduled deposit)	[OwnerUnsched]	[LicenseeUnsched]
4	Release Fee (plus NCC Escrow's reasonable expenses)	Nil	100%

Additional fees will be payable to NCC Escrow by the Licensee (unless otherwise agreed between the parties) for the following where applicable:

- Storage Fee for deposits in excess of 1 cubic foot;
- Any novation or replacement of this Agreement at the request of the Owner or the Licensee;
- Integrity Testing Fee for deposits consisting of more than 5 media items.

646

DEVELOPMENT SINGLE LICENSEE[1]

Escrow Agreement No: Dated:

Escrow Agreement Between:

(1)   [name] whose registered office is at [address] (CRN: [number]) ("the Owner");

(2)   [name] whose registered office is at [address] (CRN: [number]) ("the Licensee"); and

(3)   NCC ESCROW INTERNATIONAL LIMITED whose registered office is at Manchester Technology Centre, Oxford Road, Manchester M1 7ED, England (CRN: 3081952) ("NCC").

Preliminary:

(A)   The Owner has granted or has agreed to grant a licence to the Licensee to use a software package that the Owner is developing to the Licensee's specification pursuant to the Development Agreement.

(B)   Certain technical Information and documentation describing the software package is the confidential property of the Owner and are required for understanding, developing, maintaining and correcting the software package.

(C)   The Owner acknowledges that in certain circumstances the Licensee may require possession of the technical information and documentation held under this Agreement.

(D)   Each of the parties to this Agreement acknowledges that the considerations for their respective undertakings given under it are the undertakings given under it by each of the other parties.

It is agreed that:

I DEFINITIONS

In this Agreement the following terms shall have the following meanings:

1.1   "Development Agreement" means the agreement containing the terms and conditions relating to the development of the Package entered into between the Owner and the Licensee;

1.2   "Full Verification Service" means the appropriate tests agreed with NCC for the verification of the Material;

1.3   "Integrity Plus Testing Service" means those tests forming NCC's Integrity Plus Testing Service, in so far as they relate to the Material;

1.4   "Integrity Testing Service" means those tests forming NCC's Integrity Testing Service, in so far as they relate to the Material;

1.5   "Intellectual Property Rights" means copyright, trade secret, patent, and all other rights of a similar nature;

1.6   "Licence" means the licence granted or to be granted to the Licensee for the Package pursuant to the Development Agreement;

1.7 "Material" means the source code of the Package under development and such other materials and documentation as are necessary to comply with Clause 2.1.7; and

1.8 "Package" means the software package under development referred to in Schedule 1.

2 OWNER'S DUTIES AND WARRANTIES

2.1 The Owner shall:

2.1.1 deliver a copy of the Material to NCC within 30 days of the date of this Agreement;

2.1.2 deliver a copy of each version of the Material to NCC within 7 days of release for acceptance tests in accordance with the terms of the Development Agreement;

2.1.3 deliver a complete copy of the Material within 7 days of acceptance of the Package in accordance with the terms of the Development Agreement;

2.1.4 ensure that the Material as delivered to NCC is capable of being used to generate the latest version of the Package issued to the Licensee and shall deliver to NCC further copies of the Material as and when necessary;[2]

2.1.5 deliver to NCC a replacement copy of the Material within 3 months of the last delivery;[3]

2.1.6 deliver a replacement copy of the Material to NCC within 14 days of receipt of a notice served upon it by NCC under the provisions of Clause 4.1.5; and

2.1.7 deliver with each deposit of the Material any of the following technical information that is relevant:

2.1.7.1 Details of the deposit; full name and version details, media type, backup command/software used, compression used, archive hardware and operating system details.

2.1.7.2 Password/encryption details required to access the source code.

2.1.7.3 Directory listings of the contents of the media.

2.1.7.4 Documentation describing the procedures for building, compiling and installing the software, including names and versions of the development tools.

2.1.7.5 Software design information (e.g. module names and functionality).

2.1.7.6 Name and contact details of employees with knowledge of how to maintain and support the Material.[4]

2.2   The Owner warrants that:

    2.2.1   it owns[5] the Intellectual Property Rights in the Material and has authority to enter into this Agreement; and

    2.2.2   the Material lodged under Clause 2.1 shall contain all information in human-readable form and on suitable media to enable a reasonably skilled programmer or analyst to understand, develop (where the deposit is made prior to acceptance in accordance with the Development Agreement), maintain and correct the Package without the assistance of any other person.[6]

3 LICENSEE'S RESPONSIBILITIES

It shall be the responsibility of the Licensee to notify NCC of any change to the Package that necessitates a replacement deposit of the Material.

4 NCC'S DUTIES

4.1   NCC shall:

    4.1.1   hold the Material in a safe and secure environment;

    4.1.2   inform the Owner and the Licensee of the receipt of any copy of the Material;

    4.1.3   in accordance with the terms of Clause 9 apply the Integrity Testing Service to the Material from time to time;

    4.1.4   at all times retain a copy of the latest verified deposit of the Material; and

    4.1.5   notify the Owner if it becomes aware at any time during the term of this Agreement that the copy of the Material held by it has been lost, damaged or destroyed.

4.2   NCC shall not be responsible for procuring the delivery of the Material in the event of failure by the Owner to do so.

5 PAYMENT

The parties shall pay NCC's standard fees as published from time to time or as otherwise agreed, in the proportions set out in Schedule 2.

6 RELEASE EVENTS

6.1   Subject to the provisions of Clauses 6.2 and 6.3 and upon receipt of its release fee, NCC will release the Material to a duly authorised officer of the Licensee if any of the following events occur:

    6.1.1   the Owner enters into any company voluntary arrangement or individual voluntary arrangement or (being a company)

enters into liquidation whether compulsory or voluntary (other than for the purposes of solvent reconstruction or amalgamation) or has a receiver or administrative receiver appointed over all or any part of its assets or undertaking or a petition is presented for an Administration Order or (being an individual or partnership) becomes bankrupt, or an event occurs within the jurisdiction of the country in which the Owner is situated which has a similar effect to any of the above events in the United Kingdom; or

6.1.2   the Owner ceases to trade; or

6.1.3   the Owner assigns copyright in the Material and the assignee fails within 60 days of such assignment to offer the Licensee substantially similar protection to that provided by this Agreement without significantly increasing the cost to the Licensee; or

6.1.4   the Owner without legal justification, has defaulted to a material degree in any obligation to provide development, maintenance or modification of the Package under the Licence, Development Agreement or any maintenance agreement entered into in connection with the Package and has failed to remedy such default notified by the Licensee to the Owner.[7]

6.2   The Licensee must notify NCC of the event(s) specified in Clause 6.1 by delivering to NCC a statutory or notarised declaration ("the Declaration") made by an officer of the Licensee attesting that such event has occurred and that the Licence or Development Agreement and any maintenance agreement, if relevant, for the Package was still valid and effective up to the occurrence of such event and exhibiting such documentation in support of the Declaration as NCC shall reasonably require.

6.3   Upon receipt of a Declaration from the Licensee claiming a release event under Clause 6.1:

6.3.1   NCC shall send a copy of the Declaration to the Owner by special delivery or equivalent type of post, where the Owner is not situated in England or Wales; and

6.3.2   unless within 14 days after the date of delivery the Owner delivers to NCC a counter-notice signed by a duly authorised officer of the Owner stating that n6 such event or failure has occurred or that any such failure has been reotified NCC will release the Material to the Licensee.

6.4   Where there is any dispute as to the occurrence of any of the events set out in Clause 6 or the fulfilment of any obligations detailed therein, such dispute will be referred at the instance of either the Owner or the Licensee to the Managing Director for the time being of NCC for the appointment of an expert who shall give a decision on the matter within 14 days of the date of referral or as soon as practicable thereafter. The expert's decision shall be final and binding as between the Owner and the Licensee except in the case of manifest error.

7 CONFIDENTIALITY

7.1 The Material shall remain the confidential property of the Owner and in the event that NCC provides a copy of the Material to the Licensee, the Licensee shall be permitted to use the Material only in accordance with the confidentiality obligations contained in Clause 7.3.

7.2 NCC agrees to maintain all information and/or documentation coming into its possession or to its knowledge under this Agreement in strictest confidence and secrecy. NCC further agrees not to make use of such information and/or documentation other than for the purposes of this Agreement and will not disclose or release it other than in accordance with the terms of this Agreement.

7.3 In the event that the Material is released under Clause 6 the Licensee shall:

   7.3.1 where the Material is released to the Licensee prior to acceptance in accordance with the Development Agreement, use the Material only for the purposes of understanding, maintaining, developing and correcting the Package exclusively on behalf of the Licensee;

   7.3.2 if the development of the Material has been completed in accordance with the Development Agreement and accepted by the Licensee, use the Material only for the purpose of understanding, maintaining and correcting the Package exclusively on behalf of the Licensee;

   7.3.3 not use the Material for any other purpose nor disclose it to any person save such of its employees or contractors who need to know the same in order to understand, maintain, develop (if appropriate) and correct the Package exclusively on behalf of the Licensee. In that event the Licensee shall ensure that its employees and contractors are bound by the same confidentiality obligations as are contained in this Clause 7;

   7.3.4 hold all media containing the Material in a safe and secure environment when not in use; and

   7.3.5 forthwith destroy the same should the Licensee cease to be entitled to use the Package.

8 INTELLECTUAL PROPERTY RIGHTS

The release of the Material to the Licensee will not act as an assignment of any Intellectual Property Rights that the Owner possesses in the Material.

9 VERIFICATION

9.1 Subject to the provisions of Clauses 9.2 and 9.3, NCC shall bear no obligation or responsibility to any person, firm, company or entity whatsoever to determine the existence, relevance, completeness, accuracy, effectiveness or any other aspect of the Material.

9.2 Upon the Material being lodged with NCC, NCC shall apply its Integrity Testing Service[8] to the Material and shall provide a copy of the test report to the parties to this Agreement.

9.3 Any party to this Agreement shall be entitled to require NCC to apply its Integrity Plus Testing Service[9] to the Material or carry out a Full Verification[10]. Any reasonable charges and expenses incurred by NCC in carrying out such testing will be paid by the requesting party save that if in the opinion of the expert appointed by the Managing Director of NCC the Material is substantially defective in content any such reasonable charges and expenses will be paid by the Owner.

10 NCC'S LIABILITY

10.1 NCC shall not be liable for any loss or damage caused to the Owner or the Licensee either jointly or severally except to the extent that such loss or damage is caused by:

10.1.1 the negligent acts or omissions of; or

10.1.2 a breach of any contractual duty by NCC, its employees, agents or sub-contractors and in such event NCC's total liability in respect of all claims arising under or by virtue of this Agreement shall not (except in the case of claims for personal injury or death) exceed the sum of £500,000.[11]

10.2 NCC shall in no circumstances be liable to the Owner or the Licensee for indirect or consequential loss of any nature whatsoever whether for loss of profit, loss of business or otherwise.

10.3 NCC shall be protected in acting upon any written request, waiver, consent, receipt or other document furnished to it pursuant to this Agreement, not only in assuming its due execution and the validity and effectiveness of its provisions but also as to the truth and acceptability of any information contained in it, which NCC in good faith believes to be genuine and what it purports to be.

11 INDEMNITY[12]

Save for any claim falling within the provisions of Clause 10.1, the Owner and the Licensee jointly and severally indemnify NCC for any legal and/or related costs it incurs as a result of issuing or becoming otherwise involved in any form of dispute resolution proceedings or any litigation of any nature in relation to this Agreement.

12 TERMINATION

12.1 NCC may terminate this Agreement after failure by the Owner or the Licensee to comply with a 30 day written notice from NCC to pay any outstanding fee. If the failure to pay is on the part of the Owner the Licensee shall be given the option of paying such fee itself. Such amount will be recoverable by the Licensee direct from the Owner.

12.2 NCC may terminate this Agreement by giving 60 days written notice to the Owner and the Licensee. In that event the Owner and the Licensee shall appoint a mutually acceptable new custodian on terms similar to those contained in this Agreement. If a new custodian is not appointed within 30 days of delivery of such notice, the Owner or the Licensee shall be entitled to request the President for the time being of the British Computer Society to appoint a suitable new custodian upon such terms and conditions as he/she shall require. Such appointment shall be final and binding on all parties.

12.3 If NCC is notified of the new custodian within the notice period, NCC will forthwith deliver the Material to the new custodian. If NCC is not notified of the new custodian within the notice period, NCC will destroy the Material.

12.4 If the Development Agreement has terminated and the Licence, if granted, has also expired or been lawfully terminated this Agreement will automatically terminate on the same date.

12.5 The Licensee may terminate this Agreement at any time by giving written notice to NCC.

12.6 The Owner may only terminate this Agreement with the written consent of the Licensee.

12.7 This Agreement shall terminate upon release of the Material to the Licensee in accordance with Clause 6.

12.8 Upon termination under the provisions of Clauses 12.4, 12.5 or 12.6 NCC will deliver the Material to the Owner. If NCC is unable to trace the Owner NCC will destroy the Material.

12.9 Upon termination under the provisions of Clause 12.1 the Material will be available for collection by the Owner from NCC for 30 days from the date of termination. After such 30 day period NCC will destroy the Material.

12.10 NCC may forthwith terminate this Agreement and destroy the Material if it is unable to trace the Owner having used all reasonable endeavours to do so.

12.11 The provisions of Clauses 7, 10 and 11 shall continue in full force after termination of this Agreement.

12.12 On termination of this Agreement the Owner and/or the Licensee (as appropriate) shall remain liable to NCC for payment in full of any fee which has become due but which has not been paid as at the date of termination.

13   GENERAL

13.1 This Agreement shall be governed by and construed in accordance with the laws of England and Wales and subject to Clause 6.4 the parties submit to the exclusive jurisdiction of the English courts.

13.2   This Agreement represents the whole agreement relating to the escrow arrangements between the parties for the Package and supersedes all prior arrangements, negotiations and undertakings.

13.3   Save for Clause 6.3, all notices to be given to the parties under this Agreement shall be deemed to have been duly given or made when delivered personally or 7 days after posting or if sent by facsimile, 12 hours after despatch to the party to which such notice is required to be given or made under this Agreement addressed to the principal place of business, or for companies based in the UK, the registered office.

SCHEDULE I

The Package

The software package known as [name].

SCHEDULE 2[13]

NCC's Fees (St£)

	DESCRIPTION	OWNER	LICENSEE
1	Initial Fee (payable on commencement of work)		
2	Annual Fee (payable on completion of the agreement and on each anniversary thereafter)		
3	Scheduled Update Fee (2nd and subsequent scheduled deposits in any one year, payable on completion of the agreement and on each anniversary thereafter - NB a minimum of 3 are required in accordance with Clause 2.1.5)		
4	Unscheduled Update Fee (per unscheduled deposit)		
5	Storage Fee (and additional annual fee may be payable for deposits in excess of one cubic foot)		
6	Release Fee (plus NCC's reasonable expenses)	NIL	100%

All fees are reviewed by NCC from time to time

Signed for and on behalf of [the Owner]

Name: .... | ....

Position: .... | (Authorised Signatory)

Signed for and on behalf of [the Licensee]

Name: .... | ....

Position: .... | (Authorised Signatory)

Signed for and on behalf of NCC ESCROW INTERNATIONAL LIMITED

Name: .... | ....

Position: .... | (Authorised Signatory)

ENDNOTES

1   Under a Development Escrow Agreement, the developer is required to provide regular copies of the source code being developed for a client to The NCC Group. Once a development is complete, the Agreement can continue with reduced deposit frequencies. Thus the trigger events here are slightly different in that the client can obtain the course code if the development is not completed in accordance with the Development Agreement.

2   The Software Owner will need to ensure that the source code and other material delivered to The NCC Group is updated on a regular basis, in particular when a new version is supplied to the Licensee.

3   The NCC Group recommend that the material is replaced every three months. If this is not what is envisaged, this clause may need to be amended.

4   The obligation to deliver name and contact details of employees may be an onerous obligation on the Software Owner. In particular the Software Owner will need to ensure that he complies with the Data Protection Act before disclosing such personal data of his employees. Further, there is a risk that the Licensee may try and poach the Software Owner's employees in order to further develop the software.

5   The Software Owner needs to ensure that it does actually own the IPR rights in the Material and that they are not owned by its parent company or subsidiary.

6   The Software Owner will need to ensure that the material can be lodged in the form and on the media as set out in this clause.

7   The Software Owner should note that this clause releases the source code to the Licensee if the Licensee can show that the Software Owner was not developing or providing maintenance or other such services in breach of their agreement. However, if there is a dispute as to whether the Software Owner was in default, the parties will be able to resolve any such dispute in accordance with Clause 6.4.

8   The NCC Group carry out integrity testing on all material deposited with them. These tests are standard and check the source code to ensure that it is virus free and accessible. Any passwords and decryption keys are also verified and held by The NCC Group.

9   Integrity testing is completed in-house by The NCC Group but if either party require testing to be carried out where the source code was developed, the NCC Group provide "Integrity Plus" testing. This is a more detailed test of the source code and is carried out in the native development environment of the source code.

10 The NCC recommend that a Full Verification is carried out where the source code is either of great value to the parties (both financially and technically); or where the time taken to replace the software and re-create it (especially if it is bespoke software) would be months instead of days. Both parties need to take a commercial view as to whether a Full Verification should be carried out bearing in mind the cost of such a verification balanced with the loss that would be made if the source code deposited was incomplete or incorrect.

11 The parties should note that The NCC have limited their total liability to £500,000. If the source code (and hence the software) is worth more than this sum, then the parties should consider taking out additional insurance.

12 Note the indemnity here given by both the Software Owner and the Licensee. Again, it may be prudent to take out insurance to cover such liability.

13 The parties need to specify here what percentage of the Escrow fee is payable by the Software Owner and the Licensee.

Version: 06/01 – 206088

ESCROW SECURE[1]

Escrow Agreement No: Dated:

Escrow Agreement Between:

(1)   [name] whose registered office is at [address] ("CRN: [number]") ("the Owner"); and

(2)   NCC ESCROW INTERNATIONAL LIMITED whose registered office is at Manchester Technology Centre, Oxford Road, Manchester M1 7ED, England (CRN: 3081952) ("NCC").

Preliminary:

(A)   The Licensee has been or will be granted a licence to use a software package comprising computer programs.

(B)   Certain technical information and documentation describing the software package is the confidential property of the Owner and are required for understanding, maintaining and correcting the software package.

(C)   The Owner acknowledges that in certain circumstances the Licensee may require possession of the technical information and documentation held under this Agreement.

(D)   Each of the parties to this Agreement acknowledges that the considerations for their respective undertakings given under it are the undertakings given under it by each of the other parties.

It is agreed that:

I   DEFINITIONS

In this Agreement the following terms shall have the following meanings:

1.1   "Confirmation Agreement" means the agreement to be signed by the Licensee in the form set out in Schedule 2;

1.2   "Full Verification Service" means the appropriate tests agreed with NCC for the verification of the Material;

1.3   "Integrity Testing Service" means those tests forming NCC's Integrity Testing Service, in so far as they relate to the Material;

1.4   "Intellectual Property Rights" means copyright, trade secret, patent, and all other rights of a similar nature;

1.5   "Licence Agreement" means the licence granted to the Licensee for the Package detailed in the Confirmation Agreement;

1.6   "Licensee" means any person, firm, company or entity:

    1.6.1   to whom a licence to use the Package has been granted; and

    1.6.2   who has signed a Confirmation Agreement, forwarded the same to NCC and receipt of which has been acknowledged by NCC; reference in this Agreement to the Licensee shall be to the relevant Licensee(s) given the context in which such reference is made;

1.7 "Material" means the source code of the Package and such other materials and documentation as are necessary to comply with Clause 2.1.6; and

1.8 "Package" means the standard software package licensed to the Licensee under the Licence Agreement and referred to in Schedule 1.

2 OWNER'S DUTIES AND WARRANTIES

2.1 The Owner shall:

2.1.1 be bound by the terms of this Agreement in respect of the Licensee;

2.1.2 make the Material available to NCC within 30 days of the date of this Agreement and on each anniversary thereafter for the purposes of a Full Verification and deposit;[2]

2.1.3 at all times ensure that the Material as delivered to NCC is capable of being used to generate the latest version of the Package issued to the Licensee and shall deliver to NCC further copies of the Material as and when necessary;[3]

2.1.4 deliver to NCC a replacement copy of the Material within 12 months of the last delivery;

2.1.5 deliver a replacement copy of the Material to NCC within 14 days of receipt of a notice served upon it by NCC under the provisions of Clause 4.1.7; and

2.1.6 deliver with each deposit of the Material any of the following technical information that is relevant:

2.1.6.1 Details of the deposit; full name and version details, media type, backup command/software used, compression used, archive hardware and operating system details.

2.1.6.2 Password/encryption details required to access the source code.

2.1.6.3 Directory listings of the contents of the media.

2.1.6.4 Documentation describing the procedures for building, compiling and installing the software, including names and versions of the development tools.

2.1.6.5 Software design information (e.g. module names and functionality).

2.1.6.6 Name and contact details of employees with knowledge of how to maintain and support the Material.[4]

2.2   The Owner warrants that:

     2.2.1   it owns[5] the Intellectual Property Rights in the Material and has authority to enter into this Agreement;

     2.2.2   this Agreement is available to be taken up by any person, firm, company or entity to whom a licence to use the Package has been granted; and

     2.2.3   the Material lodged under Clause 2.1 shall contain all information in human-readable form and on suitable media to enable a reasonably skilled programmer or analyst to understand, maintain and correct the Package without the assistance of any other person.[6]

3   LICENSEE'S RESPONSIBILITIES

It shall be the responsibility of the Licensee to notify NCC of any change to the Package that necessitates a replacement deposit of the Material.

4   NCC'S DUTIES

4.1   NCC shall:

     4.1.1   be bound by the terms of this Agreement in respect of the Licensee;

     4.1.2   carry out a Full Verification of the Material as soon as possible after it is made available by the Owner, in accordance with Clause 2.1.2;

     4.1.3   hold the Material in a safe and secure environment;

     4.1.4   notify the Owner and the Licensee of the acceptance of any Confirmation Agreement;

     4.1.5   inform the Owner and the Licensee of the receipt of any copy of the Material;

     4.1.6   in accordance with the terms of Clause 10 apply the Integrity Testing Service to the Material from time to time;

     4.1.7   at all times retain a copy of the latest verified deposit of the Material; and

     4.1.8   notify the Owner if it becomes aware at any time during the term of this Agreement that the copy of the Material held by it has been lost, damaged or destroyed.

4.2   NCC shall not be responsible for procuring the delivery of the Material in the event of failure by the Owner to do so.

5   PAYMENT

The parties shall pay NCC's standard fees as published from time to time or as otherwise agreed, in the proportions set out in Schedule 3.

6   RELEASE EVENTS

6.1   Subject to the provisions of Clauses 6.2 and 6.3 and upon receipt of its release fee, NCC will release the Material to a duly authorised officer of the Licensee if any of the following events occur:

  6.1.1   the Owner enters into any company voluntary arrangement or individual voluntary arrangement or (berng a company) enters into liquidation whether compulsory or voluntary (other than for the purposes of solvent reconstruction or amalgamation) or has a receiver or administrative receiver appointed over all or any part of its assets or undertaking or a petition is presented for an Administration Order or (being an individual or partnership) becomes bankrupt, or an event occurs within the jurisdiction of the country in which the Owner is situated which has a similar effect to any of the above events in the United Kingdom; or

  6.1.2   the Owner ceases to trade; or

  6.1.3   the Owner assigns copyright in the Material and the assignee fails within 60 days of such assignment to offer the Licensee substantially similar protection to that provided by this Agreement without significantly increasing the cost to the Licensee; or

  6.1.4   the Owner without legal Justification, has defaulted to a material degree in any obligation to provide maintenance or modification of the Package under the Licence Agreement or any maintenance agreement entered into in connection with the Package and has failed to remedy such default notified by the Licensee to the owner.[7]

6.2   The Licensee must notify NCC of the event(s) specified in Clause 6.1 by delivering to NCC a statutory or notarised declaration ("the Declaration") made by an officer of the Licensee attesting that such event has occurred and that the Licence Agreement and any maintenance agreement, if relevant, for the Package was still valid and effective up to the occurrence of such event and exhibiting such documentation in support of the Declaration as NCC shall reasonably require.

6.3   Upon receipt of a Declaration from the Licensee claiming a release event under Clause 6.1:

  6.3.1   NCC shall send a copy of the Declaration to the Owner by special delivery or equivalent type of post, where the Owner is not situated in England or Wales; and

  6.3.2   unless within 14 days after the date of delivery the Owner delivers to NCC a counter-notice signed by a duly authorised officer of the Owner stating that no such event or failure has occurred or that any such failure has been rectified NCC will release the Material to the Licensee.

6.4   Where there is any dispute as to the occurrence of any of the events set out in Clause 6 or the fulfilment of any obligations detailed therein, such dispute will be referred at the instance of either the Owner or the Licensee to the Managing Director for the time being of NCC for the appointment of an expert who shall give a decision on the matter within 14 days of the date of referral or as soon as practicable thereafter. The expert's decision shall be final and binding as between the Owner and the Licensee except in the case of manifest error.

7 LICENCE

The Owner hereby grants a licence to NCC to make as many copies of the Material as may be necessary to enable NCC to comply with its obligations under this Agreement.

8 CONFIDENTIALITY

8.1 The Material shall remain the confidential property of the Owner and in the event that NCC provides a copy of the Material to the Licensee, the Licensee shall be permitted to use the Material only in accordance with the confidentiality obligations contained in Clause 8.3.

8.2 NCC agrees to maintain all information and/or documentation coming into its possession or to its knowledge under this Agreement in strictest confidence and secrecy. NCC further agrees not to make use of such information and/or documentation other than for the purposes of this Agreement and will not disclose or release it other than in accordance with the terms of this Agreement.

8.3 In the event that the Material is released under Clause 6 the Licensee shall:

8.3.1 use the Material only for the purpose of understanding, maintaining and correcting the Package exclusively on behalf of the Licensee;

8.3.2 not use the Material for any other purpose nor disclose it to any person save such of its employees or contractors who need to know the same in order to understand, maintain and correct the Package exclusively on behalf of the Licensee. In that event the Licensee shall ensure that its employees and contractors are bound by the same confidentiality obligations as are contained in this Clause 8;

8.3.3 hold all media containing the Material in a safe and secure environment when not in use; and

8.3.4 forthwith destroy the same should the Licensee cease to be entitled to use the Package.

9 INTELLECTUAL PROPERTY RIGHTS

The release of the Material to the Licensee will not act as an assignment of any Intellectual Property Rights that the Owner possesses in the Material.

10 VERIFICATION

10.1   Subject to the provisions of Clauses 10.2 and 10.3, NCC shall bear no obligation or responsibility to any person, firm, company or entity whatsoever to determine the existence, relevance, completeness, accuracy, effectiveness or any other aspect of the Material.

10.2   Upon the Material being lodged with NCC, NCC shall apply its Integrity Testing service[8] to the Material and shall provide a copy of the test report to the parties to this Agreement.

10.3   Any party to this Agreement shall be entitled to require NCC to carry out a Full Verification[9] at any time during the term of this Agreement. Any reasonable charges and expenses incurred by NCC in carrying out a Full Verification will be paid by the requesting party save that if in the opinion of the expert appointed by the Managing Director of NCC the Material is substantially defective in content any such reasonable charges and expenses will be paid by the Owner.

11 NCC'S LIABILITY

11.1   NCC shall not be liable for any loss or damage caused to the Owner or the Licensee either jointly or severally except to the extent that such loss or damage is caused by:

11.1.1   the negligent acts or omissions of; or

11.1.2   a breach of any contractual duty by NCC, its employees, agents or sub-contractors and in such event NCC's total liability in respect of all claims arising under or by virtue of this Agreement shall not (except in the case of claims for personal injury or death) exceed the sum of £500,000[10]

11.2   NCC shall in no circumstances be liable to the Owner or the Licensee for indirect or consequential loss of any nature whatsoever whether for loss of profit, loss of business or otherwise.

11.3   NCC shall be protected in acting upon any written request, waiver, consent, receipt or other document furnished to it pursuant to this Agreement, not only in assuming its due execution and the validity and effectiveness of its provisions but also as to the truth and acceptability of any information contained in it, which NCC in good faith believes to be genuine and what it purports to be.

12 INDEMNITY[11]

Save for any claim falling within the provisions of Clause 11.1, the Owner and the Licensee involved in the dispute or litigation jointly and severally indemnify NCC for any legal and/or related costs it incurs as a result of issuing or becoming otherwise involved in any form of dispute resolution proceedings or any litigation of any nature in relation to this Agreement.

13   TERMINATION

13.1   NCC may terminate this Agreement after failure by the Owner to comply with a 30 day written notice from NCC to pay any outstanding fee. Should the Owner fail to pay any fee, the relevant Licensee shall be given the option of paying such fee itself. Such amount will be recoverable by the relevant Licensee direct from the Owner.

13.2   NCC may terminate this Agreement with regard to a Licensee after failure by that Licensee to comply with a 30 day written notice from NCC to pay any outstanding fee.

13.3   NCC may terminate this Agreement by giving 60 days written notice to the Owner and the Licensee(s). In that event the Owner and the Licensee(s) shall appoint a mutually acceptable new custodian on terms similar to those contained in this Agreement. If a new custodian is not appointed within 30 days of delivery of such notice, the Owner or the Licensee(s) shall be entitled to request the President for the time being of the British Computer Society to appoint a suitable new custodian upon such terms and conditions as he/she shall require. Such appointment shall be final and binding on all parties.

13.4   If NCC is notified of the new custodian within the notice period, NCC will forthwith deliver the Material to the new custodian. If NCC is not notified of the new custodian within the notice period, NCC will destroy the Material.

13.5   If the Licence Agreement has expired or has been lawfully terminated this Agreement will automatically terminate on the same date in respect of that Licensee.

13.6   The Licensee may terminate this Agreement in respect of itself, the Owner and NCC at any time by giving written notice to NCC.

13.7   The Owner may only terminate the registration of any Licensee under this Agreement with the written consent of that Licensee.

13.8   The Owner may only terminate this Agreement with the written consent of all Licensees.

13.9   This Agreement shall terminate upon release of the Material to all Licensees in accordance with Clause 6.

13.10 Upon termination under the provisions of Clause 13.8 NCC will deliver the Material to the Owner. If NCC is unable to trace the Owner NCC will destroy the Material.

13.11 Upon termination under the provisions of Clause 13.1 the Material will be available for collection by the Owner from NCC for 30 days from the date of termination. After such 30 day period NCC will destroy the Material.

13.12 NCC may forthwith terminate this Agreement and destroy the Material if it is unable to trace the Owner having used all reasonable endeavours to do so, and there are no Licensees registered under this Agreement.

13.13 The provisions of Clauses 8, 11 and 12 shall continue in full force after termination of this Agreement.

13.14 On termination of this Agreement the Owner and/or the Licensee (as appropriate) shall remain liable to NCC for payment in full of any fee which has become due but which has not been paid as at the date of termination.

14 GENERAL

14.1 This Agreement shall be governed by and construed in accordance with the laws of England and Wales and subject to Clause 6.4 the parties submit to the exclusive jurisdiction of the English courts.

14.2 This Agreement represents the whole agreement relating to the escrow arrangements between the parties for the Package and supersedes all prior arrangements, negotiations and undertakings.

14.3 Save for Clause 6.3, all notices to be given to the parties under this Agreement shall be deemed to have been duly given or made when delivered personally or 7 days after posting or if sent by facsimile, 12 hours after despatch to the party to which such notice is required to be given or made under this Agreement addressed to the principal place of business, or for companies based in the UK, the registered office.

14.4 This Agreement does not create any right under the Contracts (Rights of Third Parties) Act 1999 which is enforceable by any person who is not a party to this Agreement.[12]

SCHEDULE I

The Package

The software package known as [name].

SCHEDULE 2

Confirmation Agreement

[A copy of this Confirmation Agreement must be returned duly signed to NCC Escrow International Limited before a Licensee can claim protection under the Escrow Agreement.]

Dated:

Between:

(1) [name] whose registered office is at [address] ("the Owner");

(2) NCC ESCROW INTERNATIONAL LIMITED whose registered office is at Manchester Technology Centre, Oxford Road, Manchester M1 7ED, England ("NCC"; and)

(3)   [Licensee's Company Name] ....
....
whose registered office is at ....
....
....
....

(Company Registration Number: [................]) ("the Licensee");

It is agreed that:

1   This Confirmation Agreement is governed by the terms and conditions set out in the Escrow Agreement Number [ ] ("EA") between the Owner and NCC.

2   This Confirmation Agreement and the EA form a binding agreement between the parties in the terms stated In the EA.

3   NCC shall record the Licensee as a party to the EA.

4   The Licensee accepts the benefits of the EA and agrees to be bound by its provisions.

Signed for and on behalf of [the Licensee]

Name .... | ....

(Authorised Signatory)

Position... |

Contact Name for Licensee .... | ....

Date of Licence Agreement for the Package .... | ....

Licensee's telephone number .... | ....

Licensee's fax number .... | ....

Licensee's correspondence address if different from above .... | ....

*VAT Registration Number: .... | .... *
*only applicable to countries within the EU.

SCHEDULE 3[13]

NCC's Fees (St£)

	DESCRIPTION	OWNER	LICENSEE
1	Escrow Secure Fee (plus NCC's reasonable travel and subsistence expenses).		
	20% payable on commencement of work.	100%	NIL
2	Escrow Secure Annual Fee (plus NCC's reasonable travel and subsistence expenses). Payable on each anniversary of the Agreement		

	DESCRIPTION	OWNER	LICENSEE
	10% discount on Escrow Secure Fee	100%	NIL
3	Licensee Annual Fee (payable on registration and on each anniversary thereafter)		
4	Minimum Annual Fee (payable in the event that there is no Licensee in any year of the Agreement)		
	Free Owner Administration Service Available.	100%	NIL
5	Scheduled Update Fee (2nd and subsequent scheduled deposits in any one year, payable on completion of the agreement and on each anniversary thereafter)		
	Free update for deposits that undergo Full Verification	100%	NIL
6	Unscheduled Update Fee (per unscheduled deposit)	100%	NIL
7	Storage Fee (an additional annual fee may be payable for deposits in excess of one cubic foot)	100%	NIL
8	Release Fee	NIL	100%

Only NCC's reasonable expenses charged (per Licensee)

• All fees are reviewed by NCC from time to time

Signed for and on behalf of [the Owner]

Name: .... | ....

Position: .... | (Authorised Signatory)

Signed for and on behalf of NCC ESCROW INTERNATIONAL LIMITED

Name: .... | ....

Position: .... | (Authorised Signatory)

ENDNOTES

1 This Agreement is similar to the Multi Licensee Agreement except that it involves a Full Verification sponsored by the software developer to be carried out at least annually. Therefore, all Licensees under the Agreement will be covered by a fully verified source code deposit and full verification test report. By subscribing to Full Verification every year, The NCC Group offer a reduced rate in its charges for this service.

2 Please note that the source code has to be made available on each anniversary for the purposes of a Full Verification. 3 The Software Owner will need to ensure that the source code and other material delivered to The NCC Group is updated on a regular basis, in particular when a new version is supplied to the Licensee.

4 The obligation to deliver name and contact details of employees may be an onerous obligation on the Software Owner. In particular the Software Owner will need to ensure that he complies with the Data Protection Act before disclosing such personal data of his employees. Further, there is a risk that the Licensee may try and poach the Software Owner's employees in order to maintain the software.

5   The Software Owner needs to ensure that it does actually own the IPR rights in the Material and that they are not owned by its parent company or subsidiary.

6   The Software Owner will need to ensure that the material can be lodged in the form and on the media as set out in this clause.

7   The Software Owner should note that this clause releases the source code to the Licensee if the Licensee can show that the Software Owner was not providing maintenance or other such services in breach of their agreement. However, if there is a dispute as to whether the Software Owner was in default, the parties will be able to resolve any such dispute in accordance with Clause 6.4.

8   The NCC Group carry out integrity testing on all material deposited with them. These tests are standard and check the source code to ensure that it is virus free and accessible. Any passwords and decryption keys are also verified and held by the NCC Group.

9   The NCC Group recommend that a Full Verification is carried out where the source code is either of great value to the parties (both financially and technically); or where the time taken to replace the software and re-create it (especially if it is bespoke software) would be months instead of days. Both parties need to take a commercial view as to whether a Full Verification should be carried out bearing in mind the cost of such a verification balanced with the loss that would be made if the source code deposited was incomplete or incorrect.

10 The parties should note that The NCC Group have limited their total liability to £500,000. If the source code (and hence the software) is worth more than this sum, then the parties should consider taking out additional insurance.

11 Note the indemnity here given by both the Software Owner and the Licensee. Again, it may be prudent to take out insurance to cover such liability.

12 This clause excludes any third parties from claiming a benefit under this Agreement. Therefore, if a Licensee has not signed the Confirmation Agreement, it will not be able to get the benefit of this Escrow Agreement.

13 The parties need to specify here what percentage of the Escrow fee is payable by the Software Owner and the Licensee. Please note that all fees in this Agreement (except the release fee and licensee annual fee) are payable by the Software Owner.

HOLDING AGREEMENT[1]

Escrow Agreement No: Dated:

Holding Agreement Between:

(1)   [name] whose registered office is at [address] (CRN: [number]) ("the Owner");

(2)   NCC ESCROW INTERNATIONAL LIMITED whose registered office is at Manchester Technology Centre, Oxford Road, Manchester, M1 7ED (CRN: 3081952) ("NCC").

It is agreed that:

I   DEFINITIONS

1.1   "Full Verification Service" means the appropriate tests agreed with NCC for the verification of the Material;

1.2   "Integrity Testing Service" means those tests forming NCC's Integrity Testing Service, in so far as they relate to the Material;

1.3   "Intellectual Property Rights" means the copyright, trade secret, patent and all other rights of a similar nature; and

1.4 "Material" means the material and documentation, including source code where required, all of which is described in Schedule 1, belonging to the Owner and to be held under this Agreement.

2 OWNER'S DUTIES AND WARRANTY

2.1 The Owner will be responsible for delivering the Material to NCC;

2.2 The Owner may make further deposits of Material as and when necessary.

2.3 The Owner shall deliver with each deposit of the Material any of the following technical information that is relevant:

2.3.1 Details of the deposit; full name and version details, media type, backup command/software used, compression used, archive hardware and operating system details and password/ encryption details required to access any source code archives.

2.3.2 A directory listing of the contents of the electronic media included in the deposit.

2.4 The Owner warrants that it owns[2] the Intellectual Property Rights in the Material and has the authority to enter into this Agreement.

3 NCC'S DUTIES

3.1 NCC shall:

3.1.1 hold the Material in a safe and secure environment;

3.1.2 inform the Owner of the receipt of any copy of the Material;

3.1.3 in accordance with the terms of Clause 7 apply the Integrity Testing Service to the Material from time to time;

3.1.4 at all times retain a copy of the latest verified deposit of the Material; and

3.1.5 notify the Owner if it becomes aware at any time during the term of this Agreement that the copy of the Material held by it has been lost, damaged or destroyed.

3.2 NCC shall not be responsible for procuring the delivery of the Material in the event of failure by the Owner to do so.

4 PAYMENT

The Owner shall pay NCC's standard fees as published from time to time or as otherwise agreed, in the proportions set out in Schedule 2.

5 RELEASE

5.1 NCC will release the Material to the Owner upon receipt of its release fee and a written request signed by a duly authorised officer of the Owner.

5.2 The Owner may re-deposit the Material at any time after release provided that this Agreement has not already been terminated in accordance with Clause 9 and payment of release fees and annual fees has been maintained.

6 CONFIDENTIALITY

NCC agrees to maintain all information and/or documentation coming into its possession or to its knowledge under this Agreement in strictest confidence and secrecy. NCC further agrees not to make use of such information and/ or documentation other than for the purposes of this Agreement and will not disclose or release it other than in accordance with the terms of this Agreement.

7 VERIFICATION

7.1 Subject to the provisions of Clauses 7.2 and 7.3, NCC shall bear no obligation or responsibility to any person, firm, company or entity whatsoever to determine the existence, relevance, completeness, accuracy, effectiveness or any other aspect of the Material.

7.2 Upon the Material being lodged with NCC, NCC shall apply its Integrity Testing Service[4] to the Material and shall provide a copy of the test report to the parties to this Agreement.

7.3 The Owner shall be entitled to require NCC to carry out a Full Verification[5]. Any reasonable charges and expenses incurred by NCC in carrying out a Full Verification will be paid by the Owner.

8 NCC'S LIABILITY

8.1 NCC shall not be liable for any loss or damage caused to the Owner except to the extent that such loss or damage is caused by:

8.1.1 the negligent acts or omissions of; or

8.1.2 a breach of any contractual duty by;

NCC, its employees, agents or sub-contractors and in such event NCC's total liability in respect of all claims arising under or by virtue of this Agreement shall not (except in the case of claims for personal injury or death) exceed the sum of £500,000.[6]

8.2 NCC shall in no circumstances be liable to the Owner for indirect or consequential loss of any nature whatsoever whether for loss of business or otherwise.

8.3 NCC shall be protected in acting upon any written request, waiver, consent, receipt or other document furnished to it pursuant to this Agreement, not only in assuming its due execution and the validity and effectiveness of its provisions but also as to the truth and acceptability of any information contained in it, which NCC in good faith believes to be genuine and what it purports to be.

9 TERMINATION

9.1 NCC may terminate this Agreement if the Owner fails to comply with a 30 day written notice from NCC to pay any outstanding fee.

9.2 NCC may terminate this Agreement by giving 60 days written notice to the Owner.

9.3 The Owner may terminate this Agreement by notifying NCC in writing.

9.4 Upon termination in accordance with Clauses 9.1 or 9.3 above, the Material will be available for collection by the Owner from NCC for 30 days from the date of termination. After such 30 day period NCC will destroy the Material.

9.5 Upon termination in accordance with Clause 9.2 the Material will be returned to the Owner.

9.6 NCC may forthwith terminate this Agreement and destroy the Material if it is unable to trace the Owner having used all reasonable endeavours to do so.

9.7 The provisions of Clauses 6 and 8 shall continue in full force after termination of this Agreement.

9.8 On termination of this Agreement the Owner shall remain liable to NCC for payment in full of any fee which has become due but which has not been paid as at the date of termination.

10 GENERAL

10.1 This Agreement shall be governed by and construed in accordance with the laws of England and Wales.

10.2 All notices to be given to the parties under this Agreement shall be deemed to have been duly given or made when delivered personally or 7 days after posting or if sent by facsimile, 12 hours after despatch to the party to which such notice is required to be given or made under this Agreement addressed to the principal place of business, or for companies based in the UK, the registered office.

SCHEDULE I

The Material

The Material known as [name]

SCHEDULE 2

NCC's Fees (St£)

	DESCRIPTION	OWNER
1	Initial Fee (payable on commencement of work)	100%
2	Annual Fee (payable on completion of the agreement and on each anniversary thereafter)	100%
3	Scheduled Update Fee (2nd and subsequent scheduled deposits In any one year, payable on completion of the agreement and on each anniversary thereafter)	100%
4	Unscheduled Update Fee (per unscheduled deposit)	100%
5	Storage Fee (an additional annual fee may be payable for deposits In excess of one cubic foot)	100%
6	Release Fee (plus NCC's reasonable expenses)	100%

● All fees are reviewed by NCC from time to time

Signed on behalf of [the Owner]

Name: .... | ....

Position: .... | (Authorised Signatory)

Signed on behalf of NCC ESCROW INTERNATIONAL LIMITED

Name: .... | ....

Position: .... | (Authorised Signatory)

ENDNOTES

1 This Agreement is used when a client requests secure storage of source code and requires the source code to be tested to a certain level. Thus this Agreement is purely between the Software Owner and The NCC Group.
2 The Software Owner needs to ensure that it does actually own the IPR rights in the Material and that they are not owned by its parent company or subsidiary.
3 Note that the source code is released merely on payment of the release fee and a written request from the Software Owner.
4 The NCC Group carry out integrity testing on all material deposited with them. These tests are standard and check the source code to ensure that it is virus free and accessible. Any passwords and decryption keys are also verified and held by The NCC Group.
5 The NCC Group recommend that a Full Verification is carried out where the source code is either of great value to the parties (both financially and technically); or where the time taken to replace the software and re-create it (especially if it is bespoke software) would be months instead of days. Both parties need to take a commercial view as to whether a Full Verification should be carried out bearing in mind the cost of such a verification balanced with the loss that would be made if the source code deposited was incomplete or incorrect.
6 The parties should note that The NCC Group have limited their total liability to £500,000. If the source code (and hence the software) is worth more than this sum, then the parties should consider taking out additional insurance.

INDUSTRIAL SINGLE LICENCEE[1]

Escrow Agreement No   Dated:

Escrow Agreement Between:

(1)   [name] whose registered office is at [address] (CRN: [number]) ("the Owner");

(2)   [name] whose registered office is at [address] (CRN: [number]) ("the Licensee"); and

(3)   NCC ESCROW INTERNATIONAL LIMITED whose registered office is at Manchester Technology Centre, Oxford Road, Manchester M1 7ED, England (CRN: 3081952) ("NCC").

Preliminary:

(A)   The Owner and the Licensee have entered into a supply agreement for the design and manufacture of the Product.

(B)   Certain technical information including but not limited to technical drawings, manufacturing processes and software that are integral to the manufacture of the Product is the confidential property of the Owner.

(C)   The Owner acknowledges that in certain circumstances the Licensee may require possession of the technical information and documentation held under this Agreement.

(D)   Each of the parties to this Agreement acknowledges that the considerations for their respective undertakings given under it are the undertakings given under it by each of the other parties.

It is agreed that:

I DEFINITIONS

In this Agreement the following terms shall have the following meanings:

1.1   "Full Verification Service" means those tests agreed between the Licensee and NCC for the verification of the Material;

1.2   "Integrity Testing Service" means those tests forming part of NCC's Integrity Testing Service, in so far as they relate to the Material;

1.3   "Integrity Plus Testing Service" means those tests forming NCC's Integrity Plus Testing Service, in so far as they relate to the Material;

1.4   "Intellectual Property Rights" means copyright, trade secret, patent, and all other rights of a similar nature;

1.5   "Licence Agreement" means the licence granted to the Licensee for the Product;

1.6   "Material" means the build, test and configuration documents, source code and proprietary object code and utilities necessary in order for the Licensee to manufacture the Product, together with the technical information described in Clause 2.1.5;

1.7   "Product" means the product referred to in the Supply Agreement and Schedule 1; and

1.8   "Supply Agreement" means the agreement between the Owner and the Licensee for the design and manufacture of the Product.

2   OWNER'S DUTIES AND WARRANTIES

2.1   The Owner shall:

    2.1.1   deliver a copy of the Material to NCC within 30 days of the date of this Agreement;

    2.1.2   at all times ensure that the Material as delivered to NCC is capable of being used to manufacture the latest version of the Product issued to the Licensee and shall deliver to NCC further copies of the Material as and when necessary;[2]

    2.1.3   deliver to NCC a replacement copy of the Material within 12 months of the last delivery;[3]

    2.1.4   deliver a replacement copy of the Material to NCC within 14 days of receipt of a notice served upon it by NCC under the provisions of Clause 4.1.5; and

    2.1.5   deliver with each deposit of the Material any of the following technical information that is relevant:

        2.1.5.1   Details of the deposit; full name and version details, media type, backup command/software used, compression used, archive hardware and operating system details and password/encryption details required to access any source code archives.

        2.1.5.2   A directory listing of the contents of the electronic media included in the deposit.

        2.1.5.3   Hardcopy parts listing of the contents of the deposit.

        2.1.5.4   Documentation describing the procedures for building, compiling and installing any software elements of the Material, including names and versions of the development tools.

        2.1.5.5   Documentation describing the processes for manufacturing the Product.

        2.1.5.6   Software and hardware design information (e.g. module names and functionality).

        2.1.5.7   Name and contact details of employees with knowledge of how to maintain and support the Material.[4]

2.2   The Owner warrants that:

    2.2.1   it owns[5] the Intellectual Property Rights in the Material and has authority to enter into this Agreement; and

2.2.2 the Material lodged under Clause 2.1 shall contain all information in human-readable form and on suitable media to enable a reasonably skilled programmer or analyst to understand, maintain and correct the Product without the assistance of any other person.[6]

3 LICENSEE'S RESPONSIBILITIES

It shall be the responsibility of the Licensee to notify NCC of any change to the Product that necessitates a replacement deposit of the Material.

4 NCC'S DUTIES

4.1 NCC shall:

4.1.1 hold the Material in a safe and secure environment;

4.1.2 inform the Owner and the Licensee of the receipt of any copy of the Material;

4.1.3 in accordance with the terms of Clause 9 apply the Integrity Testing Service to the Material from time to time;

4.1.4 at all times retain a copy of the latest verified deposit of the Material; and

4.1.5 notify the Owner if it becomes aware at any time during the term of this Agreement that the copy of the Material held by it has been lost, damaged or destroyed.

4.2 NCC shall not be responsible for procuring the delivery of the Material in the event of failure by the Owner to do so.

5 PAYMENT

The parties shall pay NCC's standard fees as published from time to time or as otherwise agreed, in the proportions set out in Schedule 2.

6 RELEASE EVENTS

6.1 Subject to the provisions of Clauses 6.2 and 6.3 and upon receipt of its release fee, NCC will release the Material to a duly authorised officer of the Licensee if any of the following events occur:

6.1.1 the Owner enters into any company voluntary arrangement or individual voluntary arrangement or (being a company) enters into liquidation whether compulsory or voluntary (other than for the purposes of solvent reconstruction or amalgamation) or has a receiver or administrative receiver appointed over all or any part of its assets or undertaking or a petition is presented for an Administration Order or (being an individual or partnership) becomes bankrupt, or an event occurs within the jurisdiction of the country in which the Owner is situated which has a similar effect to any of the above events in the United Kingdom; or

6.1.2   the Owner ceases to trade; or

6.1.3   the Owner assigns copyright in the Material and the assignee fails within 60 days of such assignment to offer the Licensee substantially similar protection to that provided by this Agreement without significantly increasing the cost to the Licensee; or

6.1.4   the Owner without legal justification, has defaulted to a material degree in any obligation to provide the manufacture, maintenance or modification of the Product under the Licence Agreement, Supply Agreement or any maintenance agreement entered into in connection with the Product and has failed to remedy such default notified by the Licensee to the Owner.[7]

6.2   The Licensee must notify NCC of the event(s) specified in Clause 6.1 by delivering to NCC a statutory or notarised declaration ("the Declaration") made by an officer of the Licensee attesting that such event has occurred and that the Supply Agreement or Licence Agreement and any maintenance agreement, if relevant, for the Product was still valid and effective up to the occurrence of such event and exhibiting such documentation in support of the Declaration as NCC shall reasonably require.

6.3   Upon receipt of a Declaration from the Licensee claiming a release event under Clause 6.1:

6.3.1   NCC shall send a copy of the Declaration to the Owner by special delivery or equivalent type of post, where the Owner is not situated in England or Wales; and

6.3.2   unless within 14 days after the date of delivery the Owner delivers to NCC a counter-notice signed by a duly authorised officer of the Owner stating that no such event or failure has occurred or that any such failure has been rectified NCC will release the Material to the Licensee.

6.4   Where there is any dispute as to the occurrence of any of the events set out in Clause 6 or the fulfilment of any obligations detailed therein, such dispute will be referred at the instance of either the Owner or the Licensee to the Managing Director for the time being of NCC for the appointment of an expert who shall give a decision on the matter within 14 days of the date of referral or as soon as practicable thereafter. The expert's decision shall be final and binding as between the Owner and the Licensee except in the case of manifest error.

7 CONFIDENTIALITY

7.1   The Material shall remain the confidential property of the Owner and in the event that NCC provides a copy of the Material to the Licensee, the Licensee shall be permitted to use the Material only in accordance with the confidentiality obligations contained in Clause 7.3.

7.2   NCC agrees to maintain all information and/or documentation coming into its possession or to its knowledge under this Agreement in strictest confidence and secrecy. NCC further agrees not to make use of such information and/or documentation other than for the purposes of this Agreement and will not disclose or release it other than in accordance with the terms of this Agreement.

7.3   In the event that the Material is released under Clause 6 the Licensee shall:

7.3.1   use the Material only for the purpose of understanding, manufacturing, maintaining and correcting the Product exclusively on behalf of the Licensee;

7.3.2   not use the Material for any other purpose nor disclose it to any person save such of its employees or contractors who need to know the same in order to understand, manufacture, maintain and correct the Product exclusively on behalf of the Licensee. In that event the Licensee shall ensure that its employees and contractors are bound by the same confidentiality obligations as are contained in this Clause 7;

7.3.3   hold all media containing the Material in a safe and secure environment when not in use; and

7.3.4   forthwith destroy the same should the Licensee cease to be entitled to use the Product.

8   INTELLECTUAL PROPERTY RIGHTS

The release of the Material to the Licensee will not act as an assignment of any Intellectual Property Rights that the Owner possesses in the Material.

9   VERIFICATION

9.1   Subject to the provisions of Clauses 9.2 and 9.3, NCC shall bear no obligation or responsibility to any person, firm, company or entity whatsoever to determine the existence, relevance, completeness, accuracy, effectiveness or any other aspect of the Material.

9.2   Upon the Material being lodged with NCC, NCC shall apply its Integrity Testing Service[8] to the Material and shall provide a copy of the test report to the parties to this Agreement.

9.3   Any party to this Agreement shall be entitled to require NCC to apply its Integrity Plus Testing Service[9] to the Material or carry out a Full Verification.[10] Any reasonable charges and expenses incurred by NCC in carrying out such testing will be paid by the requesting party save that if in the opinion of the expert appointed by the Managing Director of NCC the Material is substantially defective in content any such reasonable charges and expenses will be paid by the Owner.

10 NCC'S LIABILITY

10.1 NCC shall not be liable for any loss or damage caused to the Owner or the Licensee either jointly or severally except to the extent that such loss or damage is caused by:

10.1.1 the negligent acts or omissions of; or

10.1.2 a breach of any contractual duty by NCC, its employees, agents or sub-contractors and in such event NCC's total liability in respect of all claims arising under or by virtue of this Agreement shall not (except in the case of claims for personal injury or death) exceed the sum of £500,000.[11]

10.2 NCC shall in no circumstances be liable to the Owner or the Licensee for indirect or consequential loss of any nature whatsoever whether for loss of profit, loss of business or otherwise.

10.3 NCC shall be protected in acting upon any written request, waiver, consent, receipt or other document furnished to it pursuant to this Agreement, not only in assuming its due execution and the validity and effectiveness of its provisions but also as to the truth and acceptability of any information contained in it, which NCC in good faith believes to be genuine and what it purports to be.

11 INDEMNITY[12]

Save for any claim falling within the provisions of Clause 10.1, the Owner and the Licensee jointly and severally indemnify NCC for any legal and/or related costs it incurs as a result of issuing or becoming otherwise involved in any form of dispute resolution proceedings or any litigation of any nature in relation to this Agreement.

12 TERMINATION

12.1 NCC may terminate this Agreement after failure by the Owner or the Licensee to comply with a 30 day written notice from NCC to pay any outstanding fee. If the failure to pay is on the part of the Owner the Licensee shall be given the option of paying such fee itself. Such amount will be recoverable by the Licensee direct from the Owner.

12.2 NCC may terminate this Agreement by giving 60 days written notice to the Owner and the Licensee. In that event the Owner and the Licensee shall appoint a mutually acceptable new custodian on terms similar to those contained in this Agreement. If a new custodian is not appointed within 30 days of delivery of such notice, the Owner or the Licensee shall be entitled to request the President for the time being of the British Computer Society to appoint a suitable new custodian upon such terms and conditions as he/she shall require. Such appointment shall be final and binding on all parties.

12.3 If NCC is notified of the new custodian within the notice period, NCC will forthwith deliver the Material to the new custodian. If NCC is not notified of the new custodian within the notice period, NCC will destroy the Material.

12.4 The Licensee may terminate this Agreement at any time by giving written notice to NCC. If the Licence Agreement has expired or has been lawfully terminated then it shall be the responsibility of the Licensee to terminate this Agreement.

12.5 The Owner may only terminate this Agreement with the written consent of the Licensee.

12.6 This Agreement shall terminate upon release of the Material to the Licensee in accordance with Clause 6.

12.7 Upon termination under the provisions of Clauses 12.4 or 12.5 NCC will deliver the Material to the Owner. If NCC is unable to trace the Owner NCC will destroy the Material.

12.8 Upon termination under the provisions of Clause 12.1 the Material will be available for collection by the Owner from NCC for 30 days from the date of termination. After such 30 day period NCC will destroy the Material.

12.9 NCC may forthwith terminate this Agreement and destroy the Material if it is unable to trace the Owner having used all reasonable endeavours to do so.

12.10 The provisions of Clauses 7, 10 and 11 shall continue in full force after termination of this Agreement.

12.11 On termination of this Agreement the Owner and/or the Licensee (as appropriate) shall remain liable to NCC for payment in full of any fee which has become due but which has not been paid as at the date of termination.

13 GENERAL

13.1 This Agreement shall be governed by and construed in accordance with the laws of England and Wales and subject to Clause 6.4 the parties submit to the exclusive jurisdiction of the English courts.

13.2 This Agreement represents the whole agreement relating to the escrow arrangements between the parties for the Product and supersedes all prior arrangements, negotiations and undertakings.

13.3 Save for Clause 6.3, all notices to be given to the parties under this Agreement shall be deemed to have been duly given or made when delivered personally or 7 days after posting or if sent by facsimile, 12 hours after despatch to the party to which such notice is required to be given or made under this Agreement addressed to the principal place of business, or for companies based in the UK, the registered office.

SCHEDULE I

The Product

The product known as [name]

SCHEDULE 2[13]

NCC's Fees (St£)

	DESCRIPTION	OWNER	LICENSEE
1	Initial Fee (payable on commencement of work)		
2	Annual Fee (payable on completion of the agreement and on each anniversary thereafter)		
3	Scheduled Update Fee (2nd and subsequent scheduled deposits in any one year, payable on completion of the agreement and on each anniversary thereafter)		
4	Unscheduled Update Fee (per unscheduled deposit)		
5	Storage Fee (an additional annual fee may be payable for deposits in excess of once cubic foot)		
6	Release Fee (plus NCC's reasonable expenses)	NIL	100%

• All fees are reviewed by NCC from time to time

Signed for and on behalf of [the Owner]

Name: .... | ....

Position: .... | (Authorised Signatory)

Signed for and on behalf of [the Licensee]

Name: .... | ....

Position: .... | (Authorised Signatory)

Signed for and on behalf of NCC ESCROW INTERNATIONAL LIMITED

Name: .... | ....

Position: .... | (Authorised Signatory)

ENDNOTES

1 This is a specialist Agreement provided by The NCC Group and focuses on the protection of product design and manufacturing processes.

2 The Software Owner will need to ensure that the source code and other material delivered to The NCC Group is updated on a regular basis, in particular when a new version is supplied to the Licensee.

3 The NCC Group recommend that the material is replaced annually. If this is not what is envisaged, this clause may need to be amended.

4 The obligation to deliver name and contact details of employees may be an onerous obligation on the Software Owner. In particular the Software Owner will need to ensure that he complies with the Data Protection Act before disclosing such personal data of his employees. Further, there is a risk that the Licensee may try and poach the Software Owner's employees in order to maintain the software.

5 The Software Owner needs to ensure that it does actually own the IPR rights in the Material and that they are not owned by its parent company or subsidiary.

6 The Software Owner will need to ensure that the material can be lodged in the form and on the media as set out in this clause.

7 The Software Owner should note that this clause releases the material to the Licensee if the Licensee can show that the Software Owner was not manufacturing, maintaining or modifying the Product in breach of their agreement. However, if there is a dispute as to whether the Software Owner was in default, the parties will be able to resolve any such dispute in accordance with Clause 6.4.

8 The NCC Group carry out integrity testing on all material deposited with them. These tests are standard and check the deposited material to ensure that it is virus free and accessible. Any passwords and decryption keys are also verified and held by The NCC Group.

9 Integrity testing is completed in-house by The NCC Group but if either party require testing to be carried out where the material was developed, The NCC Group provide "Integrity Plus" testing. This is a more detailed test of the material and is carried out in the native development environment of the material.

10 The NCC Group recommend that a Full Verification is carried out where the source code is either of great value to the parties (both financially and technically) or where the time taken to replace the software and re-create it (especially if it is bespoke software) would be months instead of days. Both parties need to take a commercial view as to whether a Full Verification should be carried out bearing in mind the cost of such a verification balanced with the loss that would be made if the material deposited was incomplete or incorrect.

11 The parties should note that The NCC Group have limited their total liability to £500,000. If the source code (and hence the software) is worth more than this sum, then the parties should consider taking out additional insurance.

12 Note the indemnity here given by both the Software Owner and the Licensee. Again, it may be prudent to take out insurance to cover such liability.

13 The parties need to specify here what percentage of the Escrow fee is payable by the Software Owner and the Licensee.

MULTI LICENSEE[1]

Escrow Agreement No: Dated:

(1)   [name] whose registered office is at [address] (CRN: [number]) ("the Owner"); and

(2)   NCC ESCROW INTERNATIONAL LIMITED whose registered office is at Manchester Technology Centre, Oxford Road, Manchester M1 7ED, England (CRN: 3081952) ("NCC").

Preliminary:

(A)   The Licensee has been or will be granted a licence to use a software package comprising computer programs.

(B)   Certain technical information and documentation describing the software package is the confidential property of the Owner and is required for understanding, maintaining and correcting the software package.

(C)   The Owner acknowledges that in certain circumstances the Licensee may require possession of the technical information and documentation held under this Agreement.

(D)   Each of the parties to this Agreement acknowledges that the considerations for their respective undertakings given under it are the undertakings given under it by each of the other parties.

It is agreed that:

I DEFINITIONS

In this Agreement the following terms shall have the following meanings:

1.1   "Confirmation Agreement" means the agreement to be signed by the Licensee in the form set out in Schedule 2;

1.2   "Full Verification Service" means the appropriate tests agreed with NCC for the verification of the Material;

1.3   "Integrity Testing Service" means those tests forming NCC's Integrity Testing Service, in so far as they relate to the Material;

1.4   "Intellectual Property Rights" means copyright, trade secret, patent, and all other rights of a similar nature;

1.5   "Licence Agreement" means the licence granted to the Licensee for the Package detailed in the Confirmation Agreement;

1.6   "Licensee" means any person, firm, company or entity:

    1.6.1   to whom a licence to use the Package has been granted; and

    1.6.2   who has signed a Confirmation Agreement, forwarded the same to NCC and receipt of which has been acknowledged by NCC;

reference in this Agreement to the Licensee shall be to the relevant Licensee(s) given the context in which such reference is made;

1.7   "Material" means the source code of the Package and such other materials and documentation as are necessary to comply with Clause 2.1.6; and

1.8   "Package" means the standard software package licensed to the Licensee under the Licence Agreement and referred to in Schedule 1.

2 OWNER'S DUTIES AND WARRANTIES

2.1   The Owner shall:

    2.1.1   be bound by the terms of this Agreement in respect of the Licensee;

    2.1.2   deliver a copy of the Material to NCC within 30 days of the date of this Agreement;

2.1.3   at all times ensure that the Material as delivered to NCC is capable of being used to generate the latest version of the Package issued to the Licensee and shall deliver to NCC further copies of the Material as and when necessary;[2]

2.1.4   deliver to NCC a replacement copy of the Material within 12 months of the last delivery;[3]

2.1.5   deliver a replacement copy of the Material to NCC within 14 days of receipt of a notice served upon it by NCC under the provisions of Clause 4.1.7; and

2.1.6   deliver with each deposit of the Material any of the following technical information that is relevant:

      2.1.6.1   Details of the deposit; full name and version details, media type, backup command/software used, compression used, archive hardware and operating system details.

      2.1.6.2   Password/encryption details required to access the source code.

      2.1.6.3   Directory listings of the contents of the media.

      2.1.6.4   Documentation describing the procedures for building, compiling and installing the software, including names and versions of the development tools.

      2.1.6.5   Software design information (e.g. module names and functionality).

      2.1.6.6   Name and contact details of employees with knowledge of how to maintain and support the Material.[4]

2.2   The Owner warrants that:

2.2.1   it owns[5] the Intellectual Property Rights in the Material and has authority to enter into this Agreement; and

2.2.2   the Material lodged under Clause 2.1 shall contain all information in human-readable form and on suitable media to enable a reasonably skilled programmer or analyst to understand, maintain and correct the Package without the assistance of any other person.[6]

3   LICENSEE'S RESPONSIBILITIES

It shall be the responsibility of the Licensee to notify NCC of any change to the Package that necessitates a replacement deposit of the Material.

4   NCC'S DUTIES

4.1   NCC shall:

4.1.1   be bound by the terms of this Agreement in respect of the Licensee;

4.1.2   hold the Material in a safe and secure environment;

4.1.3   notify the Owner and the Licensee of the acceptance of any Confirmation Agreement;

4.1.4   inform the Owner and the Licensee of the receipt of any copy of the Material;

4.1.5   in accordance with the terms of Clause 10 apply the Integrity Testing Service to the Material from time to time;

4.1.6   at all times retain a copy of the latest verified deposit of the Material; and

4.1.7   notify the Owner if it becomes aware at any time during the term of this Agreement that the copy of the Material held by it has been lost, damaged or destroyed.

4.2   NCC shall not be responsible for procuring the delivery of the Material in the event of failure by the Owner to do so.

5   PAYMENT

The parties shall pay NCC's standard fees as published from time to time or as otherwise agreed, in the proportions set out in Schedule 3.

6   RELEASE EVENTS

6.1   Subject to the provisions of Clauses 6.2 and 6.3 and upon receipt of its release fee, NCC will release the Material to a duly authorised officer of the Licensee if any of the following events occur:

6.1.1   the Owner enters into any company voluntary arrangement or individual voluntary arrangement or (being a company) enters into liquidation whether compulsory or voluntary (other than for the purposes of solvent reconstruction or amalgamation) or has a receiver or administrative receiver appointed over all or any part of its assets or undertaking or a petition is presented for an Administration Order or (being an individual or partnership) becomes bankrupt, or an event occurs within the jurisdiction of the country in which the Owner is situated which has a similar effect to any of the above events in the United Kingdom; or

6.1.2   the Owner ceases to trade; or

6.1.3   the Owner assigns copyright in the Material and the assignee fails within 60 days of such assignment to offer the Licensee substantially similar protection to that provided by this Agreement without significantly increasing the cost to the Licensee; or

6.1.4   the Owner without legal justification, has defaulted to a material degree in any obligation to provide maintenance or modification of the Package under the Licence Agreement or any maintenance agreement entered into in connection with the Package and has failed to remedy such default notified by the Licensee to the Owner.[7]

6.2   The Licensee must notify NCC of the event(s) specified in Clause 6.1 by delivering to NCC a statutory or notarised declaration ("the Declaration") made by an officer of the Licensee attesting that such event has occurred and that the Licence Agreement and any maintenance agreement, if relevant, for the Package was still valid and effective up to the occurrence of such event and exhibiting such documentation in support of the Declaration as NCC shall reasonably require.

6.3   Upon receipt of a Declaration from the Licensee claiming a release event under Clause 6.1:

6.3.1   NCC shall send a copy of the Declaration to the Owner by special delivery or equivalent type of post, where the Owner is not situated in England or Wales; and

6.3.2   unless within 14 days after the date of delivery the Owner delivers to NCC a counter-notice signed by a duly authorised officer of the Owner stating that no such event or failure has occurred or that any such failure has been rectified NCC will release the Material to the Licensee.

Version: 09/01

6.4   Where there is any dispute as to the occurrence of any of the events set out in Clause 6 or the fulfilment of any obligations detailed therein, such dispute will be referred at the instance of either the Owner or the Licensee to the Managing Director for the time being of NCC for the appointment of an expert who shall give a decision on the matter within 14 days of the date of referral or as soon as practicable thereafter. The expert's decision shall be final and binding as between the Owner and the Licensee except in the case of manifest error.

7   LICENCE

The Owner hereby grants a licence to NCC to make as many copies of the Material as may be necessary to enable NCC to comply with its obligations under this Agreement.

8   CONFIDENTIALITY

8.1   The Material shall remain the confidential property of the Owner and in the event that NCC provides a copy of the Material to the Licensee, the Licensee shall be permitted to use the Material only in accordance with the confidentiality obligations contained in Clause 8.3.

8.2   NCC agrees to maintain all information and/or documentation coming into its possession or to its knowledge under this Agreement in strictest confidence and secrecy. NCC further agrees not to make use of such information and/or documentation other than for the purposes of this Agreement and will not disclose or release it other than in accordance with the terms of this Agreement.

8.3   In the event that the Material is released under Clause 6 the Licensee shall:

    8.3.1   use the Material only for the purpose of understanding, maintaining and correcting the Package exclusively on behalf of the Licensee;

    8.3.2   not use the Material for any other purpose nor disclose it to any person save such of its employees or contractors who need to know the same in order to understand, maintain and correct the Package exclusively on behalf of the Licensee. In that event the Licensee shall ensure that its employees and contractors are bound by the same confidentiality obligations as are contained in this Clause 8;

    8.3.3   hold all media containing the Material in a safe and secure environment when not in use; and

    8.3.4   forthwith destroy the same should the Licensee cease to be entitled to use the Package.

9 INTELLECTUAL PROPERTY RIGHTS

The release of the Material to the Licensee will not act as an assignment of any Intellectual Property Rights that the Owner possesses in the Material.

10 VERIFICATION

10.1   Subject to the provisions of Clauses 10.2 and 10.3, NCC shall bear no obligation or responsibility to any person, firm, company or entity whatsoever to determine the existence, relevance, completeness, accuracy, effectiveness or any other aspect of the Material.

10.2   Upon the Material being lodged with NCC, NCC shall apply its Integrity Testing Service[8] to the Material and shall provide a copy of the test report to the parties to this Agreement.

10.3   Any party to this Agreement shall be entitled to require NCC to carry out a Full Verification[9]. Any reasonable charges and expenses incurred by NCC in carrying out a Full Verification will be paid by the requesting party save that if in the opinion of the expert appointed by the Managing Director of NCC the Material is substantially defective in content any such reasonable charges and expenses will be paid by the Owner.

11 NCC'S LIABILITY

11.1 NCC shall not be liable for any loss or damage caused to the Owner or the Licensee either jointly or severally except to the extent that such loss or damage is caused by:

11.1.1 the negligent acts or omissions of; or

11.1.2 a breach of any contractual duty by NCC, its employees, agents or sub-contractors and in such event NCC's total liability in respect of all claims arising under or by virtue of this Agreement shall not (except in the case of claims for personal injury or death) exceed the sum of £500,000.[10]

11.2 NCC shall in no circumstances be liable to the Owner or the Licensee for indirect or consequential loss of any nature whatsoever whether for loss of profit, loss of business or otherwise.

11.3 NCC shall be protected in acting upon any written request, waiver, consent, receipt or other document furnished to it pursuant to this Agreement, not only in assuming its due execution and the validity and effectiveness of its provisions but also as to the truth and acceptability of any information contained in it, which NCC in good faith believes to be genuine and what it purports to be.

12 INDEMNITY[11]

Save for any claim falling within the provisions of Clause 11.1, the Owner and the Licensee involved in the dispute or litigation jointly and severally indemnify NCC for any legal and/or related costs it incurs as a result of issuing or becoming otherwise involved in any form of dispute resolution proceedings or any litigation of any nature in relation to this Agreement.

13 TERMINATION

13.1 NCC may terminate this Agreement after failure by the Owner to comply with a 30 day written notice from NCC to pay any outstanding fee. Should the Owner fail to pay any fee, the relevant Licensee shall be given the option of paying such fee itself. Such amount will be recoverable by the relevant Licensee direct from the Owner.

13.2 NCC may terminate this Agreement with regard to a Licensee after failure by that Licensee to comply with a 30 day written notice from NCC to pay any outstanding fee.

13.3 NCC may terminate this Agreement by giving 60 days written notice to the Owner and the Licensee(s). In that event the Owner and the Licensee(s) shall appoint a mutually acceptable new custodian on terms similar to those contained in this Agreement. If a new custodian is not appointed within 30 days of delivery of such notice, the Owner or the Licensee(s) shall be entitled to request the President for the time being of the British Computer Society to appoint a suitable new custodian upon such terms and conditions as he/she shall require. Such appointment shall be final and binding on all parties.

13.4 If NCC is notified of the new custodian within the notice period, NCC will forthwith deliver the Material to the new custodian. If NCC is not notified of the new custodian within the notice period, NCC will destroy the Material.

13.5 The Licensee may terminate this Agreement in respect of itself, the Owner and NCC at any time by giving written notice to NCC. If the Licence Agreement has expired or has been lawfully terminated then it shall be the responsibility of the Licensee to terminate this Agreement in respect of itself, the Owner and NCC.

13.6 The Owner may only terminate the registration of any Licensee under this Agreement with the written consent of that Licensee.

13.7 The Owner may only terminate this Agreement with the written consent of all Licensees.

13.8 This Agreement shall terminate upon release of the Material to all Licensees in accordance with Clause 6.

13.9 Upon termination under the provisions of Clause 13.7 NCC will deliver the Material to the Owner. If NCC is unable to trace the Owner NCC will destroy the Material.

13.10 Upon termination under the provisions of Clause 13.1 the Material will be available for collection by the Owner from NCC for 30 days from the date of termination. After such 30 day period NCC will destroy the Material.

13.11 NCC may forthwith terminate this Agreement and destroy the Material if it is unable to trace the Owner having used all reasonable endeavours to do so, and there are no Licensees registered under this Agreement.

13.12 The provisions of Clauses 8, 11 and 12 shall continue in full force after termination of this Agreement.

13.13 On termination of this Agreement the Owner and/or the Licensee (as appropriate) shall remain liable to NCC for payment in full of any fee which has become due but which has not been paid as at the date of termination.

14 GENERAL

14.1 This Agreement shall be governed by and construed in accordance with the laws of England and Wales and subject to Clause 6.4 the parties submit to the exclusive jurisdiction of the English courts.

14.2 This Agreement represents the whole agreement relating to the escrow arrangements between the parties for the Package and supersedes all prior arrangements, negotiations and undertakings.

14.3 Save for Clause 6.3, all notices to be given to the parties under this Agreement shall be deemed to have been duly given or made when delivered personally or 7 days after posting or if sent by facsimile, 12 hours after despatch to the party to which such notice is required to be given or made under this Agreement addressed to the principal place of business, or for companies based in the UK, the registered office.

14.4   This Agreement does not create any right under the Contracts (Rights of Third Parties) Act 1999 which is enforceable by any person who is not a party to this Agreement.[12]

SCHEDULE 1

The Package

The software package known as [name].

SCHEDULE 2

Confirmation Agreement

[A copy of this Confirmation Agreement must be returned duly signed to NCC Escrow International Limited before a Licensee can claim protection under the Escrow Agreement.]

Dated:

Between:

(1)   [name] whose registered office is at [address] ("the Owner");

(2)   NCC ESCROW INTERNATIONAL LIMITED whose registered office is at Manchester Technology Centre, Oxford Road, Manchester M1 7ED, England "NCC"); and

(3)   [Licensee's Company Name] ....
whose registered office is at ....
....
....
(Company Registration Number: [........................]) ("the Licensee");

It is agreed that:

1   This Confirmation Agreement is governed by the terms and conditions set out in the Escrow Agreement Number [ ] ("EA") between the Owner and NCC.

2   This Confirmation Agreement and the EA form a binding agreement between the parties in the terms stated in the EA.

3   NCC shall record the Licensee as a party to the EA.

4   The Licensee accepts the benefits of the EA and agrees to be bound by its provisions.

Signed for and on behalf of [the Licensee]

Name .... | ....

(Authorised Signatory)

Position... |

Contact Name for Licensee ....

Date of Licence Agreement for the Package .... | ....

Licensee's telephone number .... | ....

Licensee's fax number .... | ....

Licensee's correspondence address if different from above .... | ....
....

*VAT Registration Number: .... | ....

* only applicable to countries within the EU.

SCHEDULE 3[13]

NCC's Fees (St£)

	Description	Owner	Licensee
1	Initial Fee (payable on registration and on each anniversary thereafter)	100%	NIL
2	Annual Fee (per Licensee, payable on registration and on each anniversary thereafter)		
3	Minimum Annual Fee (payable in the event that there are fewer than two Licensees in any year of the Agreement. The minimum annual fee will be payable less any annual fees paid by Licensees within such year)	100%	NIL
4	Scheduled Update Fee (2nd and subsequent scheduled deposits in any one year, payable on completion of the agreement and on each anniversary thereafter	100%	NIL
5	Unscheduled Update Fee (per unscheduled deposit)	100%	NIL
6	Storage Fee (an additional annual fee may be payable for deposits in excess of one cubic foot)	100%	NIL
7	Release Fee (plus NCC's reasonable expenses, per Licensee)	NIL	100%

• All fees are reviewed by NCC from time to time

Signed for and on behalf of [the Owner]

Name: .... | ....

Position: .... | (Authorised Signatory)

Signed for and on behalf of NCC ESCROW INTERNATIONAL LIMITED

Name: .... | ....

Position: .... | (Authorised Signatory)

ENDNOTES

1 This Agreement is used where the Software Owner wants to licence the source code to more than one Licensee. Each Licensee has to sign the Confirmation Agreement set out in Schedule 2 in order to claim protection under the Escrow Agreement.

2 The Software Owner will need to ensure that the source code and other material delivered to The NCC Group is updated on a regular basis, in particular when a new version is supplied to the Licensee.

3 The NCC Group recommend that a replacement copy of the material is delivered to them at least annually. If the Software Owner intends to deposit more frequently, this clause may need to be amended.

4 The obligation to deliver name and contact details of employees may be an onerous obligation on the Software Owner. In particular the Software Owner will need to ensure that he complies with the Data Protection Act before disclosing such personal data of his employees. Further, there is a risk that the Licensee may try and poach the Software Owner's employees in order to maintain the software.

5 The Software Owner needs to ensure that it does actually own the IPR rights in the Material and that they are not owned by its parent company or subsidiary.

6 The Software Owner will need to ensure that the material can be lodged in the form and on the media as set out in this clause.

7 The Software Owner should note that this clause releases the source code to the Licensee if the Licensee can show that the Software Owner was not providing maintenance or other such services in breach of their agreement. However, if there is a dispute as to whether the Software Owner was in default, the parties will be able to resolve any such dispute in accordance with Clause 6.4.

8 The NCC Group carry out integrity testing on all material deposited with them. These tests are standard and check the source code to ensure that it is virus free and accessible. Any passwords and decryption keys are also verified and held by The NCC Group.

9 The NCC Group recommend that a Full Verification is carried out where the source code is either of great value to the parties (both financially and technically); or where the time taken to replace the software and re-create would be months instead of days. Both parties need to take a commercial view as to whether a Full Verification should be carried out bearing in mind the cost of such a verification balanced with the loss that would be made if source code deposited was incomplete or incorrect.

10 The parties should note that The NCC Group have limited their total liability to £500,000. If the source code (and hence the software) is worth more than this sum, then the parties should consider taking out additional Insurance.

11 Note the indemnity here given by both the Software Owner and the Licensee. Again, it may be prudent to take out insurance to cover such liability.

12 This clause excludes any third parties from claiming a benefit under this Agreement. Therefore, if a Licensee has not signed the Confirmation Agreement, it will not be able to get the benefit of the Escrow Agreement.

13 The parties need to specify here what percentage of the Escrow fee is payable by the Software Owner and the Licensee. Please note that there is a minimum annual fee which is payable in the event that there are fewer than two Licensees in any year of this Agreement.

SINGLE LICENSEE

Escrow Agreement No: Dated:

Escrow Agreement Between:

(1)   [name] whose registered office is at [address] (CRN: [number]) ("the Owner");

(2)   [name] whose registered office is at [address] (CRN: [number]) ("the Licensee"); and

(3)   NCC ESCROW INTERNATIONAL LIMITED whose registered office is at Manchester Technology Centre, Oxford Road, Manchester M1 7ED (CRN: 3081952) ("NCC").

Preliminary:

(A)   The Licensee has been granted a licence to use a software package comprising computer programs.

(B)   Certain technical information and documentation describing the software package is the confidential property of the Owner and is required for understanding, maintaining and correcting the software package.

(C)   The Owner acknowledges that in certain circumstances the Licensee may require possession of the technical information and documentation held under this Agreement.

(D)   Each of the parties to this Agreement acknowledges that the considerations for their respective undertakings given under it are the undertakings given under it by each of the other parties.

It is agreed that:

I   DEFINITIONS

In this Agreement the following terms shall have the following meanings:

1.1   "Full Verification Service" means the appropriate tests agreed with NCC for the verification of the Material;

1.2   "Integrity Testing Service" means those tests forming NCC's Integrity Testing Service, in so far as they relate to the Material;

1.3   "Intellectual Property Rights" means copyright, trade secret, patent, and all other rights of a similar nature;

1.4   "Licence Agreement" means the licence granted to the Licensee for the Package;

1.5   "Material" means the source code of the Package and such other materials and documentation as are necessary to comply with Clause 2.1.5; and

1.6   "Package" means the software package licensed to the Licensee under the Licence Agreement and referred to in Schedule 1.

2 OWNER'S DUTIES AND WARRANTIES

2.1   The Owner shall:

2.1.1   deliver a copy of the Material to NCC within 30 days of the date of this Agreement;

2.1.2   at all times ensure that the Material as delivered to NCC is capable of being used to generate the latest version of the Package issued to the Licensee and shall deliver to NCC further copies of the Material as and when necessary;

2.1.3   deliver to NCC a replacement copy of the Material within 12 months of the last delivery;'

2.1.4   deliver a replacement copy of the Material to NCC within 14 days of receipt of a notice served upon it by NCC under the provisions of Clause 4.1.5; and

2.1.5   deliver with each deposit of the Material any of the following technical information that is relevant:

2.1.5.1   Details of the deposit; full name and version details, media type, backup command/software used, compression used, archive hardware and operating system details.

2.1.5.2   Password/encryption details required to access the source code.

2.1.5.3   Directory listings of the contents of the media.

2.1.5.4   Documentation describing the procedures for building, compiling and installing the software, including names and versions of the development tools.

2.1.5.5   Software design information (e.g. module names and functionality).

2.1.5.6   Name and contact details of employees with knowledge of how to maintain and support the Material.[4]

2.2   The Owner warrants that:

2.2.1   it owns[5] the Intellectual Property Rights in the Material and has authority to enter into this Agreement; and

2.2.2   the Material lodged under Clause 2.1 shall contain all information in human-readable form and on suitable media to enable a reasonably skilled programmer or analyst to understand, maintain and correct the Package without the assistance of any other person.[6]

3 LICENSEE'S RESPONSIBILITIES

It shall be the responsibility of the Licensee to notify NCC of any change to the Package that necessitates a replacement deposit of the Material.

4   NCC'S DUTIES

4.1   NCC shall:

4.1.1   hold the Material in a safe and secure environment;

4.1.2   inform the Owner and the Licensee of the receipt of any copy of the Material;

4.1.3   in accordance with the terms of Clause 9 apply the Integrity Testing Service to the Material from time to time;

4.1.4   at all times retain a copy of the latest verified deposit of the Material; and

4.1.5   notify the Owner if it becomes aware at any time during the term of this Agreement that the copy of the Material held by it has been lost, damaged or destroyed.

4.2   NCC shall not be responsible for procuring the delivery of the Material in the event of failure by the Owner to do so.

5   PAYMENT

The parties shall pay NCC's standard fees as published from time to time or as otherwise agreed, in the proportions set out in Schedule 2.

6   RELEASE EVENTS

6.1   Subject to the provisions of Clauses 6.2 and 6.3 and upon receipt of its release fee, NCC will release the Material to a duly authorised officer of the Licensee if any of the following events occur:

6.1.1   the Owner enters into any company voluntary arrangement or individual voluntary arrangement or (being a company) enters into liquidation whether compulsory or voluntary (other than for the purposes of solvent reconstruction or amalgamation) or has a receiver or administrative receiver appointed over all or any part of its assets or undertaking or a petition is presented for an Administration Order or (being an individual or partnership) becomes bankrupt, or an event occurs within the jurisdiction of the country in which the Owner is situated which has a similar effect to any of the above events in the United Kingdom; or

6.1.2   the Owner ceases to trade; or

6.1.3   the Owner assigns copyright in the Material and the assignee fails within 60 days of such assignment to offer the Licensee substantially similar protection to that provided by this Agreement without significantly increasing the cost to the Licensee; or

6.1.4   the Owner without legal justification, has defaulted to a material degree in any obligation to provide maintenance or modification of the Package under the Licence Agreement or any maintenance agreement entered into in connection with the Package and has failed to remedy such default notified by the Licensee to the Owner.[7]

6.2 The Licensee must notify NCC of the event(s) specified in Clause 6.1 by delivering to NCC a statutory or notarised declaration ("the Declaration") made by an officer of the Licensee attesting that such event has occurred and that the Licence Agreement and any maintenance agreement, if relevant, for the Package was still valid and effective up to the occurrence of such event and exhibiting such documentation in support of the Declaration as NCC shall reasonably require.

6.3 Upon receipt of a Declaration from the Licensee claiming a release event under Clause 6.1:

6.3.1 NCC shall send a copy of the Declaration to the Owner by special delivery or equivalent type of post, where the Owner is not situated in England or Wales; and

6.3.2 unless within 14 days after the date of delivery the Owner delivers to NCC a counter-notice signed by a duly authorised officer of the Owner stating that no such event or failure has occurred or that any such failure has been rectified NCC will release the Material to the Licensee.

6.4 Where there is any dispute as to the occurrence of any of the events set out in Clause 6 or the fulfilment of any obligations detailed therein, such dispute will be referred at the instance of either the Owner or the Licensee to the Managing Director for the time being of NCC for the appointment of an expert who shall give a decision on the matter within 14 days of the date of referral or as soon as practicable thereafter. The expert's decision shall be final and binding as between the Owner and the Licensee except in the case of manifest error.

7 CONFIDENTIALITY

7.1 The Material shall remain the confidential property of the Owner and in the event that NCC provides a copy of the Material to the Licensee, the Licensee shall be permitted to use the Material only in accordance with the confidentiality obligations contained in Clause 7.3.

7.2 NCC agrees to maintain all information and/or documentation coming into its possession or to its knowledge under this Agreement in strictest confidence and secrecy. NCC further agrees not to make use of such information and/or documentation other than for the purposes of this Agreement and will not disclose or release it other than in accordance with the terms of this Agreement.

7.3 In the event that the Material is released under Clause 6 the Licensee shall:

7.3.1 use the Material only for the purpose of understanding, maintaining and correcting the Package exclusively on behalf of the Licensee;

7.3.2	not use the Material for any other purpose nor disclose it to any person save such of its employees or contractors who need to know the same in order to understand, maintain and correct the Package exclusively on behalf of the Licensee. In that event the Licensee shall ensure that its employees and contractors are bound by the same confidentiality obligations as are contained in this Clause 7;
7.3.3	hold all media containing the Material in a safe and secure environment when not in use; and
7.3.4	forthwith destroy the same should the Licensee cease to be entitled to use the Package.

8   INTELLECTUAL PROPERTY RIGHTS

The release of the Material to the Licensee will not act as an assignment of any Intellectual Property Rights that the Owner possesses in the Material.

9   VERIFICATION

9.1   Subject to the provisions of Clauses 9.2 and 9.3, NCC shall bear no obligation or responsibility to any person, firm, company or entity whatsoever to determine the existence, relevance, completeness, accuracy, effectiveness or any other aspect of the Material.

9.2   Upon the Material being lodged with NCC, NCC shall apply its Integrity Testing Service[8] to the Material and shall provide a copy of the test report to the parties to this Agreement.

9.3   Any party to this Agreement shall be entitled to require NCC to carry out a Full Verification.[9] Any reasonable charges and expenses incurred by NCC in carrying out a Full Verification will be paid by the requesting party save that if in the opinion of the expert appointed by the Managing Director of NCC the Material is substantially defective in content any such reasonable charges and expenses will be paid by the Owner.

10   NCC'S LIABILITY

10.1   NCC shall not be liable for any loss or damage caused to the Owner or the Licensee either jointly or severally except to the extent that such loss or damage is caused by:

10.1.1   the negligent acts or omissions of; or

10.1.2   a breach of any contractual duty by NCC, its employees, agents or sub-contractors and in such event NCC's total liability in respect of all claims arising under or by virtue of this Agreement shall not (except in the case of claims for personal injury or death) exceed the sum of £500,000.[10]

10.2 NCC shall in no circumstances be liable to the Owner or the Licensee for indirect or consequential loss of any nature whatsoever whether for loss of profit, loss of business or otherwise.

10.3 NCC shall be protected in acting upon any written request, waiver, consent, receipt or other document furnished to it pursuant to this Agreement, not only in assuming its due execution and the validity and effectiveness of its provisions but also as to the truth and acceptability of any information contained in it, which NCC in good faith believes to be genuine and what it purports to be.

11   INDEMNITY[11]

Save for any claim falling within the provisions of Clause 10.1, the Owner and the Licensee jointly and severally indemnify NCC for any legal and/or related costs it incurs as a result of issuing or becoming otherwise involved in any form of dispute resolution proceedings or any litigation of any nature in relation to this Agreement.

12   TERMINATION

12.1 NCC may terminate this Agreement after failure by the Owner or the Licensee to comply with a 30 day written notice from NCC to pay any outstanding fee. If the failure to pay is on the part of the Owner the Licensee shall be given the option of paying such fee itself. Such amount will be recoverable by the Licensee direct from the Owner.

12.2 NCC may terminate this Agreement by giving 60 days written notice to the Owner and the Licensee. In that event the Owner and the Licensee shall appoint a mutually acceptable new custodian on terms similar to those contained in this Agreement. If a new custodian is not appointed within 30 days of delivery of such notice, the Owner or the Licensee shall be entitled to request the President for the time being of the British Computer Society to appoint a suitable new custodian upon such terms and conditions as he/she shall require. Such appointment shall be final and binding on all parties.

13.3 If NCC is notified of the new custodian within the notice period, NCC will forthwith deliver the Material to the new custodian. If NCC is not notified of the new custodian within the notice period, NCC will destroy the Material.

12.4 The Licensee may terminate this Agreement at any time by giving written notice to NCC. If the Licence Agreement has expired or has been lawfully terminated then it shall be the responsibility of the Licensee to terminate this Agreement.

12.5 The Owner may only terminate this Agreement with the written consent of the Licensee.

12.6 This Agreement shall terminate upon release of the Material to the Licensee in accordance with Clause 6.

12.7 Upon termination under the provisions of Clauses 12.4 or 12.5 NCC will deliver the Material to the Owner. If NCC is unable to trace the Owner NCC will destroy the Material.

12.8 Upon termination under the provisions of Clause 12.1 the Material will be available for collection by the Owner from NCC for 30 days from the date of termination. After such 30 day period NCC will destroy the Material.

12.9 NCC may forthwith terminate this Agreement and destroy the Material if it is unable to trace the Owner having used all reasonable endeavours to do so.

12.10 The provisions of Clauses 7, 10 and 11 shall continue in full force after termination of this Agreement.

12.11 On termination of this Agreement the Owner and/or the Licensee (as appropriate) shall remain liable to NCC for payment in full of any fee which has become due but which has not been paid as at the date of termination.

13   GENERAL

13.1 This Agreement shall be governed by and construed in accordance with the laws of England and Wales and subject to Clause 6.4 the parties submit to the exclusive jurisdiction of the English courts.

13.2 This Agreement represents the whole agreement relating to the escrow arrangements between the parties for the Package and supersedes all prior arrangements, negotiations and undertakings.

13.3 Save for Clause 6.3, all notices to be given to the parties under this Agreement shall be deemed to have been duly given or made when delivered personally or 7 days after posting or if sent by facsimile, 12 hours after despatch to the party to which such notice is required to be given or made under this Agreement addressed to the principal place of business, or for companies based in the UK, the registered office.

SCHEDULE I

The Package

The software package known as [name].

SCHEDULE 2

NCC's Fees (St£)

NCC's Fees (St£)

	Description	Owner	Licensee
1	Initial Fee (payable on commencement of work)		
2	Annual Fee (payable on completion of the agreement and on each anniversary thereafter)		
3	Scheduled Update Fee (2nd and subsequent scheduled deposits in any one year, payable on completion of the agreement and on each anniversary thereafter)		
4	Unscheduled Update Fee (per unscheduled deposit)		
5	Storage Fee (an additional annual fee may be payable for deposits in excess of one cubic foot)		
6	Release Fee (plus NCC's reasonable expenses)	NIL	100%

• All fees are reviewed by NCC from time to time

Signed for and on behalf of [the Owner]

Name: .... | ....

Position: .... | (Authorised Signatory)

Signed for and on behalf of [the Licensee]

Name: .... | ....

Position: .... | (Authorised Signatory)

Signed for and on behalf of NCC ESCROW INTERNATIONAL LIMITED

Name: .... | ....

Position: .... | (Authorised Signatory)

ENDNOTES

1 This Agreement is used where the Software Owner is only licensing one party to the release of the source code.

2 The Software Owner will need to ensure that the source code and other material delivered to The NCC Group is updated on a regular basis, in particular when a new version is supplied to the Licensee.

3 The NCC Group recommend that a replacement copy of the material is delivered to them annually. If the Software Owner does not intend to do this, this clause may need to be amended.

4 The obligation to deliver name and contact details of employees may be an onerous obligation on the Software Owner. In particular the Software Owner will need to ensure that he complies with the Data Protection Act before disclosing such personal data of his employees. Further, there is a risk that the Licensee may try and poach the Software Owner's employees in order to maintain the software.

5 The Software Owner needs to ensure that it does actually own the IPR rights in the Material and that they are not owned by its parent company or subsidiary. The Software

697

Owner will need to ensure that the material can be lodged in the form and on the media as set out in this clause.

6 The Software Owner should note that this clause releases the source code to the Licensee if the Licensee can show that the Software Owner was not providing maintenance or other such services in breach of their agreement. However, if there is a dispute as to whether the Software Owner was in default, the parties will be able to resolve any such dispute in accordance with Clause 6.4..

8 The NCC Group carry out integrity testing on all material deposited with them. These tests are standard and check the source code to ensure that it is virus free and accessible. Any passwords and decryption keys are also verified and held by The NCC Group.

9 The NCC recommend that a Full Verification is carried out where the source code is either of great value to the parties (both financially and technically); or where the time taken to replace the software and re-create it (especially if it is bespoke software) would be months instead of days. Both parties need to take a commercial view as to whether a Full Verification should be carried out bearing in mind the cost of such a verification balanced with the loss that would be made if the source code deposited was incomplete or incorrect.

10 The parties should note that The NCC Group have limited their total liability to £500,000. If the source code (and hence the software) is worth more than this sum, then the parties should consider taking out additional Insurance.

11 Note the indemnity here given by both the Software Owner and the Licensee. Again, it may be prudent to take out insurance to cover such liability.

12 The parties need to specify here what percentage of the Escrow fee is payable by the Software Owner and the Licencee.

WEB SINGLE LICENSEE[1]

Escrow Agreement No:

Escrow Agreement Between:

(1) [name] whose registered office is at [address] (CRN: [number]) ("the Owner");

(2) [name] whose registered office is at [address] (CRN: [number]) ("the Licensee"); and

(3) NCC ESCROW INTERNATIONAL LIMITED whose registered office is at Manchester Technology Centre, Oxford Road, Manchester M1 7ED, England (CRN: 3081952) ("NCC").

Preliminary:

(A) The Licensee has been granted a licence or right to use a Website that the Owner has agreed to develop and/or maintain on the Licensee's behalf and to the Licensee's specification.

(B) Certain technical information and documentation describing the Website are the confidential property of the Owner and are required for understanding, developing, maintaining and correcting the Website.

(C) The Owner acknowledges that in certain circumstances the Licensee may require possession of the technical information and documentation held under this Agreement.

(D) Each of the parties to this Agreement acknowledges that the considerations for their respective undertakings given under it are the undertakings given under it by each of the other parties.

It is agreed that:

I DEFINITIONS

In this Agreement the following terms shall have the following meanings:

1.1 "Development Agreement" means the agreement containing the terms and conditions relating to the development of the Website entered into between the Owner and the Licensee;

1.2 "Full Verification Service" means the appropriate tests agreed with NCC for the verification of the Material;

1.3 "Integrity Plus Testing Service" means those tests forming NCC's Integrity Plus Testing Service, in so far as they relate to the Material;

1.4 "Integrity Testing Service" means those tests forming NCC's Integrity Testing Service, in so far as they relate to the Material;

1.5 "Intellectual Property Rights" means copyright, trade secret, patent, and all other rights of a similar nature;

1.6 "Licence" means the licence or right to use granted to the Licensee for the Website;

1.7 "Material" means the source code of the Website and such other materials and documentation as are necessary to comply with Clause 2.1.5; and

1.8 "Website" means the web pages of the Licensee referred to in Schedule 1.

2 OWNER'S DUTIES AND WARRANTIES

2.1 The Owner shall:

2.1.1 deliver a copy of the Material to NCC within 30 days of the date of this Agreement;

2.1.2 ensure that the Material as delivered to NCC is capable of being used to recreate the latest version of the Website used by or issued to the Licensee and shall deliver to NCC further copies of the Material as and when necessary;

2.1.3 deliver to NCC a replacement copy of the Material within 3 months of the last delivery;[3]

2.1.4 deliver a replacement copy of the Material to NCC within 14 days of receipt of a notice served upon it by NCC under the provisions of Clause 4.1.5; and

2.1.5 deliver with each deposit of the Material any of the following technical information that is relevant:

    2.1.5.1 Details of the deposit; full name and version details, media type, backup command/software used, compression used, archive hardware and operating system details.

    2.1.5.2 Website or gateway url (where applicable)

2.1.5.3 Password/encryption details required to access the source code.

2.1.5.4 Directory listings of the contents of the media.

2.1.5.5 Documentation describing the procedures for building, compiling and installing the software, rebuilding the web server and installing the Website including names and versions of the development tools and web browsers.

2.1.5.6 Documentation describing the procedures for maintaining the Website including names and versions of required web tools (e.g. html editors and ftp transfer programs).

2.1.5.7 Access details required for web server administration (ssh), Website administration (ftp) and httpd administration.

2.1.5.8 Website design information (e.g. module names, architecture and functionality).

2.1.5.9 Name and contact details of employees with knowledge of how to maintain and support the Material and contact details of remote host.[4]

2.2 The Owner warrants that:

2.2.1 it owns[5] the Intellectual Property Rights in the Material and has authority to enter into this Agreement; and

2.2.2 the Material lodged under Clause 2.1 shall contain all information in human-readable form and on suitable media to enable a reasonably skilled programmer or analyst to understand, develop, maintain and correct the Website on behalf of the Licensee only, without the assistance of any other person.[6]

3 LICENSEE'S RESPONSIBILITIES

It shall be the responsibility of the Licensee to notify NCC of any significant change to the Website that necessitates a replacement deposit of the Material.

4 NCCS DUTIES

4.1 NCC shall:

4.1.1 hold the Material in a safe and secure environment;

4.1.2 inform the Owner and the Licensee of the receipt of any copy of the Material;

4.1.3 in accordance with the terms of Clause 9 apply the Integrity Testing Service to the Material from time to time;

4.1.4 at all times retain a copy of the latest verified deposit of the Material; and

4.1.5 notify the Owner if it becomes aware at any time during the term of this Agreement that the copy of the Material held by it has been lost, damaged or destroyed.

4.2 NCC shall not be responsible for procuring the delivery of the Material in the event of failure by the Owner to do so.

5 PAYMENT

The parties shall pay NCC's standard fees as published from time to time or as otherwise agreed, in the proportions set out in Schedule 2.

6 RELEASE EVENTS

6.1 Subject to the provisions of Clauses 6.2 and 6.3 and upon receipt of its release fee, NCC will release the Material to a duly authorised officer of the Licensee if any of the following events occur:

6.1.1 the Owner enters into any company voluntary arrangement or individual voluntary arrangement or (being a company) enters into liquidation whether compulsory or voluntary (other than for the purposes of solvent reconstruction or amalgamation) or has a receiver or administrative receiver appointed over all or any part of its assets or undertaking or a petition is presented for an Administration Order or (being an individual or partnership) becomes bankrupt, or an event occurs within the jurisdiction of the country in which the Owner is situated which has a similar effect to any of the above events in the United Kingdom; or

6.1.2 the Owner ceases to trade; or

6.1.3 the Owner assigns copyright in the Material and the assignee fails within 60 days of such assignment to offer the Licensee substantially similar protection to that provided by this Agreement without significantly increasing the cost to the Licensee; or

6.1.4 the Owner without legal justification, has defaulted to a material degree in any obligation to provide development, maintenance or modification of the Website under the Licence, the Development Agreement or any maintenance agreement entered into in connection with the Website and has failed to remedy such default notified by the Licensee to the Owner. [7]

6.2 The Licensee must notify NCC of the event(s) specified in Clause 6.1 by delivering to NCC a statutory or notarised declaration ("the Declaration") made by an officer of the Licensee attesting that such event has occurred and that the Development Agreement or the Licence and any maintenance agreement, if relevant, for the Website was still valid and effective up to the occurrence of such event and exhibiting such documentation in support of the Declaration as NCC shall reasonably require.

6.3 Upon receipt of a Declaration from the Licensee claiming a release event under Clause 6.1:

6.3.1 NCC shall send a copy of the Declaration to the Owner by special delivery or equivalent type of post, where the Owner is not situated in England or Wales; and

6.3.2 unless within 14 days after the date of delivery the Owner delivers to NCC a counter-notice signed by a duly authorised officer of the Owner stating that no such event or failure has occurred or that any such failure has been rectified NCC will release the Material to the Licensee.

6.4 Where there is any dispute as to the occurrence of any of the events set out in Clause 6 or the fulfilment of any obligations detailed therein, such dispute will be referred at the instance of either the Owner or the Licensee to ! the Managing Director for the time being of NCC for the appointment of an expert who shall give a decision on the matter within 14 days of the date of referral or as soon as practicable thereafter. The expert's decision shall be final and binding as between the Owner and the Licensee except in the case of manifest error.

7 CONFIDENTIALITY

7.1 The Material shall remain the confidential property of the Owner and in the event that NCC provides a copy of the Material to the Licensee, the Licensee shall be permitted to use the Material only in accordance with the confidentiality obligations contained in Clause 7.3.

7.2 NCC agrees to maintain all information and/or documentation coming into its possession or to its knowledge under this Agreement in strictest confidence and secrecy. NCC further agrees not to make use of such information and/or documentation other than for the purposes of this Agreement and will not disclose or release it other than in accordance with the terms of this Agreement.

7.3 In the event that the Material is released under Clause 6 the Licensee shall:

7.3.1 use the Material only for the purposes of understanding, maintaining, developing and correcting the Website exclusively on behalf of the Licensee;

7.3.2 not use the Material for any other purpose nor disclose it to any person save such of its employees or contractors who need to know the same in order to understand, maintain, develop and correct the Website exclusively on behalf of the Licensee. In that event the Licensee shall ensure that its employees and contractors are bound by the same confidentiality obligations as are contained in this Clause 7;

7.3.3   hold all media containing the Material in a safe and secure environment when not in use; and

7.3.4   forthwith destroy the same should the Licensee cease to be entitled to use the Website.

8 INTELLECTUAL PROPERTY RIGHTS

The release of the Material to the Licensee will not act as an assignment of any Intellectual Property Rights that the Owner possesses in the Material.

9 VERIFICATION

9.1   Subject to the provisions of Clauses 9.2 and 9.3, NCC shall bear no obligation or responsibility to any person, firm, company or entity whatsoever to determine the existence, relevance, completeness, accuracy, effectiveness or any other aspect of the Material.

9.2   Upon the Material being lodged with NCC, NCC shall apply its Integrity Testing Service to[8] the Material and shall provide a copy of the test report to the parties to this Agreement.

9.3   Any party to this Agreement shall be entitled to require NCC to apply its Integrity Plus Testing[9] Service to the Material or carry out a Full verification[10]. Any reasonable charges and expenses incurred by NCC in carrying out such testing will be paid by the requesting party save that if in the opinion of the expert appointed by the Managing Director of NCC the Material is substantially defective in content any such reasonable charges and expenses will be paid by the Owner.

10 NCC'S LIABILITY

10.1   NCC shall not be liable for any loss or damage caused to the Owner or the Licensee either jointly or severally except to the extent that such loss or damage is caused by:

10.1.1   the negligent acts or omissions of; or

10.1.2   a breach of any contractual duty by NCC, its employees, agents or sub-contractors and in such event NCC's total liability in respect of all claims arising under or by virtue of this Agreement shall not (except in the case of claims for personal injury or death) exceed the sum of £500,000. [11]

10.2   NCC shall in no circumstances be liable to the Owner or the Licensee for indirect or consequential loss of any nature whatsoever whether for loss of profit, loss of business or otherwise.

10.3   NCC shall be protected in acting upon any written request, waiver, consent, receipt or other document furnished to it pursuant to this Agreement, not only in assuming its due execution and the validity and effectiveness of its provisions but also as to the truth and acceptability of any information contained in it, which NCC in good faith believes to be genuine and what it purports to be.

11 INDEMNITY[12]

Save for any claim falling within the provisions of Clause 10.1, the Owner and the Licensee jointly and severally indemnify NCC for any legal and/or related costs it incurs as a result of issuing or becoming otherwise involved in any form of dispute resolution proceedings or any litigation of any nature in relation to this Agreement.

12 TERMINATION

12.1 NCC may terminate this Agreement after failure by the Owner or the Licensee to comply with a 30 day written notice from NCC to pay any outstanding fee. If the failure to pay is on the part of the Owner, the Licensee shall be given the option of paying such fee itself. Such amount will be recoverable by the Licensee direct from the Owner.

12.2 NCC may terminate this Agreement by giving 60 days written notice to the Owner and the Licensee. In that event the Owner and the Licensee shall appoint a mutually acceptable new custodian on terms similar to those contained in this Agreement. If a new custodian is not appointed within 30 days of delivery of such notice, the Owner or the Licensee shall be entitled to request the President for the time being of the British Computer Society to appoint a suitable new custodian upon such terms and conditions as he/she shall require. Such appointment shall be final and binding on all parties.

12.3 If NCC is notified of the new custodian within the notice period, NCC will forthwith deliver the Material to the new custodian. If NCC is not notified of the new custodian within the notice period, NCC will destroy the Material.

12.4 If the Development Agreement has terminated and the Licence has expired or has been lawfully terminated this Agreement will automatically terminate on the same date.

12.5 The Licensee may terminate this Agreement at any time by giving written notice to NCC.

12.6 The Owner may only terminate this Agreement with the written consent of the Licensee.

12.7 This Agreement shall terminate upon release of the Material to the Licensee in accordance with Clause 6.

12.8 Upon termination under the provisions of Clauses 12.4, 12.5 or 12.6 NCC will deliver the Material to the Owner. If NCC is unable to trace the Owner NCC will destroy the Material.

12.9 Upon termination under the provisions of Clause 12.1 the Material will be available for collection by the Owner from NCC for 30 days from the date of termination. After such 30 day period NCC will destroy the Material.

12.10 NCC may forthwith terminate this Agreement and destroy the Material if it is unable to trace the Owner having used all reasonable endeavours to do so.

12.11 The provisions of Clauses 7, 10 and 11 shall continue in full force after termination of this Agreement.

12.12 On termination of this Agreement the Owner and/or the Licensee (as appropriate) shall remain liable to NCC for payment in full of any fee which has become due but which has not been paid as at the date of termination.

13 GENERAL

13.1 This Agreement shall be governed by and construed in accordance with the laws of England and Wales and subject to Clause 6.4 the parties submit to the exclusive jurisdiction of the English courts.

13.2 This Agreement represents the whole agreement relating to the escrow arrangements between the parties for the Website and supersedes all prior arrangements, negotiations and undertakings.

13.3 Save for Clause 6.3, all notices to be given to the parties under this Agreement shall be deemed to have been duly given or made when delivered personally or 7 days after posting or if sent by facsimile, 12 hours after despatch to the party to which such notice is required to be given or made under this Agreement addressed to the principal place of business, or for companies based in the UK, the registered office.

SCHEDULE 1

The Website

The website known as [name].

SCHEDULE 2[13]

NCC's Fees (St£)

NCC's Fees (St£)

	Description	Owner	Licensee
1	Initial Fee (payable on commencement of work)		
2	Annual Fee (payable on completion of the agreement and on each anniversary thereafter)		

	Description	Owner	Licensee
3	Scheduled Update Fee (2nd and subsequent scheduled deposits in any one year, payable on completion of the agreement and on each anniversary thereafter – NB a minimum of 3 are required in accordance with Clause 2.1.3		
4	Unscheduled Update Fee (per unscheduled deposit)		
5	Storage Fee (an additional annual fee may be payable for deposits in excess of one cubic foot)		
6	Release Fee (plus NCC's reasonable expenses)	NIL	100%

- All fees are reviewed by NCC from time to time

Signed for and on behalf of [the Owner]

Name: .... | ....

Position: .... | (Authorised Signatory)

Signed for and on behalf of [the Licensee]

Name: .... | ....

Position: .... | (Authorised Signatory)

Signed for and on behalf of NCC ESCROW INTERNATIONAL LIMITED

Name: .... | ....

Position: .... | (Authorised Signatory)

ENDNOTES

1 This Agreement is normally used where the software relates to website development. Thus, this Agreement requires the developer to provide regular copies of the website content, materials, development tools and security information necessary for the administration of the website being developed or maintained for the Licensee.

2 The Software Owner will need to ensure that the source code and other material delivered to The NCC Group is updated on a regular basis, in particular when a new version is supplied to the Licensee.

3 The NCC Group recommend that the material is replaced every three months. If this is not what is envisaged, this clause may need to be amended.

4 The obligation to deliver name and contact details of employees may be an onerous obligation on the Software Owner. In particular the Software Owner will need to ensure that he complies with the Data Protection Act before disclosing such personal data of his employees. Further, there is a risk that the Licensee may try and poach the Software Owner's employees in order to further develop the website.

5 The Software Owner needs to ensure that it does actually own the IPR rights in the Material and that they are not owned by its parent company or subsidiary.

6 The Software Owner will need to ensure that the material can be lodged in the form and on the media as set out in this clause.

7 The Software Owner should note that this clause releases the source code to the Licensee if the Licensee can show that the Software Owner was not developing or providing maintenance or other such services in breach of their agreement. However, if there is a dispute as to whether the Software Owner was in default, the parties will be able to resolve any such dispute in accordance with Clause 6.4.

8 The NCC carry out integrity testing on all material deposited with them. These tests are standard and check the source code to ensure that it is virus free and accessible. Any passwords and decryption keys are also verified and held by The NCC Group.

9 Integrity testing is completed in-house by The NCC Group but if either party require testing to be carried out where the source code was developed, The NCC Group provide "Integrity Plus" testing. This is a more detailed test of the source code and is carried out in the native development environment of the source code. Obviously such testing is carried out on payment of an additional fee.

10 The NCC recommend that a Full Verification is carried out where the website is either of great value to the parties (both financially and technically); or where the time taken to replace the website and re-create it would be months instead of days. Both parties need to take a commercial view as to whether a Full Verification should be carried out bearing in mind the cost of such a verification balanced with the loss that would be made if the website material deposited was incomplete or incorrect.

11 The parties should note that The NCC Group have limited their total liability to £500,000. If the source code (and hence the software) is worth more than this sum, then the parties should consider taking out additional Insurance.

12 Note the indemnity here given by both the Software Owner and the Licensee. Again, it may be prudent to take out insurance to cover such liability.

13 The parties need to specify here what percentage of the Escrow fee is payable by the Software Owner and the Licensee.

Version: 06/01 206089

28 Framework agreement

DATE:

PARTIES:

1.   [CLIENT] whose registered office is at [   ] (the 'Client'); and

2.   [SERVICE PROVIDER] whose registered office is at [   ] (the 'Service Provider').

AGREEMENT:

This Agreement is a framework agreement setting out the terms on which the Client will purchase and the Service Provider will supply software and services as agreed from time to time by the parties.

INTERPRETATION

In this Agreement:

'Acceptance'	means acceptance of Software and/or Services in accordance with the Acceptance Procedure and 'Accepted' refers to Software and/or Services in relation to which an Acceptance Certificate has been signed on behalf of the Client;
'Acceptance Certificate'	means the document signed by an authorised representative of the Client certifying Acceptance by the Client;
'Acceptance Criteria'	means Acceptance Criteria established under the Acceptance Procedure;
'Acceptance Date'	means the date on which an Acceptance Certificate is signed on behalf of the Client, or there is deemed Acceptance under the Acceptance Procedure;
'Acceptance Procedure'	means the procedure in Annex B;
'Associated Documentation'	means instructional and operating manuals, technical literature and other related materials supplied by the Service Provider to the Client in connection with Software [and listed in Annex 3];
'Charges'	means all charges by the Service Provider for Software and Services under this Agreement;
'Client Applications'	means all works created by the Client which are based upon or incorporate all or part of the Software;
'Client Group Company'	means with respect to the Client its ultimate Holding Company and any Subsidiary of such Holding Company as such expressions are defined in Sections 736 and 736A of the Companies Act 1985;

'Delivery Address'	means the place where Software is to be installed, as specified in a Purchase Order;
'Delivery Date'	means a date on which Software and/or Services are to be available for Acceptance, as set out in a Purchase Order;
'Effective Date'	means [ ];
'Installation Site'	means the location of a Server as identified in a Purchase Order;
'Intellectual Property Rights'	means all vested contingent and future intellectual property rights including but not limited to copyright, trade marks, service marks, design rights (whether registered or unregistered), patents, know-how, trade secrets, inventions, get-up, database rights and any applications or registrations for the protection of these rights and all renewals and extensions thereof existing in any part of the world whether now known or in the future created;
'Licence'	means the licence granted by the Service Provider to the Client under this Agreement to use Software and deploy Client Applications;
'Licence Fees'	means the fees payable by the Client to the Service Provider for the use of Software, as set out in Special Conditions;
'Media'	means the media on which Software and Associated Documentation are recorded or provided or otherwise contained;
'Object Code'	means the machine readable executable program code of the Software containing computer instructions translated by a compiler;
'Project'	means a discrete programme for the supply of specified Software and/or Services, subject to either one Purchase Order or a series of Purchase Orders;
'Purchase Order'	means the Client purchase order for Software and Services subject to this Agreement, including all Specifications, Special Conditions and any relevant Annexes forming part of such Purchase Order;
'Server'	means a System configured with Software installed under a Purchase Order to support an authorised number of Users;
'Service Provider Group Company'	means with respect to the Service Provider its ultimate Holding Company and any Subsidiary of such Holding Company as such expressions are defined in Sections 736 and 736A of the Companies Act 1985;
'Services'	means the professional and/or Software support services to be provided by the Service Provider to the Client pursuant to any Purchase Order;
'Service Fees'	means the fees payable by the Client to the Service Provider for Services, as set out in a Purchase Order;
'Software'	means software programs and Associated Documentation supplied by the Service Provider to the Client under any Purchase Order whose use is licensed to the Client under this Agreement;
'Source Code'	means a version of the Software in such eye-readable form that it can be compiled or interpreted into equivalent Object Code together with all technical information and documentation necessary for the use, reproduction, modification and enhancement of the same;

'Special Conditions'	means those conditions agreed between the parties in relation to any supply of Software and/or Services which are additional to the terms and conditions of this Agreement. Each Special Conditions document will be annexed to the relevant Purchase Order and will refer expressly to this Agreement;
'Specifications'	means all agreed plans, drawings, data, specifications or other information (as may be amended by agreement between the parties) relating to Software and/or Services identified as a 'Specification' in a Purchase Order;
'System'	means the operating system and associated networks in or for which the Client uses Software licensed under this Agreement;
'User'ı	means a single terminal workstation or personal computer connected to a Server operated within the Client [or by a customer of the Client to whom Software has been sublicensed by any company in the Client];
'Working Day'	means [ ], Monday to Friday inclusive, but excluding public holidays.

1. COMMENCEMENT

This Agreement shall commence on the Effective Date and subject to Clauses 10.5, 16, 22.2, 22.3 and 22.4 shall continue until terminated by mutual agreement.

2. BASIS OF PURCHASE

2.1 This Agreement together with any accepted Purchase Order and Special Conditions will form the contract between the Client and the Service Provider in connection with the Software and/or Services to be supplied.

2.2 Each Purchase Order shall be subject to written acceptance by the Service Provider. No contract shall come into being until the Service Provider has given such written acceptance to the Client.

3. SUPPLY OF SOFTWARE AND SERVICES

3.1 Purchase Order

The Service Provider shall supply the Software and Services set out in each Purchase Order.

3.2 Delivery

The Service Provider shall deliver the Software and Associated Documentation to the Delivery Address and perform the Services no later than the Delivery Date during Working Hours. the Service Provider shall install the Software upon the equipment specified in the Purchase Order.

3.3 Time

[Time shall be of the essence for the supply of all Software and Services in accordance with the Delivery Dates.] [While the Service Provider will use reasonable commercial efforts to meet delivery times, the Client's only remedy for unreasonable delay in delivery will be the right to terminate this Agreement after service of notice of breach as set out in this Agreement, plus a refund of any fees paid by the Client for no benefit.]

3.4 Title and Risk

Risk in all Media will pass to the Client upon delivery. Title to any Media will pass to the Client when the Service Provider has been paid for the related Software and Associated Documentation in full. the Service Provider may not repossess any Media delivered to the Client unless the Client has failed to pay for such Software by the due date, such payment or any part of it is not in dispute and the Service Provider is entitled to terminate the relevant Purchase Order under Clause 22.

3.5 [Compliance with Law

The Service Provider shall comply with all applicable laws, regulations or other legal requirements concerning the supply of Software and the performance of Services.]

3.6 Change Request Procedure

The Client and the Service Provider may raise requests for changes to Software or Services under the Change Request Procedure set out in Annex A.

4. CHARGES

4.1 The Service Provider's Charges shall be calculated on the basis stated in the relevant Purchase Order and shall be:-

4.1.1 exclusive of any applicable Value Added Tax (which shall be payable by the Client subject to receipt of a VAT invoice);

4.1.2 exclusive of any travel, accommodation or other expenses; and

4.1.3 inclusive of any duties, imposts or levies other than Value Added Tax.

4.2 Any increase in Charges shall be subject to written agreement of the parties.

4.3 Charges shall be expressed and payments made in Pounds Sterling unless otherwise agreed between the parties.

4.4 Unless otherwise specifically agreed in any Purchase Order the Service Provider will not charge the Client for licence or other fees paid by the Service Provider to third parties for equipment, software and services used by the Service Provider in the supply of the Software or Services to the Client.

5. PAYMENT

5.1   The Service Provider will issue invoices to the Client in accordance with any payment plan set out in the relevant Purchase Order or Special Conditions. Should no payment plan be set out the Service Provider may invoice the Client at any time after Acceptance of the Software or performance of the Services or in accordance with milestones agreed in the Project plan and forming part of the Special Conditions. Each invoice shall quote the number of the relevant Purchase Order and reflect the agreed Charges.

5.2   The Client shall pay all Charges for Software supplied and Services performed by the end of the month following the month of receipt by the Client of an invoice.

5.3   The Client shall be entitled to set off and withhold against the Charges any debt or sum indisputably owed to the Client by the Service Provider in connection with the relevant Purchase Order. For the purpose of this Clause a debt or sum will be 'indisputably' owed to the Client if at the conclusion of the Dispute Resolution Procedure in Clause 40 it is agreed that such debt or sum is so owing by the Service Provider.

5.4   Any invoice disputes shall be raised by the Client within 15 Working Days of receipt. the Client may withhold from payment on the due date under Clause 6.3 that part of the Charges which is disputed by the Client until any dispute is resolved in the Service Provider's favour.

6. PERFORMANCE

6.1   Software shall be supplied and Services shall be performed at the Delivery Address during and within Working Days unless otherwise agreed.

6.2   If Software is to be supplied or Services are to be performed by instalments the relevant Purchase Order will be treated as a single contract and not severable.

6.3   [Prior to the supply of Software or the commencement of Services, the Client may require that such supply or performance be postponed by up to 6 months without affecting the Charges, provided it gives the Service Provider reasonable prior notice. Only one postponement shall be permitted per Project.]

7. ACCEPTANCE

7.1   The Service Provider shall ensure that all Software and Services supplied comply with the relevant Purchase Order. Acceptance of Software and (if agreed) Services shall take place when the Client has signed and returned to the Service Provider an Acceptance Certificate or when the Software and/or Services are deemed to be accepted in accordance with the Acceptance Procedure set out in Annex B, whichever is the earlier. Acceptance shall be without prejudice to any of the Client's rights under this Agreement.

7.2   If no specific acceptance procedure is set out in a Purchase Order the Acceptance Procedure in Annex B of this Agreement shall apply.

8.   LICENCE

8.1   The Service Provider shall license or (as the case may be) sub-license to the Client any Software supplied under a Purchase Order subject to Licence terms contained in the Special Conditions. [Where licence terms are packaged with the media, the Client or the User will be licensed to use such Software whether provided by the Service Provider or a third party under the packaged licence terms (often referred to as a 'shrink-wrapped licence'.]

8.2   Such Licence terms shall address and/or provide for the following inter alia:-

    8.2.1   Exclusivity

    Whether the Licence is exclusive or non-exclusive, transferable or non-transferable.

    8.2.2   Term

    Whether the Licence is perpetual or term.

    8.2.3   Object Code

    Whether the Licence expressly includes the right to use the Source Code version of the Software (failing which only the Object Code will be licensed).

    8.2.4   Users

    The Licence will specify the number and type of licensed Users. Where the Licence is for a number of concurrent Users, concurrent Users shall include Users which have replaced former Users.

    8.2.5   Copying

        8.2.5.1   The Client may make so many copies of the Software as are reasonably necessary for operational security, back-up (including disaster recovery), archival purposes and use;

        8.2.5.2   Any limit on the number of copies that the Client may make shall be stated.

    8.2.6   Transfer to New Platform

    The Client may transfer any licensed Software to any new platform provided that the same number of Users will have access to such licensed Software as had licensed to that Software on the original platform. On any such transfer, the Client shall provide the Service Provider with written confirmation that the original platform is no longer in use for the purpose of the Licence.

8.2.7   Updates

Whether the Client is to receive updates, new releases and enhancements of the Software, and whether free or for a charge.

8.2.8   Modifications

Any limitation whereby the Client is permitted to reverse engineer, disassemble or decompile the Software, or allow third parties to do so.[2] In the absence of such express provision the Client shall not reverse engineer, disassemble or decompile the Software, or allow third parties to do so, except to the extent that the Service Provider cannot forbid such activities under the Copyright Designs & Patents Act 1988 (as amended) or other applicable law.

8.2.9   Assignment within the Client Group Company

The Client will be permitted to assign the benefit of the Licence to any other company in the Client Group Company.

8.2.10   Sub-Licensing

Whether the Client is permitted to sub-license the Software to its Client Group Company or its corporate or other customers and any other persons.

8.2.11   Developed Software

If it is anticipated that the Service Provider or its contractors will develop for the Client exclusively new software which incorporates portions of the Software ('Developed Software') the Licence shall provide that the Service Provider will own the Intellectual Property Rights in such Developed Software.

8.2.12   Reservation of Rights by the Service Provider and/or its licensors

Title to all Software will remain with the Service Provider or its licensors unless the contrary is expressly stated in the Licence.

8.2.13   Warranties

The Licence will include the following warranties by the Service Provider:-

8.2.13.1   a warranty that the Service Provider owns all Intellectual Property Rights in the Software or in the alternative a warranty that the Service Provider is entitled to license and/or sub-license the Software to the Client;

8.2.13.2   a 90 day warranty as to conformity to Specifications in the terms of Clause 14.1;

8.2.13.3   a 90 day warranty that the Media are free from defects in the terms of Clause 14.2;

8.2.13.4 a warranty as to statutory requirements in the terms of Clause 14.4;

7.2.13.5 a warranty of Millennium Compliance in the terms of Clause 14.5;

8.2.13.6 a warranty with regard to Data Protection in the terms of Clause 14.6; and

8.2.13.7 a warranty as regards Associated Documentation and training in the terms of Clause 14.7.

The Service Provider itself will not warrant products manufactured by a third party ('Third Party Products') which the Service Provider has resold or sub-licensed to the Client. the Service Provider will pass on to the Client the benefit of any third party warranty which will usually be supplied by a third party manufacturer as specified in the documentation provided with the Third Party Products.

9. SERVICES

9.1 Description

Subject to the payment of Service Fees, the Service Provider shall provide the following Services to the Client in respect of Software supplied to the Client:-

9.1.1 the Service Provider shall provide the Client with all standard updated releases, version enhancements and modules of Software; and

9.1.2 the Service Provider shall provide such support Services as may be specified in a Purchase Order.

9.2 Test Software

The Service Provider shall advise the Client in writing in advance of shipment of Software programs which are test Software only. the Client acknowledges that such programs do not form part of Software for the purposes of this Agreement and that such programs shall be maintained on a best efforts basis and updated as necessary for the purposes of the Project in which they are used.

9.3 No Modification or Adaptation of Software

The Service Provider is not obliged to provide Services if any Software has been modified or adapted by the Client or Software is materially affected by the Client's errors or negligence. Subject to written agreement by an authorised representative of the Client, the Service Provider may charge the Client for time spent by the Service Provider representatives in investigating or seeking to correct any problem with Software which is attributable to such causes.

9.4　Response to Reported Defects

Special Conditions may state the periods within which the Service Provider shall respond to reports of defects in the Software, the periods within which such defects will be corrected, and any reductions in the Charges resulting from any failure to respond or correct within such periods.

9.5　Termination of and Renewal of Services

Either party may terminate the Services by giving to the other party at least 30 days prior notice to such termination. Such termination shall not affect the obligations of the Service Provider to deliver Software not subject to the Services and shall not affect the Client's obligations to pay for such Services up to the date of termination.

9.6　Effect of Termination

Expiration or termination of the Services shall not limit either party from pursuing any other remedies available to it based upon events occurring prior to such expiration or termination, including the Client's obligation to pay all Service Fees.

10.　THE CLIENT'S RESPONSIBILITIES

If so required, the Client shall provide the Service Provider and (provided they have received security clearance) its staff with all office and other accommodation and facilities that the Service Provider may reasonably require to perform Services, in particular administrative support (e.g. security passes, network logons etc), access to telephone and fax communications and computer facilities. the Client shall ensure that it has appropriate back-up, security and virus-checking procedures in place for any computer facilities the Client provides. the Service Provider shall comply with the Client's reasonable virus-checking procedures relating to such facilities which the Client notifies to the Service Provider in writing.

11.　INTELLECTUAL PROPERTY RIGHTS

Neither party is granted any right, title or licence to, or interest in the other party's Intellectual Property Rights, provided however that one party may refer to the Software by the other party's Intellectual Property Rights so long as such references are truthful and not misleading. Each party acknowledges the other party's rights in such other party's Intellectual Property Rights and agrees that any and all use by it of such Intellectual Property Rights shall inure to the sole benefit of the other party. Neither party shall take any action inconsistent with the other party's ownership of its Intellectual Property Rights and agrees not to challenge the other party's ownership or use of such Intellectual Property Rights and further agrees not to attempt to register any such Intellectual Property Rights, owned or used by the other party or any other names or marks confusingly similar thereto. If at any time a party acquires any rights in, or any registration or application for any of the other party's Intellectual Property Rights by operation of law or otherwise it will immediately upon request by the other party and at no expense to the other party assign such rights, registrations or applications to the other party, along with any associated goodwill.

12. LIMITATION OF LIABILITY

12.1 The Service Provider shall indemnify the Client for personal injury or death caused by the negligence of its employees in connection with the performance of their duties hereunder, or by defects in any Software or Services supplied pursuant to this Agreement.[3]

12.2 The Service Provider shall indemnify the Client for direct damage to tangible property caused by the negligence of its employees in connection with the performance of their duties under each Purchase Order in this Agreement. The Service Provider's total liability under this Clause shall be limited to [£ (pounds)] [for any one event or series of connected events in every Purchase Order] **OR** [a sum equivalent to the total charges paid to the Service Provider (for that Purchase Order) for the Products that are the subject of the Client's claim].

12.3 Save in respect of claims for death or personal injury arising from the Service Provider's negligence, in no event will the Service Provider be liable for any damages resulting from loss of data or use, lost profits, loss of anticipated savings, nor for any damages that are an indirect or secondary consequence of any act or omission of the Service Provider whether such damages were reasonably foreseeable or actually foreseen.

12.4 [Except as provided above in the case of personal injury, death and damage to tangible property, the Service Provider's maximum liability to the Client for any cause whatsoever (whether in the form of a refund, the additional cost of remedial services or otherwise) will be for direct costs and damages only, and will be limited to, where the event is covered by the Service Provider's insurance policies, the amount which the Service Provider actually recovers from its insurers under those policies, to a maximum of [one million pounds.]

OR

[Except as provided above in the case of personal injury, death and damage to tangible property, the Service Provider's maximum liability to the Client under this Agreement or otherwise for any cause whatsoever (whether in the form of a refund, the additional cost of remedial services or otherwise) will be for direct costs and damages only and will be limited to the lesser of:-

12.4.1 The sum for which the Service Provider carries comprehensive insurance cover (subject to the Service Provider actually recovering such sum from the insurer); or

12.4.2 a sum equivalent to the price paid to the Service Provider under this Agreement for the Products that are the subject of the Client's claim [plus damages limited to 25% of the same amount for any additional costs directly, reasonably and

717

necessarily incurred by the Client in obtaining alternative products or services.]

OR

[Except as provided above in the case of personal injury, death, and damage to tangible property, the Service Provider's maximum liability to the Client for any cause whatsoever (whether in the form of a refund, the additional cost of remedial services, or otherwise) will be for direct costs and damages only, and will be limited to the lesser of:-

12.4.3   125% of the total charges paid and payable to the Service Provider for the Software and Services or services that are the subject of the Client's claim, or

12.4.4   The sum of [£].

12.5   In no event shall the Service Provider be liable to the Client for any losses whatsoever (whether lost future revenues, lost future profits, expenditure incurred to no benefit, or otherwise) suffered or incurred by the Client solely or substantially because this Agreement has been terminated.

12.6   All liability that is not expressly assumed in this Agreement is hereby excluded. These limitations will apply regardless of the form of action, whether under statute, in contract, tort, including negligence, or any other form of action. For the purposes of this Clause 'the Service Provider' includes its employees, sub-contractors and suppliers. The Client acknowledges that the Service Provider's employees, sub-contractors and suppliers shall have the benefit of the limits and exclusions of liability set out in this Clause in terms of the Contracts (Rights of Third Parties) Act 1999. Nothing in this Agreement shall exclude or limit liability for fraudulent misrepresentation.

12.7   Both parties acknowledge and agree that the limitations and exclusions of liability set out in this Clause are reasonable and have been agreed taking into account the commercial value of this Agreement to each party and the commercial standing of each party.

12.8   [No claim or action, regardless of form, arising out of this Agreement or a Purchase Order may be brought by either party more than 2 years after the cause of action has accrued.]

13.   WARRANTIES

13.1   Conformity to Specifications

The Service Provider warrants that Software will be free from defects in design, material and workmanship and will substantially conform under normal use to the specifications set forth in the Associated Documentation for a period of 90 days from the Acceptance Date. the Service Provider does not warrant that the operation of the Software will be free from minor interruptions or errors. If the Client notifies the Service Provider in writing during such warranty period of any claim that Software fails to conform to that warranty in a material respect, the Service Provider shall, without charge, take action to ensure that the Software performs substantially in accordance with such specifications. The warranties set forth herein shall not apply to any non-conformity arising out from or related to any modification or misuse by the Client.

13.2   Media Free from Defects

The Service Provider warrants that Media shall be free from defects under normal use for a period of 90 days from the Acceptance Date. During this warranty period the Service Provider will at its option repair or replace free of charge defective Media (and if necessary restore the Software thereon) or refund the purchase price of the Media which, in the Service Provider's reasonable opinion, has been damaged by accident, abuse or misapplication, or as a result of service or modification by persons other than the Service Provider. All media replaced under this warranty becomes the property of the Service Provider.

13.3   Quality of Services

The Service Provider warrants that all Services will:-

13.3.1   correspond to Specifications; and

13.3.2   be performed by adequately qualified and trained personnel, with due care and diligence and to standards appropriate to the industry.

13.4   [Statutory Requirements

The Service Provider warrants that the Software and Services will comply with all statutory and legal requirements and regulations applicable to the Service Provider but shall not be similarly liable to those applicable to the Client unless the Client notifies the Service Provider in writing of such statutory and legal requirements and regulations.]

13.5   Date Compliance

The Service Provider warrants that no Software or Services will be affected by any date and in particular:-

13.5.1   all Software and Services will behave consistently and not abnormally when using or processing any data involving dates; and

13.5.2   There will be no interruption in the operation of the Software or the provision of Services caused by the use or processing of any data involving dates; and

13.5.3   all Software will specify the century in any date in all user interface functionalities and data fields and other date related functions.

13.6   Data Protection

The Service Provider warrants that insofar as applicable to Software and Services:-

13.6.1 The Service Provider will take reasonable commercial efforts in accordance with appropriate security practice to maintain sufficient technical and organisational measures to ensure the security and integrity of its computer and other information systems to prevent the unauthorised disclosure, copying or use of confidential information or personal data and the Service Provider warrants that it will comply with the seventh principle of the Data Protection Act 1998; and

13.6.2 The Service Provider will act only on the instructions of the Client in respect of any personal data that it processes on behalf of the Client.

Both parties hereby undertake to comply with the provisions of the Data Protection Act 1998 and any related legislation insofar as the same relates to the provisions and obligations of this Agreement. Where applicable the expressions used in this Clause shall have the meanings given to them in the Data Protection Act 1998.

13.7 Documentation and Training

The Service Provider warrants to the Client that all Associated Documentation[4] and training supplied by the Service Provider will provide adequate instruction to enable the Client to make proper use of the Software.

13.8 Sole Warranties

The express warranties set forth in this Agreement are the Service Provider's sole warranties with respect to the Software, the Media and all Services provided by the Service Provider under this Agreement. the Service Provider disclaims all other warranties, terms and conditions express or implied, including any warranties, terms or conditions of satisfactory quality or fitness for any particular purpose.

14. INTELLECTUAL PROPERTY INDEMNITY

14.1 The Service Provider will defend at its expense any claim or action brought against the Client by a third party to the extent that such action is based on a claim that any Software or its use infringes such third party's intellectual property right. the Service Provider will indemnify the Client against any costs, damages and fees incurred by the Client which are attributable to such claim. the Service Provider's indemnification obligations hereunder are conditional upon the Client promptly notifying the Service Provider in writing of such claim. the Client shall permit the Service Provider to defend, compromise or settle the claim, and in such event the Client will tender such claim to the Service Provider and the Client will provide all available information, assistance and authority to enable the Service Provider to do so, provided the Service Provider reimburses the Client for such activity. the Client shall have no authority to settle any claim on behalf of the Service Provider.

14.2 Should the Client become or in the Service Provider's opinion, be likely to become, the subject of a claim of infringement of a Intellectual Property Right, the Service Provider shall at its option (i) procure for the Client, at no cost to the Client, the right to continue to use the Software; or (ii) replace or modify the Software to make its use non infringing while yielding substantially equivalent functionality.

14.3 This infringement indemnity does not cover claims arising from: the combination of Software with products or services not provided by the Service Provider; the modification of Software by any person other than the Service Provider; Software complying with or based upon: (1) designs provided by or at the Client direction (2) specifications or other information provided by or at the Client direction; or the use of Software in a manner not permitted or contemplated by this Agreement or the relevant Purchase Order.

15. FORCE MAJEURE

Neither party shall have any liability under or be deemed to be in breach of this Agreement for any delays or failures in performance of this Agreement which result from circumstances beyond the reasonable control of that party. If such circumstances continue for a continuous period of more than [6 months], either party may terminate this Agreement by written notice to the other party.

16. PROGRESS REPORTS

the Service Provider shall supply such reports on the progress of its performance of a Purchase Order in such form as the Client may reasonably require.

17. PROJECT MANAGEMENT

17.1 Project Manager

17.1.1 The Service Provider shall appoint a project manager to supervise the carrying out of the Service Provider's obligations in accordance with any Purchase Order.

17.1.2 All communications to and from the Service Provider shall be received and given by the Service Provider project manager appointed under Clause 18.1.1.

17.2 The Client Representative

17.2.1 The Client shall appoint a representative to interface with the Service Provider for the purpose of the Client's obligations under this Agreement and any Purchase Order.

17.2.2 All communications to and from the Client shall be received and given by the Client representative appointed under Clause 18.2.1.

17.3   Health and Safety

The Client shall provide the Service Provider with a safe and secure workplace and such facilities as the Service Provider may reasonably require while on the Client's premises and allow access to such premises at all reasonable times for the purpose of any Purchase Order.

17.4   [Removal of Project Team Staff

Unless stated otherwise in a Purchase Order, the Client may request at any time the removal of (and the Service Provider will remove) any Project team member if the Client; (1) reasonably believes that the individual is not performing the tasks required of that individual for the Project or does not meet the appropriate professional standards; and (2) has previously provided the Service Provider with prior written notice of the problem and a reasonable opportunity to remedy the situation and the problem has not been remedied. In such event the Service Provider will provide replacement staff as soon as reasonably practicable. Any replacement staff will have relevant experience in relation to the role they are replacing.]

18. TRAINING

Training shall be provided by the Service Provider if specified in any Purchase Order.

19. MISTAKES IN INFORMATION

19.1   Each party shall be liable for any discrepancies, errors, or omissions in the drawings and information supplied by it whether they have been approved by the other party or not, provided that such discrepancies, errors, or omissions are not due to inaccurate drawings or information furnished to supplying party by such other party, its agents, employees and sub-contractors.

19.2   The party supplying erroneous information shall at its own expense carry out any such alterations or remedial work necessitated by reason of such discrepancies, errors, or omissions detailed in Clause 20.1 and modify the drawings and information accordingly within a period of 1 month from the date of discovery of such discrepancy, error or omission, or within a period of time that is reasonable under the circumstances. If the party supplying erroneous information carries out alterations or remedial work otherwise than in respect of the matters mentioned in Clauses 20.1 and 20.2, at the request of the other party, then such other party shall bear all costs reasonably and properly incurred thereby. Any resulting changes to the Specifications shall be subject to any agreed Change Request Procedure.

20. NON SOLICITATION

Each party agrees that, during the life of this Agreement and for 6 months following completion or any termination of any Purchase Order, neither it by itself, its officers, employees or agents or otherwise howsoever and whether as a consultant, principal, partner, director, employee or otherwise, shall employ or solicit the services of any employee, officer, agent or consultant of the other party (or, as the case may be, of any Service Provider Group Company or Client Group Company) who was engaged and/or involved in providing or receiving the Software and/or Services.

21. TERMINATION

21.1 This Agreement is subject to the rights of termination in Clauses 10.5, 16, 22.2, 22.3 and 22.4. Such termination will not, however, affect the applicability of the terms of this Agreement to any Purchase Order for which the Software called for by that Purchase Order has not yet been delivered and which has not itself been terminated pursuant to Clauses 10.5, 16, 22.3 or 22.4. In addition, (i) if the Service Provider delivers the Software or commences the Services called for in a Purchase Order prior to the date of that Purchase Order, all provisions of this Agreement and that Purchase Order for the benefit or protection of either party will apply to such Services, and (ii) if any Software or Services are provided by the Service Provider while this Agreement is in effect but without execution by the parties of a Purchase Order all provisions herein for the benefit or protection of either party will apply as if such Software or Services had been subject to a Purchase Order duly executed by the parties.

21.2 Termination of Agreement

Either party may terminate this Agreement by giving the other party 90 days' prior notice of such termination.

21.3 Termination of Purchase Orders

Any Purchase Order may be terminated by the Client at any time by giving reasonable advance written notice to the Service Provider. On receipt of such a notice from the Client, the Service Provider shall cease all production and other preparations or work in respect of the Purchase Order. In full settlement the Client shall pay the Service Provider a fair and reasonable price for any Software completed and in a deliverable and operational state but not yet installed at the date of such termination, and a reasonable charge for all Services provided up to the date of termination. The termination of an individual Purchase Order will not operate to terminate any other Purchase Order or this Agreement but consequential amendments to any remaining Purchase Order may be necessary and will be agreed between the parties.

21.4 Termination for Breach and on Insolvency

Either party shall be entitled to terminate this Agreement and/or any Purchase Order without liability to the other party by giving notice to the other party at any time if:-

21.4.1 that other party is in material breach of the relevant Purchase Order or this Agreement, provided that if the breach is capable of remedy the innocent party shall not be entitled to terminate the relevant Purchase Order or this Agreement unless and until the breaching party shall have failed to remedy the breach within 10 Working Days of such notice;

21.4.2 that other party makes any voluntary arrangement with its creditors (within the meaning of the Insolvency Act 1986) or becomes subject to an administration order or goes into liquidation otherwise than for the purpose of amalgamation or reconstruction; or

21.4.3 an encumbrancer takes possession, or a receiver is appointed, of any of the property or assets of that other party; or

21.4.4 that other party ceases, or threatens to cease, to carry on business; or

21.4.5 The Client or the Service Provider reasonably apprehends that any of the events mentioned above is about to occur in relation to the other party and notifies the other party accordingly.

21.5 Accrued Rights etc

Termination of a Purchase Order or part thereof shall not affect any accrued rights or liabilities of either party nor shall it affect the coming into force or the continuation in force of any provision of this Agreement which expressly or by implication is intended to come into or continue in force on or after such termination.

21.6 Return of Property

On termination of this Agreement and any Purchase Order each party will return to the other any property of the other that it then has in its possession or control, except that solely for the Service Provider's internal audit purposes, the Service Provider may retain one copy of any documentation or software prepared by the Service Provider, or any documentation upon which the Services are based.

22. CONFIDENTIALITY

22.1 All information of a technical or business nature disclosed by one party to the other either before or after the date hereof in connection with any Software or Services or business dealings between the parties shall be regarded as confidential ('Confidential Information') and shall only be disclosed as is strictly necessary and each party shall procure that its personnel and third parties to which Confidential Information is disclosed treat such information as confidential. Such information shall be used only for the purpose for which it was disclosed and for carrying out the purposes of this Agreement and any Purchase Order and shall not without prior written consent of the disclosing party be disclosed to any third party provided that either party may disclose without consent any Confidential Information:

22.1.1 to its sub-contractors for the operation of any System or the provision of the Software or Services provided that such disclosures is on a 'need to know' basis only and the sub-contractor undertakes to keep such Confidential Information confidential; or

22.1.2 as required to be disclosed to any governmental and/or regulatory authority; or

22.1.3 to any company within the Client Group Company or Service Provider Group Company.

22.2 Information shall not be deemed to be Confidential Information where it:-

22.2.1 is authorised to be disclosed by the disclosing party to the extent of the authority given; or

22.2.2 is made public by the disclosing party or is or becomes part of the public domain other than by the default of the receiving party; or

22.2.3 is in the possession of or is known by the receiving party without any obligation to keep it confidential prior to its receipt from the disclosing party; or

22.2.4 is subsequently rightfully obtained by the receiving party from a third party; or

22.2.5 is independently developed by the receiving party.

22.3 Notwithstanding the completion or termination for whatever reason of a Purchase Order, the obligations of confidentiality shall, unless otherwise agreed, continue for a period of 5 years from such completion or termination of such Purchase Order.

22.4 Any Confidential Information referred to in Clause 23.1 shall remain the property of the disclosing party and shall be returned by the receiving party to the disclosing party if so requested.

22.5 The obligations of confidentiality set out above shall be deemed to be discharged provided that there is no intentional disclosure of the Confidential Information, that the party in question has taken reasonable efforts in accordance with best current commercial security practice to reduce the risk of accidental disclosure, and that, where accidental disclosure does occur despite the exercise of reasonable care, steps are take to minimise the risk of further accidental disclosure of the same kind.

23. INTERPRETATION

23.1 In this Agreement unless the context otherwise requires:-

23.1.1 words importing any gender include every gender;

23.1.2 words importing the singular number include the plural number and vice versa;

23.1.3 words importing persons include firms, companies and corporations and vice versa;

23.1.4 references to numbered clauses and annexes are references to the relevant clause in or annex to this Agreement;

23.1.5 reference in any annex to this Agreement to numbered paragraphs or clauses relate to the numbered paragraphs or clauses of that annex;

23.1.6 The headings to the clauses, annexes and paragraphs of this Agreement will not affect the interpretation;

23.1.7 any reference to an enactment includes reference to that enactment as amended or replaced from time to time and to any subordinate legislation or byelaw made under that enactment;

23.1.8 any obligation on any party not to do or omit to do anything is to include an obligation not to allow that thing to be done or omitted to be done;

23.1.9 any party who agrees to do something will be deemed to fulfil that obligation if that party procures that it is done.

23.2 This Agreement and any Special Conditions shall apply on an equal basis, except where there is an inconsistency between this Agreement and any Special Condition when that Special Condition shall prevail.

23.3 Where there is any conflict or inconsistency between the Specifications and any Special Condition contained in a Purchase Order, the Special Condition shall prevail.

24. AGENCY, PARTNERSHIP

This Agreement including any Purchase Order or Special Conditions shall not constitute or imply any partnership, joint venture, agency, fiduciary relationship or other relationship between the parties other than the contractual relationship expressly provided for in this Agreement.

25. AMENDMENTS

This Agreement including any Purchase Order or Special Condition may not be released, discharged, supplemented, interpreted, amended, varied or modified in any manner except by an instrument in writing signed by a duly authorised officer or representative of each of the parties hereto.

26. ANNOUNCEMENTS

No party shall issue or make any public announcement or disclose any information regarding this Agreement unless prior written consent has been obtained from the other party.

27. ASSIGNMENT

27.1 This Agreement is personal to the parties and, subject to Clause 28.2 below, neither this Agreement, any Purchase Order nor any rights, licenses or obligations under this Agreement, may be assigned by either party without the prior written approval of the other party.

27.2 Notwithstanding the foregoing, either party may assign this Agreement or any Purchase Order to any acquirer of all or of substantially all of such party's equity securities, assets or business relating to the subject matter of this Agreement or to any entity controlled by, that controls, or is under common control with a party to this Agreement. Any attempted assignment in violation of this clause will be void and without effect.

28. ENTIRE AGREEMENT

This Agreement together with any Purchase Order, Special Condition, and any subsequent amendments supersedes all prior agreements, arrangements and undertakings between the parties and constitutes the entire agreement between the parties relating to the subject matter of this Agreement. However the obligations of the parties under any pre-existing non-disclosure agreement shall remain in full force and effect insofar as there is no conflict between the same. The parties confirm that they have not entered into this Agreement on the basis of any representation that is not expressly incorporated into this Agreement.

29. NOTICES

29.1 All notices hereunder shall be in writing.

29.2 Notices shall be deemed to have been duly given:-

29.2.1 when delivered, if delivered by courier or other messenger (including registered mail) during normal business hours of the recipient; or

29.2.2 when sent, if transmitted by fax or e-mail and a successful transmission report or return receipt is generated; or

29.2.3 on the fifth business day following mailing, if mailed by national ordinary mail, postage pre-paid; or

29.2.4 on the tenth business day following mailing, if mailed by airmail, postage pre-paid in each case addressed to the most recent address, e-mail address, or facsimile number notified to the other party.

30. ANNEXES

The provisions of all the Annexes and Purchase Orders to this Agreement shall form part of this Agreement as if set out here.

31. SEVERANCE

If any provision of this Agreement is prohibited by law or judged by a court to be unlawful, void or unenforceable, the provision shall, to the extent required, be severed from this Agreement and rendered ineffective as far as possible without modifying the remaining provisions of this Agreement, and shall not in any way affect any other circumstances of or the validity or enforcement of this Agreement.

32. SUCCESSORS AND ASSIGNEES

32.1   This agreement shall be binding upon, and enure to the benefit of, the parties and their respective successors and permitted assignees, and references to a party in this Agreement shall include its successors and permitted assignees.

32.2   In this Agreement references to a party include references to a person:-

32.2.1   who for the time being is entitled (by assignment, novation or otherwise) to that party's rights under this Agreement (or any interest in those rights); or

32.2.2   who, as administrator, liquidator or otherwise, is entitled to exercise those rights;

and in particular those references include a person to whom those rights (or any interest in those rights) are transferred or pass as a result of a merger, division, reconstruction or other reorganisation involving that party. For this purpose, references to a party's rights under this Agreement include any similar rights to which another person becomes entitled as a result of a novation of this Agreement.

33. WAIVER

No delay, neglect or forbearance on the part of either party in enforcing against the other party any term or condition of this Agreement shall either be or be deemed to be a waiver or in any way prejudice any right of that party under this Agreement. No right, power or remedy in this Agreement conferred upon or reserved for either party is exclusive of any other right, power or remedy available to that party.

34. COUNTERPARTS

This Agreement may be executed in any number of counterparts or duplicates, each of which shall be an original, and such counterparts or duplicates shall together constitute one and the same agreement.

35. SUBCONTRACTING

With the prior written consent of the Client (such consent not to be unreasonably withheld or delayed) the Service Provider may perform any or all of its obligations under this Agreement through agents or sub-contractors, provided that the Service Provider shall remain liable for such performance and shall indemnify the Client against any loss or damage suffered by the Client arising from any act or omission of such agents or sub-contractors.

36. LANGUAGE

This Agreement is made only in the English language. If there is any conflict in the meaning between the English language version of this Agreement and any version or translation of this Agreement in any other language, the English language version shall prevail.

37. COSTS AND EXPENSES

Each party shall bear its own legal costs and other costs and expenses arising in connection with the drafting, negotiation, execution and registration (if applicable) of this Agreement.

38. THIRD PARTIES

The parties confirm their intent (subject to Clause 13.6) not to confer any rights on any third parties by virtue of this Agreement and accordingly the Contracts (Rights of Third Parties) Act 1999 shall not apply to this Agreement.

39. PROPER LAW AND JURISDICTION

39.1   This Agreement and all matters arising from it and any dispute resolutions referred to below shall be governed by and construed in accordance with English Law notwithstanding the conflict of law provisions and other mandatory legal provisions save that:-

   39.1.1   The Service Provider shall have the right to sue to recover its fees in any jurisdiction in which the Client is operating or has assets, and

   39.1.2   The Service Provider shall have the right to sue for breach of its Intellectual Property Rights and other proprietary information and trade secrets (whether in connection with this Agreement or otherwise) in any country where it believes that infringement or a breach of this Agreement relating to its Intellectual Property Rights might be taking place.

39.2   Each party recognises that the other party's business relies upon the protection of its Intellectual Property Rights and that in the event of a breach or threatened breach of Intellectual Property Rights, the other party will be caused irreparable damage and such other party may therefore be entitled to injunctive or other equitable relief in order to prevent a breach or threatened breach of its Intellectual Property Rights.

39.3   With respect to all other disputes which are not Intellectual Property Rights related pursuant to clauses 39.1 and 39.2 above and its special rules the following procedures in clauses 39.3 to 39.5 shall apply. Where there is a dispute the aggrieved party shall notify the other party in writing of the nature of the dispute with as much detail as possible about the deficient performance of the other party. A representative from senior management ('representatives') of each of the parties shall meet in person or communicate by telephone within five business days of the date of the written notification in order to reach an agreement about the nature of the deficiency and the corrective action to be taken by the respective parties. The representatives shall produce a report about the nature of the dispute in detail to their respective boards and if no agreement is reached on corrective action, then the chief executives of each party shall meet in person or by telephone, to facilitate an agreement within five business days of a written notice by one to the other. If the dispute cannot be resolved at board level within a further five business days, or if the agreed upon completion dates in any written plan of corrective action are exceeded, either party may seek its legal remedies as provided below.

39.4   If the parties cannot resolve a dispute in accordance with the procedure in clause 39.3 above, then they shall with the assistance of the Centre for Effective Dispute Solution, seek to resolve the dispute or difference amicably by using an Alternative Dispute Resolution ('ADR') procedure acceptable to both parties before pursuing any other remedies available to them. If either party fails or refuses to agree to or participate in the ADR procedure or if in any event the dispute or difference is not resolved to the satisfaction of both parties within [90] days after it has arisen, the matter shall be settled in accordance with the procedure below.

39.5   If the parties cannot resolve the dispute by the procedure set out above, the parties shall irrevocably submit to the exclusive jurisdiction of the Courts of England and Wales for the purposes of hearing and determining any dispute arising out of this Agreement. For the avoidance of doubt, the place of performance of this Agreement is agreed by the parties to be England.

39.6   [While the dispute resolution procedure above is in progress and any party has an obligation to make a payment to another party or to allow a credit in respect of such payment, the sum relating to the matter in dispute shall be paid into an interest bearing deposit account to be held in the names of the relevant parties at a clearing bank and such payment shall be a good discharge of the parties' payment obligations under this Agreement. Following resolution of the dispute, whether by mediation or legal proceedings, the sum held in such account shall be payable as determined in accordance with the mediation or legal proceedings, and the interest accrued shall be allocated between the parties pro rata according to the split of the principal sum as between the parties.]

Signed _____

For and on behalf of CLIENT

Signed _____

For and on behalf of SERVICE PROVIDER

ANNEX A

CHANGE CONTROL PROCEDURE

1.   If at any time either party wishes to recommend an addition, modification or change to any Software or Services supplied under a Purchase Order (a 'Modification') that party will submit a written request for the Modification (a 'Change Request') in reasonable detail to the other party.

2.   All Change Requests initiated by the Client will require authorisation in writing by the authorised representative of the Client or one of the Client's contact persons specified in the relevant Purchase Order.

3.   All Change Requests initiated by the Service Provider will require the authorisation in writing by the authorised representative of the Service Provider or one of the Service Provider contact persons specified in the relevant Purchase Order.

4.   Where the Service Provider intends to charge fees and/or expenses for the evaluation of a Change Request, the Service Provider will provide the Client with a quotation and obtain the Client's prior written acceptance.

5.   If in a party's judgement the time to evaluate and respond to one or more Change Requests, because of their magnitude, complexity or frequency, may result in a delay in Delivery Dates or otherwise impair the success of the Project, that party will notify the other party and the parties will not take action with respect to such Change Request(s) until the parties mutually agree upon an appropriate course of action.

6.   Should the parties mutually agree upon a Modification based on a Change Request, such Modification, together with any other related changes will be stated in writing and by an appropriate officer of each party The Modification so signed will be a 'Change Order'.

7.   Neither party is obliged to proceed with any Modification (or the related changes) and no Modification (or related changes) will be effective and enforceable against a party, unless and until reflected in a Change Order.

ANNEX B

ACCEPTANCE PROCEDURE

1.   The Service Provider shall prepare and submit to the Client for the purposes of each Purchase Order an Acceptance Plan which is consistent with the Specifications. The Acceptance Plan shall detail the general approach, timescales, resources and dependencies required

to demonstrate Acceptance. When the Acceptance Plan has been accepted by the Client in writing and/or incorporated in the Special Conditions all matters contained within the Acceptance Plan shall be the Acceptance Criteria.

2. Software and/or Services shall be Accepted when the Client has signed and returned to the Service Provider an Acceptance Certificate and shall be deemed to be Accepted when the Service Provider has demonstrated to the Client that the Acceptance Criteria have been met or when the Client places Software into operational use whichever is earlier.

3. The Service Provider shall give the Client reasonable prior notice of any demonstration ('Acceptance Demonstration') by the Service Provider to the Client for the purpose of demonstrating that the Acceptance Criteria have been met.

4. Unless a different time period is set in Special Conditions, the Client shall either sign and return to the Service Provider an Acceptance Certificate or give notice to the Service Provider in writing if Software and/or Services are not accepted within 30 Working Days of the Service Provider completing an Acceptance Demonstration or presenting an Acceptance Certificate to the Client for signature, whichever is the later.

5. If the Client does not notify the Service Provider within the above timescale that Software and/or Services are not Accepted, such Software and/or Services shall be deemed Accepted without the need for the Service Provider to receive a signed Acceptance Certificate.

6. The Client's notice that Software and/or Services are not Accepted shall state in reasonable detail and in a consolidated manner any failure to demonstrate that the Specifications and/or the Acceptance Criteria have been met. Acceptance or delivery of a signed Acceptance Certificate shall not be unreasonably withheld.

7. If a notice of a non-Acceptance is not sufficiently detailed to allow the Service Provider to determine why any Software and/or Services have not been accepted, the Service Provider may request in writing that the Client provides sufficient additional information. The passage of 15 Working Days from the date of such request without the provision of such additional information shall constitute deemed Acceptance without the need for the Service Provider to receive an Acceptance Certificate.

8. The Service Provider shall either fix problems reported in a notice of non-Acceptance within 10 Working Days after receipt of such notice or present the Client with a plan to fix such problems within a period of time that is reasonable under the circumstances, and shall carry out such activities at no cost to the Client. There shall be no deemed Acceptance until the Service Provider has either completed such a fix or presented such a plan.

9. Following any notice of non-Acceptance the Service Provider shall re-present the relevant Software and/or Services for Acceptance and the same procedure as set out above shall apply. In the event that

any Software and/or Services are still not Accepted on completion of such procedure, either party may escalate the Acceptance issue to the contacts nominated in the relevant Purchase Order for resolution. In such circumstances, additional development or testing shall cease until such time as a method of resolution has been agreed.

10.   Where the parties have agreed in Special Conditions that no Acceptance Plan is required, the Software and/or Services shall be deemed to be Accepted on delivery.

11.   Any Software and/or Services that have been Accepted which are inconsistent with or otherwise modify Software and/or Services Accepted previously shall supersede the Software or Services Accepted previously to the extent of the inconsistency or modification.

1   Definition of 'user': This needs to be checked against the charging structure for any software that will be supplied. Also, if the Client can sublicense software to its own customers - need to agree a charging structure for this.
2   Normally the Service Provider would want to veto this, and also copying for the purposes of error correction.
3   It is illegal to exclude such liability in the U.K.
4   This is why all Associated Documentation should be annexed, so that the Service Provider is clear about its commitment in this context.

29 Software services agreement

Date:

Parties:

1.   [ ] LIMITED whose registered office is at [   ] and whose registered
        number is [   ] ('The Customer').

2.   [ ] LIMITED a company incorporated under the laws of England and
        Wales, registered with number [   ] and having its registered office at
        [   ] (The 'Supplier')

RECITALS

(A)   The Customer has entered into several Development and Publishing
        Agreements ('the Development and Publishing Agreements') prior to
        the date of this Agreement.

(B)   The Customer intends to enter into further development and publishing
        agreement with third parties ('Future Agreements') and may require
        the Supplier to provide Additional Services as hereafter defined.

(C)   The Customer and The Supplier have agreed, that in order that the
        Customer shall fulfil its obligations under the Development and
        Publishing Agreement and any Future Agreements, the Supplier
        shall provide services to the Customer on the terms set out in this
        Agreement.

Operative provisions:

1. INTERPRETATION

Additional Services:	any services which are to be performed by the Supplier as agreed pursuant to clause 2.3;
Affiliate:	in relation to either The Customer or The Supplier, a company which is a subsidiary or holding company of it, or any company which is a subsidiary of any such holding company, 'holding company' and 'subsidiary' having the meanings ascribed to them in section 736 Companies Act 1985;

Charges:	the charges for the provision of the Services set out in Schedule 2;
Confidential Information:	means all information (whether written, oral or in electronic forms) concerning the business and affairs of one party that the other party obtains or receives as a result of the discussions leading up to or the entering into or the performance of this Agreement;
Customer Data:	all data, information, text, drawings, diagrams, images or sound embodied in any electronic or tangible medium, and which are supplied or in respect of which access is granted to The Supplier by The Customer pursuant to this Agreement or which The Supplier is required to generate under this Agreement;
Default:	in relation to either party means any breach of the obligations of that party (including but not limited to fundamental breach or breach of a fundamental term) or any default, act, omission, negligence or statement of that party, its employees, servants, agents, Sub-contractors or sub-contractors in connection with or in relation to the subject matter of this Agreement and in respect of which that party is liable to the other;
Effective Date:	the date of this Agreement;
Encumbrance:	any right or interest of any third party, including any mortgage, charge, lien, option, encumbrance, right of pre-emption of first refusal, or any agreement to create any such right or interest, other than any licence applying to any item of customer software or third party software;
Equipment:	means any equipment, facilities and/or software necessary for the provision of the Services together with any files, documents or records relating to the Services or the management, direction or organisation thereof;
Force Majeure:	means any cause not within the reasonable control of a party and which that party can not reasonably prevent or overcome, as a result of which such party is unable to perform its obligations under this Agreement but shall exclude (i) any delay or failure caused by any supplier or sub-contractor unless such supplier or sub-contractor is itself affected by an event beyond it reasonable control and which that supplier or sub-contractor cannot reasonably prevent or overcome; (ii) in the case of The Customer, any event causing a failure to pay any Charges; (iii) in the case of The Supplier any event covered by any disaster recovery or back-up service that The Supplier is obliged to provide to or for the benefit or The Customer under this Agreement or otherwise;
Intellectual Property:	means patents, design rights, trade marks and service marks, (in each case whether registered or not), domain names, Know-How, utility models, copyright, database lights, moral rights and topography rights (in each case for the full period thereof and all extensions and renewals thereof), applications for any of the foregoing and the right to apply for any of the foregoing in any part of the world and any similar rights situated in any country and the benefit (subject to the burden) of any and all agreements, arrangements and licences in connection with any of the foregoing;
Know-How:	includes all know-how, methodology, experience, data, technical and commercial information relating to any computer games or software including but not limited to the formulae, designs, drawings and mode of operation;

Parent Company:	means in relation to The Supplier or The Customer any company which is the ultimate holding company of that party and which is either responsible directly or indirectly for the business activities of that party or which is engaged in the same or similar business to that party. The term 'holding company' shall have the meaning ascribed by s.736 of the Companies Act 1985;
Relevant Employees:	means the employees, independent contractors, consultants or agents who are assigned (whether full-time or part-time) by The Supplier in the provision of the Services from time to time;
Replacement Supplier:	means a supplier which succeeds The Supplier in the provision of the Services;
Rights:	means the Intellectual Property, and any other rights, in and to the computer games and other software developed or in the process of development by the Supplier.
Services:	means the services described in Schedule 1 which are to be performed by The Supplier pursuant to clause 2.1 and all the services which are to be performed by and all the other obligations of The Supplier hereunder, including, in accordance with clause 2.3 and Additional Services;
Site:	means any premises from where the Services are provided or from which The Supplier manages, organises or otherwise directs the provision or the use of the Services and/or where the Equipment is situated;
Source Code:	means software in eye-readable form and in such form that it can be complied or interpreted into equivalent object code together with all tools, technical information and documentation necessary for the use, reproductions, modification and enhancement of such software.

1.1 Reference to any statute, enactment, order, regulation or other similar instrument shall be construed as references to the statute, enactment, order, regulation or instrument as amended by any subsequent statute, enactment, order, regulation or instrument or as contained in any subsequent re-enactment, modification or statutory extension of any of the above.

1.2 Except where the context requires otherwise the singular includes the plural and vice versa; a reference to one gender includes all genders; words denoting persons include firms and corporation and vice versa.

1.3 Headings are included in this Agreement for ease of reference only and shall not affect interpretation or construction.

1.4 References to clauses and Schedules are, unless otherwise provided, references to clauses and schedules of this Agreement.

1.5 Any negative obligation imposed on any party shall be construed as if it were also an obligation not to permit or suffer the act or thing in question and any positive obligation imposed on any party shall be construed as if it were an obligation to procure that the act or thing in question be done.

1.6 The words 'include' or 'including' shall be construed without limitation to the words following.

2. THE SERVICES

2.1 The Supplier agrees to supply the Services, in consideration of the payment of the Charges by The Customer, and upon the terms and conditions of this Agreement.

2.2 The Services shall commence on the Effective Date and shall continue during the term of this Agreement, subject to termination as provided below.

2.3 Without prejudice to clause 4, The Supplier undertakes to perform, at any time during the term of the Agreement, such Additional Services as may be agreed by the parties. Such Additional Services shall be incorporated into an addendum to Schedule 1 and signed on behalf of The Customer and The Supplier and shall be performed in accordance with and subject to the terms and conditions of this Agreement.

2.4 As part of the Services the Supplier forthwith assigns to the Customer with full title guarantee absolutely:-

2.4.1 its right title and interest in the Rights;

2.4.2 all its rights and powers arising or accrued from the Rights, including any right to see the damages and other remedies and to have the benefit of any remedy obtained in respect of any infringement of such Rights prior to the date of this Agreement; and

2.4.3 its right to apply for, prosecute and obtain other protection in any part of the world in relation to all or any of the Rights, including its right to apply for renewals and extensions of such rights,

such assignment to be deemed to have automatically taken place immediately upon the creation of any such Rights.

2.5 The Supplier agrees, at the expense of the Customer, to execute such further documents and do all such things as the customer may reasonably request to enable the Customer or its nominee to enjoy the full benefits of the Rights hereby assigned.

3. TERMS AND RENEWAL

3.1 This Agreement shall take effect on the Effective Date and shall continue thereafter until terminated by either party giving 6 months written notice to the other or this Agreement is otherwise terminated in accordance with its terms or is otherwise lawfully terminated.

4. SERVICE LEVELS

4.1 Interruptions to the Services shall only be made with the prior agreement of The Customer.

4.2 If at any time the Services are not supplied The Supplier shall, without prejudice to The Customer's other rights and remedies:

4.2.1   arrange all additional resources necessary to perform the Services as soon as possible and at no additional charge to The Customer; and

4.2.2   use its best endeavours to promptly remedy and remove the cause of non-performance; and

4.2.3   promptly remedy any Default or re-perform any non conforming Services at the request of The Customer at no additional charge.

4.3   If at any time after the Effective Date the Services are not supplied in accordance with this Agreement and such failure is not remediable The Customer shall be entitled to terminate this Agreement in accordance with clause 9.3 and obtain such other remedies as may be available to it either under this Agreement or otherwise at equity or law, including but not limited to the withholding from payment to The Supplier and/ or recovering as a sum of money due from The Supplier the Charges or any portion thereof that are allocable to the Default and/or non-continuing Services.

5.   CHARGES

5.1   In consideration of and subject to the supply of the Service in accordance with the terms of this Agreement, The Customer shall pay the charges.

5.2   Payment shall be made within thirty (30) days of receipt by The Customer of a valid invoice from The Supplier.

5.3   The Customer and The Supplier may vary the Charges upon joint agreement and such agreement shall be appended to and thereupon become a binding part of this Agreement.

5.4   In addition to the Charges and subject to receipt of a valid invoice, The Customer shall pay all applicable sales tax on the Charges at the rate and in the manner prescribed by law from time to time.

6.   THE CUSTOMER OBLIGATIONS

6.1   The Customer hereby warrants and represents to the Supplier that it will co-operate with The Supplier (without incurring any expenditure) and provide The Supplier with such information and assistance as The Supplier may reasonably require in order to enable or facilitate The Supplier duly and punctually to comply with its obligations under this Agreement.

7.   LIABILITY

7.1   Neither party excludes or limits liability to the other party for fraud nor for death or personal injury or any breach of any obligations implied by Section 12 of the Sale of Goods Act 1979 or Section 2 of the Supply of Goods and Services Act 1982.

7.2 Without prejudice to clause 7.1 in no event shall either party be liable to the other for:

    7.2.1 loss of profits (whether direct or indirect), business, revenue, goodwill or anticipated savings; and/or

    7.2.2 indirect or consequential loss or damage.

8. CONFIDENTIALITY

8.1 Each of The Customer and The Supplier hereby undertakes to the other to:

    8.1.1 keep confidential all Confidential Information belonging to the other;

    8.1.2 treat Confidential Information belonging to the other with the same degree of care that it uses for its own confidential information;

    8.1.3 not, without the prior written consent of the other, disclose Confidential Information belonging to the other in whole or in part to any other person save those of its employees, agents and subcontractors involved in the provision or receipt of the Services and who need to know the Confidential Information in question;

    8.1.4 use the Confidential Information belonging to the other solely in connection with the provision or receipt of the Services and not for its own benefit or the benefit of any third party.

8.2 Without prejudice to the generality of the foregoing The Supplier, or any person engaged by The Supplier whether as a servant or a consultant or otherwise shall not use Confidential Information belonging to The Customer for the solicitation of business from The Customer or any Affiliate of The Customer by The Supplier or by such servant or consultant or by any third party.

8.3 Each of The Customer and The Supplier hereby undertakes to the other to make all Relevant Employees aware of the confidentiality of the Confidential Information belonging to the other and the provisions of this clause 8.3 and, without limitation to this clause 8.3, to take all such steps as shall from time to time be necessary to ensure compliance by its employees, agents and sub-contractors with the provisions of this clause 8 and indemnity the other party against any breach of this clause 8.3.

8.4 The provisions of clauses 8.1, 8.2 and 8.3 shall not apply to any information which:

    8.4.1 is or becomes public knowledge other than by breach of this clause 8;

    8.4.2 is in the possession of the receiving party without restriction in relation to disclosure before the date of receipt from the disclosing party;

8.4.3 is received from a third party who lawfully acquired it and who is under no obligation restricting its disclosure;

8.4.4 is independently developed without access to any Confidential Information belonging to the other.

8.5 For the purpose of The Supplier's undertaking under clauses 8.4, 8.2 and 8.3 above, the Confidential Information shall be deemed to include all The Customer Data.

8.6 Nothing in this clause 8 shall be deemed or construed to prevent The Customer from disclosing any Confidential Information obtained from The Supplier to any consultant, contractor or other person engaged by The Customer in connection herewith, provided that The Customer shall have obtained from the consultant, contractor or other person a signed confidentiality undertaking on substantially the same terms as are contained in this clause 8.

8.7 Nothing in this clause 8 shall prevent The Supplier or The Customer from using data processing techniques, ideas and know-how gained during the performance of this Agreement in the furtherance of its normal business, to the extent that this does not relate to a disclosure of Confidential Information belonging to the other or an infringement by The Customer or The Supplier of any Rights.

9. TERMINATION

9.1 The Customer may at any time by notice in writing terminate this Agreement as from the date of service of such notice if there is a change of control, as defined by section 416 of the Income and Corporation Taxes Act 1988, in The Supplier or its Parent Company. The Customer shall only be permitted to exercise its rights pursuant to this clause 9.1 for six (6) months after any such change of control and shall not be permitted to exercise such rights where The Customer has agreed in advance in writing to the particular change of control and such change of control takes place as proposed. The Supplier shall notify The Customer within one month of any change of control taking place.

9.2 Either party may at any time by notice in writing terminate this Agreement as from the date of service of such notice if the other party passes a resolution, or the Court makes an order that the other party or its Parent Company be wound up otherwise than for the purpose of a bona fide reconstruction or amalgamation, or a receiver, manager or administrator on behalf of a creditor is appointed in respect of the business or any part thereof of the other party or its Parent Company, or circumstances arise which entitle the Court or a creditor to appoint a receiver, manager or administrator or which entitle the Court otherwise than for the purpose of bona fide reconstruction or amalgamation to make a winding-up order, or the other party or its Parent Company is unable to pay its debts within the meaning of section 123 of the Insolvency Act 1985 or any similar event occurs under the law of any other jurisdiction.

9.3   Either party may at any time by notice in writing terminate this Agreement forthwith, if the other is in Default of any obligation and if:

    9.3.1   The Default is capable of remedy and the defaulting party shall have failed to remedy the Default within thirty (30) days of written notice to the defaulting party specifying the Default and requiring its remedies; or

    9.3.2   The Default is not capable of remedy.

10. CONSEQUENCES OF TERMINATION

10.1   Upon termination of this Agreement for any reason:

    10.1.1   any outstanding Charges shall remain due and payable by The Customer to The Supplier in accordance with the terms of this Agreement or, if The Customer has paid any Charges in advance, The Supplier shall repay all such Charges other than money, in respect of any Services or part thereof properly performed in accordance with this Agreement;

    10.1.2   The Supplier shall use all reasonable endeavours to procure the assignment or novation in favour of The Customer or a Replacement Supplier of any equipment leases, maintenance agreement, support agreement or other arrangement between The Supplier and third parties as The Customer may designate which are relevant and necessary for the provision of all Services;

10.2   The Customer shall be entitled to offer any employee or contractor of The Supplier who has been involved in performing The Supplier's obligations hereunder employment or an agreement for services with The Customer and The Supplier agrees that if such person accepts such offer The Supplier shall release such person from an breach of contract with its which such acceptance may otherwise involve;

10.3   Return to The Customer or at The Customer's direction to a Replacement Supplier all Confidential Information and other Customer Data belonging to The Customer and warrant in writing that no copies of any such Confidential Information or The Customer Data have been retained. If The Supplier fails to return such information or any other property of The Customer under its care and control on or before the date of termination, The Customer shall be entitled and is hereby licensed to enter The Supplier's premises and seize the same.

10.4   Immediately upon termation of this Agreement for any reason whatsoever, The Supplier shall, at the sole option of The Customer either return to The Customer or destroy all records, documentation, Customer Data, Software and any other information and all copies thereof which are owned by The Customer.

11. CUSTOMER DATA

11.1   The Supplier acknowledges that Customer Data and all rights of whatever nature in and/or in relation to it shall at all times be and remain the sole property of Customer and The Customer hereby reserves all Rights which may subsist in Customer Data. The Supplier shall not delete or remove any copyright notice contained within or relating to Customer Data.

11.2   The Supplier and The Customer shall each take reasonable precautions (having regard to the nature of their other respective obligations under this Agreement) to preserve the integrity of Customer Data and to prevent any corruption or loss of Customer Data.

11.3   As part of the Services The Supplier shall:

11.3.1   take such steps as are necessary to ensure that, in the event of any corruption or loss of Customer Data howsoever caused, it is in a position to restore or procure the restoration of Customer Data; and

11.3.2   at the request of The Customer in the event of any corruption or loss of The Customer Data and without prejudice to any other remedies that may be available to it either under the Agreement or otherwise, restore or procure the restoration of Customer Data to its state immediately prior to the said corruption or loss.

12. PROTECTION OF PERSONAL DATA

12.1   The Supplier's attention is hereby drawn to the Data Protection Act 1998 and to Directive 95/46/EC of the European Parliament and any regulations implementing it (all referred to together as the 'Data Protection Requirements').

12.2   The Supplier and The Customer each warrant that they will each duly observe all their obligations under the Data Protection Requirements which arise in connection with the Services, Customer Data and Confidential Information.

13. TRANSFER AND SUB-CONTRACTING

13.1   This Agreement is personal to The Supplier. The Supplier shall not assign, novate, sub-contract, or otherwise dispose of this Agreement or any part thereof without the previous consent in writing of The Customer which may be withheld at The Customer's sole discretion.

13.2   The Supplier shall be liable for the acts and omissions of any sub-contractor of The Supplier. Notwithstanding the use of any sub-contractor, The Supplier shall remain solely liable to The Customer for the performance of The Supplier's obligations under this Agreement. This clause 14.2 shall not give any rights to any sub-contractor.

13.3 The Customer shall be entitled to assign novate, sub-contract or otherwise dispose of any or all of its rights and/or obligations under this Agreement to any of its Affiliates or to any person purchasing substantially the whole of the business to which the Services relate.

14. GENERAL

14.1 Entire agreement

This Agreement shall constitute the whole of the terms agreed between the parties hereto in respect of the subject matter of this Agreement provided that nothing in this clause 14.1 shall limit a party's liability for fraudulent misrepresentation.

14.2 Variation

This Agreement shall be capable of being varied only be written instrument by a duly authorised officer or other representative of each of the parties.

14.3 Severability

This Agreement is severable in that if any provision is determined to be illegal or unenforceable by any court of competent jurisdiction such provision shall be deemed to have been deleted without affecting the remaining provisions of this Agreement.

14.4 No partnership

Nothing in this Agreement shall constitute or be deemed to constitute a partnership, agency or joint venture between the parties hereto or constitute or be deemed to constitute either party the agent of the other for any purpose whatsoever and neither party shall have any authority or power to bind the other or to contract in the name of or create a liability against the other.

14.5 Waiver

Unless otherwise agreed in writing, no failure by either party to exercise any right or remedy available to it hereunder nor any delay so to exercise any such right to remedy shall operate as a waiver of it nor shall any single or partial exercise of any right or remedy preclude any other or further exercise thereof or the exercise of any other right or remedy.

14.6 Notices

Any notice to be given hereunder by either party to the other shall be in writing and delivered personally sent by prepaid recorded delivery or registered post to the addressee at the addressee's registered office for the time being or by telex or telefax and shall be deemed to be received if delivered personally at the time of receipt if sent by post at the expiration of 72 hours after being placed in the post (having been correctly addressed) whether or not received or if by telex or telefax 24 hours after despatch to the correct telex number or telefax number of the addressee.

14.7   Third party rights

No third party shall have any rights under the Contracts (Rights of Third Parties) Act 1999 or otherwise in connection with this Agreement.

IN WITNESS whereof the parties hereto have caused this Agreement to be executed by their respective representatives on the day and year first written above.

SIGNED by   )

For and on behalf of   )

Customer   )

in the presence of   )

SIGNED by   )

For and on behalf of   )

Supplier   )

in the presence of   )

SCHEDULE ONE

The Services and the Charges

1.   The Supplier shall provide such services and perform such acts and/ or tasks as shall enable The Customer to perform its obligations of the Development and Publishing Agreements.

2.   The Supplier shall provide such Additional Services as may be agreed by the parties from time to time in accordance with clause 2.3 of this Agreement.

3.   The Supplier shall charge to the Customer its costs for providing for the Services in addition to 10 per cent of the said costs.

Dated   15 December 2004

(1)   FIREFLY HOLDINGS LIMITED

And

(2)   FIREFLY STUDIOS LIMITED

SERVICES AGREEMENT

Speechly Bircham LLP

6 St Andrew Street

London

EC4A 3LX

Ref   3645889-1

Draft

30   Value added reseller agreement and licence

between

OWNER whose principal place of business is at [   ] ('Owner')

and

[   ]a company incorporated under the laws [   ]having its principal place of business at [   ]('VAR').

WHEREAS

Owner is the owner or licensee of all right, title and interest in the computer programs and related documentation described in Schedule A (referred to below as 'the ABC Programs' or 'ABC') and is willing to appoint VAR as a value-added reseller and to grant a limited license to VAR on the terms set out herein.

1.   SCOPE

1.1   Owner hereby appoints VAR as its [non] exclusive value-added reseller in the Market Sector in the Territory. VAR will develop or distribute application software ('VAR's Applications') or modify its existing applications software to run together with ABC and ABC Programs and Owner's software development ABC (SDK) as listed in Schedule A.

2.   TERRITORY

The area in which VAR is granted the right to market ABC is stated in Schedule A ('the Territory').

3.   DEVELOPMENT LICENSE

3.1   VAR is granted a non-exclusive royalty-free right to market ABC only with VAR's Applications to end-user clients within the Territory and the right to reproduce and distribute the executable files created using ABC as part of VAR's Applications PROVIDED THAT:

3.1.1   VAR includes a valid Owner copyright notice on VAR's Applications and that VAR does not otherwise use Owner's name, logo or trademarks in connection with VAR's Applications. All applications developed by VAR must make software version information easily and clearly available to the user in a substantially similar manner to the ABC splash screen and components form.

3.1.2   VAR agrees to indemnify, hold harmless, and defend Owner and its suppliers from and against any claims or lawsuits, including legal fees, that arise or result from the use or distribution of VAR's Applications;

3.1.3   VAR does not permit further distribution of such executable files by VAR's end-user.

3.2   The right granted above does not however remove the requirement for each user of ABC to acquire a license for ABC and to use ABC in accordance with the provisions of the then-current ABC license. Applications developed by the VAR under this Agreement may only be supplied to users who have a valid license to use ABC. VAR will ensure that its end-users accept all the terms and conditions of the ABC license before assuming any legal obligation to supply any VAR Application or any copy of the ABC.

3.3   Owner shall supply VAR with one set of documentation and software media.

3.4   Owner may at its sole discretion provide updates and upgrades of ABC including beta and pre-release versions of ABC that have not yet been made public. All such updates and upgrades will be supplied in accordance with the terms of the Owner maintenance agreement in Schedule B.

3.5   The right of VAR to use ABC pursuant to the ABC Development License is restricted to the site address designated by VAR and shown in the 'Designated Site Address' in Schedule A.

4.   OWNER OBLIGATIONS

4.1   Owner will provide ABC licenses for signature by end-user customers of the VAR prior to the supply of ABC to such customers.

4.2   Owner will provide a copy of the relevant documentation in [Microsoft Word] format.

4.3   Owner will provide product information to VAR, which may include information that has not yet been made public.

4.4   Owner will provide a start-up package as detailed in Schedule A including training in the development of applications for employees of VAR.

4.5   Owner will provide by phone, fax or electronic mail technical support to the VAR as detailed in Schedule A. Technical support provided by Owner to VAR under this Agreement should in no way imply responsibility for progress or results of VAR's Applications.

4.6   Where VAR is providing end user support for ABC, Owner will provide back-up to that support in accordance with the Owner standard maintenance agreement attached herewith as Schedule B. The fee for such support is defined in Schedule A.

4.7   Owner agrees to provide VAR, at the sole discretion of Owner, such marketing support as is appropriate to VAR's industry and requirements.

4.8   Owner shall provide assistance, if requested by VAR, with the preparation of a business plan pertinent to ABC.

4.9   Owner may assist VAR with the preparation and negotiation of tenders for the supply of VAR's Applications. Such assistance will be costed at the special day rate shown in Schedule A but only charged to VAR if the tender is successful.

5. WARRANTY

5.1   Warranty: Owner warrants that for a period of ninety days from delivery ABC shall perform substantially in accordance with the published specification of ABC, current at the time of installation. Further, Owner warrants that use of ABC will not to its knowledge infringe any copyright, trade secret or proprietary interest of any third party.

5.2   Warranty Exclusions: OWNER DOES NOT WARRANT THAT THE FUNCTIONS OF THE SOFTWARE WILL MEET THE ANY PARTICULAR REQUIREMENTS OR THAT THE OPERATION OF THE SOFTWARE WILL BE ENTIRELY ERROR-FREE OR THAT ALL PROGRAM DEFECTS ARE CAPABLE OF CORRECTION OR IMPROVEMENT. ALL OTHER WARRANTIES INCLUDING ANY IMPLIED WARRANTIES OF MERCHANTIBILITY, MERCHANTABLE QUALITY, SATISFACTORY QUALITY OR FITNESS FOR PURPOSE OR ABILITY TO ACHIEVE A PARTICULAR RESULT ARE HEREBY EXCLUDED. IN THE ABSENCE OF FRAUD, NO ORAL OR WRITTEN INFORMATION OR ADVICE GIVEN BY OWNER OR ITS AGENTS, DISTRIBUTORS, OR DEALERS SHALL CREATE A WARRANTY OR GIVE RISE TO ANY OTHER LIABILITY OTHER THAN IS GIVEN IN THIS AGREEMENT. LICENSEE'S STATUTORY RIGHTS AS A CONSUMER (IF ANY) ARE NOT AFFECTED BY THESE TERMS AND CONDITIONS.

6. VAR OBLIGATIONS

VAR shall:

6.1   Actively promote the sale of ABC with VAR's Applications in the Territory.

6.2   Provide end-user documentation.

6.3   Customise ABC to meet its market needs.

6.4   Provide full ABC support for its customers. All support provided by Owner will be to the VAR and not to the end user.

6.5   Provide its ABC customers with training in the use of VAR's Applications.

6.6   Provide and maintain a satisfactory level of technical and sales staff that are familiar with ABC.

6.7   For support purposes, VAR shall provide Owner with a copy of all of VAR's Applications together with documentation and ancillary material. All such software and documentation will be treated as confidential by Owner unless Owner is given a license to demonstrate any of VAR's Applications.

6.8   Where VAR provides Owner with a license to demonstrate VAR's Applications, such license will be without cost.

6.9   VAR will pay support fees as listed in the attached Schedule A.

6.10   VAR shall prepare a business plan for VAR's Applications to include sales predictions, marketing and development strategy forecasts. The business plan shall be submitted in writing, shall be for a minimum of six months and be updated on a monthly basis and should include prospect names. All such information will be subject to the requirements of confidentiality set out below.

6.11   VAR will ensure adequate product orientation and training is provided to all its ABC end users.

7.   ABC LICENSE PURCHASE PROCEDURE

7.1   When VAR has agreed to supply a licence to use VAR's Application to an end user, and in any event whenever VAR intends to make ABC available to a third party, VAR shall issue a purchase order to Owner for the required number of ABC licenses which must include:

   7.1.1   The name and address of the end user;

   7.1.2   The platform and operating system being used;

   7.1.3   The level of Software Support and Maintenance requested by the end user; and

   7.1.4   Confirmation that end user has agreed to the then-current ABC licence terms.

7.2   Owner will deliver to VAR either on suitable media or electronically by way of copy authorisation, the number of licensed copies ordered.

7.3   Owner will invoice VAR for the licenses ordered at the prices and discounts detailed in Schedule A.

8. DISCOUNTS

8.1   VAR will be entitled to a discount of 25% of the net end-user prices for a licence to use ABC as shown in Schedule A.

8.2   Owner reserves the right to change its discounts at any time before any order for particular products or services becomes binding under applicable law. During any period up to 90 days following a discount change, Owner will honour the discounts prevailing prior to the discount change if VAR has used the previous discounts as a basis for an VAR quotation, provided that the VAR quotation has a 90 days validity period or less, is binding on VAR and has been issued in good faith prior to the effective date of the Owner discount change.

8.3   Maintenance fees charged by VAR in accordance with the rates shown in Schedule A will be apportioned on the basis of one third to VAR and two thirds to Owner.

9. PAYMENT

All invoices raised by Owner to VAR are payable within 30 days of the invoice date.

10. PRICING

10.1   Local country market conditions dictate pricing for ABC licences. VAR agrees to obtain local prices for ABC from Owner when permitted by Owner to sell outside the Territory defined herein. Such permission must be obtained in writing and will not be unreasonably withheld.

10.2   Owner reserves the right to change its prices at any time before any order for particular products or services becomes binding under Texan law. During any period up to 90 days following a price change, Owner will honour the prices prevailing prior to the price change if VAR has used the previous prices as a basis for an VAR quotation, provided that the VAR quotation has a 90 days validity period or less, is binding on VAR and has been issued in good faith prior to the effective date of the Owner price change.

11. CONFIDENTIAL INFORMATION

11.1   VAR agrees that it will maintain all information disclosed to it by Owner ('Confidential Information') in confidence and will not disclose this information to any third party. Confidential Information includes any knowledge and information disclosed in connection with this Agreement directly or indirectly as well as all data derived therefrom, to the extent that such knowledge and information at the time of the said disclosure or acquisition is not, as can be established by the receiving party:

11.1.1   in the lawful and unrestricted possession of the receiving party; or

11.1.2   part of public knowledge or literature.

11.2   VAR further agrees not to make any commercial use of such Confidential Information for any purpose, or to disassemble, inspect, or perform any analysis on any material submitted hereunder except as specifically agreed to by Owner, except to the extent that Owner is unable to prevent such activities by virtue of any applicable legislation.

11.3   All documents, designs, or sample files submitted to VAR shall remain the property of Owner and shall be returned to Owner immediately upon termination of this Agreement.

12. LEGAL RELATIONSHIP

VAR is an independent contractor and not an employee, partner, joint venturer or agent of Owner, nor shall it hold itself out as such. Neither Owner nor VAR shall purport to undertake any obligation on the other party's behalf nor expose the other party to any liability or pledge or purport to pledge the other party's credit.

13. PUBLICITY

Neither party shall release publicity relating to or connected in any way with this Agreement or any resulting contracts to the news media or general public without obtaining prior approval by the other party, which approval shall not be unreasonably withheld.

14. TRADEMARKS

14.1   Each party shall refrain from any improper or wrongful use of the other's trademarks or intellectual property and each party shall use reasonable efforts to safeguard the proprietary nature of such information.

14.2   Neither party shall obtain nor try to obtain nor register for itself anywhere in the world any trade marks or trade names the same as or similar to the tradenames or trade-marks of the other.

14.3   Neither party will adopt for its own use nor for use by any third party any word or mark which is similar to or likely to be confused with tradenames or trade-marks used by the other without the other's prior written consent.

14.4   VAR shall not, in furtherance of marketing ABC, use in connection with any of VAR's trade marks any colour combinations, typefaces, or other distinctive features identical with or similar to those used by Owner in connection with its business.

15. SUB-CONTRACT

VAR may desire to sub-contract the development of VAR's Applications to third parties. In the event VAR desires to sub-contract this development it shall first obtain approval from Owner for the appointment of the sub-contractor. Owner shall only approve a sub-contractor if the person(s) undertaking the sub-contract have satisfactorily completed the Owner developer training program and the sub-contractor signs Owner's 'Software Loan Agreement'. VAR warrants and undertakes that:

15.1　The sub-contractor shall maintain the confidentiality of all proprietary information relating to ABC.

15.2　The contract for supply of VAR's Application to the end user shall remain with the VAR.

16. CHANGE OF OWNERSHIP & INSOLVENCY

Notwithstanding any provisions herein contained this agreement may be terminated forthwith by either party by notice in writing from the party not at fault if any of the following events shall occur:

16.1　The other party shall commit any act of bankruptcy, shall have a receiving order made against it, shall make or negotiate for any composition or arrangement with or assignment for the benefit of its creditors or if the other party being a body corporate, shall present a petition or have a petition presented by a creditor for its winding up or shall enter into any liquidation (other than for the purpose of reconstruction or amalgamation), shall call any meeting of its creditors, shall have a receiver of all or any of its undertakings or assets appointed, or shall cease to carry on business;

16.2　any substantially similar event to those specified in Clause 16.1 occurs under the laws of another jurisdiction;

16.3　There is at any time a material change in the management, ownership or control of the other party which creates a material conflict of interest with the party serving notice of termination.

17. OWNER INDEMNITIES

17.1　Owner warrants that it has the right to enter into and perform its obligations under this Agreement and will indemnify VAR against any loss or expense (including reasonable lawyer's fees and expenses) as a result of any claim that the normal use or possession of ABC and associated documentation infringes the intellectual property rights of any third party, provided that the claim does not arise as a result of the use of ABC and associated documentation otherwise than in accordance with the terms of this Agreement or the ABC License Agreement and subject to the following conditions:

17.1.1　VAR must promptly notify Owner in writing of any allegation of infringement.

17.1.2 VAR must make no admission without Owner's consent.

17.1.3 VAR must, at Owner's request, allow Owner to conduct and/or settle all negotiations and litigation and must give Owner all reasonable assistance at Owner's expense. The cost incurred or recovered in such negotiations and litigation will be for Owner's account with equitable allowance for pro rata offset of related VAR legal fees.

17.2 Owner will have the right to change all or part of ABC and associated documentation or to grant or obtain licences for the use of all or part of the ABC in order to avoid litigation.

17.3 Failure of VAR to notify Owner under this clause shall not relieve Owner of its obligations thereunder except to the extent that Owner is prejudiced by such failure. VAR may participate in its own defence at its own expense.

18. VAR INDEMNITIES

VAR will indemnify and defend Owner from any losses or expenses (including reasonable attorney's fees and expenses) incurred by Owner by reason of:

18.1 Any material breach by VAR of its material obligations under this Agreement, including any misrepresentation by VAR of its authority hereunder;

18.2 The manner in which VAR may market ABC, save where such marketing was in accordance with Owner marketing guidelines;

18.3 The supply by VAR of VAR's Application or of any products or services for use in conjunction with or in relation to ABC;

18.4 Any warranty offered to VAR's customers extending beyond the terms of Owner's warranty.

19. TERM AND TERMINATION

19.1 The term of this Agreement will begin on the date Owner confirms acceptance of this Agreement ('the Effective Date') and will be renewed on a yearly basis, subject to Clause 19.2 below, unless and until terminated by either party upon at least 60 days' written notice expiring on any anniversary of the Effective Date.

19.2 VAR agrees that for annual renewal of this Agreement, it must comply with Owner's then current terms and conditions - including the payment of the annual Development License fee as stated in Schedule A. Such fee shall be paid to Owner by VAR within 30 days of the renewal date.

19.3 Either party may terminate this Agreement immediately if the other fails to perform any obligation contained in this Agreement upon defaulting party receiving notice of default and failing to remedy the default before the conclusion of a 30 day cure period.

19.4 Should termination occur under the provisions of this Agreement, VAR will continue to be able to purchase additional ABC Licenses at the standard suggested list prices shown in Schedule A or as changed from time to time. This provision is to allow VAR to provide continued support to existing end users and to support any existing applications developed by VAR using ABC. VAR will return to Owner or destroy any copies of ABC and other materials supplied by Owner that are not needed by VAR for residual support activities.

19.5 Termination of this Agreement for any reason shall not affect any accrued rights or liabilities which either party shall have to the other, nor shall it affect the coming into force of any provision hereunder which is expressly or by implication intended to come into or continue in force on or after such termination.

19.6 The provisions of Confidentiality set out in this Agreement shall survive termination of this Agreement for a period of 18 months from the date of such termination.

20. INABILITY TO PERFORM MATERIAL OBLIGATIONS

Neither party shall be liable for failure to perform or delay in performing any material obligations hereunder where such failure or delay is caused solely by any circumstances beyond its control, including Acts of God, war and civil commotion, provided that if such failure to perform its material obligations hereunder, or delay in performance of its material obligations hereunder, exceeds a continuous period of 3 months, this Agreement may be terminated immediately by notice in writing from either party.

21. NO AGENCY

No agency, partnership, joint venture or other joint relationship is created hereby and neither party shall have any authority of any kind to commit the other to any legally binding obligation, nor shall it hold itself out as having such authority.

22. ENTIRE AGREEMENT

This agreement (including any amendments, exhibits, or teaming statements executed from time to time by the parties) supersedes all prior agreement, arrangements and undertakings between the parties and constitutes the entire agreement between the parties related to the subject matter hereof. All other agreements prior to the date hereof between Owner and VAR are hereby terminated. No addition to or modification of any provision of this Agreement shall be effective unless signed by an authorised representative of each of the parties. The entire contents of this Agreement are to be held confidential by both Owner and VAR. No exclusivity is provided to either party under this Agreement.

23. NOTICES

Any notice given hereunder shall be deemed to have been sufficiently served if sent in writing by prepaid certified mail, communicated by fax or my e-mail addressed to the last known address of the addressee and the same shall be deemed to have been served when in the ordinary course of transmission it would have been received.

24. CONSTRUCTION AND APPLICABLE LAW

24.1 This Agreement shall be governed and construed in accordance with the laws of [ ], save that Owner shall have the right at its absolute discretion to initiate proceedings to recover sums owing to it and/or to enforce its intellectual property rights in the courts of any jurisdiction in which VAR carries on business, in which assets of VAR are located, or in which ABC is used. If either party shall invoke legal proceedings, of any nature, to enforce the terms and conditions of this Agreement, or to impose a claim for damages against a breaching party, the prevailing party shall be entitled to recover its reasonable attorneys' fees and costs.

24.2 The headings of clauses in this Agreement are included herein for convenience and shall not be considered in construing this Agreement.

24.3 In the event that any of these terms, conditions, or provisions shall be determined invalid, unlawful, or unenforceable to any extent, such term, condition, or provision shall be severed from the remaining terms, conditions, or provisions which shall continue to be valid to the fullest extent permitted by law.

24.4 No amendment, modification, or waiver of any provision of this Agreement shall be effective unless it is set forth in writing and authorised by representatives of both parties.

25. LIABILITY

25.1 Personal Injury & Death: Owner will indemnify VAR and its end-user customers for personal injury or death caused by the negligence of its employees in connection with the performance of their duties hereunder, or by defects in any product supplied pursuant to this Agreement.

25.2 Tangible Property: Owner will indemnify VAR and its end-user customers for direct damage to tangible property caused by the negligence of its employees in connection with the performance of their duties hereunder, or by defects in any product supplied pursuant to this Agreement. OWNER'S TOTAL LIABILITY UNDER THIS CLAUSE SHALL BE LIMITED TO [ ] FOR ANY ONE EVENT OR SERIES OF CONNECTED EVENTS.

25.3 Delay: WHILE OWNER SHALL USE REASONABLE COMMERCIAL EFFORTS TO MEET DELIVERY AND SUPPLY TIMES, VAR'S

ONLY REMEDY FOR UNREASONABLE DELAY IN SUPPLYING PRODUCTS OR SERVICES WILL BE THE RIGHT TO TERMINATE THIS AGREEMENT AFTER SERVICE OF NOTICE OF BREACH AS PROVIDED FOR ELSEWHERE IN THIS AGREEMENT.

25.4   Other Exclusions: SAVE IN RESPECT OF CLAIMS FOR DEATH OR PERSONAL INJURY ARISING FROM OWNER'S NEGLIGENCE, IN NO EVENT WILL OWNER BE LIABLE FOR ANY DAMAGES RESULTING FROM LOSS OF DATA OR USE, LOST PROFITS, LOSS OF ANTICIPATED SAVINGS, NOR FOR ANY DAMAGES THAT ARE AN INDIRECT OR SECONDARY CONSEQUENCE OF ANY ACT OR OMISSION OF OWNER, WHETHER SUCH DAMAGES WERE REASONABLY FORESEEABLE OR ACTUALLY FORESEEN.

25.5   Maximum Liability: EXCEPT AS PROVIDED ABOVE IN THE CASE OF PERSONAL INJURY, DEATH, AND DAMAGE TO TANGIBLE PROPERTY, OWNER'S MAXIMUM LIABILITY TO VAR AND ITS END-USER CUSTOMER FOR ANY CAUSE WHATSOEVER (WHETHER IN THE FORM OF THE ADDITIONAL COST OF REMEDIAL SERVICES OR OTHERWISE) WILL BE FOR DIRECT COSTS AND DAMAGES ONLY, AND WILL BE LIMITED TO A SUM EQUIVALENT TO THE PRICE PAID TO OWNER FOR THE PRODUCTS OR SERVICES THAT ARE THE SUBJECT OF VAR AND ITS END-USER CUSTOMER'S CLAIM, PLUS DAMAGES LIMITED TO TWENTY-FIVE PER CENT OF THE SAME AMOUNT FOR ANY ADDITIONAL COSTS DIRECTLY, REASONABLY AND NECESSARILY INCURRED BY VAR AND ITS END-USER CUSTOMER IN OBTAINING ALTERNATIVE PRODUCTS AND/OR SERVICES.

25.6   General: All liability that is not expressly assumed in this Agreement is hereby excluded. These limitations will apply regardless of the form of action, whether under statute, in contract, tort, including negligence, or any other form of action. For the purposes of this Clause, 'Owner' includes its employees, sub-contractors and suppliers. VAR acknowledges that Owner has been appointed as the agent of its employees, sub-contractors and suppliers to agree the provisions of this on their behalf.

The undersigned affirm that they are authorised to sign this Agreement for their respective companies.

For Owner   _____   For VAR   _____

Name: _____   Name: _____

Title: _____   Title: _____

Date: _____   Date: _____

Signature: _____   Signature: _____

SCHEDULE A

ABC LICENSES

Please note that licenses will be issued only to named end-user clients. Discount levels are solely attained as shown below. All license prices are end user prices.

ABC

License Number   Price per License ($)

Discounts apply to licenses purchased by VAR with a single purchase order in the stated band of quantities.

VAR DISCOUNTS

VAR shall receive a discount deducted from the End User License Prices as follows:

Annual purchase value   Discount

Annual purchases date from the effective date of this Agreement and future anniversaries thereof. Values are the net invoice value of sales by Owner to VAR.

Discounts apply to purchases in the stated band of values.

ABC DEVELOPMENT LICENSE

Right to Develop   per annum per site

to include telephone support and upgrades

DESIGNATED SITE ADDRESS

VAR designates the following site for the use of ABC Development License:

Start up Package

Owner will provide initial training and support for VAR's personnel as follows:

Up to 10 days training at [   ] per day exclusive of expenses.

Up to 10 days Consultancy at [   ] per day exclusive of expenses.

This start up package must be agreed and purchased at the time of signing this VAR agreement.

ADDITIONAL ASSISTANCE

Additional assistance is available by arrangement with Owner at [   ] per day.

Territory   (to be agreed)

SOFTWARE MAINTENANCE AND WARRANTY

ABC is supplied with a 90-day warranty as shown in the software license agreement. After that period, all software maintenance and support is provided as detailed below.

VAR will offer software maintenance and support to its ABC customers in accordance with Schedule B on the following terms:

Full Maintenance to include Maintenance and Support with Upgrades all as detailed in Schedule B   % of the software list price.

Support Maintenance to include Maintenance and Support only. (Upgrades when available will be offered for a separate fee).   % of the software list price.

ASSISTANCE WITH TENDERS

Special deferred rate for assistance to VAR by Owner as detailed in clause 4.9 – [   ] per day

SCHEDULE B

SOFTWARE MAINTENANCE AND SUPPORT

Subject to the terms and conditions herein Owner agrees to provide the Maintenance and Support Service as described below for ABC installed at the VAR's address quoted in this Agreement or clients address advised to us, provided that the annual Maintenance and Support Service Fee for the period during which such support has been requested has been fully paid.

The Maintenance and Support Service to be provided by Owner is as follows:

The Maintenance and Support Service support shall be provided by Owner and its agents designated as qualified for the purpose by telephone, mail, E-mail or fax during normal working hours of Owner or its agents on Mondays to Fridays. Owner's normal working hours are in the period 9:00 a.m. to 5:00 p.m. from Monday to Friday but excluding public holidays.

Owner will use its reasonable endeavours to resolve any defects or 'bugs' in ABC and supply VAR with revised versions of same.

Owner will use reasonable endeavours to deal promptly with defects in ABC by making available its personnel.

When the VAR requests support on site, agreed travel, accommodation and subsistence expenses incurred by personnel working away from Owner's offices in the execution of these obligations shall be for the VAR's account and shall be payable within 30 days of invoicing of the VAR by Owner at the invoice address set forth herein.

Updates of the technical manuals relating to ABC in hard copy will be forwarded to the VAR on request as they become available, at the agreed costs of reproduction and postage. Obligations of confidence set forth in this Agreement apply to such updates.

Software Upgrades

Where VAR's customer is on Full Maintenance, they will receive at least one upgrade per calendar year included within the service covered by the maintenance fee.

Where VAR's customer has contracted for Support Maintenance only, upgrades will be offered when available for a fee, which will be quoted at the time of release.

Upgrades provided as an inclusive part of the standard software maintenance agreement will be limited to those which are within the same ABC platform architecture.

31 Standard contractual clauses (controller to processors)

Issued by EC Decision of 5th February 2010

For the purposes of Article 26(2) of Directive 95/46/EC for the transfer of personal data to processors established in third countries which do not ensure an adequate level of data protection

Name of the data exporting organisation: ....

Address: ....

Tel: .... Fax: .... email: ....

Other information needed to identify the organisation

....

(the data **exporter**)

And

Name of the data exporting organisation: ....

Address: ....

Tel: .... Fax: .... email: ....

Other information needed to identify the organisation

....

(the data **importer**)

each a **Party**: together the **parties**

HAVE AGREED on the following Contractual Clauses (the Clauses) in order to adduce adequate safeguards with respect to the protection of privacy and fundamental rights and freedoms of individuals for the transfer by the data exporter to the data importer of the personal data specified in Appendix 1.

CLAUSE I

Definitions

For the purposes of the Clauses:

(a) 'personal data', 'special categories of data', 'process/processing', 'controller', 'processor', 'data subject' and 'supervisory authority' shall have the same meaning as in Directive 95/46/EC of the European Parliament and of the Council of 24 October 1995 on the protection of individuals with regard to the processing of personal data and on the free movement of such data[1];

(b) 'the data exporter' means the controller who transfers the personal data;

(c) 'the data importer' means the processor who agrees to receive from the data exporter personal data intended for processing on his behalf after the transfer in accordance with his instructions and the terms of the Clauses and who is not subject to a third country's system ensuring adequate protection within the meaning of Article 25 (1) of Directive 95/46/EC;

(d) 'the sub-processor' means any processor engaged by the data importer or by any other sub-processor of the data importer who agrees to receive from the data importer or from any other sub-processor of the data importer personal data exclusively intended for processing activities to be carried out on behalf of the data exporter after the transfer in accordance with his instructions, the terms of the Clauses and the terms of the written subcontract;

(e) 'the applicable data protection law' means the legislation protecting the fundamental rights and freedoms of individuals and, in particular, their right to privacy with respect to the processing of personal data applicable to a data controller in the Member State in which the data exporter is established;

(f) 'technical and organisational security measures' means those measures aimed at protecting personal data against accidental or unlawful destruction or accidental loss, alteration, unauthorised disclosure or access, in particular where the processing involves the transmission of data over a network, and against all other unlawful forms of processing.

CLAUSE 2

Details of the transfer

The details of the transfer and in particular the special categories of personal data where applicable are specified in Appendix 1 which forms an integral part of the Clauses,

---

1 Parties may reproduce definitions and meanings contained in Directive 95/46/EC within this Clause if they considered it better for the contract to stand alone.

CLAUSE 3

Third-party beneficiary clause

1. The data subject can enforce against the data exporter this Clause, Clause 4(b) to (i), Clause 5(a) to (e), and (g) to (j), Clause 6(1) and (2), Clause 7, Clause 8(2), and Clauses 9 to 12 as third-party beneficiary.

2. The data subject can enforce against the data importer this Clause, Clause 5(a) to (e) and (g), Clause 6, Clause 7, Clause 8(2), and Clauses 9 to 12, in cases where the data exporter has factually disappeared or has ceased to exist in law unless any successor entity has assumed the entire legal obligations of the data exporter by contract or by operation of law, as a result of which it takes on the rights and obligations of the data exporter, in which case the data subject can enforce them against such entity.

3. The data subject can enforce against the sub-processor this Clause, Clause 5(a) to (e) and (g), Clause 6, Clause 7, Clause 8(2), and Clauses 9 to 12, in cases where both the data exporter and the data importer have factually disappeared or ceased to exist in law or have become insolvent. unless any successor entity has assumed the entire legal obligations of the data exporter by contract or by operation of law as a result of which it rakes on the rights and obligations of the data exporter, in which case the data subject can enforce them against such entity. Such third-party liability of the sub-processor shall be limited to its own processing operations under the Clauses.

4. The parties do not object to a data subject being represented by an association or other body if the data subject so expressly wishes and if permitted by national law.

CLAUSE 4

Obligations of the data exporter

The data exporter agrees and warrants:

(a) that the processing, including the transfer itself, of the personal data has been and will continue to be carried out in accordance with the relevant provisions of the applicable data protection law (and, where applicable, has been notified to the relevant authorities of the Member State where the data exporter is established) and does not violate the relevant provisions of that State;

(b) that it has instructed and throughout the duration of the personal data-processing services will instruct the data importer to process the personal data transferred only on the data exporter's behalf and in accordance with the applicable data protection law and the Clauses:

(c) that the data importer will provide sufficient guarantees in respect of the technical and organisational security measures specified in Appendix 2 to this contract;

(d)   that after assessment of the requirements of the applicable data protection law, the security measures are appropriate to protect personal data against accidental or unlawful destruction or accidental loss, alteration, unauthorised disclosure or access, in particular where the processing involves the transmission of data over a network, and against all other unlawful forms of processing, and that these measures ensure a level of security appropriate to the risks presented by the processing and the nature of the data to be protected having regard to the state of the art and the cost of their implementation;

(e)   that it will ensure compliance with the security measures;

(f)   that, if the transfer involves special categories of data, the data subject has been informed or will be informed before. or as soon as possible after, the transfer that its data could be transmitted to a third country not providing adequate protection within the meaning of Directive 95/46/EC;

(g)   to forward any notification received from the data importer or any sub-processor pursuant to Clause 5(b) and Clause 8(3) to the data protection supervisory authority if the data exporter decides to continue the transfer or to lift the suspension;

(h)   to make available to the data subjects upon request a copy of the Clauses, with the exception of Appendix 2, and a summary description of the security measures, as well as a copy of any contract for sub-processing services which has to be made in accordance with the Clauses, unless the Clauses or the contract contain commercial information, in which case it may remove such commercial information;

(i)   that, in the event of sub-processing, the processing activity is carried out in accordance with Clause 11 by a sub-processor providing at least the same level of protection for the personal data and the rights of data subject as the data importer under the Clauses; and

(j)   that it will ensure compliance with Clause 4(a) to (i).

CLAUSE 5

Obligations of the data importer[2]

The data importer agrees and warrants:

---

2   Mandatory requirements of the national legislation applicable to the data importer which do not go beyond what is necessary in a democratic society on the basis of one of the interests listed in Article 13(1) of Directive 95/46/EC: that is, if they constitute a necessary measure to safeguard national security. defence, public security, the prevention. Investigation, detection and prosecution of criminal offences or of breaches of ethics for the regulated professions, an important economic or financial interest of the State or the protection of the data subject or the rights and freedoms of others, are not in contradiction with the standard contractual clauses, Some examples of such mandatory requirements which do not go beyond what is necessary in a democratic society are, inter alia, internationally recognised sanctions, tax-reporting requirements or anti-money-laundering reporting requirements.

(a) to process the personal data only on behalf of the data exporter and in compliance with its instructions and the Clauses; if it cannot provide such compliance for whatever reasons, it agrees to inform promptly the data exporter of its inability to comply. in which case the data exporter is entitled to suspend the transfer of data and/or terminate the contract;

(b) that it has no reason to believe that the legislation applicable to it prevents it from fulfilling the instructions received from the data exporter and its obligations under the contract and that in the event of a change in this legislation which is likely to have a substantial adverse effect on the warranties and obligations provided by the Clauses, it will promptly notify the change to the data exporter as soon as it is aware. in which case the data exporter is entitled to suspend the transfer of data and/or terminate the contract;

(c) that it has implemented the technical and organisational security measures specified in Appendix 2 before processing the personal data transferred;

(d) that it will promptly notify the data exporter about:

(i) any legally binding request for disclosure of the personal data by a law enforcement authority unless otherwise prohibited, such as a prohibition under criminal law to preserve the confidentiality of a law enforcement investigation;

(ii) any accidental or unauthorised access; and

(iii) any request received directly from the data subjects without responding to that request, unless it has been otherwise authorised to do so;

(e) to deal promptly and properly with all inquiries from the data exporter relating to its processing of the personal data subject to the transfer and to abide by the advice of the supervisory authority with regard to the processing of the data transferred;

(f) at the request of the data exporter to submit its data-processing facilities for audit of the processing activities covered by the Clauses which shall be carried out by the data exporter or an inspection body composed of independent members and in possession of the required professional qualifications bound by a duty of confidentiality, selected by the data exporter, where applicable, in agreement with the supervisory authority:

(g) to make available to the data subject upon request a copy of the Clauses, or any existing contract for sub-processing, unless the Clauses or contract contain commercial information, in which case it may remove such commercial information, with the exception of Appendix 2 which shall be replaced by a summary description of the security measures in those cases where the data subject is unable to obtain a copy from the data exporter;

(h) that, in the event of sub-processing. it has previously informed the data exporter and obtained its prior written consent;

(i)   that the processing services by the sub-processor will be carried out in accordance with Clause 11:

(j)   to send promptly a copy of any sub-processor agreement it concludes under the Clauses to the data exporter.

CLAUSE 6

Liability

1.   The parties agree that any data subject, who has suffered damage as a result of any breach of the obligations referred to in Clause 3 or in Clause 11 by any party or sub-processor is entitled to receive compensation from the data exporter for the damage suffered.

2.   If a data subject is not able to bring a claim for compensation in accordance with paragraph 1 against the data exporter, arising out of a breach by the data importer or his sub-processor of any of their obligations referred to in Clause 3 or in Clause 11, because the data exporter has factually disappeared or ceased to exist in law or has become insolvent, the data importer agrees that the data subject may issue a claim against the data importer as if it were the data exporter, unless any successor entity has assumed the entire legal obligations of the data exporter by contract of by operation of law. in which case the data subject can enforce its rights against such entity.

The data importer may not rely on a breach by a sub-processor of its obligations in order to avoid its own liabilities.

3.   If a data subject is not able to bring a claim against the data exporter or the data importer referred to in paragraphs 1 and 2, arising out of a breach by the sub-processor of any of their obligations referred to in Clause 3 or in Clause 11 because both the data exporter and the data importer have factually disappeared or ceased to exist in law or have become insolvent, the sub-processor agrees that the data subject may issue a claim against the data sub-processor with regard to its own processing operations under the Clauses as if it were the data exporter or the data importer, unless any successor entity has assumed the entire legal obligations of the data exporter or data importer by contract or by operation of law, in which case the data subject can enforce its rights against such entity. The liability of the sub-processor shall be limited to its own processing operations under the Clauses.

CLAUSE 7

Mediation and jurisdiction

1.   The data importer agrees that if the data subject invokes against it third-party beneficiary rights and/or claims compensation for damages under the Clauses, the data importer will accept the decision of the data subject:

(a)   to refer the dispute to mediation, by an independent person or, where applicable, by the supervisory authority;

(b)   to refer the dispute to the courts in the Member State in which the data exporter is established.

2.   The parties agree that the choice made by the data subject will not prejudice its substantive or procedural rights to seek remedies in accordance with other previsions of national or international law.

CLAUSE 8

Co-operation with supervisory authorities

1.   The data exporter agrees to deposit a copy of this contract with the supervisory authority if it so requests or if such deposit is required under the applicable data protection law.

2.   The parties agree that the supervisory authority has the right to conduct an audit of the data importer, and of any sub-processor, which has the same scope and is subject to the same conditions as would apply to an audit of the data exporter under the applicable data protection law.

3.   The data importer shall promptly inform the data exporter about the existence of legislation applicable to it or any sub-processor preventing the conduct of an audit of the data importer, or any sub-processor, pursuant to paragraph 2. In such a case the data exporter shall be entitled to take the measures foreseen in Clause 5(b).

CLAUSE 9

Governing law

The Clauses shall be governed by the law of the Member State in which the data exporter is established, namely ....

CLAUSE 10

Variation of the contract

The parties undertake not to vary or modify the Clauses. This does not preclude the parties from adding clauses on business related issues where required as long as they do not contradict the Clause.

CLAUSE 11

Sub-processing

1.   The data importer shall not subcontract any of its processing operations performed on behalf of the data exporter under the Clauses without the

prior written consent of the data exporter. Where the data importer subcontracts its obligations under the Clauses, with the consent of the data exporter, it shall do so only by way of a written agreement with the sub-processor which imposes the same obligations on the sub-processor as are imposed on the data importer under the Clauses[3]. Where the sub-processor fails to fulfil its data protection obligations under such written agreement the data importer shall remain fully liable to the data exporter for the performance of the sub-processor's obligations under such agreement.

2. The prior written contract between the data importer and the sub-processor shall also provide for a third-party beneficiary clause as laid down in Clause 3 for cases where the data subject is not able to bring the claim for compensation referred to in paragraph 1 of Clause 6 against the data exporter or the data importer because they have factually disappeared or have ceased to exist in law or have become insolvent and no successor entity has assumed the entire legal obligations of the data exporter or data importer by contract or by operation of law. Such third-party liability of the sub-processor shall be limited to its own processing operations under the Clauses.

3. The provisions relating to data protection aspects for sub-processing of the contract referred to in paragraph 1 shall be governed by the law of the Member State in which the data exporter is established, namely ....

4. The data exporter shall keep a list of sub-processing agreements concluded under the Clauses and notified by the data importer pursuant to Clause 5(j), which shall be updated at least once a year. The list shall be available to the data exporter's data protection supervisory authority.

CLAUSE 12

Obligation after the termination of personal data-processing services

1. The parties agree that on the termination of the provision of data-processing services, the data importer and the sub-processor shall, at the choice of the data exporter, return all the personal data transferred and the copies thereof to the data exporter or shall destroy all the personal data and certify to the data exporter that it has done so, unless legislation imposed upon the data importer prevents it from returning or destroying all or part of the personal data transferred. In that case, the data importer warrants that it will guarantee the confidentiality of the personal data transferred and will not actively process the personal data transferred anymore.

---

3 This requirement may be satisfied by the sub-processor co-signing the contract entered into between the data exporter and the data importer under this Decision.

2.   The data importer and the sub-processor warrant that upon request of the data exporter and/or of the supervisory authority, it will submit its data-processing facilities for an audit of the measures referred to in paragraph 1.

On behalf of the data exporter:

Name (written out in full): ....

Position: ....

Address: ....

Other information necessary in order for the contract to be binding (if any):

Signature: ....

(stamp of organisation)

On behalf of the data importer:

Name (written out in full): ....

Position: ....

Address: ....

Other information necessary in order for the contract to be binding (if any):

Signature: ....

(stamp of organisation)

APPENDIX I

to the Standard Contractual Clauses

This Appendix forms part of the Clauses and must be completed and signed by the parties

The Member States may complete or specify, according to their national procedures, any additional necessary information to be contained in this Appendix

DATA EXPORTER

The data exporter is (please specify briefly your activities relevant to the transfer):

....

....

....

DATA IMPORTER

The data importer is (please specify briefly activities relevant to the transfer):

....

....

....

DATA SUBJECTS

The personal data transferred concern the following categories of data subjects (please specify):

....

....

....

CATEGORIES OF DATA

The personal data transferred concern the following categories of data (please specify):

....

....

....

SPECIAL CATEGORIES OF DATA (IF APPROPRIATE)

The personal data transferred concern the following special categories of data (please specify):

....

....

....

PROCESSING OPERATIONS

The personal data transferred will be subject to the following basic processing activities (please specify):

....

....

....

DATA EXPORTER

Name: ....

Authorised signature: ....

DATA IMPORTER

Name: ....

Authorised signature: ....

APPENDIX 2

to the Standard Contractual Clauses

This Appendix forms part of the Clauses and must be completed and signed by the parties.

Description of the technical and organisational security measures implemented by the data importer in accordance with Clauses 4(d) and 5(c) (or document/legislation attached):

....

....

....

....

ILLUSTRATIVE INDEMNIFICATION CLAUSE (OPTIONAL)

Liability

The parties agree that if one party is held liable for a violation of the clauses committed by the other party, the latter will, to the extent to which it is liable, indemnify the first party for any cost, charge, damages, expenses or loss it has incurred,

Indemnification is contingent upon:

(a)   the data exporter promptly notifying the data importer of a claim; and

(b)   the data importer being given the possibility to cooperate with the data exporter in the defence and settlement of the claim[4].

---

4   Paragraph on liabilities is optional.

32 Professional services agreement

This Professional Services Agreement (the 'Agreement') is entered into between the Supplier Limited ('Supplier') and the customer identified below ('Customer').

1. **Professional Services.** The Supplier will perform the professional services ('Services') and produce the deliverables ('Deliverables') described in one or more statements of work that are in a form specified by, or acceptable to, the Supplier (each a 'Statement of Work'). Each Statement of Work shall incorporate this Agreement by reference.

    A formal change control procedure will be used for all changes or revisions requested by Customer or the Supplier to the scope of work, approach, schedule, charges, or Deliverables associated with the Services. Upon submission of a change control request by the Supplier or Customer, the Supplier will complete a charge estimate and schedule impact based upon the requested change or revision and submit it to the Customer for written acceptance. If the change control request is approved by Customer, the Supplier will proceed with the Services as therein amended. If the change control request is not accepted by Customer within 10 calendar days from submittal by the Supplier, the change control will be considered null and void.

2. **Personnel.** The Supplier reserves the sole right to determine the allocation of the Supplier personnel in providing the Services.

    The Supplier personnel performing the Services will be and remain the employees of the Supplier, and the Supplier will provide for and pay the compensation and other benefits of such employees, including salary, health, accident and workers' compensation benefits and all taxes and contributions which an employer is required to pay relating to the employment of employees.

3. **Subcontractors.** The Supplier will have the right to use subcontractors in performance of its obligations under any applicable Statement of Work provided that the Supplier will remain primarily liable to Customer for any work performed by its subcontractors.

4. **Customer Responsibilities.** Customer will perform its obligations set forth in the applicable Statement of Work. In addition, to the extent reasonably required by the Supplier to perform the Services

at Customer facilities, Customer will make available to the Supplier facility access, office space, office furnishings, telephone and telecopy services, utilities, office supplies, and duplicating services. If the Services require that any software licensed or otherwise provided to Customer by third parties be disclosed to the Supplier, or used or accessed by the Supplier, Customer will, at no expense to the Supplier, obtain all consents, licenses and sublicenses necessary for the Supplier to perform the Services. Customer will defend any claim brought against the Supplier to the extent that such claim is due to Customer's failure to fulfill Customer's obligations under the preceding sentence. Customer will bear the expense of such defense and pay any damages and attorney's fees finally awarded by a court of competent jurisdiction that are attributable to such claim or that result from a settlement thereof, provided that the Supplier notifies Customer promptly in writing of the claim and allows Customer to fully direct the defence or settlement of such claim. Customer will not be responsible for any settlement or compromise made without Customer's consent. This section will survive the expiration or termination of this Agreement for any reason.

5.   **Ownership of Deliverables.**

(a) Pre-existing Software and Technology. Each party will retain all rights in any software, ideas, concepts, know-how, development tools, techniques or any other proprietary material or information that it owned or developed prior to the inception of a professional services project, or acquired or developed thereafter without reference to or use of the intellectual property of the other party.

(b) Third Party Software and Technology. All software and technology that is licensed by a party from a third party vendor will be and remain the property of such vendor.

(c) Deliverables Based on the Supplier Software and Technology. Subject to any third party rights or restrictions, the Supplier will own all intellectual property rights in or related to all deliverables that are developed and delivered by the Supplier under this Agreement, provided that they consist of pre-existing the Supplier software or the Supplier software development tools ("Supplier Tools"), modifications thereto developed as part of the Services, or works derived from pre-existing the Supplier software or the Supplier Tools developed as part of the Services.

(d) Deliverables Based on Customer's Software and Technology. Subject to any third party rights or restrictions, Customer shall own all intellectual property rights in or related to any deliverables that do not constitute pre-existing the Supplier software, the Supplier Tools, or modifications thereto or works derived therefrom, that are developed as part of the Services.

(e) License Grant for Deliverables Owned by the Supplier. With respect to deliverables owned by the Supplier, Customer is hereby granted a license to use the deliverables provided by the Supplier to Customer as part of a Services project. If the deliverable is software, it will be in object code form and Customer is authorized to load, execute, display, store and otherwise use the software. Upon payment in full for such deliverable, the license granted to Customer in this Section will be perpetual, royalty-free, non-transferable and non-exclusive and will be limited to Customer's internal use of such copy.

(f) The Services provided hereunder shall not constitute "works made for hire" under any applicable copyright laws. Ownership of work in progress under a Statement of Work shall remain with the Supplier until such time as title to a Deliverable transfers, if at all, in accordance with this Agreement.

(g) No License to Intellectual Property of the Other Party. No licenses will be deemed to have been granted by either party to any of its patents, copyrights, trade secrets or other intellectual property except as otherwise expressly provided in this Agreement. The Supplier will be free to use the ideas, concepts, methodologies, processes and know-how that are developed or created in the course of performing the Services provided that the Supplier does not use, or make reference to, the intellectual property or proprietary information of Customer.

6.   **Confidentiality and Data Protection.**

(a) The parties recognize that in the course of performing the Services, each of the parties may have access to confidential information and trade secrets belonging to the other and each desire that such confidential information and trade secrets remain confidential. Each party agrees that all confidential information and trade secrets communicated to one party by the other in any manner (the "Confidential Information"), whether before or after the date of the applicable Statement of Work, will be used by the recipient party only for the purposes of the applicable Statement of Work. The other party's Confidential Information will not be disclosed by the recipient party, other than to its employees and, in the case of the Supplier, to its consultants, agents, and contractors, without the prior written consent of the other party. Each party will advise its employees and, in the case of the Supplier, its consultants, agents, and contractors, who receive any of the other party's Confidential Information of its confidential nature. The confidentiality provisions of this Section will not apply to any Confidential Information that (i) was or becomes generally available to the public other than as a result of disclosure by the recipient party in violation of this Agreement; (ii) becomes available to the recipient party from a source other than the other party, provided that the recipient party has no reason to believe that such source is itself bound by a confidentiality or nondisclosure agreement with the other party or otherwise prohibited from disclosing such Confidential Information by a legal, contractual or fiduciary obligation; (iii) was in the recipient party's possession prior to receipt from the other party; (iv) is independently developed by the recipient party without the use of the other party's Confidential Information; or (v) is required to be disclosed by the recipient party by a governmental agency or law, so long as the recipient party provides the other party with written notice of the required disclosure promptly upon receipt of notice of the required disclosure. Upon any actual or threatened violation of this Section by either party, the other party will have the right, in addition to such other remedies which may be available to it, to seek injunctive relief enjoining such acts or attempts, it being acknowledged and agreed that monetary damages are inadequate to protect the other party. This Section will survive the expiration or termination of this Agreement for any reason.

(b) The Customer warrants that it is in compliance with The Data Protection Act 1998 (the "Act") and that it has obtained all necessary consents as required by the Act in respect of Personal Data as defined in the Act it transfers or makes available to the Supplier for processing in the course of the Services under each Statement of Work and will indemnify the Supplier in respect of all costs, claims, liabilities and demands incurred by the Supplier in respect of any breach of the Customer's warranty hereunder.

7. **Warranty.** The Supplier warrants that the Services will be performed in a professional and workmanlike manner. **EXCEPT AS EXPRESSLY SET FORTH HEREIN, THE SUPPLIER DISCLAIMS ALL WARRANTIES WITH REGARD TO ANY SERVICES OR ANY DELIVERABLES SUPPLIED HEREUNDER, WHETHER EXPRESS OR IMPLIED INCLUDING, WITHOUT LIMITATION, ALL WARRANTIES OF SATISFACTORY QUALITY, NON-INFRINGEMENT, AND FITNESS FOR A PARTICULAR PURPOSE.**

8. **Limitation of Liability.** Except in the case of death or personal injury arising out of its negligence or in the case of fraudulent misrepresentation made by it, the Supplier's entire liability for all claims or damages arising out of or related to this Agreement, regardless of the form of action, whether in contract, tort or otherwise, will be limited to and will not exceed, in the aggregate the amount paid to the Supplier under this Agreement for the specific service that caused the damage or that is the subject matter of the claim. In no event will the measure of damages payable by the Supplier include, nor will the Supplier be liable for, any amounts for loss of income, profit or savings or indirect, incidental, consequential, exemplary, punitive or special damages of any party, including third parties, even if the Supplier has been advised of the possibility of such damages in advance, and all such damages are expressly disclaimed. Neither party may make a claim under this Agreement arising out of an event or events that occurred more than two (2) years after the event is, or should have been, discovered by the party making the claim.

9. **Fees and Expenses.** Customer agrees to pay the Supplier: (i) all fees set out in each Statement of Work; and (ii) any actual, reasonable travel and out-of-pocket expenses incurred as set out in the Statement of Work.

10. **Taxes.** Customer will, in addition to all other amounts payable to the Supplier under this Agreement, remit directly to the appropriate tax authorities, or pay to or reimburse the Supplier, as applicable, all applicable taxes, assessments, duties, permits, fees and other charges of any nature or kind, now in force or enacted in the future ("Taxes"), however designated, assessed or levied, including, but not limited

to all national, foreign, local, regional, or municipal sales and/or use taxes, value added taxes, goods and services taxes, consumption taxes, personal property taxes, ad valorem taxes, custom duties, import fees, stamp duty, intangibles tax, registration fees, but not including taxes based on the net income of the Supplier. Such amounts shall also include without limitation any penalties, interest, fees, or other expenses, if any, incurred as the result of any such Taxes not being paid at the time or in the manner required by law. Taxes includes those amounts which are due based upon (i) transactions arising under this Agreement, (ii) amounts payable hereunder, (iii) the products or other services being provided to the Customer hereunder, (iv) the subsequent use of such products or services by the Customer, and/or (v) Customer's possession of such products or services.

If Customer is exempt from sales tax, uses the product or services provided hereunder in an exempt manner, or otherwise deems itself not subject to sales tax, then Customer must provide a valid and executed exemption certificate, direct pay permit, or other such government approved documentation in good faith to the Supplier.

If Customer is required by law to make any income tax deduction or to withhold income tax from any sum payable directly to the Supplier hereunder, Customer shall promptly effect payment thereof to the applicable tax authorities, and shall also promptly provide the Supplier with official tax receipts or other evidence issued by the applicable tax authorities sufficient to establish that the income taxes have been paid and to enable the Supplier to support a claim for tax credit relief for such income tax payments made on its behalf by Customer. Failure of the Customer to provide official tax receipts or other evidence of payment to the Supplier shall result in Customer paying directly to the Supplier additional amounts equal to the amounts originally deducted or withheld from the original payment and for which no documentation was provided. Customer shall also use its best efforts to work with and assist the Supplier in minimizing any domestic law withholding tax rate and, if applicable, obtain a lower withholding tax rate if one is available under the applicable tax treaty including supplying the appropriate documentation to the Supplier, assisting in its completion, providing a translation, and providing any other necessary support or documentation.

11. **Payment Terms.** Unless otherwise provided in a Statement of Work, the Supplier will invoice Customer on a monthly basis for all amounts owed under a Statement of Work. Customer agrees to pay the Supplier within 30 days of the date of each invoice. In the event that this Agreement or any Statement of Work is terminated or suspended prior to the completion of the Services or the delivery or acceptance of any final deliverable, Customer agrees to pay the Supplier for all work performed through the date of termination or suspension of the Services.

12. **Term & Termination.** This Agreement will remain in effect until terminated by either party by providing 30 days prior written notice to the other party and any additional time that may be necessary to complete any Services that are outstanding under any Statement of

Work. A Statement of Work may only be terminated in accordance with specific terms contained in the Statement of Work.

13. **Non-Solicitation of Employees.** Customer shall not, during the term of this Agreement and for a period of one year thereafter, directly or indirectly solicit, employ, offer to employ, nor engage as a consultant, any employee of the Supplier or of the Supplier subcontractor with whom Customer had contact pursuant to this Agreement.

14. **Compliance with Export Control Laws.** The Supplier's obligation to provide the Services under this Agreement is subject to the proviso that the fulfillment of these obligations is not prevented by any impediments arising out of national and international foreign trade and customs requirements or any embargoes and/or other sanctions.

This Agreement is subject to all United States government laws, regulations, orders, embargoes and or other restrictions regarding export from the United States of services, commodities, software, technology or derivatives thereof, as such laws, regulations, orders, embargoes or other restrictions may be enacted, amended or modified from time to time. Notwithstanding anything to the contrary in this Agreement, Customer will not directly or indirectly, separately or as part of a system, export or re-export any the Supplier services, commodity, software, technology or derivatives thereof or permit the shipment of same without: (i) the express written consent of the Supplier and (ii) obtaining, at Customer's sole expense, any required prior authorization from the United States Department of Commerce or other applicable authority as may be required by law.

Each party will reasonably cooperate with the other and will provide to the other promptly upon request any end-user certificates, affidavits regarding re-export or other certificates or documents as are reasonably requested to obtain approvals, consents, licenses and/ or permits required for any export or import of products or services under this Agreement.

The provisions of this Section will survive the expiration or termination of this Agreement for any reason.

15. **Entire Agreement.** This Agreement will extend to and be binding upon the successors, legal representatives and permitted assigns of the parties. However, this Agreement may not be assigned or otherwise transferred (by operation of law or otherwise) by Customer without the prior written consent of the Supplier. This Agreement constitutes the full and complete statement of the agreement between the parties with respect to the subject matter hereof and supersedes any previous or contemporaneous agreements, understandings or communications, whether written or oral, relating to such subject matter. This Agreement does not supersede any Software License Agreement (or any exhibits thereto) between the parties or any other written agreement between the parties concerning maintenance and support of the Supplier software. If Customer issues a purchase order, memorandum or other instrument covering the Services, it is agreed that all terms and conditions contained therein that are additional to or inconsistent with this Agreement and any applicable Statement of

Work will be of no force and effect. This Agreement and each Statement of Work may not be modified or amended except in writing signed by a duly authorized representative of each party.

16. **General.** This Agreement will extend to and be binding upon the successors, legal representatives and permitted assigns of the parties. However, this Agreement may not be assigned or otherwise transferred (by operation of law or otherwise) by Customer without the prior written consent of the Supplier. Customer agrees that this Agreement is not intended to confer and does not confer any rights or remedies upon any person other than the parties to this Agreement. The Supplier 's failure to insist upon or enforce strict performance of any provision of this Agreement shall not be construed as a waiver of any provision or right. Neither party will be liable for any delay in or failure to perform any of its non-monetary obligations under this Agreement if due to any cause or condition beyond their reasonable control, whether foreseeable or not. If any part of this Agreement is held invalid or unenforceable, that portion shall be construed in a manner consistent with applicable law to reflect, as nearly as possible, the original intentions of the parties, and the remaining portions shall remain in full force and effect. The parties to this Agreement are independent contractors. Nothing herein shall be deemed to cause this Agreement to create an agency, partnership, joint venture or other fiduciary relationship between Customer and the Supplier. Neither party shall not have any authority to assume or create any obligation, express or implied, on behalf of the other party and neither party shall have authority to represent itself as an agent, employee, or in any other capacity of the other party. Except as expressly provided in this Agreement, a person who is not a party to this Agreement may not enforce any of its terms under the Contracts (Rights of Third Parties) Act 1999.

This Agreement will be governed by and construed in accordance with the laws of England & Wales. and the Suppler and Customer hereby submit for the purposes of this Agreement to the exclusive jurisdiction of the English courts.

IN WITNESS WHEREOF, the parties have duly executed and delivered this Agreement as of the last date written below.

CUSTOMER:

(*insert Customer name*)

By: _____

Name:

Title:

Date:

Address:

City:

State/Zip:

SUPPLIER LIMITED.

By: _____

Name:

Title:

Date:

By: _____

Name:

Title:

Date:

Index

[all references are to paragraph number]

A

Acceptance tests
generally, 8.1.9
offsite benchmark test, 8.1.9.1
onsite objective criteria, 8.1.9.3
onsite subjective standard, 8.1.9.4
onsite ready for use, 8.1.9.2
Access software licence agreements,
2.11
Apache licences, 2.15.5.5
Application service provider licences,
2.16
Artistic Licence, 2.15.5.6
Assignment of rights clauses, 8.1.35
Audit right clauses, 8.1.44
disclosure under, guidance on, 8.1.44
Authentication, 4.8

B

Binding Corporate Rules 4.10.8
new rules for processors, 4.10.8
Bonus clauses, 8.1.4.7
Breaches of agreement
late payment, 9.1.3
termination clauses, 8.1.11.1
BSD licences, 2.15.5.5
Business secrets, 7.1.2

C

Capped payment clauses, 8.1.4.3
Change control clauses, 8.1.28
Click-wrap licence agreements
generally, 2.3.3
precedent, Appendix 3
Codes, *see* **Source codes**
Cold-site arrangement clauses,
8.1.5.13
Competition law, 4.2
Computer games development
agreement, Appendix 10
Computer programs, *see* **Software**

Confidentiality
contents of licence agreements 8.1.39
precedents
evaluation licence and confidentiality
agreement, Appendix 1
information escrow agreement,
Appendix 27.4
software evaluation licence and
confidentiality agreement,
Appendix 1
pre-contract documents, 7.1.2
Consequential damage clauses, 8.1.25
Consulting services, 8.1.16
Contamination of software, 2.15.3.9
Contents of licence agreements
acceptance tests
generally, 8.1.9
offsite benchmark test, 8.1.9.1
onsite objective criteria, 8.1.9.3
onsite subjective standard, 8.1.9.4
onsite ready for use, 8.1.9.2
assignment of rights, 8.1.35
audit right clause 8.1.44
disclosure of material, 8.1.44
availability of licensee's computer
system, 8.1.29
change control, 8.1.28
confidentiality, 8.1.39
consequential damages, 8.1.25
consulting services, 8.1.16
data protection, 8.1.41
definitions, 8.1.3
delivery, 8.1.6
development services, 8.1.16
EMU warranty, 8.1.21
enhancements, 8.1.13
entire agreement, 8.1.37
error warranty, 8.1.20
escrow, 8.1.14
force majeure, 8.1.34
governing law, 8.1.42

Index

Contents of licence agreements – *contd*
  grant of licence
    cold-site arrangement, 8.1.5.13
    duration, 8.1.5.4
    exclusivity, 8.1.5.1
    host, 8.1.5.3
    hot-site arrangement, 8.1.5.13
    introduction, 8.1.5
    licensed code, 8.1.5.7
    maintenance, 8.1.5.12
    modifications, 8.1.5.12
    number of copies that can be reproduced, 8.1.5.11
    number of licensed copies, 8.1.5.6
    payment type, 8.1.5.9
    relationship between terms, 8.1.5.5
    rights conveyed, 8.1.5.2
    scope of software, 8.1.5.10
    site, 8.1.5.3
    source code information, 8.1.5.14
    subject to other terms, 8.1.5.15
    technical information, 8.1.5.14
    territory, 8.1.5.3
    transferability of rights, 8.1.5.8
  host preparation, 8.1.7
  installation, 8.1.8
  intellectual property rights, 8.1.22
  jurisdiction, 8.1.42
  lawyer's fees, 8.1.30
  limited warranties, 8.1.18
  limitation of liability, 8.1.23
  limitation on recoverable damages, 8.1.24
  limitation periods, 8.1.31
  liquidated damages, 8.1.26
  maintenance, 8.1.12
  most favoured customer, 8.1.27
  necessary provisions
    customer's viewpoint, from, 9.2.1–9.2.4
    provider's viewpoint, from, 9.1.1–9.1.5
  notice, 8.1.36
  ongoing performance obligations, 8.1.19
  overview, 8.1
  parties, 8.1.1
  payment
    amount, 8.1.4.1
    bonus, 8.1.4.7
    caps, 8.1.4.3
    cure period for late payments, 8.1.4.4
    due date, 8.1.4.2
    increases, 8.1.4.3
    interest on late payment, 8.1.4.5
    reductions in charges or fees, 8.1.4.6
    retention against acceptance, 8.1.4.8
  recitals, 8.1.2
  recovery of lawyer's fees, 8.1.30
  remote access, 8.1.40

Contents of licence agreements – *contd*
  risk of loss or damage during transit, 8.1.32–8.1.33
  service, 8.1.12
  severability, 8.1.38
  site preparation, 8.1.7
  statute of limitations, 8.1.31
  term of agreement
    commencement before delivery of software, 8.1.10.1
    evergreen clause, 8.1.10.3
    grace period, 8.1.10.6
    introduction, 8.1.10
    limited term, 8.1.10.2
    perpetual term, 8.1.10.4
    unspecified term, 8.1.10.5
  termination
    breach, upon, 8.1.11.1
    consequences, 8.1.11.5
    expiry of term, by, 8.1.11.3
    introduction, 8.1.11
    lapse of IPR, upon, 8.1.11.4
    without cause, 8.1.11.2
  third party rights, 8.1.43
  training, 8.1.15
  updates, 8.1.12
  variations, 8.1.37
  virus warranty, 8.1.20
  warranties, 8.1.17–8.1.22
Contracts
  See also Software licensing agreements
  business secrets, 7.1.2
  confidentiality, 7.1.2
  e-signature and authentication issues, 4.8
  heads of agreement
    contract skeleton, 7.2.2
    drafting, 7.2.3
    'golden rules', 7.2.4
    introduction, 7.2.1
  pre-contract documents
    business secrets, 7.1.2
    confidentiality, 7.1.2
    introduction, 7.1.1
  sources of law, 3.6
  third party rights, 8.1.43
Copyright
  application to software contracts, recent cases, 3.3
  EC Directives, and
    rental and lending rights 4.4
    term of protection, 4.5
  legal sources, 3.3
  user manual, infringement in, 3.3
Core technology licence agreements, 2.9

Creative problem solving
introduction, 10.1
other techniques, 10.3–10.3.13
redefining the problem, 10.2
Cross-licensing agreements, 2.7
Customers
necessary contract provisions, 9.2.1–9.2.4
preparations for negotiations
acquisition structure, 6.2.5
consensus need determination, 6.2.4–
6.2.4.4
consultant-aided needs analysis and
decision, 6.2.3.1–6.2.3.3
general, 6.2.1
hiring outside help, 6.2.8
in-house needs analysis and decision,
6.2.2
leader selection, 6.2.7
management support, 6.2.6
necessary services, 6.2.4.2
personnel, 6.2.4.1
political support, 6.2.4.3
request for proposals, 6.2.3.3
review of business plans and goals,
6.2.3.3
senior management survey, 6.2.3.1
strategy, 6.2.5
support of management, 6.2.6
survey of technical personnel, 6.2.3.2
tactics, 6.2.5
team formation, 6.2.4.4

D
Data protection
background, 4.10.1
data processing precedents
agreement, Appendix 25
standard contractual clauses, Appendix
31
data security, 4.10.2
data subjects' rights, 4.10.1.1
EC Directives, 4.6, 4.10
introduction, 4.10
rights of individuals, 4.10.1.1
contents of licence agreements, 8.1.41
trans-border data flows, 4.10.5
transfer of data overseas
authorisation, 4.10.7
exceptions to general rule, 4.10.6
general principle, 4.10.3
personal data processor clauses,
4.10.8
safe harbour program, 4.10.4
trans-border data flow agreements,
4.10.8
trans-border data flows, 4.10.5
US safe harbour program, 4.10.4

Databases
commercial availability, 1.2.4
EC Directives, 4.6
legal sources, 3.3
licence agreements, 2.11
sui generis database right, 3.3
Delivery
dates, 8.1.6
necessary licence provisions
customers, 9.2.2.1
providers, 9.1.2
Demo licence, Appendix 9
Derived works, 2.15.3.3
Development
developer-publisher agreements, 2.1
precedents
computer games development
agreement, Appendix 10
services, 8.1.16
single licensee software agreement,
Appendix 27.1
Disclosure
audit rights clause, under, 8.1.44
Digital identification, 4.8
Display of software, 8.1.5.2
Distance Selling Directive, 4.9
Distribution of software
domestic distributor agreements, 2.2.1
foreign publisher-distributor licence
agreements, 2.2.2
free redistribution, 2.15.3.1
heads of agreement, Appendix 11
licence terms, 8.1.5.2
multimedia product licence and
distribution agreement, Appendix 13
open source licences, 2.15.3.7
publisher-distributor licence agreements
domestic distributors, 2.2.1
foreign distributors, 2.2.2
Documentation with software, 8.1.5.10
Domestic distributor agreements, 2.2.1
Duration of licence agreements
commencement before delivery of
software, 8.1.10.1
evergreen clause, 8.1.10.3
grace period, 8.1.10.6
introduction, 8.1.10
limited term, 8.1.10.2
perpetual term, 8.1.10.4
unspecified term, 8.1.10.5

E
EBay, 4.10.8
EC Directives
computer programs, 4.3
copyright, 4.4
harmonisation of aspects of 3.3

EC Directives – *contd*
data protection
background, 4.10.1
data security, 4.10.2
data subjects' rights, 4.10.1.1
introduction, 4.10
rights of individuals, 4.10.1.1
trans-border data flows, 4.10.5
transfer of data overseas, 4.10.3–4.10.8
US safe harbour program, 4.10.4
databases, 4.6
distance selling, 4.9
electrical and electronic equipment
inbound supply chain, 4.12.5
introduction, 4.12
key dates, 4.12.4
key elements, 4.12.2–4.12.3
supply chain, 4.12.5
type of products affected, 4.12.1
e-signatures, 4.8
lending rights, 4.4
rental rights, 4.4
software, 4.3
software patents, 4.11
term of protection of copyright, 4.5
unfair contract terms, 4.7
waste and hazardous electrical and
electronic equipment, *see* **Waste
electrical and electronic
equipment**
EMU warranties, 8.1.21
Enhancement clauses, 8.1.13
Entire agreement clauses, 8.1.37
Equipment
waste recycling, *see* **Waste electrical
and electronic equipment**
Error warranties, 8.1.20
Escrow agreements
generally, 2.4
precedents
development single licensee software
agreement, Appendix 27.1
escrow holding agreement, Appendix
27.3
information escrow agreement,
Appendix 27.4
multi licensee software escrow
agreement, Appendix 27.5
single licensee software escrow
agreement, Appendix, 27.6
single licensee software escrow
agreement (escrow secure),
Appendix 27.2
single licensee website and software
escrow agreement, Appendix
27.7
E-signature Directive, 4.8

European law, 4.1–4.11
competition law, 4.2
EC Directives
computer programs, 4.3
copyright, 4.4
data protection, 4.10–4.10.8
databases, 4.6
distance selling, 4.9
e-signatures, 4.8
lending rights, 4.4
rental rights, 4.4
software, 3.3, 4.3
term of protection of copyright, 4.5
unfair contract terms, 4.7
waste electrical and electronic
equipment, 4.11–4.11.7
overview, 4.1
status of software in EU 3.3
Evaluation licence, Appendix 1
Evergreen clauses, 8.1.10.3
Exclusivity clauses, 8.1.5.1
Exhaustion of rights, 3.3
Expiry of term, 8.1.11.3

F
Facilities management agreements,
2.13
Force majeure clauses, 8.1.34
**Foreign publisher-distributor licence
agreements,** 2.2.2
Framework agreement, Appendix 28
Free software
licences, 2.15.5.2
redistribution, 2.15.3.1

G
Gifting rights for software, 8.1.5.2
Give/get principle, 5.4
GNU
General Public Licences, 2.15.5.3
Library General Public Licences, 2.15.5.4
Goods
software classified as, 3.3
Governing law clauses, 8.1.42
Grace period for payment, 8.1.10.6
Grant of licence
cold-site arrangement, 8.1.5.13
duration, 8.1.5.4
exclusivity, 8.1.5.1
host, 8.1.5.3
hot-site arrangement, 8.1.5.13
introduction, 8.1.5
licensed code, 8.1.5.7
maintenance, 8.1.5.12
modifications, 8.1.5.12
number of copies that can be reproduced,
8.1.5.11

Grant of licence – *contd*
  number of licensed copies, 8.1.5.6
  payment type, 8.1.5.9
  relationship between terms, 8.1.5.5
  rights conveyed, 8.1.5.2
  scope of software, 8.1.5.10
  site, 8.1.5.3
  source code information, 8.1.5.14
  subject to other terms, 8.1.5.15
  technical information, 8.1.5.14
  territory, 8.1.5.3
  transferability of rights, 8.1.5.8

H
Hardware agreements
  loan agreement, Appendix 18
  maintenance, Appendix 17
  supply, Appendix 16
Hazardous substances, *see* **Waste**
  electrical and electronic
  equipment
Heads of agreement
  contract skeleton, 7.2.2
  drafting, 7.2.3
  'golden rules', 7.2.4
  introduction, 7.2.1
  software distribution precedent,
    Appendix 11
Hosting
  limitation clauses, 8.1.5.3
  preparation requirements, 8.1.7
  website hosting agreement, Appendix 21
Hot-site arrangement clauses, 8.1.5.13

I
Identification, digital
  consultation on, 4.8
Increasing payment clauses, 8.1.4.3
Installation clauses, 8.1.8
Integrity of author's source code,
  2.15.3.4
Intellectual property rights
  contents of licence agreements, 8.1.22
  copyright
    rental and lending rights 4.4
    term of protection, 4.5
    legal sources, 3.3
  moral rights, 3.8
  patents
    legal sources 3.2
    Software Patents Directive, 4.11
  registered designs, 3.7
  termination of licence agreements,
    8.1.11.4
  trademarks, 3.5
Interest payment clauses, 8.1.4.5
Invitation to tender, Appendix 19

J
Joint ventures
  licensing agreements
    generally, 2.8
    memorandum of understanding,
      Appendix 7
  software development agreement,
    Appendix 14
Jurisdiction clauses, 8.1.42

L
Late payment
  cure period, 8.1.4.4
  interest, 8.1.4.5
Lawyer's fees, 8.1.30
Leases of software
  generally, 1.5.3
  grant of licence, 8.1.5.2
  introduction, 1.5.1
Legal sources
  contracts, 3.6
  copyright, 3.3
  databases, 3.3
  European Union
    competition law, 4.2
    Directives, 4.3–4.12
    overview, 4.1
  moral rights, 3.8
  overview, 3.1
  patents, 3.2
  registered designs, 3.7
  trade secrets, 3.4
  trademarks, 3.5
Lending rights
  EC Directive, 4.4
  software
    generally, 8.1.5.2
    precedent agreement, Appendix 17
Licensing, *see* **Software licence**
  agreements
Limitation clauses
  liability, 8.1.23
  necessary licence provisions for
    providers, 9.1.4
  recoverable damages, 8.1.24
  warranties, 8.1.18
Limitation periods, 8.1.31
Liquidated damages clauses, 8.1.26

M
Mainframe software, 1.2.1
Maintenance
  contents of licence agreements, 8.1.12
  grant of licence, 8.1.5.12
  service licence agreements, 2.12, 8.1.12
Manufacturing licence agreements,
  2.6

Memorandum of understanding,
Appendix 7
Microcomputer software, 1.2.2
Minicomputer software, 1.2.1
Modification clauses, 8.1.5.12
Moral rights, 3.8
Most favoured customer clauses, 8.1.27
Mozilla public licences, 2.15.5.7
**Multimedia product licence and
distribution agreement,** Appendix 13

N
National Computing Centre, 2.4
Negotiations
body language
crossed arms, 11.3.1
eyes, 11.3.3
generally, 11.3
hand over mouth, 11.3.2
creative problem solving
introduction, 10.1
other techniques, 10.3–10.3.13
redefining the problem, 10.2
customer preparations
acquisition structure, 6.2.5
consensus need determination, 6.2.4–
6.2.4.4
consultant-aided needs analysis and
decision, 6.2.3.1–6.2.3.3
general, 6.2.1
hiring outside help, 6.2.8
in-house needs analysis and decision,
6.2.2
leader selection, 6.2.7
management support, 6.2.6
necessary services, 6.2.4.2
personnel, 6.2.4.1
political support, 6.2.4.3
request for proposals, 6.2.3.3
review of business plans and goals,
6.2.3.3
senior management survey, 6.2.3.1
strategy, 6.2.5
support of management, 6.2.6
survey of technical personnel, 6.2.3.2
tactics, 6.2.5
team formation, 6.2.4.4
ethics, 5.6
give/get principle, 5.4
introduction, 5.1
meaning, 5.2
non-verbal communication
body language, 11.3–11.3.3
introduction, 11.1
personal space, 11.4
seating positions, 11.5
silence, 11.2

Negotiations – *contd*
personal space, 11.4
preparations
customers, by, 6.2.1–6.2.8
providers, by, 6.1.1–6.1.9
provider preparations
experience, 6.1.2
fall-back positions, 6.1.7
general, 6.1.1
inter-departmental meetings, 6.1.8
internal deal structuring, 6.1.6
pre-negotiation groundwork, 6.1.5
pre-prepared contracts, 6.1.9
printed contracts, 6.1.4
sales force training, 6.1.2
standard charges, 6.1.3
standard contracts, 6.1.4
strategy meetings, 6.1.8
substantive fall-back positions, 6.1.7
tactics meetings, 6.1.8
purpose, 5.3
seating positions, 11.5
silence, 11.2
styles
generally, 5.7
introduction, 5.6
win-win deals, 5.5
Netscape public licences, 2.15.5.7
Non-contract protection, 1.2.5
Non-discrimination requirements,
2.15.3.5
Notice clauses, 8.1.36

O
Ongoing performance obligations,
8.1.19
Open Source Definition
derived works, 2.15.3.3
distribution, 2.15.3.7
free redistribution, 2.15.3.1
generally, 2.15.3
integrity of author's source code, 2.15.3.4
non-contamination, 2.15.3.9
non-discrimination requirement, 2.15.3.5
non-specific, 2.15.3.8
source code, 2.15.3.2
Open source licences
analysis
Apache licence, 2.15.5.5
Artistic Licence, 2.15.5.6
BSD licence, 2.15.5.5
free licences, 2.15.5.2
generally, 2.15.5
GNU General Public Licence, 2.15.5.3
GNU Library General Public Licence,
2.15.5.4
Mozilla public licence, 2.15.5.7

Open source licences – *contd*
  analysis – *contd*
    Netscape public licences, 2.15.5.7
    public domain, 2.15.5.1
    warranties, 2.15.5.2
    X licence, 2.15.5.5
  Apache licence, 2.15.5.5
  Artistic Licence, 2.15.5.6
  BSD licence, 2.15.5.5
  choice of, 2.15.6.1–2.15.6.4
  derived works, 2.15.3.3
  distribution, 2.15.3.7
  examples, 2.15.4
  free licences, 2.15.5.2
  free redistribution, 2.15.3.1
  future developments, 2.15.7
  GNU General Public Licence, 2.15.5.3
  GNU Library General Public Licence,
    2.15.5.4
  historical analysis, 2.15.2
  integrity of author's source code, 2.15.3.4
  introduction, 2.15.1
  Mozilla public licence, 2.15.5.7
  Netscape public licences, 2.15.5.7
  non-contamination, 2.15.3.9
  non-discrimination requirement,
    2.15.3.5
  non-specific, 2.15.3.8
  public domain, 2.15.5.1
  source code, 2.15.3.2
  warranties, 2.15.5.2
  X licence, 2.15.5.5
**Original equipment manufacturers
  (OEMs)**
  domestic distributors, 2.2.1
  foreign distributors, 2.2.2
Outsourcing
  facilities management agreements, 2.13
  services outsourcing agreement,
    Appendix 20
  software as a service (SaaS) 2.17

P
Parties to agreement, 8.1.1
Patents
  legal sources 3.2
Payment
  amount, 8.1.4.1
  bonus, 8.1.4.7
  caps, 8.1.4.3
  cure period for late payments, 8.1.4.4
  due date, 8.1.4.2
  grant of licence, 8.1.5.9
  increases, 8.1.4.3
  interest on late payment, 8.1.4.5
  necessary licence provisions for
    customers, 9.2.2.1–9.2.2.2

Payment – *contd*
  reductions in charges or fees, 8.1.4.6
  retention against acceptance, 8.1.4.8
Performance obligations, 8.1.5.2
  licensing arrangements, 8.1.5.2
  necessary licence provisions
    customers, 9.2.2.1
    providers, 9.1.2
  ongoing obligations, 8.1.19
Precedents
  click-wrap licence, Appendix 3
  computer games development agreement,
    Appendix 10
  data processing
    agreement, Appendix 25
    standard contractual clauses, Appendix
      31
  escrow agreements
    development single licensee software
      agreement, Appendix 27.1
    escrow holding agreement, Appendix
      27.3
    information escrow agreement,
      Appendix 27.4
    multi licensee software escrow
      agreement, Appendix 27.5
    single licensee software escrow
      agreement, Appendix, 27.6
    single licensee software escrow
      agreement (escrow secure),
      Appendix 27.2
    single licensee website and software
      escrow agreement, Appendix 27.7
  framework agreement, Appendix 28
  hardware
    loan agreement, Appendix 18
    maintenance agreement, Appendix 17
    supply agreement, Appendix 16
  heads of agreement for distribution,
    Appendix 11
  invitation to tender, Appendix 19
  joint software development agreement,
    Appendix 14
  licences
    demo licence, Appendix 9
    shrink-wrap licence, Appendix 2
    software licence agreement, Appendix
      4
    value added reseller agreement and
      license, Appendix 30
    website development, licensing and
      support agreement, Appendix 22
  memorandum of understanding for joint
    venture and licensing agreement
    Appendix 7
  multimedia product licence and
    distribution agreement, Appendix 13

Index

Precedents – *contd*
  services
    agreement, Appendix 29
    outsourcing agreement, Appendix 20
    professional services agreement,
      Appendix 32
  shrink-wrap licence, Appendix 2
  software
    checklist for agreement, Appendix 5
    development and licensing agreement,
      Appendix 8
    distribution agreement, Appendix 12
    evaluation licence and confidentiality
      agreement Appendix 1
    license agreement, Appendix 4
    licence code, Appendix 26
    loan agreement, Appendix 18
    reciprocal licence agreement, Appendix
      15
    support and maintenance agreement,
      Appendix 6
    trans border flow agreement, Appendix 24
    value added reseller agreement and
      licence, Appendix 30
  websites
    development, licensing and support
      agreement, Appendix 22
    hosting agreement, Appendix 21
    linking agreement, Appendix 23
Providers
  necessary contract provisions 9.1.1–9.1.5
  preparations for negotiations
    experience, 6.1.2
    fall-back positions, 6.1.7
    general, 6.1.1
    inter-departmental meetings, 6.1.8
    internal deal structuring, 6.1.6
    pre-negotiation groundwork, 6.1.5
    pre-prepared contracts, 6.1.9
    printed contracts, 6.1.4
    sales force training, 6.1.2
    standard charges, 6.1.3
    standard contracts, 6.1.4
    strategy meetings, 6.1.8
    substantive fall-back positions, 6.1.7
    tactics meetings, 6.1.8
Public domain
  display of software, 8.1.5.2
  open source licences, 2.15.5.1
Publisher-distributor licence
  agreements
  domestic distributors, 2.2.1
  foreign distributors, 2.2.2

R
Reciprocal software licence
  agreement, Appendix 15

Recitals, 8.1.2
Reduction clauses, 8.1.4.6
Registered designs, 3.7
Remote access provisions, 8.1.40
Rental of software
  Directive, 4.4
  grant of licence, 8.1.5.2
Retention clauses, 8.1.4.8
Risk
  in transit clauses, 8.1.32–8.1.33
  necessary licence provisions for
    providers, 9.1.4
Royalty payments, 8.1.5.9
Runtime licence agreements, 2.5

S
Sale of software
  Distance Selling Directive, 4.9
  force training, 6.1.2
  grant of licence, 8.1.5
  legal concepts, 1.5.2
  licences distinguished, 1.5.1
Services
  maintenance updates, 8.1.12
  precedents
    agreement, Appendix 29
    outsourcing agreement, Appendix 20
    professional services agreement,
      Appendix 32
Severability clauses, 8.1.38
Shrink-wrap licences
  generally, 2.3.2
  precedent, Appendix 2
Signature
  slectronic, 4.8
Signed licence agreements, 2.3.1
Sites
  grant of licence, 8.1.5.3
  preparation, 8.1.7
Software
  as a service (SaaS) 2.17
  copyright, application to 3.3
  EC Software Directive, 4.3
    analysis and judicial opinion on, 3.3
  conversion agreements, 2.9
  goods, classification as, 3.3
  leases
    generally, 1.5.3
    introduction, 1.5.1
  sales
    legal concepts, 1.5.2
    licences distinguished, 1.5.1
  precedents
    checklist for agreement, Appendix 5
    development and licensing agreement,
      Appendix 8
    distribution agreement, Appendix 12

Software – *contd*
precedents – *contd*
evaluation licence and confidentiality
agreement Appendix 1
loan agreement, Appendix 18
licence agreement, Appendix 4
licence code, Appendix 26
multi licensee software escrow
agreement, Appendix 27.5
reciprocal licence agreement, Appendix
15
single licensee software escrow
agreement, Appendix, 27.6
single licensee software escrow
agreement (escrow secure),
Appendix 27.2
single licensee website and software
escrow agreement, Appendix 27.7
support and maintenance agreement,
Appendix 6
Software licence agreements
See also Precedents
access software licence agreements, 2.11
application service provider licences, 2.16
central concept, 1.1
click-wrap licence agreements, 2.3.3
commercially-available databases, 1.2.4
commercially-available software, 1.2.3
contents
acceptance tests, 8.1.9–8.1.9.4
assignment of rights, 8.1.35
audit right clause, 8.1.44
availability of licensee's computer
system, 8.1.29
change control, 8.1.28
confidentiality, 8.1.39
consequential damages, 8.1.25
consulting services, 8.1.16
data protection, 8.1.41
definitions, 8.1.3
delivery, 8.1.6
development services, 8.1.16
EMU warranty, 8.1.21
enhancements, 8.1.13
entire agreement, 8.1.37
error warranty, 8.1.20
escrow, 8.1.14
force majeure, 8.1.34
governing law, 8.1.42
grant of licence, 8.1.5–8.1.5.15
host preparation, 8.1.7
installation, 8.1.8
intellectual property rights, 8.1.22
jurisdiction, 8.1.42
lawyer's fees, 8.1.30
limited warranties, 8.1.18
limitation of liability, 8.1.23

Software licence agreements – *contd*
contents – *contd*
limitation on recoverable damages,
8.1.24
limitation periods, 8.1.31
liquidated damages, 8.1.26
maintenance, 8.1.12
most favoured customer, 8.1.27
notice, 8.1.36
ongoing performance obligations,
8.1.19
overview, 8.1
parties, 8.1.1
payment, 8.1.4.1–8.1.4.8
recitals, 8.1.2
recovery of lawyer's fees, 8.1.30
remote access, 8.1.40
risk of loss or damage during transit,
8.1.32–8.1.33
service, 8.1.12
severability, 8.1.38
site preparation, 8.1.7
statute of limitations, 8.1.31
term, 8.1.10–8.1.10.6
termination, 8.1.11–8.1.11.5
training, 8.1.15
updates, 8.1.12
variations, 8.1.37
virus warranty, 8.1.20
warranties, 8.1.17–8.1.22
core technology licence agreements, 2.9
cross-licensing agreements, 2.7
database licence agreements, 2.11
developer-publisher agreements, 2.1
distributed software
commercially-available databases,
1.2.4
commercially-available software, 1.2.3
mainframe software, 1.2.1
microcomputer software, 1.2.2
minicomputer software, 1.2.1
non-contract protection, 1.2.5
escrow, 2.4
facilities management agreements, 2.13
heads of agreement
contract skeleton, 7.2.2
drafting, 7.2.3
'golden rules', 7.2.4
introduction, 7.2.1
joint venture licensing agreements, 2.8
legal concepts and characteristics
essentials, 1.5.4
introduction, 1.1
leases distinguished, 1.5.3
sales distinguished, 1.5.2
weaknesses, 1.6
'licensor', 1.1

Index

Software licence agreements – *contd*
mainframe software, 1.2.1
maintenance service licence agreements,
    2.12, 8.1.12
manufacturing licence agreements, 2.6
microcomputer software, 1.2.2
minicomputer software, 1.2.1
necessary provisions
    customer's viewpoint, from, 9.2.1–9.2.4
    provider's viewpoint, from, 9.1.1–9.1.5
non-contract protection, 1.2.5
open source licences
    analysis, 2.15.5–2.15.5.7
    Apache licence, 2.15.5.5
    Artistic Licence, 2.15.5.6
    BSD licence, 2.15.5.5
    choice of, 2.15.6.1–2.15.6.4
    derived works, 2.15.3.3
    distribution, 2.15.3.7
    examples, 2.15.4
    free licences, 2.15.5.2
    free redistribution, 2.15.3.1
    future developments, 2.15.7
    GNU General Public Licence, 2.15.5.3
    GNU Library General Public Licence,
      2.15.5.4
    historical analysis, 2.15.2
    integrity of author's source code,
      2.15.3.4
    introduction, 2.15.1
    Mozilla public licence, 2.15.5.7
    Netscape public licences, 2.15.5.7
    non-contamination, 2.15.3.9
    non-discrimination requirement,
      2.15.3.5
    non-specific, 2.15.3.8
    Open Source Definition, 2.15.3–2.15.3.9
    public domain, 2.15.5.1
    source code, 2.15.3.2
    warranties, 2.15.5.2
    X licence, 2.15.5.5
outsourcing agreements, 2.13
pre-contract documents
    business secrets, 7.1.2
    confidentiality, 7.1.2
    introduction, 7.1.1
    heads of agreement, 7.2.1–7.2.4
publisher-distributor agreements
    domestic distributors, 2.2.1
    foreign distributors, 2.2.2
purposes, 1.4.1–1.4.2
runtime licence agreements, 2.5
shrink-wrap licence agreements, 2.3.2
signed licence agreements, 2.3.1
software as a service (SaaS) 2.17
software conversion agreements, 2.9
trusted third party agreements, 2.4

Software licence agreements – *contd*
types
    developer-publisher, 2.1
    publisher-distributor, 2.2.1–2.2.2
user licence agreements
    click-wrap, 2.3.3
    shrink-wrap, 2.3.2
    signed, 2.3.1
weaknesses, 1.6
web site agreements, 2.14
Source codes
grant of licence, 8.1.5
integrity of author's source code, 2.15.3.4
open source licences, 2.15.3.2
Sources of law, *see* **Legal sources**

T
Technology
core technology licence agreements, 2.9
provision of information, 8.1.5.14
Transfer Block Exemption Regulation, 4.2
Term of licence agreements
commencement before delivery of
    software, 8.1.10.1
evergreen clause, 8.1.10.3
grace period, 8.1.10.6
introduction, 8.1.10
limited term, 8.1.10.2
perpetual term, 8.1.10.4
unspecified term, 8.1.10.5
Termination of licence agreements
breach, upon, 8.1.11.1
consequences, 8.1.11.5
expiry of term, by, 8.1.11.3
introduction, 8.1.11
lapse of IPR, upon, 8.1.11.4
without cause, 8.1.11.2
Terms of licence agreements, *see*
    Contents of licence agreements
Territorial provisions, 8.1.5.3
Third party rights, 8.1.43
Trade secrets, 3.4
Trademarks, 3.5
Training clauses, 8.1.15
Transfer of data overseas, *see* **Data**
    protection
Transferability of rights, 8.1.5.8
Treaty of Rome, 4.2
Trusted third party agreements, 2.4

U
Unfair Terms Directive, 4.7
Update clauses, 8.1.12
User licence agreements
click-wrap, 2.3.3
shrink-wrap, 2.3.2
signed, 2.3.1

User manual
  copyright infringement in, 3.3

V

Value added reseller agreement
  domestic distributors, 2.2.1
  foreign distributors, 2.2.2
  precedent, Appendix 30
Variation clauses, 8.1.37
Verification issues, 4.8
Virus warranties, 8.1.20

W

Warranties
  open source licences, 2.15.5.2
  contents of licence agreements, 8.1.17–
    8.1.22
**Waste electrical and electronic
  equipment**
  Consultation, 4.11.7
  EC Directive (RoHS) 4.11, 4.11.1
    key elements, 4.11.3

**Waste electrical and electronic
  equipment** – *contd*
  EC Directive (WEEE) 4.11, 4.11.1
    key elements, 4.11.2
    recasting of, 4.11.7
  inbound supply chain, 4.11.5
  introduction, 4.11
  key dates, 4.11.4
  outbound supply chain, 4.11.5
  type of products affected, 4.11.1
Websites
  management agreements, 2.14
  precedents
    development, licensing and support
      agreement, Appendix 22
    hosting agreement, Appendix 21
    linking agreement, Appendix 23
    single licensee website and software
      escrow agreement, Appendix 27.7
Win-win negotiations, 5.5

X
X licences, 2.15.5.5